Austrian Lives

Günter Bischof, Fritz Plasser, Eva Maltschnig (Eds.)

CONTEMPORARY AUSTRIAN STUDIES | Volume 21

UNO PRESS

innsbruck university press

Printed in the United States of America.

Book and cover design: Lauren Capone

Cover photo credits given on the following pages: 33, 72, 119, 148, 191, 311, 336, 370, 397

Published in the United States by University of New Orleans Press:
ISBN: 9781608010929
UNO PRESS

Published and distributed in Europe by Innsbruck University Press:
ISBN: 9783902811615
iup

Contemporary Austrian Studies

Sponsored by the University of New Orleans and Universität Innsbruck

Publication of this volume has been made possible through generous grants from the Austrian Ministry of European and International Affairs through the Austrian Cultural Forum in New York as well as the Austrian Ministry of Science and Research. The Austrian Marshall Plan Anniversary Foundation in Vienna has been very generous in supporting CenterAustria at the University of New Orleans and its publications series. The College of Liberal Arts at the University of New Orleans and the *Auslandsamt* of the University of Innsbruck provided additional financial support.

Table of Contents

LIVES OF THE MIND

COMMON LIVES

BOOK REVIEWS

ANNUAL REVIEW

Preface

Günter Bischof

Writing biographies (life stories) for a long time had been a male hegemonic project—writing the lives of great (white) men. Ever since Plutarch and Sueton composed their *vitae* of the greats of classical antiquity, to the medieval obsession with the hagiographies of holy men (and a few women) and saints, Vasari's lives of great Renaissance artists, down to the French encyclopedists, Dr. Johnson and Lytton Strachey, as well as Ranke and Droysen the genre of biographical writing ("the representation of self" or "the reconstruction of a human life") has become increasingly more refined. In the twentieth century male predominance has become contested and the (collective) lives of women, minorities and ordinary people are now the focus of biographical writing. The writing of lives (or lives and their times) are always situated between fact and fiction, ascertainable data and the imagination of the biographer. Leon Edel, the great American biographer of Henry James and theorist of biography, insisted that a biographer must explore and immerse him/herself in the thinking and subconscious of his subject but also know him/herself. More recent postmodern theorists such as Ira Bruce Nadel focus on the narrative technique of biographical writing.[1] The genre of biography has become so popular with the reading public that it is now applied to the lives of cities and entire nations.[2]

Biographical writing is not a *forte* of the historical profession in Austria. The reasons for this are manifold. Careers at the university level are made as quasi-"apprenticeships"; aspiring young scholars often pursue the latest methodological fashions and approaches in the historical sciences (next to serving the predilections and whims of mentors). Professors and the young

1. See the splendid *Handbuch Biographie: Methoden, Traditionen, Theorien*, ed. Christian Klein (Suttgart: J.B. Metzler, 2009) (citations 1-6, 326).
2. Simon Sebag Montefiori, *Jerusalem: The Biography* (New York: Knopf, 2011); Hank Heifetz and Enrique Krauze, *Mexico: Biography of a Power* (New York: Harper, 1998).

charges in their seminars rushed from innovations in quantitative social history in the 1960s/1970s, to the fascination with gender studies in the 1980s, to the history and memory fad in the 1990s, on to the cultural studies boom more recently. "Great men" were a negative role model through all of these historical trends. It may also be that the book market is not big enough in Austria to support independent scholars interested in writing the literate portraits of leading figures in the Austrian universe. It is astounding that some the more intriguing political figures of the two Austrian Republics (and the National Socialist past in between) have not found biographers yet. We have academic biographies of Ignaz Seipel and now of Otto Bauer[3], but no adequate scholarly biographies of Engelbert Dollfuß and Kurt Schuschnigg[4]; nor have all the "founding fathers" of the Second Republic attracted the attention of academic biographers. Leopold Figl, Julius Raab, Karl Renner, and Theodor Körner have not been the subject of abiding scholarly biographic attention[5], Adolf Schärf and Bruno Kreisky have.[6] The rest of the chancellors of the Second Republic cry out for biographic attention, not to speak of their many ministers and party elites—the political figures operating in the parliamentary arena or the battle ground of party politics. The same is true for economic tycoons and intellectual and artistic leaders. When I raised the issue of a lacunae of biographical writing among historians during the first Austrian *Zeitgeschichtetag* (Contemporary History Meeting) in Innsbruck in the spring of 1994, the response was tepid and yawning disinterest.

Across the border in Germany the interest of the reading public in biographical writing is much bigger and academia allows career paths based on writing the lives of great men and women. In fact, ever since Lothar

3. Ernst Hanisch, *Der große Illusionist: Otto Bauer (1881-1938)* (Vienna: Böhlau, 2011); Klemens von Klemperer, *Ignaz Seipel: Christian Statesman in a Time of Crisis* (Princeton: Princeton University Press, 1972).

4. Radomir Luža wanted to write a life of Schuschnigg; however, Schuschnigg and his family did not grant him access to his personal papers.

5. The contemporary biographies of Leopold Figl and Karl Renner written by journalists Ernst Trost and Jacques Hannak are dated and not based on the rich archival records. Anton Pelinka's *Karl Renner zur Einführung* (Junius Verlag, 1998) is sketchy and not based on the archival record either.

6. Karl Stadler, *Adolf Schärf: Mensch, Politiker Staatsmann* (Vienna: Europaverlag, 1982); Elisabeth Röhrlich, *Kreisky's Außenpolitik: Zwischen* österreichischer *Identität und internationalem Programm* (Göttingen: Vienna University Press, 2009); Anton Pelinka, Hubert Sickinger and Karin Stögner, *Kreisky – Haider: Bruchlinien* österreichischer *Identität* (Vienna: Braumüller, 2088) is concentrating on identity politics and not biography based on archival findings; we do have a scholarly biography of the *enfante terrible* of postwar Austrian politics Jörg Haider, see Lothar Höbelt, *Defiant Populist: Jörg Haider and the Politics of Austria* (West Lafayette, IN: Purdue University Press, 2003).

Gall's *Bismarck* and Hans-Peter Schwarz's *Adenauer* biographies one may speak of a veritable boom in academics writing biographies in Germany.[7] In the Anglo-American world and uninterrupted stream of great biographies feeds the vast reading public and keeps the publishing industry alive and well.[8] Writing the lives of Hitler, Stalin, Churchill, Roosevelt never ceases to fascinate those who like to read history. Moreover, the industry of writing presidential biographies keeps academic and popular writers busy. Stellar academic careers are made writing biography.

This volume of *Contemporary Austrian Studies* offers a cross section of Austrian lives and biographical approaches to recent Austrian history. Here are what may be called traditional biographies of leading political figures through the twentieth century. We also suggest that the intellectual biographies (lives of the mind) of thinkers and professionals are fertile soil for biographical study. Moreover, the prosopographic study of common folks in the Austrian population lifts these lives from the dark matter of anonymous masses and gives rich insights into the lives ordinary Austrians have been leading.

We present here a cross-section of political lives. It is no surprise that from John Boyer's seminar at the University of Chicago, which has been giving us seminal new insights into Austrian history in recent years, comes a fresh and fair-minded portrait by John Deak to interpret the life of the controversial Catholic priest-chancellor Ignaz Seipel.[9] Ernst Hanisch has summarized for this volume his recent biography of Otto Bauer (his book is also extensively reviewed here)—a rare attempt by one of Austria's leading contemporary historians to venture into the field of biography.[10] Gabriela Hauch and Philipp Strobl present biographies of two leading socialist activists of the interwar period—Therese Schlesinger and Joseph Buttinger. The later emigrated to the United States as a result of persecution of the Socialists by the Austro-Corporate regime and the Nazis, a fate that beset tens of thousands of Jewish Austrians and political opponents to Nazism. Johannes Koll reminds us that the life stories of leading Austrian Nazis still await the study of biographers. Arthur Seyß-Inquart, Hitler's "willing

7. Lukas Werner "Deutschsprachige Biographik," in *Handbuch Biographie*, 265-77.

8. Michael Jonas, "Britische Biographik," and Levke Harders, "US-amerikanische Biographik," in *ibid.*, 289-97, 321-30. Fittingly, there is no chapter in this handbook of biography's "regional developments" on Austria.

9. Based on his life-long deep immersion in the party politics of the late Habsburg Empire, John Boyer himself has given us a model biographic study of Karl Lueger, the iconic mayor of Vienna, see *Karl Lueger (1844-1910): Christlichsoziale Politik als Beruf. Eine Biographie* (Vienna: Böhlau, 2010).

10. Hanisch, *Der große Illusionist.*

executioner" of the "Anschluss" of Austria, was a leading figure in the occupation of Poland and the Netherlands. He was one of the Austrians who ended up in the docket in the Nuremberg War Crimes Trials and earned a sentence of capital punishment. The young German historian Elisabeth Röhrlich has been lifting the biographical study of Bruno Kreisky from the filiopietistic/frequently hagiographic approach to a more critical level of academic biographical engagement. Martin Eichtinger and Helmut Wohnout offer a first attempt of interpreting the life story of Alois Mock.[11]

The section on "Lives of the Mind" tries to capture the lives of fascinating intellectual figures in pre- and post-World War II Vienna. Deborah Holmes presents a subtle and model biographical study of the female impresario "Genia" Schwarzwald who acted as a major educational reformer, journalist, entrepreneur, and *salonière*; she maintained a notable *salon* in the interwar period where some of Vienna's leading lights regularly met and exchanged ideas. Jason Dawsey, like John Deak a recent PhD from the University of Chicago's stellar History Department, is presenting a biographical cameo the philosopher and public intellectual Gűnther Anders. Like Friedrich Heer, Anders was consistently ignored and isolated by the native chattering classes, yet was a major thinker on postwar Vienna's intellectual scene. Anders fled Nazi Germany and settled in Vienna after the war, becoming the first notable critic of the nuclear age. Dawsey concentrates on unraveling Anders role as one of the earliest critics of *Vergangenheitsbewältigung* Austrian style, namely the lie of Austrians as "first victims" of National Socialism. Timothy Pytell, on the other hand, demonstrates how the Jewish Auschwitz survivor Viktor Frankl made a career in postwar Vienna as a psychiatrist, maybe for the prize of not challenging this very "victim doctrine." There were different strategies, then, of confronting Austrians' failing memory of their World War II past. Stefan Maurer analyzes the career path or Wolfgang Kraus, one of the major literary critics and historians of the postwar era who at the same time also played a major role in the intellectual "cold wars" of Central Europe fighting the communists across the iron curtain. All of these studies show an extraordinary rich life of intellectual discourses influencing the world beyond stale and provincial postwar Austria, often contrarian thinkers whose discourses happened outside of the limelight of official "state sponsored" debates.

The approaches to writing biography taken in this volume also suggest that much work needs to be done to illuminate the lives of ordinary Austrians. While post-World War II neutralist Austria has studiously

11. See also their full-fledged biography Martin Eichtinger and Helmut Wohnout, *Alois Mock: Ein Politiker schreibt Geschichte* (Graz: Styria, 2008).

ignored the lives of millions of Austrian soldiers drafted during World War I and II and pulled into the cauldron of wars raging across Europe and the globe, three essays in this collection adumbrate the individual life trajectories of these often faceless Austrian *Soldaten*-warriors. Wolfram Dornik shows how during World War I they were stationed from front to front all over Europe and injured frequently in very difficult circumstances. Wilfried Garscha takes apart the lives of four ordinary Austrians tossed out over Nazi occupied Europe and turned into perpetrators/war criminals. One was executed for the crimes he committed during the "death marches" of Jews at the end of the war going through Eastern Austria. The other three managed to escape the retribution of the law in the years after the Austrian occupation ended and the Austrian judiciary turned soft on war criminals. Barbara Stelzl-Marx and I follow four Austrian Wehrmacht soldiers through World War II and their subsequent fate as prisoners of war of the Soviets in the East and the Americans in the West. From the millions of Austrians drafted as "cannon fodder" by their frequently ill-advised political leaders during both wars, writing the lives of soldiers in low ranks gives extraordinary agency to their lives' trajectories through "the age of extremes"(Eric Hobsbawm) and their enormous suffering on behalf of what Hitler called the *Volksgemeinschaft.* For political reasons their lives were usually silenced after both wars and they had to suffer quietly the ignominies of defeat and what today would be called "post-traumatic stress syndrome" (PTSD). These individual life stories need to be re-injected in the grand narrative of Austrian history where their roles have been ignored for a long time. More than a million *Wehrmacht* soldiers from the Ostmark were perpetrators in and victims of the Hitler state and often both. The biographic approach can do justice to the complexities of their lives' trajectories. Biographies of ordinary people compel the historians to write in hues of gray rather than in black and white.

Modern methodologies and new source materials give biographers added opportunities to explore collective lives. Hans Petschar and Herbert Friedlmeier pull the visual lives of ordinary Austrians from the rich photo collection of the United States Information Agency, deposited in the Picture Archives of the Austrian National Archives. Turning to photography as the principal source material, offers a rich menu of possibilities for biographers, especially when it comes to portraiture of ordinary Austrians. Ernst Langthaler utilizes both quantitative and qualitative records to show how farmers in Lower Austrian innovated and adjusted to changing market conditions to survive and do well through hard work in the shrinking agricultural sector. The Austrian farmer/peasant is usually ignored as actor in contemporary history and, as Langthaler demonstrates, at the peril of historians. Oliver Rathkolb and his students did an extensive survey among Austrian students today and demonstrate that the more education young Austrians have, the less prejudiced they are vis-à-vis Muslims and Jews, and the more sophisticated a view they hold about the holocaust and Austrians' role during World War II (among these youngsters the myth of Austrians as "victims" is passé). They show how survey data constitute an important historical source to understand "the lives of the mind" of the anonymous masses.

State archives usually hold the documents and written records on the people that shape the fate of nations—politicians, diplomats, military and maybe business leaders and the institutional settings in which they operate (from the ministerial and war councils to diplomatic conferences and on down). Only recently have historians begun to collect the "ego" materials of representative groups of ordinary men and women to document their life stories. The essays on ordinary Austrians in this volume use a variety of source materials to demonstrate that the biographies of common folks can be researched deeply beyond the state archives, where they are ignored as collective historical actors. Oral histories are prominently used, as are diaries and letters, as well as archival records (written and visual), data bases, polls and surveys, photographs and film. The historical profession has taken the quantitative methods of the social sciences to collect the data on vast groups of people and/or developed polls and public opinion methods to survey tens of thousands of people. All of these materials offer the historians rich source collections to write history from the "bottom up" and endow historical agency to masses of ordinary people both as individuals and group actors.

Most in this volume of our lengthy book review essays also deal with biographical approaches. Peter Berger's review of Ernst Hanisch's Bauer biography gives full credit to this complex life story and the biographer's challenges in doing justice to his/her subject matter. Alexander Lassner's review of Alfred Jansa's memoir raises issues about the genre of autobiography and the pitfalls of writing an "*apologia pro vita sua.*" Evan Bukey's book on *Jews and Intermarriage in Nazi Austria* is a prosopography of sorts as it deals with the Nazi ascription of Jewishness during World War II and the resulting game of complex identity politics as a means of survival. Regina Kecht reviews the first scholarly work on Hilde Spiel, the World War II émigré and postwar literary *grande dame* who continued the art of the Viennese *salonières* in the grand tradition of "Genia" Schwarzwald, Berta Zuckerkandl and Alma Mahler-Werfel. Thomas Nowotny's review of Rauchensteiner's Österreich *zwischen den Blöcken* is an autobiographical piece of sorts as the former staffer in Kreisky's cabinet reacts strongly to the scholarly critique of Kreisky's national security policy.

*****

I first explored the feasibility of the subject matter of this volume in May 2011 with Bernhard Fetz, the Director of the Austrian Literature Archives in his spectacular office in Vienna's Hofburg Palace. Fetz had directed a Ludwig Boltzmann Institute at the University of Vienna on writing biography, which had thoroughly theorized the writing of biography. Armed with his encouragement and good advice, some suggestions for possible authors, and a theoretical text on biography of his—a translation of which ended up providing a subtle introduction to this volume. Given the disinterest of contemporary historians in biography, Fetz's advice and my good friend Peter Berger's encouragement and suggestions for further biographies were crucial to pursue this topic. I returned to New Orleans in June and began surveying the field and inviting potential authors. The volume outline came together in the course of the summer and essays began arriving in the offices of CenterAustria at the end of the year. We are very grateful to all the authors for their agreement to contribute articles, some on very short notice, and always with grace and good cheer and mostly on time. Not all invitations to pen essays for this volume were answered. A prominent biographer of Habsburg family members did not answer my mails whether she would contribute a biographical sketch of the late Otto Habsburg who passed away recently. Win some, lose some.

Some people were particularly helpful in bringing this volume towards publication. Eva Maltschnig arrived in August as the 2011/12 Austrian Ministry of Science and Research fellow, beginning research for her dissertation on Austrian women marrying American GIs during the post-World War II Austrian occupation. She quickly immersed herself in her work as assistant to the editor and soon began to make substantive contributions towards the completion of the volume. She maintained the routine correspondence with all contributors to this collection, worked hard to obtain illustrations and copyrights for the essays, became a real expert in correcting footnotes in line with our CAS style sheet and the Chicago Manual and usually scrutinized the essays to provide a first round of corrections. She also gave some sound advice in the design of the volume. Her contributions to the volume's completion were so substantive that I promoted her to guest editor. Similarly, Inge Fink of UNO's Department of English and a native of Austria was kind enough to translate three of the essays from German into English. She did it with her usual aplomb and superior skill and in some cases turned German academese into readable English. Gertraud Griessner of CenterAustria held my back free, when important CAS work waited to be completed. Lauren Capone at UNO Press was a superb copy editor of all essays. Her good cheer turned the drudgery of editing into a joy.

This editorial team, too, represents a cross-section of sorts of Austrian lives: Inge Fink and myself represent a small cohort of Austrians who were lucky to be among the first postwar rural small town generation to receive access to higher education and profit from international student mobility. Inge Fink from Lustenau, one of the old textile capitals of Austria on the Swiss border in Vorarlberg, came to UNO more than 20 years ago to become an English instructor and a big fan of Mardi Gras. I was born in the small Alpine village of Mellau in Vorarlberg with its traditional peasant stock turned tourist entrepreneurs and lived in the U.S. for the past 30 years. Contrary to our rather unusual education backgrounds, one year research fellow Eva Maltschnig from Zell am See, Salzburg, embodies the decades of education expansion Austria has witnessed more recently. Globalization might make life experiences more universal than regionally rooted—her experiences as a graduate student in Vienna may not be so different from Isleño-American Lauren Capone's life as a creative writing MFA student at the University of New Orleans, where she also gains valuable work experience as a copy editor and book designer at UNO Press.

Editorial team of volume 21 of CAS: Lauren Capone, Inge Fink, Gűnter Bischof, Eva Maltschnig
Photo: Kimberly Edwards for CenterAustria

Bill Lavender at UNO Press and Birgit Holzner at *i*up did their share in bringing the volume towards completion. We felt that all biographies needed to be illustrated and worked hard to obtain portraits of all our subjects to help visualize their character. These pictures also provide a trajectory of sorts of Austrian portrait photography through the twentieth century. Next to the authors, a number of archivists were very kind in being cooperative with our search for images. Hans Petschar at the Pictures Archives of the Austrian National Library in Vienna has been incredibly helpful to make us obtain portraits, and so were Bernhard Fetz and the archivists at the Austrian Literary Archives of the National Library. Maria Mesner answered our queries at the Kreisky Archives and Wolfgang Maderthaner at the Austrian Labor History Association in Vienna. Without these kind and helpful colleagues this volume would not be as lavishly illustrated as it is for this journal issue.

As always, we are grateful to our sponsors for making the publication of this volume possible: at the Universities of Innsbruck and New Orleans our thanks got to Matthias Schennach of the *Auslandsamt* as well as Klaus Frantz and Christina Sturn of the UNO Office as well as Susan Krantz, the Dean of the College of Liberal Arts. We are also grateful to the new *Rektor* Tilmann Märk and President Peter Fos for their support of the UNO – Innsbruck partnership agenda. At the Austrian Cultural Forum in New York Andreas Stadler and Hannah Liko have supported our work as has Martin Eichtinger, the chief of the Cultural Division of the Austrian Ministry of European and International Affairs. In the Ministry of Science and Research and its student exchange office Őesterreichischer *Auslandsdienst* (ŐAD), we are grateful to Barbara Weitgruber, Christoph Ramoser, Josef Leidenfrost and Florian Gerhardus. Eugen Stark and the board members of the Austrian Marshall Plan Foundation have been our strongest supporters for more than a decade now. It is a great pleasure and privilege to work with them all and acknowledge their unerring support of CenterAustria and its activities.

New Orleans, April 2012

Introduction

Biographical Narrative between Truth and Lies, Production and Authenticity

Bernhard Fetz[1]

Truth and Lies

Paradoxically in biography, the dramatization of authenticity creates the biographical effect. The answer to the question of whether biographers lie depends on several factors: the biographer's interpretations of his/her role, the expectations of the audience, and the biographical genre, be that a eulogy, a *curriculum vitae*, an encyclopedia entry, a literary or a scholarly biography. In different disciplines, the gathering of biographical data has close ties to scholarship, such as the portrayal of the Other in ethnography, the transcription of autobiographical interviews in biographical sociology, or the interviewing of witnesses in Oral History. Daily life, too, constantly generates biographical evidence: police protocols, evaluative reports, entries in personnel files, or records of conversations between therapists and patients. Generally, we do not grant these documents much biographical power or dignity because they are "artless" and seemingly free of narrative manipulations. The claim to "biographical truth" fluctuates considerably in the production and reception of these texts. In police protocols, the apparent emphasis on cold facts can obscure the mendacious, denunciatory

1. This text was first published as Bernhard Fetz: Biographisches Erzählen zwischen Wahrheit und Lüge, Inszenierung und Authentizität, in: Handbuch Biographie. Methoden, Traditionen, Theorien. Herausgegeben von Christian Klein. S. 54 –60. © 2009 J.B. Metzlersche Verlagsbuchhandlung und Carl Ernst Poeschel Verlag GmbH in Stuttgart. We thank Inge Fink, Department of English, University of New Orleans, for translating this text from German to English.

character of biographical portraits created in the process. Michel Foucault planned to explore this very phenomenon—the production of authenticity in the discourse of state authority—in a collection of curriculum vitae of "infamous persons," a collection that was never realized safe for an introduction describing his intent.[2]

The following example illustrates the tension between imaginative (literary) memory and politically motivated storage memory; the confrontation between the two creates "biographical memory," consisting of facts, legends, lies, and the urge to tell the truth: The Hungarian writer Péter Esterházy had to write his father's biography twice. The first time he did so voluntarily, producing an opulent, 1000-page fantasy about the history of the legendary Esterházy dynasty, whose chronicler he considered himself to be.[3] He did not have a choice in writing the second biography, and he gave it the form of a report, which lacked all the literary imagination that distinguished the novel *Harmonia Caelestis*. Esterházy had stumbled upon his father's police files, which indicated that he had been an informant for the Hungarian secret service.[4] Many biographies had to be re-written once the Eastern European archives had been opened. The archive turned from a place of secrets and repression, a potential source of danger because it stored files on spies and those spied upon, into a place of biographical revision. The archiving of judicial, police, and medical records taught biographers—Péter Esterházy among them—that guilt cannot be wiped out through ritualistic gestures such as confessions: "Statements made in this fashion are registered, accumulated, and preserved in files and archives. The single, immediate, trackless voice making a confession, which wipes out evil because it wipes out itself, has now been replaced by many voices, which come down like a massive avalanche of documents and constitute the ceaselessly growing memory of all the evil in the world.[5]

We cannot escape the dilemma created by truth, lies, aesthetics, and morality. This is the biographer's dilemma *par excellence*. In the discussion of truth and lies with regard to biography, Friedrich Nietzsche supplies the crucial questions in his 1873 essay *On Truth and Lie in a Nonmoral Sense*: Why do people lie? Where does the desire to tell the truth come from? To what extent does language express this desire? Nietzsche argues from an anthropological standpoint: If we do not want to live like worms, i.e. if we

2. Michel Foucault, *Das Leben der infamen Menschen,* ed. and trans. Walter Seitter (Berlin: Merve, 2001).
3. Péter Esterházy, *Harmonia* Cælestis, trans. Terézia Mora (Berlin: Berlin-Verlag, 2001).
4. Péter Esterházy, *Verbesserte Ausgabe*, trans. Hans Skirecki (Berlin: Berlin-Verlag, 2003).
5. Foucault, *Das Leben der infamen Menschen*, 29.

want to prevail against weaker individuals in the "fight for existence," we must question the means we employ to do so. Unlike animals, we do not have sharp horns or a predator's teeth, which could give us direct access to truth; we have to rely on our "intellect" as a means of self-preservation. However, man has developed his "major powers through deception": "In humans, the art of deception has reached its peak: humans dissemble, flatter, lie, deceive, talk behind each other's backs, pretend to be more than they are, live in borrowed splendor, wear masks, hide behind social conventions, play a role for others and for themselves ... to the point where we must find it inconceivable that a honest and pure desire for truth could have sprouted up among the human race."[6] Man's desire for truth depends less on his impulse to combat lies than on the consequences of telling lies. We have no problems accepting comfortable truths; we do not care about "insight without consequences," but when truth becomes destructive, we fight against it.[7]

"So then, what is truth?" Nietzsche asks. For an answer, he writes the following momentous sentences not only into the biographers' family register: "A mobile army of metaphors, metonymies, anthropomorphisms, in short a sum total of human relationships, which have been poetically and rhetorically enhanced, translated, decorated, and which, after long usage, have become binding and canonical: truths are illusions, but we have forgotten that, worn metaphors deprived of any sensual power. ..."[8] The long history of trivial biography, with its fixed stereotypes and its clichés, has provided plenty of examples since the early 19th century.

Literary scholars are not the only ones who have long rejected Rousseau's Romantic notion of an authentic life *avant la lettre* and who have embraced the polyvalent and rhetorical nature of texts; however, the unquenchable desire for biographical evidence keeps (cultural) scholars, readers, and theoreticians active in their fields.

The Relativity of the Biographical Notion of Truth

The multi-faceted concept of biographical truth has been an ambivalent idea since Nietzsche's destruction and deconstruction. Biographical truth has no easy definition; it is a multi-relational construct, forever materializing

6. Friedrich Nietzsche, "Ueber Wahrheit und Lüge im aussermoralischen Sinne," in *Sämtliche Werke: Kritische Studienausgabe in 15 Bänden*, eds. Giorgio Colli and Mazzino Montinari, vol. 1, *Die Geburt der Tragödie; Unzeitgemäße Betrachtungen I-IV; Nachgelassene Schriften 1870-1873* (Munich: dtv/de Gruyter, 1999), 875.

7. Ibid., 878.

8. Ibid., 880-81.

in the interactions between the biographical narrative, its subjects, and its readers. While biographical truth is an effect created by the rhetorical nature of a text, it is always on the run from a mobile army of metaphors trying to overtake it. According to Nietzsche, the struggle for truth is a struggle between the living, graphic metaphors created by first impressions and rigid conventional metaphors.[9] Seen from this perspective, truth is subversive. It attacks outmoded ideas and dissolves them; it undercuts the foundations of one of the most powerful metaphors: the monument and the memorial. (Even Herder tries to create monuments for great men in his biographical essays, albeit living monuments, which will continue to bear witness to their lives.) We find this kind of truth predominantly in the arts, where it relies on the aristocratic "creative fact"[10] and the notion that a poet's imagination transforms fact into a higher kind of truth. The poet—and the biographer raised to the ranks of poetic nobility—frees facts from the straitjacket of their historical context and blesses them with a rebirth under new and very different conditions. Nietzsche sees truth as a linguistic convention. The "thing in itself"—we can substitute *biographical truth* here—"is inconceivable even to the artist of language. ... He only identifies the relationships between things and humans and employs the boldest metaphors in the process."[11] Similarly, Ira Bruce Nadel, the American theorist of biography, insists on the fictional character of all biographical texts: "A biography is a verbal artifact of narrative discourse."[12] However, in biography, their universal usefulness makes metaphors the mediator between a general and a specific truth "which is the recognition of universal aspects of human behavior through the particular actions of an individual life."[13]

Péter Esterházy's double biography of his father—one literary and the other quasi documentary-factual—is particularly instructive as it points out the two central concerns of biography: on the one hand, biography is an imaginative (narrative) construction; on the other, biography depends on facts, the search for truth, detective investigation, as well as the desire for mystery and the shock of discovery. The idea of biographical truth is tied to a changing notion of the subject, to the differentiation between public and private spheres, to the development of autobiographical self-

9. Ibid., 881-82.
10. Virginia Woolf, "The Art of Biography," in *Collected Essays*, vol. 4 (London: Hogarth Press 1967), 221-28, 228. The essay was originally published in 1939.
11. Nietzsche, "Ueber Wahrheit und Lüge," 879.
12. Ira Bruce Nadel, *Biography: Fiction, Fact & Form* (New York: St. Martin's Press, 1984), 8.
13. Ibid., 166.

confidence, and to the cultural relativity of the idea of biographical truth. We can see this phenomenon very clearly in a quotation from Samuel Johnson, who—as a theorist of biography and subject of one of the most famous biographies, James Boswell's *Life of Johnson*—found himself on both sides of the biographical discourse. Despite his reservations, Johnson regards self-knowledge as an advantage over the biographical insight of others because only the kind of self-investigation found in autobiography manages to resist the temptation of false praise and sycophantic flattery: "[M]any temptations to falsehood will occur in the disguise of passions, too specious to fear much resistance. Love of virtue will animate panegyric, and hatred of wickedness embitter censure. ... But he that speaks of himself has no motive to falsehood or partiality except self-love, by which all have so often been betrayed, that all are on the watch against its artifices."[14]

Where the function of biography is concerned, the genre has undergone big changes: biography as a normative-pedagogical form during the Enlightenment became a means of creating national identity in the portraits of *great men*. Especially in the 19th century, the expression of cultural norms and values oscillated between the desire for supranational balance and the production and propagation of national clichés.[15] In the 20th century, biography more or less frees itself from these constraints; instead, it tries to explain how artistic creativity, scientific and scholarly accomplishments, or political actions play out in individuals. In the same measure in which the "false" character of trivial biography becomes the subject of historical biography criticism, the demands of modern biography oscillate between literature and scholarship. Seen from a historical standpoint, the notion of the *whole* truth about a person has shifted from a moral to an aesthetic and epistemological perspective. "[A]nd while I am telling nothing but the truth, I have reminded myself that I cannot reveal the whole truth all the time," James Boswell writes in the dedication of his Samuel Johnson biography in 1791.[16] Modern biographers are challenged by precisely these gaps in biographical accounts. They see and discuss formerly taboo issues, such as sexuality, as the motors of artistic and scholarly accomplishments. Joachim Radkau's biography of Max Weber, which is subtitled "The Passion

---

14. Samuel Johnson, "The Rambler, No 69, 13. October 1750," in *Biography as an Art: Selected Criticism 1560-1960,* ed. James Clifford (London: Oxford Univ. Press, 1962), 40-45, 45.
15. Deborah Holmes and Hannes Schweiger, "Nationale Grenzen und ihre biographischen Überschreitungen," in *Die Biographie: Zur Grundlegung ihrer Theorie*, ed. Bernhard Fetz, with the assistance of Hannes Schweiger (Berlin/New York: de Gruyter, 2009), 385-418.
16. See James Boswell, *Das Leben Samuel Johnsons und Das Tagebuch einer Reise nach den Hebriden* (Leipzig: Insel Verlag, 1984; orig. 1791), 6.

of Thinking" (2005), provides an excellent example.[17] It shows that the driving force behind biographical production is not so much enlightenment as the thrill of biographical mysteries: "What is left out appears as a gap in the text and has to be filled with writing and thinking, but these gaps also make the text mysterious and interesting."[18]

The rhetoric of autobiography is a particularly important epistemological tool in the biographer's work. How can one do justice to public figures without analyzing the literary and genre-specific (self) dramatization and not consider it a part of biographical "truth"? The same holds true for psychological processes. According to Sigmund Freud's late article *Konstruktionen in der Analyse* [*Constructions in Analysis*], the goal of case histories is to reach "the conviction of truth in a construction." Freud maintains that these constructions can serve the same purpose as recaptured "authentic" memories. When it comes to one's own biography, even a surrogate memory can be effective; whether the therapeutic success is based on an illusion or a "real" memory is ultimately irrelevant.[19] This means that biographical truth can never do without a certain measure of illusion and dramatization. However, biography must reconcile a universal claim to truth with the production of truth, which is as a part of writing, and with self-dramatization, which is a part of autobiographical testimony. Artistic license in biography ends at the point where the biographer must expose biographical rhetoric, political evasion, and the attempt to hide an individual's guilt.

Authenticity and Dramatization

Biographers can take the roles of detectives, historians, their subjects' attorneys, prosecutors, or therapists. We see the same variety in the different types of biographical texts: they run the gamut from scholarly biographies, which document every detail in footnotes, to novels, which follow the biographical model and relish in its claim to truth. In his quasi-biographical novel *Flaubert's Parrot* (1984), Julian Barnes uses this technique at the very beginning when he describes a statue of Flaubert that has seen better days. His novelistic depiction of an English author who follows Flaubert's trail through France shows a lot of comical potential. Barnes's novel makes

17. Joachim Radkau, *Max Weber: Die Leidenschaft des Denkens* (Munich: Hanser, 2005).
18. Harald Weinrich, *Lethe: Kunst und Kritik des Vergessens* (Munich: Beck, 2005), 17.
19. Karl Wagner, "Glanz und Elend der Biographik," in *Spiegel und Maske: Konstruktionen biographischer Wahrheit*, eds. Bernhard Fetz and Hannes Schweiger (Vienna: Zsolnay, 2006), 58-59.

it clear that *truth* and *authenticity* are not the same thing. Statues and biographical relics such as stuffed parrots do not have to be genuine in order to appear authentic. Biographical truth relies on the suggestion of authenticity. Rousseau's notion of autobiographical truth in his *Confessions* escapes the "laws of verification": "We find ourselves no longer in the realm of *truth*, the true story, but we have crossed over into *authenticity*."[20] The production of authenticity requires imagination, the infusion of material and immaterial fragments of memory with emotions. In a culture of memory, "fantasy cannot be equated with fiction and forgery but with fabrication and invention, in short with the kind of construction that lies at the heart of all culture."[21] In this regard, individual and collective memory work resembles literature. Biography provides the link between an "atmospheric" truth, which belongs to artists, and a "factual" truth, which is the realm of historians.[22] In the words of Julian Barnes, "The past is an autobiographical narrative passing itself off as the minutes of a parliamentary session."[23]

While authors and psychoanalysts inclined toward the literary emphasize biographical narrative with all its subplots, historians and scholars in various disciplines stress the veracity of sources that have been cleansed from all manipulations: "The historian must understand and disable the power over future memory, the power of immortalization," says Jacques Le Goff, historian and biographer.[24] Historians cannot turn themselves into the assistants of a politics of memory, which operates by arranging and manipulating documents in an attempt to attain everlasting interpretative authority. They must be able to distinguish between an authentic and a fabricated source, and they must recognize whether a source is part of a controlled tradition or a *factum brutum*, a remnant and random witness of some historical fact. Their work resembles that of police investigators. However, once the historical event, the crime scene of biography, is secured, literary historians and imaginative investigators make their entrance.

"In classical mystery stories, the detective *imaginatively reconstructs scenes* from newspaper notices, conversations, and messages; he uses his own *life experiences* as a hypothesis until the *scenes* form a *sequence*, a plausible drama. The inconsistencies in his life experiences inspire him to rearrange the

---

20. Jean Starobinski, *Rousseau: Eine Welt von Wiederständen*, trans. Ulrich Raulff (Munich: Hanser, 1988), 294.
21. Aleida Assmann, *Erinnerungsräume: Formen und Wandlungen des kulturellen Gedächtnisses* (Munich: Beck, 1999), 83.
22. Ibid., 277.
23. Julian Barnes, *Flaubert's Papagei* (Munich: Heyne, 1993; orig. 1984), 128.
24. Jacques Le Goff, *Geschichte und Gedächtnis* (Frankfurt am Main: Campus, 1992), 229.

scenes until a plausible plot emerges."[25] If, in this quote from psychoanalyst Alfred Lorenzer, we substitute the detective not with the analyst but with the biographer, the family circle widens to include a third. In his analysis of Edgar Allen Poe's famous story *The Murders in the Rue Morgue*, Lorenzer contrasts the police prefect's attempts at analytical reconstruction, which is based on language and causal logic, with the detective's "scenic perception." This scenic perception translates the information gained from source analysis into the context of experience. Like the detective and the analyst, biographers must be able to confront "messages, i.e. 'linguistic formulas' with 'life experience.'"[26] Approaching truth in biography, psychoanalysis, or crime requires a critical awareness of language, that is to say, the ability to critique sources, combined with empathy and imagination. We can read the following quotation as a virtual catalogue of analytical qualities required of the biographer: "As we have seen, openness toward the outrageous must complement the critical attitude toward textual discrepancies. Critical acuity must be balanced by imagination and the ability to envision abnormal or deviant lifestyles."[27]

For the most part, the theory of biography has taken the side of imagination; it prefers the company with writers to that of strict historians. The progress of civilization becomes visible in the combination of past memory, still present in some traces, and the memory of the present: this is the humanizing effect of biography, from Johann Gottfried Herder through Wilhelm Dilthey to Leon Edel, biographer and theorist of biography. According to Leon Edel, biographers have an ethical obligation not to manipulate sources: "[A]nd the telling must be of such a nature as to leave the material unaltered."[28] His claim tallies with the demand that biography recapture (at least partially) what was once the "authentic" substance or fabric of life. The challenge consists in "[shaping] a likeness of the vanished figure."[29] However, likeness means difference, means shaping, not identity, a notion that clashes with the ethical imperative not to falsify anything. The "human element" is called upon to reconcile these seemingly contradictory demands—not to falsify sources and "to shape a likeness." In reference to Lytton Strachey, who occupies a similar position in 20th century English biography as Boswell does in the 18th century, Edel endows biography

25. Alfred Lorenzer, "Der Analytiker als Detektiv, der Detektiv als Analytiker," *Psyche* 39, no. 1 (1985): 2.

26. Ibid., 3.

27. Ibid., 7.

28. Leon Edel, *Literary Biography: The Alexander Lectures 1955-56* (London: Hart-Davis, 1957), 5.

29. Ibid.

with a humanizing function: "Humane, because, inevitably, the biological process is a refining, a civilizing—a humanizing—process."[30] Biography makes a stronger claim to "memory work" than genuine scholarly insight: "It assigns meaning, acts with partiality, and creates identity."[31] In their large collection of materials, *History and Obstinacy*, which, among many other things, contains bits and pieces of a theory of biography, Alexander Kluge and Oskar Negt present a variation on this idea: "In the manner of Levi Strauss's *bricolage*, we must recognize the subjective fragments, collect them, and reassemble them into an anthropocentric world."[32] However, when we re-assemble subjective fragments in this manner, we may risk supporting untruths when the ideal clashes with political reality; this Péter Esterházy found out to his chagrin.

Individuality and Type

Biography, in one possible definition, describes an individual's deviation from a model or type. It makes a big difference whether the individual hails from classical antiquity, the Middle Ages, or modern times. In the case of medieval persons, the biographical method might consist in creating a reconstructed normative model on one hand, and then showing the individual's deviation from this model on the other. The description of individual behavior rests on the existence of source documents that put the "truth" of the person next to social and historical "truth." The difference between role and behavior as emanations of the self would then serve as a yardstick for individuality, as an indication for *that which is biographical* in the modern sense. Literary projects like Stefan Zweig's biography of Marie Antoinette[33] demonstrate how a *role model*, an "average character," turns into a tragic figure with individual features (in Zweig, a mysterious bundle of letters plays an important role in this regard), whereby the description, the plane of presentation, depends, to a smaller or larger degree, on ideological preconceptions, cultural clichés, narratives and stereotypes, or the process of transmission.

Biography at least has the potential to capture the individual in the midst of structural connections and to describe the space the individual

30. Ibid., I.

31. Assmann, *Erinnerungsräume*, 133.

32. Alexander Kluge and Oskar Negt: *Geschichte und Eigensinn*, vol. 1, *Die Entstehung der industriellen Disziplin aus Trennung und Enteignung* (Frankfurt am Main: Suhrkamp, 1993), 151.

33. Stefan Zweig, *Marie Antoinette: Bildnis eines mittleren Charakters* (Leipzig: Insel-Verlag, 1932).

gains from these connections. Individual freedom—and the description thereof—is created by *how* the individual gains this space, be that through the therapeutic illusion of "authentic" memory in psychoanalysis, as the narrative construction of the (auto)biographical life story, or as a posthumous description of "correspondences" derived from a dead person's estate (see Sigrid Weigel's biography of Ingeborg Bachmann[34]). Writings left behind as a part of an estate are not just an archive of mightily formative discourses; they are also the place where an individual gains a voice and a face. A person's biographical truth can neither be fixed nor defined by any amount of exact reconstruction and research; this truth is negotiated anew in every biographical project.

Biography navigates between *truth* and biographical *evidence* and the notion that all biographical writing is nothing but an ideological or aesthetic construct. As the vehicle for expressing the truth of the body, the truth of ideas, and the truth of posterity, biography creates different definitions of truth. Biography is always concerned with truth, even in a fictional sense: the truth before God, the truth of the self, the truth before a court of law, the truth of a historical person, the truth of legend, the truth that goes beyond biographical mystifications, the truth of a certain life, lived in a certain social and cultural context. Biographical truth includes the truth of repression, i.e. a fundamental lie that governs a person's life and actions, as well as the textual expression of testimony in certain formats and genres.

34. Sigrid Weigel, *Ingeborg Bachmann: Hinterlassenschaften unter Wahrung des Briefgeheimnisses* (Vienna: Zsolnay, 1999).

Political Lives

Ignaz Seipel (1876-1932)

Founding Father of the Austrian Republic

John Deak

Biographies fall in and out of favor, both among publishers and in the halls of academe.[1] Historical consciousness has its own fashions and trends to be sure. Since Immanuel Kant's 1784 essay "Idee zu einer allgemeinen Geschichte in weltbürglicher Absicht," history has had pretensions of seeing through the widest lens. Kant's cosmopolitanism asked us to grapple with big pictures and movements in order to capture the long-term trajectories and sea changes. But, of course, the stories of individuals always seem to ask us to switch camera lenses from the panorama to the strongest zoom. For every major sea change, there is a biography that distills the story and makes it more accessible and more human. For every Renaissance, there is a Leonardo da Vinci and a Cosmo the Great; for every French Revolution we have our Napoleons, our Neckers, our Lafayettes. G. W. F. Hegel reminded us that these "great men," or heroes, embody the movement of the age, the spirit of the times and help us to understand how the world can change fundamentally and drastically. But Hegel gives us another conundrum with which we must deal: must prominent figures of the past embody or transcend their time? To what degree do they merely dimly reflect the light and darkness of our age? Are individuals worth studying in their own right?

For Austria's twentieth century, biography can be a ticklish subject. Biographies are all too often reminders of larger failures: the fall of the multinational Habsburg experiment; the failure of interwar democracy; the failure of international organizations; the failure of individuals to stop the slide down the slippery slope toward fascism, totalitarianism, and genocide. And while they teach us lessons about the fragility of democracy and civil society at large, twentieth-century biographies from central Europe can present us with inconvenient information. Biographies remind us all too well of what we would rather forget or re-write about the past. If the twentieth century teaches us anything in the twenty-first, it will be about the ambiguities inherent in humanity. In many ways, the fashion of historiography and Austrian studies has been to write about the Garden of Eden before the fall. The study of modernism and artistic discourses, of

1. For a recent introduction to biography and its relationship to history see the fine and readable study Barbara Caine, *Biography and history*, Theory and History (Basingstoke: Palgrave Macmillan, 2010).

Ignaz Seipel as Priest and Federal Chancellor, March 1927,
© Austrian National Library

Vienna 1900 and the cultural flowering of the old empire, are where we find Austria as a place of cosmopolitan ideas. In a way, cultural and scientific ideas have become Austria's heroes. They are less ambiguous than the humanity that biographies inconveniently put before us.

The figure of Ignaz Seipel (1876-1932), Catholic priest, politician, and Chancellor of the Austrian First Republic, is one of those inconvenient Austrian lives. August Maria Knoll, the erstwhile secretary to Ignaz Seipel who later became prominent as a left leaning Catholic and historical sociologist, asked his readers in a 1934 essay "What is Seipel's political legacy? His body of thought? His political ideas? His political journey?"[2] Knoll asked such questions as Engelbert Dollfuß's Austrofascist regime was purging institutions of the Austrian Republic in order to erect a new state. As biographers sought to answer Knoll's questions in the 1930s, they often praised Seipel as the forerunner of Dollfuß and Schuschnigg's Austro-Fascist state.[3] After the Second World War, the social democrats merely had to keep the same arguments and invert the logic of approbation into scorn. For them, Seipel was the great conniving priest who used his intellectual gifts to undermine democracy.

For all the love and hatred which Seipel evokes, we have not really come to a consensus answer on Knoll's basic questions. The last book-length biography of Seipel was published in 1972.[4] Its author, Klemens von Klemperer, is an Americanized central European who has roots in both Berlin and Vienna. Born in 1916, Klemperer found that the distance between the United States to the European continent both protected him from the slings and arrows in his work on contemporary history in Europe and provided him with historical distance to write a balanced, if conservative, biography of "one of the chief architects of the Austrian Republic."[5]

In many ways, von Klemperer's biography of Seipel is an exception. Seipel is one of those characters whose life is often seen in respect to someone else. Paired with his social democratic arch-nemesis, Otto Bauer,[6] or with the architect of Austro-fascism, Engelbert Dollfuß,[7] Seipel is defined either through his enemies and conflicts or as a precursor to the destroyers of Austrian democracy. Our stand-alone studies have likewise fallen into the extremes. "Saint Seipel" appears in hagiographic publications attesting to his superhuman qualities as a man and statesman, foiled by the

---

2. August M Knoll, *Von Seipel zu Dollfuß: Eine historisch-soziologische Studie* (Vienna: Manz, 1934), 8.
3. For instance, Knoll, *Von Seipel zu Dollfuß*; Eduard Ludwig, *Ignaz Seipel: Der Wegbereiter einer neuen Zeit* (Vienna: E. Ludwig, 1936); Franz Riedl, *Kanzler Seipel: Ein Vorkämpfer volksdeutschen Denkens* (Saarbrücken: Saarbrücker Druck und Verlag, 1935).
4. Klemens von Klemperer, *Ignaz Seipel: Christian Statesman in a Time of Crisis* (Princeton, N.J.: Princeton University Press, 1972). To this I should add that the last book-length study was the "biographical documentation," Friedrich Rennhofer, *Ignaz Seipel: Mensch und Staatsmann. Eine biographische Dokumentation,* Böhlaus zeitgeschichtliche Bibliothek 2 (Vienna: Böhlau, 1978).
5. See Klemperer's revealing and fascinating memoir, Klemens von Klemperer, *Voyage through the Twentieth Century: A Historian's Recollections and Reflections* (New York: Berghahn Books, 2009), 84.
6. Viktor Reimann, *Zu Groß für Österreich: Seipel und Bauer im Kampf um die Erste Republik*, 1st ed. (Vienna: Molden, 1968).
7. Knoll, *Von Seipel zu Dollfuß.*

hatred and party-politics of the social democrats.[8] But, on the left, Seipel assumed many forms. Walther Federn, the founder of the liberal journal of economics and politics, *Der Österreichische Volkswirt,* called Seipel in the foreword to Charles Gulick's magnum opus on the First Republic, the "evil genius of the republic," who laid the groundwork for the fall of Austrian democracy.[9] Federn merely foreshadowed what lay between the pages of Charles Gulick's two-volume *Austria from Habsburg to Hitler.*

For Gulick, who was a heterodox economics professor at the University of California at Berkley for his entire professional career, Seipel's genialness lay in the fact that he was able, through his powerful wits, to undermine democratic practice in the Republic. As such, he was Dollfuß's (and fascism's) John the Baptist—laying the groundwork for authoritarianism and the clerical-fascist state. Nearly every mention of Seipel's name among the over 1800 pages of text refers to Seipel's attempts to "exclude parliament," "throttle parliamentary committees," "increase parliamentary difficulties," or his "campaign against the constitution."[10] For Gulick, as well as countless others on the left, Seipel provided the stubborn, evil, "*Prälat ohne Milde,*" who abandoned democracy, civil rights, and embraced authoritarianism and violence.

There hardly seems much of a middle ground to understanding Seipel, or his time. Distance may help us to transcend the party-political interpretations of hagiography and demonology now that we are removed by eighty years from Seipel's death and nearly seventy-five years since the end of Austro-Fascism and the Anschluss. Of course, the focus in this volume is on "Austrian lives" and thus the underlying question is what do these biographies (not hagiographies or demonologies) of prominent politicians and thinkers, as well as biographies of groups, tell us about twentieth-century Austria? In what ways do these lives reflect the times, successes and tribulations, of Austrians who have stood at the center of the world-shaping events of the twentieth century?

Ignaz Seipel's biography resists telling us one story. Indeed the many narratives one could make out of Seipel the priest, the scholar, and the politician offer many morality tales as well as reflections on the Austrian *Mensch* and his predicament in the last century. Therefore, the difficulty

8. Gottlieb Ladner, *Seipel als Überwinder der Staatskrise vom Sommer 1922: Zur Geschichte der Entstehung der Genfer Protokolle vom 4. Oktober 1922*, vol. 1 (Vienna: Stiasny Verlag, 1964); Bernhard Birk, *Dr. Ignaz Seipel: Ein österreichisches und europäisches Schicksal* (Regensburg: G.J. Manz, 1932).

9. See Walther Federn's foreword to Charles A. Gulick, *Austria from Habsburg to Hitler* (Berkeley: Univ. of California Press, 1948), i, xi.

10. Confer the index entries for Seipel in Ibid., ii, 1895–96.

of evaluating Seipel's importance, his contributions and his failings, are ultimately worth the effort. Moreover, Seipel warrants a sustained conversation, since he reflects so much of the ambiguities and pressures of a world transitioning between absolutism and democracy, between the locally-centered economic life to a modern industrial world. He can tell us much about the transition from monarchy to republic and the changing role of the Catholic Church in public life from the nineteenth to the twentieth century. More specifically, Seipel's life reflects the major problems of the times after the fall of the monarchy: the dilemmas of Austrian conservatism; the search for the proper post-imperial scope of Austrian politics and the resistance to and acceptance of a narrowing horizon of politics and statecraft; the ambivalence to parliamentary democracy and the problematic search for alternatives to it; the distrust of party politics while at the same time becoming enmeshed in the mire of it; last but not least, Seipel can remind us of the powerful claim of Catholicism in Austrian public life.

What Seipel's life reflects then are the ambiguities of the Austrian Republic and the simultaneous, yet incompatible, identities of Austria and its peoples after the First World War and the fall of the Habsburg Monarchy. Moreover, the questions—fundamental questions—as to how the Austrian republic would make its difficult transition from being the collection some of the core provinces of the old Habsburg Empire to a state and people in its own right, how parliamentary democracy would function in a state where the tendency was for public policy to be administered by state officials rather than by parties themselves, and how the Catholic Church would function in a new republic without the implicit and explicit protection of the Habsburg dynasty, all worked to shape the inconvenient biography of Ignaz Seipel. Finally, Seipel reflects the ways in which party politics have come to dominate not only Austrian parliamentary life, but the outlook and *habitus* of Austrian public life. Seipel's political career takes the course of a setting sun, shimmering on a wide horizon of European scale. By the end of his political career, he descended into a course of hatred, of violence, and irreconcilable opposition to the social democrats. In essence, as we are forced to make sense of Seipel's descent into Austrian politics, we are forced to confront the ambiguities and rough transitions of Austria's imperial heritage, its long transition to democratic practice, and the conflict-ridden struggle to be an independent, parliamentary republic.

The main argument in this article, beyond the recognition that Seipel was a figure who reflects the deep and unresolved political problems of his times, is that eighty years after Seipel's death, we must recognize him as a founding father of both the Austrian Republic and the Austrofascist state. Even Seipel's hagiographers have recognized the ambiguities of Seipel's life and times. Such balanced criticism tends to come from the "liberal Catholic" school of thinkers who have written on Seipel. August Maria Knoll has categorized Seipel's political course into four phases or "stages" which encompass Seipel's engagement with constitutional reform in the monarchy; his engagement with the social democrats to establish a parliamentary democracy in the republic; a pragmatic capitalist period in the early 1920s when Seipel, as chancellor, worked to stabilize the Austrian economy through a major restructuring of the Austrian state; and finally, a rightist-stage, when Seipel searched for alternatives to parliamentary democracy.[11]

The criticism evident in Knoll's contemporary treatment of Seipel stems in fact from Seipel's political transitions between his taking up politics during First World War, to his death at the end of the democratic era of the Austrian First Republic. Seipel did not maintain one fixed political place—he was always engaging and moving with his political opponents and the events of the time. But Seipel's own movement from stages or positions, his weaving between two poles of a dialectic, began in the great transformations of Austrian politics long before he found himself head of the Austrian Republic.[12] In fact, his life was full of transitions and change that forced Seipel to continually reformulate his own ideas.

Early Life

Political participation expanded rapidly during the course of Seipel's early life while at the same time the city of Vienna was undergoing rapid change. The early part of Seipel's life would have seen the gradual incorporation of people like Seipel's father into the leagues of voters. At the same time, Catholicism in Austria became interwoven with the gradual opening of the political process.

Ignaz Seipel was born on 19 July 1876 in working class Rudolfsheim, Vienna, in what was then the fourteenth district. His father was a *Fiaker* coachman who got his nickname, "Deutschmeister-Karl" from his service in the 4th Infantry "Hoch-und Deutschmeister" Regiment, based in Vienna. Ignaz's mother was a farmer's daughter from Weitenegg, Lower Austria,

---

11. Knoll, *Von Seipel zu Dollfuß*, 8–10.

12. For a dialectical analysis of Seipel's phases, see the criticial intellectual biography: Ernst Karl Winter, *Ignaz Seipel als dialektisches Problem: Ein Beitrag zur Scholastikforschung*, Gesammelte Werke 7 (Vienna: Europa Verlag, 1966).

which lies on the banks of the Danube in the morning shadows of Melk's Baroque Benedictine Abbey. Ignaz's mother brought five children into the world, but Ignaz would be the only one who would survive infancy. She died of tuberculosis, three years after Ignaz's birth. Ignaz's father transferred the three-year-old boy to his mother's and sister's house in nearby Sechshaus, just south of the Westbahn train tracks. There Ignaz would spend his youth, in humble circumstances, on the border between the working and lower-middle classes, sheltered from the growing and busy city by his overbearing grandmother and aunt.[13]

Seipel was thus born into a petit bourgeois family in the Viennese suburbs but lived in the humble circumstances of the workers. As he would write to his long-time political friend and colleague Heinrich Mataja, "I come from far, far below."[14] Certainly Seipel meant this to refer to his economic situation, but one can read—as a larger take on his "Austrian life"—this language to refer to his political station as well. As such his birth and education occurred at the beginning of the constitutional era in Imperial Austria.

Seipel was born into a family that would not have the property nor the status to vote under the suffrage laws of the time. In the early years of the constitutional period in Imperial Austria, suffrage was awarded to a man of Seipel's class depending on whether he paid over ten Gulden in direct taxes. Because he was raised by his grandmother and aunt, Seipel did not likely belong to an active political household. Moreover, Seipel did not come from the legions of lower noble families or the high bourgeois. Thus, he did not benefit from educational institutions which had normally produced Austria's ministerial elite—and certainly not its Minister-Presidents.[15] In essence, Seipel's home life and his educational opportunities made him a political outsider. The young Seipel began his secondary education in 1887 at a municipal gymnasium in Meidling just as this typical worker's district underwent a municipal transformation with the regulation of the Vienna River and the connection to the streetcar network.[16] It was in this

13. Rennhofer, *Ignaz Seipel,* 3–4.

14. Quoted in Ibid., 1.

15. Gerno Stimmer, "Zur Herkunft der höchsten österreichischen Beamtenschaft: Die Bedeutung des Theresianums und der Konsularakademie," in *Student und Hochschule im 19. Jahrhundert: Studien und Materialien,* Studien zum Wandel von Gesellschaft und Bildung im Neunzehnten Jahrhundert 12 (Göttingen: Vandenhoeck und Ruprecht, 1975), 303-345. For a more thorough treatment on the education and social milieux of Austrian governmental elites in the monarchy, see Gernot Stimmer, *Eliten in Österreich 1848-1970,* Studien zu Politik und Verwaltung 57 (Vienna: Böhlau, 1997), especially vol. i.

16. Rennhofer, *Ignaz Seipel,* 1–8.

atmosphere and at this point that politics spread to the far reaches of working-and-lower-middle-class Vienna. In 1882, Count Edward Taaffe's government produced a suffrage reform that extended the suffrage to "five-gulden men"—adult males who paid more than five Gulden in direct taxes.[17]

Seipel's gymnasium and university years were thus periods of immense political change, both for Austria's working citizenry and for Austrian Catholics. Pope Leo XIII's 1891 encyclical, *Rerum Novarum*, while it condemned socialism and communism, it at the same time challenged Catholics to find ways to overcome the excesses of industrial capitalism. As John W. Boyer writes, *Rerum Novarum* "fostered a common discourse that gave European Catholics a shared starting point in dealing with industrial modernity."[18] The encyclical, through its condemnation of the capitalist instrumentalization of human beings and the urging of active forms of citizenship and participation, encouraged Catholics to work through the state to ameliorate the deleterious effects of industrialization. It fueled the fires of Catholic political participation, participation that could advocate under and against the authority of the bishops.

In this atmosphere, Austrian political Catholicism set down its roots in the city of Vienna in the form of the Christian Social Party, a party which responded to the capitalist transformation of Vienna in the late nineteenth century with anti-Semitic rhetoric and middle-and-lower class economic protest.[19] At the same time the social democrats pushed even harder for the expansion of the suffrage; and radicals and democrats in parliament agreed. In 1896 the Austrian parliament passed a third major suffrage reform, adding a fifth curia, elected by all male citizens over the age of twenty-four. Ten years later, the curial system would be completely abolished for parliamentary elections with the promulgation of equal, universal male suffrage.[20] The first elections under universal male suffrage were held in 1907, vaulting the Christian Social and Social Democratic parties respectively

17. Gustav Kolmer, *Parlament und Verfassung in Österreich* (Vienna & Leipzig: C. Fromme, 1902), iii, 137–62; Karl Ucakar, *Demokratie und Wahlrecht in Österreich: Zur Entwicklung von politischer Partizipation und staatlicher Legitimationspolitik*, Österreichische Texte zur Gesellschaftskritik 24 (Vienna: Verlag für Gesellschaftskritik, 1985).

18. John W. Boyer, "Catholics, Christians and the Challenges of Democracy: The Heritage of the Nineteenth Century," in *Political Catholicism in Europe 1918-45*, ed. Wolfram Kaiser and Helmut Wohnout, vol. 1 (London: Routledge, 2004), 25.

19. Ibid., 17–20. See also John W. Boyer, *Political Radicalism in Late Imperial Vienna: Origins of the Christian Social Movement, 1848-1897* (Chicago: University of Chicago Press, 1981).

20. For an overview of the development of suffrage and the expansion of the curial system, see above all Stanisław Starzyński, "Reichsratswahlen," *Österreichisches Staatswörterbuch* (Vienna: Alfred Hölder, 1909), iv, 871–94.

into first and second place in the Imperial parliament.[21] So as Christian socialism emerged as a strong-massed based party in Vienna through the expanding suffrage in the old Austrian state, so too did its major ideological opponent, social democracy.

Ignaz Seipel saw these changes happen as he himself entered adulthood. As the working-class suburbs of Vienna where he lived and attended school were more firmly incorporated into the Habsburg metropolis, as political life opened up to the lower classes but also took on forms of occupational and anti-Semitic protest, Seipel dedicated himself to his studies. With his *Matura* in hand, as Karl Lueger's Christian Social Party won its first major victory in Vienna's municipal elections in 1895, Seipel joined the Vienna seminary while beginning the study of Theology at the University of Vienna. There Seipel was steeped in the subject of moral theology. In 1899 Seipel was ordained a priest and spent the next four years serving the Church in a pastoral role. His first assignment was to the parish church in Göllersdorf, Lower Austria, where he ministered to 1700 people. Four months later he was transferred to Staatz, a market town near the Moravian border. Seipel would spend the next two years in the Lower Austrian countryside before being transferred back to Vienna in 1902.

In Vienna, Seipel worked not only as a chaplain and a religion teacher in a girls' school, but on a doctorate in Theology. He would receive his doctorate in December 1903. Seipel continued his academic career with a *Habilitationsschrift* on the "economic teachings of the Church fathers," which was published in 1907.[22] Two years later, he received a full professorship of Theology in Salzburg, which at that time only possessed a small theological faculty. There he taught courses on moral theology, economics, and sociology, and became involved in the struggle to reestablish a full-fledged university in the baroque city on the Salzach. In Salzburg Seipel became a thinker who used his theological knowledge to take on, and resolve, conflicts in society. Salzburg provided Seipel with a group of intellectuals with which to discuss issues of the day. As he expressed himself in literary journals or in the group of intellectuals who included literati like Hermann Bahr and legal scholars like Heinrich Lammasch, the young Seipel used his liberal brand of Catholicism as an approach to questions of government and Church policy as well as the First World War.

Seipel brought his own thinking on moral theology to bear on the world around him. His conviction that Christianity offered a firm basis

21. Ucakar, *Demokratie und Wahlrecht in Österreich*, 362.

22. Ignaz Seipel, *Die wirtschaftsethischen Lehren der Kirchenväter* (Vienna: Mayer & co., 1907).

for understanding and living in the world brought Seipel to criticize nationalist attitudes during the Great War and subsequently to publish his "expression of dissent" from mainstream Austro-German thought in an impressive tract, *Nation und Staat.* In the book, Seipel asks his reader to reflect, in the midst of nationalist feeling in the First World War, "on what our patriotism is and where it has it roots."[23] In the work he laid out the basis for a Catholic approach to European politics that was at the same time a cosmopolitan and Austrian approach. The central point for Seipel is to distinguish, rather than conflate, nation and state. For Seipel, nationalism was an exaggeration, one which rested on the chimerical idea that "belonging to a nation represented the highest good of humanity."[24] Rather, for Seipel, nations were cultural institutions, the extension of the family where one could find his place to do God's work. As bases for political organizations, however, they were unsuitable. Rivers, mountains, valleys, the natural frontiers, hardly corresponded to linguistic frontiers at all—especially in the Dual Monarchy.[25] The supranational empire, however, and its own acceptance of its supranationality, provided for Seipel the real basis for a Christian commonwealth. In many ways the book looked to reject the nation-state and see the possibilities of alternatives to it. *Nation und Staat* reflected the wide horizon of Austrian politics and Seipel's own thought before the fall of the Habsburg Monarchy, when "Austria" could be used not to denote a nation, but rather to denote a special cosmopolitanism and supranationalism. From this intellective position, Seipel became involved in circles of reformers who wanted to save the Monarchy in the midst of the hunger and deprivations of the First World War. Lectures on the themes of *Nation und Staat* drew him to Vienna and in late 1917 he took on a professorship at the University of Vienna. He would remain in Vienna the rest of his life. Seipel's descent into politics had begun.

Seipel's Political Vocation

Vienna in 1917 was a shadow of its former self. Though intellectually it remained vital and vibrant, physically it began to grow malnourished and gaunt. The food situation grew steadily worse over the course of 1918 and continued into the early years of the Austrian Republic. The *Sektionschef* (and later *Staatssekretär*) in charge of food provisioning, Hans Loewenfeld-

23. Ignaz Seipel, *Nation und Staat* (Vienna: W. Braumüller, 1916). For a discussion of the work in the context of Seipel's life, see above all Klemperer, *Ignaz Seipel,* 54–65, 54.
24. Ignaz Seipel, *Nation und Staat*, 70.
25. Ibid., 14.

Russ, noted in his memoirs that "The year 1918 showed all the symptoms of the worst sort of crisis, and the office of food provisions found itself in a perpetual state of so-called alarm for the entire year, which challenged the nerves of all its officials and functionaries." In each and every meeting of the Office of Food Provisioning, it was clear that the state was unable to cover the daily needs of the populace. "The domestic harvest fell to 50% of peacetime production. But this fact was not as decisive for the food situation as the near total cessation of food deliveries from Romania and Hungary, which...normally covered over 70% of the need of the non-self-nourishing populace and had in the course of the year sunk to about 5%." Such statistics meant complete hunger and devastation for the urban population, which now had to nourish itself using 50% of a normal harvest, no grain imports, and anything that was available on the black market.[26]

It was in this atmosphere of cold and deprivation that the first major turning point in Seipel's professional career occurred. Firstly, Seipel moved into the inner circles of politics through his advocacy of administrative and constitutional reforms of the Monarchy. Seipel was admired by the young Emperor Karl and found himself drawn increasingly into the Christian Social Party. On 22 October 1918, Seipel became the Minister of Social Welfare in the government of Heinrich Lammasch—it was to be the last ministry of "Old Austria."

When the Monarchy constitutionally crumbled between the Kaiser's manifesto on 28 October and the proclamation of a republic on 12 November, Seipel showed his political dexterity. Without abandoning his allegiance to the emperor and his idea of a multinational Catholic polity, over the next two years Seipel steered the Christian Social party—the former self-styled *Reichspartei*—into a party for parliamentary democracy and republican government, without giving up a respect for the larger "old Austrian" roots of the party and the new state. "The total collapse of Austria could have been avoided," Seipel wrote in the *Reichspost* in November 1918, "if a true democratic spirit had infused our politics."[27] What was now the task of Austria's Germans, according to Seipel, was to make sure the new state enacted a democratic constitution—and did not attempt at all to limit suffrage (even to women). Such a democratic course would provide Austria with the peace and order that Austria would need in the new Europe and

---

26. Hans Loewenfeld-Russ, *Im Kampf gegen den Hunger: Aus den Erinnerungen des Staatssekretärs für Volksernährung; 1918-1920*, ed. Isabella Ackerl, Studien und Quellen zur österreichischen Zeitgeschichte 6 (München: Oldenbourg, 1986), 94–96.

27. Ignaz Seipel, "Die demokratische Verfassung," *Reichspost* (Vienna, 21 Nov. 1918), morning edition, 1.

prevent the dictatorship of one class.[28] In essence, Seipel's articles and his political activities in the first months after the fall of the monarchy served to chart a course between a conservative rejection of the republic and parliamentary democracy and a socialist attempt to establish a revolutionary state. As such, Seipel advocated for the democratic system as the path to law and order—to prevent a dictatorship of the proletariat. Through his articles and intra-party advocacy, Seipel was able to lead his fellow Christian socials into supporting the new state. In fact, one of Seipel's major biographers, Klemens von Klemperer, takes care to emphasize that Seipel's work within the Christian Social party and in his series of articles in the *Reichspost* presented a flexible stance on parliamentary democracy. Seipel thus opened "up the possibility of a constructive conservative function within the new Austrian Republic."[29]

Seipel accompanied the political transition from Monarchy to Republic in Austria with a transformation of his own. His transition from Professor of Moral Theology to Christian Social politician brought him a rise in prominence in his new-found political career. Allowed by cardinal Piffl to stand for elections in February 1919, Seipel began his parliamentary career working in good faith with the social democrats to settle the postwar peace treaties and to write a constitution for Austria. But his connections to the Church and the moral theology of its intellectual world still tugged at him and did not let go. Seipel was elevated into the prelature in August 1919. Seipel's early political career saw him climbing two ladders at once: one in Austria's political world, the other in Austria's ecclesiastical world. Though Seipel would be tempted at least two times to become a bishop in the Catholic Church and thus commit himself fully to climbing the Church ladder, he would continually choose the political ladder as his vocation. In his own mind, this choice was one of self-sacrifice—serving God through politics instead of doing what he would prefer. Politics in Austria would become dirty and hard; Seipel's role as compromiser and Christian-cosmopolite would fade into the background.

The early years of the Republic brought Seipel two opportunities to work with the social democrats, who were led at that time by the moderate Karl Renner. The first was the approval of the draconian Treaty of St. Germain, which formalized the end of the First World War and the establishment of the Austrian Republic. The treaty set most of Austria's new narrow frontiers, which enclosed a population of 6.5 million people

28. Ignaz Seipel, "Das Volk und die künftige Staatsform," *Reichspost* (Vienna, 23 Nov. 1918), morning edition, 1.
29. Klemperer, *Ignaz Seipel*, 94–109, quote on 109.

who had once lived in an Empire of 55 million. In such a humble state, cut off from the large industrial pockets in Bohemia and the grain fields of Hungary, Austria's politicians and business class feared for the new state's economic survival. Moreover, at that time there was a strong inclination among the populace to abandon the small state solution and join the larger and more economically viable state of Germany. In this situation, Seipel worked as a coalition partner to bring the conservatives into the fold of the new Austrian state. While Renner led the socialists into supporting the small republic, Seipel continued to shepherd the Christian socials into the dual task of supporting a republican state in general and the small Austrian state in particular. This project entailed defining a new, smaller horizon for the Austrian state, and also making sure that the Austrian state put down roots and grew into something of its own. During a debate on the budget in the Constitutional Assembly in 1920, Seipel defined Austria as "a small state…a state in which everything is process, in which nothing is fixed […]. This state has no tradition of existence, of living, and such circumstances account for why any identification with the state has not welled up in the populace."[30] The work of politicians would thus be to create a state that Austro-Germans could believe in and identify with. In the years between the fall of the monarchy and the drawing up of the constitution, Seipel's vision of democracy with a new, smaller, and Christian state made him ready to work with Karl Renner to found the Austrian Republic. As such, Seipel was one of the first ranks of Austrian politicians to believe in this new state.

Such belief in the possibilities of the small Austrian state provided Seipel a good basis for pushing the constitution and finding common ground with the social democratic leadership. If the socialists feared the centrifugal tendencies of the Austrian provinces, they were right to look to Seipel for help, since he too wanted to ensure the territorial integrity of the small Austrian state. Seipel had been chosen by his fellow parliamentarians to serve on the constitutional committee as vice chairman. The chairman was none other than Seipel's future ideological opponent, the social democratic politician and Austro-marxist theorist, Otto Bauer. Here Seipel met an intellectual partner with whom he found it difficult to achieve common ground. And while the "titanic struggle" between Seipel and Bauer paved the groundwork for Austria's tumultuous political ride through the entire decade of the 1920s, one can get too wrapped up in the clash of ideological titans to see the individual "Austrian lives." Can one explain Seipel without

30. *Stenographisches Protokoll der Konstituierenden Nationalversammlung für Deutschösterreich* [hereafter SPdKN], 73. Sitzung (20 Apr. 1920), 2119.

Bauer? Such a thing is difficult.[31] For if Seipel could be flexible and able to compromise with the equally state-focused and undogmatic Karl Renner, Seipel's outlook and his practice of politics became more dogmatic and uncompromising when Otto Bauer sat across the negotiating table from him. Clearly, Bauer awakened in Seipel a competitiveness—and yes, an ideological intransigence—that Renner did not. When Karl Renner remarked that Bauer was beholden "to the same dogmatism as a left-socialist as Seipel was as a Catholic priest," Renner did not pay either a compliment.[32] But Renner sought to portray his social democratic colleague, Otto Bauer, sucked into an ideological wrestling match with Seipel, in which the rules were not to maintain a side or position so much as to throw the other opponent out of the political ring. And frankly, Bauer's evolution as an Austro-Marxist was never as flexible and open as Seipel's early liberal Catholicism. The 1920s saw Seipel drift further away from compromise and from working with the other side of the aisle. Seipel was accompanied, if not guided, on this path by Otto Bauer.

But Seipel's oppositional course was a gradual development. In May 1920, while serving on the constitutional committee with Otto Bauer, the forty-four year-old prelate published an article in the *Reichspost,* "Out with the Constitution," which expressed sympathy with the impatience of the general populace with the Constitutional Assembly at its lack of success writing a constitution for the new state.[33] But, nonetheless, Seipel cautions patience while understanding the urgency of the moment. He instructs his audience that the constitution will be important in order to resurrect the economic stability of the Austrian state and to show the world that Austria will be a worthy and solvent business partner. In order to be a viable state, Austria needs a working, viable economy. To acquire a viable economy, given the international trade context of post-war Europe, Austria needs a solid constitution. Here we see the formation of Seipel's policies for the rest of the decade: the fusing of Christian socialism with

31. In fact, understanding the competition, and yet admiration, for one another has been the subject of useful and readable studies of the 1920s Austria, for instance: Reimann, *Zu Gross;* Norbert Leser, *Genius Austriacus: Beiträge zur politischen Geschichte und Geistesgeschichte Österreichs, 2nd ed.* (Vienna: Böhlau, 1986), 141–75.

32. Karl Renner, *Österreich von der ersten zur zweiten Republik.* (Vienna: Verlag der Wiener Volksbuchhandlung, 1953), 42. For other discussions of Seipel and Bauer, see Leser, *Genius Austriacus*, 141–75; Thomas Olechowski, "Ignaz Seipel--vom k.k. Minister zum Berichterstatter über die republikanische Bundesverfassung," *Kelsen Working Papers* online-version (3 Jan. 2011): 151–56, <http://www.univie.ac.at/kelsen/workingpapers/seipelbundesverfassung.pdf.>

33. Ignaz Seipel, "Heraus mit der Verfassung!," in *Der Kampf um die österreichische Verfassung* (Vienna and Leipzig: Wilhelm Braumüller, 1930), 83-86.

capitalism.[34] Such a course put Seipel well into range of the ideological cannons of Otto Bauer and the left wing of the social democrats, but in 1920, Seipel still had the luxury of backing compromise. He ended the article by explaining that coalition government and compromise was necessary to finally bringing the constitution to the table, "To finish the constitution in good time is the aim and meaning of coalition politics. For this reason, we have upheld the coalition with great sacrifice, we have accepted some things and tolerated other things—which from our party's standpoint were difficult to do; we unceasingly with all our energy have defended what the general uncertainties would have made worse, so that we could finally give our state a constitution."[35] His article responds to the impatience, especially in the Christian-social dominated provinces, with the lack of a constitution. Although Seipel expresses sympathy with the general tenor of impatience, his article argues that a constitution will be worth the political compromises, and ultimately, the wait. This impatience had resulted in a series of conferences in which all the provinces gathered to discuss constitutional issues and the framework of the Austrian state.[36] Once again, Seipel does his part to keep the political right together and in a working pact with the social democrats.

Eventually, the constitution emerged, but not before the coalition itself crumbled on 10 June 1920. A caretaker government under the chancellorship of Michael Mayr took over the government, which was staffed with ministers from all the parties. Its task was to finish the constitution and hold the ship of state together until new elections in October of that same year. In the meantime, the constitutional committee had selected from its own membership a smaller, seven-man subcommittee to hammer out the details of the constitution. Once again, Bauer was selected to chair the body and Seipel selected as vice-chairman. The subcommittee met during the summer of 1920, but eventually ground to a halt over questions of school oversight and finances. These questions revolved around the fundamental relationships between the federal government and the provinces as well as the church and the state and had to be negotiated between the parties themselves.[37] The constitutional scholar Felix Eramacora reports that the

34. Confer what August M. Knoll calls Seipel's third "capitalist" course: Knoll, *Von Seipel zu Dollfuß, 9–10.*

35. Ignaz Seipel, "Heraus," 86.

36. The provincial conferences began in early 1920. See the *Neue Freie Presse's* [hereafter NFP] of the provincial conference in Salzburg: NFP (16 Feb. 1920), 2-3.

37. Felix Ermacora, *Quellen zum Österreichischen Verfassungsrecht (1920): Die Protokolle des Unterausschusses des Verfassungsausschusses samt Verfassungsentwürfen*, Mitteilungen des Österreichischen Staatsarchivs 8 (Vienna: Berger, 1967), 17–21.

party lines were so firmly drawn on these questions, that negotiations nearly fell apart.[38] But by the end of September, with the constitutional subcommittee working again, Seipel reported to the National Assembly that the document was finished on the 29th. On the same day, Seipel and Bauer together submitted the proposal that the "National Assembly may put to vote the attached draft of a law, which establishes the Austrian Republic as a federal state (*Bundesverfassungsgesetz.*)"[39]

Seipel's work in the early years of the republic to put the state on firm footing gave Austria a different *Entstehungsgeschichte*—a different birth narrative—than it might have had otherwise. Unlike Czechoslovakia, which founded itself as a response to the old Monarchy, which it rejected as authoritarian, militaristic, and dominated by Germans, Austria was first saddled with the status of a remnant state by the *Entente.*[40] And while some in Austria either wanted to shake loose from the past or embrace the German state instead of facing the world as a small "remnant," Ignaz Seipel rather postulated that the new republic allowed Austria's Germans to build on their past and their traditions, to make the state democratic, Christian, and stable. Not only did Seipel continue to have ties to the last emperor of the monarchy, Charles I, but he argued for continuities between the small Austrian republic and the old Austrian empire—not least of which was the appropriation of the 1867 fundamental articles on citizens' rights which were carried over into the 1920 constitution. In essence, because of Seipel, the history of Austria is different than that of its neighbors: Austria could not reject its imperial past at St. Germain, and it would not under Seipel. But, as we shall see, Seipel would not accept a republic that changed little, either.

The Party Politician

With the constitution settled and the Austrian Republic established, Seipel did not simply settle back into Church life. He became the head of the Christian Social Party in June 1921, months after it had overtaken the

38. Ibid., 20.

39. The report of the Constitutional Subcommittee is reprinted in Ibid., 547–57. The presentation to the National Assembly can be found in *SPdKN*, Sitzung 100 (29 Sept. 1920), 3375-85.

40. See, for example, the discussion of Czechoslovak state identity in opposition to the Habsburg Monarchy as militaristic, German, and authoritarian in Martin Zückert, "Antimilitarismus und soldatische Resistenz: Politischer Protest und armeefeindliches Verhalten in der tschechischen Gesellschaft bis 1918," in *Glanz - Gewalt - Gehorsam: Militär und Gesellschaft in der Habsburgermonarchie (1800 bis 1918)*, Frieden und Krieg. Beiträge zur historischen Friedensforschung 18 (Essen: Klartext, 2011), 199-218.

social democrats as the largest party in Austria. And after forging a cabinet of civil servants which was to be led by the chief of Vienna's police, Johannes Schober, Seipel himself took the reins of government nearly a year later, on 25 May 1922. It is useful to take a moment to reflect on the differences in Seipel's life between 1917, when he still was a Professor of Moral Theology in Salzburg, and 1922, when he was not only the head of a political party, but of the government. Between 1917 and 1922, Seipel's rise in the party and in Austrian politics paralleled a concomitant decline in the Austrian State. Seipel's quality as a priest, and moreover his calm determination, allowed him to collect and direct the trust of Austria's conservatives in these five years filled with crisis. But while Seipel had hitherto always been the leading voice of many, up until 1922 he had not been the leader with ultimate responsibility for both the party and the state. Now that he was, his style became more combative and his opponents, especially Bauer, more fierce. But still, in the first half of the decade Seipel still managed to focus his policies on establishing, strengthening, and founding the Austrian Republic. Moreover, he did this in the midst of (and no doubt, with the help of) a general financial crisis.

Seipel's first stint as the Federal Chancellor lasted from 25 May 1922 through 7 November 1924—898 days. From the beginning, Seipel's term in office was dominated by Austria's financial crisis. Hunger and a lack of coal did not subside with the end of the war. Rather, by 1922 it became less clear that Austria would receive the help it needed from outside. Its government had been running huge deficits and was becoming increasingly unable to buy coal or foodstuffs on the world market. Sir Arthur Salter, the head of the economic and financial section of the League of Nations, observed in a 1924 article in *Foreign Affairs* that, "Austria lived—but pitifully and precariously. She froze in winter, and a larger part of her population was hungry throughout the year. Her middle class was almost destroyed, and it was a common sight to see scientists or historians of European reputation ill-clad or obviously starved. The mortality was high and, among children, terrible."[41] Seipel took over the government in a clear crisis and it was equally clear that a determined policy and direction was needed to steer Austria out of it. As the *Neues Wiener Tagblatt* characterized this need on Seipel's ascension to the chancellorship, "A ministry with a strong hand is being formed behind the curtains. [...] A simple change in ministers without a fundamental change in the system would be worthless."[42] What Seipel

41. Sir Arthur Salter, "The Reconstruction of Austria," *Foreign Affairs 2, no. 4* (June 15, 1924): 631.
42. Quoted in Rennhofer, *Ignaz Seipel, 283–84.*

showed of himself in the years between 1922 and 1924 was an aptitude for international politics that was hitherto unobservable. Moreover, as he sought to stabilize the Austrian currency, reduce the size of the government and governmental agencies, and stabilize the state budget, Seipel moved directly into the crosshairs of the social democrats. As the rhetoric against Seipel and his role as a priest intensified, so did Seipel's eagerness to defeat the social democrats, not only at the ballot box but in parliamentary debates and at the negotiating table. Seipel the clever prelate had emerged; but Seipel the pragmatic compromiser had left the stage.

I have argued in an earlier volume of *Contemporary Austrian Studies* that Seipel's handling of the financial crisis was an important founding moment for the Austrian Republic, in which Seipel was able to cashier many of the state's civil servants while, at the same time, using the opportunity to stabilize the Austrian currency and Austria's economic viability.[43] Focusing instead here on Seipel the person, we can observe that he quickly learned to play the game of international politics. Faced with hyperinflation and most of Austria's assets already mortgaged to cover earlier loans, Seipel embarked on an international campaign to seek assistance. Highlighting Austria's financial problems not only as a humanitarian case but as a state that was near falling apart, Seipel pulled on the heartstrings of some and worried others with an impending upset in the balance of power in central Europe. By the end of the summer in 1922, the governments of Europe referred the matter to the League of Nations, where helping Austria became a matter of its own prestige. Seipel's own international reputation also grew by leaps and bounds through the process. On 6 September 1922, Seipel addressed the General Assembly of the League of Nations in his black cassock. His appeal for help was also marked by a challenge to the League to live up to its humanitarian responsibilities. Seipel the priest impressed the League delegates so much that they did not see Seipel the politician in front of them—and so Austria quickly became an important test case for the League itself. By October, Seipel's government had negotiated a series of three protocols with the governments of Great Britain, France, Italy, and Czechoslovakia, which provided 650 million gold crowns—enough to cover Austria's budget over two years.[44]

43. John Deak, "Dismantling Empire: Ignaz Seipel and Austria's Financial Crisis, 1922-1925," in *From Empire to Republic: Post-World War I Austria*, Contemporary Austrian Studies vol. XIX, eds. Günter Bischof, Fritz Plasser, and Peter Berger (New Orleans: UNO Press, 2010), 123-41.

44. For more detail on the negotiations and the terms of the Geneva Protocols, see Ladner, *Seipel als Überwinder der Staatskrise*, 123–60; Deak, "Dismantling Empire," 135–38.

The Geneva Protocols, as they came to be called, established a government program of austerity and a currency program that gave the right of note to an independent bank set up by the League. Moreover, the League appointed a commissioner to oversee the government's new austerity program, which entailed not only price hikes by the state monopolies but also the planned cashiering of 100,000 civil servants. When Seipel returned to Vienna following the negotiations with the League, the social democrats criticized him furiously for abandoning a program of self-help and, more appropriately, for not including all the parties in the negotiations. To the social democrats, Seipel had betrayed his country. Karl Renner, in measured tones that were aided by thirty-years of hindsight, remarked in his memoirs that Seipel's Geneva Protocols "sacrificed the independence of the country," they "made victims of the wide masses of the working class and wage earners with the burden of the reconstruction," and finally they "delivered the financial interests of the land into the hands of international finance capitalism." Naturally, then, the social democrats "opened a passionate campaign against both Seipel's person and his program."[45] Thirty years before, Renner claimed in parliament that a foreign commissioner to oversee the state budget was a new form of defeat for Austria's independence and parliamentary democracy.[46] After another priest, longstanding representative from Upper Austria Johann Hauser, defended Seipel's program, Karl Seitz, now a veteran member of the social democratic delegation in parliament, ridiculed the priests for preaching love and forgiveness, while at the same time advocating the "unforgivable sin" of high treason against their country.[47] The fierce debate over the Geneva Protocols ushered in a personal *Kulturkampf* in Austrian politics, one that would envelope Seipel and his social democratic adversaries for the next ten years.

Moreover, this personal *Kulturkampf* had real political consequences. As the government under Seipel followed through on many of its reforms, the conflict intensified between Seipel and the Christian socials, on the one side, and the social democrats on the other. The SPÖ started a public campaign in early 1923 that called for working-class Catholics to leave the Church—a move that would push Seipel into even sterner opposition to the socialists. As von Klemperer notes of this time in Seipel's career,

45. Renner, *Österreich*, 57.

46. *Stenographisches Protokoll des Nationalrates der Republik Österreich* [hereafter SPNR], III. Session, Sitzung 138 (12 Oct. 1922), 4414.

47. SPNR, III. Session, Sitzung 138 (12 Oct. 1922), 4433. See also Klemperer, *Ignaz Seipel*, 207–208.

the priest and politician "stopped seeing [social democracy] in terms of accommodation, and regarded it more and more, in all its doctrinarism, as anti-Church."[48] Political polarization became coupled with violence. On 1 June 1924, Karl Jaworek fired two shots from a pistol at Seipel's chest at close range. One bullet penetrated his chest on the right side and struck his lung. Rushed to a hospital, Seipel suffered from complications. The bullet stayed lodged in his chest and Seipel contracted an infection severe enough that he was administered last rites.[49]

What would have happened had Seipel died in the hospital in 1924? His legacy would have been less ambivalent than it is and quite possibly he would not be seen as the great enemy of social democracy in the First Republic. By 1924, Chancellor Seipel had—in the span of only seven years—risen to fantastic prominence in the Christian Social Party. He had participated in all of the events that put Austria on a path toward independence and self-sufficiency: the collapse of the Monarchy, the acceptance of the republican state, the passage of the Treaty of St. Germain, the drafting of the constitution, and the negotiation and implementation of the reconstruction of Austria through the Geneva Protocols. Seipel could—if Austrian historiography believed at all in heroes—be one of the founding fathers of the republic.

Of course, the lingering problem that Ignaz Seipel presents, and one that cannot be avoided, is his increasing alienation from parliamentary democracy. Seipel indeed survived the attempt on his life in 1924 and recovered slowly. By November 1924, Seipel had resigned as chancellor and left the formation of a new government in the hands of Rudolf Ramek, a Christian social from Salzburg. However, Seipel did not retreat into Church life but stayed on as head of the Christian Social Party. Additionally, he traveled throughout Europe and to North America, speaking as a priest and the former chancellor of Austria on Austria's situation and the problems endemic to postwar European politics. By October 1926, with the Christian Social Party again asking him to take the reins of government, Seipel returned as chancellor.

Over the next three years, Seipel's chancellorship would be marked by further political polarization and stalemate. Seipel formed a unity government, consisting of all the non-Marxist factions after parliamentary elections in April 1927. Less than three months later a crowd stormed the Palace of Justice on Vienna's Schmerlingplatz, in response to the acquittal of three members of the right-wing *Frontkämpfervereinigung*, who had

48. Ibid., 229–31, 231.
49. Rennhofer, *Ignaz Seipel*, 402–403.

been accused of murdering a forty-year old and his eight-year old son in Schattendorf. The crowd threw government files into the street, where they were set on fire. Soon the palace itself was set ablaze. Other fires were set in the city as well, including the editorial offices of the Christian social newspaper, *Die Reichspost.*[50] The police chief and former Federal Chancellor Johannes Schober responded by arming his police with carbines, which were then used with deadly effect against the crowd. The social democratic leadership, including Otto Bauer and Karl Seitz, appealed to Seipel to make concessions to the working classes to keep the bloodshed from spreading. But Seipel refused. In the end over ninety people died, and hundreds were seriously wounded.

While Bauer and Seitz tried to extend olive branches to Seipel and work with him to calm the situation—even offering coalition partnership—Seipel refused. He was determined not to bring peace but to politically defeat his rivals. One can get a sense of this new Seipel from the diaries of Joseph Redlich, who had served as Finance Minister in the last imperial cabinet with Seipel in 1918. Redlich had, in the meantime, taken up a professorship at Harvard University, but returning to Austria during the summer break in 1927, he met with Seipel for almost two hours in the Federal Chancellery three weeks after the riots and their brutal suppression. For Redlich, Seipel recounted the events of the July riots and the burning of the Palace of Justice and, especially, his meetings with Bauer and Seitz. Seipel relished his role as passive-aggressor, in which he encouraged the social democrats to follow their logic to the bitter end, "There is only one thing left to do," he said to Seitz and Bauer, "You really have to have a revolution!"[51] A few days earlier in parliament, on 26 July, Seipel addressed the violence which had broken out between the workers and the city police. He called the workers' actions a revolution and spoke on behalf of a "wounded republic" admonishing her ungrateful children. Toward the social democrats, Seipel accused the leadership of wasting their parliamentary authority in the eyes of the people and now using it to try to protect persons guilty of revolution. Toward the end of his speech he thundered at parliament, "Do not demand that parliament and the government show clemency toward the victims and the guilty of these fateful days, but which would be cruel to the wounded republic. Demand nothing, which would appear as a free pass for those

50. For a summary of the events surrounding the riots in Vienna in the middle of July 1927, see *NFP,* 18 July 1927 (evening edition).

51. Josef Redlich, *Schicksalsjahre Österreichs: Die Erinnerungen und Tagebücher Josef Redlichs 1869-1936*, eds. Fritz Fellner and Doris Corradini, 2nd ed., Veröffentlichungen der Kommission für neuere Geschichte Österreichs 105 (Vienna: Böhlau, 2011), ii, 649–52, 650.

who rose up."[52] Seipel the moral theologian had now become Seipel the politician. At the same time, he became the "prelate without mercy."

In this speech, the Chancellor hinted at his increasing impatience with parliamentary democracy. He blamed parliament for the workers' revolt, saying that parliament had "piece by piece, for months now, forfeited its authority, and bears responsibility" for allowing the appearance to come forward that its members do not want democracy itself.[53] But Seipel, in end effect, can be held equally guilty of the same accusation. The endless ideological confrontation with the social democrats, the burning of the Palace of Justice, and the prospect of never being able to secure outright victories in Austrian parliament, led the prelate into an intellectual search for alternative political courses. "True democracy," reminiscent of Platonic forms, became Seipel's catchphrase for a solution to Austria's parliamentary and social crises. Such thinking, a longing for a way out of the political morass, led the man to completely forget his early course of compromise and pragmatism, his commitment to living in the world.[54] As Seipel drew himself closer and closer to the *Heimwehr*, his search for a better, higher, and truer democracy latched onto this organ's own militant anti-Marxism and the physical presence of armed paramilitarism.

Seipel's Afterlife

Seipel resigned on 3 April 1929, roughly two-and-one-half years after he had taken up the chancellorship for a second time. He longed to leave politics, his health was failing, and, yet, he was only fifty-two. A year later, he would resign the chairmanship of the Christian Social Party. But, though he had taken the major steps away from politics, Seipel could not help but turn around to watch the political arena. Another stint as foreign minister followed at the end of 1930; Seipel stood for election as Federal President in 1931—and lost.

On 2 August 1932, Ignaz Seipel died, two-and-a-half months after Pius XI's encyclical, *Quadragesimo Anno.* On 5 August, his funeral train wound its way through the streets of Vienna, between St. Stephen's, the Chancellery, and Parliament—between the edifices that represented Seipel's two vocations. He was buried in Vienna's Central Cemetery—but only

52. SPNR, V. Session, Sitzung 7 (26 July 1927), 133.

53. Ibid.

54. See for instance, Seipel's speech held in 1928 at a meeting of the Graz chapter of the Christian Social Party, "Der Ruf nach echter Demokratie," printed in Ignaz Seipel, *Der Kampf um die österreichische Verfassung* (Vienna: Wilhelm Braumüller, 1930), 130–35.

rested there two years before his body was removed and interred alongside the body of Engelbert Dollfuß—the successor of Seipel as the head of political Catholicism in Austria and the architect of Austria's authoritarian, clerical-corporatist state. Together they rested as priest and martyr in the "Chancellors' Church"—in the Seipel-Dollfuß Church in Vienna's fifteenth district.[55] The National Socialists, after the annexation of Austria in 1938, took Seipel's remains back to the Central Cemetery. The three burials of Ignaz Seipel represent a real problem in Austrian historiography concerning Seipel's political legacy for the Austrian Republic. Where do his bones belong? With the graves of the Republic or with Engelbert Dollfuß and Austrofascism?

While Seipel's bones still rest in the Central Cemetery among the *Ehrengräber*, this question of Seipel's legacy and where his bones should lie have not been definitely put to rest. The Dollfuß-Schuschnigg regime had appropriated Seipel as their "founding father" as well. In August Maria Knoll's essay, quoted at the beginning of this article, Knoll asked the question, "What is Seipel's legacy?" Knoll would find his answer in Dollfuß himself. Knoll—in 1934—saw Dollfuß as Seipel's "political heir and viceroy." He continued, "in religion, in both statesmen's conceptions of fatherland, state and society, lie continuities from Seipel to Dollfuß."[56] For the Catholic-conservative camp in Austria, Seipel was a connection to Godliness, a connection that was exploited in service of a fascist regime. And though he had started on the intellectual and political path to authoritarianism himself, it was his bones—and not the man himself—that were carried there.

Otto Bauer, Seipel's opponent in many debates and the ever-present bogeyman in Seipel's political tactics and plans, honored Seipel with a moving portrait in print.[57] Calling Seipel the "by far most significant man and the only statesmen of European caliber whom the bourgeois parties have produced," Bauer recognized before the readers in the *Arbeiter-Zeitung* Seipel's strength, self-discipline, his energy, and mental acuity, which was brought to bear in "his struggle against us." But Bauer, ready to concede to the dead what he did not concede to the living, remarked that Seipel's fight against the working class "undoubtedly was led with honest inner conviction—he was as convinced of the justice of his cause as we are of

55. For a recent article on the sacralization of Dollfuß, see Lucile Dreidemy, "Austrofaschismus: Totenkult für einen Diktator," *Die Zeit*, 21 July 2011, sec. Geschichte, <http://www.zeit.de/2011/30/A-Engelbert-Dollfuss> (1 Jan. 2012).

56. Knoll, *Von Seipel zu Dollfuß*, 11, 13.

57. Otto Bauer, "Ignaz Seipel," in *Werkausgabe*, vol. 7 (Vienna: Europa Verlag, 1979), 466–70. Originally published in *Arbeiter-Zeitung*, 3 August 1932.

the justice of our own." But Bauer also recognized that Seipel had played a major role in the foundation of the Republic—a republic that he had also sought to change toward the end of his life. As Bauer recognized in Seipel a figure that, in the defense of his Church, moved from "opposition to Socialism, into passionate hatred" for it, Bauer forgot to mention the active role his party and he himself had in fostering such hatred.

But more than this, Bauer's own omissions have been superseded by new ones. Ignaz Seipel's life tells us much about the failures and the challenges of understanding the Austrian First Republic. Seipel was in many ways the founding father of the Austrian Republic. But his increasing impatience with parliamentary democracy, his growing hatred for socialism, and his willingness to embrace or use anti-democratic movements (including the National Socialists) made him into the spiritual father of Austrian clerical-fascism. Seipel is hard to reconcile with the needs of the present. But in the end, we have to ask ourselves, what is history (and thus biography) for? To judge the past, or to understand it? If our goal is to judge, we can calmly put Seipel into the category of saint or devil. If our goal is to understand, then we must accept Seipel in all his ambition, complexity, goodness, and failures, and make him relevant in our understandings of the present.

Otto Bauer (1881-1938)

Politician and Public Intellectual

Ernst Hanisch[1]

The Return of Biography

During the rise of structural and social history in the 1960s, scholars in German-speaking countries threw biography into the junk pile. Unlike their Anglo-Saxon colleagues, researchers could not boost their reputations as scholars by publishing biographies. The end of the 20th century brought a change, and biography advanced to become the "secret center" of cultural studies.[2] But this was not the old type of biography. Much of it derived inspiration from the ideas of post-structuralism and the "linguistic turn," at least in some form. Pierre Bourdieu's warning of the "biographical illusion" graced almost every introduction; the term implies that it is not possible to recreate a simple identity of a biological individual, who played a variety of different roles, without analyzing the relationship between these roles.[3]

In the case of the adult Otto Bauer, we are talking about the following social roles: author, teacher in a workers' school, secretary of the Social-Democratic parliamentary party, an officer in the Reserves, a soldier in 1914, prisoner of war in Siberia shortly thereafter; the mastermind of the party's left-wing in 1917; party leader and "minister," parliamentarian, journalist and theoretician, leading member of the "International"; a political emigrant in 1934 and then a Jewish emigrant in 1938.[4] Nevertheless, the person Otto Bauer is undeniably an individual. There are constants in his life: his support of Marxist Socialism, which began when he was a student, accompanied him for his entire life. The same is true for his role as mediator, which he had learned to perform in his immediate family before he extended it to the Social Democratic Party and the large family of other socialists. Although

---

1. We thank Inge Fink, Department of English, University of New Orleans, for translating this text from German to English.

2. Bernhard Fetz, "Die vielen Leben der Biographie: Interdisziplinäre Aspekte einer Theorie der Biographie," in *Die Biographie – Zur Grundlegung ihrer Theorie*, ed. Bernhard Fetz (Berlin: Walter Gruyter, 2009), 5, Hans Erich Bödeker, "Biographie. Annäherung an den gegenwärtigen Forschungs- und Diskussionsstand," in *Biographie schreiben*, ed. Hans Erich Bödeker (Göttingen: Wallstein, 2003), 11-63.

3. Pierre Bourdieu, "Die biographische Illusion," *Bios: Zeitschrift für Biographieforschung und Oral History* 3, no. 1(1990): 75-81.

4. Ernst Hanisch, *Der große Illusionist: Otto Bauer 1881-1938* (Vienna: Böhlau 2011).

Otto Bauer, 1929. ©Verein für Geschichte der Arbeiterbewegung, Vienna

he fought passionately for peace, the role of soldier shaped his modus operandi. Translated into the rhetoric of class warfare, military metaphors determined the mature politician's language.

Every biography has to bridge the dialectical opposition of individual and the context of a specific historical period. In general terms, this historical context is not a prison that confines people; as agents they still have a certain room for action. Leading politicians have more room for action than small party members. However, they are also capable of making bigger mistakes. Putting a biography in context thus means considering the conditions as well as the results and the side effects of a politician's actions.

It is easier to do this in retrospect, but one runs the risk of sounding like a self-righteous know-it-all.

The legacy of Otto Bauer's work consists of more than ten-thousand printed and published pages. How is a historian to interpret these texts? First, he must distinguish between the different types of texts and their respective audiences: speeches delivered at party congresses and other meetings, speeches given in parliament, propaganda leaflets, scholarly essays in "The Fight" (*Der Kampf*), a journal of theory, scholarly books, etc. The Cambridge School's concept of "intellectual history" helps in this regard. Quentin Skinner, one of the founders, gives three tips for interpreting a text: First, the interpreter must attempt to understand the meaning, the sense of a historical text. This is often much more difficult than a naïve understanding of the text leads us to believe. Second, he must include the discursive context, i.e. the contemporary discussion. Third, he has to ask what the author wants to accomplish with his argument, which position he attacks, defends, or revises.[5] A text can be a mighty sword. For example, the Linz Program (*Linzer Programm*) of 1926, written by Bauer, had a far-reaching influence on Austrian politics.

Skinner also refers to the pernicious habit of scholars of intellectual history to find coherence in different kinds of texts.[6] However, texts are written in a specific historical situation and for a specific situation. In Otto Bauer, we find that a later statement interprets a situation differently from an earlier statement. Now, which one is true? The creation of myths is another danger of historical textual analysis. Texts written before and after February of 1934 contribute to the creation of myths about the struggles, and are interpreted differently by Social Democrats after 1945. If words are deeds, the historian must pay attention to the effects of these words: How do they affect their own people? How do they affect political opponents? Last but not least, texts can acquire meaning that the author never intended. Especially complex texts contain a "surplus," which can expand beyond the author's intention. The Linz Program, again, serves as an example of this.[7]

The Jew

Otto Bauer was born on September 5, 1881 into a liberal, assimilated Jewish family of business people. His father's textile factories in Bohemia employed 800 workers. Born a Jew, Bauer remained a part of the Jewish

5. Quentin Skinner, *Visionen des Politischen* (Frankfurt/M: Suhrkamp, 2009), 79-81.
6. Ibid., 35-41.
7. Ibid., 72-76.

cultural community all of his life. This was rather unusual for a leading Marxist. But he was a non-religious Jew who still showed respect for all religions, even the Catholics. How can this be? One explanation lies in the anti-Semitic political culture in Austria, which Bauer opposed. Speaking to Ernst Fischer, he is said to have explained his commitment to Judaism in the following way: "You cannot understand this because nobody has ever mumbled 'damn Jew' behind your back."[8] Julius Raab, the "father of the Austrian State Treaty," publically shouted at him during a 1930 controversy, "A cheeky bastard you are, a cheeky damn Jew!"[9]

As a Marxist, however, Bauer expected the dissolution of traditional Judaism in the course of modernization. He wrote critical sentences about Jews, which would be rated as "anti-Semitic" today. But such a textual interpretation would be ahistorical. When Bauer heavily criticized Jewish capitalists, he meant the capitalists, not the Jews. Anti-Semitic stereotypes aim at all Jews. A latent anti-Semitism existed, without doubt, in the workers' movement.[10] It was directed against the many Jewish intellectuals in the party. This may have been one of the reasons why Bauer never strove to be the official chair of the party. However, unlike other parties, the Social Democrats never used anti-Semitic sentiments for their own political purposes.

Like many Jewish intellectuals in Austria, Bauer believed the German culture to be superior to all others. German culture, Goethe and Marx, triggered an emotional exuberance in him, the kind one otherwise rarely saw in the thinker who rarely showed emotion. This "German desire" lay at the base of his politics of annexation in 1918/19 and his justification of the annexation of Austria in 1938. Nevertheless, he was never a nationalist but always an internationalist.

What identity, then, did Otto Bauer have? First and foremost, he considered himself an international Social Democrat. He had a leading position in the Socialist International and was in constant communication with the party leaders of all European countries. A multi-lingual intellectual who had learned Russian in Siberia, he worked closely together with the emigrated Menschewiki. Being a German-Austrian constituted the second level of his identity. Until October 1918, he believed in the community of the people inhabiting the area of the Habsburg monarchy. His Jewish

8. Ernst Fischer, *Erinnerungen und Reflexionen* (Reinbek: Rowohlt, 1969), 152.

9. Stenographische Protokolle der 138. Sitzung des Nationalrates der Republik Österreich, 3. Gesetzperiode, 11.Juli 1930, 3837.

10. Robert S. Wistrich, *Socialism and the Jews: The Dilemma of Assimilation in Germany and Austria – Hungary* (London: Oxford Press, 1982).

identity came in only third, but it grew stronger with the advance of National Socialism. After Germany annexed Austria in 1938, he appealed passionately to the "conscience of the world," urging his audience to take in Jews who had emigrated or had been driven out of their homes. As an experienced politician, he knew that his appeal would not have much of a chance: "Nevertheless, it is our duty to help the latest victims of fascism and appeal to the conscience of the world time and time again.[11]

The Marxist
With Marx Beyond Marx

Otto Bauer started to read Marx when he was only a student. Later, he would talk about his "awakening": Full of curiosity he reached for Marx's works. Then came the disappointment with the difficult theoretical style of the *Kapital*, but also the consternation about the development of suffering mankind under capitalism (the world of the father), the emotional outrage, and the ethical decision to fight capitalism. But Karl Marx did not just stir his emotions. The "exact science" of Marxism satisfied his intellect and led him to theory.[12] The grand, passionate belief in Socialism and the scientific analysis of the apparent laws of history would, from now on, determine his entire life. As a theoretician, he joined the Austrian workers' movement in order to serve its cause.

Besides "the mathematical law of movement of history," which Marx is said to have discovered, he was fascinated with the "Marxist method." However, creative Marxism cannot become a formula, as in the Marxist orthodoxy of Communism, but it has to be applied as a method to ever-new work areas: "Marx's method leads beyond Marx's theses; Marx will conquer Marx."[13] In fact, the "Austro-Marxism" of the years before World War I, when Bauer was a crucial figure in the movement, distinguished itself by being open toward other contemporary social sciences.

Marxist theory strove toward political practice; it claims that pure theory is empty and that political practice without theory leads to blind pragmatism. This is how Bauer saw the dialectic of theory and practice: The task of theory is to collect, sort, and analyze experience. In addition, theory must reach the masses; it must be made popular and thus simpler. Bauer

---

11. Otto Bauer, "Ich appelliere an das Gewissen der Welt," *New Chronicle*, London, 5 July 1938. Reprinted in: Otto Bauer, *Werkausgabe* (Vienna: Europaverlag, 1975-1980) 7: 781, 784.

12. Otto Bauer, "Die Geschichte eines Buches," in *Die Neue Zeit* (1908), *Werkausgabe*, 7:927-935.

13. Otto Bauer, "Marx als Mahnung," in *Der Kampf* 16 (1923), *Werkausgabe*, 9:51.

thought it was much more important to make theory popular through pamphlets, speeches, and gatherings than to participate in noisy action: "Only theory can be the conscience of the proletarian masses; only theory can free us from the confusing influence of the bourgeois environment; only theory picks us up when the manifold experiences of the day have made us timid."[14] However, theory must prove its mettle in the course of political practice: in the struggle for power in the state, in the meetings, in the electoral movements, in parliament.

Vision of Socialism

For Bauer, Socialism was the "biggest thing we know."[15] After the crimes of Stalinism, after the break-down of "Real Socialism" (*Realsozialismus*) it is difficult to understand this belief. When Bauer adopted this philosophy during the 1890s, the vision of socialism still held an innocent charm. Its deepest emotional base lay in the desire for justice, an honorable, noble desire. And this desire could not be distracted by the formation of the Soviet Union.

Socialism tended to locate transcendence not in the hereafter but the here and now. Already in his great early opus *The Question of Nationalities and Social Democracy* (*Die Nationalitätenfrage*), Bauer specifies this (cultural) vision of socialism. He proceeds from the assumption that the working class will by and by constitute the majority of the population and thus democratically assert its desires. A socialist society will then increase the number of productive workers. Every healthy adult must work because property will no longer entitle anybody to the labor of others. His second basic assumption is that in a socialist society, everybody has a productive job. Third, only a socialist society can guarantee the full use of modern technology. And lastly, the tremendous waste of human labor in capitalism will stop because a socialist system will distribute the labor rationally among different branches of production through "central management."[16]

The core of his vision, however, consists in the creation of a "new human being." This new human differs from the "indulging idlers" and the "cultureless workers" of the last millennium. The new human will carry the naiveté of the people in his bosom like the memory of class warfare,

14. Otto Bauer, "Das Finanzkapital," in *Der Kampf* 3 (1910), *Werkausgabe*, 8:387.

15. Otto Bauer, "Acht Monate auswärtiger Politik," (Vienna: Volksbuchhandlung 1919), *Werkausgabe*, 2:189.

16. Otto Bauer, "Die Nationalitätenfrage und die Sozialdemokratie," (Vienna: Verlag der Wiener Volksbuchhandlung 1907), *Werkausgabe*, 1:156-161.

which will now end. He will create new forms of culture and new symbols. Still, he will be the heir of all previous cultures. "Whatever humans have thought and created, written and sung, now becomes the inheritance of the masses."[17]

Seen from our perspective, this vision has been falsified in almost every point by "Real Socialism." However, until 1934, Bauer's vision always depended on the structure of a democracy.

The Ambivalent Attitude Toward Communism

Bauer had been criticizing and fighting against the Communists during the First Republic, but he acknowledged the Soviet Union as an important part of the socialist family. However, he decidedly rejected its alleged dictatorship of the proletariat and kept hoping for a democratization of the Soviet Union.

In a controversy on 21 October 1932, Engelbert Dollfuß called Bauer a "Bolshevik."[18] Bauer reacted by writing an objective article in the party's newspaper, which contained the following deeply felt, monumental sentence: "What divides me from Bolshevism is much more important than all tactical considerations; it is something fundamental, something that is rooted in my understanding of human culture: my appreciation of the irreplaceable value of individual intellectual freedom."[19] This division also motivated his criticism of Stalinism.

However, in exile after the defeat of the struggles of February 1934, he shared the opinion of many intellectuals that democracy was exhausted, that it had run out of great ideas, that it was boring. He started to flirt with the dictatorship of the proletariat. This was not a completely new idea, as can be seen in the Linz Program of 1926. However, in the party program of the illegal Austrian "Revolutionary Socialist" party, Bauer pushed through the demand for a temporary "dictatorship of the proletariat," which was later replaced by the idea of a "socialist democracy." The same confusing dialectical play of language between dictatorship and socialist democracy informed his attitude toward the Soviet Union.

After the victory of National Socialism in Germany, Bauer considered World War II inevitable. If Germany wins, Europe will turn fascist; if the Soviet Union wins, Europe will become socialist. He thus thought it was

17. Ibid., 164.

18. Stenographische Protokolle, 21 Oct. 1932, 2677

19. Otto Bauer, "Wir Bolschewiken. Eine Antwort an Dollfuß," in *Arbeiter-Zeitung*, 23 Oct. 1932, *Werkausgabe*, 7:486-87.

necessary to support the Soviet Union despite Stalin. (Was the attitude of the Western Allies during the war that much different?) His criticism persisted; he regretted the loss of individual freedom and reminded his audience of the Kulaks, who had been "driven from house and home, dragged off to the forests of the far North to perform hard labor, and who had starved and frozen to death as they built the Stalin canal."[20] However, his conviction clouded his judgment, as is evident in his calling the millions of casualties of "Stalin's terrorist dictatorship" inevitable and a historical necessity; it is evident in his song of praise for Stalin, whom he calls the man with the strongest nerves, with the greatest tenacity, with the most determined abilities—Stalin, "the most successful man of our time."[21]

Stalin's constitution of 1936 spurred Bauer's hopes for democratization. However, the beginning of the "Great Terror" (1937/38), the show trials of the old Communists, plunged Bauer into deep despair. He called these crimes an "appalling disaster" for world socialism: "But we do not want to become complicit for lack of civil courage to voice our convictions to those in power in the Kremlin."[22] He really did say this, but he always found arguments for "understanding" these crimes. He held on to his concept of "integral socialism," the unification of social democracy and a transformed Communism. His untimely death in 1938 spared him the shock of the Hitler-Stalin alliance of 1939.

The Intellectual

Bauer's fellow student and later fellow politician, Joseph Schumpeter, defined the intellectual through his critical relationship with the social system in which he lived. According to Schumpeter, his role is that of a disruptive factor.[23] In the typology of intellectuals, Otto Bauer represented the "politician-intellectual" who tried to combine theory and practice. In my opinion, he was the greatest politician-intellectual in 20th century Austria. He combined multilingualism, a curiosity for contemporary science, talent as a writer, a computer-like memory, and an inexhaustible zest for work with unique intellectual energy. However, his attachment to an ultimately inflexible theory often prevented pragmatic action as a politician.

20. Otto Bauer, "Zwischen zwei Weltkriegen? Die Krise der Weltwirtschaft, der Demokratie und des Sozialismus," (Bratislava: Eugen Prager 1936), *Werkausgabe*, 4:196.

21. Ernst Hanisch, *Der große Illusionist*, 348.

22. Otto Bauer, "Das Gericht über die roten Generale," in *Der Kampf* 4 (1937), *Werkausgabe*, 9:751.

23. Joseph A. Schumpeter, *Kapitalismus, Sozialismus und Demokratie* (München: Francke, 1972), 235-251.

The Question of Nationalities and Social Democracy

As an intellectual, Bauer created four masterpieces of social science. The book *The Question of Nationalities and Social Democracy* (*Die Nationalitätenfrage und die Sozialdemokratie*) established him, then in his mid-twenties, as a top-notch Marxist-Social-Democratic theoretician.[24] He had the courage to tackle the core problem of the Habsburg monarchy. However, his Marxist convictions forced him into a corset and repeatedly enticed him to make predictions that eventually proved false.

Naturally, many of Bauer's ideas seem antiquated now: his static, essentialist definition of a nation as a "community of people knit together by their common fate into a community of character;"[25] his attempt to project his idea of a nation onto the ancient Germanics; the distinction he makes between "history-less" and "historical" nations. However, he presented new ideas in his analytical combination of economic development, social structure, politics, and cultural experience—the depiction of all possible dimensions of a society.

However, the political volatility of his book lay in his suggestions for the renewal of Austria: he replaced the personal principle with the territorial principle. Nations should have cultural autonomy, which he expected would defuse nationalism. His ultimate goal was to save the multi-ethnic empire. For Bauer, there was only one choice: a state consisting of multiple nations or the collapse of the empire. In the long run, Bauer was thinking of the "United States of Europe," a model which he thought could only be realized under socialism.[26]

The Austrian Revolution

As a leading politician, Bauer was instrumental in founding and developing the republic. A short time later, Bauer the historian wrote the classical work of this era: *The Austrian Revolution* (*Die österreichische Revolution*).[27] The scope of his work transcended Austria to include central Europe and South-West Europe. He used Slavic sources because he spoke Czech as well as Russian. In contrast to the prevailing historical and positivist

---

24. Otto Bauer, "Die Nationalitätenfrage und die Sozialdemokratie," (Vienna: Verlag der Wiener Volksbuchhandlung 1907), Werkausgabe 1.Bd., 49-622.

25. Ibid., 194.

26. Ibid., 569.

27. Otto Bauer, "Die Österreichische Revolution" (Vienna: Volksbuchhandlung, 1923), *Werkausgabe*, 2:490-866.

Vienna School of writing history, his book did not solely focus on politics, but he included economics, social structure, and culture in its analysis. He presented the events of 1918-1920 as grand drama; its actors were not the "great men" but social classes, nations, parties, the masses. According to Bauer, the Austrian revolution lacked "heroic deeds," but its very poverty and powerlessness accounted for its strange grandeur. "Because poverty and powerlessness kept us from creating a strong revolutionary force, we had to rule the masses by intellectual means."[28]

Bauer supported his theoretical ideas with terse and precise social-historical analyses. For example, he said about the bourgeoisie: "Inflation impoverished the old Viennese patrician class, the leaders of the Austrian intelligentsia, and large parts of the middle and lower bourgeoisie. The latter had been the actual ruling class of the Habsburg monarchy. They had furnished the Habsburg monarchy with clerks and officers. They were the pillars of Austrian patriotism and the old Austrian tradition. For a century, they had carried on a specifically Austrian culture, Viennese literature, Viennese music, and Viennese theatre. They were the true losers of the war. It was their empire that collapsed in October of 1918. And with their empire they had also lost their wealth."[29]

Bauer distinguishes between three types of revolution: the national, the democratic, and the social. His analysis was a part of his theory that revolution will establish balance between the social powers, a theory that had a certain appeal. But it also provoked criticism. For one, if we think of social classes as compact units, we lose any internal differentiation. On the other hand, the constant talk about the "bourgeois republic" sounded too denunciatory after the end of the revolution. It went against the constitutional state, as Hans Kelsen pointed out. Democracy is not about rulers and subjects but about the conflict of interests, which has to be negotiated according to the rules of the constitutional state.[30]

The Struggle for Forest and Meadow

Bauer knew that other social groups outside of industrial regions needed to be addressed if democratic elections were to determine political power. The Social-Democrat Workers' Party (*Sozialdemokratische Arbeiterpartei*, SDAP) designed an agrarian program for this purpose. In preparation for this program, Bauer wrote his third master piece of social history: *The*

28. Ibid., 741.
29. Ibid., 757.
30. Ernst Hanisch, *Der große Illusionist*, 199.

Struggle for Forest and Meadow (*Der Kampf um Wald und Weide*)[31] in which he depicted Austrian history not as the history of the Habsburgs but as the history of the people. A complete stranger to the agrarian lifestyle, Bauer worked his way into the field in the shortest time possible. He conducted intensive research into sources and literature. He used a differentiated model of the class struggle as his guide: ruler versus landlords; ruler versus peasants; landlords versus peasants; peasants versus rural underclass. He examined this struggle not just from the top down but also from the bottom up. Again, he played up his scholarly strength in linking theoretical ideas with exact data analysis. His political purpose was to alleviate the peasants' fear of the "Reds." The Social Democrats never meant to dispossess peasants; they only wanted to socialize large rural properties.

The Problem of Rationalization

In the midst of the global economic crisis, Bauer wrote his fourth masterpiece, *Rationalization and Mis-Rationalization* (*Rationalisierung und Fehlrationalisierung*).[32] His book offered an answer to the crisis. He focused not on Central Europe but on the United States and the Soviet Union. He referred not so much to Marx and Engels but to F.W. Taylor, Henry Ford, and Herbert Hoover. He took the second industrial revolution at the beginning of the 20th century as his point of departure, considering new energy sources such as electricity and oil and new materials for industrial production. For Bauer, rationalization meant a scientific approach to labor distribution and social issues, an intensified work force, and scientific business managment.[33] This would also lead to a change in thinking. Bauer envisioned a new type of human being who thought rationally and was distanced from nature, a type embodied in the engineer, the hero of the era. A modern culture of mass consumerism developed simultaneously, at least in the USA. The automobile changed space and time; film and radio reduced the difference between town and country. Thanks to new media like radio and film, advertising made its way into every family.

While rationalization increased production, it created technological unemployment as well. This, to Bauer, was the deepest contradiction of capitalism: rampant unemployment, along with an increase in mental

31. Otto Bauer, "Der Kampf um Wald und Weide. Studien zur österreichischen Agrargeschichte und Agrarpolitik," (Vienna: Volksbuchhandlung, 1925), *Werkausgabe*, 3:32-248.
32. Otto Bauer, "Rationalisierung – Fehlrationalisierung," (Vienna: Volksbuchhandlung, 1931), *Werkausgabe*, 3:721-914.
33. Ibid., 825.

illness among assembly-line workers on one hand, and the expulsion of superfluous workers from the labor process on the other. While rationalization increased business profits, society would have to bear the cost through mis-rationalization.

Only socialism would bring about a higher form of rationalization: in the planning of economy and society. Bauer staked his hopes on the Soviet Union's first five-year-plan (1928/29-1932/33), on the gigantic, massive development of heavy industry. However, he saw the victims—the starved peasants, the poverty of the workers, the total control, the terror, the dictatorship. He found solace in history. In England, the early years of industrialization claimed many human victims as well, he argued, but in the future, once the emergency is over, the "terrorist dictatorship" could be dismantled. This was another of Bauer's grand illusions.

The Politician

Otto Bauer had a passion for politics. However, he lacked the politician's tenacious, determined will for power. As a politician, the bold theoretician was intimidated by power; he was hesitant—the Hamlet of Austrian politics. The intellectual was handicapped by the responsibility for the "mothers of the country." Bauer could be demagogical, of course, but in the end, uncertainty and thinking in terms of alternatives always prevailed. As much as he loved the revolutionary phase, as a person he was not a revolutionary, something Leo Trotzky identified correctly.[34] The result was a politics of on-the-one-hand/on-the-other-hand.

This difference comes out clearly in a comparison with the Christian Socialist Ignaz Seipel, his big political opponent. Both were the leading thinkers of their parties; both were intellectuals; both were theoreticians, Seipel a Catholic theologian, Bauer a Marxist. Both owed their careers to great institutions—Seipel to the Catholic Church, Bauer to the social democracy. Both were doctrinarians, but, in the end, Seipel emerged as the better, more flexible politician who had mastered the art of intrigue and the tactical gamesmanship necessary to attain power. Both led modest private lives, believed—albeit in different ways—in social justice, which was the goal of their politics.

They both respected each other even though they battled mercilessly in the public forum. Bauer expressed his respect for Seipel in his famous 1932 obituary.[35] They were on an equal footing with each other; Bauer

34. Ernst Hanisch, *Der große Illusionist*, 106.
35. Otto Bauer, "Ignaz Seipel," in *Arbeiter-Zeitung*, 3 Aug. 1932, *Werkausgabe* 7:466-470.

rather despised most of the political "two-bit lawyers" from the bourgeois camp. A new source provides insight into Seipel's attitude toward Bauer. Josef Redlich, politician and historian (who also taught at Harvard), made a note of a conversation in his well-known diary on August 6, 1927. After the dramatic events of July 15, 1927, the fire in the Vienna court house (*Justizpalast*), Seipel declared that Bauer did not intend this riot. According to Redlich, Seipel characterized Bauer as a person "for whose character and knowledge he had a lot of respect," as a party leader who lives exclusively in theories, even when political action is called for. Faced with any political action, he examines the theory "in his mind," measuring it against great historical revolutions of the past.[36] This was a fitting characterization of the leader of the Social-Democratic party.

Seipel's respect for Bauer probably dated back to the years 1918/19. Seipel, at first, led the Catholic Church successfully into the democratic republic; Bauer stabilized the parliamentary democracy against the attacks of radical leftists, his greatest political achievement without doubt. In those days, he saved Austria from civil war, from leftist terror and successive right-wing terror, if we consider the example of Hungary a realistic paradigm. He managed to prevent the splitting-up of the social democracy—as happened in many European countries—and reduced the Communists to a marginal political power. However, he paid the price of his revolutionary gesture in theory; the radical left called him a "social traitor" as a result of his ambivalent actions.

In addition to his accomplishments, Bauer made some serious mistakes, easily recognized in retrospect. His first mistake was his uncompromising politics of annexation when he was "Secretary of State." The real problem is not that he considered unification with Germany: the collapse of the Habsburg monarchy, the prospect of a small state, of life as a "poor peasant state," triggered the hope of unification with Germany in intellectuals and all political parties. The real problem was that Bauer, as the leader of Austrian foreign policy, had maneuvered himself into a general contradiction: On the one hand, he faced the Allied Forces as a beggar pleading for food and financial help; on the other he proclaimed unification with Germany, which, for France, was a completely unacceptable demand.[37]

An additional mistake was his rejection of the Geneva Convention of 1922. He railed against the treaty, calling it a "crime" and "treason"! Seipel never forgave him. The Social Democrats did not want to take responsibility for the treaty nor shoot it down. In fact, by supporting the

36. Fritz Fellner and Doris A. Corradini, eds., *Schicksalsjahre Österreichs: Die Erinnerungen und Tagebücher Josef Redlichs 1869-1936* (Vienna: Böhlau, 2011), 2:649-651.
37. Ernst Hanisch, *Der große Illusionist*, 157-161.

creation of a special cabinet (without the participation of parliament), the party indirectly supported the treaty.[38]

Bauer made his next political mistake when it came to writing the Linz Program of 1926.[39] Bauer was at the height of his influence in the Social-Democratic party—and he was playing with fire. Seen from a Marxist perspective, the Program sketched a grandiose panorama of past, present, and future, a "grand narrative," buoyed by passion and intellectual brilliance. However, he threatened dictatorship if the bourgeoisie were to hinder the socialist transformation of society. The term "dictatorship" was stock-in-trade in the Marxist tradition and was intended as a defense strategy. However, what could remain an abstract concept in theoretical writings gained a different status in a party program. In the political controversy, the term became a death sentence; the bourgeoisie and the peasantry interpreted it as a sign that the socialists intended dictatorship. However, the dictatorship cliché was disputed inside the party as well. And Bauer knew very well what violence meant in the context of civil war, and he understood that the captains of industry and the Catholic Church would not give up their property peacefully. Yet, he still wrote dictatorship into the party program. He frivolously evoked doom and gloom at a relatively peaceful time and thus handed his political opponents a strong weapon of propaganda. After the defeat of February 1934, the dictatorship of the proletariat became the programmatic goal of the illegal Revolutionary Socialists as well. It became an embarrassment for the Austrian Socialist Party after 1945 and was thus never talked about.

Could Bauer and the Social Democrats have prevented the Austrian dictatorship of Engelbert Dollfuß? Hardly! All of Europe experienced a swing to the right. In countries where democracy had only weak social roots, where the global economy had plunged people into despair, authoritarian governments offered treacherous solutions. However, the Social Democrats, by their refusal to compromise, handed the government a powerful argument: social democracy has no social consciousness, no responsibility for society; Social Democrats only have the workers' interests in mind. They should have tried to prevent the entrance of the mostly fascist home guard (*Heimwehr*) at any price, maybe by means of indirectly supporting the democratic government before Dollfuß became chancellor.

The February uprising of 1934 broke out against Otto Bauer's will. When the fighting began, he showed weak leadership and fled to Czechoslovakia

38. Ibid., 214-218.

39. Klaus Berchtold, ed., *Österreichische Parteiprogramme 1868-1966* (Vienna: Verlag für Geschichte und Politik, 1967), 247-264.

on February 13 before the fighting had ceased. This definitely damaged his reputation with parts of of the labor class.

The Human Being

A critic of my biography of Otto Bauer remarked that my "portrayal of his life" remained "strangely bloodless."[40] He is right. The reasons lie in the lack of sources (a historian is no writer of literature, after all) and in the fact that Bauer had almost no private life; his life and his work overlapped almost completely. One can only trace feeble indications of the person he was in a few letters, in public speeches, books, and pamphlets.

He was a rather shy person, given to depression, from which he rescued himself by believing in the theory of the legitimacy of history. Busy with his work from morning until late at night—in parliament, in committees, as a party leader, journalist, propagandist, and author—he rarely gave himself a break. A rather humorless person, he had few friends. His daily life was organized by his wife, a fellow scholar, who was ten years his senior. A Viennese who rarely went to the theatre or a concert, he avoided large gatherings but went to see a movie once in a while. He remained a stranger to the enjoyments of life, with one exception: while he was a strict teetotaler, he was a chain smoker, which contributed to his early death.

This richly gifted politician, endowed with superior intelligence and versed in many scholarly fields, far outstripped his political opponents. He showed off his superiority during controversies, which earned him the respect of his fellow party members but triggered pure hatred among the mediocre politicians on the other side. However, he approached the simple working man and the industrious peasant with great understanding. He despised the nepotism in Austrian politics—the politics of the wine glass—and remained entirely free of corruption. Intellectually, he was a political nonpareil with a stern moral sense who failed in the end but who, even in exile, continued the political fight.

40. Kurt Scholz, "Heimat bist du … Über die Kunst Lebensgeschichten zu erzählen," in *Die Presse*, 10 May 2011, 27.

"Against the Mock Battle of Words"

Therese Schlesinger, neé Eckstein (1863-1940), a Radical Seeker

Gabriella Hauch [1]

Interests, preferences, and aversions, with all their contradictions, unite or divide people; they form the chemistry between them, providing that which cannot be expressed in words but which can still be lived and can define reality. Behind all of this, we find an ambiguous variety of experiences, character traits, conscious decisions and unconscious predilections. Like a sounding board, this complexity amplifies the biographer's interest in approaching a historical person. Life stories are never logical and goal-oriented chains of events, and we must abandon the illusion of coherence, which is a product of retrospective wishful thinking. Like we do in friendships, biographers need to open themselves to breaks and affirmations to accommodate a multi-dimensional web of cause and effect. The life and influence of the biographical subject, his or her character idiosyncrasies, individual talents, and characteristics illustrate the process of biographical construction, which is based on scholarly research. We cannot determine how a person "really" was or is. "Biographical truth cannot be found," wrote Sigmund Freud to Arnold Zweig in 1936, "and if we had it, we would not be able to use it."[2]

Meaning in the Context of the Past

We meet the human subject at the center of biographical research in texts, maybe photographs, films, or audio-recordings, which create a network of ideas and images and allow us to "recognize" this specific person.[3] The biographer's emerging interest in dedicating him/herself to someone's life for an extended period of time is embedded in multiple contexts. Walter Benjamin described the attachment of any historical interest to the present when he noticed that the "image of the past" threatens to "disappear in every confrontation with the present, which does not recognize itself in this

---

1. This article was translated by Inge Fink, Department of English, University of New Orleans, special thanks to her and to Michaela Neuwirth, University of Vienna, for help with the bibliography.
2. Sigmund Freud to Arnold Zweig, 31 May 1936, in *Sigmund Freud, Arnold Zweig, Briefwechsel*, ed. Ernst L. Freud (Frankfurt am Main: Fischer, 1984), 137.
3. Toril Moi, *Simone de Beauvoir. Die Psychographie einer Intellektuellen* (Frankfurt am Main: Fischer, 1996), 21-22.

Therese Schlesinger in the 1920s, ©Kreisky Archiv, Vienna

image."[4] Certain themes, events, or facets of different pasts fluctuate like economic statistics in the memory of the public. Some scholarly work creates interest where none existed before. This interest can be shared by individual groups or the general public. In our highly technological media and information society, it is possible to trigger or amplify a boom in interest. As a result, Walter Benjamin's theory that mechanical reproduction destroys the exclusive originality of art and culture can be applied, in a modified form, to scholarly work and its discoveries.[5] In the past few years, for example, we have observed how the dormant interest in

4. Walter Benjamin, "Über den Begriff der Geschichte," in *Illuminationen: Ausgewählte Schriften* (Frankfurt am Main: Suhrkamp, 1980), 251-62, 257. This essay was originally published in 1939.

5. Walter Benjamin, "Das Kunstwerk im Zeitalter seiner technischen Reproduzierbarkeit," in *Drei Studien zur Kunstsoziologie*, 12th ed. (Frankfurt am Main: Suhrkamp, 1981), 7-44. This essay was originally published in 1935/36. Sigrid Weigel, *Entstellte Ähnlichkeit: Walter Benjamins theoretische Schreibweise* (Frankfurt am Main: Fischer, 1997).

National Socialism coincided with an increase in Germany and Austria of movies and TV-series with similar themes. The simultaneous tendency to historicize and excuse provokes criticism[6] and points to the paradox that the current loss of political interest in the Liberal Arts coexists with a heavy demand for "history."[7] The term *Zeitgeist* (Ernst Bloch) indicates an emerging—and often sub-conscious—readiness for different topics. As a result, we must ask how history is constructed as scholarship, with what interests it is connected, what effect it has on individuals, and what its relationship is with the re/production of power dynamics. The interest in certain topics means that people "recognize" themselves in some way in the history represented by these topics. Scholars are involved in this process as they produce the "image of the past" onto which people project this "recognition" of themselves.

The choice of a biographical subject depends on the same process. Biographers can never claim a neutral authorial position in the way that was expected in the bourgeois novel of initiation. The process of scholarship makes visible the scholar's interests, predilections, and aversions because nobody "has" a biography; a biography is created in a social process, at the crossroads between personal and social factors, between the individual and society.[8] The "mirror effect" between narrator and subject is intensive, complicated, and multi-layered. "The person whose story is told becomes the mirror, through which the narrator understands and interprets herself," says Seyla Benhabib as she describes Hannah Arendt's method in the latter's work on Rahel Varnhagen.[9] This brings her close to Liz Stanley's argument for using the term "auto/biography," which attempts to capture the involvement of biographers in their material and emphasizes the close connections between biography and autobiography as the person writing

6. On the history of women and gender: Johanna Gehmacher, "Frauen, Männer, Untergänge: Geschlechterbilder und Gedächtnispolitiken in Darstellungen zum Ende des 'Dritten Reiches,'" in *Frauen- und Geschlechtergeschichte des Nationalsozialismus: Fragestellungen, Perspektiven, neue Forschungen,* eds. Johanna Gehmacher and Gabriella Hauch (Innsbruck: Studienverlag, 2006), 240-56; Johanna Gehmacher, „Im Umfeld der Macht: populäre Perspektive auf Frauen der NS-Elite," in *Nationalsozialismus und Geschlecht,* eds. Elke Frietsch and Christina Herkommer (Berlin: Transcript, 2008), 7-25.

7. Brigitte Studer, "Geschichte schreiben: Moralischer Auftrag, lohnendes Geschäft, szientistischer Erkenntnisgewinn oder intellektueller Selbstzweck? Positionen und Politiken," *Österreichische Zeitschrift für Geschichtswissenschaften* 17, no. 1 (2006): 169-78.

8. Reinhard Sieder, "Gesellschaft und Person: Geschichte und Biographie; Nachschrift," in: *Brüchiges Leben: Biographien in sozialen Systemen, Kultur als Praxis 1,* ed. Reinhard Sieder (Vienna: Turia und Kant, 1999), 234-64.

9. Seyla Benhabib, *Hannah Arendt: die melancholische Denkerin der Moderne* (Hamburg: Suhrkamp, 1998), 39; Hannah Arendt, *Rahel Varnhagen: Lebensgeschichte einer deutschen Jüdin aus der Romantik,* 9th ed. (Munich: Piper, 1997).

and the person written about position themselves (or are positioned) in a social context.[10] In her 1929 biography of Rahel Varnhagen, Hannah Arendt attempts "to tear Rachel's life and legacy out of her husband's claws," as Benhabib puts it.[11] In her rejection of the husband as biographer and his masculine power of definition, philosopher Hannah Arendt—not a feminist by definition—approaches the realm of women and gender studies, a field that has always understood itself as an identity-giving project by and for women.[12] Seen from this perspective, the past was not the explicit focus of the biographer's work, which was undertaken to serve as a "guide for the interest in women's liberation," as Herta Nagl-Docekal put it, a term that reduces the heterogeneous field of feminist scholarship to a common denominator.[13] History has long been the leading science of feminist studies because it has provided "useful" historical arguments against the claim that women's scope of action was supposedly determined by nature.[14] As feminist scholars investigated the historical genesis of concepts, laws, and institutions and examined the discourses that legitimate and reproduce women's inclusion in and exclusion from social structures, they exposed the changeability of the constructs that constitute modern society. Feminist biographical scholarship emerged from the same connection between the biographers' epistemological interest and the persons they studied. By focusing on an individual, the biographer turned her subject into a thinking, acting, and feeling woman, whose story became a feminist counterpoint to the "biographical hero as masculine hero."[15] However, according to feminist historians of the 1990s, this early approach in feminist scholarship underestimated the influence of gender dynamics and gender codes that are woven into the structure of scholarship and society because biographers reproduced the hero as a "figure in a structurally masculine position" in

10. Liz Stanley, *The auto/biographical I: The theory and practice of feminist auto/biography* (Manchester: Manchester University Press, 1992).

11. Benhabib, *Arendt*, 32-33.

12. Conference Report "3. Historikerinnentreffen" in Bielefeld, April 1981, *beiträge zur feministischen theorie und praxis*, no. 5 (1981).

13. Herta Nagl-Docekal, Feministische Geschichtswissenschaft: ein unverzichtbares Projekt, *L'Homme. Zeitschrift für Feministische Geschichtswissenschaft* 1, no. 1 (1990): 7-18, 18.

14. Referring to the much-quoted essay by Joan W. Scott, Regina Wecker, "Vom Nutzen und Nachteil der Frauen- und Geschlechtergeschichte für die Gender Theorie; oder Warum Geschichte wichtig ist," *L'Homme. Zeitschrift für Feministische Geschichtswissenschaft* 18, no. 2 (2007): 27-52, 37.

15. Ann-Kathrin Reulecke, "Die Nase der Lady Hester: Überlegungen zum Verhältnis von Biographie und Geschlechterdifferenz," in *Biographie als Geschichte*, ed. Hedwig Röckelein (Tübingen: Dicord, 1993), 117-42, 134; Christine Thon, *Frauenbewegung im Wandel der Generationen: Eine Studie über Geschlechterkonstruktionen in biographischen Erzählungen* (Bielefeld: Transcript, 2008), 87-117.

every person they wrote about, "exceptional individuals" and "unknown women" alike.[16] Despite this fundamental criticism, feminist interest in individual women's life stories did not disappear. However, the demand for speaking about and reflecting on the process by which figures "emerge/ are made" in biography has gained importance.[17] Given our awareness of the problems with scholarly methods and theories, we can discover and explain the contradictions in auto/biographical narratives and understand the mechanism by which biography creates heroines.[18]

If we make visible female experience and scope of action in the life stories of historical activists who devoted themselves to the emancipation of the underprivileged, the minorities, and the socially marginalized, it will not be difficult to find an "image of the past" that bestows current meaning on the triumphs and failures of female emancipation. This image, this meaning, has also evoked distrust and has changed the continuing scholarly interest in researching and writing about persons. While biographers in the past worried about solving the problems of correctly interpreting sources about their subjects, they now emphasize these very concerns. Monika Bernold and Johanna Gehmacher, for example, assembled hundreds of letters, diaries, correspondences, and essays by Mathilde Hanzel-Hübner, an activist in the Old Feminist Movement in Austria, not into "a biography" but into an "annotated biographical edition."[19] Toril Moi, too, who fulfilled her long-held wish to write about Simone de Beauvoir, created an alternative concept to biography which she called "genealogy." According to Moi, biography is concerned with linearity, origin, finality, and the attempt to make visible an autonomous identity; genealogy, on the other hand, is "open" and wants to make us "conscious of the process

16. Reulecke, *Nase*, 134.

17. Moi, *Simone de Beauvoir*, 27.

18. I tried to demonstrate this process by using the example of Adelheid Popp, a pioneer of the social-democratic women's workers' movement and author of two autobiographical memoirs, and of Käthe Leichter, social democrat, political scientist, and founder of Austrian feminist scholarship: Gabriella Hauch, "Käthe Leichter, geb. Pick. Spuren eines Frauenlebens," in *Frauen bewegen Politik: Österreich 1848-1939* (Innsbruck: Studienverlag, 2009), 225-248. This essay was originally published in 1992. Gabriella Hauch, "Adelheid Popp, 1869-1939: Bruchlinien einer sozialdemokratischen Frauen-Karriere," in *Frauen bewegen Politik: Österreich 1848-1939* (Innsbruck: Studienverlag, 2009), 27-51. This essay was originally published in 1998. See also: Hanna Hacker, "Wer gewinnt? Wer verliert? Wer tritt aus dem Schatten? Machtkämpfe und Beziehungsstrukturen nach dem Tod der 'großen Feministin' Auguste Fickert, 1910," *L'Homme. Zeitschrift für Feministische Geschichtswissenschaft* 7, no. 1 (1996): 97-106.

19. Monika Bernold and Johanna Gehmacher, *Auto/Biographie und Frauenfrage: Tagebücher, Briefwechsel, Politische Schriften von Mathilde Hanzel-Hübner, 1884-1970* (Vienna: Böhlau, 2003), 18.

of emerging or being created," thus illustrating the complex combination of different kinds of power in determinants and discourses. When working with terms like "I" and "subject," Toril Moi regards them indications of a "personal" genealogy.[20] Seyla Benhabib, too, asked *why Hannah Arendt in particular* in the introduction to her biographical work, in which she reflects on her decades-long enthusiasm about Arendt's writings, explains her understanding of Arendt's lack of feminism, and concludes that her grappling with Arendt's theoretical writings turned into a "very personal book".[21]

I am plagued by a similar project. Throughout my research on the feminists of the Old Women's Movement of the Habsburg monarchy and the *discrete charm of the sub-contradiction* (*Nebenwiderspruch*), which seduced the social-democratic women's movement during the years before the first World War, in the course of my research on the gender of the councils' movement and the women parliamentarians of the First Republic in Austria, on the fate of female intellectuals during the Nazi regime up to a project called *gender housing*[22]—time and time again, I kept running into a person who stopped me in my tracks, irritated, and fascinated me: Therese Schlesinger.[23] Her actions and statements, as they have come down to me, showed me a contrarian, a theoretician who was open for ideas and far off the beaten track of party discipline and mainstream positions, a political strategist very much aware of the workings of power, who knew when it was time to compromise. For her, all of her work was a means

20. Moi, *Simone de Beauvoir*, 27.

21. Benhabib, *Arendt*, 9-28, 23.

22. Gabriella Hauch, "Der diskrete Charme des Nebenwiderspruchs. Zur sozialdemokratischen Frauenbewegung vor 1918," in *Frauen bewegen Politik: Österreich 1848-1939* (Innsbruck: Studienverlag, 2009), 101-118. This essay was originally published in 1988. Gabriella Hauch, *Vom Frauenstandpunkt aus: Frauen im Parlament 1919-1933*, (Vienna: Gesellschaftskritik, 1995); Gabriella Hauch, "Gender = Geschlecht: Einführende Überlegungen zu einem komplexen Gegenstand," in *gender housing: Geschlechtergerechtes bauen, wohnen, leben; Theorie und Praxis*, eds. Christina Altenstraßer, Gabriella Hauch and Hermann Kepplinger (Innsbruck: Studienverlag, 2007), 19-38.

23. I plan to write an extensive biography of Therese Schlesinger and her writings, her family, and the social settings and networks in which she moved. See the more methodical essay, Gabriella Hauch, "Therese Schlesinger, geb. Eckstein, 1863-1940, Schreiben über eine Fremde," in Österreichische Zeitschrift für Geschichtswissenschaften 19, no. 2 (2008): 98-117, and other preliminary writings: Gabriella Hauch, "Schlesinger, Therese, 1863-1940," in *A Biographical Dictionary of Women's Movements and Feminisms: Central, Eastern and South Eastern Europe; 19th and 20th Centuries*, eds. Francisca de Haan, Krassimira Daskalova and Anna Loutfi (Budapest: CEU Press, 2006), 479-83; Gabriella Hauch, "Schlesinger, Therese geb. Eckstein: Theoretikerin der Frauenbewegung," in *Wissenschafterinnen in und aus Österreich: Leben – Werk – Wirken*, eds. Brigitta Keintzel and Ilse Korotin (Vienna: Böhlau, 2002), 650-55.

to an end, the creation of a more just—and thus more women-friendly—society, and it brought women into the party leadership of the Austrian Social-Democratic Workers' Party (SDAP) and into the National and Federal Council of the Austrian parliament. I am interested in Therese Schlesinger's gender-specific analyses and social-political positions, as well as in her way of dealing with institutional power and her own personal tragedies. In many ways, I am removed from this woman, who died in exile in France in 1940, at the age of 77, but in some of the questions she asked herself as a woman intellectual, I recognize my own: In her meditations on the women's movement and feminist politics, on the position of the intellectual woman in an institutional environment, on the penetration of sexual politics in all aspects of life, in her questions concerning the power of the subconscious and the role of psychoanalysis 'beyond the couch.' I also find myself agreeing with Schlesinger's insight that the discussion and analysis of gender-based power must always include other factors besides gender. However, I must reflect critically on my understanding of Therese Schlesinger's image, which I formed as I read her writings and the memories her contemporaries had of her, as well as the few letters of hers that have been found in the estates of those who knew her. This critical stance is the only way to reconcile getting involved and simultaneously remaining aloof and to achieve a balanced "strangeness in convergence"[24] without projecting my own life story onto a (re)constructed life.

"There was nothing to do but 'to stick it out'"[25]: The Feminists in the Social-Democratic Workers' Party

Therese Schlesinger got politically involved relatively late in her life. At the age of 31, she became a member of the General Austrian Women's Association (*Allgemeiner Österreichischer Frauenverein*, AÖFV), which had at last been founded by Auguste Fickert, Marie Lang, and Rosa Mayreder after a three-year wait imposed by the police. Therese Schlesinger's decision to get involved in an organized and public struggle for women's emancipation seems to have been influenced by two aspects: her family's social situation and personal tragedies she suffered during the mid-1890s. As the daughter of business magnate Albert Eckstein, she grew up in a liberal, bourgeois, Jewish household. Her family subscribed to the ideals

24. Gabriella Hauch, *Frau Biedermeier auf den Barrikaden: Frauenleben in der Wiener Revolution 1848*, (Vienna: Gesellschaftskritik, 1990), 6 ff.

25. Therese Schlesinger, "Die Stellung der Intellektuellen in der Sozialdemokratie," *Der Kampf: Sozialdemokratische Monatsschrift* 16, no. 8 (1923): 264-72, 270.

of the Enlightenment, the French Revolution and the Revolution of 1848, which induced them to provide reduced hours and health insurance for the workers in the family factory. Therese Schlesinger remembered herself, at the age of 15, as a teenager inspired by an "emotional socialism" and the "romantic dreams" connected with it.[26] When she joined the AÖVF, she was already a widow and mother of a five-year old daughter, Anna; she was also suffering from impaired mobility as the result of a measles infection she contracted during childbirth. She saw her public engagement as an opportunity to "lift herself above her personal misfortunes and participate in the great struggles of [her] time."[27]

Today, the AÖFV would be regarded as part of the autonomous women's movement: its demands for an end to the legal and social discrimination of women coincided with the necessity of structural changes in society to achieve greater justice, not just for women but for all under-privileged social groups. Having received a comprehensive private education, Therese Schlesinger worked in the AÖFV's legal protection department, wrote articles for the weekly supplement of the "People's Voice" (*Volksstimme*) owned by the democrat Ferdinand Kronawetter, joined the ranks of the organization's officer as its vice president, and rose to the rank of keynote speaker at AÖFV meetings. In the summer of 1896, she participated in the first international women's congress in Berlin as a delegate of the AÖFV, where she was to speak about the results of the "inquiry into the situation of female workers in Vienna"[28] and about the Austrian women's movement. However, when she reported too positively about the activities of the Social Democrats, the chairman bid her be silent. It took some persuasion to keep her from leaving the congress and going home immediately. However, she had caught the attention of Social Democrats of both genders, and they started courting her. A year later, in the summer of 1897, she yielded to their entreaties; as she explained to Auguste Fickert in elaborate letters, she had decided in favor of a clearer program and the social structure of the

26. Therese Schlesinger, "Mein Weg zur Sozialdemokratie," in Gedenkbuch: Zwanzig Jahre österreichische Arbeiterinnenbewegung, *Eine handschriftliche und gedruckte Ausgabe*, ed. Adelheid Popp (Vienna: Wiener Volksbuchhandlung, 1912), 125-39, 125. In addition: Marina Tichy, "'Ich hatte immer Angst unwissend zu sterben': Therese Schlesinger; Bürgerin und Sozialistin," in *"Die Partei hat mich nie enttäuscht…": Österreichische Sozialdemokratinnen*, ed. Edith Prost (Vienna: Gesellschaftskritik, 1989), 135-84; Gabriella Hauch, "Schlesinger Therese, geb. Eckstein," in *Wissenschafterinnen in und aus Österreich: Leben – Werk – Wirken*, eds. Britta Keinzel and Ilse Korotin (Vienna: Böhlau, 2002), 650-55.

27. Schlesinger, "Mein Weg," 126.

28. *Die Arbeits- und Lebensverhältnisse der Wiener Lohnarbeiterinnen: Ergebnisse und stenographisches Protokoll der Enquete über Frauenarbeit in Wien 1.3.-21.4.1896*, (Vienna: Erste Wiener Volksbuchhandlung 1897).

Social Democrats. However, she still tried to reorganize the AÖFV into a "Social-Democratic organization, which we can manage autonomously," but Fickert rejected this idea.[29] Both women continued their discussion in the fall in the "People's Voice," but their tone became sharper. When Schlesinger called the AÖFV's refusal to align itself with any political party "ridiculous," Fickert countered that the vision of socialism was not the same as that of the Social-Democratic Party (*Sozialdemokratische Partei*, SDAP) and that there would not be any "future consummation" without the "women's movement, so much scorned by the SDAP."[30]

Fickert's assessment followed Schlesinger, a former member of the "much-scorned women's movement," throughout her career as a Social Democrat. As a member of the AÖFV, she never had to "hold back or disguise her convictions in any way," as she told her mentor and friend, the socialist Karl Kautsky, shortly after she joined the party in 1898. All this changed now that she was a Social Democrat. When she spoke out in favor of the autonomous political organization of women and the development of women-specific policies, she was accused of "separatism." However, neither of these strategies had been invented by women. While the Jacobins forbade women's political engagement in the French Revolution in 1793, during the 1848 Revolution in Europe, men and women were organized in separate political groups. In Vienna, men organized the "Democratic Club" while women founded the "First Viennese Democratic Women's Club" later. After the defeat of the 1848 revolution, paragraph 30 of the new *Vereinsgesetz*, the law codex for associational groupings, locked in the stigmatization of women by declaring them a special case. Until 1918, women were forbidden to become politically active, on their own or in conjunction with men. As a result, all women's organizations during the Habsburg monarchy, including the AÖFV and the various Social-Democratic women's clubs, declared themselves "apolitical" because that was the only way for women to act publicly. While the SDAP strove to organize a legal party for both genders, the "proletariat," a gender-neutral concept that applied to skilled (male) workers, remained at the center of politics.[31]

In this context, Therese Schlesinger, a feminist Social-Democrat from

29. Therese Schlesinger to Auguste Fickert, 30 August 1897, Nachlass Auguste Fickert, Handschriftensammlung, Stadt- und Landesarchiv, Vienna.

30. Therese Schlesinger-Eckstein, "Zur Frauenfrage," *Volksstimme* (Vienna), 31 Oct. 1897: 6.

31. Gabriella Hauch, "Arbeite Frau! Die Gleichberechtigung kommt von selbst"? Anmerkungen zu Frauen und Gewerkschaften in Österreich vor 1914," in *Frauen bewegen Politik: Österreich 1848-1939* (Innsbruck: Studienverlag, 2009), 105-28. This essay was originally published in 1991.

the Jewish bourgeoisie, met with distrust and rejection. The SDAP was not a place of safety and solidarity, as was stated decades later, with regret but without apology, on the occasion of its 70th birthday in 1933. Anna Boschek, first female union employee and specialist in Austrian women's issues since 1893, admitted, "Especially the women comrades criticized the 'bourgeois woman' and did not trust her all the way."[32]

Since the turn of the century, various records of party conventions, women and union conferences, reveal an increasingly rational discussion of women's demands among Social-Democratic politicians. The question whether women's political demands should take precedence over those made by unions, which concerned mostly men but were defined as general politics, emerged as a major issue. Schlesinger took the women's side and thus provoked criticism from her own party at all levels. At the 1900 party convention, the unchallenged party leader Victor Adler carped, "You are not as emancipated as you would like us to think. You propose that we should not forget about women's suffrage when we initiate action to reform the election laws. I have no problem with that. But tell me: don't we have other things to worry about?"[33] And three years later, the chair of the Social-Democratic free unions, Anton Hueber, opined that, confronted with Schlesinger's demands, he felt "compelled to drop customary gallantry and say a few stern words." Both Adler's and Hueber's speeches reflect the patriarchal notion—anchored in paragraph 91 of the Austrian Law Codex—of man's dominion over his wife and children in (party) politics.

Therese Schlesinger knew that she was the focus of the SDAP men's distrust towards women's rights and that, because her demands always went a step beyond, she had become a—subconsciously welcome—scapegoat for Social-Democratic women who yearned for approval. When the news of the Russian Revolution broke during the 1905 SDAP party convention and 250,000 people demonstrated for their right to vote in the streets of Vienna, she compromised by retrieving the demand for women's right to vote so as not to endanger the general suffrage for men.[34] Schlesinger did not garner any noticeable respect. A few months later, in March of 1906, she wrote to Auguste Fickert,"I am presently hated, defamed etc. in the party.... The matter is based on personal envy and baseness."[35] Despite their differences in opinion, her old political comrade had remained

32. "Anna Boschek über Therese Schlesinger," *Die Frau*, no. 7 (1933): 5.

33. *Verhandlungen des Parteitages der Deutschen Socialdemokratie Oesterreichs: Graz 2 -6 September 1900,* (Vienna: Volksbuchhandlung, 1900), 84.

34. Hauch, "Der diskrete Charme."

35. Schlesinger to Fickert, 6 March 1906, Nachlass Auguste Fickert, Handschriftensammlung, Stadt- und Landesarchiv, Vienna.

her confidante. A few years before, Schlesinger had thanked her for her successful cooperation in the AÖFV because, not that she found herself among the Social Democrats, she was no longer "so spoiled but rather a bit inured."[36] In the years before World War I, women all over Europe who thought of themselves as feminists but were thought of as radicals believed that women's liberation could only be achieved in a social system different from the modern capitalist, bourgeois society. At the same time, many European countries were still a long way from bourgeois liberties and democratic conditions.

Therese Schlesinger answered the negative treatment she received from the Social Democratic party with an attempt to analyze the insult at an abstract level. In her 1919 pamphlet "The Intellectual Working Woman and Socialism," Schlesinger, the pacifist, claimed that the place of wage-earning women doctors and teachers must be in a social democracy, and she warned about the problems that would result from the clash of different social milieus and their cultural differences. She emphasized that the "rough manners of the working classes, the lack of culture in the milieu in which the proletariat is forced to live, understandably repels" intellectual women.[37] In her 1923 article "The Position of Intellectuals in a Social Democracy," she went a step further.[38] After the publication of two books by and about the German social democrat Lily Braun, Schlesinger talked about the little-appreciated contributions of intellectuals to the establishment of the so-called workers' movement. Lily Braun, an intellectual of aristocratic descent, failed to "stick it out" and left the party. According to Schlesinger, "deviant opinions" are tolerated much more readily if they are voiced by "comrades who hail from the working class" than by "academicians." And the fact that the latter are "more skilled in disputation" than the workers "turns us against them even more."

By the time this article appeared, the 60-year-old Therese Schlesinger was already one of the first and, more importantly, most influential women members of the National Council. In cooperation with Christian Socials Hildegard Burjan and Olga Rudel Zeynek and the German Nationalist Emmy Stradal, she had prevailed in the fight to allow girls access to boys' high schools and thus higher education—with the votes of all the parties,

36. Schlesinger to Kautsky 10 February 1898, Nachlass Karl Kautsky, Internationales Institut für Sozialgeschichte, Amsterdam; Schlesinger to Fickert, 23 September 1899, Nachlass Auguste Fickert, Handschriftensammlung, Stadt- und Landesarchiv, Vienna.

37. Therese Schlesinger, *Geistige Arbeiterin und der Sozialismus*, (Vienna: Hugo Heller, 1919), 16.

38. Therese Schlesinger, "Die Stellung der Intellektuellen in der Sozialdemokratie," *Der Kampf: Sozialdemokratische Monatsschrift* 16, no. 8, (1923): 264-72.

including the strictly anti-co-educational Christian Socials and German Nationalists.[39] To give women the chance to engage in creative work, Therese Schlesinger had stuck it out, the outsider in the center: "for long years, I had to fight hostility and overcome my own feelings of inferiority."[40]

Caring for the Human Soul: Theoretical Positions

The birth of the Republic coincided with a personal tragedy in Therese Schlesinger's life. Her 30-year-old daughter Anna had committed suicide in February of 1920. "Annerl," as Therese Schlesinger called her, had been a high-school teacher and an activist in the Socialist Youth Movement. Both mother and daughter belonged to the party's so-called "left fringe" during World War I.[41] Her daughter's death plagued Therese Schlesinger throughout her life like a wound that would not heal. It is remarkable that during the years of the First Republic, she focused on fundamental questions concerning those who suffered from their cultural and social circumstances. In doing this, she developed a clear position about the responsibilities of a social democracy, beyond issues like wage increases, housing, social security, and (continuing) education for all. In essence, she strove for "moral and aesthetic refinement," the development of the "nobler self,"[42] the "human soul" which had been "hitherto neglected" and which "needed urgent care."[43] For her, the soul was located in the tensions between outside conditions and psychological impulses rooted in the subconscious.[44] The human soul, proclaimed Schlesinger, must be the concern of a social democracy if it wants to advance the promise of "redeemer socialism" and the project of a "new humanity." The Social Democrats, in their cult of the proletariat as the revolutionary subject, had counted on mobilizing the goodness, solidarity, compassion, and discipline of the lower social orders

---

39. Gabriella Hauch, "Oszillierende Allianzen: Die ersten Politikerinnen und ihre Politik zur höheren Mädchenbildung im inner- und außerparlamentarischen Raum der Ersten Republik Österreichs," in *Frauen bewegen Politik: Österreich 1848-1939* (Innsbruck: Studienverlag, 2009), 171-80. This essay was originally published in 1997.

40. Schlesinger to Karl Kautsky, 3 June 1933, Nachlass Karl Kautsky, Internationales Institut für Sozialgeschichte, Amsterdam.

41. It was in this milieu, which formed as a result of the SDAP's position on war politics, that Anna Schlesinger met her husband Josef Frey (1889-1957), Trotsky's Austrian agent, a lawyer and editor of the *Arbeiter-Zeitung* (The Austrian Socialist Party's daily newspaper) and chair of the *Wiener Arbeiter- und Soldatenrat* (Vienna Workers' and Soldier's Council).

42. Therese Schlesinger, "Zur Evolution der Erotik," *Der Kampf: Sozialdemokratische Monatsschrift* 16 , no. 11 (1923): 368-71, 371.

43. Therese Schlesinger, "Ein Volksbuch über die Freudsche Lehre," *Der Kampf: Sozialdemokratische Monatsschrift* 20, no. 4 (1927): 191-95, 194.

44. Ibid., 192 and 194.

as soon as their basic existential needs had been met and they had a chance to improve their lives—however, this did not turn out to be true. As before, certain sub-cultures were cast in the role of the Other to serve as a foil to "Red Vienna," the showcase of Social-Democratic politics in Austria. These social groups continued to function as projection screens for deviance and lack of order, for misery and moral depravity, even though they constituted the social basis for the SDAP's social and political reforms.[45] The War and the Austrian Revolution had brought about a constitution, the elimination of gender as a reason for exclusion, middle-class liberties—in short, democracy and a republican government. However, Schlesinger saw the devastation of World War I as the cause for the ongoing brutalization of man.[46]

Schlesinger's articles written during the time of the First Republic testify to the broadening and deepening of her expansive mind and her multi-layered understanding of politics—including the ruptures in her own political and private views: they track her career, which ran the gamut from being a feminist intellectual and outsider in the SDAP, to being the speaker of the "left opposition" during the war in Austria, to being the delegate at council conventions and a member of the National Council; in addition, her writing touches on the death of loved ones—her brother Gustav died in 1916, her daughter in 1920, her mother in 1921, and her sister Emma in 1924.

As early as 1912, Therese Schlesinger had developed the project Communal Housing (*Genossenschafts-Wohnbau*) from the insight that humans need a satisfactory, energy-sustaining environment if they were to become interested in education and develop the imagination for a life of culture.[47] Her idea went beyond putting an end to the housing shortage; she envisioned central kitchens, community laundry services, kindergartens, and "youth centers" in order to ease women's burdens and make the state responsible for some of the work involved in reproduction. The problem of reconciling job, parenthood, political and cultural activity, an everyday reality for women, ran like a red thread through Schlesinger's ideas on gender dynamics.

Schlesinger emphasized the role of boys, men, and fathers as a central concept in her work on gender dynamics. In a 1921 article, she presented her views of "domestic education," suggesting that both boys and girls should learn to "supervise younger siblings" and do "superfluous household

45. Wolfgang Maderthaner and Lutz Musner, *Die Anarchie der Vorstadt: Das andere Wien um 1900,* 2nd ed. (Frankfurt am Main: Campus, 2000), 9-16.

46. Schlesinger, "Zur Evolution," 371.

47. Therese Schlesinger, "Eine Aufgabe der Arbeiter-Baugenossenschaften," *Der Kampf: Sozialdemokratische Monatsschrift* 1, no. 6 (1912): 131-35.

chores." Her ideas went beyond relieving the mother as she focused on the formation of the male character, claiming that her method was the "best way to forestall male arrogance, a habit that is often hard to break in grown men." In addition, she concluded that the "mis-education of men, in particular, is often the reason that men and women cannot work together" in politics "without friction."[48] When discussing the "psychological bond" between mother and baby, which could foster positive "powers" so important for the baby's welfare, she also included the "father instinct" as an equal factor. However, given the "current conditions, the father instinct develops only rarely." Her solutions included a universal insurance for mothers, which would allow every woman to choose between raising her child on her own or, through a reduction of working hours, together with the child's father.[49] On the subject of the gender-specific division of labor, she quipped, "All the jobs we view as the natural responsibility of women can become men's jobs as soon as we pay for them." At the same time, she regretted that, when both parents work outside of the home, the husband would not do his share of housework. If this had been the case, men, who sit at the controls of power, would have lost no time to make the job easier through technology and better management: "Since women are doing the work, however, men lack any incentive for innovation."[50]

Schlesinger's theory did not agree with the seemingly crude differentiation between "women" and "men." While she defined gender dynamics as a power structure in its own right, she demanded the inclusion of other "interdependencies" such as class and nation—termed "categories of difference" in today's women and gender studies—in the social and scholarly analyses.[51] She saw the power dynamics in all three categories as essential for the development of "character differences." Given the way gender differences work, she ascertained that it would be almost impossible to determine how much the social construction of gender has overlaid the "natural causes of this differentiation." Addressing her scientific inquiries to psychologists, she demanded the exclusion of the "sexual component" and the inclusion of women on research teams. Transposed to contemporary scholarly research, this would mean that we have to eschew the androcentric

48. Therese Schlesinger, *Wie will und wie soll das Proletariat seine Kinder erziehen?* (Vienna: Vlg. Frauen- Reichskomitee, 1921), 20f.

49. Therese Schlesinger, "Zum Problem der Mutterschaft," in *Der Kampf: Sozialdemokratische Monatsschrift* 20, no. 10 (1927): 475-79, 478.

50. Therese Schlesinger, "Bericht der Frauenprogrammkommission," in: *Frauenarbeit und Bevölkerungspolitik: Verhandlungen der sozialdemokratischen Frauenreichskonferenz 29. und 30. Oktober 1926 in Linz* (Vienna: Vorwärts, Wiener Volksbuchhandlung n.d.), 10.

51. Therese Schlesinger, "Zur Psychologie der Geschlechter," *Der Kampf: Sozialdemokratische Monatsschrift* 18, no. 6 (1925): 225-29, 226.

fallacy of seeing the masculine as gender-neutral and universal and, at the same time, take into account the power of reproduced gender dynamics and gender-specific attributions. She claimed it was the "the undisputed result of recent research" that made us understand that "male and female individuals are more alike intellectually than different" and that other differences within one gender group would be more important.[52] In the 1920s, Therese Schlesinger saw psychoanalysis as a way to solve the gender problem. Because psychoanalysis attempts to bring these "people from the murky subconscious into the bright light of consciousness," its representatives must be "theoreticians and supporters of women's emancipation."[53]

The connection between Therese Schlesinger and psychoanalysis had many layers. In the 1890s, her sister Emma, two years her junior and also active in the AÖFV, was one of Freud's first patients and students, and Freud knew her older brother Friedrich.[54] From about 1889/90 on, Therese Schlesinger was friends with the psychoanalyst Paul Federn,[55] who was eight years younger than she and who treated her daughter Anna, who suffered from depression.[56] After Anna's tragic suicide, Schlesinger did not turn her back on psychoanalysis; on the contrary, her friendship with the Federns grew even closer—they started spending their summer holidays together in Aussee, Salzkammergut—and, as she pondered in 1930, she intensified her intellectual interest in psychoanalysis, without, however, undergoing analysis herself.[57]

New Ways: Political Concepts

When, in 1923, 60-year-old Therese Schlesinger left the National Council for the Federal Council, she began to devote more time to her publications. In the area of women and gender issues, she was responsible for the women's part of the SDAP's Austro-Marxist "Linz Program" of 1926, which meant that she had to coordinate the ideas of the program

---

52. Ibid., 227.
53. Ibid., 226.
54. Wolfgang Huber, "Emma Ecksteins Feuilleton zur Traumdeutung," *Jahrbuch der Psychoanalyse* 19 (1986): 90-106; Friedrich Eckstein, *Alte unnennbare Tage: Erinnerungen aus 70 Lehr- und Wanderjahren* (Vienna: Severus, 1988). This essay was originally published in 1936.
55. Letters from Therese Schlesinger to Wilma Bauer (later Wilma Federn), Paul Federn Archive, Library of Congress, Washington D.C.; Bernhard Kuschey, *Die Ausnahme des Überlebens: Ernst und Hilde Federn; Eine biographische Studie und eine Analyse der Binnenstruktur des Konzentrationslagers* (Gießen: Psychosozial, 2003), 1:77.
56. Kuschey, *Die Ausnahme*, 194.
57. Schlesinger, "Strafjustiz und Psychoanalyse," 39.

commission and its sub-groups and make them into a brochure.[58] During her preparations for "women's work and population issues," a central issue that touched upon the declining birth rates of the First Republic, Schlesinger already investigated ways to reconcile motherhood, career, and political and cultural activity, a problem still very much part of the contemporary feminist discourse on migration. Privileged women "buy" their "freedom" from childrearing labor by engaging under-paid—and mostly uninsured—women to perform these services.[59] The second strand of Schlesinger's intellectual work in the 1920s consisted in examining the usefulness of psychoanalysis in solving the problems of the time; she was convinced that "every fruitful thought, regardless of where it crops up, must in the end furnish new power for our movement," an idea that included both ideas and utopias.[60] After working on gender problems, and in preparation for the above-mentioned party program,[61] Schlesinger turned to writing about psychiatry, child education, and the judicial system.

Schlesinger believed that the public should not only be made aware of the intellectual potential of psychoanalysis in various scientific fields, but that Freud's "therapeutic methods" should become available to as many people as possible through national health insurance and not be restricted to the affluent classes.[62] She believed that "psychologically endangered children and youths (with behavioral problems)," criminals, and mental patients should be treated "according to the psychoanalytical method," and she included in this idea judges and jury members, who would "be prepared as well as possible for their difficult responsibilities through psychoanalytical education"—at least "until they have to make way for doctors and caretakers."[63] 67-year-old Schlesinger was convinced that psychoanalysis constituted "the first promising method to fight those asocial behaviors," which would not disappear with a change in the social system or in ownership structures. In the course of a life marked by social breakdowns

58. Therese Schlesinger, *Die Frau im sozialdemokratischen Parteiprogramm*, (Vienna: Vorwärts, 1928); Therese Schlesinger, "Forderungen der arbeitenden Frauen an Gesetzgebung und Verwaltung," in: *Handbuch der Frauenarbeit*, ed. Kammer der Arbeiter und Angestellten Wien, Schriftleitung Käthe Leichter, (Vienna: Kammer für Arbeiter und Angestellte, 1931), 663-70.

59. Therese Schlesinger, "Der psychologische Faktor in der Bevölkerungsfrage," *Der Kampf: Sozialdemokratische Monatsschrift* 18, no. 10 (1924): 447-51, 451.

60. Schlesinger, "Ein Volksbuch," 194.

61. Therese Schlesinger, "Der psychologische Faktor" and "Zur Psychologie der Geschlechter" and "Zum Problem der Mutterschaft."

62. Schlesinger, "Ein Volksbuch," 192.

63. Schlesinger, "Strafjustiz und Psychoanalyse," 39; Therese Schlesinger, "Zur Befreiung der Irren," 226.

and revolutionary changes, as well as personal tragedies, Schlesinger learned to acknowledge the power of the subconscious and the central position of sexuality.[64] The latter especially separated her from her contemporaries—even the Social Democrats.

Apocalypse at the End of her Life—"Yes, let's do it!"

Schlesinger's intensive preoccupation with psychoanalysis took place in an increasingly critical political situation. The verdicts of the Schattendorf trial, the torching of the Vienna courthouse, the disorientation of the SDAP, and brutal police action against demonstrators on July 15, 1927 reveal the fragility of the young republic, which was ushered into the world by a social revolution and which ended in civil war in February of 1934. For 71-year-old Schlesinger and many of the pioneers of a democratic social system, the end of civil liberties and the 1934 establishment of an authoritarian government of Catholic origins under chancellor Engelbert Dollfuß meant the defeat of all their hopes at the end of their lives.

For twenty years, Therese Schlesinger has been living in a different milieu than most of her contemporaries. Since World War I, when she resolutely opposed the war and represented the "left wing" in the Social-Democratic party, she was viewed as standing on the "far left" but also as being the "conscience of the party."[65] Through the agency of her daughter Anna, Schlesinger, a (grand)mother figure but open for young people's radical impatience during World War I, became the center of a group of young women who had "no real relationship" with the concept of a social democracy and who lived (it up) in revolutionary circles," as Käthe Leichter put it, but who trusted Therese Schlesinger because "she herself had always been a seeker."[66] Part of this group, which became a kind of intellectual daughter's circle during the 1920s, were Marianne Pollak and Stella Klein-Löw, who remembered her as "initially almost timid and shy," an impression that disappeared as soon as the discussion started: "Nothing was taken for granted. We had a real discussion, not just a mock battle with words and sentences."[67] Since the death of her sister, Schlesinger had been living by

64. To sum up: Schlesinger, "Strafjustiz und Psychoanalyse," 35.

65. For example: Martha Tausk, in: *Frauenarbeit und Bevölkerungspolitik*, 20. Martha Tausk, a delegate from Styria, defined herself as "very much the left, like comrade Schlesinger..." when she petitioned for paragraphs 144-146 to be repealed.

66. Käthe Leichter, "Therese Schlesinger und die Jungen," *Die Frau*, no. 7 (1933): 6.

67. Stella Klein-Löw, "Therese Schlesinger," in *Werk und Widerhall: Große Gestalten des österreichischen Sozialismus*, ed. Norbert Leser (Vienna: Volksbuchhandlung, 1964), 353-62, 353.

herself in the spacious apartment on Liniengasse in Vienna, which she turned into an intellectual and political "house of refuge." "If one does not know where to turn, if one is haunted by doubt, if one questions whether one has taken the right path, if one is not lukewarm about expressing one's ideas, one heads for Theres's," said Käthe Leichter, political scientist and then-director of the women's department of the Vienna Chamber of Labor, as she expressed her affection and gratitude on the occasion of Schlesinger's 70th birthday.[68] Like other young women and like Schlesinger twenty years before, she herself had painfully experienced the crude treatment in store for the members of the first generation of female academics, who profited from the women's movement, and for women of Jewish descent.[69] In addition, Oskar Pollak, Julius Braunthal, and his sister Bertha Braunthal were regular participants in the discussions at Schlesinger's house.

By the early 1930s, a more radical group had joined the circle in Schlesinger's home, a group carried by the grandchildren's generation and concerned with the growing authoritarian and fascist trends. Therese Schlesinger, who had a big heart for juveniles with a criminal record or psychiatric patients, was adamant on this question: "Of course, we cannot reform or educate political enemies. We must incapacitate them."[70] This was the kind of language the young people liked, among them her declared "adopted grandson"[71] Ernst Federn, the son of Paul and Wilma Federn, the secretary of the Protective Association, Karl Heinz or Peter Strasser, the son of Isa and Josef Strasser. As Federn recalled, she insisted that he graduate high school and not get himself lost in party politics. Schlesinger knew that "only too often will we measure the attainability of a goal by the zeal with which we pursue it."[72] Federn obeyed and enrolled in law school. As a result of the Social Democrats' policies of retreat in the face of growing authoritarian and anti-democratic trends, young people from various Social-Democratic organizations in Vienna staged a massive protest at the beginning of the 1930s, among them Karl Stavarits, who, in 1968, became professor for modern history at the Johannes Kepler University in Linz after decades in exile as Karl R. Stadler, as well as Christian Broda, legendary Austrian reform minister of justice in the 1970s. "Theres" was said to have predicted the disaster and to have understood the young people

68. Leichter, "Therese Schlesinger," 6.
69. Hauch, "Käthe Leichter."
70. Schlesinger, "Strafjustiz," 418.
71. Interview Ernst Federn 10 July 1982, interviewed by Hans Schafrank, Sammlung erzählte Geschichte, Dokumentationsarchiv des Österreichischen Widerstandes, Vienna.
72. Schlesinger, "Mein Weg," 137.

who sought more radical political ways. Ernst Federn, however, remained a Social Democrat all of his life.

In 1929, Therese Schlesinger gave the 15-year-old Federn Leo Trotsky's biography, *My Life*, which had just been published in German and which, in her opinion, was one of the "most crucial books."[73] He associated this episode in his memory with meeting Julius Metsch in Schlesinger's circle after February 1934. Four years older than Federn and a major in German language and literature, Metsch showed him the appeal for the foundation of the (Trotskyist) Fourth International and inspired him to become active inside the clandestine follow-up organization of the illegal SDAP, the Revolutionary Socialists, and to contact Trotsky. Schlesinger approved of Metsch's suggestions: "'Yes,' she said, 'Let's do it. I will write to Fritz Adler.'"[74] Apart from the grandchildren in Schlesinger's circle, other Revolutionary Socialists who were concerned about Stalinism and National Socialism and disappointed with Social-Democratic politics, such as Carl and Aline Furtmüller, became enthusiastic about the analyses and perspectives of Trotsky, who himself was threatened by persecution and lived in exile. The group was discovered in 1936, and Federn was arrested. When he got out of jail after four months, he ended his clandestine activities but continued to attend meetings at "Theres's."

By dint of her age, Therese Schlesinger embodied the kind of authority and radical tradition sought by the young intellectuals born between the turn of the century and the First Republic, the partially Jewish elite of the Viennese Social-Democratic movement. In the memories of Käthe Leichter, Marianne Pollak, or Stella Klein-Löw, she emerges as the approving and thus exonerating mentor in their individual lives. She took the part of Ernst Federn, when, shortly after his release from prison, Käthe Leichter, who was 19 years his senior, challenged him on his Trotskyist phase: "'But, Käthe, we, too, embraced radical ideas in our day. Ernst is completely right.'" This "settled" the issue, as Ernst Federn remembered.[75] Both Käthe Leichter and Ernst Federn were arrested and deported to concentration camps after the Nazis took power. Käthe Leichter was murdered; Ernst Federn survived.[76]

73. Kuschey, *Die Ausnahme*, 109.

74. Ibid., 173-87. Friedrich Adler, son of SDAP party founder Victor Adler and secretary of the Socialist International at the time, had shot Prime Minister Graf Stürgkh in 1916 to protest against the war politics of the Habsburg state.

75. Ibid., 232.

76. Ernst Federn died after his life's odyssey—seven years in concentration camps, immigration to the USA, called back by Minister of Justice Christian Broda—shortly after his 93rd birthday in July 2007 in Vienna; Bernhard Kuschey, "Nachruf auf Ernst Federn, 1914-2007," *Werkblatt. Zeitschrift für Psychoanalyse und Gesellschaftskritik* 24, no. 2 (2007):

We have not been able to determine how Therese Schlesinger managed to flee to France in 1939. Marianne Pollak welcomed Therese Schlesinger, who was sick and had grown more and more infirm as a result of several falls and abdominal and lower back pain, at the Gare de L'Est in Paris. A year later, Therese Schlesinger died on July 5, 1940 in a sanitarium in Blois near Paris, one day before her 78th birthday and six days before the invasion of Paris by German troops.

Therese Schlesinger's ideas, whose goal it was to make possible a joyful existence for all in a society that embraced universal fairness and thus was friendly to women, did not re-enter the discourse until the 1970s. This is how long the specter of the destruction of freedom of opinion at the hands of the National-Socialists and Dollfuß's corporate state remained alive in the young Austrian democracy. At the beginning of the 21st century, we lack those social utopias, those social models based on "liberty-equality-sisterhood," which were discredited in the face of Stalinist crimes and the so-called real, existing socialism. Unlike many of her intellectual and artistic contemporaries, Therese Schlesinger never departed from the straight and narrow.

Intimate Stranger

Being aware of the "misinterpretation" of a biographical life story, we must acknowledge that we cannot know or show what somebody—Therese Schlesinger, in this case—was "really" like. Therese Schlesinger's public activities and her published ideas and opinions offer many opportunities to tighten the focus and pin her down to an identity, such as the active and theoretical feminist, the critical-yet-loyal Social Democrat, the successful parliamentarian, and the woman of Jewish descent. In my biographical approach, I try to avoid limiting her to any of these narratives. As I said in the beginning, my interest in researching a historical personality, apart from personal reasons, originated in the meaning a person's life takes on in a specific historic context. Current interest in Therese Schlesinger's person revolves around the desire to construct a female individual without contradictions. Schlesinger's life offers much inspiration to modern women to think and do something about their status as members of a disadvantaged gender group in a precarious political, social, cultural, and economic world. Schlesinger's determination not to isolate herself after personal tragedies but to create new social ties, an extended family, so to speak, can become an important connection with modern women, who are struggling with

117-22.

the dissolution of traditional social relationships. Schlesinger's philosophy, her ideas and concepts, which sprang up around her goal to create a joyful existence for all in a society that is fair to women, also resonate with modern women and give meaning to her life. Schlesinger's ideas re-entered the discourse in the 1970s.[77] This is how long the destruction and loss of her *world* through the corporate state and National Socialism haunted the young Austrian democracy. However, her thoughts and concepts still move us, which makes Therese Schlesinger an intimate stranger.

77. Please find Therese Schlesinger's bibliography in progress at <http://www.univie.ac.at/biografiA> (11 Aug. 2011).

Thinking Cosmopolitan or How Joseph Became Joe Buttinger

Philipp Luis Strobl [1]

Introduction

> "Mr. Buttinger was such a hero that if he had returned he would have become Chancellor."
>
> The former Austrian Chancellor Bruno Kreisky on Joseph Buttinger [2]

On May 27, 1932, the Austrian parliament approved a new government that should change the democratic course the country had pursued since the end of the First World War. The new chancellor Engelbert Dollfuß now was in charge of the country's leadership. On October 1, he used a so-called "emergency degree," a wartime relict, to rule the country without the approbation of the Austrian parliament.[3] That was the hour of birth of Austria's first dictatorship. The consequences for the people were fatal. *Unliebsame Personen* as "unpleasant" persons were called at that time had more and more problems living a normal life. Particularly intellectuals who were engaged in the ideas of psychoanalysis, neopositivism, or austromarxism (socialism) had to fear reprisals from the government.[4] Life became very hard for the government's opponents, but for most of these persons, the situation turned from bad to worse with the incorporation of Austria into Hitler's German Reich in 1938. So-called "enemies of the government" were forced to emigrate and many of them did so. According to a 1941 Office of Strategic Service memorandum, more than 40,000 Austrians had immigrated to the United States during the three years since the Anschluss in 1938.[5]

---

1. I would like to thank the Botstiber Foundation for its generous support of my work at the University of New Orleans. I would also like to thank my mentor at UNO Günter Bischof for his advice in the writing of this paper and for inviting me to UNO to participate in his "Quiet Invaders" research project supported by the Botstiber Foundation.

2. Bruce Lambert, "Joseph A. Buttinger, Nazi Fighter And Vietnam Scholar, Dies at 85," *New York Times*, 8 Mar. 1992.

3. Joseph Buttinger, *In the Twilight of Socialism: A History of the Revolutionary Socialists of Austria* (New York: Frederick A. Praeger, 1953), 3.

4. Alfred Poser and Friedrich Stadler, *Die verbrannten Bücher* (Vienna: author's edition, 1983), 30.

5. Peter Eppel, *Österreicher im Exil: USA 1938-1945; Eine Dokumentation*, vol 1 (Vienna: Österreichischer Bundesverlag, 1995), 29.

Joseph Buttinger, © Dokumentationsarchiv des österreichischen Widerstandes (DÖW)/Fotosammlung

This paper is about one of those who emigrated as a result of ideological reasons. It describes the life of the former Socialist leader, International Rescue Comitee (IRC) founding member and writer, Joseph Buttinger, who had to flee his native country to start a new life in an unfamiliar continent like many of Austria's "unpleasant persons." The main intention of this paper is to depict how and why Buttinger integrated into his new homeland and when he became a "real American." The description of his difficult and eventful youth when he worked his way up from a poor agricultural servant with little perspectives to a respected leader of one of Austria's largest parties is also of interest here. On the one hand it will help us find answers on the paper's primary purpose. On the other hand a biography about a person with a strong will such as Buttinger possessed is not possible without a description of his fascinating personal background that characterized the development of his exceptional personality.

A further task of the paper is to ask whether he came to the United States as a so-called "quiet invader" as E. Wilder Spaulding named those Austro-Americans who integrated "so quietly and with so little to say about the glories of the old monarchy or the charm of the young republic that Americans are surprised to learn that they were ever anything but American."[6] Another point of interest is whether it was easy for Buttinger to immigrate into the States. In this context, immigration laws of the United States during the sensitive period of the Anschluss era are also of great interest.

Rural Poverty—Buttinger's Childhood

Joseph Buttinger's youth was a time full of hardship and poverty. His father Anton came from a poor rural family from the village of Lohnsburg in the Austrian state of Upper Austria. Life was hard in the countryside at the turn of the 19th to the 20th century. Most of the numerous members of rural families lived together in a single house. There were no "modern" amenities such as electrical light or indoor plumbing. Peasants lived from what they could harvest from their fields. Goods such as salt, pepper and sugar were rare on the farmers' tables. Coffee, if ever, was served only on holidays.[7]

Buttingers father Anton was one of twelve children. This was not unusual in the Austrian countryside. The region of Upper Austria belonged to an agricultural area characterized by the growing of cereals. In that region peasants needed fewer servants than in other more labor-intensive agricultural branches.

There was no chance for Buttinger's father to find a job on the parental farm, for only the oldest male child was entitled to inherit the farm. Anton Buttinger hence had to do odd jobs wherever he could find them. Like his brothers he worked as agricultural servant before he got a job in the road building business bringing him to the neighboring German province of Bavaria.[8] In the spring of 1905 he met his later wife, a poor Bavarian orphan who already had a child. She was employed at a local farm. He fell

---

6. E. Wilder Spaulding, *The Quiet Invaders: The Story of the Austrian Impact Upon America* (Vienna: Österreichischer Bundesverlag, 1968), 1.

7. Ernst Hanisch, *Der Lange Schatten des Staates: Österreichische Gesellschaftsgeschichte im 20. Jahrhundert* (Vienna: Ueberreuter, 1994), 20.

8. Joseph Buttinger, *Ortswechsel: Geschichte meiner Jugend* (Frankfurt: Verlag neue Kritik, 1979), 9.

in love with her and married her after a few weeks. The marriage resulted in the birth of three children. The first was Joseph, born on April 30, 1906.

Anton's salary barely sufficed to feed the family.[9] The family's Nutrition consisted mainly of potatoes and bread.[10] His efforts to grant his family a better life by accepting various different jobs brought the Buttingers to several places in Germany during Joseph's youth.[11] In his memoires, he stated that poverty was omnipresent during these years. He wrote how he went barefooted through German streets collecting horse manure to dung his mother's small vegetable garden.[12] Buttinger described his childhood before the war as a very annoying time. Because of the family's impecuniousness they could not buy toys or books. So there was not much for the children to do except play in the dirty streets.

August 1914 changed the life of the family dramatically. Like millions of other males in Austria-Hungary and her wartime ally Germany, Joseph's father was drafted to serve in the Austrian Army during the First World War. During the first war year when he, as an Austrian citizen, was employed in a German mine he was lucky enough not to be detected by the authorities. But in July 1915 the German draft board apprehended him and sent him to the Austrian army. One year later, his family was sent back to the native village of Joseph's father.

The war years were full of deprivations. Nearly everything was rationed and the Buttinger family experienced desperate poverty.[13] Joseph described that time as particularly hard. The family had barely enough to eat and insufficient clothing; shoes for the children were only available in wintertime.[14] They also did not have enough money for Christmas or birthday presents. In Austria where living conditions were much worse than in Germany, the Buttingers made ends meet, but barely so. Before the war, the mining company Anton Buttinger worked for provided them with a flat comprising three bedrooms, a kitchen, and a toilet. The house even contained a hand-operated washing machine.[15] In Waldzell in Upper Austria, however, the Buttingers were crowded together in a simple single room apartment in a small building extension of an old farm.[16]

9. Muriel Gardiner and Joseph Buttinger, *Damit wir nicht vergessen: Unsere Jahre 1934-1947 in Wien, Paris und New York* (Wien: Verlag der Wiener Volksbuchhandlung, 1978), 25.

10. Buttinger, *Ortswechsel*, 10.

11. Gardiner and Buttinger, *nicht vergessen*, 25.

12. Buttinger, *Ortswechsel*, 14.

13. Ibid., 21.

14. Gardiner and Buttinger, *nicht vergessen*, 26.

15. Buttinger, *Ortswechsel*, 19.

16. Ibid., 24.

In 1916, Anton Buttinger was wounded on the Italian front. Lousy medical care and undernourishment led to his death in March 1917 in a military asylum in Linz.[17] During these desperate years, young Joseph, for the first time, felt deep anger with the political system. He later observed that he had recognized at that point that "for poor people the fatherland often is the real enemy."[18]

The loss of the only wage earner worsened the family's deprivation. There were many days when the members of the family had nothing to eat. The Buttingers, like many other Austrians in the last year of the war, experienced disastrous food shortages. The population was particularly affected by cuts in the flour ration, caused by peace expectations following the talks of Brest-Litovsk in early 1918.[19] The small widow's pension of Mrs. Buttinger did not suffice to feed all of the family's mouths. The Buttinger children had to go begging in the neighborhood. Years later, Buttinger described street beggary as a deeply shaming experience. According to historian Ernst Hanisch, begging was a common institution and not unusual for poor agricultural laborers at that time. According to Hanisch, begging children appealed to the "maternal duty of wealthier farmers' wives."[20]

Joseph's childhood was characterized by his strictly conservative Catholic surroundings and he began to develop enthusiasm for the church. He served as an altarboy whenever it was possible. Besides the small compensation altarboys could earn for their services, there was another incentive for him—it was the only escape from the monotonous daily life characterized by hard physical work, no access to consumer goods, a rigid hierarchical social structure, and last but not least strict social control by the village community and the church.[21] During his entire four years in rural Waldzell, young Joseph never experienced the pleasure of reading a book or watching a stage play or a concert apart from listening to organ music in the church.[22]

When he turned thirteen, he started a job as an agricultural servant on a local farm[23], which was common in the countryside.[24] Now at least his worries about food came to an end. But new problems emerged. He

---

17. Gardiner and Buttinger, *nicht vergessen*, 26; Buttinger, *Ortswechsel*, 28.
18. Buttinger, *Ortswechsel*, 29.
19. Hanno Scheuch, "Austria 1918-55: From the First to the Second Republic," *The Historical Journal* 32, no. 1 (1989): 177-199, 178.
20. Hanisch, *Österreichische Geschichte*, 97.
21. Ibid., 93.
22. Buttinger, *Ortswechsel*, 62.
23. Gardiner and Buttinger, *nicht vergessen*, 26.
24. Hanisch, *Österreichische Geschichte*, 97.

described unspeakable working conditions. Corporal punishment still was regularly administered in rural Austria. It even was accepted as the rule in the official regulations for the treatment of agricultural servants, the so-called *Dienstbotenordnungen*.[25] After a while, Buttinger developed neurotical symptoms (bedwetting, spasmodic winking)[26] showing the enormous stress the teenager was under. Moreover, three month before his thirteenth birthday he had to drop out school against his will.[27]

First Contacts with the Social Democratic Movement

Although he lived in a strictly conservative catholic rural environment, he came in to contact with the ideas of the Socialist party. At the turn of the century, voters in the countryside tended entirely to be in favor of the conservative Christian Social party. The leftist Social Democrats usually gained about twelve percent of the rural vote.[28] The revolutionary mood at the end of World War I was characterized by Social Democratic attempts to strengthen their political influence by mobilizing the masses.[29] In the countryside they began to organize conservative agricultural workers with some success. In Waldzell, young religious conservative Joseph not only witnessed two of these organizational attempts but also recognized the unjust violent reaction Social Democratic activists were facing from rural landowning conservatives.[30] He began to sympathize with the ideas of the Social Democrats. In his memoirs, he described a demonstration organized by the Social Democrats in Waldzell in January 1921. This became a turning point in his life. He began to realize "to where he belongs."[31]

The Buttinger family was fortunate to escape the economic and mental dead-end of their situation in Waldzell. Negotiated through a wealthy influential relative, the Buttingers got the chance to move to the industrial village of Schneegattern a few miles away from Waldzell. Joseph arrived there on February 2, 1921. In Schneegattern everything was different. While conservative catholic farmers dominated Waldzell, Schneegattern was dominated by a sizable Social Democratic anticlerical population

25. Ibid.
26. Buttinger, *Ortswechsel*, 54.
27. Gardiner and Buttinger, *nicht vergessen*, 26.
28. Lewis Gavin, "The Peasantry, Rural Change and Conservative Agrarianism: Lower Austria at the Turn of the Century," *Past & Present* 81, no 1 (1978): 119-143, 123.
29. Scheuch, "Austria 1918-55," 178.
30. Buttinger, *Ortswechsel*, 60.
31. Ibid., 61.

(about ninety percent of all residents).[32] Wages still were not very high, but people had the chance to experience a new life with new and unknown possibilities. At fifteen years old Joseph read his first book there, browsed through his first newspaper, and ate his first orange.[33]

Buttinger and his older half-brother Anton found a job in a factory that produced glassware. Apart from encountering new treasures (books, fruits) Buttinger in Schneegattern experienced a further achievement of a modern society—regular working hours. In contrast to his former work as a rural servant when he labored regularly through sixteen-hour workdays, he now had a forty-eight-hour workweek in the glass factory, introduced by the Socialist led postwar Austrian government two years earlier.[34] This eight-hour workday, together with the free access to information and education in the workers' library, allowed the studious adolescent to acquire more and more knowledge. Buttinger soon found a new home within the Social Democratic party organizations. Besides his largely autodidactic studies, Buttinger's leisure time was governed by activities organized by the party.

Soon after his arrival in the new workers' environment, young Joseph joined several leftist party organizations such as the *Naturfreunde* who regularly organized hiking tours and lectures about geography and life in other countries. He also became a member of the Social Democratic party and of the trade union for glassworkers.[35] In his memoires he wrote, that he "always will be grateful for the possibilities the party, the labor union, and the workers' cultural associations offered him."[36]

A year or so after the beginning of his new life as a worker in Schneegattern, the former religious adolescent turned away from the Catholic Church. According to his new socialist perspective, he considered the Roman Catholic Church not only as a false faith (like most Social Democrats at that time), but also a tool "to enslave the poor and exploited population."[37] He delved into studying the history of religion along with political history, philosophy and psychology.

In February 1922, not quite sixteen years old, Buttinger was elected chair of a local group of the Socialistic Workers Youth.[38] Since alcoholism

32. Ibid., 59.
33. Gardiner and Buttinger, *nicht vergessen*, 27.
34. Peter Jabornegg, *Interessenskampf um die Arbeitszeit: Die Arbeitszeit in der Arbeitsrechtentwicklung*, AK-Konferenz: Die Arbeitszeit human gestalten, June 2006, 11.
35. Buttinger, *Ortswechsel*, 85.
36. Ibid., 86.
37. Ibid., 80, 91.
38. Gardiner and Buttinger, *nicht vergessen*, 27.

was a huge problem in the Austrian working class[39], Buttinger, driven by the Socialist ideology[40], decided to do something about it. He founded a local group of the socialistic workers abstinence association, the so-called *Arbeiter Abstinenzverein*. According to contemporary social researcher Marie Jahoda, who knew him well, Buttinger's excellent organizing skills made him widely accepted within the local party circles.[41] He soon started giving talks to socialistic youth organizations throughout his home district of Wels.[42]

Buttinger's financial and personal situation improved steadily. In 1923, he even managed to afford a pleasure trip to Italy; something the average working class Austrian could not do until the beginning of the *Wirtschaftswunder* (economic miracle) in the 1950s.[43]

In December 1924 his financial situation worsened as a result of his company's closing due to the postwar economic downturn. The decommissioning of the factory affected the entire industrial village. Almost the whole population of Schneegattern lost their jobs.[44] As a consequence, many workers left the village. Among them were Joseph's half-brother Anton as well as his stepfather, the man his mother had married shortly after the family arrived in Schnegattern. The eighteen-year-old Buttinger decided to stay in his village although it was impossible for him to find a job. He now profited from the newly created public unemployment insurance the Austrian postwar government had introduced two years before.[45] Buttinger's next two years were characterized by intensive self-studies and participation in several Socialist Party events. Shortly after he became unemployed, he started learning English on his own—no one in his village was able to teach him or even spoke any English. It is very unlikely that he intended to emigrate to the United States or Great Britain at that point.

---

39. Robert J. Wegs, "Working Class Respectability: The Viennese Experience," *Journal of Social History* 15, no. 4 (1982): 621-635, 628.

40. Many socialist believed, alcoholism, like religion was a capitalist means to enslave the working class.

41. Marie Jahoda, *Ich habe die Welt nicht verändert: Lebenserinnerungen einer Pionierin der Sozialforschung* (Frankfurt: Campus Verlag, 1997) 53.

42. Buttinger, *Ortswechsel*, 92.

43. See: Axel Schildt, "From Reconstruction to 'Leisure Society': Free Time, Recreational Behavior and the Discourse on Leisure Time in the West German Recovery Society of the 1950's," *Contemporary European History* 5, no. 2 (1996): 191-222.

44. ATSV Schneegattern, "85 Jahre ATSV Schneegattern: 1922 – 1997," in *ATSV Schneegattern.com*, 2009 <http://www.atsv-schneegattern.com/index.php?option=com_content&view=article&id=51&Itemid=55&showall=1> (16 Apr. 2010).

45. Das Rote Wien. Lexikon der Wiener Sozialdemokratie, "Ferdinand Hanusch," in *dasroteWien.at, 2005* <http://www.dasrotewien.at/online/page.php?P=11548> (15 Apr. 2010).

He did not mention such intentions in his memoirs. His English studies rather were part of a self-driven personal general education program that also included the disciplines of economics, natural history, and philosophy.[46] He even mentioned in his memoirs that, for a long time, he had prejudices towards "the quality of American literature."[47] Buttinger most certainly also was influenced by a common leftist view characterizing the United States of America as a capitalistic, unsocial country.[48]

Buttinger's Political Career in the Making

A further turning point in Buttinger's life took place in April 1926 when he found employment in a small glassware factory in the upper Austrian city of Wels. Unlike the villages of Schneegattern or Waldzell with about 1,000 inhabitants, Wels was one of the biggest towns in Upper Austria. A 1923 census pointed to a total population of 24,248.[49] A few weeks after his arrival, he was elected into his first important political position. Hardly twenty years old, he became chairman of the Social Democratic Party for the political district of Wels.[50] He now came into contact with the leaders of the party as well as with socialist intellectuals who supported him with books and advice to continue his autodidactic studies.

The closing of the factory two months after he started to work did not really affect him too much this time because his party friends had already organized a job for him in the administration of Upper Austria's provincial capital of Linz. One month before he started his new job, he got the chance to participate in a workshop in Vienna about the principles of socialist education. Already in the first week of his stay, he attracted the attention of the course organizer who offered him a job as manager and educator in a Social Democratic youth center in Carinthia, in the south of Austria, starting in September 1926.[51]

He remained in that position for four years until January 1930. That time period was among the happiest of his life. He had a chance to make

46. Buttinger, *Ortswechsel*, 102.
47. Ibid., 117.
48. Günter Bischof, "Two Sides of the Coin: The Americanization of Austria and Austrian Anti-Americanism," in *The Americanization of Europe: Culture, Diplomacy, and Anti-Americanism after 1945*, ed. Alexander Stephan (New York: Berghan Books, 2006), 147-184, 167.
49. Statistik Austria, "Ein Blick auf die Gemeinde Wels," in *statistik.at*, 2010, <http://www.statistik.at/blickgem/blick1/g40301.pdf> (15 Apr. 2010).
50. Buttinger, *Ortswechsel*, 106.
51. Ibid., 107.

enormous progresses in his continuous autodidactic studies thanks to an abundant workers' library and his contacts to many educated socialists in his new residence city of St.Veit/Glan or the nearby provincial capital of Klagenfurt.[52] In 1928, when he took a pleasure trip to Paris and London, he heard English spoken by a native for the first time. This was a shock for him; never before had he heard how English words were pronounced—he hardly understood a single sentence.[53]

During the last year of his time in Carinthia, he decided to write a book "combining the whole knowledge of his studies."[54] *Vom Urnebel zum Zukunftsstaat* (from the primeval fog to the state of the future) was characterized by "frightening dogmatism and intellectual arrogance" as Buttinger himself stated years later.[55] Nonetheless, the book attracted attention among higher party officials in Vienna. In 1930 he became secretary of the Social Democratic Party in the district of St.Veit/Glan.[56]

Before he started in St.Veit, he was sent to the Social Democratic *Arbeiterhochschule*, an intensive political preparation course in the party academy. The course was held in the city of Vienna and lasted for six months. Its founding can be seen as a short lasting (1926 to 1933) party attempt to create an alternative education track for future party elites.[57] The course level corresponded with the level of a sophisticated secondary school.[58] Among his fellow students were future party leaders such as Franz Jonas (a later president in Austria's Second Republic).[59] Buttinger left the party academy with "enormous self-confidence and high-flying political ambitions"[60] and was willing to address the problems and tasks of his party position.

By the time Buttinger entered his new position, Austrian Social Democrats (or democracy generally speaking) faced huge problems. The economic crisis unleashed by black Friday in New York in October 1929 had repercussions not only on the economic situation of the entire country, it also had huge negative effects on the political climate.[61] Austria's

---

52. Ibid., 115.
53. Ibid., 128.
54. Christian Reder, "The Twilight of Socialism: Drei Biographien zu Österreichs Zeitgeschichte," *Falter*, Nr. 20 (1983).
55. Buttinger, *Ortswechsel*, 118.
56. Gardiner and Buttinger, *nicht vergessen*, 28.
57. Gernot Stimmer, *Eliten in Österreich: 1848-1970* (Vienna: Böhlau, 1997), 628.
58. Ibid.
59. Buttinger, *Ortswechsel*, 132.
60. Jahoda, *Lebenserinnerungen*, 53.
61. Emmerich Tálos and Walter Manoschek, "Zum Konstituierungsprozeß des Austrofaschismus," *Austrofaschismus: Beiträge über Politik, Ökonomie und Kultur 1934-1938,*

conservative and right wing parties more and more embarked on an anti-democratic course in order to save their position of power.[62] They began to use the apparatus of state against their opponents.[63] Unpopular budget restoration actions as well as the bankruptcy of the biggest Austrian bank led to an increasing influx of voters to the opposition parties.[64] There were not only Social Democrats who gained more votes. The newly emerged Nazi movement became stronger and stronger in those years. In April 1933, provincial elections in Vienna, Lower Austria and Salzburg had shown that about a third of the former Christian Social Party voters had gone National Socialist.[65] The former Austrian Socialist emigrant Adolf Sturmthal described the situation as extremely critical. Each of the three bigger parties fought "a war of life and death."[66] Buttinger and his party members saw the new movement as much more dangerous for Austrian democracy than the conservatives who turned increasingly undemocratic.[67] In these difficult times, when his party literally and physically was "fighting" a war on two frontiers, Buttinger constantly tried to gain more and more voters in his district. Ambitiously, he started to reorganize the party apparatus and to find talented people representing the Social Democrats in the particular villages.

But the years from 1930 to the outlawing of his party in 1934 above all were characterized by his war against "Nazism." In his memoirs, Buttinger described that he used "all his power and his political knowledge to expose the real nature of the movement."[68] In the summer of 1933 he had saved enough money to take a further pleasure trip. He decided to go to France for several weeks to "improve his French," as he wrote in his memoirs.[69] Based on the critical political situation in Austria as well as on the election of the NSDAP in Germany on January 30, one might assume that the trip was not all pleasure. Maybe Buttinger, who was neither welcomed by the Nazi party nor by the conservative Christian Social Party, had an inkling of what might happen in the following years and had begun to consider emergency

eds. Emmerich Tálos and Walter Neugebauer (Vienna: Literaturverlag, 2005), 31-52, 36.

62. Ibid., 37.

63. Emmerich Tálos, "Das Herrschaftssystem 1934 – 1938: Erklärungen und begriffliche Bestimmungen. Ein Resümee," *Austrofaschismus: Beiträge über Politik, Ökonomie und Kultur 1934-1938,* eds. Emmerich Tálos and Walter Neugebauer (Vienna: Literaturverlag, 2005), 267-286, 274.

64. Ibid., 275.

65. Buttinger, *Twilight of Socialism*, 3.

66. Adolf Sturmthal, *Zwei Leben: Erinnerungen eines sozialistischen Internationalisten zwischen Österreich und den USA* (Wien: Böhlau, 1989), 131.

67. Buttinger, *Ortswechsel*, 142.

68. Ibid., 143.

69. Ibid., 149.

emigration plans. In his memoirs he also mentioned that he had started to prepare himself and some of his colleagues for the "expected illegality."[70] He spent four months in St.Rémy Les Chevreuse, a small village close to Paris, where he made contact with the socialist family Coissac. In 1938, when he was forced to emigrate, he profited from these months and his relationship to the French family, even though, at that time, he already was financially secure through his relationship to his later wife Muriel "Mary" Gardiner.[71]

The Road into the "Illegality"

On March 4, 1933, a few months before Buttinger's trip to France, the Christian Social chancellor Engelbert Dollfuß used discordances in parliament to dissolve it. That step de facto dismantled democracy in the Austrian republic.[72] On a party congress shortly afterwards, Buttinger found himself among the most vehement critics of the party leadership's decision not to intervene.[73] "One of the most important failures of the party before its dissolution was the lacking preparation for its illegal work," he later wrote in an expose.[74] The Austrian government used the period from 1933 to 1934 to transform the former Republic into a fascist one-party state. In May 1933 the fast growing Nazi party was outlawed after launching a couple of assaults. At the same time Austria's chancellor Dollfuß successively began to dismantle the Social Democratic party structures. On May 31, the *Republikanische Schutzbund*, the Socialist party's militia, was prohibited. Soon afterwards, the government banned the traditional May ceremonies, and weakened the party's position in different important state institutions (social insurance, etc.).[75]

Buttinger, in his position as party secretary of St.Veit/Glan, prepared himself for an "emerging civil war."[76] He tried to convince the party leaders of the necessity of a strong-armed resistance, worked meticulously on plans for harassments in his home district in case of a civil war, and as mentioned before, tried to prepare himself and other party members for

70. Ibid., 153.
71. Jahoda, *Lebenserinnerungen*, 53.
72. Nationalsozialismus.at, "Die Ausschaltung des Parlaments," in *nationalsozialismus.at: Demokratie braucht Wissen*, 10 July 2003, <http://nationalsozialismus.at/Themen/Austrofasch/parlament.htm> (05 May 2010).
73. Buttinger, *Ortswechsel*, 149.
74. Dokumentationsarchiv des Österreichischen Widerstandes [hereafter cited as DÖW] Archive, File Number: 7523, Dokumente und Entwürfe über die Programme und Arbeiten der RSÖ.
75. Tálos and Manoschek, "Konstituierungsprozess," 44.
76. Buttinger, *Ortswechsel*, 152.

partisan activities underground.[77] Buttinger, who, up until that moment in time, owed everything in his life to the Socialist party, was willing to defend it by all means. His cold-blooded determination was clearly analyzed by Marie Jahoda criticizing his "frightening determination" during the "illegal years" of the party.[78] But the intentions towards war and peace of the party's leadership around Otto Bauer differed greatly from Buttinger's expectations. The main goal of the Social Democrat's majority was to avoid a military clash between the party militia and governmental troops.[79] That strategy worked until February 12, 1934, when state troops attacked several party offices in Upper Austria, Styria, and Vienna. This unleashed an intensive but short lasting burst of resistance of local, armed party members.

Interestingly, Buttinger did not participate in these resistance fights. He claimed in his memoirs that he did not get promised munitions in time and therefore decided to hide from the state executive, which "likely would have put him into prison."[80] When Buttinger realized that the government did not prosecute lower party functionaries from districts that had not participated in the February fights he left his hiding-place. Now, the party profited from the underground structure he had organized before. He began to print pamphlets critical of the government and even a weekly magazine, and started to paint anti-fascist messages on walls all around his district.[81] His intensive underground work soon attracted the suspicious country's government. His flat became increasingly suspect and attracted house searches. Finally, in May 1934, he was thrown into prison for the possession of illegal propaganda material.[82]

Going Underground: Buttinger's Career as the Leader of the Revolutionary Socialists

The local security police kept him in a jail in the city of Villach for more than three months. He only was released because he agreed to leave the state of Carinthia.[83] He decided to move to the capital city of Austria where the leadership of the illegal socialist party was situated. He arrived in Vienna on August 20, 1934.[84] Because of the steady arrests of members of the socialist

77. Ibid.
78. Jahoda, *Lebenserinnerungen*, 53.
79. Buttinger, *Twilight of Socialism*, 10.
80. Buttinger, *Ortswechsel*, 152.
81. Ibid., 154.
82. Ibid., 155.
83. DÖW Archive, File Number: 2761, Erlebnisbericht und Lebenslauf des österreichischen Historikers Josef Buttinger.
84. Joseph Buttinger, *Am Beispiel Österreichs: Ein Geschichtlicher Beitrag zur Krise der*

party,[85] there was an urgent need of devoted activists. Buttinger proved to be a "master of the tactics of conspiracy" escaping arrest again during this dangerous time working underground in Vienna.[86] Within a short time, he became an important player in the illegal party network. He entered the so-called *Zentralkomitee*, a successor organization of the Socialist Party leadership. One month after his arrival, he became spokesman of the body's provincial organization. In this position, he tried to change the course of the party. He increasingly became one of the most important inner party critics. In order to save the party's existence, he demanded a total change of the party's structures and therefore criticized the leading position of the emigrated party leadership across the Austrian border in the Czechoslovakian city of Brno.[87]

A further wave of arrests, following a secret party conference in December 1934, eliminated nearly the whole managerial level of the Socialist Party.[88] The lack of leaders favored Buttinger's further advancement in the party. He and four other party members, who were lucky enough not to be caught by the authorities, took over the orphaned party leadership on February 17, 1935. They began to centralize what remained of the formerly biggest party of Austria,[89] which once had gained more than two thirds of all Austrian votes.[90] Along the lines of Buttinger's former demands, the new management changed the shape of the Socialist Party now called the "Revolutionary Socialists of Austria." According to Lenin's principle of a "democratic centralism," the new members of the *Zentralkomitee* privileged themselves with dictatorial power.[91] They also changed the structure of the inner party organization. According to an article describing the new design of the socialistic workers movement, the whole organization was downsized and much more tightly organized.[92] Buttinger also demanded a much more visible delimitation of the leftist block consisting of the Revolutionary

sozialistischen Bewegung (Cologne: Verlag für Politik und Wirtschaft, 1953), 235.

85. Everhard Holtmann, *Zwischen Unterdrückung und Befriedung: Sozialistische Arbeiterbewegung und autoritäres Regime in Österreich 1933-1938* (Vienna: Verlag für Geschichte und Politik, 1978), 144.

86. DÖW Archive, File Number: 2761, Erlebnisbericht und Lebenslauf des österreichischen Historikers Josef Buttinger.

87. DÖW Archive, File Number: 7523, Dokumente und Entwürfe über die Programme und Arbeiten der RSÖ.

88. Holtmann, *Unterdrückung und Befreiung*, 201.

89. Ibid.

90. Sturmthal, *Zwei Leben*, 177.

91. DÖW Archive, File Number: 7523, Dokumente und Entwürfe über die Programme und Arbeiten der RSÖ.

92. Ibid.

Socialist and the Austrian Communist Party.[93] Several days after the new leadership seized power, it broke up the existing confederation with the Communists.[94] This was necessary since the Communists attempted to appear as the only real alternative for leftist voters.[95] His description in one of his letters from that time that he had intensive "contact with the *Zentralkomitee* of the Communist Party" does not fit the official course of the Revolutionary Socialists of Austria. Both organizations published some political statements, agreed to a mutual action program against the government, and decided to establish "companionable relations."[96]

His years in the country's most important socialistic organization brought a significant insight to the successful social climber. Buttinger recognized that it is much easier to criticize from the margin than rule at the center. "In that time, I experienced numerous really desperate moments," he later observed.[97] That feeling of desperation as well as his realization that sometimes change is not possible, might be seen as one of the causes for his quick withdrawal from politics after his wealthy wife Muriel Gardiner introduced him to a different life and society with broader possibilities in the United States.

Buttinger and his comrades had to fight on two fronts. On the one, hand they fought the political enemy tooth and nail (the fascist government, National Socialists); on the other hand, they struggled to keep the workers mobilized. The latter proved to be more difficult than expected. Numerous half-hearted protest campaigns showed the workers' increasing lack of interest in Socialist affairs.[98] From 1935 to 1938, Buttinger in his role as member of the party's leadership, worked on numerous publishing projects. He issued the *Informationsdienst*, the *Zentralkomitee's* weekly magazine, published numerous fliers and articles in illegal socialist workers journals, and was in charge of the publication of various brochures.[99]

The End of Buttinger's Life in Austria: First Connections to the United States

In February 1934 Buttinger entered the most important position within the Socialist Party. He became a member of a group in charge of the

93. Buttinger, *Am Beispiel Österreichs*, 261.
94. Holtmann, *Unterdrückung und Befreiung*, 214.
95. Ibid., 208.
96. DÖW Archive, File Number: 7523, Dokumente und Entwürfe über die Programme und Arbeiten der RSÖ.
97. Buttinger, *Am Beispiel Österreichs*, 266.
98. Holtmann, *Unterdrückung und Befreiung*, 205.
99. DÖW Archive, File Number: 7523, Dokumente und Entwürfe über die Programme und Arbeiten der RSÖ.

movement's future direction. However, his political rise was not necessarily connected to an improvement of his financial situation. That would happen only after he met his later wife Muriel Gardiner. Muriel was born in 1901 as the fourth child of the wealthy Morris family who owned one of the largest butcher shops and meat packing businesses in Chicago.[100] After earning a bachelor degree from Wellesley College in 1922, the wealthy American heiress moved to Europe to continue her studies.

One of Gardiner's trips brought her to Vienna where she became fascinated by psychoanalysis. She decided to stay there to be analyzed. In 1926 she married Julian Gardiner, a music student from Great Britain with whom she had one child, her daughter Connie. The marriage was only short-lived and the couple divorced a few years later.[101] While staying in

Muriel Gardiner, © Dokumentationsarchiv des österreichischen Widerstandes (DÖW)/Fotosammlung

100. Gardiner and Buttinger, *nicht vergessen*, 10.
101. Ibid., 18.

Austria studying medicine, Muriel became involved in Austrian politics. She advanced into an invaluable position of the antifascist Austrian underground, supporting Revolutionary Socialist activists with money and a hiding place when they had to hide from the police.

Gardiner owned a house in the small village of Sulz in the Vienna Woods not far away from the capital city of Vienna. That place became one of the secret meeting places of the illegal *Zentralkomitee*.[102] At one of these meetings, probably in 1935, she met Joseph Buttinger. Immediately she felt sympathies for him, as she later wrote in her memoirs.

Buttinger at that time still lived a modest life full of deprivations. He regularly had to hide out at various places to avoid being caught by the Austrian police. The relationship to Muriel Gardiner changed his entire life. "Wieser [Joseph Buttinger] had only the clothes he was wearing [....]: a pair of black striped trousers and a tight-fitting brown jacket, obviously city clothes and in any case too small for him," Gardiner noted in her first impression of her latter husband.[103] His relationship to the wealthy American woman brought important changes to his daily life. She bought him new clothes that were better fitting, and gave him shelter in one of her flats in Vienna as well as in her house in Sulz. Buttinger, being accustomed to poverty and deprivations, began to experience a life he never had known before—and he enjoyed it too.

In the summer of 1935 the couple was planning their first vacation to London, where Muriel introduced him to her stepfather Francis Nelson, formerly a member of the British parliament.[104] Back in Vienna, she began to introduce him to her American and British academic friends. In the summers of 1936 and 1937, she took him along with a group of American academics to the Salzburg music festival. Buttinger enjoyed every moment of these trips. He was fascinated by the friends of his American girlfriend and immediately settled down in this new life with intelligent well-traveled people, summer trips to Salzburg and winter journeys to the Swiss ski resort of Arosa.[105]

At the end of 1937, the persecution of the Socialist movement by the Austro-Fascist government reached a final climax before the Anschluss. After months of detailed preparations, the police launched a massive raid against the party's leadership. Within three days following November

102. Muriel Gardiner, *Code Name "Mary": Memoirs of an American Woman in the Austrian Underground* (New Haven: Yale University Press, 1983), 57.
103. Ibid., 71.
104. Ibid., 75.
105. Ibid., 79.

27, the police arrested about forty top-level functionaries.[106] Buttinger was abroad at that time and was lucky to escape the police raids.[107] With only a few top functionaries at large, the work of the party's leadership was reduced to wasting time in hiding while being on the run. Given this critical situation, Buttinger and his later wife saw the handwriting on the wall and made the hard decision to leave the country for a while. Muriel rented a room in a beautiful hotel situated in the snow-covered mountains of Arosa, Switzerland.

In early 1938, German pressure on Austria further increased. The German *Führer* Adolf Hitler summoned Austria's chancellor Kurt Schuschnig to a meeting in the Nazi mountain retreat in Berchtesgaden on February 11, 1938, dictating him numerous demands. One of these was an amnesty for imprisoned National Socialists.[108] Schuschnig answered with the release of all political prisoners, not only National Socialists but also Social Democrats. A few days later, Buttinger returned to Austria. "Vienna was seething with uncertainty and unrest," Muriel Gardiner later wrote. Buttinger had no doubt in his mind that the National Socialistic German Reich soon would annex Austria. Through numerous reports of their German party friends, Austrian Socialists knew very well what they had to expect in the case of the "Anschluss."[109] The majority of the Austrian Socialists elite however decided to stay in the country. According to Helene Maiman, most of them "hoped for better days" while they temporarily relinquished their political activities.[110] Buttinger recognized the perilous situation and spent his next weeks convincing his colleagues to emigrate immediately.[111] "None of his comrades were prepared for emigration," he later wrote.[112] The expected hopelessness of the Socialists' situation in Austria following the "Anschluss" effected another change in Buttinger's political career. He now took the view that the illegal Socialist Party, with its inflexible structures, had no chance fighting an underground war against the well-organized secret State Police, the Gestapo. Besides the external menace, the doubtful future provoked consistent ideological struggles between the different party

106. Holtmann, *Unterdrückung und Befreiung*, 265.

107. Gardiner and Buttinger, *nicht vergessen*, 68.

108. Francis L. Carsten, *Faschismus in Österreich: Von Schönerer zu Hitler* (Munich: Wilhelm Fink Verlag, 1977), 288.

109. Wolfgang Benz, "Fliehen vor Hitler: Einleitende Bemerkungen zum sozialdemokratischen Exil," in: Marianne Loring, *Flucht aus Frankreich 1940: Die Vertreibung deutscher Sozialdemokraten aus dem Exil* (Frankfurt: Fischer, 1996), 9-24, 9.

110. Helene Maimann, *Politik im Wartesaal: Österreichische Exilpolitik in Großbritannien 1938-1945* (Vienna: Böhlau, 1975), 9.

111. Gardiner, *"Mary,"* 84.

112. Maimann, *Politik im Wartesaal*, 10.

wings.[113] Buttinger therefore advocated a complete dissolution of the party in Austria.[114] In one of his later books he compared the party after the annexation to an "obsolete, embattled warship unfit for action."[115]

In Exile: The Stateless Refugee Buttinger

The expectation that the German Reich had plans to annex Austria became clear even to the greatest skeptics by early March 1938. Already before the official "Anschluss," illegal Austrian National Socialists had seized local control in many important cities such as Graz, Linz, and Innsbruck on March 11.[116]

Masked as a British vacationer planning a ski holiday in Switzerland, Buttinger left Vienna the next morning. He used the typical escape route to France via Switzerland that had been used by many Jews at that time.[117] Muriel Gardiner's young daughter Connie and one of her British friends accompanied him strengthening his camouflage.[118] Muriel herself remained in Austria for a few more months, finishing her medical studies. It was a time when she, recognizing the hopeless situation of many of her Austrian friends, began to help numerous people leaving the country. Most of the Austrian Socialist leaders were not as lucky as Buttinger and the small number of other refugees who left the country in the last minute. Within very short time, the new German authorities captured and arrested the rest of the Socialist underground.[119]

Buttinger meanwhile went to Paris, where most of the Austrian Socialists emigres lived for the time being. As soon as he arrived in Paris, he became entrapped in the various inner party struggles about the future direction of the Austrian Socialist movement. Because of the poor preparation for their flight, "Austrian Socialists went into emigration without a political concept." This resulted in "an aimless activism" and uncertainty about the future party direction.[120]

Soon after his arrival in April 1938, he was elected chairman of the Foreign Board of the Austrian Socialists and one of the editors of the

---

113. Ibid, 35.
114. Buttinger, *Am Beispiel Österreichs*, 543.
115. Ibid.
116. Carsten, *Faschismus*, 294.
117. Maimann, *Politik im Wartesaal*, 10.
118. Gardiner and Buttinger, *nicht vergessen*, 68.
119. Walter Wisshaupt, *Wir kommen wieder! Eine Geschichte der Revolutionären Sozialisten Österreichs 1934-1938* (Vienna, Verlag der Wiener Volksbuchhandlung, 1967), 223.
120. Maimann, *Politik im Wartesaal*, 36.

socialists' emigration magazine *Der sozialistische Kampf* (The Socialistic Struggle).[121] In this leading position, he faced the challenge of settling numerous daily disputes between the infighting party functionaries.[122] He increasingly became unhappy with the situation. "Joe was worried and often gloomy, not the cheerful, active, even-tempered person I had known in Austria," Muriel Gardiner later remembered.[123] In one of the letters he wrote in 1942, Buttinger offered some insight into his thoughts of that time. He argued that he had never really been advised to found the Foreign Board; he did not believe in the success of the "old social-democratic policy."[124] In fact one may assume that during that time, Buttinger had already embarked on pursuing other goals in his life. All evidence suggests that he did not want to be part of the Socialist emigration any longer, with its endless infighting over stale doctrine and policy. In one of his letters, he even stated that he had recognized he did not see "further use of his time and his energy within the Socialist Party."[125] He realized that he had to change his life in order to achieve success in other fields. Muriel shared his opinion and tried to convince him of a better use of his time and his capabilities.[126]

Shortly after Muriel arrived in Paris, he proposed marriage to her.[127] It probably did not entirely come out of a spontaneous feeling of love. Both, Muriel and Joseph never really believed in the importance of marriage as a legitimated life partnership.[128] In the end, both agreed to enter the marriage to ease their life situation. Buttinger had given up his Austrian citizenship shortly after his arrival in Paris. Now he was a stateless person. At that time, he most likely envisioned the "new continent" for a better future. One might gather how well prepared Buttinger was for his new life in America when reading one of his letters. Only two weeks after his arrival in New York, he noted that he was immediately familiar with the multicultural metropolis of the city of New York and his social interaction with Americans.[129]

The biggest problem for people wanting to leave Europe for the United States was getting an immigration visa.[130] Most European immigrants

121. DÖW Archive, File Number: 2761, Erlebnisbericht und Lebenslauf des österreichischen Historikers Josef Buttinger.

122. For interesting insights concerning Buttinger's occupation during that time see: DÖW, File Number: 7601, Auslandsvertretung der österreichischen Sozialisten, Paris.

123. Gardiner, *"Mary,"* 132.

124. DÖW Archive, File Number: 2761, Erlebnisbericht und Lebenslauf des österreichischen Historikers Josef Buttinger.

125. Ibid.

126. Gardiner and Buttinger, *nicht vergessen*, 116.

127. Ibid., 117.

128. Ibid., 118.

129. DÖW Archive, File Number: 7824, Briefe J. Buttinger, N.Y. 1939-1940.

130. Sturmthal, *Zwei Leben,* 163.

learned the hard way in a hurry. The European stereotype of America as an efficient and fast moving society was not really true.[131] Since a 1921 Congressional Quota Act, all persons intending to immigrate to the States had to organize a so-called "affidavit of support," guaranteeing the U.S. authorities that the would-be-immigrant had a sponsor taking care of him/her so he/she would not become a "public charge."[132] In addition, their immigration efforts had to match a very restrictive quota system. The 1921 Quota Act, passed by Congress, placed ceilings on the number of immigrants admitted from each country. The quota for Austria, counted as part of the Eastern Europe quota, was set at 7,442 immigrants to the United States per year.[133] In May 1924, the Johnson-Reed Act limited the total European immigration to 150,000 per year, and reduced each nation's quota to two percent of the population that had entered the United States in 1890.[134] In the census of 1890, significantly fewer Southern and Eastern Europeans had been recorded than in the 1920s when the law was passed. This effectively reduced immigration from these regions while making more room for immigration from Western Europe.

As a result of the 1924 quota restrictions, the immigration quota for Austria was limited to a meager 785 persons per year.[135] Although these quota limits were not very high, interestingly neither gross nor net immigration ever used up the full quota during the 1930s.[136] Yet American nativism provoked massive paranoia about masses of immigrants flooding the American homeland. Therefore the President and most members of Congress were averse to accept higher numbers of immigrants from areas of Europe, where the situation was precarious for many people persecuted by the Nazis. Given this nativist domestic climate "nothing much was done" in the United States to make the immigration process bureaucratically easier and smoother to save tens of thousands of refugees in Europe.[137] Only after the fall of France, did Franklin D. Roosevelt and the State

131. Ibid., 167.

132. Walter Dujmovits, *Die Amerikawanderung der Burgenländer* (Stegersbach: author's edition, 1975), 55.

133. US Bureau of the Census, Statistical Abstract of the United States: 1960 (81st edition.), Washington D.C., 1960, 91.

134. Mae M. Ngai, "Race, Nation, and Citizenship in Late Nineteenth-Century America: 1878-1900," in: *Race and Ethnicity in America. A Concise History,* ed. Ronald H. Bayor (New York: Columbia University Press, 2003), 96-130, 22.

135. US Bureau of the Census, Statistical Abstract of the United States: 1970 (91st edition.), Washington D.C., 1970, 91.

136. Roger Daniels, *Coming to America: A History of Immigration and Ethnicity in American Life* (New York: Harper Perennial, 1991), 300.

137. Ibid., 301.

Department, pressured by numerous human rights activists (including Joseph Buttinger[138]), reluctantly issue 3,268 emergency visas to "those of superior intellectual attainment, of indomitable spirit, experienced in vigorous support of the principles of liberal government and who are in danger of persecution or death at the hands of autocracy."[139] But here again, the slow bureaucratic authorization process only resulted in about a third of the quota being utilized.[140]

Being married to an American citizen, "Joe" as Joseph Buttinger soon became known, intended to get a special visa and the permission to enter the United States, without being hindered by the severe restrictions of the quota system and the bureaucratic formalities preceding an application.[141]

Yet Joe and his soon-to-be wife had to wait about one year to get permission to marry from the French authorities. During that time, the couple faced numerous bureaucratic hurdles. Muriel even travelled to New York, spending a lot of time with her family's lawyer in order to find other ways to get Joe into her country. But all other possibilities apart from a marriage in France proved to be impossible.[142] Through the mediation of the former Socialist French Prime Minister Léon Blum, Buttinger finally got the required documents and the Buttingers got married on August 1, 1939.[143]

Besides his activity on the exiled Austrian Socialists' Foreign Board, he learned more about the activities Muriel was pursuing. After she returned from Vienna, Muriel continued her efforts to help down and out desperate Austrians to leave their country, now a small province in the National Socialistic German Third Reich.[144]

Buttinger entered his future field of occupation in humanitarian refugee aid as a result of two factors. One was the shining example of his generous wife who began to support Austrian refugees as early as 1938.[145] Joe started his new vocation in life soon after his arrival in America.[146] The second important reason for Buttinger's turn towards international refugee aid was

138. Gardiner and Buttinger, *nicht vergessen*, 154.
139. Daniels, *Coming to America,* 301.
140. Ibid.
141. Gardiner and Buttinger, *nicht vergessen*, 131.
142. Ibid., 133.
143. Ibid.
144. See Gardiner, *"Mary,"* 132.
145. Ibid., 86.
146. DÖW Archive, File Number: 2761, Erlebnisbericht und Lebenslauf des österreichischen Historikers Josef Buttinger.

his own experience in a dismal French internment camp.[147] As a so-called "enemy alien" he, like many other Austrian and German Nazi refugees, was interned for many weeks after the outbreak of World War II in the fall of 1939. He described the conditions in these internment cages as absolutely unbearable. The internees were jammed together on a wet meadow in tents insufficient to protect them from wetness or coldness.[148] While Joe suffered in the internment camp, Muriel organized his visa as well as the tickets and transportation to the new world. She was desperately trying to get him out of his internment. Her efforts finally succeeded on October 20, 1939, when some of the leaders of the Austrian Socialists were released from the camps.[149] Joe's and Muriel's last weeks in Europe were marked by the couple's attempts to get one of the rare shipping tickets out of a continent descending into its most horrible war. After many complications and delays, the Buttingers finally embarked on the *S.S. Manhattan*, crossing the Atlantic Ocean in early November 1939.[150] Buttinger quickly put Europe and its miseries behind him.

Buttinger: The New American Citizen

Buttinger came to the United States very well prepared for his new life. His long relationship with his American partner had introduced him to many of her friends and he learned how to deal with his future compatriots. Muriel rented a spacious flat in New York on Central Park West, which also doubled as temporary lodging for needy new refugees arriving daily from war-torn Europe. During this time, the Buttingers also accommodated important guests such as the Austrian Socialist leaders Otto Bauer and Friedrich Adler.[151]

Buttinger fit the image of the typical Austrian and German immigrant who came to America during the early years of the Second World War. This cohort of immigrants to America was made up of well-educated people who usually integrated and assimilated quickly into their new homeland. Compared to their size, this group of people contributed disproportionately to the progress of American society and culture.[152] A Bureau of the Census statistical abstract of the year 1940 shows that out of 70,794 people of age

147. DÖW Archive, File Number: 7824, Briefe J. Buttingers, New York, 1939-1940.
148. Gardiner and Buttinger, *nicht vergessen*, 151.
149. Ibid., 144.
150. DÖW Archive, File Number: 7824, Briefe J. Buttingers, New York, 1939-1940.
151. Gardiner and Buttinger, *nicht vergessen*, 155.
152. Daniels, *Coming to America*, 301.

sixteen or above coming to the United States in 1939, only 9,137 were unskilled workers.[153] The rest were highly educated professionals with great skills. It is often forgotten that these refugees from Hitler's Europe in most cases took their life's savings with them. In the year 1939, 24,954 persons (ca. thirty-five percent of all immigrants) came to the United States with more than $1,000 in their pockets.[154] That meant that these people brought at least the total of twenty-five million dollars with them.

Shortly after Buttinger's arrival in the United States, he made an important step to let his Austrian compatriots know that he was finished and done with his service to the Socialist Party. He resigned his position as chairman of the Foreign Board of the Austrian Socialists.[155] Two years later, he quit his membership in the Socialist Party. Buttinger's resignation and withdrawal was characteristic for the future development of the Radical Socialist wing he had led and represented. The reformist part of the Socialist Party leadership disintegrated and disappeared in exile, or returned to the less radical traditional prewar party line during their emigration.[156]

Buttinger's ambitions soon emerged. He was fascinated by the new and unknown opportunities the United States offered a restless and dynamic person like him. He wanted to become a part of this fascinating new world as soon as possible. The enthusiasm of his language in his first letters to his friends in Europe offers some telling insights into his first impressions. "It is a great pleasure to speak with these people [Americans] about our [his and his wife's] and your [the Austrian Socialists] worries," an enthusiastic Joe Buttinger wrote to friends in Europe only two weeks after his arrival.[157] He added: "These kinds of relations to Americans are much more important to me than everything else. I certainly will not waste my time for different kinds of immigrant groups." He also enthused about New York as a "great city that exceeds all imagination."[158]

As his first activity after his arrival in November 15, 1939, he launched a massive public attack against the unbearable conditions in the French internment camp he had experienced, where a lot of German and Austrian Antifascists still suffered imprisonment.[159] To achieve his goals, he began

153. US Bureau of the Census, Statistical Abstract of the United States: 1940 (51st edition.), Washington D.C., 1940, 100.
154. Ibid.
155. DÖW Archive, File Number: 2761, Erlebnisbericht und Lebenslauf des österreichischen Historikers Josef Buttinger.
156. Maimann, *Politik im Wartesaal*, 36.
157. DÖW Archive, File Number: 7824, Briefe J. Buttingers, New York, 1939-1940.
158. Ibid.
159. Gardiner and Buttinger, *nicht vergessen*, 152.

to establish relations to major newspaper such as the *Jewish Daily Forward*, *The New York Times*, and the weekly magazine *The Nation*.[160] The *left Nation* printed his first article attacking French internmentpolicy of refugees from Nazi occupied Europe, after *The New York Times* had turned it down.[161]

Muriel and Joe also tried to promote their cause with different influential people. They established excellent contacts with Robert Maynard Hutchins, president of the University of Chicago and a good friend of President Roosevelt's.[162] They also invited the first lady Eleanor Roosevelt to their apartment in New York to discuss the overwhelming bureaucracy of visa application and authorization in U.S. consulates abroad and the State Department.

Buttinger also started to deliver public lectures about the situation in Europe. The "League of Industrial Democracy" organized his first presentation on January 7, 1941.[163] While Buttinger tried to help desperate new refugee arrivals from Austria and Europe, he chose not to join the emigrant organizations, as he wrote in one of his letters. He turned down numerous requests by his Austrian émigré compatriots to join their organizations.[164] Instead, he became a member of and participated in many American clubs and societies. In January 1941, he joined a leading American aid organization, the International Relief Organization now known as International Relief Committee (IRC).[165] After Hitler's defeat and the subsequent occupation of France, Buttinger and numerous influential Americans founded the "Emergency Rescue committee" (ERC).

The goal of the ERC was to rescue as many refugees as possible from Southern France.[166] Buttinger later wrote that he got support from Jewish Organizations as well as first lady Eleanor Roosevelt in the White House.[167] Once these organizations succeeded in bringing refugees out of Europe, his wife Muriel played an important role in helping them launch their new existence in the United States. Muriel rented twenty apartments and several single rooms in New York to offer lodging to the new arrivals.[168]

160. DÖW Archive, File Number: 7824, Briefe J. Buttingers, New York, 1939-1940.
161. Gardiner and Buttinger, *nicht vergessen*, 152.
162. Ibid.
163. DÖW Archive, File Number: 7824, Briefe J. Buttingers, New York, 1939-1940.
164. See DÖW Archive, File Number: 7893, Briefe aus der Emigration der österreichischen Sozialisten.
165. Gardiner and Buttinger, *nicht vergessen*, 152.
166. Bruce Lambert, "Joseph A. Buttinger, Nazi Fighter And Vietnam Scholar, Dies at 85," *New York Times*, 8 Mar. 1992.
167. Gardiner and Buttinger, *nicht vergessen*, 153.
168. Ibid., 154.

She also supported many of them generously with interest free loans as well as presents.

The Buttingers spent much of their time organizing visas for the flood of displaced Europeans streaming into the U.S.. Muriel wrote hundreds of letters to "all sorts of people," persuading them to write affidavits in support of refugee immigrants. An affidavit implied a financial guarantee from these sponsors. The Buttingers were confronted with many disappointing rejections to their pleas for help. Muriel never gave up and ended up offering many refugees her own guarantee and assurances, offering her personal financial backing for those who had none.[169]

Joe Buttinger found his new mission in life in the organization of refugee aid and in the process quickly became an American. He embarked on his new occupation with the same gusto he had formerly devoted to the Socialist Party in Austria. After World War II, the situation in Europe was catastrophic. Millions of people were dead, wounded, or displaced by the war. Millions of houses were destroyed. After 69 months of war and bombing, the infrastructure of the European economy had collapsed.[170] On October 3, 1945, the "IRC" dispatched Buttinger to Europe to give support to desperate people, especially those Antifascists and racially persecuted who had spent years in Nazi concentration camps.[171] During that time, he rose to the position of the European Director of the IRC in charge of organizing aid deliveries to the countries of France, Italy, Germany, Austria, Switzerland, Sweden, Belgium, Holland, and Turkey.[172] At the end of 1945, the Buttingers launched another important project with their own funds. They began to send "care packages" to poor and destitute people in France, Germany, and Austria in want of everything. The project lasted until 1950 and brought thousands of American care packages to Europe.[173] During the immediate postwar years, these care packages were the differences between life and death for countless individuals.

By the 1950s the situation in Western Europe had improved and stabilized. Now the "IRC" dispatched the experienced humanitarian and refugee expert Joe Buttinger into other danger zones. After the Hungarian Crisis in 1956/57, he was put in charge of coordinating aid for more than 100,000 Hungarian refugees.[174] Like in the years before, the Buttingers

169. DÖW Archive, File Number: 18886/2, Buttinger Material (USA/Schweden).

170. On the devastations of post war Europe, see Tony Judt, *Postwar: A History of Europe Since 1945* (New York: Penguin Press, 2005), 13-63.

171. Gardiner and Buttinger, *nicht vergessen*, 159.

172. DÖW Archive, File Number: 18904/3, Buttinger Materialien.

173. Gardiner and Buttinger, *nicht vergessen*, 162.

174. DÖW Archive, File Number: 2761, Erlebnisbericht und Lebenslauf des

generously supported numerous people not only with official "IRC" financial backing but also with funds out of their own pocket. Joe Buttinger also managed to use his excellent contacts with his former Socialist party comrades now back in power to convince the Austrian government "to open fully the door for the refugees of the Hungarian Revolution," as Andreas H. Pongany, President of the World Federation of Hungarian Freedom Fighters later asserted.[175]

Next to his refugee work, Joe Buttinger continued his intellectual pursuits. In 1953 he published his first ambitious history book *In the Twilight of Socialism*—his personal and painful analysis of the history of the Revolutionary Socialists during the Austrofascist era.

In 1954 the "IRC" sent him to Vietnam for two months to build up a relief agency for refugees from the Communist northern part of the divided country.[176] He worked with many refugees with an intellectual background[177] and immersed himself in the history, culture and politics of Vietnam. He founded a new organization—the "American Friends of Vietnam"—and became a personal friend of Ngo Dinh Diem, the later president of South Vietnam.[178] Later, disillusioned with Diem's dictatorial regime and upset about American Vietnam policies after 1965, he resigned from the "Friends of Vietnam" he had founded.

During these years he became a respected authority of Vietnamese history and culture when there were few available in the U.S.. In 1958, he published *The Smaller Dragon: A Political History of Vietnam,* a history of Vietnam.[179] In 1967, 1972, and 1977 he wrote three mere books on Vietnamese history.[180] *Encyclopedia Britannica* commissioned him to write a history of Vietnam for its fifteenth volume. This gave him additional stature and standing as a respected expert of Vietnamese history. He collected an important and rare library including 7,000 books concerning the history of Indochina, which he later donated to Harvard University.[181]

österreichischen Historikers Josef Buttinger.

175. Ibid.

176. Ibid.

177. Ibid.

178. Bruce Lambert, "Joseph A. Buttinger, Nazi Fighter And Vietnam Scholar, Dies at 85," *New York Times*, 8 March 1992.

179. See Joseph Buttinger, *The Smaller Dragon: A Political History of Vietnam* (New York: Praeger, 1958).

180. See Joseph Buttinger, *Vietnam: A Dragon Embattled* (New York: Praeger, 1967), Joseph Buttinger, *A Dragon Defiant: A Short History of Vietnam* (New York: Praeger, 1972), Joseph Buttinger, *Vietnam: The Unforgettable Tragedy* (New York: Horizon, 1977).

181. DÖW Archive, File Number: 2761, Erlebnisbericht und Lebenslauf des österreichischen Historikers Josef Buttinger.

Joe Buttinger's life trajectory from European poverty to American prosperity was remarkable but not unrepresentative of the World War II cohort of refugees from Nazi Germany to the United States. As early as the 1940s, the former Austrian agricultural serfe Joseph Buttinger had

Buttinger, the Expert of Vietnamese History, © Dokumentationsarchiv des österreichischen Widerstandes (DÖW)/Fotosammlung.

fully assimilated into American society. He gave numerous lectures on American university campuses; he wrote books and articles on Vietnam for American audiences; he became a great humanitarian and assisted refugees in Europe and Asia as a leader in American relief agencies. The Buttingers no longer spent their annual ski holiday in the Austrian or Swiss Alps. In the 1950s they began to frequent the new American ski Eldorado of Aspen, in the Colorado Rockies.[182] By the 1950s Joseph Buttinger, the self-made Austrian Socialist leader, had transformed into Joe Buttinger, the American humanitarian and refugee official and respected "Vietnam Scholar."[183]

The American Joe with his Wife Muriel, © Dokumentationsarchiv des österreichischen Widerstandes (DÖW)/Fotosammlung.

Conclusion

Joseph Buttinger's life trajectory took him from a small rural village in interwar Austria to wealthy New York, one of the world's great metropolises. He was from a poor background and he lacked formal education beyond the sixth grade. His means to break away from the rural environment

182. DÖW Archive, File Number: 18904/6, Buttinger Materialien.
183. Bruce Lambert, "Joseph A. Buttinger, Nazi Fighter And Vietnam Scholar, Dies at 85," *New York Times*, 8 March 1992.

with little hope was a strong will. On the one hand, Buttinger set himself ambitious targets in life. On the other hand he had the discipline to pursue these targets successfully. He learned quickly that a solid education is a key to success in life anywhere. He was never idle and he always wanted to extend his knowledge. Because of his lack of financial means he never had the opportunity to finish secondary education, let alone embark on a university career. He was eager to acquire more knowledge and studiously continued his autodidactic studies at a time when there were few avenues towards a high school and university education for poor Austrians with rural backgrounds. His intense educational efforts towards self-improvement were so successful that he later graduated to become the premier American expert on Vietnam, even writing memoranda for the White House and advising Presidents.

For Buttinger, narrow nationalism or patriotism did not count for much. He was a new type of modern cosmopolitan, not bound to a single state or nation. He lived for his personal ambitions and to further humanity, not for a state or a homeland. Given these cosmopolitan attitudes emerging early as an official reared in socialist internationalism, his flight to France and his emigration to America were not difficult steps for him. It may well have been in his nature to emigrate without being forced to do so by fascist regimes and the scourge of war. He was on the run during his whole life. In his childhood, he moved to Germany, first to Bavaria, then to the Rhineland. His family came back to Austria during the dislocations of World War I and he returned to Upper Austria. Once he joined the Socialist movement, he moved to Carinthia and then to Vienna as a party functionary. The "Anschluss" forced him to leave Vienna for Paris. From there he finally moved to his final refuge, the United States. While in Europe, Buttinger never lived in a place for a long period of time. It was his restless life in desperate poverty that led him towards cosmopolitanism.

Surely his greatest fortune in life was to meet the generous American heiress and humanitarian Muriel Gardiner who became his love. She made his rapid integration and seamless assimilation into American society possible. She supported him financially, gave him shelter to protect him from police goons, introduced him to her influential American friends, helped him organize and finance his various humanitarian projects, and organized his escape from Hitler's Europe to build a new life in America.

Buttinger quickly embarked on new careers in America. As a young Austrian socialist, emigration to America was not on his radar. On his trips to Italy, France, and Great Britain he began to experience a world beyond the confines and provinciality of his native Austria. After his steep career ascent in the Socialist Party, he launched a new life as a humanitarian and scholar in the United States. He abandoned his work in the Socialist Party. He felt that the infighting in the party would have held him back from achieving new goals and launching new careers. In the United States an active and a productive newcomer like him quickly was accepted as an American. He did not want to wallow in emigrant politics on the margins of American society. He preferred joining American organizations and contributing to American causes. In fact, Buttinger saw himself as an American as soon as he entered the United States. His numerous letters to his Austrian friends bear witness to it.

His marriage to Muriel Gardiner made his naturalization easy. Buttinger's immigration was a rare case of a European wartime refugee whose entry into the United States was easy and quick. Less prominent refugees without American spouses or sponsors experienced more difficulties getting visas for America.[184] Buttinger's biggest challenge came in France. He was interned and waited nearly one year for an official permission to marry Muriel Gardiner so he could apply for a visa to the U.S.. With his marriage came his passage and entry into the United States and a new beginning.

184. Daniels, *Coming to America*, 300.

From the Habsburg Empire to the Third Reich: Arthur Seyß-Inquart and National Socialism

Johannes Koll[1]

Biographical research and National Socialism

During the past two decades, biographical research connected with National Socialism abounded.[2] This boom is the more remarkable since especially in the German-speaking academic world biographies were long regarded with suspicion. Due to their characteristic focus on individual lives, they were considered of no great use for the analysis of historical structures and general developments of the past—unlike quantitative social history and structural history which were held in high esteem from the 1960s well into the 1980s.[3] Especially among contemporary historians the conviction was widely shared that biographies were not capable of procuring solid scholarly contributions to the understanding and interpretation of historical processes like the emergence and growth of fascism and their significance for modernity. Interest in biographical research came back in the wake of the "cultural turn" and the ascent of "history from below" and oral history. From the 1990s onwards, many outstanding biographical works effectively helped to dispense of the idea of the categories "structure" and "person" as being allegedly mutually exclusive, and to reveal the relatedness between individual actions and dispositions on the one hand and super-individual structures or general conditions on the other. With regard to the Third Reich, Ulrich Herbert's and Ian Kershaw's biographies of Werner Best and Adolf Hitler, the collective biography of the "ordinary men" of a police unit by Christopher Browning and Michael Wildt's investigation of the fanatic personnel of the *Reichssicherheitshauptamt* can justifiably claim pioneering status.[4]

---

1. I am grateful to the Austrian Science Fund and the Gerda Henkel Foundation for subsidizing my research. Furthermore I am grateful to Peter Berger for correcting my English.

2. Johannes Koll, "Biographik und NS-Forschung," *Neue Politische Literatur* (forthcoming).

3. Hans Erich Bödeker, "Biographie: Annäherungen an den gegenwärtigen Forschungs- und Diskussionsstand," in *Biographie schreiben*, ed. idem (Göttingen: Wallstein, 2003), 9-63.

4. Ulrich Herbert, *Best: Biographische Studien über Radikalismus, Weltanschauung und Vernunft 1903-1989*, 2nd ed. (Bonn: J.H.W. Dietz Nachfolger, 1996); Ian Kershaw, *Hitler*, 2 vol. (London: Allen Lane, 1998 and 2000); Christopher R. Browning, *Ordinary Men. Reserve Police Battalion 101 and the final solution in Poland* (New York: HarperCollins, 1992); Michael Wildt, *Generation des Unbedingten. Das Führungskorps des Reichssicherheitshauptamtes* (Hamburg: Hamburger Edition, 2002).

Reich Commissioner Arthur Seyß-Inquart wearing a SS-uniform with decorations and the badge of the NSDAP, 1943.

It is important to note that biographical research into the era of the Third Reich is not restricted to the upper echelons of the National Socialist regime. It also deals with the middle and lower ranks of the NSDAP, different levels of the public administration, the armed forces, and actors in the social, economic and cultural domains like scientists and scholars, artists, businessmen, lawyers or physicians. On the whole, the biographies published in recent years cover a broad range of personalities, not only perpetrators but also victims of the regime, members of resistance organizations and dissidents within Germany or those sections of Europe which were occupied or annexed by the Greater German Reich during the Second World War. Provided the relationship between the respective protagonist(s) and the social environment was duly taken into account, the biographical approach managed to establish itself as a theoretically and empirically valid mode of delivering significant contributions to the history of society.

Austrians, the *Anschluss* of 1938, and the Greater German Reich

Historical research so far has failed to close significant gaps in our knowledge of the role played by Austrians in the preparation of the Anschluss, in the general history of the Greater German Reich from 1938 to 1945, and in the functioning of National Socialist regimes of occupation in wartime. In particular, the widely held assumption that Austrians contributed excessively to crimes committed under the swastika[5] requires further testing by means of quantitative social history and qualitative biographical research likewise. Collective biographies of Austrian National Socialists,[6] or of soldiers from the *Ostmark* serving in the German army[7] can help to assess the extent and shape of the contribution made by Austrians (deliberately or under constraint) to the establishment and day-to-day business of the National Socialist regime. The same holds true for Austrian participation in resisting the brutal implementation and deployment of the National Socialist "New Order" in Europe.[8] Also, we need more research into the lives, attitudes and mentalities of thousands of Austrian National Socialists

5. Ernst Hanisch, "Der Ort des Nationalsozialismus in der österreichischen Geschichte," in *NS-Herrschaft in Österreich: Ein Handbuch*, ed. Emmerich Tálos et al. (Vienna: öbv & hpt, 2002), 18. See also Bertrand Perz, "Die österreichische Beteiligung an NS-Verbrechen: Anmerkungen zur Debatte," in *Österreichische Nation–Kultur–Exil und Widerstand: In memoriam Felix Kreissler*, ed. Helmut Kramer, Karin Liebhart, and Friedrich Stadler (Vienna: LIT, 2006), 223-34.
6. Gerhard Jagschitz, "Die österreichischen Nationalsozialisten," in *Österreich, Deutschland und die Mächte: Internationale und österreichische Aspekte des „Anschlusses" vom März 1938*, ed. Gerald Stourzh and Brigitta Zaar (Vienna: Verlag der Österreichischen Akademie der Wissenschaften, 1990), 229-69 and the following remarks by Bruce F. Pauley, in ibid., 271-76.
7. Bertrand Michael Buchmann, *Österreicher in der deutschen Wehrmacht: Soldatenalltag im Zweiten Weltkrieg* (Vienna: Böhlau, 2009).
8. For an overview on the political spectrum see Evan Burr Bukey, *Hitler's Austria: Popular sentiment in the Nazi era, 1938-1945* (Chapel Hill: The University of North Carolina Press, 2000), part II and Robert Kriechbaumer, *Die großen Erzählungen der Politik: Politische Kultur und Parteien in Österreich von der Jahrhundertwende bis 1945* (Vienna: Böhlau, 2001).

who zestfully prepared the political unification of their home country with Hitler's Germany, sometimes many years before the Anschluss became a fact. Recently published studies on the "Austrian Legion" and the Viennese SS may be regarded as substantial contributions to this research gap.[9]

One of those Austrians whose life and contribution to the history of National Socialism have not as yet been explored sufficiently is Arthur Seyß-Inquart (1892-1946).[10] For several reasons the absence of an in-depth, source-based biography of this Viennese lawyer and National Socialist politician must be deplored. Seyß-Inquart played a decisive part in laying the groundwork for the Anschluss. He was one of the very few Austrians enjoying Hitler's personal appreciation. Even though he failed to acquire a reliable power base within the NSDAP, he rose to a key position in the Greater German Reich which he managed to defend until the final stages of World War II. While his name appears in every handbook, and in numerous detailed studies on the Third Reich and the Second World War, little is known about the life and career of Seyß-Inquart. In what follows I will briefly sketch the outlines of his biography, attempting an answer to the following pivotal questions: Why did Seyß-Inquart join National Socialism, and what drew him to the Third Reich? How did his career develop? And how did he succeed in remaining one of the high-ranking National Socialists right to the end of the war within the highly polycratic and competitive power structures of the Greater German Reich? Answers to these questions should help us assess the relevance of Seyß-Inquart for European history during the first half of the 20th century, and to identify specific patterns of ideological attitudes and political actions explaining his active role in the Holocaust and in German aggression against Poland and the Netherlands.

Seyß-Inquart's road to National Socialism

There is no reason to believe that Seyß-Inquart's liaison with National Socialism, let alone his role in the Eastern war of extermination and the

9. See Hans Schafranek, *Söldner für den "Anschluss": Die Österreichische Legion 1933–1938* (Vienna: Czernin, 2010) and Christiane Rothländer, *Die Anfänge der Wiener SS* (Vienna: Böhlau, 2012).

10. For existing literature on Seyß-Inquart see Wolfgang Rosar, *Deutsche Gemeinschaft: Seyss-Inquart und der Anschluß* (Vienna: Europa Verlag, 1971) and H.J. Neumann, *Arthur Seyss-Inquart* (Graz: Styria, 1970, first published in Dutch in 1967). Below common academic standards is the biography by Wilco Gieling, *Seyss-Inquart* (Soesterberg: Aspekt, 2011). At present, I am preparing a scholarly biography on this Austrian National Socialist. Here further references to literature and sources will be found.

Holocaust were preordained. Born on the 22th of July 1892 in the small village of Stonařov near the German linguistic enclave of Jihlava, he grew up in the Habsburg Crown land of Moravia. In their childhood years and as youths, neither Arthur nor his four brothers and sisters showed signs of outspoken anti-Semitism or hostility against the Czech or Slovak people. We can take it for granted that both Arthur's Carinthian mother Auguste and his father Emil, principal of the German grammar school at Olomouc, conferred upon him a feeling of German cultural superiority not uncommon in regions where ethnic Germans and Slavs lived and worked side by side. However, father Seyß-Inquart is known to have held liberal convictions. He seems to have been a politically moderate, Catholic Austrian patriot who repeatedly expressed friendly feelings towards Jewish pupils of his school. At home, Arthur cannot have adopted or developed a radical ideology. Rather, we have indications to the contrary. In a letter dated September 1910, the young high-school graduate talked about the "struggle of our people for its existence." But he explicitly rejected any form of aggressive German nationalism "which denies the right of existence to members of other nations."[11]

Despite all this, there is a high probability that the young Arthur Seyß-Inquart sensed the sphere of national tensions characteristic of a traditionally bilingual area of the Habsburg Empire. Many times in his political career under National Socialism, he stressed his origins from the multinational area of Moravia. Confronting the judges of the International Military Tribunal at Nuremberg, he sought to explain his conversion to National Socialism in retrospect by emphasizing that he had been brought up in what he considered a contested borderland, where everyone was aware of the social and political relevance of national issues at an early stage of life.[12] And isn't it notable that apart from Seyß-Inquart, several other fervent National Socialists like Odilo Globocnik, Karl Hermann Frank or Dr. Hugo Jury originated from multinational borderlands and binational areas? Nevertheless, it is impossible to determine whether Seyß-Inquart's retrospective testimonies about the formative impression of the ethnically mixed Sudetenland accurately mirrored the thoughts, feelings and beliefs of the period of his adolescence.

We know, however, that the young Arthur increasingly got in touch with organizations of the radical Right. One of them was the Singers'

11. Arthur Seyß-Inquart, Nationale Arbeit der Hochschüler, September 1910, Arthur Seyß-Inquart, H.I.N. 205.784/14, manuscript department of the Wienbibliothek im Rathaus, Vienna.

12. See his statement during the sitting of the International Military Tribunal of 10 June 1946, *Der Prozess gegen die Hauptkriegsverbrecher vor dem Internationalen Militärgerichtshof, Nürnberg, 14. November 1945 – 1. Oktober 1946*, vol. 15 (Nuremberg, 1948), 665.

Association at the Austrian municipality of Baden, where the Seyß-Inquarts found a new home after Emil's retirement from school service in 1908. The *Gesangverein Baden* was one of those nationalist associations that explicitly excluded Jews as "Non-Aryans" from membership long before the First World War.[13] At the same time, Arthur took part in activities of the *Verein Südmark* which saw itself in the vanguard "for the preservation and advancement of Germandom" in the German-speaking parts of the Habsburg Empire[14] and aggressively opposed Czech and Jewish influence in public life. Similar objectives were shared by the student leagues which attracted future prominent National Socialists like Ernst Kaltenbrunner and others.[15] Whether Seyß-Inquart was also member of one of the *Burschenschaften* cannot be said with certainty.

For Arthur's private life, his professional career and his political and ideological development, World War I and its aftermath were extremely important. On the one hand, he volunteered as cadet and managed to move up the career ladder up to the rank of first lieutenant in the course of the war. Like many of his contemporaries, he regarded military service as an obligation self-evident for a young citizen. At the same time, he sought to continue, with the approval of his superiors, his law studies at the University of Vienna, originally taken up in autumn 1910. At one occasion, while taking a furlough in Vienna in December 1916, he married his fiancée Gertrud Maschka, the daughter of a high-ranking officer of the Austro-Hungarian Ministry of War. A half year after his marriage he earned his doctoral degree,[16] and in September 1917 his wife gave birth to the first of their three children. In May 1915, Seyß-Inquart suffered a serious injury at the Galician front, but his letters to Gertrud do not really give evidence of his being appalled at the unprecedented manslaughter during the battles of the war.[17] But, following the defeat of the Central Powers, the war gained a specific significance for him: the comradeship-in-arms of Germany and Austria in 1914-18 intensified his pan-Germanic feelings which were

13. See Johann Walter, *Festschrift zur Feier des 50jährigen Bestandes des Gesangvereines Baden* (Baden: Verlag des Gesangvereines Baden, 1912), 50 and 54.

14. *Was will der Verein Südmark in Wien und Niederösterreich-Land?* ([Graz]: Verlag des Vereines Südmark, [1912]), 1-2.

15. Peter Black, *Ernst Kaltenbrunner, Vasall Himmlers: Eine SS-Karriere* (Paderborn: Schöningh, 1991), 62-63; the American edition was published in 1984.

16. See Promotionsprotokoll der Juridischen Fakultät, Universitätsarchiv Wien, M 32.8, nr 342.

17. Arthur's letters to Gertrud are stored at the manuscript department of the Austrian National Library, Vienna, Autogr. 1019. For his injury see Karl Raschin Edler von Raschinfels, *Die Einser-Kaiserjäger im Feldzug gegen Rußland 1914–1915: Auszug aus dem Tagebuche des Regimentsadjutanten* (Bregenz: J.N. Teutsch, 1935), 179.

to become the cornerstone of his political ideology. The solidarity of the Austrian Doctor of Laws with the Germans grew even stronger when the harsh terms of the 1919 peace treaties of Versailles and Saint Germain-en-Laye were imposed on Germany and Austria by the victorious Entente Powers. Until the end of his life, Seyß-Inquart considered these treaties to be highly unjust. He did not so much bemoan the loss of vast territories, including his native province, Moravia, which for centuries had belonged to the Habsburg monarchy. In the first instance, he objected to those clauses in the treaties which prohibited unification of Austria with Germany. In his view which totally conformed with Austrian and German public opinion these articles violated the right of national self-determination, solemnly proclaimed in January 1918 by US-President Woodrow Wilson as the basis for a political post-war order in Europe, and generously applied in support of Czech, Polish, or Italian (but not of German and Austrian) claims. Like many of his contemporaries, Seyß-Inquart actively propagated the Anschluss idea throughout the interwar period via speeches and published articles, based on his genuine belief that both the German and Austrian populations shared the same historical, cultural, and racial foundations and therefore formed one nation.[18] An important platform for his fight against the "discriminatory" articles of the Paris peace treaties was provided by the *Österreichisch-Deutscher Volksbund.* It is important to note that in its early days this "Austrian-German People's Association" was a supra-party institution, welcoming membership of Social Democrats, Christian Socials, Pan-Germans and anti-Semites of all shades. It was only after the NSDAP had come to power in Germany in January 1933 that Austrian Social Democrats officially shelved their demand for an Anschluss. From then onward, the concept of Austro-German political unification became the exclusive domain of the political Right.

Seyß-Inquart's affiliation with Austria's radical Right antedated Hitler's assuming the post of Reich Chancellor in Germany. Already in 1931 he made financial contributions to the NSDAP. In the same year he joined the *Steirischer Heimatschutz.* Led by Walter Pfrimer, armed forces of this paramilitary, semi-fascist organization attempted a putsch in September 1931 to topple Austria's democratically elected government and replace it with a dictatorial, corporatist regime.[19] The abortive uprising seems to

18. Rolf Steininger, "12 November 1918-12 March 1938: The Road to the Anschluß," in *Austria in the Twentieth Century*, ed. Steininger, Günter Bischof and Michael Gehler (New Brunswick: Transaction Publishers, 2002), 85-114.

19. On the history of the *Heimwehr* see John T. Lauridsen, *Nazism and the Radical Right in Austria, 1918-1934* (Copenhagen: The Royal Library and Museum Tusculanum Press, 2007).

have left a strong impression with Seyß-Inquart, and may have spurred his enthusiasm to enter the ranks of this radical branch of the polymorphic Austrian *Heimwehr* movement. At all events, he strongly advocated political cooperation between the *Heimwehr* movement and the ever-growing National Socialist movement of Austria. Behind the scenes he lobbied to bridge the gaps between conflicting nationalistic, conservative and National Socialist currents, with the aim to establish a strong National Right in Austria. His legal profession provided good opportunities for social and political networking. Yet it seems that from the early 1930s on, the legal career and his prosperous lawyer's office right in the center of Vienna no longer satiated Seyß-Inquart. His ambition now was directed towards assuming political responsibility. In this area he pursued two interrelated goals, firstly to end the fragmentation of the political Right in Austria, and secondly to promote and ultimately realize the Anschluss.

What did he think about the putsch which, in July 1934, culminated in the murder of Austrian Chancellor Engelbert Dollfuß by National Socialists? Unfortunately, it is not possible to exactly determine the degree of Seyß-Inqart's personal involvement in the aborted insurrection. What we do know, however, is that he in no way objected to Hitler's seizure of power in Germany in 1933. More than that, it seems that he regarded a powerful National Socialist government in Berlin as the perfect ally (and presumably the only one available) in the struggle for revision of the peace treaties of 1919, and for the ensuing unification of Germany and Austria. The Anti-Semitism and anti-Parliamentarianism displayed by National Socialists did certainly not repel him. Long before the coming of the Anschluss, Seyß-Inquart repudiated democratically elected parliaments, and he joined anti-Semitic associations like the *Verband deutsch-arischer Rechtsanwälte in Österreich* (Union of German-Aryan Lawyers in Austria) which lobbied for the removal of Jewish lawyers from the bar associations.

Seyß-Inquart's role in the preparation of the *Anschluss*

Despite his close contacts with some of the insurgents of July 1934, Seyß-Inquart disapproved of Nazi acts of violence or terrorism which at that time were endemic in Austria. Instead, he advocated a two-step strategy of reconciliation, first of all the self-styled "national groupings" active on Austrian soil, and then of Germany and Austria altogether. In June 1937 he was offered an opportunity to promote effective collaboration of Catholic conservatives, the *Heimwehr* movement and National Socialists as a newly appointed member of the Privy Council. The appointment was an initiative by Kurt Schuschnigg, the Christian Social politician who in the summer of 1934 had succeeded Dollfuß as head of the Austrian government. In his capacity of a *Staatsrat* Seyß-Inquart was to assume the task of leading Austria's various organizations of the political Right into the fold of the Christian Corporate State, whose institutions slowly took shape after 1933. In his attempt to merge the "national groupings" into the *Volkspolitisches Referat*, a subdivision of the all-encompassing "Patriotic Front," Seyß-Inquart enjoyed both the support of the Schuschnigg regime and of influential circles within the Third Reich. During his tenure as Privy Counselor, Seyß-Inquart intensified contacts with leading politicians and functionaries of the German Reich. Since he considered himself a "bridge builder" between Schuschnigg and Hitler and their respective countries, he felt entitled and even obliged to improve the relationship between Vienna and Berlin for the sake of all Germans living in Austria and Germany. This proved a difficult task. Earlier attempts to reconcile the "national groupings" in Austria and to restore harmony between Germany and Austria after the putsch of July 1934 had failed. Chancellor Schuschnigg and his "Patriotic Front" feared (with good reason) that Austria's powerful northern neighbor might resort to open aggression and ultimately annex Austria. Therefore neither the "National Action" initiated by the National Socialist Anton Reinthaller nor the idea to install a "German Social People's League" (*Deutsch-Sozialer Volksbund*) in Austria received official authorization.[20] While stepping up the frequency of his exchanges with German as well as Austrian interlocutors, Seyß-Inquart made sure that everybody received the right signals. Following a journey to Berlin in summer 1937 he reported to Schuschnigg that the Germans were about to pledge "active noninterference" with Austrian internal affairs. Joachim von Ribbentrop was assured somewhat enigmatically that Seyß-Inquart's talks with members of the German government were expected to bring about "useful results for the German people and our two states as soon as possible."[21]

From the time when this statement was made, it took no more than a few months for the merger of Austria and Germany to be accomplished. This was due to an effective combination of military force, diplomacy, and propaganda. When Hitler began to radicalize German politics at the end of 1937 and the beginning of 1938, both the Reich Chancellery in Berlin and the German ambassador in Vienna, Franz von Papen, believed that Seyß-Inquart, given his tactfulness and diplomatic skills, was the right man

20. Rosar, *Deutsche Gemeinschaft*, 75-82 and 108-17.

21. Seyß-Inquart to Schuschnigg and to Ribbentrop, 3 resp. 14 July 1937, Bundesarchiv Koblenz, N 1180/8.

to successfully undermine the Austrian corporate state in a pseudo-legal manner. Accordingly Hitler, during his ominous talks with Schuschnigg in Berchtesgaden in February 1938, demanded from the Austrian Chancellor that Seyß-Inquart be appointed Minister of the Interior and Security. Competing aspirations of other Austrian National Socialists, among them the leader of the illegal Austrian NSDAP Josef Leopold, were intentionally frustrated by the "*Führer.*"

As Minister of the Interior, a post he held since 16 February 1938, Seyß-Inquart was in charge of the national security portfolio, a position of utmost importance for the arrangement of the Anschluss. He used his influence to avert an untimely insurrection by the impatient illegal National Socialist rank and file in the Austrian provinces, and to preserve law and order until the German government and army were ready to accomplish the Anschluss "from above." On the other hand, he was capable of blackmailing the Schuschnigg-regime due to his being in control of the police forces. At this stage it was already perfectly clear that Seyß-Inquart had given up the intermediary position of Austro-German "bridge builder." It was signifying that the freshly appointed member of the Austrian Cabinet paid his first official visit to the German capital. In Berlin Seyß-Inquart was given the opportunity to talk to leading figures of the National Socialist regime including Hitler, Ribbentrop, Hermann Göring, Rudolf Heß, and Wilhelm Frick. Also with Heinrich Himmler he had "a long conversation."[22]

One month later, Arthur Seyß-Inquart did exactly what Hitler and Göring expected of him: in March 1938, he loyally cooperated in preparing the invasion of Austria by the German army, and smoothed the political and juridical implementation of the Anschluss.[23] From 11 March onwards, he assumed the office of Austrian Chancellor for a couple of days. Furthermore, he was temporarily endowed with the prerogatives of a Federal President. There are indications that he would have preferred to avoid German military intervention, and that he originally opted for the preservation of limited autonomy of Austria within the Greater German Reich. But in the process he went along with the political demands of the German leadership, and accepted the invasion of the *Wehrmacht* as well as the total incorporation of Austria by Germany. From now on his political career was tied to the fate of the National Socialist regime, for better or worse.

---

22. *Liverpool Daily Post*, 18 Feb. 1938. Contemporaries observed attentively and amazed that within not even twenty-four hours the newly appointed Austrian Minister of Interior had conversations with a considerable number of high-ranking politicians. See *Pester Lloyd*, 19 Feb. 1938.

23. For details see Rosar, *Deutsche Gemeinschaft*, in particular 262-98. For the general context see Erwin A. Schmidl, *Der "Anschluß" Österreichs: Der deutsche Einmarsch im März 1938* (Bonn: Bernard & Graefe, 1994).

In the service of the Greater German Reich—Austria, Poland, and the Netherlands

On 15 March 1938, Hitler appointed Seyß-Inquart Reich Governor of Austria, thus rewarding him for his assistance in facilitating the Anschluss.[24] As *Reichsstatthalter* Seyß-Inquart was charged with the dismantling of the institutions of the defunct Austrian state, and with laying the groundwork for Austria's transition to the status of some kind of province of the Greater German Reich. In this task to transform Austria into the nazified *Ostmark* he was expected to collaborate with Reich Commissioner Joseph Bürckel and other German and Austrian functionaries.[25] When on 1 May 1939 the law on the *Ostmark* entered into force, Seyß-Inquart's functions of Reich Governor and head of the Austrian Land Government automatically expired. As compensation—or consolation—for the loss of these functions he became Reich Minister (however without portfolio), and a member of the disempowered German parliament, the *Reichstag*. Both positions were prestigious ones, but none of them provided Seyß-Inquart with the power he aspired to. He had to wait until Germany unleashed the Second World War. This moment provided him with new opportunities to underscore his value for Hitler and the Greater German Reich.

Starting from September 1939, Seyß-Inquart's chance for sharpening his profile lay in Poland. At first Hitler appointed him civilian chief executive in the military district of Cracow.[26] One week later Himmler subordinated to him all police forces of the same district. His official title became *Höherer SS-und Polizeiführer*.[27] Finally, on the 26th of October, Seyß-Inquart got promoted to the rank of Deputy General Governor under Hans Frank, following Hitler's decision to replace military administration in occupied Poland with a civilian regime.[28]

It is difficult to determine what exactly Seyß-Inquart's activities in the Polish theatre were, and particularly in Cracow. Plenty of documents were

---

24. See the letter of appointment in Bundesarchiv Berlin, R 43 II/140, fol. 17.

25. Hermann Hagspiel, *Die Ostmark: Österreich im Großdeutschen Reich 1938 bis 1945* (Vienna: Braumüller, 1995).

26. See Hitler's edict of 25 September 1939, published in *"Führer-Erlasse" 1939-1945. Edition sämtlicher überlieferter, nicht im Reichsgesetzblatt abgedruckter, von Hitler während des Zweiten Weltkrieges schriftlich erteilter Direktiven aus den Bereichen Staat, Partei, Wirtschaft, Besatzungspolitik und Militärverwaltung*, ed. Martin Moll (Stuttgart: Steiner, 1997), Doc. 10, 97-99.

27. Bundesarchiv Berlin, former Berlin Document Center, SSO Arthur Seyß-Inquart, fol. 12 (5 October 1939).

28. For Hitler's edict of October 12, 1939, see *Reichsgesetzblatt* I/1939, vol. 2, 2077-2078.

destroyed during the war, and neither Frank's well-known diary[29] nor the official journals of the General Government, the *Krakauer Zeitung* and the *Warschauer Zeitung*, allow for a detailed reconstruction of Seyß-Inquart's ventures. This is the more regrettable as the first months of the Second World War did not just mark a decisive turning point in European history. They also represented a dividing line in Seyß-Inquart's biography. For the first time, he was part of a reckless occupying regime which could not even be justified in terms of a racially founded Pan-Germanic ideology. In Poland, the issue was not the liberation of a German Diaspora from foreign rule and the pursuit of a Greater German concept on racial terms. The issue was plain and simple conquest, and subsequent ethnical cleansing.[30] It must be taken for granted that Seyß-Inquart was well-informed on all aspects of German politics in the General Government including persecution of the Jews, suppression of any organized resistance, and economic exploitation of Polish manpower and natural resources—not to mention the theft of numerous treasures of art. It is beyond doubt that Seyß-Inquart actively stimulated and helped put into effect National Socialist policies in the General Government. During an inspection mission in November 1939 he unmistakably set out the principles of German rule in occupied Poland. According to him, nothing but the concerns of the Reich mattered: "By means of a strong-handed and impeccable administration, this region must be made into an asset for the German economy. To avoid inappropriate acts of clemency it suffices to bring to one's mind the undesired consequences of the incursion of the Poles (*Polentum*) into the German living space." On the same occasion, he implicitly supported a proposal of the Governor of Lublin, Friedrich Schmidt, to take preparatory steps for the settlement of non-native Jews in the Lublin district, a measure that was known to lead to "a significant reduction in numbers" of those affected.[31] Seyß-Inquart belonged to the group of National Socialist office holders who agreed with the commander of the Security Police and Security Service, SS-*Brigadeführer* Bruno Streckenbach, that Frank's plan to liquidate thousands of members of the Polish intelligentsia by means of the infamous

29. Bundesarchiv Berlin, R 52 II/174 ff. and the editions *Das Diensttagebuch des deutschen Generalgouverneurs in Polen 1939-1945*, ed. Werner Präg and Wolfgang Jacobmeyer (Stuttgart: Deutsche Verlags-Anstalt, 1975) and *Hans Franks Tagebuch*, ed. Stanisław Piotrowski (Warsaw: Polnischer Verlag der Wissenschaften, 1963).

30. Jochen Böhler, *Auftakt zum Vernichtungskrieg: Die Wehrmacht in Polen 1939* (Frankfurt on the Main: Fischer, 2006).

31. *Trial of the Major War Criminals before the International Military Tribunal, Nuremberg 14 November 1945 – 1 October 1946*, vol. 30 (Nuremberg, 1948), doc. 2278-PS, 84 and 95 (17 and 20 November 1939).

Außerordentliche Befriedungsaktion ("Special Action of Pacification") would help warrant "safety, calm and order in the country."[32] So far, no evidence exists that Seyß-Inquart ever opposed the murderous plans conceived by Hans Frank or other leading National Socialists. His room for maneuver, however, was limited, since Frank jealously guarded his prerogatives as General Governor and tolerated no one next to himself. Due to the authoritarian style of leadership applied by Frank, Seyß-Inquart from the very beginning of his tenure apparently was deprived of any possibility to take autonomous political action in the General Government.

This changed completely when he was given the post of Reich Commissioner in the Netherlands after the German army's *Blitzkrieg* against the Dutch in May 1940.[33] In two respects his position in The Hague significantly differed from the situation in Cracow: 1) For the first time Seyß-Inquart was chief executive in a given administrative district of the Greater German Reich. Reporting directly to the "*Führer*," the *Reichskommissar* was freed from unwelcome interference both of equals in rank and of superiors in the civilian hierarchy. 2) In accordance with the racial foundations of National Socialist ideology, the people of the Netherlands were regarded as ethnically close to Germans. Starting from this assumption both Seyß-Inquart and Hitler arrived at policy prescriptions very different from those applied in Poland. While the allegedly "subhuman" Slavic population in Poland suffered treatment as helots, the "Germanic" population of the Netherlands was thought capable of and destined to adopt National Socialism more or less voluntarily.[34] Against this ideologically motivated background, a process of what can be termed "guided self-nazification" of the Dutch population, discretely overseen by the occupying power, was initiated. In line with this strategy, the Reich Commissioner patronized and supported indigenous fascists, notably the Dutch "National Socialist Movement" founded in 1931 by Anton Adriaan Mussert. But other than his Norwegian counterpart Vidkun Quisling, whose *Nasjonal*

---

32. Präg/Jacobmeyer, *Diensttagebuch*, 203 (16 May 1940). On the whole, between 4,000 and 6,500 Polish people lost their lives due to the "extraordinary action of pacification," ca. 20,000 people were transferred to concentration camps. See Hans-Jürgen Bömelburg, "Die deutsche Besatzungspolitik in Polen 1939 bis 1945," in *Die polnische Heimatarmee: Geschichte und Mythos der Armia Krajowa seit dem Zweiten Weltkrieg*, ed. Bernhard Chiari (Munich: Oldenbourg, 2003), 76 with footnote 79.

33. Hitler's edict dating from 18 May 1940 in *Reichsgesetzblatt* I/1940, 778.

34. Still basic is Gerhard Hirschfeld, *Fremdherrschaft und Kollaboration: Die Niederlande unter deutscher Besatzung 1940-1945* (Stuttgart: Deutsche Verlags-Anstalt, 1984, English translation published in 1988). Irregardless of the underlying moralizing approach, the 14 volumes of *Het Koninkrijk der Nederlanden in de Tweede Wereldoorlog* by Louis de Jong still are indispensable for the history of German occupation of the Netherlands.

Samling movement was allowed to formally rule Norway subject to Reich Commissioner Josef Terboven,[35] Mussert never rose to premiership in the Netherlands. Although in 1941 his *Nationaal-Socialistische Beweging* (NSB) received authorization as Holland's sole political party; and despite Mussert's being awarded the—completely irrelevant—title of "leader of the Netherlandish nation" one year later, Seyß-Inquart was eager to keep pulling the strings so long as the war's outcome was not decided. To this end the Reich Commissioner effectively fought all non-fascist political movements in the Netherlands and eventually prohibited them. Trade unions, the media and religious communities suffered strict German control designed to force Dutch society and public life into line with the German National Socialist system.

Seyß-Inquart's concept of gradually synchronizing (*gleichschalten*) and nazifying institutions in the Netherlands, however, faced a number of obstacles. To begin with, Dutch civil servants on the national and local levels of administration were often reluctant to execute German policy.[36] Also, the "National Socialist Movement" was and remained at the margins of Dutch society, and within this party considerable frictions became manifest. Whereas Mussert and the majority of NSB's top figures favored national autonomy for their country within a confederation of "Germanic states" under the auspices of Berlin,[37] a radical fraction led by Meinoud Marinus Rost van Tonningen openly propagated annexation of the Netherlands by the Greater German Reich.[38] Even more cumbersome for Seyß-Inquart's policy of guided self-nazification was the growing reticence which the overwhelming majority of Dutch population displayed towards National Socialism and the *Reichskommissariat*. As the occupation regime turned into routine, the initial wait-and-see attitude on the part of the Dutch people gave way to expressions of dissent.[39] Hostility towards the National Socialist regime manifested itself not just in acts of sabotage and aggression

35. For Norway, see Robert Bohn, *Reichskommissariat Norwegen: "Nationalsozialistische Neuordnung" und Kriegswirtschaft* (Munich: Oldenbourg, 2000).
36. Peter Romijn, *Burgemeesters in oorlogstijd: Besturen onder Duitse bezetting* (Amsterdam: Balans, 2006).
37. *Vijf nota's van Mussert aan Hitler over de samenwerking van Duitschland en Nederland in een bond van Germaansche volkeren 1940-1944*, ed. Adolf Emile Cohen ('s-Gravenhage: Nijhoff, 1947).
38. *De SS en Nederland. Documenten uit SS-archieven 1935-1945*, ed. Nanno Klaas Charles Arie In 't Veld, 2 vol. ('s-Gravenhage: Nijhoff, 1976), passim. See also David Barnouw, *Rost van Tonningen. Fout tot het bittere eind* (Zutphen: Walburg Pers, 1994).
39. J.C.H. Blom, "Nederland onder Duitse bezetting 10 mei 1940 – 5 mei 1945," *Geschiedenis van het moderne Nederland. Politieke, economische en sociale ontwikkelingen* (Houten: De Haan, 1988), 481-516.

against German institutions, soldiers of the *Wehrmacht*, functionaries of the civil administration, or Dutch collaborators. Repudiation of German rule became particularly obvious in three remarkable instances. In February 1941, April-May 1943, and from September 1944 onwards intensified persecution of the Jews, introduction of Dutch forced labor, and internment of thousands of soldiers of the demobilized Netherlands army, infuriated the public. All of these instances gave rise to strikes in different parts of the country—the latter together with the Dutch desire to facilitate the advance of the Allied forces in the wake of D-day. All of them were put down brutally, each crushing of resistance bringing about a further hardening of the German attitude and, in turn, increased repression—a vicious spiral.

Right from the start, the Jews were a target of oppressive measures by the occupation regime. As in the Reich, they were considered the primary obstacle of a specifically National Socialist "New Order" designed for the whole of continental Europe. It is striking that the number of Jews deported from the Netherlands was higher than in any other Western European country under National Socialist rule. France and Belgium witnessed 25 and 43%, respectively, of their Jews being removed during the Second World War. The Jewish population of the Netherlands got reduced by 76%. On the whole, more than 107,000 children, men, and women were channeled via the detention camp at Westerbork to the concentration and extermination camps throughout Eastern Europe.[40] Though formal responsibility for this crime against humanity rested with *Höherer SS- und Polizeiführer Nordwest* Hanns Albin Rauter, Reich Commissioner Arthur Seyß-Inquart made a point of keeping the expropriation, socio-economic segregation and deportation of the Jews under his control. He did so by issuing a whole string of anti-Jewish decrees, by assigning responsibilities to his subordinate officials in order to speed up the genocide, by installing a "Special Representative for the Persecution of the Jews," and by personally signing lists of deportation. Furthermore he participated in creating an anti-Semitic atmosphere conducive to the persecution of the Jews. In March 1941, for example, he publicly announced in Amsterdam: "We will hit the Jews wherever we reach them, and whoever goes along with them, will have to bear the consequences. The *Führer* has declared that the Jews' game in Europe is over, and hence it is over."[41]

40. Wolfgang Seibel, "The Holocaust in western Europe," in *The Routledge History of The Holocaust*, ed. Jonathan C. Friedman (Oxon: Routledge, 2011), 224-25 and Bob Moore, *Slachtoffers en overlevenden: De nazi-vervolging van de joden in Nederland* (Amsterdam: Bert Bakker, 1998, English edition London 1997).

41. Cited from Arthur Seyß-Inquart, "Versammlung des Arbeitsbereiches der NSDAP. Amsterdam, 12. März 1941," in idem, *Vier Jahre in den Niederlanden: Gesammelte Reden*

Regarding the persecution of Jews as well as other activities under the Reich Commissioner's jurisdiction, Seyß-Inquart was compelled to cooperate closely with National Socialist instances in the Reich and in the occupied Netherlands. Since he belonged to the upper part of the middle ranks of the regime, his job was to mutually reconcile the objectives of various agencies and power factors. Concerning the "Final Solution" and the deportation of gypsies, for example, he had to reckon with Himmler and the *Reichssicherheitshauptamt* in Berlin. For his economic policy, the recruiting of foreign workers and the exploitation of Dutch industry, agriculture, and art resources Seyß-Inquart kept in touch with Göring as Hitler's Commissioner for the Four Year Plan, with Ministries of the Reich, and the General Plenipotentiary for the Employment of Labor, Fritz Sauckel, to name but a few relevant persons and institutions. In all these matters—and in several others—he also regularly consulted with the Reich Chancellery under Hans Heinrich Lammers and the Chancellery of the NSDAP. At the same time, Seyß-Inquart did everything in his power to block the encroachment of central instances of the Reich on "his" territory by pointing time and again to his immediate subordination under the "*Führer*." In this sense, cooperation and coordination implied permanent definition and regulation of the proper competences within the polycratic and dynamically floating structures of the National Socialist system.

Furthermore the Reich Commissioner had to communicate his proposed actions to the staff members of the *Reichskommissariat*, and to harmonize the guidelines issued by his office to the Dutch organs that would then put them into practice. In some cases, working relationships with subordinate German employees were without any difficulty. Old friends from Austria like DDr. Friedrich Wimmer (General Commissioner for Administration and Justice) and Dr. Hans Fischböck (General Commissioner for Finance and Economy) supported Seyß-Inquart's policy in The Hague effectively and smoothly. The Salzburg art historian Dr. Kajetan Mühlmann efficiently organized the theft of art works to the complete satisfaction of the Reich Commissioner. Seyß-Inquart relied on his services already in the era of the Anschluss and during his tenure as Deputy General Governor in Poland.[42] In other instances, however, coordination of occupation policies was difficult to achieve because time and again personal rivalries and conflicts

(Amsterdam: Volk und Reich, 1944), 57.

42. Jonathan Petropoulos, "The Importance of the Second Rank: The Case of the Art Plunderer Kajetan Mühlmann," in *Austro-Corporatism: Past-Present-Future*, ed. Günter Bischof and Anton Pelinka, Contemporary Austrian Studies, vol. 4 (New Brunswick: Transaction Publishers, 1996), 177-221.

of competence between various agencies of the Reich like the party and the SS threatened the progress of civil administration in the Netherlands. Frequently Seyß-Inquart was compelled to settle disputes between Rauter, who styled himself first and foremost as Himmler's lieutenant in The Hague, and General Commissioner Fritz Schmidt, who acted as representative of the NSDAP in the Netherlands. While Rauter pleaded for a rapid and complete annexation of the Netherlands, Schmidt resolutely championed setting up a domestic government formed by the NSB. Despite their obvious incompatibility, Seyß-Inquart managed to blend some of the views of Rauter and the SS on the one hand and Schmidt and the party on the other into his day-to-day policies.

His talent to successfully go along with different agencies and to reconcile opposing points of view certainly was a prerequisite for being entrusted with delicate assignments within the scope of the Greater German Reich. The intriguing question is what power techniques Seyß-Inquart was capable of applying to establish and sustain his positions in Vienna, Cracow and The Hague.

Power techniques—surviving in a pool with sharks

Arthur Seyß-Inquart is one of those bureaucratic perpetrators who by conviction bound their career completely to National Socialism. From the middle of the 1930s onwards he was on the fast track. Starting as a political nobody, he continuously worked his way up within just a few years. As Austrian Privy Counselor, Minister and Chancellor he paved the way for the Anschluss Österreichs, as Reich Governor, Deputy Governor, Reich Commissioner and Reich Minister he essentially contributed to the efforts of nazification and *Gleichschaltung* of Austria, Poland, and the Netherlands. In the very last days of the war, Hitler, in his so called "Political Testament," decreed that Seyß-Inquart be Foreign Minister in the cabinet of Admiral of the Fleet Karl Dönitz.[43] Furthermore Seyß-Inquart was made SS-*Gruppenführer* by Himmler right after the German takeover of Austria. Three years later he was promoted to *Obergruppenführer*. After the Anschluss, some politically minor but nonetheless prestigious posts were conferred to him. In July 1938, for example, he was appointed leader of the German Alpine Association,[44] and in 1944 he became president of

43. Bundesarchiv Koblenz, N 1128/23.

44. Johannes Koll, "Aufbau der 'Volksgemeinschaft' durch Vereinspolitik: Arthur Seyß-Inquart und der Alpenverein 1938-1945," *Zeitschrift für Geschichtswissenschaft* 60, no. 2 (2012): 124-45.

the *Deutsche Akademie* charged with propagating German language and culture in foreign countries. The accumulation of professional and honorary functions signaled to his contemporaries that Seyß-Inquart was one of those National Socialists who, despite their absence from the innermost circle of Hitler's confidantes, had to be taken seriously.

All this said, it is reasonable to ask why Seyß-Inquart remained in power beyond the point of realization of the Greater German idea, in other words why his upward path continued after Germany had accomplished the incorporation of Austria and the Sudetenland in 1938. What particular methods helped Seyß-Inquart, the "Austrian," "survive" and succeed on a high level within a political system that was characterized by internal competition and structural rivalries among its leaders? In two respects, circumstances militated against him. Firstly, many remunerative career posts were already filled by German National Socialists before Seyß-Inquart was able to speed up his own political career in the spring of 1938. Secondly, Seyß-Inquart did not possess a power base within the NSDAP. This was a serious deficiency given the party's faith in the "soldiers of the first hour," men who partook in Hitler's struggle for a Third Reich right from its inception in the early 1920s. Seyß-Inquart could not claim the status of *alter Kämpfer*, and he failed to command a following among the party's senior members. Both handicaps placed him in a difficult position when quarreling with long-serving party warhorses like Joseph Bürckel and others.[45]

As a compensation, Seyß-Inquart meticulously cultivated his personal relationship with Hitler. He more or less regularly reported to the "*Führer*" on his activities, plans and ideas. From 1938 onwards, both men congratulated each other on the occasion of their birthdays, and Seyß-Inquart met Hitler several times for confidential conversations. As a final proof of recognition the "*Führer*," shortly before committing suicide in his Berlin bunker, included Seyß-Inquart's name in the last cabinet list of the Third Reich. At that point of time former pillars of the regime like Göring and Himmler had already lost all their credit with the "*Führer*." But Hitler continued to have confidence in Seyß-Inquart. On the whole, Seyß-Inquart seems to have been among the very few Austrians whom Hitler really esteemed. Given the importance attached by the National Socialist regime to the Leader Principle (*Führerprinzip*), it was of utmost importance for a leading functionary to get along with Hitler. In this respect Seyß-Inquart obviously succeeded in striking the right note.

---

45. On this see Radomír Luža, *Österreich und die großdeutsche Idee in der NS-Zeit* (Vienna: Böhlau, 1977), 98-102.

Another important element in Seyß-Inquart's career-promoting strategy after the Anschluss consisted in entertaining friendly relations with a number of men close to Hitler, like Lammers, Martin Bormann, or several of the Reich's cabinet Ministers. Among the men Seyß-Inquart courted, Heinrich Himmler stands out in importance. His friendship with the Reichsführer-SS warranted his inclusion into the powerful network of the *Schutzstaffel*. For Seyß-Inquart, alignment with the mighty SS certainly held the potential of compensating for the lack of power within the NSDAP. Himmler's and Seyß-Inquart's sympathy for each other was rooted in their common *Weltanschauung*. Both men shared a deep-seated hatred of Jews and a willingness to promote radical ethnic cleansing, both advocated the use of force in creating the 'New Order', and both believed in the necessity of an elitist organization like the SS to do the dirty work. On the basis of these common attitudes, their relationship was one of mutual respect, and Seyß-Inquart's affiliation into the SS helped both men to benefit from each other.

This, however, does not mean that Seyß-Inquart unilaterally favored the SS at all times. Rather, he skillfully played on existing tensions between various agencies of power like the SS, the *Wehrmacht*, ministries of the Reich, rivaling party organizations, indigenous collaborators in the occupied countries, and his own offices of the *Reichsstatthalterei* in Austria and the *Reichskommissariat* in the Netherlands. It is noteworthy that, in the Netherlands, Seyß-Inquart constantly supported the local fascist movement. On several occasions he defended the "National Socialist Movement" and its leader Mussert against Himmler and Rauter, who both were skeptical about the NSB's ability and enthusiasm to substantially contribute to the nazification of Dutch society, or to the effective incorporation of the Netherlands into a future "Germanic Reich." Despite his affiliation with the network of the SS-complex, regardless of his good personal relationship with Himmler, and in contrast to his own Greater Germanic aspirations, Seyß-Inquart steadfastly endorsed Mussert and the *Nationaal-Socialistische Beweging*. Though Mussert was not given the permission to act as head of a Dutch government, the Reich Commissioner constantly hoped to win over Dutch society for National Socialism by backing the NSB. In the end, Seyß-Inquart's expectations as to the "self-nazification" of the Netherlands were frustrated. Still his efforts to cooperate with all relevant power factions in his realm and to prevent one of them from becoming predominant are clearly evidenced by a large number of documents.

Essential for his political "survival" was also his readiness to radicalize his political attitude. He played an important part in the execution of the

Holocaust, he encouraged the economic exploitation of territories under German rule, and he assisted in the brutal repression of local resistance, whether spontaneous or organized. His unconditional commitment to Nazism and the radicalization of his political beliefs and attitudes estranged him from Catholicism which, up to the Anschluss, had had a strong impact on his views of the world. Not before the Nuremberg trials did he show signs of returning into the Catholic fold. Between 1938 and 1945, he presented himself as a National Socialist fanatic dedicated to the establishment of a "New Order" based on German superiority, and on the conviction that the power of the Christian churches need be contained. In the Netherlands, he supported the security forces in their attempt at undermining the existing legal system. When, for example, in November 1942 Seyß-Inquart presented to Himmler his draft of a decree on police jurisdiction, he explicitly pointed out that in certain cases police courts-martial (which, by definition, were largely exempted from legal restrictions) might act even without prior promulgation of martial law.[46] With this flat denial of any rule of law, the former attorney Seyß-Inquart sought to adapt the Dutch situation to that in the Reich or even to turn "his" Netherlands into a model for Greater Germany. In this sense, Seyß-Inquart was not a victim of the process of radicalization inherent in National Socialism during World War II. In quite a few instances he rather belonged to the driving forces of this process.

Despite his willingness to actively take part in the radicalization of National Socialist politics, Seyß-Inquart proved to be flexible when negotiating matters of wartime food supply with representatives of the Dutch government in exile, with members of the Dutch administration in the occupied Netherlands, or with the Allied Supreme Command in the very last weeks of the war. These negotiations were facilitated by his explicit choice to ignore Hitler's "scorched earth" strategies. Did his decision reflect a realistic judgment of German military weakness in the final stages of the War? Was it plain altruism that motivated Seyß-Inquart's efforts to mitigate the consequences for the Western Netherlands of the "hunger winter" of 1944-45, causing thousands of deaths from starvation?[47] Or did he naively expect the victorious Allied Powers to give him credit for his attempts at feeding the Dutch once the war would be over?

There are good reasons for being critical of Seyß-Inquart's role in the hunger winter episode. His intervention on behalf of the Dutch people

46. Seyß-Inquart to Himmler, 30 November 1942, Bundesarchiv Berlin, NS 19/2860, fol. 260-61.

47. Gerard M.T. Trienekens, *Tussen ons volk en de honger: De voedselvoorziening 1940-1945* (Utrecht: Matrijs, 1985), 398-407.

came very late. To a certain degree, armed German units sabotaged the deal struck between him and US-General Walter Bedell Smith. And from a technical point of view, Seyß-Inquart's participation in the negotiations failed to make much sense. With hindsight, though, the incident once again reveals an important aspect of the way he used his powers, betting on several horses at the same time. When entering into confidential negotiations on food supply in spring 1945, he simultaneously launched a public appeal to German and Dutch National Socialists to continue their struggle against the Allied forces until the bitter end. Seyß-Inquart's answer to the demand for German unconditional surrender issued by the Yalta Conference came during a political rally in March 1945, when he said: "An iron will to persist helps us endure everything except a disgraceful surrender without a fight."[48] For Seyß-Inquart, battling to the last breath obviously did not exclude the dismissal of Hitler's politics of the "scorched earth," nor did his desperate moves to entrench the National Socialist regime in the Netherlands exclude cooperation with the enemy in the last weeks of the war. By trying to preserve a choice of options for himself, he made it difficult for contemporaries and historians alike to unveil his real intentions. The same pattern of behavior can be detected in numerous other phases of his political career. Time and again he publicly spoke in favor of an autonomous Dutch administration, while his *Reichskommissariat* hardly left any freedom of movement to indigenous functionaries and politicians. And didn't Seyß-Inquart's early career run on double-tracks? In the era preceding the Anschluss he presented himself as a more or less neutral "bridge-builder" between Schuschnigg and Hitler, while in the actual process of Austro-German unification he clearly acted as Hitler's Trojan horse.

Setbacks

All these strategies and techniques of political conduct helped Seyß-Inquart to remain in relatively powerful and influential positions from March 1938 up to his capture by Canadian soldiers in May 1945. But it is also true that his career suffered several setbacks, and some of his plans were foiled by competing currents. In April 1942, for example, he founded the "Germanic Research Institute" designed to become *the* central institution for scholarly research on and in the Low Countries. Since the SS considered Seyß-Inquart's brainchild an unwelcome rival

48. Arthur Seyß-Inquart, *Warum Nationalsozialismus?*, cited from the *Deutsche Zeitung in den Niederlanden*, 10 and 11 Jan. 1945 (Bundesarchiv Koblenz, ZSg 103/8644).

to its own research organization *Das Ahnenerbe*,[49] it was doomed from the beginning. In Poland in 1939-40, General Governor Hans Frank successfully nipped Seyß-Inquart's political aspirations in the bud. But it seems that the period between May and September 1939 was the least promising stage of Seyß-Inquart's career, when, following the end of his tenure as Reich Commissioner in Austria, he tried to convince Hitler and other leading National Socialists of his capacities as an expert on cultural policy and on East and South-East European politics. Failing to be entrusted with an important task, he contributed behind the scenes to the gradual destruction of the Czechoslovak state and the creation of the Protectorate of Bohemia and Moravia. To this end, Seyß-Inquart worked to foment secessionist tendencies among Sudeten Germans and Slovaks in 1938–39. Being a native Sudeten German himself, he took pride in being present at the spot when Hitler welcomed "the new citizens of the Greater German Reich" in Brno on 17 March 1939.[50] In fact, however, his efforts to acquire a job in the fields of culture or of (South-)East-European politics delivered no results. For nearly a half year, in which the Greater German Reich vigorously prepared territorial expansion, Seyß-Inquart justifiably felt that he was sidelined, being no more than a Reich Minister without portfolio and member of the powerless German parliament. Neither of these posts afforded an opportunity for the deployment of proper political or administrative energies. In this situation, the lack of a power base within the NSDAP proved cumbersome, while being on friendly terms with Hitler and Himmler did not help much, either. Early in 1939, the "*Führer*" even withdrew his assent to naming Seyß-Inquart the German representative in Slovakia. Hitler's decision was based on the advice of his Minister of Foreign Affairs, Ribbentrop, who feared that the government in Bratislava might overestimate its significance for the Greater German Reich should a high official like *Reichsminister* Seyß-Inquart be appointed ambassador.[51]

There were other reasons as well for Seyß-Inquart to lose faith in the loyalty of his fellow National Socialists. In the spring and summer of 1939, several of his close associates died under circumstances that never

49. For the *Germanisches Forschungsinstitut* see Nanno Klaas Charles Arie In 't Veld, "Inleiding," in *De SS en Nederland*, ed. idem and archival materials in NIOD. Instituut voor Oorlogs-, Holocaust- en Genocidestudies, 20/633 and 77/21. For the *Ahnenerbe* see Michael H. Kater, *Das "Ahnenerbe" der SS 1935-1945: Ein Beitrag zur Kulturpolitik des Dritten Reiches*, 4th ed. (Munich: Oldenbourg, 2006).

50. Cited from *Hitler: Reden und Proklamationen 1932-1945*, ed. Max Domarus, 4th ed. (Leonberg: Pamminger, 1988), vol. 3, 1101.

51. Hans Heinrich Lammers to the *Adjutantur des Führers*, 16 June 1939, Bundesarchiv Berlin, NS 10/26, fol. 165.

were clarified in a satisfactory way. It seems that the *Schutzstaffel* had a finger in the pie when Seyß-Inquart's right hand man, SS-*Sturmbannführer* Dr. Franz Hammerschmid, his friend and informant Dr. Fritz Flohr, and Dr. Wilhelm Wolf, the Minister of Foreign Affairs in Seyß-Inquart's *Anschlusskabinett*, lost their lives. Be that as it may, the fact that several people with whom Seyß-Inquart had intimately collaborated in the era of the Anschluss Österreichs passed away within a couple of weeks, pointed at some internal rivalry among National Socialist factions. Notwithstanding his good personal relations with Himmler and his affiliation with the SS, the fatalities reminded Seyß-Inquart once more of the absence of a genuine power base. It looked as if his political career had come to an end in 1939. In fact, he had to wait until the beginning of the Second World War to find new opportunities for political and professional advancement.

Conclusion

On account of his deep involvement in the National Socialist regime, Seyß-Inquart was tried as one of twenty-four major war criminals and ultimately sentenced to death by the International Military Tribunal in Nuremberg.[52] Failing to have shown signs of regret or feelings of guilt in the face of unparalleled atrocities committed by National Socialism and the Greater German Reich, he was hanged on 16th October 1946 together with nine other perpetrators. Thereafter, American soldiers burnt the corpses, and the ashes were poured into a small tributary of the Isar. This procedure was deliberately chosen to exclude any possibility of gravesites becoming a place of worship for National Socialists or likeminded people.

What does Arthur Seyß-Inquart's biography tell us in retrospect? Undoubtedly he was one of those bureaucratic perpetrators (*Schreibtischtäter*) who belonged to the middle stratum of the National Socialist hierarchy. His ambition propelled him to seek ever further advancement, but both his successes and failures were determined by the structure of the National Socialist state, and its elites. Within this general framework, Seyß-Inquart skillfully worked his way up until the Greater German Reich finally collapsed in May 1945. From the 1930s onwards, he knowingly and deliberately chose for a career under National Socialist auspices, disregarding other options of Greater German orientation. Once embedded, he smoothly followed all the twists and turns of the regime, and more than once he

52. In recent years, abundant literature on the Nuremberg trials has been published by historians, political scientists and legal experts. See e.g. *Nazi Crimes and the Law*, ed. Nathan Stoltzfus and Henry Friedlaender (Cambridge: Cambridge University Press, 2008).

delivered contributions to the radicalization of National Socialist politics. By adroitly making use of the techniques of power politics outlined above, he managed to "survive" in high positions with considerable success. In the end, though too late for any practical effect to follow from it, he witnessed the fulfillment of his highest aspirations: he got appointed Minister of Foreign Affairs of a by now defunct German Reich. It would be misleading to assume that Seyß-Inquart's career rested exclusively on opportunism and tactical suppleness. All his letters, articles and proclamations reveal a great portion of idealism. In National Socialist thought he obviously recognized the appropriate expression of Greater German nationalism. Deeply rooted anti-Semitic and racist feelings combined with his rejection of communism, liberal democracy and parliamentarianism were further ideological components which firmly tied him to Hitler and his movement.

It goes without saying that Seyß-Inquart shared his beliefs with many contemporaries in Austria and Germany. Furthermore, he was far from alone in his desire to benefit from the establishment of a "New Order" in state and society. In this respect his biography may be regarded as a typical "Austrian life" of the first half of the 20th century. What makes him a special case, however, is the fact that no other well-known Austrian succeeded in gaining and preserving Hitler's favor, and no other Austrian National Socialist managed to "survive" almost continuously in high positions within the Greater German Reich. In this sense, Seyß-Inquart's biography is certainly not representative of Austria at the same time. On all accounts, regardless of his biographical singularity Seyß-Inquart may be taken as a striking example of innumerable Austrians who opted for National Socialism. His active involvement in the Anschluss Österreichs and his subsequent career within the Greater German Reich convincingly falsify the belief that Austria had been no more than the first victim of Nazi aggression. Though rebutted by professional historiography for a long time, the widespread *Opferthese* has led a long-lasting life after World War II.[53] Biographical research on perpetrators of all ranks, by contrast, has the potential to demonstrate that National Socialism has to be considered as an integral part of Austrian history of the 20th century.

53. Heidemarie Uhl, "Österreich: Vom Opfermythos zur Mitverantwortungsthese: Die Transformationen des österreichischen Gedächtnisses," in *Mythen der Nationen: 1945 – Arena der Erinnerungen*, ed. Monika Flacke, vol. 2 (Mainz: Philipp von Zabern, 2004), 481-508; see also the essay by Winfried Garscha on ordinary Austrian war criminals in this volume.

A Century in a Lifetime: Biographical Approaches to Bruno Kreisky (1911-1990)

Elisabeth Röhrlich

If Austria had a Mount Rushmore, Bruno Kreisky most likely would be sculpted in it. He was the longest standing Austrian federal chancellor in the history of the Second Republic, and the thirteen years of his government (1970-1983) mark a period of societal reforms, liberalization, and internationalization. In retrospect, the picture of Kreisky's chancellorship seems to shine even brighter, and it is often recalled as a golden era. More than that, Kreisky's appearance, his way of talking, and the fact that he cultivated the friendship of many artists, musicians, and businessmen, made him the subject of numerous anecdotes. Almost every Austrian seems to know at least a few of these little stories in which Kreisky is the main character and that describe his personality and nature. The anecdotes continue to be narrated in countless ways and, for instance, point to the fact that the Austrian chancellor was listed in Vienna's telephone directory, that people could call him at home, and that they even got through to him. At the heart of most anecdotes lies the complexity of Kreisky's character: the stories describe him as a sometimes ready witted, sometimes enraged man, as a grand statesman and yet a down-to-earth politician. As a matter of fact, lots of these anecdotes have a true core and have often been verified by former staff members of Kreisky.[1]

The brightest picture of the Kreisky era has been drawn in 2011, when Kreisky would have been a hundred years old. The Austrians commemorated their former chancellor like they never had before: exhibitions, talks, books, TV shows, and plays were focusing on the life and times of the famous social democrat.[2] During Kreisky's chancellorship his politics were by no means without controversy, but now, they often become a model for the present. "What would Kreisky do today?" journalists, intellectuals, and politicians keep asking.[3] To handle the challenges of the present they refer to Kreisky's famous slogans, political concepts, and key words. Kreisky had coined many of them already in his early career and had echoed them throughout his

1. Elisabeth Röhrlich, *Kreiskys Außenpolitik: Zwischen österreichischer Identität und internationalem Programm* (Göttingen: Vienna University Press, 2009), 344.
2. The complete program is accessible at: <www.kreisky100.at> (25 Dec. 2011).
3. Thomas Nowotny, "Und wenn jetzt ein "neuer Kreisky" käme," *Der Standard*, 8. / 9. Jan. 2011.

political life—a phenomenon that, in the words of the former Austrian foreign minister Peter Jankowitsch, could be called "Kreisky vintage."[4]

The booking photograph shows Bruno Kreisky after being arrested in January 1935.
© Bruno Kreisky Archives Foundation, Vienna

Nonetheless, the 2011 anniversary alone is not the explanation for the ongoing fascination with Kreisky. A major part of the reason why he is still so popular today can be found in Kreisky's personality and, closely linked to that, in his biography. His appearance was that of a gentlemanly, urbane, and self-assured man, a cosmopolitan and an intellectual, but he had experienced deep ruptures during his life: two world wars, imprisonment, and exile. Both the main continuities and the main discontinuities in the history of the twentieth century in Europe—and particularly in the history of Austria—had affected Kreisky's life and his political career. The biographical approach—without overvaluing its explanatory power—can offer revealing insights into Kreisky's life and thus explain some of the chancellor's key strengths and weaknesses.

When Kreisky was born in Vienna in 1911, his hometown was still the capital of the huge multi-ethnic Habsburg Monarchy. Like many of their contemporaries Kreisky's parents had migrated from the Habsburg crown lands; the family of Kreisky's father Max Kreisky was from Bohemia, Kreisky's mother, Irene Felix, came from Moravia. Kreisky's parents were assimilated Jews, Kreisky himself resigned from the Viennese Jewish

4. Peter Jankowitsch, "Zum Phänomen Bruno Kreisky als Außenpolitiker" (book presentation and panel discussion at the University of Vienna), 19 Nov. 2009.

Community (*Kultusgemeinde*) when he was twenty years old.[5] As a young boy, during World War I, he witnessed the carrying of the wounded to the military hospital in Vienna. His father had been a soldier in the war too.[6] During Kreisky's school years Austria became a republic, and during his time as a university student the country came under the rule of the clerico-fascist Dollfuss-Schuschnigg regime. Kreisky's *Rigorosum* coincided with Hitler's invasion of Austria in March 1938. He had to leave Vienna and spend his exile years in Sweden. When Kreisky came back to Austria in 1951, the country was still under the control of the four occupying powers. The autobiography of the German born U.S. historian Fritz Stern is called "Five Germanys I have known"[7]—likewise there were at least five Austrias that Kreisky had known during his lifetime.[8]

One could argue, that—as a result of his remarkable biography—Kreisky virtually had to become a politician. That was how Kreisky himself, too, explained his way into politics. In his autobiographical texts he frequently referred to certain key experiences that had made him a political person—experiences such as the July revolt in 1927 (*Justizpalastbrand*), the Austrian civil war of 1934, his imprisonment, the so-called Anschluss in 1938, Kreisky's years in exile in Sweden, or his participation in the negotiations for the Austrian State Treaty in Moscow in April 1955.

However, since Kreisky's vita was that outstanding, the opposite could have been just as true. How, after all, was it possible that a person with such an exceptional life could finally end up as Austria's federal chancellor? If the characterization of Austria as a "paradoxical republic"[9] is right, then the fact that Bruno Kreisky was the country's longest-standing chancellor can be described as even more paradoxical: he was a Jewish chancellor in a country with strong anti-Semitic tendencies, a former victim of the Nazi persecution who became a leading politician in a country that thought of itself as "Hitler's first victim." Moreover, he was a social democrat with an upper-class behavior in a widely catholic and predominately agrarian country, and a cosmopolitan who aimed to strengthen Austria's patriotism. According to the contemporary historian Oliver Rathkolb "as with no chancellor of the Second Republic before him, all the internal political structural conditions spoke against Kreisky, but all the social and international trends weighed in his favour."[10]

5. Röhrlich, *Kreiskys Außenpolitik*, 52.
6. Ibid., 379.
7. Fritz Stern, *Five Germanys I have Known* (New York: Farrar, Straus & Giroux, 2006).
8. Röhrlich, *Kreiskys Außenpolitik*, 27.
9. Oliver Rathkolb, *The Paradoxical Republic: Austria 1945-2005* (New York: Berghahn Books, 2011).
10. Rathkolb, *The Paradoxical Republic*, 112.

In 1974, an internal C.I.A. memorandum named the Austrian chancellor an "Austrian Horatio Alger, at least in terms of his rise to political prominence."[11] Referring to the prolific American novelist Horatio Alger whose characters were mostly young men who struggled upward from a poor background, the U.S. report referred to Kreisky's astonishing political success. Albeit Kreisky came not from a poor family but from an upper middle-class background, the comparison to the ambitious and determined characters of Horatio Alger's novels indeed hit the mark. Even in his own party Kreisky's way to the top was not easy and had often demanded persistence.

Bruno Kreisky's Austrian Life

Kreisky was a typical Austrian, and yet he was not. His early life was shaped by a series of changes in the political and economic system of the country, the first of which was the disintegration of the Habsburg Empire. Even though Kreisky was only a young boy when the multiethnic empire collapsed, the Danube Monarchy had left an imprint on his youth. His parents had moved from the crown lands to Vienna; Kreisky's maternal grandparents, the Felix family, had a family-owned enterprise based in Southern Moravia. Many summers the young Kreisky spent amid his relatives in Znaim, where the domicile of the family business was. The Kreisky household in Vienna employed domestic maids from Bohemia, with whom his parents, as Kreisky later recalled, spoke Czech.[12]

Notwithstanding his upper middle-class family background Kreisky's way into politics was a socialist one. In 1924, a schoolboy from Vienna committed suicide after he had to suffer the torments of his teacher—a bitter event that the Austrian writer Friedrich Torberg later transformed into a novel.[13] When students from all over Vienna, organized by the socialist youth organization for high school students (*Sozialistische Mittelschüler*) took to the streets to protest against the state of the Austrian educational system, Kreisky joined them, and in doing so, attended his first political demonstration. From then on Kreisky regularly participated in the meetings of the socialist youth organizations. First, he joined the *Sozialistische Mittelschüler*, but soon he switched to the Socialist Working

11. "Memorandum: Subject: Austria Today, from 25 October 1974," 20 July 2012, CIA-RDP 85T00353R000100100010-4, CIA Records Search Tool (CREST), National Archives and Records Administration, College Park, MD.

12. Bruno Kreisky, *Zwischen den Zeiten: Der Memoiren erster Teil* (Vienna: Kremayr & Scheriau, 2000), 61-102.

13. Friedrich Torberg, *Der Schüler Gerber hat absolviert* (Vienna 1930).

Youth (*Sozialistische Arbeiterjugend*). In Kreisky's eyes the latter was less intellectual and, moreover, at the base of the working class. To cover his political activities he wore his best suit when leaving for the group meetings, telling his mother that he would attend classes at Vienna's most famous dancing school Elmayer.[14]

At least that is what Kreisky tells us in his memoirs. This autobiographical work, published in 1986, is the most comprehensive historical source for Kreisky's youth and for his first steps into politics. Whereas his exile years in Sweden as well as his political career in the Second Republic are documented very well, we lack detailed historical information about Kreisky's early political socialization. This is due to the fact that at the beginning of his political activities Kreisky only held minor positions in the youth organizations of the Social Democrat Party. In 1986 though, Irene Etzersdorfer and Oliver Rathkolb were able to edit some sources about Kreisky's early political socialization.[15] But since there are hardly any documents dating from his first twenty years, for that period we depend on the information given in Kreisky's memoirs. These, on the other hand, are a subjective source and, in addition, can only offer a retrospective view. In essence, this problem applies to most forms of autobiographical texts, and it will be examined more closely in the second part of this essay.

After Kreisky had finished school, he went to the University of Vienna to study law. In doing so he acted on the advice of the leading Austrian socialist Otto Bauer who, as Kreisky later recounted, had told him that the Social Democrat Party needed good attorneys.[16] To study in Vienna in the 1930s also meant to experience rising political radicalism and unveiled anti-Semitism. For Kreisky it was even worse. When the Socialist Democrat Party was forbidden by the Austro-fascist regime after the Austrian civil war of 1934, the Socialists had to operate as an illegal underground group. In a wave of arrests Kreisky was detained.

Kreisky was almost a year and a half under arrest. An exceptional historical source dates from this period of Kreisky's life—the journal he kept during his imprisonment. Even more exceptional than the mere fact that Kreisky kept a journal during his arrest is the way this outstanding source has come down to us. For almost twenty years the original document was considered to be lost, and it was only available as a fading copy. Nevertheless, in 2009 the Bruno Kreisky Archives Foundation decided to

---

14. Kreisky, *Zwischen den Zeiten*, 103-42.
15. Irene Etzersdorfer and Oliver Rathkolb, eds., *Der junge Kreisky: Schriften, Reden, Dokumente, 1931-1965* (Vienna: Schriftenreihe der Stiftung Bruno Kreisky Archiv, 1986).
16. Kreisky, *Zwischen den Zeiten*, 161.

publish Kreisky's diary on the basis of the existing copy.[17] An anonymous addresser, probably lead by his guilty conscious, thereupon sent a package with the journal's original copy to Kreisky's longtime assistant Margit Schmidt. Thus, on the verge of the journal's publication, the original copy had found its way back into the holdings of the Kreisky Archives. Besides this adventurous history of the sources' origin, what makes Kreisky's journal an important source for historians is that it gives in-depth insights into the experiences and the mind-set of the young Kreisky.

In his journal, Kreisky writes about the daily routine in prison, about how he gets along with cellmates, and about the discipline he needs to endure his imprisonment. Furthermore, the journal is a revealing source about Kreisky's intellectual background. This is particularly true for the literature Kreisky read during his imprisonment. In his journal, he lists the books he reads while under arrest, among them studies on racial issues, Zionism, and Jewry. The list shows that already in his twenties Kreisky intellectually dealt with these subjects—subjects he continued to occupy himself with throughout his political career.

But the imprisonment during the Dollfuß-Schuschnigg was not the only time that Kreisky had to spend in prison. The next time it was the Nazi regime that brought him into jail. Only on condition that he would leave the country Kreisky finally was released in August 1938. He took refuge in Sweden, having left Vienna via Berlin and Copenhagen with a copy of Robert Musil's novel *Der Mann ohne Eigenschaften* in his coat pocket—an anecdote that Kreisky later often repeated and with which many Austrians therefore still are acquainted.[18] Like other little stories about Kreisky it illustrates the close entanglement of biographical facts and Kreisky's own autobiographical statements with which historians are confronted.

Unlike many of his fellow Austrian emigrants Kreisky soon was able to establish himself in Stockholm. Although he had some financial difficulties in the beginning, the hard times did not last long. He got a job with the Swedish consumer cooperative and worked as a freelance correspondent for several international newspapers. Kreisky established close bonds with leading social democrats in Stockholm and, by marrying the Swede Vera Fürth, he could improve his social status even more. Despite his good position in Sweden, Kreisky's attention centered on Austria and the country's future after the war. This becomes very clear when looking at Kreisky's political activities during his exile in Sweden. He participated in both Austrian

17. Ulrike Felber, ed., *Auch schon eine Vergangenheit: Gefängnistagebuch und Korrespondenzen von Bruno Kreisky* (Vienna: Mandelbaum Verlag, 2009).
18. Kreisky, *Zwischen den Zeiten*, 313.

and international exile groups: the Club of Austrian Socialists (*Klub österreichischer Sozialisten*, KÖS) and the non-party Austrian Association in Sweden (*Österreichische Vereinigung in Schweden*, ÖVS) on the one hand, and the *International Group of Democratic Socialists* on the other hand. Unlike Austrian socialist exile groups in other countries the KÖS always argued for an independent Austria. The association had held this view even before the release of the Moscow Declaration in November 1943, in which the allied forces had committed themselves to an independent postwar Austria. Although the Austrian social democrat party traditionally favored a greater Germany including Austria, Kreisky—and with him large parts of the younger socialists—dissented from this point of view.[19] For the ÖVS and the KÖS alike the future independence of Austria was a major postwar goal that was emphasized through an extensive cultural program including for instance Austrian literary evenings and concerts. The socialist KÖS, under its president Kreisky, unabashedly employed traditional elements of Austrian high culture and the country's monarchic past to underscore its political aim of Austrian independence and mixed it with elements of socialist culture, like songs of the working class.[20] Certainly, this was not only a political strategy to promote the Austrian interests in Sweden but also a means to cope with the emigrants' homesickness and nostalgia. But in the context of the socialist KÖS and the non-party ÖVS—both groups were lead by Kreisky—he developed for the first time a policy of combining traditional with modern images of Austria. After 1945, Kreisky followed this political pattern again when he for example reopened the Diplomatic Academy in the early 1960s or when he argued for a new international conference center in Vienna in the 1970s and 1980s.

The *International Group of Democratic Socialists* in Stockholm consisted of social democrats from varying national backgrounds, including European emigrants, international diplomats, and Swedish politicians. It therefore has been often referred to as "The Little International."[21] It was in this group where Kreisky got to know the German social democrat Willy Brandt. They became close political and personal friends, and in the 1970s both had great impact on the reformation of the Socialist International. Some of the political ideas Kreisky and Brandt brought forward later were

19. Röhrlich, *Kreiskys Außenpolitik*, 171.
20. Elisabeth Röhrlich, "Donauweisen und Arbeiterlieder: Zur österreichischen Kulturpolitik im schwedischen Exil," *Exil: Forschung, Erkenntnisse, Ergebnisse*, no. 1 (2008): 47-58.
21. Klaus Misgeld, *Die Internationale Gruppe demokratischer Sozialisten in Stockholm 1952-1945: Zur sozialistischen Friedensdiskussion während des Zweiten Weltkrieges* (Uppsala: Verlag Neue Gesellschaft, 1976).

developed in these early years. This was particularly true for the global focus that characterized the activities of the Socialist International in the 1970s. About thirty years back, the "Little International" of Stockholm had anticipated this direction: "The possibilities to get in closer touch and strengthen the ties with the labor movement in North and South America, in the British Dominions, China, India, in the Near East and the African and Asiatic colonies should be carefully examined."[22]

Throughout his lifetime Kreisky remained closely connected with Sweden. This was not only true for his wife's family and his friends from exile days, but also for leading political and public figures of Sweden. For example the Swedish longtime Director General of the International Atomic Energy Agency (IAEA) in Vienna, Sigvard Eklund, became a good friend of Kreisky—the Eklund and the Kreisky families spoke with each other in Swedish. When it came to Sweden and the country's social democrat party, Kreisky—who was friends with Prime Minister Olof Palme—usually did not hesitate to show his opinion. In view of the election defeat of the Swedish social democrats in 1976, Kreisky immediately called the party headquarters in Stockholm in order to recommend what Palme should do now.[23]

Notwithstanding Kreisky's close ties with the Swedes and despite his successful integration into Stockholm's social democratic life, he never seriously thought about staying in Scandinavia. After the end of the war his main goal was to establish himself in Austrian politics. However, the postwar socialist party was not very eager to integrate the remigrees, neither to provide them with significant political positions. Since the *Sozialistische Partei Österreichs* (SPÖ) wanted to shed its prewar image as a "Jewish party," it was particularly hard for Jews to find their way back into the party.[24] Kreisky was sent back to Stockholm to build up the Austrian Embassy there. He did not come back to Austria until 1951. Although the appointment in Stockholm did not meet Kreisky's expectations for his postwar political career, the new job in Sweden turned out to be an important part of Kreisky's political vita. It was his first professional engagement with Austrian foreign policy—a political issue that later became his favorite field of activity.

Back in Austria, Kreisky firstly held the position as an advisor to the Austrian Federal President Theodor Körner (SPÖ). Shortly after he made

22. Bruno Kreisky, *International Debate in Stockholm*, Jun.-Jul. 1943, Bruno Kreisky Archives Foundation, 1.2.-1.2., Box 8.

23. Klaus Misgeld, "Politik för Österrike: Bruno Kreisky och Sverige ," *Arbetarhistoria* 135, no. 1 (2008): 8-17 (17).

24. Oliver Rathkolb, "Der Fall Kreisky: Grenzgänge zwischen Politik, Wissenschaft und Kunst," *Austriaca* 6 (2003): 36-45.

a big jump in his career: Kreisky became Austrian under secretary of state for foreign relations (1953-1959). This position carried him right into the center of international politics, including the state treaty negotiations in Moscow. Already as under secretary of state Kreisky developed a political style that was very self-confident and often out of the ordinary. This can be exemplified by his mediation attempts during the Berlin Crisis in spring 1959. Kreisky, at that time only under secretary, had the idea to set up a personal meeting between Nikita Khrushchev and Willy Brandt, then Mayor of West Berlin. In his efforts to set a date Kreisky acted hastily; he neither waited for Brandt's approval to the plan nor did he reassure himself with his own boss, Foreign Minister Leopold Figl (*Österreichische Volkspartei*, ÖVP). And, worse yet, Kreisky informed Khrushchev that Brandt had already consented to the plan when the mayor was still pondering. Finally Kreisky's plan failed. Only toward the end of his efforts the Austrian under secretary realized that his own political career was at stake. Afterwards Kreisky's friendship with Brandt cooled down for a while.[25]

Kreisky's objective during the Berlin Crisis was to establish a direct dialog between East and West. From his point of view this was also a means to foster Austria's neutrality. Nonetheless, Kreisky never left a doubt that he was a man of the West. In speeches, talks, and papers he often used typical Cold War rhetoric like the persistent reference to the "free world"—most notably during the 1950s.[26] Another revealing example for Kreisky's orientation toward the ideological West can be found in his collaboration with the so-called *Meraner Kreis* (Circle of Meran), a group of people that tried to organize a counter-program to the communist world youth festival that took place in Vienna in summer 1959. Federal Chancellor Julius Raab (ÖVP), who was known for his often Soviet-friendly interpretation of Austria's neutrality, had officially invited the festival's organizers to Vienna. In order to counter the communist festival Bruno Kreisky and a few other political and public figures set up several working meetings, the first of which took place in a hotel in Meran (hence the name of the group).[27] Alongside Kreisky the circle included the socialists and members of parliament Christian Broda and Peter Strasser, the German Catholic and Adenauer-intimate Klaus Dohrn, the financier Georg Fürstenberg, and the American C.D. Jackson, vice president of Time Life and former advisor to President

25. Hanns Jürgen Küsters, "Konrad Adenauer und Willy Brandt in der Berlinkrise 1958-1963," *Vierteljahreshefte für Zeitgeschichte* 40, no. 4 (1992): 483-542.

26. Röhrlich, *Kreiskys Außenpolitik*, 133-39.

27. Ibid., 143-51; Oliver Rathkolb, *Washington ruft Wien: US-Großmachtpolitik und Österreich 1953-1963; Mit Exkursen zu CIA-Waffenlagern, NATO-Connection, Neutralitätsdebatte* (Vienna: Böhlau, 1997), 100-101.

Eisenhower—he added an international dimension to the group. Together they drafted an extensive program to counter the communist initiative and even achieved that the Western press did not report on the youth festival. The *Meraner Kreis* is an early example for Kreisky's approach to networking in which he often went beyond the boundaries of party affiliations.

In 1959, Kreisky became Austria's foreign minister. Traditionally, the foreign ministry was an office of the federal chancellery, but under Kreisky it had been elevated to full cabinet rank for the first time since World War II. This modification had been Kreisky's condition to accept the office, a plan that was backed by many members of the Foreign Ministry, among them also conservatives.[28] During the years as foreign minister (1959-1966), Kreisky pursued his goal to consolidate Austria's westernization. A U.S. observer of that time described Kreisky as follows: "A brilliant intellectual with an international reputation, Kreisky is pro-Western and less addicted to the opportunism that Raab frequently tended to inject into Austria's relations with the Communist bloc in the past." Kreisky aimed to strengthen Austria's position in international relations by giving the neutrality of the state a new and more active profile. In the 1960s, he therefore pursued the West-oriented foreign policy but underlined Austria's neutrality. The U.S. report continued: "On the other hand, Kreisky has tended to feel that Austria's neutrality—required by law only in the military field—should be patterned after the broader Swiss concept. This and his dislike of West German economic influence in Austria have made him oppose Austrian membership in the Common market in a broader economic association."[29]

Next to the East-West-relations and to the European integration process, Kreisky put a major emphasis on development politics as well as on Austrian-Italian relations, notably South Tyrolean affairs. The latter was also a means for the Jewish socialist Kreisky to prove his patriotism. In his memoirs Kreisky explained: "In addition to the obvious political considerations, I also had a strong personal reason for wanting to be viewed as active in the matter of South Tyrol; I had to prevent people from assuming that because of my commitment to socialism and my inclination towards cosmopolitism (which was sometimes attributed to my Jewish background), I would not pursue this matter with the necessary energy ..."[30] Moreover,

---

28. Journal of Martin Fuchs, 4 Apr. 1959, Archiv des österreichischen Instituts für Zeitgeschichte, DO 834/File 43.
29. "Current Intelligence Weekly Summary, from 16 July 1959," 20 July 2012, CIA-RDP 79-00927A002300090001-8, CIA Records Search Tool (CREST), National Archives and Records Administration, College Park, MD.
30. Matthew Paul Berg (ed.), *The Struggle for a Democratic Austria: Bruno Kreisky on Peace and Social Justice* (New York: Berghahn Books, 2000), 355.

since the question of South Tyrol was discussed before the United Nations, it was a significant step of internationalization.

Kreisky also showed a particular fascination for the United States. He admired New York. He visited the city yearly to attend the United Nations General Assembly, and he was greatly interested in new trends in American literature, sciences, and the arts. He spoke frequently to U.S. politicians, diplomats, and intellectuals and was keen on knowing what was new in America. In order to stay updated he often talked to friends and journalists in the United States who became important sources of information. In October 1963, one month before the assassination of President Kennedy, Kreisky, who had been recommended to Kennedy by former president Harry S. Truman, was invited to the White House. In fall 1965, Kreisky visited the United States to attend the so-called Austrian Fortnight in Dallas—the event was a means of cultural politics—and to give a talk at Yale University about Eastern Europe and political "Changes in the Danubian Area."[31] Already in the late 1950s, more than a decade before the Conference on Security and Cooperation in Europe (CSCE) took place, Kreisky developed a new policy toward Eastern Europe, the so-called *Nachbarschaftspolitik*. In Kreisky's opinion, Austria and its Eastern neighbors were linked with each other through the shared past of the Danube Monarchy.[32]

When the ÖVP succeeded in the elections of 1966 and thenceforth formed a one-party government, Kreisky was thrown back upon his seat as a simple member of parliament. In party politics he was more successful: in 1967 Kreisky became chairman of the SPÖ and was responsible for developing a new party program. Kreisky promoted the new program with the slogan that it had been prepared by "1,400 experts"—a number that was obviously exaggerated. But Kreisky had indeed established a close dialog with different experts to create the new party program. In doing so, Kreisky was able to show that modern politics could take advantage of the social sciences and other disciplines. Probably he was also influenced by his Swedish experiences. In the context of the *International Group of Democrat Socialists* Kreisky had worked together with Alva and Gunnar Myrdal, noted Swedish scholars and politicians who had linked economics, sociology, and politics.

Only a few years later, the elections of 1970 sent the SPÖ back to power and Kreisky became federal chancellor in a minority government. In 1971, a new government was formed after snap elections, this time

---

31. Bruno Kreisky, "Is the Cold War over? Changes in the Danubian Era," New Haven, 14 Oct. 1965, in Kreisky: *Reden*, vol. 1 (Vienna: Österreichische Staatsdruckerei, 1981), 647-55.
32. Röhrlich, *Kreiskys Außenpolitik*, 221.

Kreisky's SPÖ had received an absolute majority. Kreisky's chancellorship (1970-1983) was an epoch of domestic and foreign successes, but one of international and inner-Austrian crises as well. While Kreisky succeeded in strengthening Austria's position in international relations and while his government initiated far-reaching social reforms, the Kreisky era was also marked by serious domestic political conflicts. Austria's foreign and defense policies, which in the first decades of the Second Republic were based on a broad political consensus, now more and more became a field of conflict between SPÖ and ÖVP. Also within the SPÖ arose conflicts, as the emotion-laden clash between Kreisky and his former protégé Hannes Androsch showed in the 1970s.

A recurring theme during Kreisky's chancellorship was the question of this Jewish origin—a question that referred to both his political activities as well as to his biography. In his foreign policy, Kreisky had set a major emphasis on the Mideast Conflict. Although he always manifested his absolute loyalty toward Israel, Kreisky's Jewish background did not lead to an uncritical position toward the state. Instead, he became a committed advocate of the Palestinians. Kreisky's most important political initiatives in this domain were the fact-finding missions which he led in 1973, 1974, and 1975. Already during the previous years Kreisky had consistently called for dealing with the Mideast on an international level. Following the Yom Kippur war of 1973 the international attention for Kreisky's ideas increased and he finally was put in charge by the Socialist International to conduct three fact-finding missions to the Mideast on behalf of the organization. It was during these missions that Kreisky met several leading and often controversial politicians of the Arab world, including Yasser Arafat or Muammar Gaddafi. Kreisky always aimed to establish new relations between politicians from different political and national backgrounds and, in doing so, often chose unorthodox methods. In the early 1980s, for instance, he established a connection between Gaddafi and the German Greens, among them Otto Schily.[33] In recent years, new research on the transnational terrorism in the 1970s and 1980s has shed new light on Kreisky's mediation attempts in the Mideast Conflict.[34]

When the SPÖ lost the absolute majority in the elections of 1983, Kreisky resigned as chancellor and was succeeded by Fred Sinowatz. As an

33. Ijoma Mangold, "Die Grüne Internationale," *Die Zeit*, 10 Oct 2011.

34. Thomas Riegler, *Im Fadenkreuz: Österreich und der Nahostterrorismus, 1973-1985* (Göttingen: Vienna University Press, 2010); Matthias Dahlke, *Demokratischer Staat und transnationaler Terrorismus: Drei Wege zur Unnachgiebigkeit in Westeuropa, 1972-1975* (München: Oldenburg, 2011).

elder statesman Kreisky continued his international activities and, among other things, chaired the Kreisky Commission on Employment Issues in Europe. For Kreisky, who had experienced the World Economic Crisis and high unemployment in his youth, this issue was of special relevance. In August 1990 he died in Vienna.

Writing Kreisky's Biography(s)

It is not surprising that Kreisky's multifaceted life and his long chancellorship have drawn interest on his biography—neither that this interest is still lasting. The first biographies on Bruno Kreisky appeared at the beginning of his chancellorship in the early 1970s. The manuscripts had been written in close collaboration with him. In 1972, Victor Reimann, a columnist of the Austrian tabloid *Kronen Zeitung*, published a first comprehensive biography, entitled "Bruno Kreisky: The Portrait of a Statesman."[35] Two years later, in 1974, the journalists Paul Lendvai and Karl Heinz Ritschel released a second Kreisky-biography that was published under the same title.[36] As Lendvai later recalled, Kreisky and his close intimate Marietta Torberg observed the work of the journalists throughout the book's development and, in addition, provided the authors with autobiographical material as well as with historical sources about the Kreisky family. In his memoirs, Lendvai described the great influence that Kreisky had on the biographers and called it "problematic."[37]

Up to the late 1990s, writing biographical texts about Kreisky was an endeavor primarily conducted by Kreisky's fellow politicians, his former associates and political admirers, and journalists. Among these books were *The Kreisky Era*, published in 1983 and edited by Kreisky's fellow politicians Erich Bielka, Peter Jankowitsch, and Hans Thalberg.[38] Another example is Wolfgang Petritsch's *Biographical Essay* on Kreisky.[39] Petritsch has started his political career as Kreisky's secretary and published an extended version of the essay with his 2011 monograph *Bruno Kreisky: Die Biographie*

35. Victor Reimann, *Bruno Kreisky: Das Porträt eines Staatsmannes* (Vienna: Molden, 1972).
36. Paul Lendvai and Karl Heinz Ritschel, *Kreisky: Porträt eines Staatsmanns* (Berlin: Econ, 1974).
37. Paul Lendvai, *Mein Österreich: 50 Jahre hinter den Kulissen der Macht* (Salzburg: Ecowin, 2007), 133.
38. Erich Bielka, Peter Jankowitsch, and Hans Thalberg, eds., *Die Ära Kreisky: Schwerpunkte der österreichischen Außenpolitik* (Vienna: Europaverlag, 1983).
39. Wolfgang Petritsch, *Bruno Kreisky: Ein biographischer Essay* (Vienna: Kremayr & Scheriau, 2000).

(Bruno Kreisky: The Biography).[40] Herbert Pierre Secher's monograph *Bruno Kreisky: Chancellor of Austria*, however, made an important and early exception to this.[41] Secher put an emphasis on the Jewish aspect—an approach that enabled him to develop a new perspective on Kreisky's biography.

In the 1990s, further scholars started to ask for fresh perspectives on Kreisky's biography. The Austrian contemporary historian Peter Malina pointed out that, until then, most biographers had shown a lack of theoretical and methodological reflection toward their subject: "There is the remarkable fact that hardly any of Bruno Kreisky's biographers have tackled the fundamental issue as to whether and how it is still possible to write a "great" biography today. It is taken for granted that the course of his life represents a sequence of chronologically ordered periods, the same ones being mentioned time and time again: his political experiences in Austria in the 1920s and 1930s, his enforced exile in Sweden, his return to Austria, his rise within the party hierarchy, his election success in 1970-71 and his appointment as federal chancellor."[42] Here Malina refers to theoretical and methodological debates in history that have been affected by the social sciences and that challenged the belief that "great men make history." Malina's essay was published in this very series in 1994, in the second volume of the *Contemporary Austrian Studies* that focused on *The Kreisky Era in Austria*.[43]

Also scholars of literature, like the American specialist in German Studies, Jacqueline Vansant have shed new light on Kreisky's biography. Vansant focuses on Kreisky's autobiographical works, notably his memoirs, and points to the links between Kreisky's individual biography and more general aspects of Austrian identity formation. She reads Kreisky's memoirs as a book that clearly refers to the Austrian collective. She writes about Kreisky's and other Austrian emigrees' memoirs: "Political and religious affiliations, among others, have shaped these writers' interpretations of the past and have led them to fit their lives into the narrative of the group with which they identify."[44] In which way did Kreisky fit his life into this Austrian narrative?

40. Wolfgang Petritsch, *Bruno Kreisky: Die Biographie* (St. Pölten: Residenz, 2011).

41. Herbert Pierre Secher, *Bruno Kreisky: Chancellor of Austria; A Political Biography* (Pittsburgh: Dorrance, 1993).

42. Peter Malina, "'Imagination Is More Than Knowledge.' Bruno Kreisky's Life as Biography," in *The Kreisky Era in* Austria, Contemporary Austrian Studies vol. 2, eds. Günter Bischof, Fritz Plasser, and Oliver Rathkolb (New Brunswick, NJ: Transaction Publishers, 1994), 205-21, 207.

43. Bischof, Plasser, and Rathkolb, *The Kreisky Era in Austria.*

44. Jacqueline Vansant, "Challenging Austria's Victim Status: National Socialism and Austrian Personal Narratives," *The German Quarterly* 67, no. 1, 1994: 38-57, 51.

To answer this question it is essential to begin with a closer look at the genesis of Kreisky's memoirs. In his fascinating monograph *In Command of History: Churchill Fighting and Writing the Second World War* David Reynolds has demonstrated how fruitful the historical investigation of the genesis of a political memoir can be.[45] The first volume of Kreisky's memoirs was released in 1986, in 1988 a second followed. The third and final volume appeared in 1996, six years after Kreisky's death, and had been compiled on the basis of numerous interviews, speeches, and essays.[46] Whereas the second and third volumes are structured thematically and focus on the different fields of Kreisky's political activities, the first volume proceeds chronologically. The book starts with Kreisky's family background and his youth, continues with his first steps in politics, his imprisonment and exile years, and it ends with the conclusion of the Austrian State Treaty, an event that Kreisky describes in his memoirs as his greatest political success and the most beautiful day in his political life.[47] Because of this chronological structure the first volume, which is entitled *Zwischen den Zeiten* (Between the Times), is the most revealing one when asking for the characteristics of Kreisky's autobiographical work. Besides, it was a great commercial success and had sold more copies than any other Austrian book since 1945.[48]

Kreisky had a group of historians and publishers to assist him with the book. First of all, there was his publisher from Berlin, Wolf Jobst Siedler, who had founded his own publishing house *Siedler Verlag* only a couple of years before. One of Siedler's major publishing activities was the book series *Die Deutschen und ihre Nation* (The Germans and their Nation), which appeared since 1982. His publications were part of a new trend toward dealing with history of the German national consciousness and processes of German identity formation. Siedler represented the Berlin upper middle-class and embodied all aspects of a typical *Großbürger*. So too did Joachim C. Fest, the author of an influential biography on Adolf Hitler and like Siedler an advisor to Kreisky's book project. At the first glance, the thematic focus of the *Siedler Verlag*, as well as what Siedler stood for, were an antagonism to the memoirs of a leading socialist. But it was not the first time that

45. David Reynolds, *In Command of History: Churchill Fighting and Writing the Second World War* (London: Penguin, 2004).

46. First editions: Bruno Kreisky, *Zwischen den Zeiten: Der Memoiren erster Teil* (Berlin: Siedler, 1986); Bruno Kreisky, *Im Strom der Politik: Der Memoiren zweiter Teil* (Berlin: Siedler, 1988); Bruno Kreisky, *Der Mensch im Mittelpunkt: Der Memoiren dritter Teil* (Vienna: Kreymayr & Scheriau, 1996).

47. Kreisky, *Zwischen den Zeiten*, 476.

48. <http://www.randomhouse.de/siedler/bucherfolge.jsp?men=1496&submen=1499> (14 Dec. 2011).

Kreisky, who himself wore custom-made shoes and suits, collaborated with conservative representatives of the upper middle class, as his activities with the *Meraner Kreis* had proved. With the choice of his publishing house Kreisky again underlined his affection for the *Bürgertum*, and, what is more important, he placed his memoirs thematically in a context of nation building and identity-formation.

The text of the book resulted from numerous talks with Kreisky. In the first interview sessions Siedler and Fest questioned Kreisky; later the team was lead by the young Austrian historian, Oliver Ratholb. The team included further members, for instance Kreisky's secretary, Margit Schmidt. The German editor Thomas Karlauf turned the oral interviews into a written text, which Kreisky then reworked. Kreisky wanted his memoirs to express his personal experiences and thoughts, but it was of the utmost importance to him that all historical dates and events were quoted correctly. Oliver Rathkolb's extensive archival research and fact checking was therefore an important part of the book project.

The stories he told and the stories he was

Throughout his political career Kreisky's "Austrianess" has been subject to many debates. When he ran for chancellorship for the first time in 1970, the slogan of the ÖVP rival candidate was: "Josef Klaus: a real Austrian." Klaus' campaign clearly had an anti-Semitic undertone that alluded to Kreisky's Jewish origin, to his exile in Sweden, and to socialist internationalism in general. For Kreisky his memoirs therefore were also a means to prove his "Austrianess." In order to show that his ancestors had been loyal servants of the Habsburg Monarchy, Kreisky quoted historical sources of his family in detail—going back to the Seventeenth Century.[49] He emphasized that he had left Austria in 1938 as a political, and not as a Jewish refugee, and he underscored that he had only left Austria when no alternative remained. With his memoirs Kreisky, a victim of the Nazi regime, indirectly reinforced the so-called victim theses, that is the belief that Austria had been Hitler's first victim. There are many more examples for this Austrian narrative in Kreisky's memoirs. They all have one thing in common: when dealing with Bruno Kreisky's autobiographical texts, we can never completely entangle the stories he told and the stories he was.[50]

The Kreisky anniversary in 2011 has shown that the life and times

49. Kreisky, *Zwischen den Zeiten*, 90.

50. I took the liberty to use a phrase from: William L. Randall, *The Stories We Are: An Essay on Self-Creation* (Toronto: University of Toronto Press, 1995).

of Bruno Kreisky still form a major field of interest for the Austrians. According to Peter Malina "any biography of Bruno Kreisky is surely an indication of how the Austrian society treats a 'great man,' of how it comprehends his biography as 'its own,' and of how it can incorporate this individual history in collective history. It is the 'greatness' of Kreisky that induces his biographers to study his person."[51] It seems that it has been this very "greatness" that for many years has held historians from writing critical biographies about Kreisky. Maybe with the "Kreisky Year" this development has reached its peak and the anniversary has cleared the way for the historization of Austria's longest serving chancellor. For even though the 2011 festivities have been dominated by the voices of Kreisky's admirers and companions, in the last years a younger generation has come to the fore. Austrian historians who have grown up after the Kreisky era took a fresh look at the former chancellor. They focused on individual aspects of Kreisky's politics instead of seeking the reason for his "greatness."[52] This trend can also be found in the arts. In 2011, a young theater company from Vienna premiered the play *Die Quadratur des Kreisky: Eine Diskurs-Revue* (Squaring Kreisky: a Discursive Revue) and thereby used theatrical means to approach the life and times of Kreisky.[53] For this younger generation, the question "What would Kreisky do today?" becomes less and less important.

51. Malina, "Imagination," 216.
52. See annotation 34.
53. Kosmos Theater Wien / Tanja Witzmann, *Die Quadratur des Kreisky: Eine Diskurs-Revue*, Vienna 2011.

Alois Mock—Pioneer of European Unity

Martin Eichtinger and Helmut Wohnout

In 2009, Austria joined her neighboring countries in celebrating twenty years of the Fall of the Iron Curtain and the demise of communism, a true shift in paradigms in European and global history. For many Austrians, the picture that best sums up the events of 1989 is a photo of Alois Mock with his Hungarian colleague Gyula Horn wielding wire shears to cut the much hated barbed wire, which so often in the history of the twentieth century had brought death and injury to people trying to escape from the oppressive communist regimes of the Warsaw Pact.

The ability to define historical moments belongs to great politicians and statesmen. Alois Mock has defined a number of these moments: when he handed over Austria's application for accession to the European Union (then the European Community), when he symbolically helped dismantle the Iron Curtain, when he paid the first-ever visit of a Foreign Minister to newly independent Croatia and Slovenia or when he announced the successful conclusion of Austria's negotiations with the EU. From an early date, Alois Mock's heart had really belonged to foreign politics. For that passion to bear fruit in the momentous changes that occurred during his tenure as foreign minister (1987-1995) and in which he played a prominent role, he first had to prove his skills in Austrian domestic politics.

A Christian Democratic Reformer—
Alois Mock's Political Career up to 1989

Alois Mock's political career began in earnest in 1969. On 2 June, shortly before he turned 35, he was sworn in as minister of education. Until that date Federal Chancellor Josef Klaus's chief of cabinet was virtually unknown to the public at large, even though he had already left his mark on the inner circles of Vienna's political scene.

Alois Mock was born near Amstetten on 10 June 1934 into a rural middle class family with a background in trade. His father having died before his birth, Alois was brought up by his mother on Catholic principles and in strict opposition to Nazism. At school at Seitenstetten Monastery he impressed everyone with his fledgling interest in international politics and his talent for languages. On completion of his legal studies at the University of Vienna he spent a post-graduate term at the European Center of Johns Hopkins University in Bologna before joining the Department of University

Alois Mock and Gyula Horn, the Foreign Ministers of Austria and Hungary, cut through the Iron Curtain on 27 June 1989, © Bernhard J. Holzner, HOPI-MEDIA, Vienna/Austria

Administration at the Ministry of Education. After a year in Brussels in 1960 he returned to a position in the Department of International Economic and Trade Affairs in the Austrian Federal Chancellery. In 1962 Mock was despatched to the Austrian OECD mission in Paris; after two years he was recalled to become personal assistant to Federal Chancellor Josef Klaus. After the ÖVP (Österreichische Volkspartei – Austrian People's Party) had won the absolute majority of votes in the 1966 general elections and formed a solo government, Mock, who had already established a reputation for himself through his capacity for hard work and his dedication, was made Klaus's chief of cabinet.[1]

At around that time the professionalization—inspired by the US model—of aides and advisors in the entourage of Austria's leading politicians set in. This involved the creation of staffs of personal aides and advisors who first became active under Josef Klaus in the triangle formed by

1. See Martin Eichtinger and Helmut Wohnout, *Alois Mock: Ein Politiker schreibt Geschichte* (Wien: Styria, 2008) 14-28.

the civil service bureaucracy, political elites and the public.[2] As was also the case with Alois Mock, membership in a political cabinet often proved the first step for many an aspiring novice's political career ladder. In addition to this, Mock benefited from the political father-son relationship that had developed over time between Josef Klaus and himself. His dedication, his single-mindedness, his command of languages, his morally impeccable and unassuming lifestyle, all these appealed to Klaus—qualities, incidentally, that were eminently associated also with the Federal Chancellor himself. What left a particularly deep impression on Klaus was the fact that, while coping with the rigors of a cabinet job, Mock had prepared for—and passed with flying colors—the demanding Foreign Office entrance exam without so much as even mentioning it to anyone; he wanted to prepare for a diplomatic career.[3] This goes to show that Mock's political initiation—at government level to boot—in fact came as a surprise to him, regardless of his personal closeness to Josef Klaus.

The welcome the media gave to Alois Mock as minister of education was anything but friendly. The newly appointed minister, who had no political powerbase to support him other than the Chancellor's goodwill, was considered a stopgap, necessitated by the unexpected resignation of his predecessor, Theodor Piffl-Perčević, who had been unable to unite his own party behind him in a matter of educational policy, the addition of another year to the grammar schools' traditional eight-year curriculum.[4] To make matters worse, the overall political situation had gradually turned against the government after its electoral victory in 1966 and there were only ten months to go before the next general elections. Mock nevertheless made good use of his time as minister of education. Being the very incarnation of optimism and youthful dynamism, he seemed to personify the type of politician needed to keep the spirit of innovation alive that was beginning to make itself felt in Austria's educational policy in the 1960s. New schools and educational facilities were being built, the general level of education was being raised, women were enrolling in record numbers in universities and other institutions of higher learning and students were beginning to sense change in the air. Mock initiated a slew of reforms both in schools and in universities, showed great interest in new directions and developments in educational pedagogics and was soon perceived as an

2. Heinrich Neisser, "Zwischen Technokratie und Management: Politikberatung als Aufgabe," in *Politik für das dritte Jahrtausend: Festschrift für Alois Mock zum 60. Geburtstag,* eds. Erhard Busek, Andreas Khol and Heinrich Neisser (Graz: styria medienservice, 1994), 61, 68.

3. Josef Klaus, "Vorwort" in *Ibid,* 13.

4. see Eichtinger and Wohnout, *Mock,* 36.

asset for the government. However, the public image of the ÖVP in the campaign for the general elections in 1970 was not determined by him but by Josef Klaus, on whom politics was visibly beginning to take its toll, by Vice Chancellor Hermann Withalm, who was asserting himself more and more, and possibly by the minister of finance, Stephan Koren. "Sincere, punctilious and bit out of touch," that was the general verdict on the ÖVP's "enlightened conservativism," which cut no ice in the general elections on 1 March 1970 against the liberal, leftist zeitgeist harnessed with consummate skill for his social democratic project by Bruno Kreisky.[5]

The ÖVP's loss of its parliamentary majority and Kreisky's formation in April 1970 of an SPÖ minority government supported in parliament by the FPÖ meant that the ÖVP now found itself in the role of the opposition. Alois Mock, having won a seat in the general elections, remained in politics. Initially a member of the foreign policy and the education committees, he soon championed causes typically associated with parliamentary opposition, inveighing against a billowing state bureaucracy and the waste of public funds. Such themes were visibly to his taste and until 1986 he continued to find variations on those themes, some of which were not without a dose of populism. The years 1970 and 1971 saw him taking a brief excursion into local politics. Mock, who always enjoyed the direct contact with the populace, added a short spell of the mayorship of his Lower Austrian home town Euratsfeld to his parliamentary mandate. In spring 1971 he became the head of the ÖVP's Confederation of Employees, the ÖAAB (Österreichischer Arbeiter- und Angestelltenbund), which is one of the ÖVP's three powerful confederations (the other two representing entrepreneurs and farmers). This meant Mock had now arrived in the inner circle of party leaders, with a seat and a vote in all decision-making bodies.

The early 1970s presented the ÖVP with a novel and difficult situation. For the first time in the history of the party, i.e. since 1945, the ÖVP was not part of the federal government. This required some getting used to. As the ÖVP put up the governors in six out of nine of Austria's provinces and was playing an important role in the so-called social partnership via its Confederation of Entrepreneurs, the weight of the responsibilities it had to shoulder was somewhat at odds with its role as an opposition party. This was made even more difficult by the figure of Bruno Kreisky, whose SPÖ, in a historic first, had won an absolute majority in the general elections in autumn 1971. Kreisky went on to dominate the 1970s in Austria. While it is true that the ÖVP, at more than 40% of the popular vote, managed to

5. Ernst Hanisch, *Der lange Schatten des Staates: Österreichische Gesellschaftsgeschichte im 20. Jahrhundert* (Wien: Ueberreuter, 1994), 461.

retain a high level of voter acceptance, the chancellorship remained out of its reach. No ÖVP party leader was in sight who would have been capable of taking on Kreisky in the chancellor stakes.

In this situation Mock became a driving force within the Austrian People's Party. In a volume edited by him he pleaded already in 1971 for the party to open itself to the progressive center, which would enable it to benefit from the new societal developments signaled by the turmoil of 1968.[6] As Mock and others in the younger generation of the party saw it, this was a precondition for the ÖVP to become again attractive for the new middle classes and to regain the majority of votes. At the same time Alois Mock advocated a Christian conception of the world and of man's role in it, based on the encyclicas of John XXIII., notably *Pacem in terris,* which provided the ground in which to anchor the natural law inspired organizing principles of Catholic social teaching without further qualification, in the sense of making human rights a key concern of modern democracy. Mock always attached crucial importance to the concepts of the inviolability of the human person and of individual responsibility for social life.[7]

As the leader of the Arbeiter- und Angestelltenbund Mock was responsible for proposals weighted in favor of employees relating to family policy and taxation, such as the extension of the legal minimum annual leave, the introduction of parity in terms of labor law between part time and full time employees, the cost-of-living linkage of the family allowance or the extension of the entitlement to maternity allowance to the completion of the child's third year of life. At the time, these demands and other similar ones, today part and parcel of Austria's social and family legislation, earned Mock in his party the reputation of "being more socialist than the Socialists."[8]

When ÖVP party leader Karl Schleinzer died in a traffic accident in 1975 only a few weeks before the general elections, Mock was one of the candidates for his succession but had to give way to Josef Taus. By way of compensation Mock was appointed chairman of the ÖVP parliamentary group in 1978, which ranks as one of the top jobs of a party in opposition after the posts of party leader and secretary general. When Josef Taus

6. Alois Mock, ed., *Die Zukunft der* Volkspartei: *Eine kritische Selbstdarstellung* (Vienna: Molden, 1971), 12.

7. See Alois Mock, "Politische Verantwortung im Wohlfahrtsstaat," in: *Verantwortung in Staat und Gesellschaft*, eds. Alois Mock and Herbert Schambeck (Vienna: Europaverlag, 1977), 13-15, as well as Mock's inaugural speech when he was elected party leader. Stenographisches Protokoll des 21. außerordentlichen Bundesparteitags der ÖVP, 7.7.1979, Archiv des Karl von Vogelsang-Instituts, Vienna, 228f.

8. See Eichtinger/Wohnout, *Mock*, 60f.

lost the next general election in spring 1979 against Bruno Kreisky, who was even able to increase his absolute majority, Mock was an obvious candidate for Taus's succession. When Taus, who sought to implement a comprehensive reform of the ÖVP as a reaction to repeated electoral defeat, failed to overcome the opposition of the party's grandees in the provinces and in its confederations, he handed in his resignation. At a convention of the federal party in July 1979 Mock was elected as new party leader. As chairman of the ÖVP parliamentary group Mock had already favoured tactics of tough opposition to the ruling SPÖ and he was not averse to personal confrontation in parliamentary debates, a style he remained faithful to as a party leader. He managed to consolidate the party and give it a more sharply defined profile as opposition. In the years up to 1986 the ÖVP presented a picture of unity the likes of which one had not seen from 1970 onward. What helped him in his dealings with the SPÖ was the first signs of attrition that were becoming visible in the party after more than ten years in power; the climax of Bruno Kreisky's string of political successes was already a thing of the past. Both facts became obvious when major corruption scandals connected to the SPÖ could not be contained, such as the one in connection with the construction of the new general hospital (Allgemeines Krankenhaus) in Vienna or the intra-party conflict between Kreisky and his vice chancellor and heir-presumptive, Hannes Androsch. Another factor that was to shape the incipient electoral campaign in 1983 was Bruno Kreisky's visibly deteriorating health; by now he was dependent on dialysis. Mock by contrast presented himself as a youthful and energetic challenger, who also acquitted himself well—and better than his predecessor—in TV confrontations with the Chancellor.

In the meantime "the social democratic decade" of the 1970s had run out of steam worldwide.[9] In Great Britain, a conservative prime minister, Margaret Thatcher, was already in office; in the Federal Republic of Germany Helmut Kohl had become federal chancellor in autumn 1982; and in the U.S.A. Ronald Reagan moved into the White House in 1980. Mock too made increasingly use throughout the 1980s, for the definition of his own programmatic position, of neo-conservative thinking, which was being championed as the new model particularly in the Anglo-Saxon world. It was through an emphasis on the value of private ownership and on

9. See Bernd Faulenbach, *Das sozialdemokratische Jahrzehnt: Von der Reformeuphorie zur neuen Unübersichtlichkeit; Die SPD 1969-1982* (Bonn: J:H:W. Dietz, 2011); with respect to Austria see for example the chapter „Das lange sozialistische Jahrzehnt" in Peter Berger's History of Austria in the 20th century. Peter Berger, *Kurze Geschichte Österreichs im 20. Jahrhundert*, 2nd ed. (Vienna: Fakultas, 2008), 326-67.

downsizing the role of the state that he wanted to sharpen his party's profile in opposition to the SPÖ.

The 1983 general elections were to become Alois Mock's greatest success in terms of domestic politics. Not only did the ÖVP again prove able to win votes and parliamentary seats—for the first time since 1966—, it was also able after almost twelve years to deprive the SPÖ of its absolute majority in Parliament. Even though Kreisky resigned the night following the elections, the SPÖ entered into a coalition with the FPÖ, forcing the ÖVP to continue in the role of opposition. The new government had problems getting started, the two main obstacles being the nationalized industries, which were running up huge losses, and the conflict with a newly formed ecological movement, which had found a catalyst in the construction of the power station on the Danube at Hainburg. The ÖVP in its role of sole opposition party kept on hammering the government in parliament. Opinion polls had the party repeatedly in the number one slot. Alois Mock was secure in his positions as leader of the party and leader of the opposition; the office of chancellor seemed to be within his reach. This was the situation in spring 1986, before Austria's presidential elections. Mock had cast an eye on Kurt Waldheim, the former secretary general of the United Nations, as the ÖVP's candidate; he had served with Waldheim under Josef Klaus, when Waldheim was foreign minister. He was convinced the diplomat's international renown would decide the elections. Rumours about Kurt Waldheim's wartime past were initially ignored by the ÖVP, and when the debate on the candidate's alleged involvement in war crimes erupted at the beginning of the campaign's hot phase, the party found itself totally unprepared. Should he retire Waldheim as candidate? This was not an option for Mock, who from the beginning saw the SPÖ's hand behind the international attacks on Waldheim.[10] The party decided to present Waldheim as the victim of an internationally orchestrated campaign of character assassination—and carried the day. Waldheim was elected in June 1986, after a campaign of unparalleled acrimony also on the part of the ÖVP; however, the recriminations launched against Waldheim both from within Austria and from abroad continued to flare. In Austria, Bruno Kreisky's somewhat uncharismatic successor as chancellor, Fred Sinowatz, was retired by the SPÖ in early summer 1986 and replaced by the minister of finance, Franz Vranitzky. When Vice-Chancellor Norbert Steger was ousted as party leader of the FPÖ in September 1986, under tumultuous circumstances, by the far right-wing Jörg Haider, Chancellor Vranitzky dissolved the coalition and called early elections.

10. See Eichtinger and Wohnout, *Mock*, 104-111.

For Alois Mock this meant a complete reversal of the political starting situation. From 1983 onward, his counterparts had been two party leaders who had cut a rather poor figure as heads of government. Now he himself was already 52 and his opposite numbers were new figures, younger, more telegenic and more vigorous than he was, and could look back on a rapid rise to the top. Mock was beginning to feel the toll that 17 years in politics were taking on him. Occasionally he gave the impression of being erratic and overworked. He had always refused to take it easy at least temporarily, before important appearances, and had simply ignored what his advisors had to say on the topic. In the election Mock presented a classic center-right platform: less state, more market, encouragement of private initiative and hard work, privatizations and tax reform. It dawned on him at this stage that the elections of 1986 were his best—and at the same time probably his last—chance to achieve his great aim of becoming chancellor. This caused great inner tensions in him. In the televised debate with Franz Vranitzky he initially gave the impression of being absent minded and lost valuable time before he was able to focus again. Altogether, the election campaign unfolded, from the ÖVP's point of view, in an unsatisfactory way in several respects and was overshadowed towards the end by an untimely, altogether mistaken and self-inflicted discussion about a possible grand coalition. When at the end of the election day the ÖVP turned out to have again been beaten to the post by the SPÖ, if only narrowly, Mock, having put himself through a marathon programme in the days leading up to the elections, suffered a dizzy spell and presented himself to the TV cameras "like a boxer who had been knocked out on his feet."[11] It is possible that those were the first warning signs of the disease that later came to trouble him.

Even though Mock soon recovered from the shock of the election night, his days as ÖVP party leader were numbered from that time onward. His project of forming a center-right coalition under his leadership with Jörg Haider's FPÖ found no favor with the ÖVP party grandees, a majority of whom favored collaboration with the SPÖ. Much as he detested doing so, he was forced to enter into talks with the SPÖ, where the presumable outcome was the role of junior partner in a grand coalition under a social democratic chancellor. In the coalition talks Mock proved himself a savvy, tough negotiator who was capable of extracting maximum concessions from the other side both in terms of policy and in ministerial portfolios. He achieved parity with the SPÖ in the distribution of ministerial posts, securing, among others, the newly created Ministry of Economic Development with its multiple competencies and the Ministry of Foreign Affairs. Not content with the post of vice chancellor for himself and choosing to ignore the

11. *Kurier*, 25 Nov. 1986.

tremendous workload this implied, he added the particularly demanding, if prestigious, Ministry of Foreign Affairs to his personal portfolio.

On 21 January 1987 the Vranitzky/Mock government was sworn in by the Federal President. This meant Alois Mock was returning to the Council of Ministers after 17 years. While seeking to establish a constructive climate in his dealings with the coalition partner, Mock never failed, if at all possible, to emphasize his party's share in the work of the government; this, and his tenacity as a negotiator, did not endear him to the SPÖ. Alois Mock and his ÖVP ministers acted with competence from the first days of the new government and were indeed able to point to a number of achievements, such as the tax reform that entered into force in 1988 and the first privatizations; the very fact that the latter were considered acceptable signaled a change of the political paradigm. It was unfortunate that these achievements were not sufficiently perceived as such by the public. The reason for this lay largely in intra-party tensions, such as the conflict about the stationing of the Saab Draken interceptors delivered in 1987, which resulted in a deep rift between the federal party and the Styrian ÖVP. To make matters even worse, there was the escalation of developments centering on Federal President Kurt Waldheim, who was put on the so-called Watch List by the US authorities in April 1987. For months on end debates about the head of state overshadowed the political process in Austria and paralyzed Mock in his activities. He had been the driving force behind Waldheim's candidacy in the first place and now considered it his duty to throw his weight behind him. It speaks to his integrity and his personal loyalty that he refused to drop Waldheim in a situation where the President was shunned internationally.[12]

The ÖVP's setbacks in regional elections inevitably led in the spring of 1989 to an escalation of the leadership crisis in the party, which had been going on, if on the back burner, from the 1986 elections onward. True to his character, Mock ignored calls from inside the party for him to step down. It was only when some of his closest political associates began to distance themselves from him that he agreed to resign from the post of party leader; he retained the Foreign Ministry and was made honorary party chairman, which guaranteed him a certain amount of influence on the party. On 24 April 1989 Mock's former minister of agriculture, Josef Riegler, was sworn in as the new vice-chancellor; Riegler also succeeded Mock as party leader in May 1989. Having held the post of ÖVP party leader for almost ten years, Alois Mock had served the party the longest in this function at the time; he had even overtaken Julius Raab, who had more than eight years in

12. See Eichtinger/Wohnout, *Mock,* 133f.

that function to his credit. It was only Wolfgang Schüssel with his almost twelve years at the helm of the ÖVP who was to go one better. In his last TV "Pressestunde" ("Meet the Press") in his capacity as party leader Alois Mock compared himself to a political marathon runner, who through sheer staying power was ultimately able to bring his political ideas to fruition, whereas short distance runners were no more than a flash in the political pan.[13] Even though he could not have known it at the time, the greatest moments of his political career were still lying ahead of him.

Already during his years as parliamentary group leader of the ÖVP, Alois Mock held a major international position as president of the EDU (European Democrat Union). At the founding congress of the IDU (International Democrat Union) in 1983 in London, in which prominent conservative and Christian-Democratic politicians such as Prime Minister Margaret Thatcher, German Chancellor Helmut Kohl, Vice-President George H.W. Bush and Jacques Chirac, then mayor of Paris and later president of France, participated, Mock was also elected IDU president, a position he held until 1987 (he held the position of EDU chairman from 1979 until 1998).[14] Alois Mock devoted much time and effort to the expansion of the EDU/IDU network. He saw it as a counterweight to the Socialist International (SI), which had come to prominence in the 1970s under the Socialist triumvirate of Willy Brandt, Bruno Kreisky and Olof Palme.

In addition to putting its international connections at Mock's disposal, the IDU/EDU's network enabled Alois Mock to acquaint himself with all international issues and conflicts and to act as leader of international observer missions, even to remote destinations in Africa, Asia and Latin America. Even more importantly, he was able to use his international party connections later in his career, in particular during the Austrian negotiations for EU accession.

After the Austrian general elections of November 1986, when the ÖVP eventually decided to enter into a grand coalition with the SPÖ, Alois Mock was faced with the question of what portfolio to choose in addition to vice chancellor (deputy prime minister) in the government of Chancellor Franz Vranitzky, as already mentioned earlier. After a protracted period of deliberation in which several options were tossed around, Mock secured the Foreign Ministry,[15] despite fierce opposition from former Chancellor

13. *Der Standard*, 3. Apr. 1989.

14. See Eichtinger/Wohnout, *Mock*, 145-57.

15. Alois Mock: "...die Interessen unseres Landes vertreten," Zeitzeugengespräch mit Michael Gehler und Helmut Wohnout, in *Demokratie und Geschichte: Jahrbuch des Karl-*

Bruno Kreisky, who resigned from his position as honorary chairman of the SPÖ to protest it. Mock's constant presence in the media and the high profile foreign policy issues ensured to him in the following, turbulent years, proved him right. The combination of the positions of vice-chancellor and foreign minister was also chosen by two of Mock's successors, Wolfgang Schüssel and Michael Spindelegger.

Mock felt very comfortable in the position of foreign minister. Due to his long-time involvement in international relations and his language skills (Mock speaks fluent English and excellent French; he has always been considered a Francophile, a reputation he owes to his studies in Belgium, his time at the OECD in Paris, his love of French literature—Edmond Rostand's *Cyrano de Bergerac* being his favorite play—and his daily reading of *Le Monde*). But it was only after his resignation as chairman of the ÖVP in April 1989 that Mock was able to devote all his energy to foreign affairs. It was this period in his life which put him in the position to write history as Austria's "Mr. Europe."

The following sections will attempt to outline the key foreign policy issues that shaped Alois Mock's tenure as foreign minister (1987-1995). Several of them overlapped in time, but all will be dealt with separately to make it easier to understand events as they unfolded. These chapters include Mock's involvement in preparing Austria's application for EU/EC membership, the Fall of the Iron Curtain and its consequences for Austrian foreign policy, the resolution of the conflict with Italy on South Tyrol, the dissolution of Yugoslavia and Austria's negotiations for accession to the EC/EU and their successful conclusion.

Austria's Application for EC/EU Membership

The two parties of Austria's post-war grand coalition differed in their position vis-à-vis European integration. In the ÖVP one-party government of Chancellor Josef Klaus, Vice-Chancellor Fritz Bock spearheaded an effort to reach an association agreement with the European Community. The attempt failed due to Italian and French vetoes. The SPÖ favored a membership in the European Free Trade Area (EFTA), arguing that the EC constituted a "bourgeois block."[16] As Chief of Cabinet of Chancellor

---

von-Vogelsang-Instituts zur Erforschung der christlichen Demokratie in Österreich, ed. Helmut Wohnout, vol. 5 (Vienna: Styria, 2002), 44.

16. Martin Hehemann, "Die SPÖ und die Anfänge der Europäischen Integration 1945-1959," in *Österreich und die europäische Integration 1945-1993*, eds. Michael Gehler and Rolf Steininger (Vienna: Böhlau, 1993), 342.

Josef Klaus, Alois Mock was certainly influenced by Klaus' strong convictions regarding a European Parliament and Government. According to Chancellor Klaus, such a European Government "would have to be entrusted in addition to economic and social affairs with a common financial, foreign and cultural policy."[17]

In the 1970s, there was broad political consensus regarding the conclusion of a Free Trade Agreement of EFTA, to which Austria adhered since its foundation in 1960, and the European Economic Community (EEC). There was little movement in Austria's policy towards the European Community in the late 1970s and early 1980s. The incompatibility of the status of Austria's permanent neutrality with a full membership in the EC, which had been defined by international law experts following a Swiss interpretation of the concept of permanent neutrality, was not challenged.

The situation took a sudden turn when the Commission of the EC published in 1985 a White Book on the completion of the EC's internal market. Worried by the analysis of economic experts regarding the negative consequences of an internal EC market for non EC-members and in particular for EFTA members, politicians in the ÖVP started to advocate a full membership of Austria in the EC.[18] In December 1985, ÖVP MPs with full support of its group leader Alois Mock submitted a draft resolution calling for bilateral treaties or a special Europe treaty to be negotiated between Austria and the EC and a tailor-made cooperation of Austria in the project of a united Europe. The resolution was rejected by the governing small coalition of SPÖ and FPÖ. However, some prominent members of the SPÖ voiced support for a closer relationship of Austria with the EC or did not rule out the idea of membership. A driving force for a full membership of Austria in the EC was the Federation of Industry which commissioned a study on the neutrality aspects of an Austrian participation in the process of European integration.[19]

In February 1987, shortly after the swearing into office of the new grand coalition government, the Council of Ministers approved a report by Alois Mock, establishing a Working Group for European Integration which included representatives of all ministries, the social partners and the National Bank. Consequently, Alois Mock promoted the concept of a "global approach" for the relationship between Austria and the EC, which

17. Beatrice Weinmann, *Josef Klaus: ein großer Österreicher* (Vienna: Molden, 2000), 217.

18. See Andreas Khol, „Im Dreisprung nach Europa: Kooperation-Assoziation-Union, in *Europäische Rundschau* 13, no. 3 (1985), 28.

19. Waldemar Hummer and Michael Schweitzer, *Österreich und die EWG: neutralitätsrechtliche Beurteilung der Möglichkeit der Dynamisierung des Verhältnisses zur EWG* (Vienna: Signum, 1987).

should allow Austria full participation in all four freedoms of the EC's internal market. The concept which was developed by Alois Mock's chief EC diplomat Manfred Scheich was met with quite some doubts by the partners in Europe. However, it served well as a vehicle to move the agenda forward.

At the traditional ÖVP New Year's meeting of the party leadership in January 1988, the ÖVP declared full membership in the EC as the party's goal. Already in November 1987, the powerful Governors Conference (Landeshauptmännerkonferenz) had taken a unanimous decision that Austria should become a full member of the EC while maintaining her status of permanent neutrality. The ÖVP decision encountered strong criticism from the Russian side. The Russian Ambassador protested against the goal of full membership, calling it a violation of international law and the State Treaty of 1955.[20]

Already in March 1988 in a private meeting, Alois Mock and Chancellor Franz Vranitzky agreed on the goal of full membership in the EC and not only in the EC's internal market. From there, it took more than a year to convince all the opinion leaders and interest groups in both governing parties to agree on the submission of a membership application. Franz Vranitzky encountered considerable resistance in his party. Mock had to quell the concerns of the agricultural sector, a core electorate of the ÖVP, that was afraid of the competition coming from large agricultural companies in the EC. In April 1988, Mock declared in a public speech which he delivered at the second Europe Congress of the ÖVP that he wanted to reach a government decision on a membership application in 1989.[21]

Later in 1988, Alois Mock and Franz Vranitzky paid separate official visits to Moscow. Mock's Chief of Cabinet, Emil Staffelmayr, summed up his impressions of the meeting of Alois Mock with Foreign Minister Eduard Shevardnadze in Moscow in his personal memoirs: "The atmosphere was dominated by the style of the 'new thinking' in the Soviet Union. Diverging opinions were voiced calmly without any exertion of pressure....Soviet concerns were put forward in the form of questions—they related to possible military aspects of EC integration; there was much understanding for the economic necessity of Austria's integration into the EC's internal market." Highly interesting from hindsight was Shevardnadze's statement that with a sustained détente and a continuation of the radical changes, our ideas could be realized in the 1990s, about the middle of the 1990s (note:

20. See Eichtinger/Wohnout, *Mock,* 178-79.
21. *Austrian Press Agency*, no. 165, 22 Apr. 1988.

Austria joined the EU on 1 January 1995).[22] Franz Vranitzky's encounter with Soviet Prime Minister Nikolai Ryzhkov was "not very pleasant," as the Chancellor put it to accompanying journalists. Ryzhkov officially stated that a membership of Austria in the EC would infringe on Austria's neutrality. However, the Chancellor did not want to dramatize it, as he had explained to Ryzhkov that Austria would not deviate from her neutrality.[23]

Around the turn of the year 1988/89, the domestic political situation heated up over the role that the two parties played in the preparation of the membership application. Mock was clearly seen as the driving force for the application, while Vranitzky tried to secure his role in the political process. There was also more resistance to be overcome domestically and the European Community made a surprise move: in January 1989, Commission President Jacques Delors presented the new concept of a European Economic Area, which could be seen as a possible waiting room for potential future membership candidates such as Austria.

Eventually, Mock's political insistence lead to the result he had wished for. However, it came along with a big personal disappointment for Mock: the day of the decision in the Council of Ministers to submit an official letter to the European Commission in which Austria applied for full membership in the EC, the 17 April 1989, was the day in which the ÖVP's governing board agreed on a new party chairman: Alois Mock handed in his resignation from his position as party leader and Vice-Chancellor. On 17 July 1989, Alois Mock officially handed over the Austrian membership application to the then President of the EC, the French Foreign Minister Roland Dumas. Mock insisted that the letter should be dated 14 July 1989 as an homage to the French Presidency's National Holiday.

The Fall of the Iron Curtain and Its Consequences for Austrian Foreign Policy

There was no politician in Europe or elsewhere who claimed to have foreseen the Fall of the Iron Curtain and the end of the Warsaw Pact when the "triumph of the unexpected," as it was labeled by journalists, happened. When he took office as Foreign Minister, Alois Mock insisted that his visits to Eastern-bloc countries also included meetings with dissidents. He met with the late Václav Havel in Prague and Andrei Sakharov in Moscow. In the EDU, developments in the Warsaw Pact were carefully observed,

22. Emil Staffelmayr, "Private Memoirs" (unpublished), private archive of Martin Eichtinger, 244.
23. *Austria Press Agency*, no. 297, 10 Oct. 1988, and no. 209, 12 Oct. 1988.

however, even when Alois Mock and Gyula Horn got international attention for cutting the barbed wire at the Iron Curtain, nobody believed that the demise of communism would follow suit in such a rapid way.

The photo of the two Foreign Ministers abolishing the most visible sign of the European divide which came to embody the shift of paradigms in Europe's and the world's post-World War II political landscape has a peculiar history to it: Mock's photographer, Bernhard Holzner, was disappointed that his pictures of Hungarian soldiers dismantling the Iron Curtain were not printed by the Austrian press. When he complained to Mock's spokesman who in turn informed Mock, the Foreign Minister decided to invite his Hungarian colleague to make this welcome sign of détente an official event. It took some time until the Hungarian side agreed, but eventually the event took place on 27 June 1989 and drew an enormous crowd of journalists to the border between the two countries. The historic photo appeared in hundreds of newspapers worldwide and was aired around the globe.[24]

Austria, which geographically formed a wedge into the Warsaw Pact, played a special role in the events of 1989. On 19 August 1989, the Pan-European Movement organized a Pan-European Picnic for which a border-crossing was temporarily opened: more than 600 East-Germans took advantage of this opportunity and fled to the West. The night of 9 November 1989 found Mock in Brussels where he watched the live broadcast from Berlin reporting on the Fall of the Berlin Wall at the Residence of the Austrian Ambassador. In a comment to the press, he declared that this meant in fact the end of Europe's division at Yalta.

Mock always supported an enlargement of the European Union to the countries of Central and Eastern Europe. At the conclusion of Austria's negotiations for EU membership, Mock declared that Austria's membership should pave the way for the new democracies in Europe's East to adhere to the Union. While Austria was seen by many citizens of Central and Eastern Europe during the communist era as the "lighthouse" of the democratic West in Europe, the new democracies saw Austria as an advocate of their integration into the European political structures. Alois Mock was certainly prepared to offer the expected support. For Austria, the developments of 1989 meant nothing less than moving from a geographic and political cul-de-sac during the Cold War into the center of European developments after the end of the 40-year standoff between East and West.

In this turbulent period, Mock implemented a whole series of foreign policy and foreign cultural policy programs: together with a group of

24. See Eichtinger/Wohnout, *Mock,* 192-93.

advisors (among them poets such as György Sebstyén, Wolfgang Kraus, journalists like Hans Magenschab, or dedicated officials in his Ministry, such as Bernhard Stillfried) he started bilingual school projects in Budapest and Prague, increased the number of Austrian diplomatic and cultural representations in the former communist countries, established a network of Austrian libraries (today they number 61), set up a program for Austrian professors and language teachers at East European universities, increased scientific co-operations and co-initiated the Working Group of Danubian countries.[25] Already prior to the Fall of the Berlin Wall, Mock together with his colleagues from Hungary, Yugoslavia and Italy had founded the Quadragonale (today's Central European Initiative), an organization for regional co-operation which in its beginning was the first organization to include an EC country, a Neutral & Non-aligned (N&N) member state, a Warsaw Pact member and a neutral country.

It is certainly correct to say that Alois Mock never wavered in his political support for the countries of Central and Eastern Europe. His foreign policy and foreign cultural and scientific policy activities in the new democracies help pave the way for the success story of Austrian business investments in these countries which today have all either become full EU members or are in a cooperation or association relationship with the Union.

The Conclusion of the Conflict with Italy over South Tyrol

The 1946 Gruber-De Gasperi-Agreement between Austria and Italy was meant to settle all questions regarding the status of autonomy for South Tyrol which had become part of Italy after World War I as a reward for Italy's joining the allied forces in 1915. As the implementation of the Agreement did not advance, Foreign Minister Bruno Kreisky seized the United Nations with the conflict in 1959. As a result, Austrian Foreign Minister Kurt Waldheim and Italian Foreign Minister Aldo Moro signed an "operations calendar," a schedule for the implementation of measures regarding the establishment of South Tyrol's autonomy, in 1969.

Still, the implementation dragged on and the final declaration of settlement of the conflict as foreseen in the operations calendar was a distant goal when Alois Mock took over the Austrian Foreign Ministry. Mock had closely followed the South Tyrol issue since his days in the Cabinet of

25. Martin Eichtinger, "Österreichs Außenpolitik in Zentral- und Osteuropa nach dem Annus mirabilis 1989: Das Engagement des österreichischen Vizekanzlers und Außenministers Alois Mock nach dem Zusammenbruch des Kommunismus," in *Viribus Unitis: Festschrift für Bernhard Stillfried aus Anlass seines 70. Geburtstages*, eds. Ilona Slawinski and Joseph Strelka (Bern: Peter Lang, 1996), 103-122.

Chancellor Josef Klaus. He could also rely on a number of experts in his own party, such as Ludwig Steiner, Andreas Khol and Felix Ermacora, as well as the support of foreign policy experts of other parties who had been involved in the negotiations, like Peter Jankowitsch, Mock's predecessor as Foreign Minister, or the Third President of the Austrian Parliament (National Council), Siegfried Dillersberger. He also enjoyed the confidence of the South Tyrolean leadership, in particular of former Governor Silvius Magnago and Governor Luis Durnwalder.

Quite naturally, the negotiations became more difficult in the final phase when the most challenging issues had to be tackled. It was certainly due to Mock's tireless efforts and his political skills that he managed to rally all parties behind a final compromise on all outstanding issues. Although the Italian domestic political situation had not been stable in the 1980s (the 1980s saw twelve Italian Governments in office), Prime Minister Giulio Andreotti and Foreign Minister Gianni de Michelis managed to reach a positive decision with the Italian Government in 1992.

On 21 June 1992 the Ambassadors of Austria and Italy submitted identical diplomatic notes to the Secretary General of the United Nations, thus ending a 32-year conflict brought before the United Nations. Alois Mock always considered this declaration of the settlement of the South Tyrol conflict a major accomplishment of his tenure as foreign minister. Its importance also lay in the fact that the settlement paved the way for an Italian consent to Austria's EU accession.

The Dissolution of Yugoslavia

At the end of the twentieth century and further into our century, Yugoslavia and its successor states had been a constant center of conflicts. When Marshal Josip Broz Tito died in 1980, many political experts expected a breakup of Yugoslavia. After all, Yugoslavia was a "state without Yugoslavs." At the 1981 census, only 1.2 million inhabitants of an overall population of 22.4 million declared themselves Yugoslavs.[26]

The events of the *annus mirabilis 1989* did not stop short of Yugoslavia. The Serb dominated Central Government in Belgrade rejected democratic reforms which were demanded by Croats and Slovenes. Serb leader Slobodan Milosevic reconfirmed Serbia's historic claims of the province of Kosovo. Kosovo's autonomy was abolished in 1989, its provincial parliament dissolved in 1990.

26. See Paul Lendvai, "Jugoslawien ohne Jugoslawen. Die Wurzeln der Staatskrise," in *Europa Archiv* 19 (1990): 574.

Earlier than most European politicians, Mock had reached the conclusion that Yugoslavia as a multi-ethnic state would not be viable in the future. He started to use all foreign policy tools in order to alert the international community about the imminent dissolution of Yugoslavia, while he tried to contribute to a peaceful transition to democratic successor states. Already in the years 1987-1989, Mock had launched a joint initiative with Norway for the creation of an EFTA-Fund for Yugoslavia: a sound economic development should pave the way for economic liberalization and democratic reforms. Mock also supported the inclusion of Serbia in the Working Group of Danubian countries.

As a reaction to human rights violations in Pristina/Kosovo at the beginning of 1990 which claimed the deaths of several dozens of people, Mock initiated the first stage of the CSCE human dimension mechanism (request for information). In May 1991, Austria triggered the second stage of the mechanism, requesting a bilateral meeting over the situation in the Kosovo.

While the United States remained committed to a solution of the national conflicts within a single, democratic Yugoslav state,[27] Mock saw a dissolution of Yugoslavia as an unavoidable consequence of the bloody conflicts in ethnically mixed territories. He remembers that this became clear to him when clashes resulted in the first casualties at the Plitvice lakes on 1 April 1991.[28] As more clashes occurred and the number of victims rose, Mock suggested the creation of an international Council of Wise Men which should be composed of European elder statesmen who could mediate between the Yugoslav Republics. The proposal was rejected by the Serb Prime Minister who insisted that Yugoslavia would solve its problems alone.

In addition, Mock pleaded for the deployment of a European peace-keeping force in order to avoid a civil war in Yugoslavia. An escalation of the situation occurred when the election of Stipe Mesić to become the regular President of Yugoslavia, according to the Yugoslav constitutional principle of a rotating presidency, failed due to a negative vote of Serbia and its provinces (with Montenegro abstaining). The United States responded to the vote and continuing human rights violations with a reduction of economic support for Yugoslavia. After a visit to Yugoslavia at the end of May 1991, the EC leadership (Presidencies of the Council and the Commission) voiced its fear of an imminent dissolution of Yugoslavia.

27. A letter containing this message by US President George H.W. Bush was handed over to Serb Prime Minister Ante Marković by US Ambassador Warren Zimmerman on 28 Mar. 1991 (*Austria Press Agency*, no. 321, 28 Mar. 1991).

28. Mock: "*...die Interessen unseres Landes vertreten,*" 47.

The EC announcements of more financial aid and the perspective of an association agreement came too late.

On 25 June 1991, the Parliaments of Slovenia and Croatia passed a declaration of independence of their republics. As a response, the Yugoslav National Army launched an attack on the territory of Slovenia and tried to secure the border stations. Serbia was of the opinion that it had received a green light from the United States, even for military action, in order to prevent a dissolution of Yugoslavia. Foreign Minister James Baker, who visited Belgrade just a few days earlier, had declared that maintaining a federal state was the best way to secure human rights and international economic aid for Yugoslavia.[29] In this phase, Mock was involved on several levels. He initiated the CSCE mechanism on unusual military activities. He conferred with the EC Presidency and his European colleagues and he was in constant contact with Slovenia's political leadership. Croatia asked for a special session of the UN Security Council, however, Belgrade rejected such a request. Austria stationed 6,500 troops at the Slovenian border. The ten-day war in Slovenia ended with the Brioni Agreement brokered by the EC. The civil war continued in Croatia for many months and claimed many casualties, particularly also among the civilian population. On 25 September 1991, Austria demanded a special session of the UN Security Council to deal with the Yugoslav conflict. On this occasion, Mock warned that the conflict could spread to Bosnia and Herzegovina.

In the following months, the domestic policy debate in Austria heated up over the question of diplomatic recognition of Slovenia and Croatia. While Mock and the ÖVP, but also the FPÖ and the Greens strongly supported such a move, the SPÖ opposed it vehemently. A report to the Council of Ministers on the recognition of the two countries filed by Mock was rejected by Chancellor Vranitzky on 3 September 1991. Vranitzky declared on that occasion that "the efforts of the international community of states for a termination of the military conflict in Yugoslavia have to be carried on ... the instrument of recognition would not constitute a guarantee that peace and order would prevail in Yugoslavia."[30]

Mock insisted that the conflict between the peoples of Yugoslavia could no longer be regarded as an internal affair. According to Mock, a recognition of the two republics would allow to invoke the Security Council of the United Nations, a step which had always been opposed by the Yugoslav Central Government as an interference in internal affairs of Yugoslavia.[31]

29. *Austria Press Agency*, no. 351, 21 June 1991.
30. *Austria Press Agency*, no. 108, 3 September 1991.
31. See Eichtinger/Wohnout, *Mock*, 218.

Mock kept pushing for diplomatic recognition of Slovenia and Croatia all throughout the end of 1991, but he failed to convince his coalition partner.

Austria eventually officially recognized Slovenia and Croatia as independent states on 15 January 1992, at the same time as the European Community member states agreed on such a decision. On 18 January 1992, Mock paid an official visit to independent Slovenia and Croatia; it was the first official visit of a foreign minister. Some European politicians and American media argued that the recognition happened prematurely and that it triggered the conflict in Yugoslavia. Mock always pointed to the report of the international Badinter Commission which confirmed in December 1991 that, indeed, the dissolution of the Yugoslavia Federation in its constituent parts was taking place. That the conflict turned bloody was due to the decision of the Serb leadership to use the Yugoslav People's Army to achieve its objectvies.[32] "It was not the war which followed a hasty recognition, but the long-delayed recognition followed a war in full swing."[33]

Mock stayed diplomatically active in the continuing conflicts in the Balkans. Already at the end of 1991, he suggested dispatching UN troops to Bosnia and Herzegovina. UNPROFOR was deployed, however, initially only in Croatia. After diplomatic recognition of Bosnia and Herzegovina by the international Community occurred in April 1992, a civil war erupted there as well. In many meetings and with many demarches, Mock tried to reach a decision on the establishment of security zones (safe havens) for the civilian population in Bosnia and Herzegovina (Mock took similar zones for the Kurds in Northern Iraq during the Second Gulf War as a model). Such zones were established by a Security Council resolution in May 1993. However, due to a lack of troops and equipment, the security of the civilians could not be adequately protected, nor could these zones prevent the massacre of Bosniaks in Srebrenica in 1995.

In December 1992, Mock organized a visit by four foreign ministers of the Central European Initiative to the White House in Washington. The outgoing US President George H.W. Bush listened to the plea of the ministers to lift the arms embargo in Bosnia and Herzegovina for the Bosniaks who were severely disadvantaged in the armed conflict. Bush's successor, Bill Clinton, made good on his promise in his election campaign and involved the United States in the efforts to stop the killing in the Balkans. It was only in November 1995 that the Dayton Peace Accord

32. Albert Rohan, "The Conflict in Former Yugoslavia," in *EDU Yearbook 1993* (Vienna: n.p., 1994), 271-82.

33. Peter Michael Lingens, "Das Märchen von der Mitschuld Mocks," *Der Standard*, 16 Aug. 1995.

ended the civil war in Bosnia. The conflict then moved further south to the Kosovo region. During the war in Bosnia and Herzegovina, Austria welcomed more than 80,000 refugees and organized a widely acclaimed and successful humanitarian aid program "Neighbor in Need" for which Austria was commended by President Bill Clinton.

Alois Mock's active involvement in the Yugoslav conflict was often criticized. His political opponents accused him of having contributed to the outbreak of the conflict and later criticized him for not having been able to avoid the dreadful bloodshed. Mock justified his action by pointing to the fact that as a responsible politician, he could not close his eyes before severe infringements of human rights in Europe and in Austria's neighborhood without resorting to action. The warnings which he issued long before anyone else were unfortunately disregarded by the international community (Mock always speaks of the international reaction as "too little and too late"). While involving himself in the search for a peaceful solution to the crisis, Mock stayed within the framework of international law and used all diplomatic means which were at his disposal. In Croatia and Slovenia, Mock has entered the history books as a decisive supporter of the countries' independence.

Austria's Negotiations and Successful Conclusion of the Negotiations for Accession to the EC/EU

In the years 1993-1994, Alois Mock's agenda was to a large extent filled with the negotiations for Austria's accession to the European Union. The Commission had decided to start negotiations only after the date of the official entering into force of the internal market (1 January 1993) and once a group of candidate countries had gathered. This was the case, as Finland, Norway and Sweden had officially filed their membership applications. Among these countries, of which all except Norway wanted to join the EU as neutral states, Austria was the only one which had applied already before the demise of communism.

The crucial question of the compatibility of Austria's neutrality with the future development of the EU was solved in the fall of 1993. Austria's neutrality was defined in its core elements: no participation in wars, no membership in military alliances and no foreign military installations on Austrian territory. This interpretation of Austria's neutrality was confirmed by a decision of the Council of Ministers and complemented by a declaration that "Austria would actively participate in the development of security policy structures as envisaged by the Treaty of the European Union."[34]

Austrian journalists noted that Alois Mock had reached a new quality in his position in domestic politics: "Alois Mock is no longer the unlucky Chairman of the ÖVP.... He has moved above daily politics.... As he had to deal for quite some time primarily with issues, such as European integration and the conflict in former Yugoslavia, Austria's Foreign Minister Alois Mock inevitably had to mutate to some sort of an superior authority in political philosophy and morale, i.e. to a living myth."[35]

Without going into the details of the negotiations which would exceed the limits of this article, it should be stated that their success was by no means granted. The European Commission judged Sweden and Finland as easy cases and calculated that Austria would be a tough problem to solve. Key issues in the negotiations were the question of second residences by EU citizens in Austria, the support for Austria's agriculture taking into account its unique challenges (mountainous land, small family structures), and the question of limitations for the transit traffic, in particular in Tyrol.

It the evening hours of 1 March 1994, Alois Mock, who headed the Austrian delegation, was able to announce the successful conclusion of the negotiations. Alluding to the famous words by Austrian Foreign Minister Leopold Figl at the signing of Austria's State Treaty in 1995 ("Austria is free"), Alois Mock declared: "The road for Austria to the EU is free."[36] The success of the negotiations added to Mock's reputation as Austria's "Mr. Europe." The ensuing nationwide campaign for a "yes" vote in the referendum on the accession was supported by all major political forces in Austria. The referendum brought an overwhelming support for Austria's EU membership: 66.58% of the votes were cast in favor.

Only in February 1995, Mock informed the public that he was suffering from Parkinson's disease thus ending long-lasting speculations about his state of health. On 4 May 1995, Alois Mock handed over the Foreign Ministry to his successor, Wolfgang Schüssel, and to State Secretary Benita Ferrero-Waldner. An era in Austrian foreign policy had ended. Mock's disease prevented him from assuming an international position for which he would have been highly qualified. Mock has rightfully earned a prominent place in Austrian history. While he could not reach his ultimate domestic policy goal to become Austrian Federal Chancellor, he was highly successful in shaping Austria's foreign policy. His tenure was characterized

34. Manfred Scheich, *Tabubruch: Österreichs Entscheidung für die Europäische Union* (Vienna: Böhlau, 2005), 70.

35. Michael Fleischhacker, *Kleine Zeitung*, 28 Nov. 1993.

36. Franz Vranitzky, *Politische Erinnerungen* (Vienna: P. Zsolnay, 2004), 317.

by a historic change in Europe, the Fall of the Iron Curtain and the demise of Communism, and by a war in Austria's immediate neighborhood. While the Balkans stayed a crisis region for long after his mandate, Austria has secured her role in the European Union as a reliable partner in the process of European integration.

Alois Mock's great strengths lay in his integrity as a politician, in his clear principles and visions for Austria and Europe. Andreas Unterberger, a prominent Austrian journalist and expert in international affairs said about Mock: "With all his excellent education, Alois Mock was never a brilliant intellectual or an eloquent speaker. However, to the end of his political career he had a healthier political instinct and a clearer vision than many others."[37] Heinz Fischer, Austrian Federal President and a political opponent, conceded Mock great diligence and engagement: "[He is] a convinced parliamentarian and a politician with clear positions. That he proved as foreign minister and in the preparation of Austria's EU accession."[38]

Mock received international recognition and praise for his lifetime achievements. He was awarded high and highest decorations and holds several honorary doctor's degrees. As of late, his disease does not allow him to be often where he has always felt best: among ordinary people. Wherever he goes, he is met by a wave of sympathy and admiration.

37. *Die Presse* (Andreas Unterberger), 24 April 1995.
38. Heinz Fischer, *Überzeugungen*, (Vienna: Styria, 2006), 307.

Lives of the Mind

"Genia" Schwarzwald and Her Viennese "Salon"

Deborah Holmes

The basic facts of Eugenie Schwarzwald's biography can be summed up in a few lines. Born Eugenie Nussbaum to Jewish parents on 4 July 1872, she spent her early childhood in Eastern Galicia. The family moved to Czernowitz in the Bukowina sometime during her teenage years. In 1895, she left home to go to Zurich University, graduating in July 1900. In December of the same year, she married the aspiring civil servant Hermann Schwarzwald and settled in Vienna, where she lived and worked until the Anschluss. Schwarzwald was active in the education reform movement, founding pioneering girls' and primary schools. She kept an open house, now generally referred to as her "salon," through which she maintained close links to major Modernists—Adolf Loos, Oskar Kokoschka and Egon Wellesz in particular, but also Peter Altenberg, Arnold Schönberg and others. During World War I and the interwar period, she founded and ran a series of co-operative restaurants and children's holiday camps. She is also remembered for *Pension Seeblick*, the "Ferienheim für geistige Arbeiter" she founded in 1920 in Grundlsee in the Styrian Salzkammergut. Schwarzwald died in exile in Zurich on 7 August 1940.

The basic contours of her life story follow instantly recognizable historical patterns—movement from East to West, from lower to upper middle class, from nineteenth-century Liberalism to Modernist reform. Given the culturally prestigious company she kept, her individual contribution to these patterns of progress also seems relatively easy to classify on first sight. Although she herself may not be the best-known of Vienna's fin-de-siècle figures, the period of her greatest achievements is extremely well-documented. Using what we know about her contemporaries and milieu as a guide, we might feel as though we can extrapolate her own aspirations and motivations with a reasonable degree of accuracy. As she supported a number of artists and writers who came to define the Viennese fin de siècle, she often features in footnotes to their works and the standard secondary literature.[1] However, these brief descriptions can do little more than generalize

---

1. For example, in the footnotes to Hermann Broch, *Briefe: Dokumente und Kommentare zu Leben und Werk. 1. 1913 – 1938* (Frankfurt am Main: Suhrkamp, 1981), 218-19 and 506, or in the explanatory notes to Thomas Mann, *Tagebücher 1935-36* (Frankfurt am Main: Fischer, 1978), 607-8; *Tagebücher 1937-39* (Frankfurt am Main: Fischer, 1980), 549-50 and *Tagebücher 1940-43* (Frankfurt am Main: Fischer, 1982), 685. See also the aside on Schwarzwald in Karl Corino, *Robert Musil: Leben und Werk in Bildern und Texten* (Reinbek: Rowohlt, 1988), 268.

Eugenie Schwarzwald, mid-1920s, wearing her trademark Reformkleid.

and the very fact that they are subsidiary in character perpetuates an impression of her as an essentially minor figure, a kind of handmaiden of greatness. A further familiar cast given to Schwarzwald's biography is that of the exceptional female figure who was ahead of her times and broke down social conventions. In this biographical model, uniqueness itself paradoxically becomes a category that irons out difference by encouraging superlatives and generalizations. Rather than perpetuating either of these interpretative paradigms, the present article seeks to investigate some of the pitfalls of "biography of the gaps," of biographical naming conventions and gender assumptions, using Schwarzwald as a case study.

Naming conventions

Eugenie Schwarzwald—Frau Dr. Schwarzwald, Frau Doktor, Genia, Genka—went under several names. She was Genia, a female "genius", to her intimates and contemporaries; Genka, in the Slavic diminutive, to the husband who knew her from her youth in the Eastern Habsburg provinces; Frau Doktor, or simply Fr. Dr., to several generations of pupils and protégés in Vienna. The first portrayals of her penned after her death in 1940 tended to be written by close friends, who inevitably still referred to her as "Frau Doktor" or "Genia." Many professional historians who have worked on her since have however continued to use these nicknames, creating an immediate and yet deceptive sense of familiarity.[2] Anyone writing biography must of course accept that they will add to the meanings associated with the name of their subject. As Jean-François Lyotard points out, a name is never saturated: its past associations influence its future significance and vice versa.[3] For this very reason, proper names and their variations should be used with due care: historical empathy, even when coupled with the most meticulous study of the sources available, should not encourage the biographer to write as if it were possible to know the person behind the names.

Such an approach is particularly common when it is a woman's life that is being studied. First names are far more likely to be used in biographies of female subjects than those of men, as though women, even after death, automatically retain greater (emotional?) accessibility. "Virginia," "Marie Antoinette" or "Cleopatra" would surely hardly have approved of the informality that often results. In some cases of course, using a first name or nickname is quite simply a way of avoiding confusion. Historically

---

2. See Beatrix Schiferer, "'Fraudoktor' Eugenie Schwarzwald," in Robert Streibel, ed., *Eugenie Schwarzwald und ihr Kreis* (Vienna: Picus, 1996), 13-18; Beatrix Schiferer, *Vorbilder: Kreative Frauen in Wien 1750-1950* (Vienna: Verband Wiener Volksbildung), 81-92; René Freund, *Land der Träumer: Zwischen Größe und Größenwahn – verkannte Österreicher und ihre Utopien* (Vienna: Picus, 2000), 101-115; Heike Herrberg and Heidi Wagner, *Wiener Melange: Frauen zwischen Salon und Kaffeehaus* (Berlin: edition ebersbach, 2002).

3. Jean-François Lyotard, "Le nom et l' exception," in *Tod des Subjekts?*, ed. Herta Nagl-Docekal and Helmuth Vetter (Vienna: Oldenbourg, 1987), 43-53, here 52.

speaking, women's names have been particularly liable to change through marriage or the adoption of a pseudonym: "Woolf" will not do for "Virginia" in the period when she was still Virginia Stephen, for example. A woman may have had a succession of names—Schwarzwald's contemporary Alma Schindler-Mahler-Gropius-Werfel immediately comes to mind—or else become known in public by a name that had little to do with her private or legal identity.[4] Viennese fin-de-siècle feminist Rosa Mayreder, for instance, much admired by Schwarzwald for her work with the *Allgemeiner Österreichischer Frauenverein*, nevertheless found it expedient to publish her art criticism in the press under the male pseudonym Franz Arnold. Lyotard claims that "toute crise d'identité [...] est une crise de nomination";[5] if the inverse is also true, then naming conventions have routinely subjected women to identity crises for centuries.

Eugenie Schwarzwald's case seems simple by comparison. However, having quitted her maiden name in the conventional manner upon marriage, she made consistent and effective use of her new name, making it into something approaching a trademark or institution in her adopted home city of Vienna. Her appearances in the public sphere, whether in person or in print, were invariably heralded by the full appellation Frau Dr. Phil. Eugenie Schwarzwald. Despite the official sounding ring, this name posed a double challenge to the status quo. Not only was it still virtually unheard of for a woman to have graduated from university, but Schwarzwald also refused to go through the rigmarole of having her Swiss degree recognized by the Habsburg authorities.[6] She was therefore using her academic title illegally, as the *Ministerium für Kultus und Unterricht* vainly pointed out to her on numerous occasions. Flaunting it in public was an act of overt defiance in the more or less open conflict that rumbled on for years between Schwarzwald, the Ministry and the *Landesschulrat für Niederösterreich*. The series of girls' and coeducational schools she began to found in 1901 were known as the *Schwarzwald'sche Schulanstalten*, and bore her contested title in full on the front page of their annual reports; her charity and self-

4. Further examples include Caroline Schlegel-Schelling, Hester Lynch and Thrale Piozzi, see Stephanie Bird, *Recasting historical women: Female identity in German biographical fiction* (Oxford: Berg, 1998), also Franziska Meyer, "Die Konkurrenz der Biographen: Der Fall Caroline Michaelis-Böhmer-Schlegel-Schelling," *Querelles. Jahrbuch für Frauenforschung* 6 (2001): 85-102.

5. Lyotard, "Le nom et l'exception," 49.

6. "Nostrifizierung" involved renewed examination, long waits, and expensive official stamps. The 1896 law detailing this process was moreover openly sexist: women candidates were expected not only to produce academic "Zeugnisse" but also "den Nachweis eines einwandfreien Vorlebens." See Renate Göllner, *Kein Puppenheim: Genia Schwarzwald und die Emanzipation* (Frankfurt am Main: Peter Lang, 1999): 122-23.

help initiatives were bound together under the organizational umbrella of the *Schwarzwald'sches Wohlfahrtswerk*; the co-operative restaurants she founded and ran from 1917 throughout the 1920s were known simply as the *Schwarzwaldküchen*. In this way, she built up a corporate identity for her enterprises at a time when it was still very unusual for women to make such a name for themselves at all. The pursuits that she chose—education, welfare, supporting the arts—were deemed acceptable occupations for a female, but only within limits. Her projects were unique in *fin de siècle* Vienna in their ambition and in the amount of self-publicity that they involved. According to one of her admirers, Jakob Wassermann, the mere mention of Eugenie Schwarzwald was enough to alarm the public; it was, he claimed, a name that constantly kept tongues wagging.[7]

Visible woman...?

Schwarzwald was, therefore, not an "invisible" woman of the type whose lives were led in the shadow of their menfolk, or carefully kept out of the public eye only to be uncovered in retrospect by painstaking detective work on the part of their biographers.[8] Not for her the helpmeet role, nor that of the mysterious muse: for nearly forty years, she was prominent in her own right in the social and cultural life of her adopted city. Her articles became fixtures in Vienna's big liberal dailies, and three generations of its intelligentsia sent their children to her to be educated, entertained and given a social conscience. The money for her initiatives came partly from sizeable loans and partly from Hermann Schwarzwald's income as a senior civil servant, but she also financed them herself with her writing, fundraising and business ventures, such as a taxi company, a market garden and a beauty parlor.[9] She was impresario, entrepreneur, director, manager—all epithets that, if used at all in Schwarzwald's Vienna, were applied exclusively to

7. Jakob Wassermann, „Eugenie Schwarzwald," *Neue Freie Presse* 21 June 1925, 1-3, here 1.

8. For an example of this type of biography see Claire Tomalin, *The Invisible Woman: The Story of Nelly Ternan and Charles Dickens* (London: Penguin Books,1991). Jean Strouse coined the term "semiprivate" to describe the biographies of women led in subservience to famous husbands or fathers and their careers, see "Semiprivate Lives," in *Studies in Biography*, ed. Daniel Aaron (Cambridge, 1978), 113-29 and recent discussion of the term by Caitríona Ní Dhúill, "Biographie von ‚er' bis ‚sie': Möglichkeiten und Grenzen relationaler Biographik," in *Die Biographie: Zur Grundlegung ihrer Theorie*, ed. Bernhard Fetz (Berlin: de Gruyter, 2009), 199-226, here 214.

9. Hans Deichmann, *Leben mit provisorischer Genehmigung: Leben, Werk und Exil von Dr. Eugenie Schwarzwald* (Vienna: Guthmann-Peterson,1988), 143. Lisa Fischer, "Die Kunst des Lebens oder die Meisterin sozialer Kreativität: Eugenie Schwarzwalds flüchtige Kreationen," in Streibel, *Eugenie Schwarzwald und ihr Kreis*, 19-28, here 25.

men. Those of her male friends and acquaintances who are now considered central to the canon of Viennese Modernism—and one could add Robert Musil, Sigmund Freud, Hermann Broch and Karl Kraus to those already mentioned above—are never referred to by their first names in secondary literature, let alone by diminutive forms thereof.

Once Schwarzwald had moved to Vienna and embarked on her public career, she began to leave a substantial paper trail of official documentation in her wake, from files on her schools at the Ministry of Education, including her own often impassioned petitions, to planning permission for the icehouse Adolf Loos designed for the first *Schwarzwaldküche*, the *Akazienhof* in Vienna's ninth district. Satirized by Alfred Polgar and Egon Friedell, photographed by Madame D'Ora, dressed by Klimt's protégées the Flöge sisters, published by the liberal *Neue Freie Presse* and attacked by both the left-wing *Arbeiter-Zeitung* and the right-wing *Reichspost,* the public Schwarzwald can be made to epitomize many of the cultural and social paradigms of her times. From the early 1930s, the familiarity that characterizes the contours of her biography takes on a sickening turn. Financial hardship and political extremism gradually put paid to her schools and welfare organizations; exile came suddenly if not entirely unexpectedly.[10] Schwarzwald left Vienna for a lecture tour of Denmark at the beginning of March 1938 and was urged not to return by her family and friends. She never saw Austria again, succumbing to breast cancer in Zurich in August 1940. As she faced her final illness, it seemed increasingly likely that Hitler would stage a successful invasion of Switzerland: having championed tolerance and civil society all her life, Schwarzwald died thinking that both would soon be impossible throughout continental Europe. Research on her biography therefore opens a series of intriguing perspectives on some of the most turbulent years of Central Europe's history. She not only experienced but influenced and commented on events within her many spheres of activity, as a pedagogue, a woman and an acculturated Jew.

However, the fact that Schwarzwald fits into a number of categories that have become reasons in themselves for researching a biography—female, Jewish, a victim of Nazism—has paradoxically resulted in a lack of clarity as to some of the central details of her life story. Over the past two decades in particular, a proliferation of derivative mini-biographies

10. On 11 April 1938, Schwarzwald wrote to Alice Herdan-Zuckmayer from the first stage of her exile in Copenhagen "Alles, was geschehen ist – ich bin grossartig informiert – habe ich schon in Dezember gewusst, und immer wieder versucht, H.[ermann] und M.[arie Stiasny] zur Liquidierung unserer dortigen [i.e. in Vienna] Existenz zu bewegen. Seit dem 12. ii [*Berchtesgadener Abkommen*] habe ich für diese keinen Heller mehr gegeben." DLA Marbach, A: Zuckmayer, 56.6.2651/9.

has sprung up, often following predetermined agendas and propagating inaccuracies or generalizations that border on the inaccurate.[11] Contrary to what has sometimes been claimed, Schwarzwald was not the first Austrian woman to attend university; she did not open the first ever school in Austria to prepare girls for the *Matura*, nor was her teaching staff made up of Modernist iconoclasts.[12] She was neither fabulously wealthy, nor desperately poor;[13] she invented neither the "Gemeinschaftsküche" nor the "Ferienkolonie" and none of her initiatives were open to all comers.[14] She was however the first Austrian woman to attain a doctorate—*summa cum laude*—in German Language and Literature. She also founded the first girls' *Realgymnasium* and the first co-educative primary school in what was then the Austrian half of the Habsburg Empire. Her model for welfare during the First World War was one of middle-class self-help, not charity. As for Modernist iconoclasts, they certainly feature in her story, but in more diffuse and complex ways than has previously been suggested. Schwarzwald's relationship to her Jewishness has also often been subjected to polemical simplification.[15] Taking anyone as a representative figure—of their times, ethnicity or sex—is a fraught enterprise *per se*, but can become dangerously misleading if the biographical details used are unreliable.

Contrary to the conventions of traditional biography—in particular commercial biography—social, political or cultural developments can seldom be linked in a straightforward manner to any one individual. Conversely, biographical research, by its very definition, should subvert and exceed the categories of social, political or cultural history. The designations available to us for Schwarzwald—headmistress, welfare pioneer, friend of

11. See for example the presentation of Schwarzwald's biography as a "typical" lesbian trajectory in Ines Rieder, *Wer mit wem? Berühmte Frauen und ihre Liebhaberinnen* (Munich: DTV, 1997).

12. Steven Beller, *Vienna and the Jews 1867-1938: A Cultural History* (Cambridge: Cambridge University Press, 1989), 40-41 and 209.

13. Philipp Blom, *The Vertigo Years: Change and Culture in the West 1900-1914* (London: Weidenfeld and Nicolson, 2008), 240. Peter Drucker, *Adventures of a Bystander* (New York: Harper Collins, 1978), 46-60.

14. Alison Rose, "The Jewish Salons of Vienna," in *Gender and Modernity in Central Europe*, ed. Agatha Schwartz (Ottawa: University of Ottawa Press, 2010), 119-32, here 126.

15. Manès Sperber, who took part in some of Schwarzwald's summer colonies, claimed in his autobiography "...von ihr wußte man alles – sogar das einzige Detail, das sie unbedingt verheimlichen wollte: nämlich, daß sie eine Jüdin aus dem südöstlichen Randgebiet der Monarchie war." *Die vergebliche Warnung: All das Vergangene ... II*, (Vienna: Europaverlag, 1975), 118. Taking their cue from him, later commentators assumed that she must have repudiated her origins, and to have been baptized, which was not the case. Still others have implied that she consciously represented a Jewish element in Viennese society, see for example Rose, "The Jewish Salons," 130.

the arts, businesswoman, social reformer, teetotaller, *Ostjüdin*, even simply that of Austrian—all come with reservations and limitations attached. As applied within the diverse academic disciplines that have shown interest in Schwarzwald's activities, these labels also tend to separate out her activities, to cordon them off from each other in a way that threatens to diminish them. Schwarzwald is not considered enough of a writer to merit attention in her own right by literary scholars, neither did she set down enough of a recognizably new pedagogical theory to merit attention by mainstream historians of education.[16] Her welfare work has often passed under the radar of social history, presumably due to its often personal and localized nature.[17] What falls through the gaps between these categories is however crucial to biography. And this is before we have even begun to consider what Lyotard refers to as "l'inflation des significations" attached to names, not just by the language of academic research and cognition, but by the nebulous, heterogeneous speech acts of everyday usage.[18]

...or invisible woman?

Despite the difficulties of fitting Schwarzwald and her names into a disciplinary box and the perils of biographical generalization, it is however—thankfully—no longer necessary, as it was in the 1990s, to preface comments on her life with a reference to her shameful neglect.[19] A number of projects over the past two decades, in particular those of the historian Robert Streibel and the education specialist Renate Göllner, have made more information available on Schwarzwald's life and works than ever before.[20] In the early

16. Renate Göllner stresses that she was a practical, not a theoretical pedagogue, and belittles her written oeuvre, *Kein Puppenheim*, 67. She nevertheless criticizes Helmut Engelbrecht's five volume *Geschichte des österreichischen Bildungswesens* for failing to even mention Schwarzwald, ibid., 12.

17. She is for example nowhere to be found in Maureen Healy's accounts of self-help and war welfare in *Vienna and the Fall of the Habsburg Empire: Total War and Everyday Life in World War I* (Cambridge: Cambridge University Press, 2004).

18. Lyotard, "Le nom est l'exception," 48.

19. See Wilhelm Rochester, "Dr. Eugenie Schwarzwald," in *West-östlicher Divan zum utopischen Kakanien: Hommage à Marie-Louise Roth,* eds. Annette Daigger, Renate Schröder-Werle and Jürgen Thöming (Bern: Lang, 1999), 333-49, also Erik Adam, "Eugenie Schwarzwald und die Reformpädagogik: eine Skizze über eine bislang übergangene Pionierleistung in der Geschichte des österreichischen Bildungswesens," in *Eugenie Schwarzwald und ihr Kreis*, ed. Streibel, 47-53.

20. See Streibel, *Eugenie Schwarzwald und ihr Kreis*. Streibel also runs a permanent exhibition on Schwarzwald at the Volkshochschule Hietzing in Vienna, which opened in 2001. In the 1990s, he set up regular meetings between former pupils of the Schwarzwald Schools and recorded numerous interviews with them. Renate Göllner wrote her doctoral dissertation on Schwarzwald, "Mädchenbildung um Neunzehnhundert: Eugenie Schwarzwald und ihre Schulen," PhD. diss., University of Vienna, 1986, followed by her 1999 biography, *Kein Puppenheim.*

stages of her research, Göllner worked together with Hans Deichmann, one of the younger generation of Schwarzwald's closest friends, on the creation of a Schwarzwald Archive. This invaluable collection consists of copies from other archives, Deichmann's personal papers, and memoirs that he collated on Schwarzwald. It was donated it to the *Wiener Stadt und Landesarchiv* in 1990 and 1995, and as Deichmann well knew, is the only archive to offer anything approaching a comprehensive insight into both Schwarzwald's professional and private life. Due to the circumstances of her exile, Schwarzwald left no actual *Nachlass*, and very little documentary evidence remains of her obviously immense skills as a net worker. Despite her comparative visibility during her lifetime, therefore, this aspect of her biography does in fact fit her for a subsection of the category "invisible women." Her material and written legacy was abruptly wrested from her; her traces on Austria's archival landscape are a mere fraction of what she would have left had she been able to live out her days at home. And of course, not only was Schwarzwald herself affected, but countless aspects and inhabitants of the world she knew and lived with fell victim to Nazi violence.[21]

Therefore, although Schwarzwald may have been well-known among her contemporaries, anyone wishing to write her life story still needs to carry out investigative research around and about the known sources. Her ubiquity and notoriety in certain Viennese circles, followed by the obliteration of so much that she experienced and worked for, has encouraged a tendency to rely on assumptions about her personality and motivations rather than to seek for further evidence. Biography is, of course, always fragmentary: every biography has to select, and every biography has unavoidable gaps. Nevertheless, a surprising number have been left to stand in Schwarzwald's case, in particular as regards her interaction with renowned male contemporaries. These lacunae tend to be filled in one of two unsatisfactory ways. Some of her chroniclers choose to give misplaced weight to works of literature written during her lifetime that used her as a model for fictional characters. Kraus's Hofrätin Schwarz-Gelber, Musil's Diotima, Bettauer's Dr. Eugenia Harz, Weinheber's Frau Doktor Mania or Dörmann's Selma Boskovits-Silbermann are illuminating illustrations of how Modernist Vienna portrayed socially and culturally active females, but are not reliable sources of information on the historical Schwarzwald's life,

21. As well as Jewish associates, close friends such as Hans Deichmann's brother-in-law Count Helmuth James von Moltke, who took part in the resistance, died at the hands of Hitler's henchmen.

private or otherwise.[22] The other solution is to stop the gaps in her biography with preconceived notions of how men and women related to one another during the period. Clichés such as "schillernde Figur" or "charismatische Persönlichkeit" have become a substitute for trying to determine how her initiatives may actually have worked, in particular her "salon."[23] There are many accounts listing the well-known artistic and intellectual figures who frequented Schwarzwald, but very few that pay any attention to chronology or to the ways in which she and her guests influenced each other beyond the mere fact of their being there together.

The works of these famous, mostly male friends are of course more immediately recognizable as belonging to an accepted canon of individual creativity. Much of what Schwarzwald did—educating, comforting, motivating, challenging, feeding, clothing—belongs to the so-called reproductive rather than the productive sphere, considered intrinsically inferior by many artists and writers of the period.[24] The terms used by Schwarzwald's contemporaries to describe her activities implicate her in the debates on genius and the nature of the artist that so preoccupied fin-de-siècle Vienna.[25] Attitudes to her were inevitably colored by Weiningerian misogyny and the burgeoning Schopenhauer reception of the day, influential currents of thought that rejected any notion of female creativity out of hand.[26] However, fin-de-siècle Vienna also offered an alternative

22. For example, however carefully the literary scholar Arno Rußegger tries not to identify Musil's figure of Diotima in *Der Mann ohne Eigenschaften* with Schwarzwald on a one-to-one basis, his attempt eventually breaks down when he compares Diotima's relationship with her husband, "Giovanni" Tuzzi, to the Schwarzwalds' marriage, see Arno Rußegger, "'Der Zeus von Tarnopolis' Eugenie Schwarzwald als Figur in Robert Musils 'Der Mann ohne Eigenschaften'," in Streibel, *Eugenie Schwarzwald*, 29-40, here 37-40. For a more differentiated discussion of the same material, see Karl Corino, "Musils Diotima: Modelle einer Figur," in *Literatur und Kritik* 149/159 (1980): 588-98.

23. For example, Edith Friedl, *Nie erlag ich seiner Persönlichkeit: Margarete Lihotzky und Adolf Loos; Ein sozial- und kulturgeschichtlicher Vergleich* (Vienna: Milena, 2005), 52.

24. Referring to these activities in an unpublished letter, Herdan-Zuckmayer remarks that figures such as Loos, Kokoschka and Schönberg "litten an einem bedeutenden Geld und Anerkennungsmangel. Sie wurden in jeder Weise genährt im Hause Schwarzwald." Herdan-Zuckmayer to Hilde Frankenstein, 1969, DLA Marbach, A: Zuckmayer.

25. For instance, see Paul Stefan's somewhat defensive description of her: "Ihr Helfen und Retten ist nicht minder Kunst, nicht minder Genietat als Dichtung, Musik, Bildnerei, wenn das Verschiedene auch nicht wahrhaben wollen," *Frau Doktor: Ein Bildnis aus dem unbekannten Wien* (Munich: Drei Masken, 1922), 27. Wassermann also referred to her directly as "ein unbequemes Genie der Hilfeleistung," "Eugenie Schwarzwald", 2.

26. Weininger believed women to be the absolute opposite of genius, see David S. Luft, *Eros and Inwardness in Vienna: Weininger, Musil, Doderer* (Chicago: Chicago University Press, 2003), 69-74. Descriptions of Schwarzwald as an unintelligent, irritating gossip by young Modernists such as Elias Canetti owe much to these ideas: Canetti, *Das Augenspiel* (Frankfurt am Main: Fischer, 1988), 178.

model of genius that was better suited to her methods and achievements. At the opening lecture of Vienna's first *Frauenclub* in November 1900, Rosa Mayreder referred to „eine […] spezifisch weibliche Genialität […] die Genialität des geselligen Verkehrs, die Gabe, die eigene Persönlichkeit durch die Umgangsformen zum Ausdruck zu bringen."[27] Eugenie Nussbaum, soon to become Schwarzwald, had arrived in the capital a few months previously; by February 1901, she herself would be holding a lecture on one of her favorite authors, Gottfried Keller, at the *Frauenclub*. However, this proved to be a short-lived forum that folded in 1902 for financial reasons. Female "geniuses" such as Schwarzwald were therefore thrown back once again onto a more traditional platform for female intellectual and social brilliance: the salon.

The Viennese salon in the fin de siècle

Opinions are divided in the secondary literature as regards the state of the Viennese salon when Schwarzwald arrived in the capital in 1900. Some believe its heyday to have ended with the death of Josephine von Wertheimstein in 1894; they argue that it had been rendered obsolete by the rise of the coffee house, the solipsistic nature of Modernist discourse and an increasing tendency to see cultural activities as potential business ventures.[28] Others claim that the fin de siècle witnessed a new blossoming of the salon, and interwar Vienna its unique, final flowering.[29] The social institution of the aristocratic salon may have perished along with the Habsburg Empire, these commentators note, but the salon as a cultural and intellectual meeting place was able to modernize and diversify. Women finally had the vote, access to higher education and more professional freedom. As a result, Vienna's surviving salons were able to exercise far more direct influence on public life than had previously been the case, and their hostesses were more often identified with concrete cultural and social aims.[30] The central characteristics of the salon are considered to have

27. Rosa Mayreder, "Das Weib als Dame," in *Zur Kritik der Weiblichkeit: Essays* (Mandelbaum: Vienna 1998), 126.

28. Karl-Heinz Rossbacher, *Literatur und Bürgertum: Fünf Wiener Jüdische Familien von der Liberalen Ära zum Fin de Siècle* (Vienna: Böhlau 2003) 113; Michael Pollak, *Wien 1900: Eine verletzte Identität* (Constance: Universitätsverlag, 1997), 163.

29. By contrast, Barbara Hahn points out that, post-World War I, there were no more Jewish salon hostesses in Berlin, "Encounters at the margins: Jewish salons around 1900," in *Berlin Metropolis: Jews and the New Culture 1890-1918*, ed. Emily Bilski (New York: Jewish Museum, 2000), 188-203, here 202.

30. Isabella Ackerl, "Wiener Salonkultur um die Jahrhundertwende: Ein Versuch," in *Die Wiener Jahrhundertwende: Einflüsse, Umwelt, Wirkungen*, ed. Jürgen Nautz (Vienna: Böhlau

remained the same, however: a strong, female personality as focal point and a private house as main venue. Three names are habitually mentioned in this context: Alma Mahler (-Werfel), Berta Zuckerkandl and Eugenie Schwarzwald, presented as a new, if somewhat staggered, generation of Viennese *salonières* who rose to prominence during the fin de siècle and continued to be influential throughout the period 1918-1938.[31]

Alma Mahler (1879-1864) is best known to posterity as a somewhat unscrupulous *femme fatale* who used her charms to attract a circle of important artists to her home. It was however not only the renown of her first husband, Gustav Mahler, that attracted leading lights of the avant garde to her side, but also her own musical talent and training. Arrested in her development as a composer by Mahler's insistence that his music come first, she remained an accomplished performer and discerning critic. By contrast, Alma Mahler's older friend, Berta Zuckerkandl (1864-1945) did not give up her intellectual pursuits upon marriage, neither would her husband, Emil Zuckerkandl—anatomy professor and champion of women's education—have expected her to. Since her earliest youth, Zuckerkandl had played a role in the newspaper empire of her father Moriz Szeps. Following a successful career on the *Wiener Presse* and *Wiener Morgenpost*, Szeps founded the influential *Neues Wiener Tagblatt* in 1867, a newspaper aimed at the liberal (upper) middle classes. His daughters were educated at home, as was the young Alma Schindler. Unlike the Schindlers, however, the Szeps family spared no expense and no subjects were favored or neglected. Berta was therefore well prepared to perform secretarial duties for her father. She also later claimed to have acted as a secret go-between, facilitating the publication of anonymous articles by the progressive heir to the throne, Crown Prince Rudolph.[32] Zuckerkandl married in 1889, and began to open her home to prominent cultural, literary and political figures. Her salon is now celebrated as one of the birthplaces of the Viennese Secession and the *Wiener Werkstätte*, as a forum where Hermann Bahr, Arthur Schnitzler and Hugo von Hofmannsthal met with Gustav Klimt, Otto Wagner, Josef Hofmann and the artists of the Nötscher Circle. Zuckerkandl was not only a talented hostess and networker, but also became an influential cultural critic with an appetite for controversy. As art and culture columnist, first for the *Wiener Allgemeine Zeitung*, then the *Neues Wiener Journal*, she worked as

1993) 694-709, here 707.

31. Rose, "The Jewish Salons," 204.

32. Olaf Herling, "Berta Zuckerkandl oder die Kunst weiblicher Diplomatie," in *Das alles war ich: Politikerinnen, Künstlerinnen, Exzentrikerinnen der Wiener Moderne*, ed. Frauke Severit (Vienna: Böhlau, 1998), 53-74, also Michael Schulte, *Berta Zuckerkandl: Saloniere, Journalistin, Geheimdiplomatin* (Zurich: Atrium, 2006), 28-40.

a professional journalist at a time when women's names were seldom if ever to be found under serious newspaper articles.

By comparison to both Zuckerkandl and Mahler-Werfel, Eugenie Schwarzwald was an exception as a salon hostess even during this period of general transformation. Zuckerkandl was undeniably a woman of great wit and taste; nevertheless, she owed her social status and press contacts to her family, in particular to her newspaper mogul of a father.[33] She grew up in a *Palais* that had been built especially for the Szeps in the ninth district, and had been accustomed to mixing with Vienna's cultural and political elite from childhood. The frequent assumption of much secondary literature on the salon, that hostesses must have been creatures of luxury, "schon vom Elternhaus her ziemlich begütert bis sehr reich," is certainly true in her case, as is the claim that they were brought up to take on "die Führung eines mehr oder weniger großen Haushaltes—natürlich an einer eleganten Wohnadresse."[34] Alma Mahler was born into less luxurious circumstances, but her father belonged to a well-established Viennese dynasty of artists, and her first husband left her both fame and fortune. In contrast, Schwarzwald's biography is very much that of a self-made woman.

Schwarzwald—an unusual *salonière*

No direct documentation has survived of Eugenie Nussbaum's childhood or youth: apart from her own memoirs, the only clues to be gleaned come from sources on the male members of her family: her brothers' school reports and adverts for her father's business. It seems that the Nussbaum family moved around continually during her early youth, and eventually settled in Czernowitz in the Bukowina in the mid- to late 1880s. Eugenie's father Leon gave his profession as "Gutsverwalter" or "Ökonom" on his son's school records in the 1870s, whereas Czernowitz address books for the 1890s list him as the owner of a "Vermittlungs- und Plakatirungsbüro".[35] Schwarzwald herself later claimed to have attended the state "Lehrerinnenbildungsanstalt" in Czernowitz, but as she never

33. Bettina Spoerri, "'Auf meinem Diwan wird Österreich lebendig' Die jüdische Journalistin Berta Zuckerkandl-Szeps und ihr Wiener Salon," in *"Not an Essence but a Positioning." German-Jewish Women Writers (1900-1938)*, eds. Andrea Hammel and Godela Weiss-Sussex (Munich: Martin Meidenbauer, 2009), 163-80.

34. Ackerl, "Wiener Salonkultur," 707.

35. Isidor Nussbaum's school reports are to be found in the records of the Czernowitz Gymnasium in the city archives, holding 228, box 3, files 30-35. The address and adverts for Leo Nussbaum's business are to be found in *Dr. Nussbaum's Allgemeiner Wohnungs-Anzeiger nebst Handels- und Gewerbe-Adressbuch für die Landeshauptstadt Czernowitz und Vorstädte. Erster Jahrgang* (Czernowitz, Selbstverlag, 1895), 124 and 178.

graduated, her name is not to be found in the school's annual reports.[36] The first reliable information on her individual biography dates from 1895, when she departed from the female norm to register at the Philosophy Faculty of Zurich University.[37] We can only speculate as to why and how exactly she studied for university entrance. Her uncle Joachim Nussbaum was a *Gymnasiallehrer* in Suczawa and Czernowitz, and both of her (surviving?) brothers graduated in law from Czernowitz University; they may have helped her prepare. Who financed her studies is also unclear: in articles she later published on the subject, Schwarzwald looked back to her student days as a time of happy privation, remembering badly paid translation work and private lessons as her main source of income.[38] It is certainly true that she selected the cheapest courses available to complete her degree.[39] None of the evidence available suggests that this future *salonière* grew up a creature of luxury.

Eugenie's husband Hermann Schwarzwald was also Jewish, a native of Czernowitz. After having married and settled in Vienna, the couple threw themselves into making careers and earning a living—no signs of inherited ease here either. Hermann, whose degree was in law and economics, offered his services as private consultant on the side while climbing the ladder of the Habsburg civil service. Eugenie continued to give private lessons to begin with, and also taught for a session at the newly founded *Volksheim* in Ottakring.[40] In 1901, she took over Eleonore Jeiteles' *Mädchenlyzeum* in Franziskanerplatz in Vienna's first district. At that time in Austria-Hungary, secondary schools for girls had to be private institutions; with the exception of a handful of teaching training colleges, there was no state provision for educating females beyond the age of fourteen.[41] Schwarzwald's

36. Compare the "Vita" at the end of Schwarzwald's published dissertation, Eugenie Nussbaum, *Metapher und Gleichnis bei Berthold von Regensburg* (Vienna: Rieper, 1902) with the *Bericht der k.k. Lehrer- und Lehrerinnenbildungsanstalt in Czernowitz* (Czernowitz: Selbstverlag, 1896).

37. Matrikeledition der Universität Zürich (http://www.matrikel.uzh.ch/pages/0.htm , last accessed 29 Feb. 2012), Eintrag 10993 phil. WS 1895, Nussbaum, Eugenie.

38. Eugenie Schwarzwald, "Zürcher Studentenleben um 1900," *Neue Freie Presse*, 13 July 1931, 1-2.

39. The courses that Eugenie Nussbaum took, or at least paid for, can be deduced from the "Kollegiengeldkarten" of Zurich University for the years 1895-1900, Staatsarchiv Zürich, Universitätsarchiv UU 25. I analyze these in depth in chapter three of my forthcoming biography of Schwarzwald, *Langeweile ist Gift: Das Leben der Eugenie Schwarzwald* (St Pölten: Residenz, 2012).

40. *Jahresbericht des Vereins Volksheims in Wien* 2 nos 6/7 (April 1901- April 1902), 6.

41. Helmut Engelbrecht, *Geschichte des österreichischen Bildungswesens: Erziehung und Unterricht auf dem Boden Österreichs*, vol 4: *Von 1848 bis zum Ende der Monarchie* (Vienna: Österreichischer Bundesverlag, 1986), 286-89.

school, therefore, was not only an expression of what she saw as a cultural mission, but—unavoidably—a business venture. While Berta Zuckerkandl fought in the press on behalf of the Viennese Secession, Schwarzwald struggled with the Ministry and the School Board for permission to vary the official syllabus, pushing back the frontiers of women's education. The number of pupils at her schools grew rapidly over her first decade in Vienna from around 200 in 1901 to over a thousand during World War I.[42] From the very beginning, she provided extra-curricular courses to prepare her pupils for the Matura; from 1909, she advertised a section of the school as a *Realgymnasium*. This type of school was revolutionary *per se* for either sex, its curriculum of modern languages and science subjects representing a break with the traditions of classical education. Schwarzwald not only opened one of the first of such institutions, but hers was for girls, an innovation that threw Ministry and School Board into a positive panic.[43]

1909 was also the year in which the Schwarzwalds were able to afford to begin renting a miniature, two-story Baroque *Palais*, hemmed in by new apartment buildings at Josefstädterstraße 68 in the eighth district. This became the venue for their "at homes," held on a Sunday evening like those of both Mahler-Werfel and Zuckerkandl. Rivalry was thus pre-programmed, not so much between Zuckerkandl and Alma Mahler-Werfel as between Zuckerkandl and the *arriviste* Schwarzwald. Zuckerkandl was fifteen years older than Mahler-Werfel and had helped launch her into Viennese artistic society as a precocious teenager. The age gap between Zuckerkandl and Schwarzwald was much smaller, and the latter had come to town as an ambitious, opinionated twenty-eight-year-old, highly educated, yet a no-name in Viennese society. Adolf Drucker also later suggested that Schwarzwald was automatically at a disadvantage—according to the prevailing views of the time—due to the "Schlacken ihrer Herkunft" as an Eastern Jew.[44] And indeed, although there were overlaps between some of the main protagonists of Mahler-Werfel, Zuckerkandl and Schwarzwald's salons, there were also definite differences, amounting sometimes and in some cases to opposing camps. The writers who had been

42. Approximate numbers can be deduced from the *Jahresberichte* the school published 1902-1913, although not every issue contains a list of all the pupils. Available online: http://www.literature.at/default.alo, last accessed 29 Feb. 2012

43. Amalia Mayer and Hildegard Meissner, eds., *Geschichte der österreichischen Mädchenmittelschule* (Vienna, Österreichischer Bundesverlag, 1952), vol 1, 59. Hans Deichmann publishes part of the letter exchanges between Schwarzwald, Ministry and Schools Board in *Leben mit provisorischer Genehmigung*, 70-72.

44. Adolf Drucker and Trude Fleischmann, 9. August 1964. Excerpts are quoted by Deichmann, *Leben mit provisorischer Genehmigung*, 19; a photocopy of the whole letter can be found in the Wiener Stadt und Landesarchiv: Schwarzwaldarchiv 2.8.

known as "Jung Wien" did not frequent the Schwarzwalds, for example. Schnitzler, although a minute chronicler of fin de siècle society, seldom mentions her in his letters or diaries, and when he does, his comments are disparaging.[45] There are no records of contact between Hofmannsthal and Schwarzwald, but Hofmannsthal's daughter Christiane later described working for Schwarzwald's welfare organizations after World War I as a welcome opportunity to break out of the milieu in which she had been raised.[46]

While one section of Viennese Modernism kept its distance from Schwarzwald, however, others maintained intimate links to her. The architect and cultural theoretician Adolf Loos was one of her closest friends. He not only attended her salon, but lived at her house and holiday homes for extended periods. They also worked together: he designed interiors for the building her schools moved into in 1913 and for the *Schwarzwaldküchen*. Loos's second wife, the dancer Elsie Altmann, was a pupil at Schwarzwald's *Lyzeum*; they first met at a Schwarzwald "at home."[47] Oskar Kokoschka came to Schwarzwald through Loos, but was also welcome *chez* Zuckerkandl, not least because of his links to the Secession. He disappeared from Schwarzwald's salon for the duration of his notorious affair with Alma Mahler, only to reappear again after Alma rejected him. Schwarzwald's guests also included the composer Egon Wellesz, whose wife, the art historian Emmy Stross, had been one of her first pupils.[48] Other regulars were the actress Ida Roland, the soprano Emmy Heim and the dancers Grete, Berta and Elsa Wiesenthal, although records of the Wiesenthal sisters attending Schwarzwald's "at homes" are

45. Indeed, no mention of Schwarzwald is to be found in Schnitzler's diaries until after the First World War. In 1922, he considered working together with her on a fundraising tour to Sweden, but the idea came to nothing and the experience was obviously unsatisfactory for both, see Arthur Schnitzler Tagebuch 1920-22 (Vienna: Österreichische Akademie der Wissenschaften, 1993), 282-3 and 286.

46. This account by Christiane Zimmer (née von Hofmannsthal) is to be found in the unpublished typoscript of an early biography on Schwarzwald now preserved in the papers of Alice Herdan-Zuckmayer. Trude Fleischmann, *Magische Blätter: Ein Erinnerungsbüchlein an Frau Doktor Genia Schwarzwald*, 78 in DLA Marbach, A: Zuckmayer.

47. Some of these details emerge from the standard secondary literature on Loos, for example Burkhard Rukschscio and Roland Schachel, *Adolf Loos: Leben und Werk* (Salzburg: Residenz, 1982), 154, 165, 178. The extent of Loos's private contact to the Schwarzwalds only becomes apparent in unpublished correspondence between members of Schwarzwalds' inner circle. See for instance a letter from Hermann Schwarzwald to the singer Emmy Heim, 18 July 1911, detailing Loos's physical afflictions and the way he has taken refuge in the Josefstädterstraße. Karin Michaelis Archive, 35. Royal Danish Library, Copenhagen.

48. Egon Wellesz, *Egon Wellesz: Leben und Werk* (Vienna: Zsolnay, 1981), 48, 68-69. See also Emmy Wellesz's memories of her school days, as described in a private letter to Alice Herdan-Zuckmayer, 30 December 1979, DLA Marbach, A: Zuckmayer, 56.6.2172/16, also in Deichmann, *Leben mit provisorischer Genehmigung*, 101, 131.

no longer to be found during the interwar period.[49] The actor, cabaret artist and writer Egon Friedell frequented both Zuckerkandl and Schwarzwald, but disagreements over money in the 1930s led to a break with the latter and an ostentatious turn to the former.[50] Other influential Modernists such as Arnold Schönberg, Peter Altenberg and Karl Kraus were linked to Schwarzwald as much via Loos as on their own behalf, but all three made use of the infrastructure and connections she had at her disposal. Kraus is believed by some to have satirized Schwarzwald in encrypted form in the figure of Hofrätin Schwarz-Gelber in *Die letzten Tage der Menschheit*, although opinions in the secondary literature vary.[51] There is certainly no evidence for a lasting break or animosity between Kraus and Schwarzwald following the play's publication—quite the opposite, in fact: during the interwar period, Kraus practiced his Offenbach performances in the main hall of her schools, and she continued to send him fan mail.[52] By way of comparison, there can be no doubt as to Kraus's dim view of Zuckerkandl: his slighting comments on her activities were always made very much *ad personam*.[53]

Schwarzwald's schools fed into her "salon" and vice versa: she put especial emphasis on literature, art, theatre and music both during lessons and in the extra-curricular activities on offer. She encouraged artist friends to give courses without official permission or teaching qualifications. She was however careful in the final instance not to jeopardize either her

49. For lists of artist regulars, see Johann Dvořák, "Intellektuelle Avantgarde in Wien und das Schulreformwerk von Eugenie Schwarzwald," in *Das Kind ist entdeckt: Erziehungsexperimente in Wien der Zwischenkriegszeit*, eds. Charlotte Zwiauer and Harald Eichelberger (Vienna: Picus, 2001), 291-314.

50. Once again, clues have to be ferreted out of unpublished correspondence, sometimes between third parties. See for example Egon Friedell to Maria Lazar, undated letter, Karin Michaelis Archive, 35. Royal Danish Library, Copenhagen.

51. Those who hold the Schwarz-Gelbers to be a parody of the Schwarzwalds include Renate Göllner, *Kein Puppenheim*, 12 and Rene Freund, *Land der Träumer*, 109-110. Edward Timms believes the lawyer and politician Rudolf Schwarz-Hiller von Jiskor and his wife Erna to be more likely candidates, see *Karl Kraus: Apocalyptic Satirist* (New Haven, Conn.: Yale University Press, 1986), vol. 1, 429.

52. The Offenbach rehearsals were documented by Kraus's accompanist, Georg Knepler, who was also invited to Schwarzwald's at homes, see Georg Knepler Archive 427, Akademie der Künste, Berlin. See also letters from Hans Deichmann to Knepler, 16 April 1985 and Knepler's reply, 10 June 1985, Wiener Stadt und Landesarchiv: Schwarzwaldarchiv 6.22. for an example of a fan letter, see Eugenie Schwarzwald to Karl Kraus, 27 November 1931: "als ich heute Abend Ihre Stimme hörte, begriff ich zum ersten Mal den Wert der Erfindung des Radio." Wien Bibliothek, Handschriftenabteilung, I.N.138.770.

53. Contrary to Philipp Blom's claim that Kraus "mercilessly" and "obsessively" poked fun at Schwarzwald in *Die Fackel*, she is in fact never mentioned there, at least by name, whereas Zuckerkandl frequently is. Early examples include criticism of Zuckerkandl's support for the Secession in *Die Fackel* 43 (1900), 26, persiflage of her art reviews in *Die Fackel* 87 (1901) 28, an accusation of nepotism in *Die Fackel* 149 (1903), 27.

standing with her pupils' parents or her schools' official recognition as "öffentlich rechtlich"—a powerful marketing tool. The courses her "salon" guests gave were mostly an addition to the official curriculum—such as the series of lectures Loos offered on architecture and modern living in 1911/2, or Schönberg's composition seminars, held in 1903/4 and again from 1918 into the early 1920s.[54] Kokoschka was one of the few to have been engaged as a "regular" teacher, for drawing classes given to the lower grades of the Lyzeum in late 1911 and early 1912. His employment at the school caused controversy among parents and at the Ministry, and was of very short duration. Nevertheless, general osmosis between Schwarzwald's "salon" and schools was on-going. Regular guests were not only active at the schools, but selected pupils were invited to the "at homes." And thanks to Hermann Schwarzwald's steady career progression, both the "salon" and the schools had close links to men who went on to make up the upper echelons of the civil service.[55] Hermann worked alongside figures such as Adolf Drucker (father of the American management guru Peter Drucker), Robert Scheu and Hans Kelsen, who were not only civil servants, but also academics, writers and social reformers. Drucker and the legal scholar Kelsen both married Schwarzwald pupils.[56] *Chez* Schwarzwald, radical Modernism met the cream of the Habsburg bureaucracy met precocious, day-dreaming schoolgirls. This heady mix made up the unique character of Eugenie Schwarzwald's open house.

When is a salon not a salon?

In the late eighteenth and early nineteenth century, the salon functioned as an ersatz university for women wishing to further their education. The conversations that they were able to conduct with scholars, writers and artists in this private, if not entirely domesticated atmosphere, were the equivalent of the tutorials (*Privatissimen*) that male students were offered by their professors. During one of the many clashes between Schwarzwald and

54. For Loos's participation in the *Fortbildungskurse*, see *Jahresbericht der Schulanstalten der Frau Dr. phil. Eugenie Schwarzwald in Wien* (Vienna: Selbstverlag, 1912), 101. Loos also used rooms in the Schwarzwald schools over several years to hold lectures for his *Bauschule*, see Rukschcio and Schachel, *Adolf Loos*, 170. For details on Schönberg's compositions seminars, see Wellesz, *Leben und Werk* 48-9, also Hans Heinz Stuckenschmidt, *Schönberg. Leben. Umwelt. Werk* (Zurich: Atlantis, 1974), 75 and 224 and Deichmann, *Leben mit provisorischer Genehmigung*, 110-117.

55. For details of Hermann's career, see Deichmann, *Leben mit provisorischer Genehmigung*, 205-213.

56. Deborah Holmes, "Die Schwarzwaldschule und Hans Kelsen," in *Hans Kelsen: Leben – Werk – Wirksamkeit*, eds. Robert Walter, Werner Ogris and Thomas Olechowski (Vienna: Manz, 2009), 97-109.

the Ministry during the early years of her schools, an inspector remarked sardonically that her aim seemed to be "aus ihrem Lyzeum [...] eine Universität für Mädchen [zu] machen."[57] Schwarzwald would no doubt have taken this as a compliment. The close links and overlaps between her business—her schools—and her private, but open, house were in the best traditions of higher education. The first Viennese *salonière* with an academic degree and her own girls' *Realgymnasium* saw absolutely no contradiction in this combination. She did however have her problems with the term "salon" itself. Although this has become the accepted way of referring to gatherings at the Josefstädterstraße 68, Schwarzwald never used it, nor did she ever refer to herself as a "Salondame." In this respect, she took her lead at least in part from Vienna's fin de siècle feminists. In her opening lecture to the *Frauenclub* in 1900, Rosa Mayreder had been adamant about the limitations of the salon:

> In demselben Maß, wie der Abstand zwischen der männlichen und der weiblichen Bildung zunimmt, verengert sich die Sphäre, die der Dame eingeräumt ist. Alle großen und ernsten Probleme des Lebens sind daraus verbannt; der Salon, in dem die Dame herrscht, ist nicht viel mehr als ein modernisiertes Gynaeceum, bewohnt von eleganten Puppen, deren oberste Aufgabe ist, sich zu schmücken, um zu gefallen.[58]

By 1900, the traditional advantage or attraction of the salon for women—its private, informal nature—was seen as a potential disadvantage in some quarters, as attitudes to women's emancipation and professional lives underwent fundamental change. At a time when the borders between the private and the public were shifting, any would-be *salonière* had a difficult balance to maintain. Some persisted in presenting dilettantism and informality as a liberating force—Zuckerkandl, for example. Born into a milieu in which (high) culture formed an unquestioned part of everyday life, she considered a girl's formal schooling to be far less important than her upbringing within the family circle. In her view, "mangelhafte Bildung" did not automatically preclude "Verständnis für Culturerscheinungen"—quite the opposite, so long as young ladies were trained from childhood "zur Aufnahme allgemeiner, unpersönlicher Fragen." She admitted that the private nature of this type of education ran the risk of formlessness: mothers in particular were advised by Zuckerkandl to ban "das öde Salongeschwätz"

57. Report of School Inspector Vrba, submitted to Ministry on 30 April 1908 (Z:20226). AVA Staatsarchiv, U2 2562 Wien 1. Bezirk M.Sch. Schwarzwald bis 1927.
58. Mayreder, *Kritik der Weiblichkeit*, 132.

from their houses and dining tables.[59] The principle problem that she saw in this negative version of "Salongeselligkeit" was "[d]er Persönlichkeitscultus, welcher in den Wienern steckt [...]. Beinahe immer fällt dem sogenannten Tratsch der Löwenantheil der Unterhaltung zu. Wenige nur kennen den köstlichen Werth einer die geistigen Vibrationen der Gegenwart streifenden Discussion."[60] However, only a few lines later in the same article, Zuckerkandl praises the salon as one of the birthplaces of the Enlightenment and women as mediators of this new Weltanschauung, not because of any newly acquired academic or philosophical training, but rather because they were free of such formal education:

> Der philosophisch-ethische Dilettantismus der Frau des achtzehnten Jahrhunderts war für den Durchbruch der grossen socialen Umwälzung von weittragender Bedeutung. Ihr Bildungsgrad reichte oft kaum bis zur Orthographie. Trotzdem war ihr Gedankenflug hoch und eigen, Freiheit und Sinnesfeinheit erfüllte ihre Seele. Von ihrer Kaminecke, aus ihrem Salon strömte die befreiende Lehre eines Rousseau, eines Voltaire und Diderot. So wie damals die Lehren einer neuen Weltordnung durch die enthusiastische Intuition der Frauen bis in das feinste Geäder der Volksseele geleitet wurde, sollte jetzt die culturell sociale Umwandlung – in welche die Emancipation des weiblichen Geschlechtes eine so grosse Rolle spielt – durch geistig mitstrebende, congenial empfindende Frauen propagirt werden.[61]

Dr. Phil. Eugenie Schwarzwald, educational pioneer and founder of schools, naturally saw the matter differently. The formal education of women was both her mission in life and her main source of income. Zuckerkandl considered "der geistige Genuss" as a refined and worthy leisure-time activity, almost as a moral duty for well-situated women: by exercising their intellect in this manner, they were helping their less fortunate sisters to an at least theoretical recognition of women's equal rights to the kingdom of the mind. Schwarzwald, by contrast, had only been able to secure her place in the (upper) middle class by means of formal education. To her, "Cultureller Dilettantismus"—for such is the self-confident title of the article by Zuckerkandl quoted above—was a specter to be exorcised, a

59. Berta Zuckerkandl, "Cultureller Dilenttantismus," *Documente der Frauen* 1, no. 9 (July 1899), 231-33, here 231.
60. Ibid., 232.
61. Ibid., 233.

potential reproach to all educated women that had to be firmly repudiated. From 1902 onward, she offered "Wissenschaftliche Fortbildungskurse" at her school to fill in the gap between the final year of the *Lyzeum* and university entry: courses in literary and art history, the sciences, economy, law and philosophy. The description published in the *Jahresbericht* of her schools goes to great pains to stress their legitimacy as intellectual training:

> Die Kurse sind durchweg besonders qualifizierten Dozenten anvertraut. Sie können auch einzeln belegt werden; doch verpflichtet die Einschreibung zu regelmäßiger Frequentation und aktiver Teilnahme an den seminaristisch gehaltenen Vorträgen, um jeglichen Dilettantismus zu vermeiden. Die Vorträge sind nach einem wohlüberlegten Plane zusammengestellt und behandeln in dreijährigem Turnus die wesentlichen Bestandteile moderner Bildung. Sie sollen den jungen Mädchen nicht äußerlich Gedächtnisstoff bieten, sondern vornehmlich zu selbstständigem Denken, Arbeiten und Lesen anregen.[62]

Memoirs of Schwarzwald's "at homes" suggest that they were in fact often much more informal and unorthodox in nature than those organized by either Zuckerkandl or Alma Mahler; nevertheless, it is clear why she should shun the particular associations of informality and dilettantism that still clung to the term salon.

Despite their differences, Zuckerkandl and Schwarzwald were nevertheless united in opposing the willful abandonment of all the traditional characteristics and prerogatives of womanhood. That meant "alles […] lernen, was die Männer wußten, und dabei lieb, bescheiden, mädchenhaft und hausfraulich bleiben"[63] in Schwarzwald's case, and in Zuckerkandl's, claiming partisanship as a feminine virtue, not only as regards personal friendships but also in cultural criticism. Zuckerkandl wrote of her own journalism: „Als Frau bin ich mit Leidenschaft subjektiv; mit Begeisterung einseitig."[64] Research on Schwarzwald's biography is still caught up in the tensions created by these constant negotiations between public and private, intellectual and emotional, traditional gender roles and models of emancipation. In many ways, *salonière* seems to be one of

62. *Jahresbericht des Mädchen-Lyzeums am Kohlmarkt* (Vienna: Selbstverlag, 1905), 51.

63. As quoted by Hilde Spiel, *Die hellen und die finsteren Zeiten: Erinnerungen 1911-1946* (Munich: List, 1989), 56.

64. As quoted by Andrea Winklbauer, "Wien muss der Kunst erobert werden: Berta Zuckerkandl als Kunstkritikerin um 1900," in *Beste aller Frauen: Weibliche Dimensionen im Judentum*, ed. Gabriele Kohlbauer-Fritz (Vienna: Jewish Museum, 2007), 120-26, here 122.

the few designations that comes close to encompassing the variety of her activities and the nature of her influence. However, it still requires careful, comparative consideration and tailoring; otherwise it sits as loosely over her life story as the *Reformkleid* that she favored, obscuring her idiosyncracies and individual achievements.

Where Hitler's Name is Never Spoken: Günther Anders in 1950s Vienna

Jason Dawsey[1]

Introduction

Although he lived in Vienna for the last four decades of his very long life (1902-1992) and did his most important theoretical and political work there, the technology critic and anti-nuclear militant Günther Anders has rarely been included in treatments of the intellectual and cultural history of modern Austria. The growth of a rich secondary literature on Anders has occurred primarily in the fields of philosophy and *Germanistik*.[2] Historians of contemporary Austria and Germany have recently begun to discover Anders' astonishing philosophical writings. Understandably, these historians have mainly focused on his trenchant analyses of the nuclear threat.[3]

1. My thanks to Ke-chin Hsia, Andrew Sloin, and Jim Walsh for their feedback.

2. Sustained scholarly interest in Anders only began in the late 1980s. For the most important general studies on Anders in German, see Micha Brumlik, "Günther Anders: Zur Existenzialontologie der Emigration," in *Zivilisationsbruch: Denken nach Auschwitz*, ed. Dan Diner (Frankfurt am Main: Fischer, 1988); Jürgen Langenbach, *Günther Anders: Eine Monographie* (Munich: Raben, 1988); Gabriele Althaus, *Leben zwischen Sein und Nichts: Drei Studien zu Günther Anders* (Berlin: Metropol, 1989); Eckhard Wittulski, *Kein Ort, Nirgends: Zur Gesellschaftskritik Günther Anders'* (Frankfurt am Main: Herchen, 1989); Werner Reimann, *Verweigerte Versöhnung: Zur Philosophie von Günther Anders* (Vienna: Passagen, 1990); Elke Schubert, *Günther Anders: Mit Selbstzeugnissen und Bilddokumenten* (Reinbek bei Hamburg: Rowohlt, 1992); Ludger Lütkehaus, *Philosophieren nach Hiroshima: Über Günther Anders* (Frankfurt am Main: Fischer, 1992); Konrad Paul Liessmann, ed., *Günther Anders kontrovers* (Munich: Verlag C.H. Beck, 1992); Margret Lohmann, *Philosophieren in der Endzeit: Zur Gegenwartsanalyse von Günther Anders* (Munich: Fink, 1996); Konrad Paul Liessmann, *Günther Anders: Philosophieren im Zeitalter der technologischen Revolutionen* (Munich: Verlag C.H. Beck, 2002); Christian Dries, *Günther Anders* (Paderborn: Wilhelm Fink, 2009); Raimund Bahr, *Günther Anders: Leben und Denken im Wort* (Vienna: Edition Art & Science, 2010). The only monograph on Anders in English is Paul van Dijk, *Anthropology in the Age of Technology: The Philosophical Contribution of Günther Anders*, trans. Frans Kooymans (Atlanta: Rodopi, 2000).

3. For some prominent examples, see Holger Nehring, "Cold War, Apocalypse and Peaceful Atoms: Interpretations of Nuclear Energy in the British and West German Anti-Nuclear Weapons Movements, 1955-1964," *Historical Social Research* 29, no. 3 (2004): 150-70; Benjamin Ziemann, Introduction, in Ziemann, ed., *Peace Movements in Western Europe, Japan and the USA during the Cold War* (Essen: Klartext, 2007); idem, "The Code of Protest: Images of Peace in the West German Peace Movements, 1945-1990," *Contemporary European History* 17, no. 2 (2008): 237-61.

Günther Anders, New York, 1945. © Literary Archives of the Austrian National Library

In this essay, I argue that Günther Anders should be considered as a key figure in post-1945 Austrian intellectual history. This argument is supported through extensive use of his "philosophical journals" from 1950-1951.[4] These texts, which have received minimal attention in the secondary literature on Anders, are among the most salient of the numerous works he

4. The central text I analyze is: "Wiedersehen und Vergessen," first published in its entirety in *Die Schrift an der Wand: Tagebücher 1941 bis 1966* (Munich: Verlag C.H. Beck, 1967), and also available in *Tagebücher und Gedichte* (Munich: Verlag C.H. Beck, 1985), hereafter TG. In this piece, I have used the latter and supplemented it with materials from Anders' *Nachlass*.

wrote before the 1956 publication of the first volume of his *magnum opus* on modern technology's increasing independence from human control, *The Obsolescence of the Human Being*.[5] These journals contribute significantly to a symptomology of what I call post-fascism. The concept of post-fascism is a crucial, if undeclared, category of Anders' philosophical writings from 1950 on. In Anders' case, "post-fascism" refers to a host of noxious socio-psychological and ideological strategies for repressing, distorting or minimizing the horror from the fascist era.[6] What Anders himself labeled, much later, fascism's "afterlife," covered the tendencies to elevate Austrians (or Germans) to an equal status of victimhood with Jews, if the latter's claims were recognized at all, to restore former Nazis to places of authority, and to seek comfort in memories of a pre-*Anschluss* past.

The texts examined in this article evince Anders contending with the "after" to Hitler and the Holocaust in its quotidian aspects in Vienna. Left-wing intellectuals, like himself, had to face a most reactionary "normalization" in Austrian Second Republic (and the new Federal Republic of Germany) in the wake of catastrophic war and genocide. Anders witnessed and challenged the consolidation of the victim myth.[7] He became a most prescient critic of the form of post-fascist national identity which solidified in Austria in the early Cold War and his "philosophical journals" merit careful attention from scholars exploring the history of Austrian memory.

---

5. *Die Antiquiertheit des Menschen*, Volume 1: *Über die Seele im Zeitalter der zweiten industriellen Revolution* (Munich: Verlag C.H. Beck, 1956). The second volume was not published until almost a quarter-century later: *Die Antiquiertheit des Menschen*, Volume 2: *Über die Zerstörung des Lebens im Zeitalter der dritten industriellen Revolution* (Munich: Verlag C.H. Beck, 1980).

6. My own conception of post-fascism owes a great deal to the work of Theodor W. Adorno, especially his "The Meaning of Working Through the Past" (1959), and "Education After Auschwitz" (1965), both in *Critical Models: Interventions and Catchwords*, trans. Henry Pickford (New York: Columbia University Press, 1998). The full import of these two extraordinary pieces has not yet been absorbed by European historians. Also helpful for the framing of this chapter were the two excellent essays by Roger Griffin, "Europe for the Europeans: Fascist Myths of the European New Order 1922-1992" and "Fascism's New Faces (and New Facelessness) in the 'Post-Fascist' Epoch" in his *A Fascist Century: Essays by Roger Griffin*, ed. Matthew Feldman (New York: Palgrave Macmillan, 2008).

7. For some works addressing the victim myth, see Günter Bischof, "Victims? Perpetrators? Punching Bags of European Historical Memory? The Austrians and Their World War II Legacies," *German Studies Review* 27, no. 1 (February 2004): 17-32; Peter Utgaard, *Remembering and Forgetting Nazism: Education, National Identity and the Victim Myth in Postwar Austria* (New York: Berghahn, 2003); Hella Pick, *Guilty Victim: Austria from the Holocaust to Haider* (London: I.B. Tauris Publishers, 2000); Meinrad Ziegler and Waltraud Kannonier-Finster, *Österreichs Gedächtnis: Über Erinnern und Vergessen der NS-Vergangenheit* (Vienna: Böhlau Verlag, 1993); Günther Bischof, "Die Instrumentalisierung der Moskauer Erklärung nach dem 2. Weltkrieg," *Zeitgeschichte* 20, no. 11/12 (1993): 345-66.

"Homecoming"

With a life that encompassed almost the entire twentieth century, Anders lived through or witnessed from afar most of its crucial moments. Frequently, he declared his philosophical writings to be efforts to catch up, at the level of thought, to the century's events. His friendships and relationships tied him to many of that century's most significant intellectuals and artists. Born Günther Stern (Anders was a pseudonym he first began to use in the early 1930s) in Breslau in July 1902, he was the son of the eminent psychologists, William and Clara Stern. Walter Benjamin was a distant cousin. In the 1920s, Anders studied with the most important philosophers in Weimar Germany: Ernst Cassirer, Edmund Husserl, Martin Heidegger, and Max Scheler. He was also Hannah Arendt's first husband (they were married from 1929-1937), a participant in Weimar leftist circles that include Bertolt Brecht and George Grosz, and an acquaintance of the members of the Frankfurt School of Critical Theory. Anders, too, must be counted as part of the exodus of artists, scientists, and writers who fled Nazi Germany for the United States after January 1933. Spending the first three years after Hitler's assumption of power in Paris, he emigrated to the U.S. in 1936. Anders lived in New York and southern California for fourteen difficult years and did a variety of "odd jobs" (factory work, screenplay writing, dishwashing) to make ends meet. The final years of the Second World War changed Anders' thinking forever. He first heard reports of mass killings of Jews in 1943, reports confirmed the following year. When he heard of the obliteration of Hiroshima over the radio in New York City in August 1945, he claimed that the news left him totally speechless.[8] These events forced a turn to a more explicitly historical form of theorizing. For the remainder of his life, he would develop and elaborate a philosophy capable of grasping the Shoah and the nuclear threat within the framework of a critique of contemporary technology.

Throughout his time of exile, Anders long imagined his return to Europe. In 1950, he finally departed the United States and relocated to Austria. The pressures behind this move were both personal and political. Anders' second wife, Elisabeth Freundlich, sorely wanted to go back to her *Heimatstadt*, Vienna, after twelve years in exile. By her own account, she had nursed such wishes since the war's end, but delayed in order to hold American citizenship

8. The most detailed biographical treatment of Anders is Bahr, *Günther Anders*. See also Liessmann, *Günther Anders*, 14-29, as well as Paul Van Dijk, *Anthropology in the Age of Technology*, Ch. 2.

for the one year required to leave the country.[9] There were crucial political issues which informed their decision as well. She and Anders shared a very bleak assessment of the situation in their adopted country. The activities of the House Un-American Activities Committee, which had investigated many of their friends, including Brecht and Hanns Eisler, would soon be overshadowed by the even more paranoid anti-communism of Wisconsin Senator Joseph McCarthy. With the onset of the Korean War in June 1950, the already existing climate of surveillance, denunciation, and persecution for leftists of all stripes and national backgrounds worsened.

For Anders and Freundlich, this course of events bespoke an indigenous American fascistization.[10] One experience with an extreme turn to the right was enough for both of them. Freundlich persuaded Anders to give up his position as lecturer at the New School for Social Research and leave America behind for good.[11] Her parents, despite their own deep attachments to New York City, followed them. They departed New York on the *Queen Mary* in April 1950. Following stops in Paris and Zürich, the former being especially poignant for Anders, they reached Vienna in May.[12] His first journal entries on arriving measured his immediate emotional reactions against the expectations he had harbored. Setting foot on Austrian soil was not exactly the homecoming he had envisioned for 17 years. Anders, retaining though a sense of humor, observed laconically of his "return," how "incapable of separating myself right away from the familiarity of being foreign (*Fremdseins*), from the habit of the years-long exile life," having "come back to a country in which I have never lived before."[13] If he had desperately wanted to write in German and for a Germanophone readership, he now contended each day with an unfamiliar Viennese dialect.[14] His journey back to the Old World would indeed be one of perpetual and, at least in its early stages, usually unpleasant, discovery.

---

9. Elisabeth Freundlich, *The Traveling Years*, trans. Elizabeth Pennebaker (Riverside, California: Ariadne Press, 1999), 97.
10. See ibid., 98.
11. Elisabeth Young-Bruehl, *Hannah Arendt: For Love of the World*, 2nd Edition (New Haven: Yale University Press, 2004), 250. A sign of Anders' continuing good relations with Hannah Arendt, the lectureship was taken over by Arendt's second husband, Heinrich Blücher.
12. *TG*, 95-106. Among the many sights that moved Anders so much upon his trip to Paris was a stop at the shop where he had last spoken to Walter Benjamin in 1936. For this, see ibid., 100. Freundlich indicated that their journey to Vienna also included stops in Frankfurt and Munich. Freundlich's parents did not return to Vienna, however. Instead, they took up in residence in Zurich. Freundlich, *Traveling Years*, 98.
13. *TG*, 107.
14. Ibid., 108.

In their first few years in Vienna, Anders and Freundlich tried a number of locations before establishing themselves in the city's fourth district in late 1952 or early 1953. He lived there for most of the decade, even after his separation from Freundlich in 1955. During this phase of (re)settlement, first with Freundlich, then with his third wife, the American-Jewish musician Charlotte Zelka, Anders finally won recognition as an independent writer and philosophical thinker. For much of his first decade in Vienna, Anders continued to be, as Margret Lohmann has described him, a "boundary-crosser (*Grenzgänger*)."[15] Until the late 1950s, Anders still pursued an amazing diversity of interests—i.e. literary and film criticism, fiction and poetry writing. Anders was quickly dismayed, however, by the paltry number of publishing outlets available in the Austrian capital. He regularly complained in his correspondence of the moribund state of cultural life in Vienna. In one instance, he described it to Karl Löwith as a "city without philosophy, publishing houses, and journals," and "intellectually, everything other than satisfying."[16] Anders complained to Helmuth Plessner that "here in Vienna" the "university leads a life of an oyster hermetically sealed against the outside world, which can only be induced to open its shell through the incantations of the political parties."[17] Until at least 1957, Anders considered moving again, even after he acquired Austrian citizenship in 1951.

Consequently, he found new fora for his voluminous writings in the Federal Republic of Germany and inquired about teaching opportunities there as well. With the release of his controversial *Kafka—Pro und Contra* in 1951, he began a forty-year partnership with the Munich publisher C.H. Beck.[18] He contributed regularly, from 1952 on, to *Merkur*, the new self-styled "German journal for European thought." The publication of *The Obsolescence of the Human Being* in 1956 earned him plaudits as a major critical voice in debates about the impact of modern technology and ushered in a remarkable period of involvement with European, American, and Japanese peace politics. The success of these books lifted him out of anonymity. Soon thereafter, the release of his correspondence with Claude Eatherly, the American pilot who had given the "go-ahead" signal to the *Enola-Gay* to drop the atom bomb on Hiroshima, reinforced his growing reputation as a thinker who not only wrote but "acted" as well. After declining in 1957 an offer for a teaching position at the Free University in

15. Margret Lohmann, *Philosophieren in der Endzeit*, 14.
16. Günther Anders to Karl Löwith, January 26, 1952, Österreichisches Literaturarchiv der Österreichischen Nationalbibliothek, Vienna, Nachlass Günther Anders 237/04, hereafter ÖLA-ÖNB, NGA 237/04. The original German is far better—"in der Stadt der Philosophie-, verlags- und Zeitschriftenlosigkeit."
17. Günther Anders to Helmut Plessner, April 16, 1953, ÖLA-ÖNB, NGA 237/04. .
18. *Kafka—Pro und Contra: Die Prozess-Unterlagen* (Munich: Verlag C.H. Beck, 1951).

West Berlin, he fully embraced the subjectivity of the "committed" writer as outsider, of, quite literally, being *anders* ("different").[19]

Conditions in Austria both contributed to Anders' identification with the figure of the outsider and were the focus of one of his first post-exile writing projects. For years, Austrians largely ignored Anders' books. Overwhelmingly, his new acclaim was a German (and later international) phenomenon. As he described it to an interviewer in 1979, after thirty years in the country, "I have not earned a single penny" in Austria and "my existence here is totally unknown."[20] As a result, Anders came to view his new home in the city of Vienna merely as a base of operations for writing and speaking engagements elsewhere not as a source of support and inspiration.[21] Keeping the apartment in Vienna was purely utilitarian for him. In a response to Herbert Marcuse, he bluntly dubbed it "the local village (*das hiesige Dorf*), which I use simply as 'headquarters' without making the slightest use of the local 'cultural life.'"[22] Despite his unflaterring opinions of Vienna, he never, despite entreaties, relocated. Gradually, he reached a sort of *modus vivendi* with his anonymity there, a situation which has since changed radically.[23] Undoubtedly, once Anders funneled his energies into anti-nuclear praxis, the Second Republic's official neutrality also made the country more palatable. He also found political developments in the Federal Republic of Germany, especially the threat of a neo-Nazism, far more menacing than Austria's brand of reaction.

Austria's quite troubled relation to its Nazi past was one of the first subjects that Anders analyzed upon his return to Europe. His deep disappointment about how Nazism had been vanquished and his trepidation about what would succeed it received frightening confirmation in the Austrian context. Soon after his arrival in Vienna, Anders investigated whether Austrians had moved forward out of the shadow of catastrophic warfare and genocide by confronting their enthusiasm for Hitler, support for the National Socialist regime's criminal war, and their own anti-Semitism. Through a detailed set of philosophical journals, Anders charted how Austrians were doing the exact opposite.

---

19. Anders discusses his decision to refuse this offer in his 13 Oct. 1990 interview with Konrad Paul Liessmann, contained in Liessmann, *Günther Anders zur Einführung*, 2nd Edition (Hamburg: Junius, 1993), 162.

20. See his 1979 interview with Mathias Greffrath, "Wenn ich verzweifelt bin, was geht's mich an?," in *Günther Anders antwortet: Interviews & Erklärungen*, ed. Elke Schubert (Berlin: Edition Tiamat, 1987), 41.

21. The troubled relationship between Anders and Vienna was already thematized by Ursula Pastwerk in her foreword to Liessmann, ed., *Günther Anders kontrovers*, 13-14.

22. Günther Anders to Herbert Marcuse, January 27, 1967, ÖLA-ÖNB, NGA 237/04.

23. In 1979, Anders was awarded the Austrian State Prize for Cultural Writing. Thanks largely to the efforts of Konrad Paul Liessmann, Dirk Röpcke, and Raimund Bahr, Vienna has become, in the last two decades, the focal point for critical discussion, inside and outside the academy, on Anders and his legacy.

The Critical Ethnographer

Günther Anders was an unacknowledged chronicler and interpreter of the Austrian Fifties, especially the early years of the Cold War until the 1955 State Treaty. Upon his arrival in the country, he immediately joined in a discursive struggle over the lessons to be drawn from the Third Reich. Anders' extraordinary writings from this period have yet to be integrated into scholarly accounts of the history of Austrian *Vergangenheitsbewältigung*.[24] In this section, I attempt to at least partially correct this oversight through a focus on Anders' trenchant observations on the lived experience of past persecution, guilt, and privation, and present dynamics of selective remembrance and collective forgetting in the Second Republic.[25] Just half a decade after the war's end, he documented, as an outsider, exculpatory forms of narrativization operating in Vienna.

Anders and Freundlich moved to a city whose inhabitants regarded them and other rémigrés with suspicion. Still divided in 1950 between American, British, French, and Soviet zones, Vienna had not yet recovered from the bombing, streetfighting, and mass rape that marked the city's fall to the Red Army in April 1945. Surprisingly, Anders and Freundlich's status as outsiders did not prevent many Viennese from confiding in them their anecdotes and opinions. He recorded his early impressions of Vienna in his journals between May 1950 and July 1951, but only published them in their entirety in 1967 and, then again, in 1985. Far more extensive and philosophically ambitious than Freundlich's memoir, they, too, reflected on everyday encounters and conversations with an outsider's perspective.[26]

---

24. A similar complaint was made recently by Raimund Bahr in his "Annäherungen an die Biographie: Günther Anders im Blick," in *Zugänge: Günther Anders: Leben und Werk*, ed. Raimund Bahr (Vienna: Edition Art & Science, 2007), 81. Subsequently, Bahr analyzed this period of Anders' life in his *Günther Anders*, 231-51. Although my treatment of Anders here goes into much greater detail about his journals than does Bahr, his approach is comparable. He also provides a great deal of interesting biographical detail about Freundlich. For some earlier attempts to integrate Anders' writings on the topic, see Hans-Martin Lohmann, *Geisterfahrer: Blanqui, Marx, Adorno & Co.: 22 Portraits der europäischen Linken* (Hamburg: Sammlung Junius, 1989), 110-12; Schubert, *Günther Anders*, 60-68.

25. Unfortunately, I can only deal briefly here with Freundlich's memoir. I plan to write a longer piece on her place in these Austrian debates in the future.

26. Her marriage to Anders disintegrated shortly thereafter. They separated and divorced in 1955. After their split, Freundlich continued to write fiction. She participated with Anders in the Symposium on Research on Austrian Exile Literature in June 1975, an event which earned them both long-overdue attention in Austria. They reconciled and Anders drew close to her again when his third marriage ended that same year. He praised her "very important book on the devastation of Stanislau," a project on the eradication of a Jewish community in Galicia. This book, *Die Ermordung einer Stadt namens Stanislau: NS-Vernichtungspolitik in Polen 1939-1945* (Vienna: Paul Zsolnay Verlag, 1986), prefigured the recent "regional turn" in Holocaust studies.

Anders' journals supplied a critical impressionistic ethnography of Viennese life in the first decade after Nazism. He acted as an ethnographer—asking questions, gathering anecdotes, making notes, and submitting his own philosophical and political commentaries. The crucial collection of entries called "Returning and Forgetting (*Wiedersehen und Vergessen*)" documents, from May 1950-July 1951, how a thinly veiled post-fascist mentality endured in Vienna. In a most insightful letter to Thomas Mann, he described his purpose in compiling these "philosophical journals." "After my return," he wrote, "I recorded right away my daily conversations with the local population, their stories and arguments, and attempted in appended commentaries to depict the moral condition of the postwar and post-Hitler soul and to more closely define the spiritual vacuum (as a non-entity scarcely visible to the locals)."[27] These commentaries not only recorded the still common word of praise for Nazism as well as strategies for avoiding or confronting the Nazi past, but also attempted to account for them historically and psychologically. Anders' journals critically examined subjectivities "on the ground" in Vienna as the victim myth solidified into an official state ideology.

In these entries, Anders never named his conversation partners, preferring to give only initials and brief biographical details. The exchanges in "Returning and Forgetting" took place across and outside the city, though several, interestingly, happened in the western area of Hietzing, known for the Habsburg summer palace of Schönbrunn and its many luxurious homes. Most of the entries involved him probing the opinions, anecdotes, memories and mannerisms of others. More generally, they typified the mode of philosophical-literary analysis he had adumbrated in the 1940s—the fusion of phenomenological attention to quotidian comments, memories, gestures, silences, objects, and spaces with sharp but terse critical analysis of the bigger pathologies these micro-phenomena revealed. Philosophically subtle, stylistically beautiful, and packed with haunting stories, "Returning and Forgetting" was among the very best works Anders authored in his long career. As an avowedly political collection, he designed the journals to be an obstruction to the suppression of Austria's place in the history of the Third Reich. "Every moment," Anders wrote, "one is in danger of forgetting it, and not even for an instant may one forget it (*Jeden Augenblick ist man in Gefahr, es zu vergessen, und keinen Augenblick lang darf man es vergessen*)."[28] The "it" in this passage did not substitute for a specific event but, instead, for

27. Günther Anders to Thomas Mann, 23 Sept. 1952, ÖLA-ÖNB, NGA 237/04.
28. *TG*, 160.

a period he titled simply "the critical years."[29] In the Austrian context, this meant the temporal rupture of 1938-45.

The confrontation, avoidance or denial of this rupture manifested itself in very different ways that Anders mapped. First, he described the "normal" habitus of the émigré—where the blackest hatred for the Nazi dictatorship instilled fortitude. In the journals, he analyzed what happened to this rancor in the postwar period. Anders spoke about how twenty years before (1930), he and so many of his contemporaries would have refused to hate. Falling prey to hatefulness would have been perceived as combating a situation with the heart instead of thinking (*Einsichten*) or insight.[30] "And the single thing that we would have allowed ourselves to hate," he added, "was the thought of hating something with one's entire soul and entire heart."[31] The catastrophes of 1933 and 1938 had upended such noble sentiments. Loathing for the Brown Revolution became a means of sustenance. Out of fear that people would not face the ugly necessity of such hate, Anders utilized words such as "task," "single nourishment," "sole strength," and "the single fire which kept us active," to hammer the point home.[32] These statements concur with the de-romanticized image of the emigrant he sketched in other writings.[33]

Among this group of exiles, in Anders' telling, were an especially hardened minority who steadfastly clung to the old, undiluted animus and its objects. With a kind of religious fervor, "they could not live without their daily horrors of the already long dead Hitlers and Himmlers."[34] Anders did not leave out how troubling he and others found these individuals, yet he concluded that their recalcitrance may have rested on rational foundations. These "true believers" in their hatefulness cautioned "that tomorrow the same thing could happen? Who forgets yesterday, forgets tomorrow."[35] The failure to break with the Nazi past would be ominously evident in the young Austrian republic and, consequently, the devotion of the "true believers" all the more legitimate.

He pointed out how the hatred of the exiles like himself, nurtured for at least a dozen years, crashed into the radically different emotional

29. Ibid.
30. Ibid, 112-113.
31. Ibid, 113.
32. Ibid.
33. See, for example, "Der Emigrant," *Merkur* 16, no. 7 (July 1962): 601-622. The essay is also reproduced in *TG* under the title, "Post festum," 64-93.
34. *TG*, 114.
35. Ibid., 114-115.

imaginary of "those who had stayed behind (*die Zurückgebliebenen*)."[36] The chasm between the returning exiles and the Austrian population could not have been wider. The émigrés, he contended, would not relinquish their fixation on the primordial year—1933.[37] For those who stayed behind, the primal catastrophe for the exiles had been "buried under the fullness and under the ruins of wider events: the pseudo-blooming (*Scheinblüte*) of the Third Reich, of war, of victory, of defeat, of invasion, of collapse."[38] The privation of the immediate postwar period, which he did not emphasize, could also be appended to this claim. If one accepts Anders' descriptions, the two groups, quite asymmetrical in numbers, inhabited fundamentally different cognitive worlds with distinct temporal frames of reference. For him, these worlds could not and should not have been reconciled. However, in his new role of the returning exile as social dissident, Anders labored to record, understand, and explain the perspectives of "those who stayed behind" on the "critical years."

The enmity and suspicion between the exiles and Vienna's population that Anders experienced and recorded was tremendously complicated by a crucial third group: Austrian Jews who had lived through the Nazi period in Austria in hiding (the so-called "U-boats"), and the survivors from concentration or extermination camps, Jew and Gentile, who had made their way home. In several places in his journals, Anders detailed their reestablished presence in the Austrian capital and some of their heartrending stories. He also paid tribute to those Jews who did not survive, and what the eradication of the city's once remarkable Jewish community meant for a politics of memory.

What these three groups (the exiles, the survivors, and those who remained) held in common was a shared urban space, the rebuilding city of Vienna. The new Vienna Anders portrayed was a mournful replica of the cosmopolitan city it had once been. Since the war's end, the Viennese had sunken into a unique provincialism all their own. Anders noted how insulated from global problems the Viennese appeared to be. Trips through local bookstores and cafes produced no German journals or books. It was, he wrote, as if Metternich's sentinels still sealed the country's borders from dangerous print materials.[39]

Yet something "much bleaker than provincialism" marred Vienna's postwar character.[40] He reminded his readers that the inhabitants of a province always know whose province it is and where its center of gravity is. The self-enclosed state of Viennese life did not fit this model.

36. Ibid., 115.
37. Ibid.
38. Ibid.
39. Ibid., 119.
40. Ibid., 126.

Alternatively, he suggested, "an answer is then only possible if one expands the meaning of the word 'province.' Vienna is namely a province in a purely historical sense: *province of its own splendid, far-distant past* (*Provinz seiner eigenen, glaenzenden, weitentfernten Vergangenheit*)."[41] The city's unique provincialism could be captured then under the slogan—"*Vienna wants under no circumstances to remain back behind Vienna.*"[42] The very streets of Vienna, Anders added, seemed to become "museum pieces" as well.[43] There was nothing accidental, though, about the emergence of this self-provincialization. For Anders, this "splendid, far-distant past" became a refuge for a citizenry in flight from a horrendous, recent past.

He detected this retreat in the quotidian language of greetings and titles. The intemperate politeness of the Viennese amazed him. In his own case, he pointed to how often the appellation "Herr Doktor" was granted him by people who knew nothing of his academic past. Such courtesy could not be accepted as a remnant from the Habsburg past, as one person claimed.[44] Its "prerequisites" like the "feudal lord-serf relation and the pyramid rising over the ranks of the officials and the nobility to the palace no longer exist. The K. and K. world finally collapsed more than thirty years ago."[45] Anders understood that the Austrian Social Democrats and then the Nazis had intervened, with varying degrees of success, in the sphere of interpersonal conduct. Factoring in, too, the devastating experiences of the war, he asked why the tenacity of this politeness. Anders contended that fear and suspicion were its covert motivations. His conclusions, then, took a surprising twist, however.

Anders did not believe the pleasantries he experienced any longer masked anxiety about the recent past. On the contrary, they indicated fear about the future, the future of a country that was now powerless. "One can never know. Never know," he wrote, "what tomorrow will be like. Who will be master tomorrow."[46] Thus, the uncertainty about tomorrow induced the Viennese to practice a realistic caution with regard to strangers. For a populace that simply wanted to be left in peace, extremely courteous behavior could be an alibi if a new turn in the nation's political course occurred. This also meant, Anders thought, maintaining a distance from the dangerous world of politics. "One is unpolitical in order to demonstrate tomorrow that

41. Ibid., 127. Italics in the original.
42. Ibid. Italics in the original. In Anders' view, Vienna, in fact, could not, at the time, compare, culturally, to many small cities or states.
43. Ibid., 131.
44. Ibid., 168.
45. Ibid.
46. Ibid., 169.

one has been unpolitical yesterday. *The rebirth of politeness from the spirit of mistrust.*"[47] Perhaps correcting his own first inclination to view the formal friendliness as only futural, he ended this entry from November 1950 with the observation that the holdovers from the k and k period covered over the now most unpleasant "reality of the Hitler intermezzo."[48]

One of the vital tasks Anders undertook in the journals was to transcribe the unsaid. What was not expressed frequently counted as much if not more than the spoken word. Anders recorded how, after months in Vienna, he never heard Hitler's name spoken.[49] He considered this silence, especially among younger Austrians subjected for seven years to the cult of personality surrounding Hitler, to be menacing. Anders wondered if the reluctance to utter the name in public actually meant that the dictator had become an object of private reverence. He worried, too, as did many of his contemporaries on the Left, "whether the time of quiet is not a threatening period of latency (*eine bedrohliche Latenzzeit*), in which he [Hitler] ripens into a perhaps depoliticized prestige of a savior."[50] Anders legitimately feared the inception of a new Hitler myth within the Austrian populace and he suspected that its first manifestation might be a taboo on voicing the dead *Führer's* appellation.[51]

In many of the entries, though, Anders gathered the stories of others. Several of his oral histories detail incredible, post-war encounters between persecuted and persecutor. With the official N., Anders witnessed an example, different from his own experience, of the bond between politeness and mistrust. During a walk with N. the official exchanged ostentatious greetings with a neighbor. Subsequently, N. claimed the man he had addressed, a Dr. R., had denounced him during the Nazi years for not flying a flag (presumably a swastika) at his home. Anders could not believe that N. would even acknowledge such a person. His disbelief was not diminished when N., in response to Anders' tough questioning, asked what good could come from behaving in a "more unchristian" way than had Dr. R.[52] Dr. R. did not hold on to this past and neither would he. Anders suspected that the real reasons motivating N.'s reticence were his anxiety about spoiling currently smooth relations with people with whom he had a past grievance and, second, that he "probably more or less clearly recognizes his omission as guilt."[53]

47. Ibid. Italics in the original.
48. Ibid.
49. Ibid., 179.
50. Ibid.
51. Ibid.
52. Ibid., 146.
53. Ibid., 146-47.

Anders marveled as well at the case of M. M was an actor who had been sentenced to a concentration camp after being denounced for unspecified activities. In the early postwar period, he resumed his old job. For four years, M told Anders, he had worked alongside two of those men who had denounced him. When relating this, he spoke of his situation only in positive terms. Things were fine with him. "Such steadiness," Anders wrote, "would require a *double life*; and a double life one may expect from a very few."[54] Consequently, he concluded that "*only virtuosos of abstraction*" could live with the same detachment as had M. They displayed their virtuosity in how decently they treated their accusers, while inwardly, abstracting from their behavior, they condemned them as "rotten people" or "murderers" for their vile deeds.[55]

The most unforgettable example of the juxtaposition of former enemies Anders discovered was his "After All, I Was Only Seventeen," a brief excerpt from these journals published by *Commentary*.[56] In this piece, Anders transmitted a story told to him by an Austrian-Jewish architect L., whose family had been murdered at Auschwitz. Himself an inmate in unnamed camps, he had returned to Vienna in 1948. L.'s account dealt with one of his employees, a twenty-nine year old draftsman named Huber, who had worked for him for two years. Huber wanted to leave Austria for more promising work in Australia, but was not granted an exit visa. Huber then sought L.'s advice on what to do next. As L. discovered, Huber had served in the SA in the late 1930s, had, along with his comrades, "cleaned out a Jewish house," and later saw combat with Rommel's Afrika Korps at the Battle of Tobruk.[57] L. conveyed to Anders his horror upon learning Huber's past.

> "A clever type, very useful, skillful draftsman, a big hulk of a man, bony, with the face of a theological student from the country. He dragged his left foot a little. Even that had given

54. Ibid., 187. Italics in the original.
55. Ibid. Italics in the original.
56. "After All, I Was Only Seventeen: A Story," trans. Francis Golffing, *Commentary* XIV (September 1952): 254-58. The German original can be found in *TG*, 150-60. The English translation omits, for reasons I have not been able to ascertain, Anders' brief commentary on L.'s story. It can be found on pp. 159-60 of *TG* and my explication of the story includes this commentary.
57. "After All, I Was Only Seventeen," 254-55. Most likely, Huber meant the Battle of Tobruk that occurred in eastern Libya in April 1941, where British, Australian, Polish, and Czechoslovak troops successfully held Tobruk against what was, actually, a series of attacks by German and Italian forces.

> me confidence in him, I don't know exactly why. All in all, I found him a sympathetic character; every once in a while we joked with each other. And now all of a sudden he was one of *them*. And had been all along."[58]

In the course of the story, the reader learns that Huber had been tried for his activities in the SA by an Austrian People's Court and spent a short period in prison. Due to this prison sentence, he had been denied the exit visa. The revelations led to an extraordinary exchange between the two men. At first, L. questioned whether Huber knew that his boss was a Jew and squarely blamed him for the agony he went through. The draftsman answered yes to the question and was incredulous about the accusation.[59] L. spoke as well of his sisters, who had been murdered at Auschwitz. He told Huber, "You people expect to be treated as though nothing had happened, because the wrong is irreparable anyhow."[60] Huber ascribed his Nazism to youthful ignorance. "But, Herr Doktor," he told L., "after all I was only seventeen!"[61] Huber's old self, the stormtrooper, had supposedly ceased to exist, at least until he met with a former superior in the SA.

The meeting came about due to Huber's request for an exit visa. As L. relayed it to Anders, Huber audaciously described this encounter with a man who had recruited him to be a stormtrooper and who had given him orders. This "old comrade," now a civil servant "side-whiskered like old Franz Joseph," pretended he did not know him. After being subjected to a formal series of questions, Huber was dismissed by his one-time commander upon seeing information about his appearance before the People's Court. Shockingly, Huber seemed to have expected sympathy from L. When he did not get it, he spoke sarcastically to L. of "you people" who allowed the SA officer to hold such a position. L. interpreted "you people" as meaning "all of us who had fought against Hitler and beaten him, and now have let the victory slip through our fingers."[62] In its abbreviated English rendering, the story ended with L. conversing with Anders over the moral ambiguities of the situation. What should one do with the cases of people like Huber?

Prompted by his own question, the architect arrived at a nuanced characterization of lower-level Nazis of the Huber variety:

---

58. Ibid., 254. The story relates how the dragging of the foot was the result of a wound Huber suffered at Tobruk.
59. Ibid., 255.
60. Ibid., 256.
61. Ibid., 255.
62. Ibid., 257.

> "Simply an ordinary man, caught in the crush of history, who wasn't over-fastidious in his choice of means when it was a question of survival. Seeking advice from a Jew wasn't a sign of turpitude, but simply a lack of moral sensitivity. His outbursts, though they might look suspicious, were genuine, I think. Mediocrity does not protect you from despair, and it's no proof of dishonesty either. After all, Huber had every reason to feel desperate. And the question whether a man of thirty should be held accountable for what he committed at the age of seventeen—under duress, besides—remains a valid question, no matter what moral stuff the 'victim' is made of."[63]

The German version, however, does not indicate that L. made this characterization. Rather, it appears that these were actually Anders' conclusions about the Huber case. The English translation also omits Anders' final remarks to the story:

> "Of course Huber's question is not answered. Just as little the moral question of the one who has returned, with which the 'scene' closes. What I wrote down is mere recording (*Mitschrift*). But the recording itself seems important to me, because already tomorrow or the day after tomorrow the huge absurdities, which have resulted from the local situation, will be forgotten or denied."[64]

This striking story that Anders transcribed encapsulates several of his philosophical-political concerns after 1950. How should an individual deal with former Nazis when they had already been permitted by the society to resume normal lives? Should low-ranking, former NSDAP members like Huber be forgiven for their role in despicable, if not criminal, actions when they were very young? Did Huber's mediocrity, his averageness, require less severe moral condemnation even if he did not seem to be particularly contrite? What responsibility did one have to the victims of National Socialism, such as L.? What course of action could an anti-fascist take in the midst of the early Cold War, when the goals of purging fascists from social and political life had generally been abandoned?

Equally prominent among the "huge absurdities" Anders confronted was the distorting role of the Allied bombing in Viennese collective memory. Here, he entered a sphere of remembrance often dominated in Central Europe by right-wing apologetics (e.g. the repeated targeting of

63. Ibid., 258.
64. *TG*, 160.

German and Austrian civilians by British and American planes equaled, if not surpassed, anything comparable carried about by the Luftwaffe; that Germans and Austrians were victims just like Jews, Poles, Russians, etc.).[65] In one of the more impressive moments of empathy in the journals, Anders sincerely tried to comprehend the experiences and mindset of those who had endured the air attacks. He realized that, in the Austrian and German contexts, the rage, helplessness, deprivation, and dying which adults and children underwent during saturation bombing would feed directly and powerfully into national myths of victimization. Combined with memories of the Allied occupation and then subsequent reconstruction of the ruined cities (still not complete when Anders wrote), a counter-narrative to that put forward in trials and exposes of Nazi war criminals could be constructed around the trauma of aerial devastation, a counter-narrative based on very real suffering.

Anders was among the first to anticipate how the *Luftkrieg* could and did divert anger away from "the truly guilty," "Hitler and his circle."[66] Though he never, as far as I can tell, sanctioned the area-bombing strategies employed by the Royal Air Force and U.S. Army Air Force against the Third Reich, he concerned himself with demonstrating that the essential, quite human, aspects of this area of Austrian wartime memory bolstered a pernicious variant of forgetting of Nazism's victims. Moreover, he thought that a critical evaluation of the recollections of these raids might help explain why the Hitler dictatorship was not overthrown from within. In this section of the text, Anders grounded his remarks on the experience of bombing in a philosophical anthropology of the merely human, the "human, all too human," to use a familiar phrase. Anders had theorized the limits of humanity for many years already. The contact with Viennese who survived the bombing raids pushed him to reconsider more fully the political and moral consequences of these limitations in light of a type of terror that he and the exiles (or, at least, most of them) never passed through.

---

65. In the last ten years, there has been massive public interest in Germany in the air war and the suffering of German civilians. Works by W.G. Sebald and Jörg Friedrich contributed to the renewed fascination with Allied bombing. For Sebald, see his *Luftkrieg und Literatur* (Frankfurt am Main: S. Fischer, 2001). Friedrich's most important contribution to this discussion was *Der Brand: Deutschland im Bombenkrieg 1940-1945* (Munich: Propyläen, 2002). These books have also meant that this subject is no longer solely the terrain of the German Right. See the analyses by Lothar Kettenacker, ed., *Ein Volk von Opfern? Die neue Debatte über den Bombenkrieg, 1940-1945* (Berlin: Rowohlt, 2003); Mary Nolan, "Air Wars, Memory Wars," *Central European History* 38, no.1 (2005): 7-40; Gilad Margalit, *Guilt, Memory, and Suffering: Germany Remembers its Dead of World War II*, trans. Haim Watzman (Cambridge, Mass.: Harvard University Press, 2010).

66. *TG*, 117.

The basic anthropological supposition in Anders' examination of the Austrian victims of the Allied air war involved a claim about the moral insufficiency of "mere knowing." Why had civilians in Vienna or in German towns targeted by British, American or Soviet warplanes not reacted to the raids with contempt for and perhaps real opposition to the dictatorship which had instigated the conflict? This question stood behind all of his commentary. First, in answering this question, he asserted that the bombings produced a type of solidarity. Since the "bombs threatened and annihilated *all* without distinction of person, the 'good' and the 'bad,'" a community of suffering resulted where the "internal boundary between the humane and the infamous (*Binnengrenze zwischen Humanen und Infamen*)" was eviscerated.[67] Did any among the Viennese have the "inhuman and supernatural power of moral abstraction (*unmenschliche und übernatürliche moralische Abstraktionskraft*)" to hail the pilots as comrades? Anders realized he had come close to asking the impossible of them. "Those who could do it," he noted, "deserve, in any case, the greatest admiration. Those who could not were *only human*."[68]

An average person seeking shelter from an air attack, Anders thought, focused solely on those who immediately endangered them and their families. They would seldom follow the chain of responsibility for the air war up to the policies of their own leaders. They could not divide their rage between two totally different objects.[69] In one of his most perceptive moments, Anders presented a succinct epistemology of the bombing victim.

> "Possible, that this one and that one in burning Berlin, Dresden or Cologne yet knew *why* the bombs fell, and *who* had originally provoked them; but, of course how ineffective and how unreal such mere knowing (*blosses Wissen*) remained. The heart knows instead only the immediate, never the cause which remains back far behind in the past. *Causality is foreign to the heart.* Thus it happened that the criminals were forgotten, to some extent buried under the terrible consequences of their crimes."[70]

That men and women loathed their attackers and lost sight of the real criminals was to be expected then, was "only human" for Anders. The hatred, the "true hate," the "hate against the *cause* and against the *guilty*," mustered

67. Ibid., 116.
68. Ibid., 116-117. Italics added.
69. Ibid., 117.
70. Ibid. Italics in the original.

by the exiles, Anders thought, looked, in comparison, "almost a luxury."[71] Nevertheless, his entries on the air war and victimization unmistakably indicate the limits of his empathy. The merely human in this context was to be rigorously criticized and transcended. As I will show in the final part of this section, he entrusted to exiles, like himself, with their deeper mode of knowing, the task of challenging the suppression of the Nazi leadership's guilt.

Subsequently, this relatively abstract analysis of the psychological impact of the bombing became much more concrete. Anders related the case of a landlady and her son in the city center, who discussed the air assaults on Vienna with him. He told her how Warsaw, London and Rotterdam, not to mention German cities, had suffered far worse damage from air raids than Vienna. The landlady's facial expressions, he claimed, radiated shock that these foreign locales would even be brought up.[72] Her son acknowledged the devastation of the Polish and British capitals and the Dutch port-city, but he astonished Anders with his reply. He merely gestured through a window to a destroyed building nearby, without explaining the meaning of the gesture. Anders understood it all too well: the air assaults on these cities were revenge actions for the damage done to Vienna![73] Anders realized that for the young man, the "local ruins stand so absolutely in the foreground, they are so primary, that they have become a *temporal primum*; if Warsaw or London are devastated, it is because *they* knocked down our homes."[74] Essentially, for this kind of thinking, the Luftwaffe had justly retaliated because of the damage done to Vienna. The bewildering reversal of "earlier" and "later" he heard was guided by the principle of "*Proximum; ergo primum est*" (nearest, therefore first).[75] This extreme example of perverse recollection, even worse than the "selective remembering" researched so thoroughly by Robert Moeller, betrayed an absolute refusal to concede the Nazi regime's responsibility for the war and its crimes against civilians, or sympathize with human beings who had experienced similar tribulations.[76]

According to Anders' description of the encounter, the landlady's son (who obviously made a lasting impression on him) unconsciously adhered to a skewed chronology of the war which permitted him to judge the

71. Ibid. Italics in the original.
72. Ibid., 135.
73. Ibid.
74. Ibid, 135-36.
75. Ibid., 136
76. Robert Moeller coined this phrase as an alternative to the notion of collective amnesia in his *War Stories: The Search for a Usable Past in the Federal Republic of Germany* (Berkeley: University of California Press, 2001).

inhabitants of Warsaw, Rotterdam, and London as having gotten just what they deserved. Although he acknowledged that the young man's "inversion" was "*no conscious trick*," Anders maintained that the son was "sly enough to know where it is advantageous not to know; and cautious enough to be able to decide where it pays to remain 'unconscious.'"[77] In the conclusion to this entry from August 1950, he explained why he did not regard the mother and son as marginal figures. The palpable, if frightening, absurdity of this case was symptomatic of a general outlook on the war and typified the response to a whole set of burning political questions such as the problem of collective guilt. Austrians appealed constantly to their very real privation as a means of total exoneration. Thus, Anders noted, the invariable response to any discussion of war, war crimes, and responsibility was the "reference to one's own misery; as if the crimes which not only preceded this misery temporally, but also have finally produced it, are explained and excused by this."[78]

Just as historians would do later, Anders posed questions about the limits of compliance with the Nazi worldview and the possibilities for opposition. He revisited his earlier question—whether there had been any Viennese who welcomed, in spite of all the suffering they unleashed, the bombing raids and the sounds of Soviet artillery drawing closer. He speculated whether some were "objective enough" to celebrate the attacks as portending the Nazi regime's downfall.[79] Such progressive defeatism he found in two women, the first a pediatrician, the second a housewife. Both had lost loved ones in the war and held no love for the dictatorship that waged it. The two women admitted to Anders that they struggled to contain their excitement about the falling bombs. One of them, a Frau B., conducted "inspection tours" of the results of the raids with her husband.[80] This showed that cases of fervent, yet private, opposition existed under National Socialism, yet he knew they were exceptional and marginal.

Anders' important reflections on the bombing of German and Austrian cities should be read against his later theory of technology. In his writings after *The Obsolescence of the Human Being*, pilots, especially Claude Eatherly, who gave the "go-ahead" signal to the *Enola-Gay* to drop the atom bomb on Hiroshima and suffered serious psychological difficulties because of his role in the attack, personified the dilemmas of "mere knowing," guilt,

77. *TG*, 136. Italics in the original. Afraid of misunderstanding, Anders also assured his readers that the use of the psychoanalytic vocabulary of the "unconscious" in no way was intended to exonerate the young man.

78. Ibid.

79. Ibid., 186.

80. Ibid. Anders made clear in this entry that "inspection tours" were "*her* words."

and responsibility in the Atomic Age.[81] The American, British, and Soviet men flying the aircraft across Central European skies did not seem to pose, however, a pressing ethical problem for Anders in "Returning and Forgetting." Whether because they carried out their missions in the pre-atomic era or perhaps from concern that he would sound like the reactionaries in West Germany and Austria who dominated discussion of the bombing, he devoted no time there to the moral status of the Allied pilots.

Finally, Anders' journals present extensive and grim accounts of widespread anti-Semitism in 1950s Vienna, an urban center where Jewish life existed largely as a memory. He confided to Hannah Arendt how the "Jewlessness of the world here is hardly bearable. But I try to make virtues of necessities, and, not entirely in vain."[82] The existence of such virulent racism in a situation where there were so few actual Jews will not come as a shock for historians, but its depth and malleability, as indicated in these stories, still mortify. He tired of hearing the remarks of locals about Jews who had been deprived of their property without ever acknowledging the persecution, forced emigration, and eventual annihilation of much of the country's Jewish population after the *Anschluss*.[83] Right after his arrival in Vienna, Anders and Freundlich stayed in an apartment that, he later discovered, had been "Aryanized."[84] Afterwards, he attempted to capture the plight of Jews seeking to reacquire apartments or houses that had been confiscated by the Nazis. Most memorably, they were portrayed in "Returning and Forgetting" as unwelcome, ghostly presences.[85] Just how unwelcome they were comes through in Anders' reporting on the "compensation sums (*Entschädigungssummen*)" local authorities compelled Jewish rémigrés to pay before expropriated possessions were turned back over to their original owners.[86] A wild miscarriage of justice, these payments compensated the people who benefited from Aryanization for the renovations to the property they had made since its seizure. In effect, Anders exposed how the Austrian legal system penalized the Jewish *Rückkehrer* for having survived.

81. Anders corresponded extensively with Eatherly and regarded him as a representative figure of the era. Their correspondence is available as *Burning Conscience: The Case of the Hiroshima Pilot, Claude Eatherly, Told in Letters to Günther Anders* (New York: Monthly Review Press, 1962).

82. Günther Anders to Hannah Arendt, 20 Feb. 1956, Correspondence File, 1938-1976, Hannah Arendt Papers, Manuscript Division, Library of Congress, Washington, D.C..

83. This distinction in German is difficult to render in English—"1938 *beraubte* Juden erwähnt man mir wiederholt; *geraubte* Juden kaum je." *TG*, 111.

84. Ibid., 107-108.

85. Ibid., 148.

86. Ibid.

In numerous cases, however, the claims for restitution were flatly denied. Anders wrote about those instances where the second occupier refused to vacate the property. Asserting his property rights, he often would mobilize his friends and neighbors to back him. Anders spoke of a "flame of indignation" that ignited whenever Jews submitted the claims.[87] The old Austrian anti-Semitism lived again, expressed popularly in the organizing against the nullification of "Aryanization" measures. "Many," he noted, "greet with enthusiasm the occasion to allow free rein to his anti-Semitic impulses, dormant for years, in an entirely official function."[88] If any of the returning Jews had wished to placate the Viennese by abandoning their wishes for some form of compensation, they could not possibly succeed, no matter their course of action. Anders summarized their situation: "Whatever the returning person (*Rückkehrer*) does, is false. Who does *not* report his claims comes across as suspicious: either as cowardly; or as one whose case is fishy; or, since he places so little value on his property, as a Communist. But who does report his claims is a thief."[89] From the standpoint of such totalizing mistrust, the expropriation of Jews appeared legitimate. The recalcitrance of Viennese anti-Semitism was captured in one especially vicious comment. "Please, Herr Doktor, hand on heart, was Hitler so absolutely wrong here?"[90] Elsewhere in the journals, Anders conceived a fitting maxim for the cruelty of this milieu: "*Who has misfortune thereby demonstrates that he deserves nothing better.*"[91] His descriptions of such bitterness toward returning Jews, those who had exited Austria before the Final Solution and those who survived the camps, impart an image of a culture where defeat and occupation had not dispelled ideas of racial exclusion.

The most powerful evidence for defiance of Nazi racial ideology he produced was the improbable tale of five Jewish women in an air-raid shelter. Anders committed this story to paper after hearing it from Frau F., a Jew married to an "Aryan." She and four other Jewish women had been employed in early 1943 in a munitions factory. During the regular bombings of Vienna which began that fall, they were denied entry into the shelter. Anders relayed how "already after a few days, the [factory] personnel declared they would refuse to go below, if the prohibition for the Jews was not lifted."[92] On the following day, the prohibition was in fact removed.

87. Ibid., 147.
88. Ibid., 148.
89. Ibid., 149.
90. Ibid.
91. Ibid., 112. Italics in the original.
92. Ibid, 170.

From this one story, Anders squeezed a great deal of importance. He argued that the support exhibited by the munitions workers for the five proved that "in the time of terror it was thus possible to protest and to set conditions without being punished; and even possible to implement conditions. And this could happen simultaneously with the systematic extermination of the Jews, in the interests of some Jewish women, with whom one even, at odds with all of the false solidarity of National Socialism, could feel solidarity."[93] This "so impressive and so admirable" case, this "shining example," of the munitions workers standing by Jewish colleagues Anders mustered as "counter-evidence" against nay-sayers that "non-compliance (*Nichtmitmachen*)" occurred during the darkest stretches of the war.[94] Frau F.'s story is indeed remarkable and most admirable, but, again, Anders' own investigations (not to mention later scholarly research) signal how exceptional such open dissent in Austria really was. Interestingly, Anders said little about Frau F.'s non-Jewish husband, a marriage which likely guaranteed her a measure of legal protection others would not hold.

The sobering rarity of such instances of defiance was underscored in Anders' investigation of the motives of many who felt bitterness towards the Third Reich. For example, of all the people he had met in Hietzing, none had been National Socialists. On the contrary, Anders observed, they had never truly adopted Nazism as their cause.[95] These men and women espoused a very traditional conservatism foreign to the mass politics of fascism. "Seen historically," he argued, "they are the last descendants of the world of Metternich."[96] By invoking the name of Prince Clemens Metternich, the Austrian arch-conservative foreign minister and architect of the counter-revolutionary Restoration after 1815, Anders recalled an era when Austria exerted tremendous influence among the European great powers. The invocation of Metternich also recalled a period of renunciation by the masses in political participation. To these latter-day Restorationists, "their first civic duty consisted of 'quiet' ('*Ruhe*'); and they saw their virtue still in steady and steadily declared non-opposition... whereby it absolutely did not matter *whom* they did not oppose."[97] Because of their attitude of non-participation, some of these individuals drew the attention of the regime. Only when faced with a persecution they could not comprehend, did they turn against the Third Reich. Hence, Anders placed a clear boundary between

93. Ibid.
94. Ibid.
95. Ibid., 172.
96. Ibid., 173.
97. Ibid. Italics in the original.

the late Metternichians and the authentic anti-fascist. What the former "emphasize is their own fundamental innocence," while, in distinction, the latter "emphasize, as well as the enemy's guilt, their own, because he has 'done' too little."[98] The "dull fury against the regime" demonstrated by those who did not embrace Nazi ideology hardly encouraged the advocates of a total purging of Nazism.[99] Their quite modest opposition arose at all only because the Nazis refused to accept their non-opposition as a sufficient sign of loyalty. An Austrian anti-fascist Left could absolutely not depend, Anders' analysis suggested, on the inheritors of Metternich's worldview.

Although his ethnography hovered very close to the ground and utilized conversations, anecdotes, and physical gestures as its material, Anders tackled the necessary issues of totality. By this, I mean issues of collective guilt, collective remorse, and collective remembrance. In these sections of "Returning and Forgetting," his tone sharpens considerably. Anders referred there to ongoing public discussions of forgiveness. He dismissed them as farcical. What lay behind these debates was the desire for amnesty not forgiveness.[100] The binary of remorse and forgiveness derived from the sphere of interpersonal ethics. It was a reciprocal action; forgiveness usually followed genuine contrition. Anders maintained that in interactions between individuals, a person could forgive the other, even when the latter did not appeal for it. Remorse was not always required.[101] "But on a collective scale," he insisted, "there is nothing of the like. No situation is more ridiculous than when one group offers forgiveness to another which disputes its own wrongdoing. Already *who* are actually the partners in such a transaction remains obscure. *Pardon in the plural is an absurdity*."[102] In one place, he admitted he had no enthusiasm for the phrase "collective guilt."[103] Elsewhere, his perspective moved closer to that very view. Collective forgiveness could only legitimately be broached when a sense of collective penitence had emerged. Therefore, "from these situations where millions have made themselves complicit through participation (*Mittun*) only two roads lead. Education or forgetting."[104] Faced with the tenacity of forgetting in Vienna, and with a political climate which enabled a selective remembering, he conceded that forgetting was a much easier, and more likely, path.[105]

98. Ibid.
99. Ibid.
100. Ibid., 162.
101. Ibid.
102. Ibid. Italics in the original.
103. Ibid., 136.
104. Ibid., 162.
105. Ibid.

For those, like Anders, who refused to forget, the language of the pardon had to be exposed as a pretext for a whitewashing of the past. He cited the coverage of the "problem of forgiveness" in a local periodical. The author, whose name went unmentioned, evidently complained of those who had not learned the meaning of Christian forgiveness. The referent could not be mistaken. The writer blamed the Jews for not embracing this most important virtue from Christianity.[106] Indignant that such vileness could still be said publicly in the Second Republic, Anders exclaimed, "one risks after the murder of six million Jews and even in the discussion of forgiveness to make the Jews again the scapegoat; this time those who accidentally survived, the accidentally not exterminated Jews."[107] A hideous reversal had taken place in the Austrian discourse on forgiving. "Not the one who struck the blows (*der Schläger*) is guilty—who presumably no longer recalls the murder—but rather the one who received the blows (*der Geschlagene*): because he cannot forget the blow, who struck it, and who received it."[108] The Jews, according to this line of reasoning, must shoulder the blame for not yielding to amnesia about the Shoah and the stages of persecution leading to it. Anders' vituperative comments on the Austrian scene anticipate the much-quoted statement that the Germans will never forgive the Jews for Auschwitz.

As the sequence of entries in "Returning and Forgetting" unfold, a deeper trepidation becomes prescient. Anders feared that the scale of the Shoah would surpass any effort, no matter how sincere, to come to terms with it. The horror of his realization grabs the reader immediately. Even those like himself, who had escaped death, struggled to understand the magnitude of the Judeocide. "I doubt," he wrote," that there is a human heart whose capacity suffices to even only 'grasp' ('*fassen*') several millions gassed. *What one cannot 'grasp,' this one cannot also forgive.*"[109] All too presciently, he "feared, for this reason, it will also be universally forgotten. Buried under its own size."[110] These remarks show Anders caught between, on the one hand, the imperative to remember and do justice to the murdered, and, on the other, the problem of the basic fragility of empathy, mourning, and imagination. The goal of a radical transformation of a once Nazified culture appeared far more difficult to obtain than he had believed. If a confrontation with the Holocaust stood at the center of an *Anderschen* politics of remembrance,

106. Ibid., 163.
107. Ibid.
108. Ibid.
109. Ibid. Italics in the original.
110. Ibid., 164.

his anthropology of the feeble human powers of comprehension always complicated any stringent demands to mourn. Needless to say, for Anders, attention to human limitations did not excuse Austrians and Germans from the strenuous labors of facing the Nazi past. Rather, he believed his philosophical reflections on the human being enabled a much more thorough confrontation with that history.

In such circumstances, Anders defended the critical properties of the émigrés' old hatefulness. The "exile heart," for all its difficulties, had much to teach.[111] Anders insisted "that our hatred, as stubborn as it might have looked, had been an act of strength, fidelity, and reason."[112] The émigrés should not cede the sphere of remembrance to the narratives of victimization circulating in the country. The qualities of desperation, revulsion, and determination which had maintained them after their expulsion by the Nazis could prove their worth to a reconstituted Left in Austria. Anders was grateful, that the hostility had not evaporated.[113] If he, at some points, despaired whether the Viennese were "really changed people," the recalcitrance of the exiles inspired him.[114] "We have to plant our passion in them," in the people of Vienna, he argued.[115] If he worried it was already too late to forge a deep-seated anti-fascist consciousness there, the sight of a little boy playing beneath his window, a child with no knowledge of Hitler, reminded him that the future was at stake.[116]

Conclusion

By parsing the recollections the Viennese foregrounded and those which they suppressed, Anders' "philosophical journals" uncovered an ideology which operated most fully at the level of ordinary life and seemed quasi-independent of direction from political parties or other elites. This ideology was composed of four central, intertwined features: 1) a desperate striving for normality which, in its most extreme moments, even induced one-time victims to renounce redress for the wrongs inflicted on them 2) the bombing and siege of Vienna as the basis for a corollary to the Moscow Declaration's gift of victimhood to the Austrians 3) pre-1938 cultural traditions as markers of national pride and simultaneous escapes from

111. Ibid., 116.
112. Ibid., 118.
113. Ibid.
114. Ibid., 193.
115. Ibid., 117-18.
116. Ibid., 118.

national shame 4) a resurgent anti-Semitism motivated less by a resentment that surviving Jews were living reminders of the brutality, expulsion, and eradication submerged under the mythology of victimhood.

What I have called Anders' "critical impressionistic ethnography" remains a neglected theorization of post-fascist Vienna. Therein, Anders challenged repeatedly the "selective remembering" which prevailed in Austria and the Federal Republic of Germany during the 1950s. Although his observations do not wield the vivid dramatic intensity of that decade's best-known intervention, Günter Grass' Oskar Matzerath, with his tin drum and glass-shattering scream, they preserved actual voices and narratives from perpetrators, victims, and bystanders that could have easily disappeared.[117] It must also be pointed out that Anders resumed his career as a writer in a country bereft of its most stalwart critical voices. Joseph Roth, Robert Musil, and Stefan Zweig had all died in exile during the war years, Hermann Broch in 1951. Among the most intriguing of the country's young authors, the poet Ingeborg Bachmann decided to depart Austria for Italy in 1953. Their neglect notwithstanding, Anders' ruminations in the early 1950s on Austria and its Nazi past filled a void before new talents like Thomas Bernhard, Peter Handke, and Elfriede Jelinek emerged.

Furthermore, his philosophically-subtle remonstrances against forgetting merit inclusion in the history of the formation of a larger Central European culture of memory. Undeniably, however, Anders' disengagement from the then unimpressive literary sphere in Austria in favor of West German or American periodicals separated him from the very audience most in need of his critique. Excepting the small segments that appeared in *Commentary*, *Aufbau* and *Merkur*, he did not finally publish "Remembering and Forgetting" until 1967.[118] Even then, the book appeared with his old Munich publisher C.H. Beck. That Anders' trenchant analyses have exerted so little impact on the production of histories of Austria's "politics of the past" has not a little to do with the deeply conflicted relationship to the city and country in which he resided for more than four decades.[119] Viewed within the longer trajectory of his career, Anders' ethnography of

117. For one recent assessment of Grass, see Nicole Thesz, "Dangerous Monuments: Günter Grass and German Memory Culture," *German Studies Review* 31, no. 1 (February 2008): 1-21.

118. Besides "After All, I Was Only Seventeen,“ see also "Vom Vergeben, Vergessen, Schuld, Sühne, " *Aufbau*, no. 20, 29 April and 13 May 1960, 30; "Vor elf Jahren: Aus dem Tagebuch eines Rückwanderers," *Merkur* 15, no 6 (June 1961): 597-600.

119. My use of the term "politics of the past" echoes the title of a crucial book by Norbert Frei on the West German case. See his *Vergangenheitspolitik: Die Anfänge der Bundesrepublik und die NS-Vergangenheit* (Munich: Verlag C.H. Beck, 1996).

the "post-Hitler soul" in Vienna represented a new phase of philosophical investigation for him that continued through his 1979 essay on the reception of the American television series "Holocaust."[120] Even after he channeled his theoretical and political energies into a critique of modern technology, the arc of forgetting and remembering he had exposed so powerfully in the Austrian context was constantly in view.

120. The essay, "Nach 'Holocaust' 1979," along with his journals from his visit to Auschwitz and a long recollection of his childhood home in Breslau, is contained in his *Besuch im Hades* (Munich: Verlag C. H. Beck, 1979).

Viktor Frankl: The Inside Outsider

Timothy Pytell

> To be a Jewish citizen of Austria puts one in danger of being impaled on one horn of a dilemma or the other.[1]

Viktor Frankl had a fascinating "all-too-Austrian life." He was born in Leopoldstadt the Jewish section of Vienna on March 26, 1905. He died of heart failure in Vienna on September 2, 1997 at the age of 93. His parents were both assimilated Jews and his father was a member of the civil service with socialist political leanings. From these humble beginnings Frankl eventually developed an international reputation as Holocaust survivor and the founder of his own school of psychotherapy—logotherapy.

As a teenager Frankl developed an interest in psychology and was initially taken with Freudianism in the early 1920s. He quickly found the Freudian worldview disenchanting and joined Adler's circle in 1924, embraced the socialism of Red Vienna and became involved in youth counseling. However, with the break-up of Adler's circle in 1928, Frankl allied with two of the older and more conservative departing members; Rudolf Allers and Oswald Schwarz. In 1928 Frankl also began working under Otto Pötzl who had replaced Wagner Juaregg at the University of Vienna; the next year he designated Pötzl as "Honorary President" of his burgeoning youth counseling movement.[2] In the early 1930s, apparently under the guidance of Pötzl and Allers, Frankl initially formalized logotherapy and his prescription for youth impacted by economic distress was a call for them to find a "mission."[3] In 1996, Frankl described Pötzl as "the true genius," ranking him above both Freud and Adler.[4] This praise for Pötzl by Frankl is curious because Pötzl claimed to have paid Nazi party dues from 1930-33, and he eventually joined the Nazi party in December of 1943.[5] After receiving his medical degree in 1930, Frankl practiced as a doctor, first under Pötzl, and then under Dr. Joseph Gerstmann at the Maria

---

1. Paul Grosz, "A Jewish View of the Anschluss and the Second Republic," in *Austria, 1938-1988: Anschluss and Fifty Years*, ed. William Wright (Riverside, Calif.: Ariadne Press, 1995), 264.
2. See Frankl, "Selbstmordprophylaxe und Jugendberatung," *Münchner Medizinische Wochenschrift*, 4 Oct. 1929: 1675.
3. Viktor Frankl, "Wirtschaftskrise und Seelenleben vom Standpunkte des Jugendberaters," *Sozialärztliche Rundschau*, no.3 (1933): 45.
4. Viktor Frankl, *Was nicht in meinen Büchern steht* (Munich: Quintessenz, 1995), 48.
5. For unknown reasons, Pötzl had his application reconsidered and redated to January 1941. See, Pötzl's Nazi Party file available at the Dokumentationsarchiv des österreichischen Widerstandes.

Viktor Frankl, about 1975. © Austrian National Library

Thersien-Schlössel. From 1933 until 1937 Frankl worked in the female suicide ward at the state hospital Am Steinhof.[6] In 1936-37 he participated as a commentator in all four seminars conducted by the Austrian Landesgruppe (branch) of the International General Medical Society for Psychotherapy.[7] The International General Medical Society was under the leadership of Carl Jung. The German General Medical Society (Göring Institute) was the largest of the national groups, and beginning in 1934 was under the leadership of Henri Mathius Göring the cousin of Hermann Göring. In the Landesgruppe Jews were not allowed to present papers but until 1938 could be commentators.[8] The central journal of the Göring Institute was the *Zentralblatt für Psychotherapie* and in 1937 Frankl published an article on the "spiritual problem in psychotherapy" in the

6. See, Index of Psychiatric Krankenhaus Baumgartnerhöhe 1934-1938, Wien Landes Stadt Archiv.

7. See *Zentralblatt für Psychotherapie,* no. 10 (1937): 7-8.

8. See Geoffrey Cocks, *Psychotherapy in the Third Reich: The Göring Institute* (New York: Oxford University Press, 1985), 116.

Zentralblatt.[9] In this article Frankl reframed the notion of having a mission as one of accepting responsibility. In the article Frankl embraced the Göring Institute's "spiritual" anti-Freudian turn along with the subsequent focus on world-views and the therapeutic aspects of will and responsibility. But he also took an adamant stance against the Göring Institute's agenda of creating a Nazi form of psychotherapy with his argument that the therapist was in no position to determine the content of the sense of responsibility. Also, in January 1938, two months before the Anschluss with Germany, Frankl connected his logotherapeutic focus on world-views to the work of some of the leading Nazi psychotherapists.[10] It is important to note that despite the affirmative statements about the focus on world-views, Frankl once again took a stance against the imposition of world-views in therapy. Also, Frankl published the article in *Der christliche Ständestaat*, which was anti-Nazi and a steadfast supporter of the Catholic authoritarian state.[11]

In the early 1940s, Frankl worked as a Jewish Specialist at the Rothschild hospital which was one of the last places Jews could work in Vienna under the Nazis. At Rothschild Frankl conducted medical research in order to revive Jews that had attempted suicide in response to the trying circumstances—which was often deportation orders. These experiments included the application of amphetamines through the use of lumbar puncture and brain trepanation. For some Frankl's medical efforts are heroic and capture the desperation of a doctor acting in unfathomable circumstances to save Jewish patients, others tend to focus on the ethically questionable medical experiments that had no basis in clinical experience and under the circumstances of Nazi occupation were possibly a way for Frankl to ingratiate himself with the regime. Another issue of concern is that in the circumstances of Nazi oppression suicide was often considered a viable option if not a form of resistance, and he was therefore undermining the choice of people who made such a difficult decision.[12]

In September 1942 Frankl was deported to the ghetto Theresienstadt along with his wife and parents. He spent two trying years in Theresienstadt working in the so-called mental hospital, three anxious days "in depot"

9. Viktor Frankl, "Zur Geistigen Problematik der Psychotherapie," *Zentralblatt für Psychotherapie*, no. 10 (1937): 33-45.

10. Viktor Frankl, "Seelenärztliche Selbstbesinnung," *Der christliche Ständestaat*, 30 Jan. 1938: 8.

11. See Timothy Pytell, "The Genesis of Viktor Frankl's Third Viennese School of Psychotherapy," *The Psychoanalytic Review* 88, no. 2 (April 2001): 311-34.

12. See Timothy Pytell "The Missing Pieces of the Puzzle: A Reflection on the Odd Career of Viktor Frankl," *Journal of Contemporary History* 35, no. 2 (2000): 281–306, specifically 291-95.

in the unfinished "Mexico" section of Auschwitz Birkenau, before being transferred to Dachau. He spent nearly seven horrendous months working first as a laborer (5 months in Kaufering III), then as a doctor (2 months in Türkheim) in two sub-camps of Dachau. After his release in April 1945 Frankl eventually returned to Vienna. He already knew his father had died in Theresienstadt, and he now learned his mother was gassed at Auschwitz and his wife had died near the end of the war at Bergen Belsen. Deeply depressed and suicidal, Frankl nevertheless began to put his life back together. He began revising an earlier version of the manuscript that had been taken from him in the camps, *The Doctor and the Soul.*[13] In the Fall of 1945 he dictated his famous Holocaust testimony in nine days.[14] The next year he wrote *The Unconscious God* which argued there is a religious sensibility in everyone's unconscious depths. For most observers Frankl's logotherapy, as well as his heroic and redemptive version of surviving the Holocaust affirms god and religion. In February of 1946 Frankl reestablished his professional career by becoming Director of Vienna's Policlinic and worked there until his retirement. His personal life came back together when he met a young catholic nurse, Eleonore Schwindt. They married in 1947 and had one daughter.

During the latter 1960s and early 1970s Frankl spent significant time in America, and his ideas about god, religion and Western culture became extremely popular. Frankl's survival of the Holocaust, his reassurance that life is meaningful and his conviction that god exists, served to make him an early master of the self-help genre. Finally, Frankl was a professor of neurology and psychiatry at the University of Vienna, Distinguished Professor of Logotherapy at the U.S. International University and visiting professor at Harvard, Duquesne University and Southern Methodist University. He also received twenty-eight honorary doctorates from universities throughout the world, and the American Psychiatric Association awarded him the Oskar Pfister Award.

A western diplomat once quipped that post-war Austria was "an opera sung by the understudies." There is a great deal of truth in the claim since in 1919 Vienna had lost its status as an Imperial capital, during the 1930s and early 1940s most of the city's Jews either fled or were deported, and many of the more celebrated cosmopolitan citizens had left as well. Observers of post-war Austria also describe the onset of a crisis of national identity. The

13. Apparently his good friend Paul Polak had kept an original copy of the unfinished manuscript in hiding during the war and gave it to Frankl upon his return.

14. Frankl claimed he dictated *Man's Search for Meaning* in nine days. See Frankl, *Was nicht in meinen Büchern steht*, 83.

historical roots of this crisis are traced to construction of "Austria" by the resolutions and compromises amongst the great powers.[15] Subsequently, up until 1933, if not 1938, the majority of Austrians held a conviction about the unfeasibility of Austria as an independent nation. In the inter-war years most Austrian politicians, socialists included, clamored for an "Anschluss" with Germany.[16] But after the disastrous war, and the experience of Nazi "oppression" for seven years, the cultural reference with Germany changed. Rather than a look of envy or sympathy, most Austrian's felt disdain, if not outright disgust and hate of Germany. Consequently, after 1945 any philo-Germanism was perceived as neo-Nazi.

The foundation stone in the construction of Austrian national identity was the victim clause of the 1943 Moscow agreement. In this agreement, the three allied powers established that Austria was the first victim of Nazi Germany. The declaration also mentioned that Austria had to take responsibility for fighting the war at the side of Nazi Germany. But in the political climate of the cold war, and especially after the communist coup in Czechoslovakia in 1948, both Austria and the allies had reasons to ignore the latter point.[17] The "myth" of Austrians as victims of the Nazis, was necessary for the constitution of a westward and liberal leaning Austria.[18] In order to create a bulwark against the Soviets, Austria, Western Europe and America all tacitly agreed to sustain the mendacious view that Austria was a victim of the Nazis. But the truth that everyone knew was that Hitler, along with many of the leading Nazis came from Austria, and there were over 600,000 Austrian Nazi party members at the end of the war. The point

---

15. In 1918, with the treaty of St. Germain, and in 1943, with the Moscow Agreement, (the latter claimed Austria was the first victim of Nazism) the "state" of Austria was determined by diplomatic resolutions amongst the victorious powers.

16. In May 1933, after Hitler's seizure of power in Germany, the socialists removed the clause for a union with Germany from their platform. But as the archive footage reveals, there was little or no resistance to the 1938 "Anschluss" by the Austrian people. For an excellent discussion of these issues see, Richard Mitten, *The Politics of Anti-Semitic Prejudice* (Boulder, Co.: Westview, 1992), 12-17. Also see Evan Bukey, *Hitler's Austria: Popular Sentiment in the Nazi Era, 1938-1945* (Chapel Hill: University of North Carolina Press, 2000).

17. For an excellent discussion of these issues see, Günter Bischof, "Victims? Perpetrators? 'Punching Bags' of European Historical Memory? The Austrians and Their World War II Legacies," *German Studies Review* 27, no. 1 (2004): 17-32. Also the earlier, Fritz Fellner, "The Problem of the Austrian Nation after 1945," *Journal of Modern History* 60, no. 2 (1988): 264-89.

18. On why Stalin failed to gain control of Austria, and the political motivations behind America's accepting the "myth" of Austria's victimization, and the subsequent abandoning of the de-Nazification of Austria, see, Harry Piotrowski, "The Soviet Union and the Renner Government of Austria, April-November 1945," *Central European History* 20, no. 3-4 (1987): 246-79.

is that "Austria" was formed on rather tenuous foundations.[19] Nevertheless, Austria's post-war economic success, along with the "invention of a tradition," led to the instilling of a national sentiment in the majority of the people and the "myth" of Austrian victimization by the National Socialists was widely accepted well into the 1990s.

Austria was the only European country once occupied by Soviet troops to attain full independence after 1945. Once Austrian sovereignty was achieved, internal differences between political parties were glossed over, and the post-war political culture of Austria was characterized by a desire for stability. After experiencing the cultural trauma of civil war in the thirties, and "abuse" by the Nazi "occupation," Austria established a system of social peace. With the state treaty in 1955, and subsequent withdrawal of the allied occupation forces, a more or less "corporate system" was constructed. In this system parliament played little or no role in decision making. Instead, political party leaders controlled a system of patronage and issues between capital and the workers were resolved in back room meetings. From 1955 until 1999 this form of political power was shared essentially between the People's Party (Christian Conservatives) and the Socialists.

However, the first crack in the stability of both the "social peace," and the tenuous Austrian national identity appeared with the Waldheim affair and the end of the Cold War. With the revelation that presidential aspirant Kurt Waldheim lied about his wartime activities, and his resume "overlooked" his pre-war membership in National Socialist clubs, the myth began to crumble.[20] Since the Waldheim affair, Austria has been in a process of self-questioning that has led to a slow recovery of a buried and forgotten past. But discovering the malaise and ambiguity that lay behind the comfortable post-war political and cultural synthesis—a synthesis built on a repression of the past—has had many ramifications.

---

19. The longstanding political conservatism in Austria is exemplified by Dollfuß' subduing of the workers in February 1934, and the defeat of the Nazi coup by the Austrian state after Dollfuß's assassination in July of 1934. In both events the forces for an "Austrian order" defeated the political aspirations of both the left and right. In sum, the absence of a positive democratic tradition makes the political foundations of the second republic very shaky. For a useful overview see Melanie Sully, *A Contemporary History of Austria* (New York: Routledge, 1990), 110-15. Also Oliver Rathkolb, *The Paradoxical Republic: Austria 1945-2005* (New York: Berghahn Books, 2010) especially "Peculiarities of Austrian Democracy," 30-54.

20. For an excellent discussion of these issues see, Mitten, *The Politics of Antisemitic Prejudice*, especially "When 'the Past' Catches Up," 246-61. Also see Peter Utgaard, *Remembering and Forgetting Nazism: Education, national Identity and the Victim Myth in Postwar Austria* (New York: Bergahn Books, 2003) especially "Part III: The End of the Austria-as-Victim Myth? Official Memory Since 1986," 161-97.

Given the repressed and ambiguous past, it is not surprising that in the 1990s the Freedom party (FPÖ led by Jörg Haider attempted a renewed interest in trying to find a "usable" tradition.[21] Rather than denying the Nazi past, Haider attempted to recast the Waffen SS as "decent men" of spiritually superior character. Along with these and numerous other outrages, Haider described Nazi employment policies as "sound," and Nazi extermination camps as "punishment camps."

As a Jew, Holocaust survivor, and founder of the third school of Viennese psychology, Frankl had a peculiar role in post-war Austria. On the issue of the ambivalent past, Frankl chose the part of reconciler. This attitude of reconciliation eventually led to his success in a society placing a premium on "social peace." But to be honest, in post-war Austria, Frankl had few other options, and in many ways his decisions mirror Bruno Kreisky's who was chancellor in the 1970s and also Jewish. For both Kreisky and Frankl it seems professional success required downplaying the crimes of the Holocaust and supporting the myth of "Austrian-as-victims." No doubt the fact that the deeply imbedded Austrian anti-Semitism lingered on in society and culture even after the Holocaust impacted their attitudes. In postwar Austria there was also a tendency to deny or at least downplay the atrocities committed against the Jews so neither Frankl nor Kreisky would ingratiate themselves to their fellow Austrians by reminding them of the crimes against the Jews.[22]

As a survivor of Auschwitz, Frankl spoke publically on the Holocaust and the Nazis with moral authority. And, in the post-war Austrian culture of denial and repression it goes without saying that Frankl was one of the few voices "describing" Auschwitz. Not surprisingly, Frankl was essentially

21. The FPÖ was originally the League of Independents formed in 1949. The League was made up of ex-Nazis, Monarchists, and other right leaning figures. Most commentators considered Haider a political opportunist and not a neo-Nazi. But there was a political philosophy that was seemingly anti-democratic, anti-capitalist and authoritarian behind his opportunism. For example his disdain for "foreigners," his hatred of "corrupt" government, his proclaimed desire to remain isolated from the European union, his call for a third republic were all suggestive of an extreme agenda. See, Jörg Haider, *Die Freiheit, die ich meine* (Vienna: Ulstein, 1993). For a discussion of these issues and a history of the party see, Max Riedlsperger, "FPÖ: Liberal or Nazi?," *Conquering the Past: Austrian Nazism, Yesterday and Today*, ed. Fred Parkinson, (Indiana: Wayne State University, 1989), 257-75. Also see Tony Judt, "Austria & the Ghost of the New Europe," *New York Review of Books,* 15 Feb. 1996, 22-25. For a more moderate and sympathetic view of Haider see Lothar Höbelt, *Defiant Populist: Jörg Haider and the Politics of Austria,* (West Lafayette, Indiana: Purdue University Press, 2003).

22. On these issues see Robert Wistrich, *Austrians and Jews in the Twentieth Century: from Franz Joseph to Waldheim* (New York: St. Martin's Press, 1992), especially Robert Knight, ""Neutrality," not Sympathy: Jews in Post-War Austria," 220-33, and in the same volume Robert Wistrich, "The Kreisky Phenomenon: A Reassessment," 234-51.

overlooked by his fellow Austrians. Nevertheless, Frankl's chosen role of reconciler represented a peculiar example of how post-war Austria failed to come to terms "honestly" with the past. Frankl therefore had a role in downplaying the Nazi atrocities and the horrors of the Holocaust. He was also used to legitimize those with an ambiguous past. But again and to be fair, this engagement in white-washing of the past was the only possibility in the post-war Austrian culture of denial and arguably Frankl's own choices in the 1930s colored his strategy for coming to terms with the past.

Forgetting and Forgiving

Upon his return to Vienna in 1945 Frankl expressed a strong desire to help his old friend Otto Pötzl. Along with providing written testimony on behalf of Pötzl in his denazification hearings, Frankl's 1946 genealogy of Viennese doctors designated Pötzl as the „leading brain surgeon."[23] Ironically, when Frankl made this claim Pötzl was being dismissed from his university position. Frankl also contributed to his *Festschrift*.[24] But exactly why he wanted to help Pötzl was never fully explicated. The sense of debt, likely centered on their medical work and proclaimed sabotaging of euthanasia in 1941 that is the central statement of support in Frankl's contribution to Pötzl's denazifcation file. Also, Pötzl might have played the role of Frankl's protector.[25]

We can therefore assume that in his play *Synchronisation in Birkenwald* (1946) Frankl had protecting Pötzl in mind when he described feeling the "responsibility" to make up a "mercy list ... of people whose life will be in danger during the first waves of hate." He wanted to protect those who did "a lot of good, secretly ... including some who are wearing uniforms," because "here and there still beats a human heart."[26] Frankl apparently felt a "responsibility" to return to Vienna to protect those he described as "good"

23. Viktor Frankl, "Wien und die Seelenheilkunde," *Wiener Kurier*, 23 March 1946, 11.

24. See Viktor Frankl, "Über Lehrbarkeit und Lernbarkeit der Psychotherapie," *Neurologie und Psychiatrie: Festschrift zum 70. Geburtstag von Otto Pötzl*, ed. Hurbert Urban (Innsbruck: Wagner, 1949) 222-29. In this piece Frankl claimed that the school of psychotherapy was of less importance than the personality of the physician and his approach to the patient.

25. Although, Else Pappenheim, who worked at the university clinic under Pötzl *until the Anschluss*, recalled no special relationship between Frankl and Pötzl. This information was given by Else Pappenheim during an interview with the author on 15 July 1996 in New York City.

26. Viktor Frankl, "Synchronisation in Birkenwald," translated by Joseph Fabry (unpublished manuscript, available at Graduate Theological Union, Berkeley), 25. Also see Viktor Frankl "Synchronisation in Birkenwald," *Gesammelte Werke*, vol. 2, eds. Alexander Batthyány, Karlheinz Biller and Eugenio Fizzotti (Vienna: Böhlau, 2006) 39-72.

Nazis. For example he described hiding a "medical colleague in his apartment" in order to protect him from prosecution.[27] Frankl's urge toward reconciliation eventually mirrored the post-war climate of social peace. Not surprisingly, in Austria de-nazification of party members was curtailed, and as Frankl's comments revealed, there was a tendency to view ex-Nazis as victims.

Frankl described how Emil Tuchman helped him upon his return to Vienna by connecting him with Bruno Pitterman. Pitterman was a long standing socialist that Frankl knew from the 1920s when he was member of the socialist student organization. Apparently Pitterman gave Frankl a Remington typewriter and also "had him sign a blank form" which was then used as an application for a position at the Vienna Policlinic Hospital.[28] As mentioned, in February of 1946 Frankl began work in the small city hospital and for the next 25 years he was the head of the neurology department.

Frankl recognized that it was rather ironic that a man in his position should come out in 1946 against recognizing a collective guilt.[29] But as an Auschwitz survivor, Frankl felt he had the authority to pardon the perpetrators. For example, in 1946, Frankl spoke against collective guilt in the French occupied zone. The next day a former SS officer came to him "with tears in his eyes." He asked Frankl "where he found the courage to take a stand against collective guilt." Frankl told him: "You can't do it, you would be speaking out of self-interest. But I am the former prisoner No. 119104, and so I can do it....People will listen to me..."[30] According to Alexander Batthyány the Director of the Viktor Frankl Archive in Vienna Frankl's convictions were based in his logotherapeutic belief that assigning guilt to a collective was impossible because guilt is particular to each individual and accusing the totality "contradicts what constitutes the nature of freedom and responsibility."[31]

In a speech given at the Vienna Rathausplatz on March 10, 1988, on the 50th anniversary of "the occupation of Austria by the troops of Hitler's Germany," Frankl repeated his argument against collective guilt that he first made in 1946.[32] Once again, he claimed "there are only two races of men:

27. Frankl, *Was nicht in meinen Büchern steht*, 81.

28. Frankl, *Was nicht in meinen Büchern steht*, 82. Also see Haddon Klingberg, *When Life Calls Out to Us: The Love and Lifework of Viktor and Elly Frankl* (New York: Double Day, 2001), 156.

29. Ibid., 80-81.

30. Ibid.

31. Alexander Batthyány, *Mythos Frankl?: Geschichte der Logotherapie und Existenzanalyse 1925-1945; Entgegnung auf Timothy Pytell* (Vienna: LIT Verlag, 2006), 10.

32. See Viktor Frankl, *Logos und Existenz* (Vienna: Amandus-Verlag, 1951), specifically, "Die Existenzanalyse und die Probleme der Zeit (1946)," 24-31.

those who are decent people, and those who are not." Frankl universalized this "distinction" as in "every nation, and within nations right through every political party..." He then extended this distinction to the "concentration camps" and the "more or less decent people who belonged to the S.S. And in the same way there were also scoundrels amongst the prisoners."[33]

Peter Gay has described this strategy as a sidestepping of responsibility through "comparative trivialization."[34] That is, since there were some good SS and some bad prisoners we cannot make distinctions between them. From Gay's perspective Frankl's claims served to pacify guilt, and avert focus on the point that some people chose to accommodate the Nazis while others took paths of resistance. While many others, were indecent people, who decided to join the party and carry out its program fully aware it was an immoral, anti-democratic political agenda that worked by terrorizing certain people.

Frankl also didn't attach his rejection of collective guilt to a condemnation of the Austrian Nazis. Nor did he condemn the role the anti-democratic, Christian, authoritarian state played in paving the way for Nazism. Instead, he affirmed the victim clause of the Moscow Agreement, and side-stepped Austrian responsibility, by claiming "Ladies and Gentlemen, it was National Socialism which inflicted the scourge of racial persecution on us."[35] Frankl extended these apologetics, and again side-stepped the issue of Austrian responsibility by blaming the "regime or system which brings the scoundrels to the top....Therein lies the true peril." This distancing of responsibility excused everyone on the basis of the system. That is, everyone was just an insignificant cog, caught in the totalitarian system. This version served to deny responsibility and soothe the guilty conscience. Frankl also diffused responsibility for the Holocaust by claiming "in principle any country is capable of perpetuating the Holocaust."[36]

Taking a different tack, Karl Jaspers argued that all Germans shared a "political liability" for the Nazi period. Writing in 1947, Jaspers was challenging the Germans to found their political outlook and new state, by being honest about the crimes perpetuated in the name of Germans by the Nazi regime.[37] Unlike Jaspers, Frankl opted to not confront Austrian responsibility for taking the anti-democratic turn that led to the Fatherland

33. Viktor Frankl, "There is no Collective Guilt," *Austrian Information* 41, no.6 (1988): 5.

34. See Peter Gay, *Freud, Jews and Other Germans: Masters and Victims in Modernist Culture* (Oxford: Oxford University Press, 1978), XI-XII.

35. Ibid.

36. Ibid.

37. See Karl Jaspers, "The Question of German Guilt," in *Karl Jaspers: Basic Philosophical Writings* trans. and eds. Edith Ehrlich, Leonard H. Ehrlich, and George B. Pepper (New Jersey: Humanities Press, 1986), 396-408.

Front and ultimately Nazism. For Frankl the vacuous "system," not the people, was responsible for Nazism and the Holocaust.

Since he was helping commemorate the 50th anniversary of the Nazi occupation—which coincided with the Waldheim affair—Frankl also argued against making people "feel guilty or even ashamed ... unless they were determined to drive the young people today into the arms of the old-style Nazis or neo-Nazis.[38] Frankl's point is well taken. Burdensome guilt upon preceding generations could possibly lead to a neo-fascist reaction.[39] Even so, Jaspers pointed-out that there is a type of metaphysical guilt that every human community has—a responsibility for what was done in the name of ancestors. In this limited sense, every generation of Austrians, and more broadly, the community of the West, has a responsibility for the legacy of fascism and the Holocaust. Not a responsibility for, but a responsibility to remember in order to guard against the reoccurrence. But Frankl claimed the present generation shouldn't be held responsible for "something their parents or grandparents had to answer for." The contradiction is that the victim clause of the Moscow agreement viewed everyone as victims postwar.

Frankl also argued against collective guilt in a memorial speech held upon request of the Society of Physicians in Vienna on March 25, 1949 for the members who died in the years 1938-45. In this speech, he also "blamed the system that brought some men to guilt and which brought others to death." He then asserted an authoritative voice by articulating the experience of the victims. Frankl claimed "in their last words there was not a single word of hate—only words of longing came from their lips, and words of forgiveness..."[40] As a Holocaust survivor Frankl claims about the dying probably seemed believable. He therefore used his authority to place words of forgiveness on the lips of those who died. Clearly this version would soothe the guilty conscience; regardless of whether the guilt was attributable to crimes committed, passivity or perhaps simply survival. Everyone was pardoned by the dead according to Frankl.

Frankl's personal desire to reconcile—with ex-Nazis—and resolve guilt, dovetailed with Austrian needs. As a persecuted Jew he seemed the perfect spokesperson. One could argue that Frankl's "benevolent" forgiveness was a form of passive aggression that allowed him to humble his former oppressors. On some level this might be true. Nevertheless, by excusing

38. Frankl, "There is no Collective Guilt," 5.

39. This claim for an unburdened past is similar to Hannah Arendt's notion of "natality" where each generation has the opportunity to start anew. For an interesting insight into the psychology of guilt, Germans, and the Nazi past see Peter Sichrovsky, *Born Guilty* (New York: Basic Books, 1993).

40. Frankl, "In Memorium," *The Jewish Echo: Periodical of Jewish Intellectuals* 5, no.6 (1949): 1.

the perpetrators, and by claiming to voice the dead's sentiments, he was stretching his newly acquired authority because no one has the right to forgive an offense that has been done to someone else.

Frankl ended the speech, which was published in *The Jewish Echo*, with comments that could be read as autobiographical. Frankl described the "personal guilt of a man who has 'done nothing' wrong, but who has failed to do 'something' right." Frankl attributed this failure to "apprehension for himself or anxiety for his family." But he deflected the judgement of the gathered physicians by stating "whoever wishes to condemn such a man as a coward needs first to prove that in the same situation he himself would have been a hero....But it is prudent not to sit on judgement of others."[41] Frankl knew there were few heroes but as a survivor of Auschwitz everyone gathered knew he was a victim. Therefore, it was "prudent" not to judge him. But what did he exactly mean by the statement that no one can sit in judgement on those who have "done nothing right?" It appears Frankl was deflecting coming to terms with guilt. But this was the guilt that Jaspers honestly faced when he stated "we are alive—that is our guilt ... we preferred to stay alive, on the feeble, though correct, ground that our death could not have helped anyone."[42]

As survivors, everyone in Frankl's generation had some elemental guilt. Everyone was in need of self-examination. No one was pure. The time for judgement has certainly passed. Not surprisingly, shortly after Frankl's death in 1997 Austria began a serious confrontation with the buried past that culminated with Chancellor Wolfgang Schüssel's (2000-2007) policies of restitution (especially for former slave laborers) and a "memory year in 2005" where the National Socialist past was confronted openly and honestly for the first time.[43] The thrust behind this confrontation with the past was a long time coming and has many causes but most significant was the Waldeim Affair that broke in 1986.

Reconciling

Frankl had a small almost insignificant role in the affair, but his actions reflect the peculiar position he played in Austrian public life. On the September 9, 1988 a picture of Frankl with Waldheim was printed in the

41. Ibid.
42. Jaspers, *The Question of German Guilt*, 400.
43. On the Schüssel Era see Günter Bischof, Fritz Plasser, eds., *The Schüssel Era in Austria*, Contemporary Austrian Studies vol. 18 (New Orleans: University of New Orleans Press, 2010), especially Günter Bischof and Michael S. Maier, "Reinventing Tradition and the Politics of History: Schüssel's Restitution and Commemoration Policies," 206-234.

Neue Kronen Zeitung.[44] "President Waldheim" handed Frankl, the former "concentration camp prisoner ... that in the hell of National Socialism had lost his entire family, the Große silberne Ehrenzeichen mit dem Stern," (Great Silver Badge of Honor with the Star). Frankl looked directly into the camera, while his wife, standing in the background averted her eyes. Waldheim, smiling, towered over Frankl and appeared polished, genteel and happy. And why should he not? Frankl was helping in the "domestic rehabilitation" of Waldheim. That Frankl took the medal from Waldheim in these circumstances shocked many Austrians.[45]

For the newly elected Waldheim, Frankl was useful for his 'rehabilitation' on a number of levels. First, because Frankl represented a survivor who apparently had no animosities toward "good" Nazis like Waldheim. Therefore his appearance with Waldheim had the effect of a defacto reduction of Waldheim's culpability for Nazi crimes, and represented a moral and political legitimation. More broadly, Frankl's conciliatory actions can be viewed as soothing Austria's wounded identity. And, by appearing with the ex-Nazi, he was also serving to reaffirm Austria's victimization myth. For his part, Frankl appeared heroic and gracious—big enough—to be capable of forgiveness.

There was also another layer to their relationship. Some of Waldheim's defenders resorted to a covert anti-Semitism by claiming he was being slandered by the World Jewish Congress (WJC). One example of a crude right wing defense of Waldheim was Carl Hödl's attack on President Bronfman of the WJC. Hödl, the deputy mayor of Linz and member of the conservative, Christian-democratic Austrian People's Party (ÖVP) compared the attacks on Waldheim with the crucifixion of Jesus—and framed the debate in terms of Christians versus Jews. He also attacked the placing of Waldheim on the "Watch list" and Bronfman's description of Waldheim as "part of the [Nazi] death machinery." Interestingly, Hödl cited Frankl's rejection of collective guilt to buttress his defense of Waldheim.[46] According to Hödl, Frankl's attitude of a reconciling, reasonable, good Jew was the correct attitude toward the Nazi past.[47]

Frankl had other uses for the political right in Vienna. His coronation with an "*Ehrenbürgerschaft*," (Honorary citizenship of Vienna) came

44. The *Neue Kronen Zeitung* was the largest selling daily paper, and has a strong rightist orientation.

45. According to Klingberg the Frankl's and Waldheim's were "social acquaintances." Klingberg, *When Life Calls Out to Us*, 301.

46. See Carl Hödl, *Leben ist nicht Zufall: ein Kaleidoskop mit bunten und lebendigen Bildern aus dem Leben eines Linzer Kommunalpolitikers, der seine Meinung immer offen vertreten hat* (Vienna: Trauner, 1990) 141-77.

47. On the WJC and Waldheim, see Mitten, *The Politics of Antisemitic Prejudice*, 119-37.

surprisingly at the hand of Haider and the Freedom Party (FPÖ). Frankl's ties to the FPÖ apparently began in 1981. His philosophy of meaning, to be found in a "great idea" or in "giving to humanity" was cited by the party theorist, Fritz Wolfram.[48] But Frankl's reconciling spirit and subtle downplaying of Nazi atrocities was the center of his appeal for the FPÖ. As mentioned, the attempt to find a usable past was one of Haider's, who described himself as a "good friend" of Frankl, main goals. Frankl's claims that there is "no collective guilt," "there were good Nazis and bad Nazis," "good prisoners and bad prisoners," and most significantly, "good SS and bad SS," fit nicely with the FPÖ agenda.[49] For many observers Frankl's willingness to fraternize with Haider and the FPÖ was puzzling since it went a step beyond reconciliation and seemed to legitimize the FPÖ's agenda to whitewash if not outright deny the Holocaust.

The FPÖ did not have an easy time getting Frankl nominated. The Christian Conservatives thought the award should go to a Catholic university professor. The Socialist Party (SPÖ) was willing to go along with the nomination, although the leftist intellectuals were demanding a detailed resume from Frankl. For their part, the SPÖ tried to undermine the FPÖ's efforts by offering Frankl another, although less esteemed, citizenship award. Frankl declined, and at this point the FPÖ forced the issue by going public with the nomination and started a petition campaign. In these circumstances the other parties ended up bequeathing the "Ehrenbürgerschaft" on Frankl.[50] The vote was a unanimous 99-0.

Interestingly, the famed Nazi hunter Simon Wiesenthal was nominated for the award exactly at the same time as Frankl. But the FPÖ voted against the nomination because the Wiesenthal Center had hung Haider's photo next to the right-wing extremists, Jean Le Pen and David Duke at the museum of tolerance. For his part Wiesenthal viewed the FPÖ "no votes as a badge of honor, and said that his name and the prize would have no meaning if extremists voter (sic) for him."[51]

48. Fritz Wolfram, "Die Problematik einer weiteren Arbeitszeitverkürzung und Freizeitvermehrung," *freie argumente: Freiheitliche Zeitschrift für Politik*, no.2 (January 1981): 29.

49. Frankl made this last claim first in his 1963 edition of *Man's Search for Meaning*, 136 (footnote), repeated it in *Was nicht in meinen Büchern steht*, 80, and once again on a nationally broadcast television interview in 1994, Wolf Interview, (FPÖ). Dr. Rüdiger Stix, FPÖ member and in the Defense Ministry claimed they nominated Frankl based on the 1993 interview. Significantly, in 1993 the more liberal "leftist" members of the FPÖ left the party to form the Liberal Forum. Frankl seemed to be useful in the attempt to legitimize and rehabilitate a rightist group.

50. The information on the politics behind Frankl's nomination comes from my interview with Dr. Rüdiger Stix of the FPÖ in Vienna, 15 June 1996.

51. See *Simon Wiesenthal Center News Release*, 29 June 1995.

Frankl eventually "distanced" himself from Haider, and had "little understanding" for Haider's speaking to the Waffen SS.[52] But Rüdiger Stix, a leading member of the FPÖ and supporter of Frankl's nomination, bitterly pointed-out that this remark by Frankl seemed disingenuous, because Frankl, like Haider, often claimed there were good SS. Frankl's daughter, Gabriele Vesely-Frankl also reiterated the claim of "distance" from Haider. She described the accidental grounds of Haider's and Frankl's "friendship" and defended her father with the claim he is "no politician."[53] Nevertheless Frankl made his political positions public. For one interesting example, in January 1993 Frankl was interviewed on television by Johannes Kunz. Frankl claimed there was a necessity "for a dialog with the right extremists," because the cultural crisis was attributable to a sense of meaninglessness and a lack of a rewarding life. Therefore dialog and democratic tolerance was the best way to avoid "terrorist actions."[54]

In the post-war political culture of reconciliation, Viktor Frankl came to be recognized as a "leading citizen" of Vienna.[55] After the war Frankl assumed the moral high ground for himself and the Austrian people. His claims about collective guilt seemed legitimate because the call came from a person "morally purified" by the oppression of Auschwitz. The plight of Frankl, and Austria deserves our respect. Life under the Nazis was treacherous and besieged with extenuating circumstances. For sure, Austrian suffering at the hands of the Germans in a limited sense does redeem them from responsibility. In addition, Austria's occupation until 1955 by the allies, along with the myth that she was the first victim of the Nazis, conveniently ruled out a self-induced moral purge. But with Waldheim and in some sense culminating with the Schüssel Era, Austria achieved the long overdue process of introspection. In his monumental *Postwar* Tony Judt argued "Today the pertinent European reference is not baptism. It is extermination....Holocaust recognition is our contemporary European entry ticket."[56] Based on Judt's contention it appears Austria has earned its European entry ticket by successfully creating "a dense landscape of World War II memorials" and is no longer "the black sheep of

52. See "Viktor Frankl distanziert sich von F-Chef Haider," *Der Standard*, 13 Jan. 1996, and "Frankl an Haider: Verärgerung über den 'Freund,'" *News*, 3 Mar. 1996.

53. Gabriella Vesely-Frankl, "Lasst Frankl aus dem Spiel!" *profil*, 22 Jan. 1996, 70-71.

54. See "Viktor Frankl für echten Dialog mit den Rechtsextremisten," *Politik*, no.6, 26 Jan. 1993.

55. Frankl's world-wide renown was exemplified by the fact he gave the keynote address to the first World Congress of Psychotherapy held in Vienna July, 1996.

56. Tony Judt, *Postwar: A History of Europe Since 1945* (New York: Penguin Books, 2005), 803.

Europe."[57] Frankl didn't live to see Austria come to terms with its past. And it is doubtful whether the "good humanist" Frankl was even fully conscious of his role in the burial of the past. Frankl's argument against collective guilt, that served to foreclose notions of collective responsibility, fit the Austrian milieu after the war. It was also likely key to his success on both a professional and psychological level, to help his fellow Austrians bury the past. This became his "use" of his survival. By 1988 Frankl could claim "that the only people who are justified" in saying "people should have preferred imprisonment to compromise or coming to terms with the Nazis ... are people who ... did indeed allow themselves to be incarcerated in a concentration camp rather than betray themselves or their convictions."[58] Frankl overlooked the fact that some people compromised with the Nazis and were still sent to the camps. By 1988, Frankl's survival of Auschwitz had placed him beyond reproach. After pardoning individual ambiguous actions, he could use his badge of survival to pardon Austria.

Not surprisingly some Austrians and Jews in particular were disappointed by Frankl's cultural role. For example his biographer Haddon Klingberg depicted how Frankl's reconciling attitude and stance on collective guilt ultimately led to a frayed relationship with other Viennese Jews.[59] Frankl's attitude of reconciliation was also not well received by the American Jewish community. Klingberg also describes how in 1978, Frankl gave a lecture at the Institute of Adult Jewish Studies at Congregation B'nai Jeshurun on the upper east side of New York City that led to an outburst of boos from the audience and Frankl was called a "Nazi Pig."[60] It appears although Austria eventually mastered the horrendous past, Frankl's personal history that included a connection to the Nazi Psychotherapy movement, mentoring by Pötzl, and culminated with his interaction with Waldheim and Haider in the last decade of his life, left his own past—a multi-dimensional all-too-Austrian Jewish tragedy—unmastered.

57. See Günter Bischof, "Victims? Perpetrators?," 24.
58. Frankl, "There is No Collective Guilt," 5.
59. Klingberg, *When Life Calls Out to Us*, 229.
60. Ibid., 230

Wolfgang Kraus: Impresario of Austrian Literature and Cold Warrior

Stefan Maurer[1]

Introduction

The ambivalence which accompanies Wolfgang Kraus (1924-1998) as one of the most important public figures of literary life in Austria's Second Republic is astonishing: "Kraus dictated the [Austrian] politics of literature with unrivalled self-aggrandizement, something which was rare even in the totalitarian satellite states of the Soviet Union,"[2] states Thomas Rothschild in an article about the canon of the *Österreichische Gesellschaft für Literatur* (Austrian Literary Association; hereafter referred to as ÖGL). On the other hand the writer Hans Weigel (1908-1991), the unifying figure of Austrian literature after the second World War, acknowledges him as an unmistakable institution and explains, that Kraus was "the center, the outpost, the incarnation—not of our literature, but of literary life. He is contestable—certainly!—but he is of unspoken importance. He is indispensable."[3] The essayist Franz Schuh (born in 1947) depicts the part Kraus played in the literary field of Austria as as critical as Rothschild, and posits Kraus had "diverse, unique, distributed positions and assignments, that were interrelated and that formed a kind of net, in which a lot got entangled, and that should be the target of extensive interpretation, because this net contains in pure form the paradigm of sociology of literature in Austria."[4] Kraus, who was aware of his unique role as an intermediary in Austrian literary life, stressed at one point in his journal: "Liaisons, intermediaries, interpreters between statesmen, politicians and intellectuals, writers and artists, characters of the cultural life and the mass media—the search of which has been neglected, even omitted for centuries (since 45). This was my role in Vienna."[5]

1. This is a revised and enhanced version of an article published together with Michael Hansel in *Kalter Krieg in Österreich: Literatur – Kunst – Kultur,* eds. Michael Hansel and Michael Rohrwasser (Vienna: Zsolnay ,2010). Translations of german sources by the author.
2. Thomas Rothschild, "Die besten Köpfe: Der Kanon der Österreichischen Gesellschaft für Literatur," in *Die einen raus – die anderen rein: Kanon und Literatur; Vorüberlegungen zu einer Literaturgeschichte Österreichs*, eds. Wendelin Schmidt-Dengler, Johann Sonnleitner, and Klaus Zeyringer (Berlin: Erich Schmidt, 1994), 126-133, 130.
3. Hans Weigel, "Ein Kolumbus namens Kraus," *Wiener Journal*, no. 41, Feb. 1984.
4. Franz Schuh, "Literatur und Macht am Beispiel Österreichs der siebziger Jahre," in ibid. *Liebe, Macht und Heiterkeit: Essays* (Klagenfurt: Ritter, 1985): 175-202, 199.
5. Journal entry of Wolfgang Kraus, 9 July 1986, Literary Estate of Wolfgang Kraus, ÖLA

Wolfgang Kraus, 1975.

Although Kraus is rarely mentioned in more modern literary histories of Austria[6], his national and international legacy still remains in the form of the *Anton Wildgans-Preis* der österreichischen Industrie, as well as the *Österreichische Staatspreis für Europäische Literatur*, and the *Manès-Sperber-Preis* which he initiated, the *Österreich Bibliotheken*[7], and of course the ÖGL which played an important role as a forum for Austrian literature throughout the sixties and is now headed, since Kraus' retirement in 1994, by the writer Marianne Gruber (born in 1944).

The following essay focuses on the early years of Kraus and the ÖGL, in particular Kraus' part in the cultural cold war, and his alliance with members of the Congress for Cultural Freedom (hereafter referred to as CCF), as well as his participation in the covert book distribution-program by the

63/97, Literary Archive of Austrian National Library, Vienna.

6. e.g. in newer literary histories like Klaus Zeyringers *Österreichische Literatur seit 1945: Überblicke, Einschnitte, Wegmarken* (Innsbruck: Haymon, 1999).

7. Helmut Buchhart, "Die Österreich-Bibliotheken des Bundesministeriums für Auswärtige Angelegenheiten, Wien," *Biblos: Beiträge zu Buch, Bibliothek und Schift* 41 (1992): 191-92.

CIA. The essay hereby tries to take Gilles Scott-Smith's recommendation into account, that "the starting point for interpreting the CCF … should not be the outlook of the CIA but the view of post-war intelligentsia…,"[8] to which Kraus belonged.

Born 13 January 1924 in Vienna, Kraus attended elementary school in *Katholischer Schulverein*, and afterwards a catholic high school *Zu den Schotten* in Vienna, which was closed down following the Anschluss in 1938. He finished high school on 23 March 1942. Kraus was drafted to the Wehrmacht, developed an heart condition during basic military training and was discharged on 10 June 1943. He studied German and literature at the University of Vienna, and received his PhD in July 1947. Kraus himself describes his youth during the Nazi-era as an "inner emigration" pointing out that books and theatre, music and visual arts revealed to him, that "this hellish situation, in which I undeservedly found a rather quiet corner was not the normality of life itself."[9] He was employed at the Viennese Publishing house Ullstein as a freelancer where he was a subordinate of Edwin Rollett (1889-1964), literary program manager of the publishing house, who not only acted as president of *Verband der freien Schriftsteller und Journalisten Österreichs* (Union of free writers and journalists of Austria), but also as chairman of the *Austrian Schriftstellerverband* (Writers Union).[10] In 1949 Kraus changed from Ullstein to the publishing house of Paul Zsolnay, where he rose to the position of chief editor then to chief press officer and sales manager. In 1956 he left this job and worked as a freelance journalist, writing for Austrian, German, and Swiss newspapers. From 1959 on he frequently travelled to the countries of "real socialism," to report about "cultural and political life in the East."[11] In a résumé, he notes that he never received an official invitation, and that he financed these ventures himself. Kraus was later to benefit from his experiences in Eastern Europe. Following the establishment of the ÖGL in 1961, one thematic priority

8. Gilles Scott-Smith, *The Politics of Apolitical Culture: The Congress for Cultural Freedom, the CIA and post-war American Hegemony* (London: Routledge, 2002), 22, 56. W. Scott Lucas, "Beyond Freedom, Beyond Control: Approaches to Culture and the State-Private Network in the Cold War," in *The cultural Cold War in Western Europe: 1945–1960*, eds. Giles Scott-Smith and Hans Krabbendam (London: Routledge, 2003), 53-72.

9. Speech on the 50th anniversary of matriculation (Vortrag zum 50jährigen Maturajubiläum) on 4 Apr. 1992, Literary Estate of W. Kraus, ÖLA 63/97, Literary Archive of the Austrian National Library, Vienna.

10. See Karin-Heidi Hackenberg, "Der Kritiker, Journalist und Schriftsteller Edwin Rollett: Ein Beitrag zur Wiener Theaterkritik im 20. Jahrhundert," PhD. diss, University of Vienna, 1985.

11. Profile (Kurzbiographie) W. Kraus, Literary Estate of W. Kraus, ÖLA 63/97, Literary Archive of the Austrian National Library, Vienna.

of the ÖGL was the communication between East and West, in particular with writers from the former Danube Monarchy.

The Literary Field of Austria in the 1960s and the Founding of the ÖGL

Since the end of World War II literary life in Austria had been dominated by such conservative figures, as writer Rudolf Henz (1897-1987), who was not only a member of the Austrian *Kunstsenat* (Senate of Arts), and director of broadcasting station *RAVAG*, but also editor of the official literary magazine *Wort in der Zeit*, subsidized by the Austrian Ministry of Education. His political stance can be summed up as catholic, anti-modernist and of course anti-communist.[12] The adage of the writer Alexander Lernet-Holenia (1897-1976), that "we have only to continue where our dreams were disrupted by the madmen Hitler"[13] found a broad echo within the political officials and the protagonists of literary life. During the *longue durée* of the dark 1950s, avant-garde writers such as the *Wiener Gruppe*, who opposed traditional writing standards were excluded and their performances scandalized.[14] Austrian Minister of Education Heinrich Drimmel (1912-1991) only supported writers and artists, whose work had been published during the time of the First Republic of Austria and also those, who were active in the literary field during the Nazi era. This matter was covered up and excused, as long as these writers fitted into the cultural policy of the Drimmel era, which unified baroque and catholic Austrian traditions in a backward-looking *Austriazistik*. Therefore between 1945 and 1965 there were two competing literary concepts, one that was of content and stylistic departure, which had been dominant in the immediate post-war period, and which reappeared in the 1960s. The other concept was one associated with traditional values, which prevailed, at least officially parallel.[15] Contemporary Austrian literature was very under-represented and a critical article by Wolfgang Kraus about the *Österreichische*

12. See Karl Müller, *Zäsuren ohne Folgen: Das lange Leben der literarischen Antimoderne Österreichs seit den 30er Jahren* (Salzburg: Otto Müller, 1990), 227.

13. Alexander Lernet–Holenia, "Gruß des Dichters," *Der Turm* 1, no. 4-5 (1945): 109.

14. See Kristina Pfoser–Schewig, and Ursula Seeber, "'...der spiesser fühlt sich auf sein wiener schnitzel getreten...': Die Wiener Gruppe; Literatur und Avantgarde in den fünfziger Jahren," in *Die ‚wilden' fünfziger Jahre: Gesellschaft, Formen und Gefühle eines Jahrzehnts in Österreich*, eds. Gerhard Jagschitz and Klaus–Dieter Mulley (St. Pölten: Niederösterreichisches Pressehaus, 1985), 284-88, 284.

15. See Karl Müller, "Zur Kontinuität österreichischer Literatur seit den dreißiger Jahren," in *Kontinuität und Bruch: 1938 – 1945 – 1955; Beiträge zur österreichischen Kultur- und Wissenschaftsgeschichte*, ed. Friedrich Stadler, (Vienna: Jugend & Volk, 1988), 181-215.

Buchwoche (Austrian book week) in 1958 provides an insight into the reality of the literary scene: "In this prestigious exhibition of the Austrian Book Week one is searching in vain for crucial representatives of Austrian literature—e.g. [Hugo von] Hofmannsthal, [Arthur] Schnitzler, [Franz] Kafka, [Rudolf] Kassner, [Franz] Werfel, [Hermann] Broch, [Robert] Musil, Joseph Roth, [Stefan] Zweig, [Fritz von] Hermanovsky–Orlando, [Heimito] von Doderer and Ferdinand Bruckner are at least found on photographic portraits, even though their books are nowhere to be seen, not to mention the forthcoming books of younger writers, such as Herbert Eisenreich, Jeannie Ebner, Humbert Fink. … An outsider might be led to believe that Austria is ashamed of them and excludes them in their own country from the promotion for creative intellectuality of Austria."[16] Since the work of the above mentioned writers was published by West German publishing houses, their reception in Austria was minimal. Referring to the international literary scene, the writer Milo Dor spoke of a "paper curtain," that affected economic, legal, and political matters of bilateral cultural contact between Austria and the GDR, that continued until shortly before the end of the occupation period in 1955.[17]

Attempts were made to escape from the parochialism which had dominated the Austrian literary field before the inception of the ÖGL. There was no organized literary scene, with literary events, readings by authors or book presentations. The genuine role the ÖGL played in the early 1960's in establishing a literary scene is surprising by today's standards, where a variety of literary events take place in Vienna, for example by Alte Schmiede, Literaturhaus and Büchereien Wien. The ÖGL had its precursor in the *Grillparzer Institut*, founded in 1956, which was lead by the Grillparzer-Association, whose president, the writer Kurt Frieberger (1883-1970) also acted as vice-president of the Austrian P.E.N.-Club. This Institute had as its task the promotion of Austrian literature in foreign countries, and was intended by Alfred Weikert and Hans Brunmayr, of the Austrian Ministry of Education, who were two of its most avid supporters to become a kind of Austrian Institute for Culture. These two were also pivotal for the establishment of the ÖGL.[18] In a letter to Rudolf Henz in June 1960, only five months before the ÖGL was officially founded as an association[19], Weikert regrets that the establishment of the Grillparzer-

16. w. k. [Wolfgang Kraus], "Am Rande notiert," *Die Presse*, 12 Nov. 1958, 6.
17. See Joseph McVeigh, "'Lifting the Paper Curtain': The opening of Austrian Literary Culture to Germany after 1945," *German Studies Review* 19, no. 3 (1996): 479–99, 481.
18. See Victor Suchy, "Hundert Jahre Grillparzer Gesellschaft," *Jahrbuch der Grillparzer–Gesellschaft* 18, (Vienna: Hora, 1992), 123.
19. See Polizeiprotokoll, Schreiben der Sicherheitsdirektion Wien an die

Association had been unsuccessful, even the inception of an association, concerned with Austrian Literature and the Austrian author, because that would be, as Weikert points out, the "much desired, long arm of the Ministry of Education."[20] Therefore it was only a matter of time before the government's idea for an institution to promote Austrian literature took shape: the opening speech, delivered by Kraus at the inauguration of the ÖGL on 18 November 1961, detailed the intentions of the Association in ten articles, for example a sponsorship for novelists, the supply of foreign Universities and research institutes with Austrian literature, a large-scale program of lectures and the promotion of scientific exchanges with writers from the former Danube Monarchy, which were now satellites of the Soviet Union. Kraus and the ÖGL started their activities, which also included inviting exile Austrian authors such as Erich Fried (1921-1988), Fritz Hochwälder (1911-1986), Max Brod (1884-1968), Robert Neumann (1897-1975) and Elias Canetti (1905-1994), something which Austrian officials and government had failed to do since 1945[21]. As Canetti pointed out, until 1962 "no one came up with the idea to invite me to Vienna. In Spring 1962 Wolfgang Kraus did visit me [in Hampstead], and in February 1963 I held a reading in Vienna for the first time.... The literary Association has done something crucial for me regarding Austria."[22] By inviting Canetti to Vienna the ÖGL ensured increased public recognition: in 1966 Canetti received the *Preis der Stadt Wien* (Award of Vienna) and 1967 the *Großen Österreichischen Staatspreis*, and in November of the same year his play *Die Befristeten* premiered in theater in der Josephstadt.[23]

That the political agenda of the ÖGL reflected Austrian foreign policy true to party principles is illustrated by an incident surrounding the prize-giving ceremony of the Alma Johanna Koenig-Award in 1962, that was intended to take place on the premises of the ÖGL. The award, in remembrance of an authoress, who had been murdered by the Nazis, was given to the writer Johannes Bobrowski (1917-1965). Bobroswki however could not be officially invited by the ÖGL, because he was a citizen of the

---

Bundespolizeidirektion Wien (Police Departement in charge of registered societies in Austria to Federal Police Headquarters), 30 Nov. 1960, Archive of the ÖGL, Vienna.

20. Letter from Alfred Weikert to Rudolf Henz, 30 June 1960, Literary Estate of Rudolf Henz, box 19/V, Dokumentationsstelle für neuere österreichische Literatur im Literaturhaus, Vienna.

21. In his autobiography Viktor Matejka, former city councillor in charge of cultural affairs, reports that he had tried to invite the emigrants, but had failed because of the indifference of both the Federal government and the federal state government of Vienna, see Viktor Matejka, *Widerstand ist Alles: Notizen eines Unorthodoxen* (Vienna: Löcker, 1984), 192.

22. "Der optimistische Elias Canetti," *Die Presse*, 24-26 Dec. 1971.

23. See Sven Hanuschek, *Elias Canetti: Biographie* (Munich: Carl Hanser, 2005), 490.

Federal Republic of Germany (FRG). The FRG was not recognized as a state by the Austrian government, and reference was made to "political doubts," despite the fact that Bobrowski's work was known for its "unpolitical" powerful eloquence.[24]

In retrospect, the organization of international congresses throughout the 1960s are among the most important events and accomplishments of the ÖGL. They created an international stir and are "a legend even today" as Kraus remarked in his journal in 1977: "There is no chance to re-enact them. Gone. All for the want of a whit of money."[25]

Wolfgang Kraus and the Networks of the Cultural Cold War in Europe

The three international congresses hosted by the ÖGL during the 1960s, "Present Theater—Presence of Theater" (22 to 24 March, 1965), "Our Century and the Novel" (25 to 27 October, 1965), and "Literature as Tradition and Revolution" (24 to 26 April, 1967) were announced as round–table–discussions and did not only result from the idea that the "soil of neutral Austria was ideal for a cultural dispute between East and West"[26] and corresponded with the tradition of the once multinational state, but served in fact as an extension of one of the most powerful and influential organizations of the post-war period. To a great extent the implementation and success of these congresses owed much to the support of members of the Congress for Cultural Freedom (CCF), to which Kraus stood in a close relationship. Founded in 1950 the CCF served as a counterweight to the pro-soviet Peace-Congresses, opposing totalitarianism and functioned as a high impact political-cultural instrument of the CIA during the Cold War. The CCF was an "apparatus of the cold war,"[27] and encompassed a network of different groups and organizations within Europe. Members of the CCF were primarily recruited from the non-communist left and former communists, who had turned away from communism after the show trials held in Moscow in 1937 and the Stalin-Hitler-Pact in 1939. Communist and bourgeois "anti-fascists" as well as émigrés and dissidents from communist-reigned countries in Eastern Europe were among the

24. See Marcel Atze, "Wien in Klammern: Johannes Bobrowski an Gerhard Fritsch," in *"Aus meiner Hand dies Buch": Zum Phänomen der Widmung*, eds. Volker Kaukoreit, Marcel Atze, and Michael Hansel (Vienna: Turia + Kant, 2006), 308–313, 309.

25. Journal entry of Wolfgang Kraus, 8 Jan. 1977, Literary Estate of Wolfgang Kraus.

26. Einladung zur Konferenz (Invitation to the Conference), Archive of the ÖGL, Vienna.

27. Ernst Nolte, *Deutschland im Kalten Krieg* (Munich, 1974), quoted in Michael Hochgeschwender, *Freiheit in der Offensive: Der Kongreß für kulturelle Freiheit und die Deutschen*, 1st ed. (Munich: Oldenburg, 1998), 17.

members. Between 1951 up until his withdrawal in 1967, the CIA-agent Michael Josselson (1908-1978) was the "heart and soul" of the congress. He distributed monetary allowances through a number of the US-foundations, for example the Fairfield Foundation and the Ford Foundation, which served as a front to obscure the flow of the money. Together with Nicolas Nabokov (1903-1978) secretary general of the CCF, and cousin of the famous writer Vladimir Nabokov, he tried to contain the influence of hardcore anti-communists and to intellectualize and culturally strengthen the organization. The main idea was to oppose the East on a spot where it was most vulnerable: art and science. The CCF tried to promote the interests of democracy based on the American format by "calling attention to innovation and freedom in the cultural and political spheres characteristic of Western democracies."[28] Josselson's political program was directed at the intellectual elite of Eastern Europe and more effective through an "intelligent anti-communism"[29] as well as pro-Americanism. Parallel to the internationally initiated congresses, cultural exchanges, lectures and working groups took place. Another important aspect of the cultural cold war, which had waged in Europe since the late 1940s was the founding of and funding of magazines in France, Italy, Great Britain, the GDR, and Austria, and which addressed the intellectual elite in their respective countries. The CCF-magazine in Austria was the *FORVM*, founded in 1953 by writer Friedrich Torberg (1908-1979)[30], which was seen as an ideological counterweight to the communist magazine *Tagebuch*, edited by politician and writer Ernst Fischer (1899-1972), and also as a bridge-builder to German-speaking dissidents in Hungary. Other magazines edited and financed by the congress were for example *Monat* in western Germany, and *Encounter* in Great Britain. François Bondy (1915-2003), editor of French congress-gazette *Preuves* was at the same time responsible

---

28. Felix Tweraser, "Paris Calling Vienna: The Congress for Cultural Freedom and Friedrich Torberg's Editorship of Forum," *Austrian Studies* 13 (2005), 158-72, 164.

29. Volker Berghahn, *Transatlantische Kulturkriege: Shepard Stone und die Ford Foundation*, 1st ed. (Stuttgart: Franz Steiner, 2004), 170.

30. Torberg, who re-migrated from America to Austria in 1952 and was known as a sworn anti-communist often depicted as the Austrian version of US–senator Joseph McCarthy, used denunciation to harm literary rivals, e.g. the exile-writer Hilde Spiel (1911-1990), who was—through her first husband Peter de Mendelsohn—associated with *Monat.* See Ingrid Schramm, "Heimersatz und Schauplatz des 'Kalten Krieges': Hilde Spiel und der P.E.N.," in *Hilde Spiel. Weltbürgerin der Literatur*, eds. Hans A. Neunzig and Ingrid Schramm, (Vienna: Paul Zsolnay, 1999), 125-32; Michael Hansel: "'…ein Lackerl Geifer zu erzeugen': Friedrich Torberg als Vermittler und Verhinderer von Literatur," in: *Die "Gefahren der Vielseitigkeit": Friedrich Torberg 1908–1979*, eds. Marcel Atze and Marcus G. Patka, (Vienna: Holzhausen, 2008), 121-42; see Herbert Tichy, *Friedrich Torberg: Ein Leben in Widersprüchen*, 1st ed. (Salzburg: Otto Müller, 1995) 241-47.

for the coordination of all CCF-publications and brought a "modest liberal anticommunist perspective into the French debates."[31] Polish writer Kontanty (Kot) Jeleński (1922–1987), another mastermind of the CCF[32] and editor of the Polish exile-magazine *Kultura*, played an important role within this cultural cold war, which was conducted via Paris.

Kraus' contacts to the officials of CCF came as a result of Manès Sperber (1905-1984), with whom he had a strong friendship having first met him in Sperber's bureau in the Parisian publishing house of Calmann-Lévy, where Sperber worked as an editor. Sperber, who drew up the "Manifest für freie Menschen" ("Manifest for free People")[33] together with Arthur Koestler (1905-1983), which was read at the first CCF conference in June 1950, was—in addition to Eugen Kogon (1903-1987), Denis de Rougemont (1906–1985) and Ignazio Silone (1900-1978)—as a member of the executive committee, one of the main protagonists of the congress in Europe. The fact that the administrative headquarters of the CCF was moved to Paris in 1951, made it possible for Sperber to participate energetically in the process of planning and organization and was challenged as organizer, communicator and generator of ideas.[34] Sperber had been always true to the Viennese line of thought, radically anti-communist and methodically suspicious of communism.[35] He was always aware of his mission and put all his energy into fighting the supremacy of the Soviet Union in Eastern Europe. His main interest was hereby to convey a message, and he not only appealed to the mind, but also to sentiments. He decided to do this not only by persuading friends or enemies, but by convincing them.[36] Sperber and François Bondy both identified with the ideas of Charles de Gaulles Minister of Culture, André Malraux, and also of Raymond Aron, who had broken with the majority of French leftists surrounding Jean-Paul Sartre "to advocate a policy of European integration and the preservation of democracy."[37]

---

31. Peter Coleman, *The Liberal Conspiracy*, 53, quoted in Berghahn, *Transatlantische Kulturkriege*, 180.
32. see Berghahn, *Transatlantische Kulturkriege*, 338.
33. Michael Hochgeschwender, *Freiheit in der Offensive: Der Kongreß für kulturelle Freiheit und die Deutschen* (Munich: Oldenburg, 1998), 17.
34. Mirjana Stančić, *Manès Sperber: Leben und Werk*, 1st ed. (Frankfurt/Main: Stroemfeld, 2003), 463.
35. Gerald Stieg, "Manès Sperber im Kalten Krieg der französischen Intellektuellen," *Wortverbunden – zeitbedingt: Perspektiven der Zeitschriftenforschung*, eds. Wolfgang Hackl and Kurt Krolop, (Innsbruck: Studienverlag, 2001), 207-218, 209.
36. See Anne-Marie Corbin-Schuffels, "Von Berlin nach Berlin: Manès Sperber und der Kongreß für kulturelle Freiheit (1950–1960)," *Manès Sperber als Europäer. Eine Ethik des Widerstands,* eds. Stéphane Moses, Joachim Schlör and Julius H. Schoeps (Berlin: Edition Hentrich, 1996), 90-119, 114.
37. Tweraser, "Paris Calling Vienna," 161.

In 1960 the CCF moved into a new phase and wanted to extend its activities all over the world. However contrary to Sperber, Kraus did not belong to the inner circle of the CCF.

Correspondence between Kraus and Sperber exemplifies how the ÖGL congress was organized: for the "Round table" talk, "Our Century and its novel" in October 1965, Kraus discussed with François Bondy "everything in minute detail, … the list of participants, the usages for the conference, was determined, and that everyone had to present a paper which had to be submitted in written form in advance. The fact that the invitation does not mention this is for psychological reasons, because I do not want to deter any of the very sensitive gentlemen."[38] Kraus compiled a "wish-list" of "names" for the discussion and requested Bondy to let him know, "upon which gentlemen on the list you have influence and where you find an invitation promising and meaningful."[39] Finally the congress came up with a variety of grand persons: the Slovakian writer Ladislav Mňačko (1919-1994), who was a critic of the political system of his country, the Czech writer, translator and psychiatrist Josef Nesvadba (1926-2005), the German writer Hermann Kesten (1900-1996) and the literary scholar Hans Mayer (1907-2001) all of whom attended the conference. Elias Canetti and Erich Fried came from England and both had already been invited to read in the ÖGL. The literary voices of France were represented by the father of *Nouveau Roman* Alain Robbe-Grillet (1922-2008) and Manès Sperber. Even the Polish literary scholar of German Roman Karst (1911-1988) was on the list of attendees. He had attended a conference on Franz Kafka in Liblice Castle near Prague in May 1963, where he had tried to encourage the works of Kafka in communist countries, together with other intellectuals such as Roger Garaudy, Eduard Goldstücker and Ernst Fischer. Hungary was represented by Tibor Déry (1894-1977) and Géza Ottlik (1912-1990). Déry, who had been imprisoned because of his participation in the Hungarian Uprising in October 1956, and whose works had been banned up to 1962 in Hungary, had kept in touch with Kraus, since his first reading in the ÖGL in 1963. Kraus invited him to read in his Association, provided him with books, and wrote reviews in prestigious journals and magazines. As contributors for Austria the writers Fritz Habeck (1916-1997), Hans Lebert (1919-1983) and Peter von Tramin (1932-1981) participated.

For the next conference "Literature as Tradition and Revolution" Kraus also received support from the Parisian bureau of the CCF. He was aware,

38. Letter from Wolfgang Kraus to Manès Sperber, 14 January 1965, Literary Estate of Wolfgang Kraus.
39. Letter from Wolfgang Kraus to Manès Sperber, 12 May 1965, Literary Estate of Wolfgang Kraus.

that his conferences could only benefit from this: “Incidentally [François] Bondy managed to persuade Marcel Reich-Ranicki to participate. The ‘Congress for Cultural Freedom’ is mighty”.[40] However a problem arose prior to the organization of the conference in 1966, as the literary scholar and critic Reich-Ranicki remarked in German newspaper *Die Zeit*, after it became apparent that the conference hade been postponed. The original date coincided with the tenth anniversary of the Hungarian Revolution and the “Polish October” in 1956, and since the conference theme was also “Literature as Tradition and Revolution,” the East suspected that the Viennese could be up to some mischief, maybe a political demonstration or even a sturdy provocation.” Reich-Ranicki mentioned that the cancellation would exacerbate the mediation between East and West that was “even in the sphere of literature an ungrateful and hard business” and defended the ÖGL as “a friendly and even cozy organization”: “I don’t think that Kraus is up to abuse the neutrality of Austrian soil for provoking activities.”[41]

As Kraus remarked in a letter, he had noticed the “unpleasant fact,” that “for different reasons … most of the participants from the socialist states who had already bindingly committed had withdrawn.” He criticized the absurdity of conducting a “talk without a counterpart, that could not fulfil the original concept of our enterprise.”[42]

A further advantage which arose from Kraus’ connection with the Parisian bureau of the CCF was the “Comité des écrivains et des éditeurs pour une entr’aide intellectuelle européenne,” founded in 1957, which was headed by Bondy and Jeleński. It concentrated its activities on supporting Hungarian intellectuals who had been persecuted since 1956. The program involved symposia, they shipped books that were only available in the West to writers in communist reigned countries, and assisted them with opportunity for publication of their books in western publishing houses. The Comité did not turn to official institutions in Eastern Europe, but rather to individuals, to ensure the authenticity of the exchange.[43] How the support for East European writers worked can be shown quintessentially in case of the Hungarian playwright and spokesman of the Hungarian Uprising in 1956, Julius Háy (1900-1975), who had spent three years in prison. In November 1963 Kraus contacted Sperber with the plea, to assist

40. Letter from Wolfgang Kraus to Herbert Zand, July 1965, Literary Estate of Herbert Zand, ÖLA 1/89, 1/B30/4, Literary Archive of the Austrian National Library, Vienna.

41. Marcel Reich–Ranicki, “Wiener Kongreß 1966 abgesagt,” *Die Zeit*, no. 42, 1966.

42. Letter from Wolfgang Kraus to Heimito von Doderer, 30 Sept. 1966, Autograph Collection of the Austrian National Library, Vienna.

43. See Ulrike Ackermann, *Sündenfall der Intellektuellen: Ein deutsch–französischer Streit von 1945 bis heute*, 1st ed. (Stuttgart: Klett–Cotta, 2000), 107f.

Háy, who intended "after infinite difficulties to travel" to foreign countries in the West: "Hay will bring three new, yet unpublished plays with him to the West [and] will come to Paris probably in early December and it would be most amiable, if you could greet him. As far as I can asses, he has an attitude closely related to ours, and it would be important to provide contacts for him in the West."[44] Sperber stepped in "so your protégé Julius Hay [sic] will be welcomed by CCF in Munich, honored and introduced to intellectuals in Munich. The matter that François Bondy, who knows the Magyar from his early days of theater, was sent from Paris to Munich, to hold an effective introductory speech, is implicitly your work as well."[45]

The ÖGL and the "Marshall Plan for the Mind"

Furthermore there were other points of contact of the ÖGL with American organizations financed by the CIA. In the request for funding of the Association to the Ministry of Education in the year of its founding, under article five, the intent turned up, that various institutions all over the world, like German Seminars, University libraries, broadcasting stations, theaters, professors, lecturers and PhD candidates should continuously be informed about Austria, it's literature and art. To this propaganda belonged the official literary magazines *Wort in der Zeit* and its successor *Literatur und Kritik*, whose editorial departments were located within the rooms of the ÖGL. Those mailings, especially to Eastern European countries should later continue on a much broader scale and with financial aid. From a journey to the United States in late September 1967 Kraus wrote from New York to his proxy and confident in the ÖGL, the writer Herbert Zand (1923-1970): "Today I had a dainty lunch with Minden and it has been very pleasant. He is a man of the world and an aesthete. By the way, he descended from Bukarest."[46] This "man of the World and aesthete" was no one other than George C. Minden (1921-2006), head of Free Europe Press and later president of the International Literary Center, an organization, which for more than twenty years functioned implicitly through a widely ramified European network of book and magazine publishers as well as unsuspicious cultural organizations such as the ÖGL. Between 1956 and 1991 more than 10 million western books and publications found their

44. Letter from Wolfgang Kraus to Manès Sperber, 5 Nov. 1963, Literary Estate of Wolfgang Kraus.
45. Letter from Manès Sperber to Wolfgang Kraus, 30 Nov. 1963, Literary Estate of Wolfgang Kraus.
46. Letter from Wolfgang Kraus to Herbert Zand, 15 Sept. 1967, Literary Estate of Herbert Zand, ÖLA 1/89, Sign. 1/B30/24, Literary Archive of the National Library, Vienna.

way to the communist reigned countries. The goal of the "book-mailing program" was to "communicate Western ideas to Soviet citizens by providing them with books—on politics, economics, philosophy, arts, and technology—not available in the Soviet Union."[47] Minden wanted to help prevent a communication breakdown like the one that had happened in the 1920s and 1930s, to interpret the democratic values of the West to East Europeans, to oppose boredom, irrationality, mediocrity and provincialism, to help create an open society, and to show the interest of the West in the intellectual and spiritual life of the East Europeans.[48] Even before his involvement in Minden's program, Kraus was a modern day "knigonoshi," a term that refers to the "book torchbearers" of czaristic times, and indicated Russians, who travelled to the west and came back with forbidden books "by bribing border guards to avoid government controls on the import of foreign literature."[49] The Russian writer and Germanist Lev Zalmanovich Kopelev (1912-1997), for example thanks Kraus in a letter dated November 1963 for the "rincley gift—of five volumes [Heinz] Kindermann, works by Karl Kraus and Hermann Brochs *Schlafwandler*—trilogy: the joy you brought me with that can hardly be verbalized."[50]

The contact of the ÖGL with Minden can be proven since 1964, as in an internal memo the visit of "Mr. Minden, US–Project, in July 1964" has been recorded. Minden agreed to cover all expenses for foreign books as well as Austrian literature, if it was of political relevance, like Franz Kafka, Robert Musil and Hermann Broch. Eventually he even paid a travel grant for up to five writers "à $200" from Romania and declared himself ready to pay half of the salary of an employee, who worked only on this project.[51] Kraus started working on this project immediately and presented as early as December 1964 a list of non-Austrian books in English and French as well as "suitable examples from the Austrian production," that he intended to send to "authors, translators, scientists and literary critics whom we either know personally, or who have been recommended to us as open minded and

47. Lowell Schwartz, *Political Warfare against the Kremlin. US and British Propaganda Policy at the Beginning of the Cold War*, (Basingstoke: Palgrave Macmillan, 2009), 197.
48. See George C. Minden, "The Book Project: A Presentation," prepared by George C. Minden, Director, Publications and Special Projects Division, Free Europe, Inc., 18 July 1969, 1, quoted in John P. C. Matthews, "The West's Secret Marshall Plan for the Mind," *International Journal of Intelligence and Counter Intelligence* 16, no. 3 (2003): 409-427, 419.
49. Yale Richmond, *Cultural Exchange and the Cold War: Raising the Iron Curtain*, (Univ. Park Pa.: Pennsylvania State University Press, 2003), 136.
50. Letter from Lew Kopelew to Wolfgang Kraus, 25 Nov. 1963, Archive of ÖGL, Vienna.
51. This was confirmed by the International Advisory Council Inc., in a Letter from Ethel C. Schroeder to Wolfgang Kraus, 2 Nov. 1964, Archive of the ÖGL, Vienna.

nonconformist representatives."[52] He also proposed to supply university libraries in Hungary and Czechoslovakia with books, "to provide professors and students with an opportunity of forming a more accurate picture of the western world."[53] Minden's organization also paid the annual subscription fee for the official Austrian literary magazine *Wort in der Zeit*, that was sent to addresses in the satellite countries of the Soviet Union.[54] One year later Kraus reported, that "every book we send to the East has an extraordinary impact. Thus we sent the mailings to people and institutions known to us, a maximal effect is granted. I can determine on my continuous travels to the East, that these book mailings play an important part in the intellectual progression of writers, literary scholars, and people working on the theater. No one can asses what we contribute to a more liberal growth."[55]

For Kraus' plans, financial aid was of the essence: "We need money, money, money, and forces to use it in a meaningful way. We have to heard possibilities for scholarships to the East." Kraus who neither lacked "ideas nor energy," often spent sleepless nights—how he remarked in a letter to Minden—because he didn't quite know, how he "could raise the money for his schemes."[56] Minden promised he would take care of the financial problems: "I hope money or the absence there of will not stand in the way of similar projects in the future."[57] Kraus suggested starting an operation, through which every addressee, who got books from us, should now get four works which reflect the Western point of view in order to make our eastern friends aware of such important books."[58] To "avoid the appearance of a propaganda campaign," Kraus intended not to send everyone the same books, but to "vary them from a larger assembly of books."[59] So that the Association would not be discredited in the East, Kraus had to utilize the books of Austrian writers as a backup, because he made no mistake, that "if we appear in a crooked light, the books will not be let trough by censorship."[60] On the lists assembled by Kraus, among politically charged books like Karl Poppers *The open Society and its Enemies* (1946), there were

52. Letter from Wolfgang Kraus to Mrs. Ethel Schroeder, International Advisory Council Inc, New York, 1 Dec. 1964, Archive of the ÖGL, Vienna.
53. Ibid.
54. Letter from Hella Bronold [secretary of the ÖGL] to Mrs. Ethel Schroeder, 14 Sept. 1965, Archive of the ÖGL.
55. Letter from Wolfgang Kraus to George C. Minden, 14 Dec. 1965, Archive of the ÖGL.
56. Letter from Wolfgang Kraus to George C. Minden , 4 Jan. 1966, Archive of the ÖGL.
57. Letter from George C. Minden to Wolfgang Kraus, 21 Dec. 1965, Archive of the ÖGL.
58. Letter from George C. Minden to Wolfgang Kraus, 4 Jan. 1966, Archive of the ÖGL.
59. Letter from Wolfgang Kraus to George C. Minden, 4 Jan. 1966, Archive of the ÖGL.
60. Letter from Wolfgang Kraus to George C. Minden, 3 Jan. 1968, Archive of the ÖGL.

always titles of Austrian authors like Thomas Bernhards *Frost* (1963), Hermann Brochs *Die Schlafwandler* (1931-1932) or works of Franz Kafka. So the ÖGL participated in a covert CIA-operation that went down in history as the "Marshall Plan for the Mind." Because of Minden's ingenious covert operations, these circumstances became apparent only after Mindens death in 2006.[61]

Despite all of his achievements in the cultural cold war, Kraus had reason for complaints. Shortly after the publication of his first collection of essays *Der fünfte Stand* (1966), he wrote to Sperber, that the Slavist and translator Peter Urban had released a "huge pamphlet against my books" in *Literatur und Kritik*: "It teems of boast and ill concealed communist aggression."[62] For the "departure of intellectuals in West and East," that Kraus tried to outline in terms of the history of ideas, he got international recognition and praise. Content wise, Kraus referred to the origin, structure, as well as the part of intellectuals in Eastern and Western European countries. By his knowledge and outlook across the Eastern European countries and their respective intellectual climate, Kraus tried a depiction of the intellectual state and confronted the leading ideologies with each other. For the critic Friedrich Heer (1916-1983) the book portrayed the "overcome of the Cold War in the intellectual and spiritual space of central Europe,"[63] and the Swiss philosopher and political theorist Arnold Künzli (1919-2008) verified, that the relationship of East and West had rarely been depicted in such a "factual, wise and dialectic" manner.[64]

But for his essay Kraus also earned critique. The already mentioned Peter Urban alleged Kraus, that he had "downright uncritically used the terms of Springer-Press" and that "each and every chapter could stand apart as pamphlets in magazines of the West committed to cultural policy," but they would not result in a "framework."[65] Urban criticized the terms Kraus applied, because he wrote of "the East under soviet control," of "communistic Eastern Europe" and "of countries, that were monitored by Moscow."[66] Even in *Österreichische Osthefte* Kraus' thesis was attacked

61. See Martin Douglas, "George C. Minden, 85, Dies; Led a Cold War of Words," *New York Times*, 23. Apr. 2006.
62. Letter from Wolfgang. Kraus to Manès Sperber, 15. Apr. 1967, Literary Estate of W. Kraus, ÖLA 63/97, Literary Archive of the Austrian National Library, Vienna.
63. Friedrich Heer, "Der fünfte Stand: Aufbruch der Intellektuellen," *Wiesbadner Kurier*, 17 Dec. 1966.
64. Arnold Künzli, "Review of Wolfgang Kraus: Der fünfte Stand," *Gewerkschaftliche Monatshefte* (Cologne), May 1967, 113.
65. Peter Urban, "Zur Diskussion über 'Der fünfte Stand' von Wolfgang Kraus," *Literatur und Kritik* 2, no. 14 (1967): 247.
66. Ibid.

by Kurt Marko, who labeled the book as "eastwardly inspired" and "a self portrait of Western crudeness." At the same time Marko apostrophized the "pale decalcomania pictures of communist chimeras,"[67] that Kraus had brought into the game. In this context, another controversy from the late 1970s shall be mentioned. Kraus had in an article titled "Die Normalität der Intellektuellen" ("The normality of the intellectuals") written in *Der Tagesspiegel* about the internment of oppositional intellectuals in mental institutions that grew common in the Soviet Union.[68] This caused the Soviet writer Alexander Kriwitzki to publish a counter-statement in which he blamed Kraus for writing his article, "as if everything he had invoked, was familiar and needed no proof." Kriwitzki stated that Kraus felt in the "atypical situation of the 'cold war' as right as rain."[69]

As an answer to bewildered Kraus, Sperber replied: "What happened to you on behalf of this Urban is gods just punishment. You have been far to kind and forgiving towards the procurers of Stalinism."[70]

The ÖGL and the End of the CCF

The CCF had over the years evolved into a transnational platform and an interface between the East and West had reached its zenith between 1964 and 1966. Then a phase of unrest and destabilization began, and the CCF found its inglorious end in 1966, when CIA-funding was made public in a series of newspaper articles in the New York Times. Among the CCF members only a few had known about this covert financial aid. Even for Sperber the scandal surrounding the CCF was a huge personal disappointment. In a letter to Kraus he states, that the activity of the CCF had been "utterly disparaged."[71] Following the exposure severe conflict arose within the committee of the congress and the editorial teams of those journals, associated with the Congress. Especially Michael Josselson came under fire from all sides. For the anti-totalitarian left-wing intellectuals the scandal surrounding the CCF was a huge disappointment. Given the

67. Kurt Marko,"Ein fünfter Stand?" *Österreichische Osthefte: Mitteilungen des Österreichischen Ost– und Südosteuropa–Instituts* 9, no. 3 (1967): 246-51.

68. Alexander Kriwitzki, "Das Syndrom Wolfgang Kraus," in *Bundesrepublik Deutschland – Sowjetunion. Offenheit gegen Offenheit. Meinungen – Kontroversen – Dialoge*, ed. Friedrich Hitzer (Colonge: Pahl Rugenstein, 1978), 258-61.

69. Wolfgang Kraus, "Die Normalität der Intellektuellen," in Hitzer, *Bundesrepublik Deutschland,* 257–58.

70. Letter from Manès Sperber to Wolfgang Kraus, 25 Apr. 1967, Literary Estate of Wolfgang Kraus, ÖLA 63/97.

71. Letter from Manès Sperber to Wolfgang Kraus, 5 July 1968, Literary Estate of Wolfgang Kraus.

students, civil rights and anti-war-movements of the time, the members of the CCF were politically discredited. The extent to which the exposure of the CCF continued to have an effect, is reflected in a letter from Sperber to Josselson in 1976, in which Sperber reports about the completion of his autobiography and even nine years later, his approach in respect of the involvement of the CIA, is still extremely cautious: "In the third volume of my recollections, which I'm working on, so it can be published in summer, I'm talking about the congress, to which I pledge myself explicitly. Of course I have to, even in brief, mention the question regarding the CIA. ... I would like to know, if you'd wish or refuse the mentioning of your name—not only in regard to this episode, but because of your activity as general secretary, about which I could say a lot of good things. Of course I can't mention the one thing without the other, which means I can't state your name as general secretary and than leave the CIA–incident anonymous."[72]

Josselsons successor was the journalist, historian and diplomat Shepard Stone (1908-1990), who oversaw the follow–up organization of CCF, the International Association for Cultural Freedom (IACF). Stone was anxious to campaign further against the East through intellectual means and to defuse the powerful political and military confrontations, so they would not lead to a nuclear war.[73] Stone strove with financial support of the Ford Foundation to counteract the loss of importance of the CCF.

However in the beginning of 1967, only a few months before the scandalous reveal of the CIA-financing of CCF, Sperber arranged a meeting between Wolfgang Kraus and Michael Josselson in Geneva: "The conversation with you was immensely important to me, and I wanted to thank you for your invitation, that gave me the opportunity to meet you in person. Mr. Sperber is now residing in Vienna, and we are going to talk about some of the broached issues,"[74] Kraus wrote to Josselson.

As early as 1965 Kraus had met in person with Shepard Stone in Vienna and encountered him repeatedly in the course of the second half of the 1960s. Kraus was also on hand with help and advise on the occasion of Stones visit in the CSSR: "You will probably approach a whole series of official institutions. Certainly these are all facilities shaped by the sheer communistic ideology. We ourselves behave distant towards these facilities and only have as much linkage with them as is necessary for the handling of our contacts. As a precaution, we are wary about inviting official

72. Letter from Manès Sperber to Michael Josselson, 2/B1720/6, Literary Estate of Manès Sperber, Literary Archive of the Austrian National Library, Vienna.

73. Berghahn, *Transatlantische Kulturkriege*, 256.

74. Letter from W. Kraus to Michael Josselson, 16 Jan. 1967, Michael Josselson Papers, Harry Ransom Center, Austin/Texas.

personalities among writers, critics, and editors or such, who are regarded as spokespeople true to party principles. We are avoiding this because the invitees will be granted a consolidation of their position."[75]

In the same letter Kraus guessed that it would be much harder for Stone, to bring "a non-official writer from the CSSR to the US or to the West, than for the neutral state of Austria," and offered to invite "various writers, literary scholars, directors and personalities, who stand somehow in relation to literature, on Stones orders, whereby his institution should not appear on the invitation."

That there were "things possible in Vienna, which yet were inoperable in Berlin," became clear in 1968, when after the Russian invasion in the CSSR, about 200 intellectuals, who had fled to Vienna, among them the writer Milan Kundera (born in 1929), knocked on the door of the ÖGL. Kraus, whose bureau was "crowded with Czech writers, whom I'm trying to help, as best as I can,"[76] in spite of the conversations he had had with Stone concerning the refugees, "not a dime had been made available for these people and the supporting measures had spring-fed only from Austrian resources." Kraus was disappointed in "the way things turned out" and asked himself, if there had been an "ideological cue, which had led to such a complete policy shift."[77]

However the literary scholar Eduard Goldstücker (1913-2000) did not forget Kraus' commitment to the Czech and Slovakian intellectuals "who were not in favor of the regime and the all around moral and material support," which Kraus had granted them. In the beginning of the 1990s he suggested to Václav Havel (1936-2011), the ex-president of former CSSR, to honor Kraus with a medal, which was presented to him on the fourth of December 1991 in celebration of the thirty year anniversary of the ÖGL.[78]

In a letter to Sperber in the 1970s, Kraus concluded, that Austria was not as important for the East-West encounter anymore, because other countries (France and the GDR) had surpassed Austria in this role, and as far as Kraus was concerned, in a "towering eagerness."[79] In his journal too, Kraus later commemorated this time of his greatest achievements: "How long the successful time of the East-West congresses dates back! Back then I thought it would always go on like this, even up higher."[80]

75. Letter from Wolfgang Kraus to Shepard Stone, 13 Dec. 1965, Archive of the ÖGL.

76. Letter from Wolfgang Kraus to Heinrich Böll, 16 Sept. 1968, Archive of the ÖGL.

77. Letter from Wolfgang Kraus to George C. Minden, 15 Jan. 1969, Archive of the ÖGL.

78. See copy of a letter from Eduard Goldstücker to Vaclav Havel, Literary Estate of Wolfgang Kraus.

79. Letter from Wolfgang Kraus to Manès Sperber, 28 Dec. 1970, Literary Estate of Wolfgang Kraus.

80. Journal Entry of Wolfgang Kraus, 29 Mar. 1972, Literary Estate of Wolfgang Kraus.

Conclusion

On 20 February 1969, in the office of Federal Chancellor Josef Klaus, the "Fest der Harmonie" ("Festival of Harmony"), named ironically by Hans Haider, was established as proof of Kraus' unifying abilities. This event, organized by the ÖGL, gathered writers persecuted by the Nazi regime and opportunists, as well as neo-classicists and "Sprachzertrümmerer" with political references between Christian-conservative and communistic.[81] As Kraus remembered this appearance of all the important "dramatis personae" of the literary scene: "Thomas Bernhard was charmingly and animatedly chatting with Josef Klaus, Wolfgang Bauer, Alfred Kolleritsch, Hilde Spiel stood aside Friedrich Torberg, Franz Nabl, Max Mell, Alexander Lernet-Holenia, Felix Braun, Franz Theodor Csokor beside Herbert Zand, Friedrich Heer, Ernst Jandl and Friedericke Mayröcker. Ingeborg Bachmann, dressed in a white pantsuit, was talking to Christine Busta, Hans Lebert was there, Barbara Frischmuth, Andreas Okopenko, Fritz Habeck, Milo Dor, Otto Gründmandl."[82]

However with the shift in the political constellation in the Austrian Government and the one-party government of the SPÖ a number of things changed for Kraus. While he had been on friendly terms with Minister of Education, Heinrich Drimmel and his head of department Alfred Weikert (who was sentenced to prison for four years for embezzling funds), Kraus had difficulties finding common ground regarding cultural policy with social democratic politician Fred Sinowatz (1929-2008), Minister of Education and Arts from 1971 to 1983.[83] From 1971 to 1975 Kraus found shelter in the "Europa Verlag" of the Austrian trade union federation, where he was responsible for its literary program. Although critics did remark that he tended to support only his prestigious journalist friends, the works of authors

81. Hans Haider, "Der Kartonismus' 1965: Ende und Wende; Ein Streifzug durch die Literatur- und Kulturpolitik der Zweiten Republik," in *Österreich – 90 Jahre Republik. Beitragsband der Ausstellung im Parlament*, ed. Stefan Karner (Innsbruck: Studienverlag, 2008), 421-28.

82. Ibid. 427; see Wolfgang Kraus, "Zwischen Trümmern und Wohlstand: Das literarische Leben in Österreich von 1945 bis zur Gegenwart; ein Essay," in *Geschichte der Österreichischen Literatur von den Anfängen bis zur Gegenwart*, vol. 7, ed. Herbert Zeman (Graz: Akadem. Druck- u. Verlagsanstalt, 1999), 539-636, 601.

83. Journal Entry of Wolfgang Kraus, 3 Feb. 1974, Literary Estate of Wolfgang Kraus. "Freitag war ich bei Kulturminister Sinowatz, der mir auch nicht gerade Sympathien entgegenbringt. Es liegt mir nicht, bei so schweren Problemen ... im österreichischen Kulturleben den Mund zu halten. Die Sozialdemokraten sind nach wie vor voller Misstrauen und vertragen ... keine leiseste Kritik. ... Wenn ich bedenke, wie hart ich [die] ÖVP–Spitzen in Gesprächen kritisiert habe, muß ich staunen."

like Julien Green (1900–1998), Manès Sperber, Mircea Eliade (1907–1986), François Bondy, E. M. Cioran (1911–1995) and Lewis Mumford (1895–1990) were published.[84] In 1975 Kraus was given the assignment that reinforced his position within the "field of power" (Bourdieu) and not only made him "importer" but also "exporter" of Austrian literature. In this official capacity Kraus took responsibility for the content of the cultural activities of all ten of the *Kulturinstitute* (Institutes of Culture) of the Republic of Austria abroad, and was accountable to no one other than the Foreign Minister Erich Bielka (1909-1992), who had offered Kraus this position.[85] Kraus held this bureaucratic position until 1981, when the department was closed. In the late 1970 he was repeatedly under fire from diverse (political) directions, because of his accumulation of various key-professions within literary life, that led to a "singular concentration of power,"[86] as a telegram of the *Grazer Autorenversammlung* (GAV) claimed. The GAV founded in 1973, which saw itself as an "anti-PEN" and was the manifestation of real change within the literary scene,[87] received from 1974 on, almost the same amount of public fundings as Austrian P.E.N.-Club. The founding of the GAV had been a sort of "collateral campaign" to the boom of social democracy, in which the "sozialpartnerschaftliche" [social-partnership] re-organization of the literary scene took place.[88]

Just two years before the break up of the Soviet Union Kraus had one of his last coups. The idea for the Österreich Bibliotheken in 1988, with "their associated scholarships."[89] His idea was realized initially in Bratislava and Brno, followed by branches in Kiev, Olmouc, Mocow and St. Petersburg. By 1995 some 37 libraries had been established in the post-communist countries, and Kraus still dealt with the invitations, despite having resigned from the ÖGL in 1994.

84. See *50 Jahre Europa Verlag: "Aus dem Drangsal in ein neues Europa."* (Vienna: Europa Verlag, 1983), 20.

85. See journal entry of W. Kraus, 17 Aug. 1974, Literary Estate of Wolfgang Kraus. "Gestern Nachmittag zu Bielka gekommen. Er hatte mich von hier aus in Wien angerufen, ich solle kommen wegen der Situation der Kulturinstitute. Bietet mir an, zu versuchen, die Sektionsleitung für mich durchzusetzen oder die Leitung der Clearing-Stelle."

86. wespennest. Zeitschrift für brauchbare Texte, no. 36 (1979): 53. "Die GAV macht darauf aufmerksam, daß es im literarischen Leben Österreichs zu einer einmaligen Machtkonzentration auf eine Person gekommen ist."

87. Evelyne Polt-Heinzel, "Kulturskandale der 1970er Jahre: Lauter kleine Staatsoperetten," in *Staatsoperetten: Kunstverstörungen; Das kulturelle Klima der 1970er Jahre*, ed. Ibid., (Vienna: Dokumentationsstelle für neuere österreichische Literatur, 2009), 9-42, 12.

88. see Roland Innerhofer, *Die Grazer Autorenversammlung (1973-1983): Zur Organisation einer "Avantgarde"* (Vienna: Böhlau, 1985).

89. Wolfgang Kraus to François Bondy, 6 January 1995, Literary Estate of Wolfgang Kraus.

When Kraus died on 19th September 1998, various obituaries were published in most of the major domestic newspapers and even abroad, claiming his merits in the field of literature, the literary émigrés and his commitment to East European intellectuals. They also stated, that he had been "not particularly popular"[90] in Vienna, and that he "long ago had to make place for a new type of official of the literary scene."[91]

90. u.we., "Der große Kommunikator," *FAZ*, 22 Sept. 1998.
91. Hans Haider, "Ein altmodischer Literaturfreund," *Die Presse*, 21 Sept. 1998, 21.

Common Lives

Torn apart between time and space?

A Collective Biography of Austro-Hungarian Military Personnel on the Eastern Front, 1914-1918

Wolfram Dornik

Our idea of the First World War is still dominated by the trench warfare at the Somme, at Ypres or other famous war scenes of the Western Front. Ernst Jünger, Erich Maria Remarque and the published memories of hundreds of others who fought at this part of the war have painted our picture: trenches, tanks, shock troops, the bone mills and the *Stahlgewitter* shape this narration. But this was not the common experience of Austro-Hungarian soldiers. Most of them fought on at least two or more fronts, and they experienced a wide variety of terrain: from the highly mobile warfare in Serbia, the great plains of Eastern Europe with long and cold winters and short but very hot summers, to the dry and bleak karst of the Isonzo/Soča Valley, to the extreme conditions in the high alpine mountains of Tyrol and Carinthia. But one of these war theaters dominated the experience of most of the military personnel, because masses of men and materials were deployed there, and the unimaginable dimensions of its war scene (twice as long as the Western Front!) were extraordinary, too—the Eastern Front.[1]

While we have initial studies on the war experience on the Italian and Serbian Fronts,[2] similar ones for the Eastern Front have been limited so far.[3] The war between the Baltic Sea and the Black Sea, with its very different

---

1. The following paper has been written as part of the "Beyond the Trenches. War Memories of German-speaking Soldiers of the Austro-Hungarian Army on the Eastern Front of the First World War" project, funded by the Austrian Science Fund (P 23070-G15). The project is led by the author of this paper, and will run at the Ludwig Boltzmann-Institute for Research on the Consequences of War until 2014.

2. See for example: Hermann J. W. Kuprian, and Oswald Überegger, eds., *Der Erste Weltkrieg im Alpenraum: Erfahrung, Deutung, Erinnerung* (Innsbruck: Universitätsverlag Wagner, 2006); Daniela Schanes, *Serbien im Ersten Weltkrieg: Feind- und Kriegsdarstellungen in österreichisch-ungarischen, deutschen und serbischen Selbstzeugnissen* (Frankfurt/Main: Peter Lang Verlag, 2011); Oswald Überegger, *Der andere Krieg: Die Tiroler Militärgerichtsbarkeit im Ersten Weltkrieg* (Innsbruck: Universitätsverlag Wagner, 2002); etc.

3. Some of the following books refer to the war experience on the Eastern Front: Wolfram Dornik et al., *Die Ukraine zwischen Selbstbestimmung und Fremdherrschaft 1917–1922* (Graz: Leykam Verlag, 2011); Richard Lein, *Pflichterfüllung oder Hochverrat? Die tschechischen Soldaten Österreich-Ungarns im Ersten Weltkrieg* (Münster: LIT-Verlag, 2011). In terms of the German experience in the Baltics, the following book is still a benchmark: Vejas Gabriel Liulevicius, *Kriegsland im Osten: Eroberung, Kolonisierung und Militärherrschaft im Ersten Weltkrieg* (Hamburg: Hamburger Edition, 2002).

kinds of experience—heavy fighting followed by longer phases of silence, occupation and exploitation of huge, foreign territories, and confrontation with alien, heterogeneous cultures—formed their picture of Eastern Europe. To focus too narrowly on the doubtless extreme conditions on the Isonzo Front would distort our understanding of the war experience of millions of soldiers, who had to suffer years of war, displacement and social upheaval. It is also important to keep in mind that the war did not end here in November 1918, but at the earliest in 1921/22 with the territorial consolidation of the newly emerged states as a result of the Peace Treaties of Riga.[4]

In terms of the individual war experience, we have a pretty good picture of the political and military elites, and the officers of the Habsburg Empire.[5] But there has been little research on John and Jane Doe.[6] Through the war biographies of five Austro-Hungarian soldiers, NCOs and low level officers, this paper intends to give an insight into what they experienced and how this shaped their understanding of the war and Eastern Europe. The collective biography approach allows us to avoid a tedious listing of the

4. See for this: Jerzy Borzęcki, *The Soviet-Polish Peace of 1921 and the Creation of Interwar Europe* (New Haven: Harvard University Press, 2008). See also the unpublished paper of the author: Wolfram Dornik, "A Question of Nation, Territory and Ideology: Intervention and Occupation in Eastern Europe 1914-22," in *Russia's Great War and Revolution, 1914-1922: The Centennial Reappraisal*. Vol. 1/2: The Russian Civil War (in preparation).

5. See especially: Peter Broucek, ed., *Theodor Ritter von Zeynek: Ein Offizier im Generalstabskorps erinnert sich* (Vienna: Böhlau Verlag, 2009); István Deák, *Der K.(u.)K. Offizier 1848-1918* (Vienna: Böhlau Verlag, 1991); Georg Reichlin-Meldegg, *Der Löwe von Limanowa: Josef Roth Freiherr von Limanova-Lapanów – Ein Leben zwischen den Epochen* (Graz: Ares Verlag, 2005); Gergely Romsics, *Myth and Remembrance: The Dissolution of the Habsburg Empire in the Memoir Literatur of the Austro-Hungarian Political Elite* (New York: Columbia University Press, 2006); Albert Pethö, ed., *Belagerung und Gefangenschaft: Von Przemyśl bis Russisch-Turkestan; Das Kriegstagebuch des Dr. Richard Ritter von Stenitzer 1914-1917* (Graz: Ares-Verlag, 2010); Ursula Prutsch, and Klaus Zeyringer, eds., *Leopold von Andrian (1875-1951): Korrespondenzen, Notizen, Essays, Berichte* (Vienna: Böhlau Verlag, 2003); etc.

6. For this, see for example: Hannes Leidinger, and Verena Moritz, eds., *In russischer Gefangenschaft: Erlebnisse österreichischer Soldaten im Ersten Weltkrieg* (Vienna: Böhlau Verlag, 2008); Angelique Leszczawski-Schwerk, "'Amazonen, emanzipierte Frauen, Töchter des Volkes': Polnische und ukrainische Legionärinnen in der österreichisch-ungarischen Armee im Ersten Weltkrieg," *Glanz – Gewalt – Gehorsam: Militär und Gesellschaft in der Habsburgermonarchie (1800 bis 1918)*, eds. Laurence Cole, Christa Hämmerle, and Martin Scheutz (Essen: Klartext Verlag, 2011), 55-76; Alon Rachamimov, "Normalität als Travestie: Das Theaterleben der k.u.k. Kriegsgefangenenoffiziere in Russland, 1914-1920," in *Glanz–Gewalt–Gehorsam*, eds. Cole, Hämmerle, and Scheutz, 101-126; Martin Scheutz, "'Frontangst,' 'Frontrisiko' und 'Frontdrang': Die Korrespondenz der Historiker Heinrich Ritter von Srbik, Wilhelm Bauer und Hans Hirsch im Ersten Weltkrieg," in *Glanz–Gewalt–Gehorsam*, eds. Cole, Hämmerle, and Scheutz, 77-99; Oskar Dohle, ed., *Constantin Schneider: Die Kriegserinnerungen 1914-1919* (Vienna: Böhlau Verlag, 2003); etc.

individual chronology.[7] Thus, we will follow the individual experience of each person analyzed across the most important cross-sections: space and time, fear and despair, identity and culture, and body and mind. Of course, in a paper like this, we cannot follow every possible aspect, but we can gain an initial insight into common experiences as well as individual differences by examining the chosen aspects. This will give us the chance to get a better idea of which experiences and consequences they shared and which were unique to the individual. This paper will also try to offer a brief insight into the development of mentalities within the interwar years, during which veterans had a vital influence on the public and political discussions on Eastern Europe.

Of course, the five individuals are not representative of the nine million soldiers of the Habsburg army. The individuals chosen were born between 1888 and 1894, and they are mainly German-speaking. Nonetheless, an attempt has been made to cover a wide range of geographical, socio-economic and political backgrounds: there is thus a Galician Jewish artillery man, Theofil REISS, born in 1889[8]; an NCO (June 1916: *Feldwebel*/sergeant) from the heart of what is today Austria (Weißenbach/Enns), Alois PROKOSCH, born in 1888[9]; a social democratic infantryman from Vienna, Karl SCHOVANEZ, born in 1894[10]; a low-level officer (Aug. 1916: *Leutnant*/second lieutenant; Aug. 1917: *Oberleutnant*/first lieutenant) from Linz, Josef BRUCKNER, born in 1892[11]; and an infantryman from rural Eastern Styria, Karl SCHABERL, born in 1893, who spent most of

---

7. Here I draw on the concept of a group/collective biography, which gives us the opportunity to explore a small group of persons who define themselves as a group, at least for a short period of time. See for group/collective biography and prosopography: Levke Hardes, Hanns Schweiger, "Kollektivbiographische Ansätze," in *Handbuch Biographie: Methoden, Traditionen, Theorien,* ed. Christian Klein (Stuttgart: Verlag J.B. Melzer, 2009), 194-98.

8. A copy of Theopil Reiss' diary is stored at the Universität Wien, Institut für Wirtschafts- und Sozialgeschichte, Dokumentation Lebensgeschichtlicher Erinnerungen (DOKU). I would like to thank Mag. Günter Müller for his help during my research.

9. Alois Prokosch kept a diary throughout the war, which he drew on to produce seven handwritten booklets in the early 1950s (last one in 1955). They are stored in the Provincial Archives of Styria in Graz. I would like to thank Dr. Wolfgang Weiß for his support.

10. Karl Schovanez wrote handwritten memoirs of his entire life for his family under the title *Im Zwielicht der Jahrzehnte* between 1960 and 1969. For this paper, I have focused on the parts covering his childhood up to the early Interwar Period. A copy of this is stored in the DOKU. I would like to thank Günter Müller once again for his assistance.

11. Josef Bruckner left a couple of loose diary entries and notes, which were compiled by his widow with a couple of letters. A copy of this compilation is stored in DOKU, thanks to Günter Müller.

the war in Russian captivity.[12] Their social background not only determined their rank, but also their educational level and subsequently their ability to express their feelings and thoughts. They all survived the war, although most of them were wounded or in critical physical conditions at least once. They had all served in a wide range of war theaters on at least two fronts. But their most important and longest war experience had been in Eastern Europe.

The main sources for the analysis are *ad hoc* or retrospective written remains (diaries, letters, memoirs, curricula vitae etc.). The problem with these sources is that there are few originals, and we have to rely on copies of the originals and transcripts by the authors themselves or family members. Using a careful and critical approach based on textual hermeneutics, I tried to approximate the *ad hoc* point of view or contextualize it in the relevant time frame. Of course, this is a shortcoming of this type of source, but nonetheless a careful use of these materials allows us to achieve a point of view closer to the original and more free of (self) censorship than other individual sources (especially field post).[13]

All of these sources were written with the intention of preserving a particular image of the authors for following generations—in some cases, via the filter of a loved one. A central aspect of the writing, regardless of whether it took place at the time or years afterward, which is not reflected in the texts themselves, is that the process of writing was also a way of coping with their experiences: to find a place for the things they experienced in their understanding of life. What most of the authors emphasize is that their experiences were not unique to them, but were shared by others: they saw themselves as part of a big mass. By entering the army, they had to give up their individual freedom of choice (*ade zivil*). They were now drilled (*abgerichtet*), transported in masses across half of Europe, and they suffered and died in masses at the front.[14] This feeling of deindividualization can also be observed in higher ranks. Franz Conrad von Hötzendorf, the head of

12. Karl Schaber wrote his reminiscences in a small booklet in 1922, which his son transferred from Gothic to modern script, and which was digitalized by his grandson in the 1990s. A copy of these memoirs has been handed over to me by a friend of the family, Johann Praßl, whom I am grateful for his support.

13. For more methodological and empirical questions on field post (especially the papers from Christian Heuer and Elke Scherstjanoi), see: Veit Didczuneit, Jens Elbert, and Thomas Jander, eds., *Schreiben im Krieg. Schreiben vom Krieg: Feldpost im Zeitalter der Weltkriege* (Essen: Klartext Verlag, 2011).

14. This fundamental loss of individuality has been described in detail: DOKU, Karl Schovanez, *Im Zwielicht der Jahrzehnte*, unpublished manuscript, 1969, 280-91.

the Austro-Hungarian General Staff for nearly two-thirds of the war, also described himself after the war as being just a small cog in a larger machine, with limited possibilities of influencing the course of events.[15]

Of course, a collective biography which deals with a qualitative and not a quantitative approach has to consider the question of representativity.[16] Another question is authenticity: sources have passed through different "hands," and a lot of details could have been changed, left out or added. Particularly the changing contexts of their lives could also have altered their interpretations of what happened before 1918. Therefore, we have to be careful in working with these sources. Nonetheless, this paper could provide us with an initial insight into the individual biographies of soldiers who fought in Eastern Europe.

Space and Time

In his groundbreaking book "The Culture of Time and Space, 1880-1918" (first published in 1983), the cultural historian Stephen Kern analyzed the transformation of time, space and society because of innovations such as the telegraph, the railroad, the bicycle, the automobile and the cinema in the critical years around the Fin de Siècle. The First World War also plays an important role in his book, accelerating and increasing processes observable since at least the last quarter of the 19th century.[17] This can be seen in the biographies of our five individuals. The new technologies shaped their individual pace of life in war. During their time as soldiers they traveled huge distances through Central and Eastern Europe, in one case,

15. This was also a common way of denying responsibility and guilt: Lawrence Sondhaus, *Franz Conrad von Hötzendorf: Architect of the Apocalypse* (Boston: Humanities Press, 2000), 244.

16. See the introduction of Bernhard Fetz in this volume. In addition, see the following two comprehensive overviews on history and discourse, and on collective biography and prosopography: Wilhelm Heinz Schröder, "Kollektivbiographie: Spurensuche, Gegenstand, Forschungsstrategie," in *Historische Sozialforschung: Kollektivbiographie als interdisziplinäre Methode in der Historischen Sozialforschung; Eine persönliche Retrospektive*, ed. Wilhelm Heinz Schröder, Supplement 23 (Cologne: Zentrum für Historische Sozialforschung, 2011), 74-152; Thomas Winkelbauer "Plutarch, Sueton und die Folgen: Konturen und Konjunkturen der historischen Biographie," in *Vom Lebenslauf zur Biographie: Geschichte, Quellen und Probleme der historischen Biographik und Autobiographik; Referate der Tagung "vom Lebenslauf zur Biographie" am 26. Oktober 1997 in Horn*, ed. Thomas Winkelbauer (Horn: Waldviertler Heimatbund, 2000), 9-46.

17. Stephen Kern, *The Culture of Time and Space, 1880-1918* (Cambridge: Harvard University Press, 2003). On "movement" from a military perspective during the First and Second World War, see: Alexander Meschnig, *Der Wille zur Bewegung: Militärischer Traum und totalitäres Programm; Eine Mentalitätsgeschichte vom Ersten Weltkrieg zum Nationalsozialismus* (Bielefeld: transcript Verlag, 2008).

even through parts of Asia. Within a relatively short time, they saw places, which the average citizen of the Habsburg monarchy before 1914 had never seen before, and which would have been unimaginable in previous wars. Only a small class of trades people, scientists, scholars, artists, high ranking military officers, and the political elite ever crossed distances like these. Alois Prokosch, for instance, enlisted in Leoben in August 1914, and then traveled to Przemyslany and Kolomea via Graz, Fehring, Győr, Budapest, and Stryj. Exactly one year later he was sent to the Isonzo front, then to Coldonaro in March 1916 and finally he was moved back to fight in the 12th Insonzo battle in October 1917. Theofil Reiss, who was born in Lemberg but grew up in Vienna, fought in Western Galicia, where he was wounded and brought back to Vienna. After this, he spent some weeks in staging areas. Since he felt bored, he volunteered once again for the front and was sent to Belezyce, where he became severely ill and had to be brought back to Vienna once again for recovery. In the following months, he spent a lot of time on vacation, escorting prisoners, or in staging areas. Starting in early October 1916, he once again found himself at the front near Chadky-Bzresani and Dolna, where he once again fell ill. From October 1917 until February 1918 he was at the front in Germanovka and Rarancze. Starting in late April 1918 he fought at Marter and Manduello, Barikata and Montelongara on the Tyrol Front, where he got shell-shock (*Granaterschütterung*) in a heavy artillery attack. In mid-June he was brought back to Vienna, where he stayed throughout the summer. But he was not done yet. He was sent to Tarnow at the beginning of October, where we lose track of his movements. But Karl Schaberl covered the longest distances: the young man from a farm in Eastern Styria, near Feldbach, was deployed in August 1914 and sent to the Eastern Front, where he participated in the retreat to the Carpathian passes. He was caught by Russian troops at Mezőlaborc in late November. He was then sent to a camp in Borisovka near Lake Baikal via Lviv, Brody, Kiev, Moscow, Voronezh, and Novonikolayevsk (today Novosibirsk). From there, they sent him to Bjelowodsk east of Starobilsk (in what is today Eastern Ukraine), where he worked on farms or in private houses. In April 1918, he was liberated by the invading German troops and brought back to Austria-Hungary[18], where he arrived in his home garrison on June 18. After reintegrating his unit and a short vacation (which he tried to extend by faking an illness), he was sent to the Tyrol Front in late October, and on the way there he experienced the breakdown of the Habsburg monarchy.

Our five individuals also got used to most of the new technologies, which helped them to overcome space: telegraphs transported their orders

18. On the occupation of the Ukraine by the Central Powers, see: Dornik et al., *Die Ukraine*:

from headquarters to the foremost frontlines; trains transported them and their supplies through half of Europe and made short vacations at home possible during the war; bicycles, cars, trucks and armored vehicles accelerated individual military transport behind the frontline; airplanes and captive balloons completely changed notions of distance and introduced air space into military thinking.

However, all five individuals also experienced periods of limited movement: Josef Bruckner spent two and a half months in front line positions on the Eastern Front at the end of 1915 and the beginning of 1916 and later nearly three months in a small, quiet post in the Alps, restricted to just a few square meters and seldom excursions into the staging area. On November 14, 1915, he noted in his dugout behind the front line near Chalupki: "Evening: kicking back and taking it easy by candlelight. Read a little Ibsen and then surrendered myself to the peace of sleep without a care in the world. It seems to me like one is more in touch with oneself out here and not so fragmented like back home in the city."[19] He read dozens of books during this time: Johann W. Goethe, William Shakespeare, Henrik Ibsen, Arthur Schopenhauer, Ferdinand von Saar, Edward George Earl Lytton Bulwer, Tristam Shandy, and Paul Rohrbach. He spent weeks in a hospital in a small room with a small bed. Karl Schaberl's freedom of movement was greatly restricted during his more than one year in the POW camp in Berisovka. He and his comrades were hardly ever allowed to leave their barracks, which could have helped them improve their inadequate supplies, because they did not have any proper clothes. Alois Prokosch, Teofil Reiss and Karl Schovanez experienced long periods of trench warfare in Eastern Europe, which were dominated by short periods of heavy fighting and longer periods of more calm situations. During this time, they were restricted to the small trenches, except for short stays in the staging area.

The long distances they traveled, on the one hand, and confinement within small places for long period of times, on the other, heavily influenced their perception of time. Phases of heavy shelling, and the wearisome pursuit of or retreat from the enemy compressed their individual sense of time. Alois Prokosch noted on October 17, 1914: "Many days and nights of nearly uninterrupted attack and counterattack with heavy artillery, M.G. and infantry fire. We didn't eat, we just shot and fought. Many dead, friend and foe lying on the mounds. Plus the cholera was raging. We lost track of time. We didn't know the day of the week or the date. I no longer remember

19. DOKU, *Kriegstagebuch meines lieben Mannes Sepp Brunner*, entries from 26 Oct. 1915- 6 Jan. 1916.

which day it was that we ran out of ammunition ...."[20] Bruckner and Schaberl experienced the dramatic, physically and mentally, extraordinary situation of fast retreat or advance.

On the other hand, individual time frames were also stretched, particularly during silent observation posts, boring back line service, residences in camps, or convalescence in hospitals. These different forms of time experience were captured best by Karl Schaberl, one of the most poorly educated of those investigated, when he wrote: "The war ended as quickly as it had begun (although four years have passed in the meantime, I mean that it began suddenly and ended rapidly). We have had the desired peace now for years. Who could have believed at the beginning that such a modern war could have lasted so long, especially in the snowfields of Galicia and Russia during a Russian winter ... But the soldier in the cold trench ponders, while his superiors sit by the warm stove and give orders."[21] We can even observe this stretching and compressing of time and space in the style and content of the memories of the soldiers. Alois Prokosch, who experienced the Eastern, Isonzo and Tyrol Fronts, stopped describing the countryside when he came to the Isonzo. The heavy shelling, the permanent stress of machine gun fire, the artillery attacks, the air reconnaissance, as well as the constant infantry attacks forced him to only concentrate on the limited space of the trench. Once he was sent to the Tyrol Front, he once again started to pay attention to the space around him. Even his grammar and sentence construction highlights this: on the Eastern and Tyrol Fronts, he uses long descriptions and a lot of adjectives to explain everything he saw, but on the Isonzo Front, his writing is characterized by short sentences, superlatives and the use of industrialised terms.[22]

Fear and Despair

The question arises of how soldiers who experienced the horrors of fighting in heavy snowfall and minus twenty or thirty degrees Celsius without sufficient supplies and food for days, who had to stand on guard in the long nights of the Carpathian winter, or who had been wounded several times could cope with fear and despair, and how they maintained their morale.

---

20. Steiermärkisches Landesarchiv (StmkLA), Sammlung 20. Jahrhundert, HS 1832, Tagebuch von Alois Prokosch, vol. 2, 146f. See a couple of other examples in volumes two and three, where he lost his sense of time.
21. Private collection of Dornik, Sammlung Ego-Dokumente, Karl Schaberl, 86.
22. StmkLA, Prokosch, vol. 4, 343-60.

Beginning in the summer of 1914, our individuals describe the exuberant cheering as they left home. Known as the *Augusterlebnis*, this has long been part of the narration on the outbreak of the war.[23] Our sources present us with an ambivalent picture of this: most of the men describe being cheered with flowers and songs by hundreds if not thousands when they enlisted or at the train stations when they left for the front. But they also describe the reflectiveness and sadness they experienced as they were ripped out of the life they knew so far. The Viennese worker, Karl Schovanez, wrote that only the men, especially the officer corps between 19 and 45 years old, had been enthusiastic. Prokosch described similar scenes in Styria: "Crowded rows of people lined the street to the train station. You could see people waving scarves, and hear people crying and shouting goodbye, which drowned out our march music. A train decorated by the women of Leoben was ready to board at the train station ... At every train station we stopped, people gave us charitable donations."[24] In late summer, Schovanez also described how women pressured younger men who had not joined the military yet. They were angry, because their husbands were already at the front, but the young men were still at home.[25]

Austro-Hungarian soldiers experienced despair and fear very early on: not only were soldiers and officers surprised by their first fighting experience (*Feuertaufe*) as well as the way of fighting[26], they were also confronted with military failure and retreat. Alois Prokosch noted on September 19, 1914: "This kind of retreat is horrible: Broken wagons lay upturned in the roadside ditch, and swollen carcasses of shot horses were scattered about with bared teeth and their tongues hanging out of their mouths. But the most gruelling part was when a comrade lay alongside the road completely exhausted and his fading eyes bid us last ones farewell as we gave him the last sip of water

23. This has recently been questioned by more and more scholars, although it seems that the war had been widely heralded in Austria-Hungary as a way of solving the inherent problems of the monarchy: Manfried Rauchensteiner, *Der Tod des Doppeladlers:* Österreich-Ungarn und der Erste Weltkrieg (Graz: Styria Verlag, 1994), 100-106; for a more nuanced view of this, see: Überegger, *Der andere Krieg*, 256-60. In terms of Germany, the *Geist von 1914* was at least an urban bourgeois phenomenon, which also attracted leftist workers, and was instrumentalized by the propaganda at the time: Jeffrey Verhey, *Der "Geist von 1914" und die Erfindung der Volksgemeinschaft* (Hamburg: Hamburger Edition, 2000); Meschnig, *Der Wille zur Bewegung*, 109-21.

24. StmkLA, Prokosch, vol. 1, 12f. For similar experiences, see: private collection of Dornik, Schaberl, 9f.

25. DOKU, Schovanez, *Im Zwielicht der Gezeiten*, 276-79.

26. StmkLA, Prokosch, vol. 1, 27; DOKU, Schovanez, *Im Zwielicht der Gezeiten*, 302-309; private collection of Dornik, Schaberl, 13-15. In terms of their sense of helplessness in the face of artillery, see: StmkLA, Prokosch, vol. 2, 163.

in our canteen. It broke my heart not being able to help. But duty didn't allow us to stop because the enemy was advancing rapidly."[27]

Thus, we can already observe the disillusionment and despair of most of the biographies examined by the beginning of 1915.[28] In these precarious situations, even minor incidents could lead to a personal breakdown, as we see in Prokosch's entry from the beginning of January 1915: "My ripped shoes let in snow which soaked my good Christmas socks. I wanted to dry them. .... I sat down on the large rocks around me, took my shoes off, and laid the wet socks on the warm rocks surrounding the embers. After constantly turning them over, they were nearly dry. How I looked forward to putting them on soon, when by misfortune, a strong gust of window blew the nearly dry sheep's wool Christmas socks into the embers. Although I grabbed them quickly, a big hole was burnt into each sock. I was close to despair, because I didn't have any other socks and now had to put on the holey socks again in the gaping shoes. I felt so miserable back then that tears ran down my cheeks, tears that the cold biting wind froze in place. At the time, I envied my fallen comrades."[29]

During the war the soldiers realized that even the situation at home was getting worse. The soldiers emphasized these instances of despair, particularly in retrospective interpretations.[30] Examples of this can also be found in *ad hoc* entries: Josef Bruckner wrote in his diary on the second day of 1917: "We have lost any hope of peace. We know that more fighting is coming."[31] News about the worsening strategic situation could lead to even more desperation and growing hatred. In his diary, Bruckner described the USA's entry into the war in the following way: "People in New York are supposedly cheering! Yeah, we did the same thing. All the things they were shouting about in Vienna back then! But we soon learned the terrible meaning of the word 'war.' All the sacrifices people have had to make in the last three years! We didn't know at the beginning that it could ever come to this. But the fact that a people could experience joy in the imminent declaration of war after three horrible years of fighting just goes to show how low the state of culture of these peddlers and shopkeepers has sunk."[32] This last clause displays an Anti-Semitic tendency, which we can find in his diary in other places, too.

27. StmkLA, Prokosch, vol. 2, 101-103.
28. Ibid., vol 3, 245-49, 273.
29. Ibid., vol. 3, 254-56.
30. Ibid., vol. 6, 468f.; DOKU, Schovanez, *Im Zwielicht der Gezeiten*, 343.
31. DOKU, Bruckner, entry from 2 Jan. 1917.
32. Ibid., entry from 7 Feb. 1917.

Desperation was also an important factor for those, who faced captivity instead of the front. Schaberl described his fear of sickness and poor medical assistance, the danger of cold temperatures without proper clothing and adequate shelter, and threat posed by camp guards. Another reason for his desperation was the complete lack of information on his family, the situation at home, and the uncertainty concerning his future. In this situation, rumors played a decisive role, capable of sending a whole barrack into depression, or breaking into cheers of joy about possible repatriation.[33] If this came together with a critical physical situation, it could be lethal.

Identity and Culture

The fact that the individuals soon found themselves covering long distances in a short period of time led to a situation where they were confronted with foreign cultures, but without the time or help necessary to develop ways of coping with these experiences. Regardless of whether these confrontations took place in their own country or in foreign countries, they ultimately led to a fundamental questioning of one's own position within these identity discourses.

At the beginning of the war, the soldiers and officers had to undergo a process of deindividualization through their integration into the military system. Any plans for the individual future had to be put on hold, they had been transformed into their troops, and they had to follow a daily routine, which was not theirs, but the army's.[34] The *Frontgemeinschaft* (the community of soldiers/veterans of the front) slowly developed, which separated the ones who had experienced the front from those at home or in the staging area. Poems and songs were important expressions of these new communities. Binge drinking together with comrades was a significant ceremony of underscoring this new group identity, and promotions and medals were its visible signs of acceptance.[35] Veteran organizations kept these communities after the war.

Although there were different forms of exchange between soldiers and their loved ones at home and soldiers got the opportunity to observe the situation at home first hand during holidays, there was a growing sense of alienation and misunderstanding between them.[36] Even Austro-

33. Private collection of Dornik, Schaberl, 22-77.
34. DOKU, Schovanez, Im Zwielicht der Jahrzehnte, 284-91.
35. StmkLA, Prokosch, vol. 1, 4; ibid., vol. 2, 3; DOKU, Reiss, 22 Feb. 1916, 7 Mar. 1916, 7 Apr. 1917, 22 Apr. 1917, 5-23 Dec. 1917, 29 Dec. 1917.
36. DOKU, Reiss, entries from 20 Jan. 1916, 25 Mar. 1916, 25 Mar. 1916; DOKU, Bruckner, entry from 27 Mar. 1917.

Hungarian statehood or religion could not provide everyone with a sense of togetherness. In this situation, language and national identities played an ever more important role. The state or military leaders were seen as corrupt and not connected to the people. The church was also considered part of this system.[37]

In particular, German-speaking individuals from the West of Cisleithania held the population of Galicia to be underdeveloped, weird or suspicious.[38] Ukrainian-speaking inhabitants were generally suspected of being Russophiles. Their contact with the orthodox Jews of Eastern Galicia, in particular, confused them and provoked refusal and aggression.[39] Josef Bruckner described in his diary entry of June 29, 1915: "Tarnogrod. Today we are in a place made up of low, dirty, whitewashed shacks that stink to high heaven. There are Jews here and what great specimens they are, too! They are even better than the caricatures in 'Kikeriki.'"[40] This alienation could even lead to the willingness to use violence: A few months later, he noted: "It frequently happens that Jews are struck by soldiers. Anyone who knows these eternal peddlers will agree that this is the best way to deal with them .... Incidentally, the Jews would rather take a beating than stop their profiteering."[41] The German language and culture became the main way for Josef Bruckner and Karl Schaberl to describe and identify themselves However, at this point, Germaneness was not expressed in terms of superiority to other national identities (Bruckner appreciates non-German literature), but through economic backwardness.[42]

A sense of togetherness grew amongst soldiers in captivity due to the time they shared. When they lived outside the camp, they met weekly to talk about their experiences, their feelings, culture and everyday politics in Russia. When they were sent home, they realized that they felt alienated from their families at home as well as from the community of veterans of the front, which was bound together even stronger in the years following the fighting. This can be seen several times during the repatriation process of Karl Schaberl: "On May 9 [1918], we arrived in Yekaterinoslav and

37. DOKU, Schovanez, *Im Zwielicht der Gezeiten*, 268-275, 300, 335; DOKU, Bruckner, entry from 27 Mar. 1917; private collection of Dornik, Schaberl, 78. Favorable entries on the Emperor were seldom: DOKU, Bruckner, 15 May 1917.
38. StmkLA, Prokosch, vol. 2, 112-114; ibid., vol. 3, 240f.; DOKU, Bruckner, entry from 20 Oct. 1915.
39. StmkLA, Prokosch, vol. 1, 13-18, 46-48; DOKU, Bruckner, entry from 5 Oct. 1915.
40. DOKU, Bruckner, entry from 29 June 1915.
41. Ibid., entry from 18 Oct. 1915.
42. DOKU, Bruckner, entries from 20 Oct. 1915; private collection of Dornik, Schaberl, 32, 81.

saw the first [Austro-Hungarian] occupation troops there. They seemed foreign to me and my comrades, and they had completely different uniforms and equipment than at the beginning of the war in 1914. They also wore steel helmets. The chests of the officers, NCOs and almost all the troops were covered in medals or other badges of honor, which hardly any of us had. Everything had changed and even our own countrymen were strangers to us."[43] He and his comrades had to recognize that all the POWs repatriated from Russia were constantly being watched under suspicion of being supporters of Bolshevism and revolutionary ideas. This was a bitter experience, which resulted in a couple of awkward situations between former POWs and the filtration and reintegration staff.[44] After the war, they maintained their own *Heimkehrer* (returnee) communities, with separate clubs, newspapers etc.[45]

In one case, his war experience led to a stronger religious identification: Theofil Reiss strongly identified with the emperor; he had a neutral position towards the German language (he wrote his diary in German); and he was very critical towards other nations (especially Poles, Ukrainians and Czechs) because he feared they were disloyal. The result was that he tended more and more towards Jewishness. He even tried to cook kosher food in the harsh conditions behind the front. Reiss celebrated Pesach, and he maintained loose contact with a rabbi.[46]

In the writings of Karl Schovanez, who was shaped by a typical working class job and ideology even before 1914, we can find no growing sense of Germanness. On the contrary, he emphasized that soldiers and workers lived under similar conditions on both sides of the fronts.[47] Except when it came to the Italian "enemy," for which he used propagandistic terms such as (*Zschusen* [dagos], *Katzelmacher* [wops]). In Bruckner's notes, they also are depicted as *treulos* (treacherous), *schlampig* (slovenly) and *faul* (lazy).[48] Alois Prokosch noted on August, 13 1914: "The regiment now faces new missions in the southern theater of war against a new enemy, the treacherous

43. Private collection of Dornik, Schaberl, 73.
44. Ibid., 76-84.
45. See for example the magazines of the Austrian former POWs: Der *Kriegsgefangene als Erzähler: Zeitschrift des Reichsverbandes ehemaliger Kriegsgefangener des Mannschaftsstandes Deutschösterreichs*, November 1923 - July 1927.
46. DOKU, Reiss, entries from 15 Jan. 1916, 17 Apr.1916, 7 Aug. 1916, 15/16 Feb. 1918.
47. However, concerning the "Asian" or "Mongolian" troops in the Russian army, large parts of his memoirs are dominated by pejorative terms (they were "brutal," "stupid" and "war enthusiasts"): DOKU, Schovanez, *Im Zwielicht der Gezeiten*, 372. These remembrances may have been influenced by the National Socialist era and experiences he had during the Second World War, especially those in Eastern Austria in spring 1945.
48. DOKU, Bruckner, entry from 6 Jan. 1917.

Italians. The news was greeted by cheers, because now we were defending our immediate homeland."[49]

Schaberl developed a more nuanced picture of the "enemy": on the one hand, he described the Russians as *faul*, *träge* (lazy) and *liederlich* (wanton), but on the other hand, he was fascinated by their culture and language, which he learned pretty well, and the friendliness and cordiality of some whom he got to know better.[50] Nonetheless, "Russia" became Schaberl's metaphor for his three years of captivity, hard work, coldness, illness and poor treatment: "Now, after years of captivity as prisoners of war, we had left miserable and accursed Russia and Siberia behind us and were on Austrian soil again. Who could have been happier than we were? Of finally achieving that which we had so often longed for and that which we had already given up hope of ever attaining."[51] His refusal was not based on racist ideology, but on the fact that he was held captive in this country. He tried to adopt a more nuanced point of view towards the Russian people. A sense of superiority cannot be found in his writings.

We also do not find expressions of bitterness, hatred or superiority towards the Russian "enemy" in the other diaries: Alois Prokosch noted: "I have often noticed that Russian soldiers are brave, but as soon as they are taken prisoner they make no efforts to escape."[52] And on Easter 1915 he wrote: "Early Easter Sunday an officer and several Russian soldiers left their trench across from the 1st Company and approached us unarmed, and with peaceful intentions. The commandant of the 1st Company, First Lieutenant Wagner, went out to meet them with the same number of soldiers. When they met, they exchanged Easter kisses which are customary in Russia and gave each other presents. Neighboring companies on both sides of the front liked the idea and did the same. It seemed as if everyone had forgotten about the war. Then the order came from the brigade to take cover quickly and to stress this order the artillery began to speak with its iron tongue. The Easter peace had been broken and the war continued on its way."[53] Karl Schovanez described similar experiences of officers trading liquor, knives and razor blades across the front line in 1917 and 1918.[54]

The "Cossacks" was a very important metaphor for the Russian enemy. They were characterized as "brutal" and "blundering" hordes. On September

49. StmkLA, Prokosch, vol. 4, 312f.
50. Private collection of Dornik, Schaberl, 24-74.
51. Ibid., 74.
52. StmkLA, Prokosch, vol. 3, 222f.
53. Ibid., vol. 3, 276-78.
54. DOKU, Schovanez, 372.

3, 1914, Alois Prokosch wrote: "… that the Cossacks do not take prisoners, but kill and rob everyone. Since they are always in a hurry, they simply cut the pockets off from the clothing of the dead and put these including all of their contents, into their large saddlebags, which are perfect for raiding. Besides, they couldn't have taken prisoners on their swift rides."[55] Or as Josef Bruckner wrote on October 5, 1915: "We will arrive soon in Rava-Ruska. Heavily hit. Nearly everything Jewish. Most of the Ruthenian inhabitants have left with the Russians. There was a Cossack commandant here for some time; almost all the young women pregnant."[56] This picture of looting and raping Cossacks also shows up in the official propaganda, particularly in depictions of the war in newspapers in the early years of the war.[57]

Body and Mind

The climate and weather, food and supplies (especially clothing), physical violence, or mental conditions could affect an individual's body and mind. It is difficult to rank these factors in terms of importance, but climate was definitely one of the most often mentioned topics in the texts analyzed. The changing weather, extreme hot or cold, sunshine or long periods of rain had a dramatic impact on the body of someone, who was confronted with these conditions without proper shelter. Muddy streets, the fight against frost, or water in accommodations (regardless of whether these were a dugout, shelter or simple barracks) could result in cold and/or wet feet for days; frostbite, sunburns, and dirt and could thus lead to illness or severe damage to the body. These conditions could lead soldiers to fall into a deep depression, whereas sunny phases could also lighten their mood and morale, as Bruckner described during his time at a quiet alpine post, where the weather conditions were part of his daily entries.[58]

Karl Schaberl noted that he got severe frostbite on his feet while waiting in a dugout in full gear to follow the others in retreat. After this, he could hardly walk and only very slowly with great pain. The following night he started to fall back and was captured by Russian troops.[59] In captivity, he

55. StmkLA, Prokosch, 85f.
56. DOKU, Bruckner, entry from 5 Oct. 1915.
57. See for example: *Wiener Bilder*, 11 Oct. 1914, 9; ibid., 18. April 1915, 5.
58. DOKU, Bruckner, entries from 30.12.1916-12.3.1917.
59. For more on captivity on the Eastern Front, see: Hannes Leidinger, and Verena Moritz, *Gefangenschaft – Revolution – Heimkehr: Die Bedeutung der Kriegsgefangenenproblematik für die Geschichte des Kommunismus in Mittel- und Osteuropa 1917-1920* (Vienna: Böhlau Verlag, 2003); Alon Rachamimov, *POWs and the Great War: Captivity on the Eastern Front* (Oxford, New York: Berg, 2002); etc.

received two kinds of treatment: the first escort (infantrymen) treated him and the other prisoners well, whereas the second one (Cossacks) beat him with whips. Employing a trick, he could flee and join a medic train. In Kiev, the people gave him food and he was treated in a hospital.[60] Even when Austro-Hungarian soldiers were treated in their "own" medical system, the situation was not necessarily adequate: the food supply in some hospitals was very poor, not as a result of shortages, but because of corruption and mismanagement.[61]

As we can read in Theofil Reiss' diary, the condition of the daily food supply was essential: good and warm food or alcohol gave them the chance to relax and enjoy themselves and served as a kind of flight from reality. For Reiss, who was responsible for the kitchen, making his comrades happy also made him feel accepted in the regiment and gave him a feeling of success.[62] In general, the supplies were very important to the soldiers. Alois Prokosch noted in the beginning of October 1914: "Bad weather. Inspection of the reserve rations, clothing and equipment. Anything missing or in bad shape is collected, repaired, cleaned etc. They are turning us into soldiers again."[63] Later on he stressed that they got *Schwarmöfen* (small ovens used on the frontline), which could be used for heating or warming up food.[64] On the other hand, periods of hunger and bad food could not only worsen the soldiers' physical condition, but their psychological one, too. As a prisoner of war, Karl Schaberl had experienced longer periods of hunger and unsanitary conditions in the camp. This was why many of his comrades fell ill (dysentery, typhus, cholera etc.). They tried to cope with the hunger and home sickness by talking about which foods from home they would like to eat.[65]

Particularly at the beginning of the war or during retreat, the supply chain of the troops could break down, resulting in large numbers of losses due to illness. During retreat in October 1914, Alois Prokosch reported that 600 men in his regiment were ill (mainly dysentery and cholera), whereas a similar number were killed (200) or wounded (400).[66] When supply chains were inefficient or broke down completely, he and his comrades had to rely on themselves: "Cooking has become the favorite pastime of soldiers. The

60. Private collection of Dornik, Schaberl, 19-21.
61. DOKU Reiss, entries from 13 Feb.1915 and 6 Aug.1915.
62. Ibid., entries from 21 Jan.1915, 5 July 1915, 22 and 25 Feb. 1916, 21 Oct. 1916, 7 Apr. 1917.
63. StmkLA, Prokosch, vol. 2, 130f.
64. Ibid., vol. 3, 270f.
65. Private collection of Dornik, Schaberl, 22-42.
66. StmkLA, Prokosch, vol. 2, 177.

order to rest merely seconds old, every company would already have a fire burning. Unfortunately, most of the time we didn't have anything to cook."[67]

Of course, weapons are the most dangerous thing for bodies in wartime. Infantry fire, small assaults and sniper attacks were part of the daily routine on the front, even in quiet sectors of the front. In our chosen sample, Alois Prokosch was the only one who was never injured or fell seriously ill, although he fought three years on three different fronts. In one of his first encounters with the enemy in August 1914, he had nearly unimaginable luck: "Recently we charged forward. I moved to the left as ordered, encountered heavy infantry fire, and bullets whizzed by, barely missing my head. My marksmanship lanyard was shot off, a bullet passed through my cap and my bullet pouch took a hit."[68] Theophil Reiss fell ill several times due to poor supplies and food conditions, and he got shell-shock after a heavy artillery attack during his last deployment on the front. Karl Schovanez was heavily wounded on his shoulder, and he got a serious skin disease on his feet at the end of the war. Josef Bruckner was wounded three times: shot through the thigh in July 1915, shot through the upper arm in May 1916, and multiple injuries to the face and legs because of a hand grenade in June 1917.

The soldiers on the Eastern Front also had to cope with the industrialized war, particularly in the form of the machine gun and heavy shelling.[69] During these attacks not only the shrapnel and explosions themselves were lethal, but nature could also be dangerous, too: "August, 30 [1914] The Battle of Przemyśl. We are suffering terribly from the shelling of the heavy artillery. Big trees including oaks exploded, shattered into matchsticks, branches and treetops went flying through the air and fell on comrades, burying them or skewering them to the ground. Crashes and explosions amidst cries for help from injured comrades. This went on almost without interruption .... We retreated back along the hill and saw the burning town down below surrounded by farms engulfed in flames. What a horrible image. Then someone called us, it was General Schmid. Our Captain answered, and the General screamed, what the hell are you doing retreating, turn about face right now, you have to hold your position until my artillery is ready to pull back."[70]

---

67. Ibid., vol. 2, 109.
68. Ibid., vol. 1, 35.
69. See on this: Meschnig, *Der Wille zur Bewegung*, 161-74; Peter Wilding, "Krieg – Technik – Moderne: Die Eskalation der Gewalt im 'Ingenieur-Krieg'; Zur Technisierung des Ersten Weltkrieges," in *Aggression und Katharsis: Der Erste Weltkrieg im Diskurs der Moderne*, eds. Petra Ernst, Sabine A. Haring, and Werner Suppanz (Vienna: Passagen Verlag, 2004), 163-86.
70. StmkLA, Prokosch, vol. 1, 57f.

But those soldiers who were sent to the Isonzo Front soon realized the difference between their previous war theater and the new one: "The new enemy [note: the Italians] fought differently than the Russians, especially the excessive amount of ammunition fired by its artillery. The shelling in karst terrain was much more effective in terms of the range of damage caused by impact than in the deep soil of Galicia. ... We slowly got used to the nearly constant booming from the nearby battlefield. The only time we pricked up our ears was when a particularly heavy shell hit, for instance, an Italian 28 cm. A sense of how heavy the new fighting would be went through our ranks. All the more columns of wounded filed past."[71] The secondary effect of artillery shelling was even more dangerous here than the explosions in the muddy earth of Eastern Europe: stone splinters were a common danger, especially for soldiers' heads.[72] The sound of the war at the Isonzo itself had a deep physical and psychological impact on the soldiers: Alois Prokosch only used the phrase *"Gebrüll der Schlacht"* ("the roar of battle") to speak of the Isonzo fighting. He never used this term to speak of the Eastern or Tyrol Fronts.[73] The result of this warfare was the diagnosis of a new disease: shell-shock.[74]

Besides shell-shock, high losses or a lost battle were dangerous to the morale of soldiers: "September 12 [1914] Physically and mentally demoralized we started to retreat. We had done everything in our power. How many of our wounded, helpless comrades did we have to leave behind in their misery and how many died a hero's death? Losses we can never replace. Whatever follows will be second best."[75] To leave wounded comrades behind takes a heavy mental toll on the retreating soldiers, but they try to understand this from a strategic point of view. Much more difficult to cope with was violence within one's own military regime. In Austria-Hungary, the punishment of *Anbinden* (where a soldier was tied to a tree in such a way that his feet did not touch the ground and thus the soldier's entire body weight rested on the rope) or *Schließen in Spangen* (where the right wrist and the left ankle were bound by a kind of iron shackle for several hours) were performed until mid-1917 (in some special cases, until the end of the

71. Ibid., vol. 4, 314-318.
72. Ibid., vol. 5, 402f.; DOKU, Reiss, entries from 19 June 1918.
73. StmkLA, Prokosch, Vol. 4, 317-335.
74. For a groundbreaking paper on the Austro-Hungarian perspective of shell-shock and the medical discourse of this disease, see: Georg Hofer, "'Nervöse Zitterer'. Psychiatrie und Krieg," in *Krieg, Medizin und Politik. Der Erste Weltkrieg und die österreichische Moderne*, ed., Helmut Konrad (Vienna: Passagen Verlag, 2000), 15-134.
75. StmkLA, Prokosch, vol. 1, notes on the last page of the envelope.

war), especially in cases of desertion or cowardice in the face of the enemy.[76] This punishment was feared because of the pain and humiliation in front of comrades. Alois Prokosch himself received two hours of *Anbinden*, because he ate the emergency reserves. In February 1915, he saw a whole squadron of the 97th Infantry Regiment *angebunden* because of cowardice in the face of the enemy.[77] One result of this special type of punishment was a loss of loyalty within the army, because it became a weapon in the long-lasting national discourse of the Habsburg monarchy. The officers, who carried out these punishments, were usually part of the hegemonic national groups, whereas the soldiers punished were part of the "suppressed nations."

Sexual violence in wartimes is taboo up to this day. Whether as an official strategy or as a tolerated secondary effect, rapes underscore the claim to power in a foreign country through the bodies of women. And women in this moment become victims twice over: once due to the physical act of violence done to them and a second time because they have now been stigmatized as a disgrace to their family and their nation.[78] Owing to the fact that the materials analyzed were meant for their own family members and were supposed to project a certain image in the future, it may come as no surprise that we find very little mention of this topic. Only Karl Schovanez wrote in one place: "From the top brass all the way down to the infantry, everyone was horny as hell for women … and the women for the men."[79] It is not clear if Schovanez is referring to informal prostitution or rape, but based on the context it would seem to refer to front brothels or informal prostitution. Although there has not been enough research on this so far, it is clear that sex with women was used to maintain morale and was seen as a kind of reward. But the strict Catholic state leadership was against this "immoral" behavior. Moreover, it was a physical danger for the whole unit, because venereal diseases could spread through a whole front section within a short period of time, and thus weaken the strength of the military.

Re-entering society not only meant a change in veterans' daily routines, but it was also a process of reinventing themselves as individuals and members of civil society. Hundreds of thousands had to cope with physical

76. Emperor Charles banned this punishment in 1917. It was only used in special cases: Hans Hautmann, "Sittenbilder aus dem Hause Habsburg im Weltkrieg," *Mitteilungen der Alfred Klahr Gesellschaft* 15, no. 2 (June 2008) Vienna: 10-14.

77. StmkLA, Prokosch, vol. 2, 106f.

78. For this see the quote above by Bruckner on October 15 about the pregnant girls in Rava-Ruska. For more detailed information on rape and sexuality in World War One, see: Tammy M. Proctor, *Civilians in a World at War, 1914-1918* (New York: New York University Press, 2010), 124-51.

79. StmkLA, Prokosch, Vol. 4, 317-335.

or mental disabilities, which limited their individual possibilities and had a massive impact on their economic situation.[80] In terms of Josef Bruckner, Karl Schovanez and Theofil Reiss, we know that they came out of the war with disabilities and long-lasting psychological problems. In addition to blindness in one eye, Bruckner also had to cope with severely limited vision in his other eye, and other injuries to his body. He managed to get a relatively good job in the Austrian post administration during the interwar years. Later he joined the National Socialists and became a counter-intelligence officer at the postal administration. After 1945, he had to undergo US denazification. He continued with his job in the postal administration from 1947 until 1951 and died in 1958.[81] Schovanec worked various jobs for a short period of time before he got a job with the railroad administration. There he developed a strong worker's identity, although he sided with the Christian-conservative *Ständestaat* dictatorship, and later with the National Socialists. His life went relatively smoothly, without big breaks in his career, until retirement and he died in 1987.[82] Reiss stayed in Vienna after 1918, and had two boys with his wartime bride. He must have come into a certain amount of wealth, because he founded a temple and a Torah school in 1931, where he worked as headmaster without pay until March 1938. After the Anschluss of Austria to Nazi Germany, he was detained and deported to Nisko, Poland in October 1939. There he managed to flee across the Soviet-German demarcation line. The Soviet administration deported him to a labor camp in Siberia, where he fell seriously ill after two years of hard labor and deprivations. He was then taken to Ferghana, Uzbekistan, where he died on February 7, 1942.[83]

Conclusion

After the collapse of the Habsburg Empire, most of the soldiers returned home, but it was difficult for them to orient themselves in their greatly changed home country. Alois Prokosch summed up his feelings in 1955 in the following way: "The homecoming was sad and grim. The monarchy was broken up, and the loss of South Tyrol, Southern Carinthia and Southern

80. See in particular: Verena Pawlowsky, and Harald Wendelin, "Die normative Konstruktion des Opfers: Die Versorgung der Invaliden des Ersten Weltkrieges," in *Glanz – Gewalt – Gehorsam*, eds. Cole, Hämmerle, Scheutz, 359-83. In terms of the war blinded, see: Barbara Hoffmann, *Kriegsblinde in Österreich, 1914-1934* (Graz: Verein zur Förderung der Forschung von Folgen nach Konflikten und Kriegen, 2006).
81. DOKU, Bruckner, 128-40.
82. DOKU, Schovanez, supplement.
83. DOKU, Reiss, supplement.

Styria was particularly bitter. Access to the sea via Trieste had been cut off. The slogan was "never again war," and people spit on and defiled anything that reminded them of the monarchy's military tradition. It was only years later that soldiers got together in associations to revive and maintain the old noble manly virtues of camaraderie and sense of duty as a role model for future generations. Even if these men were not distinguished by any visible luster, it should be kept in mind that every participant of the war deserves the highest honor."[84] And Karl Schaberl wrote in his conclusion in 1922: "Let us now consider the consequences of the war. What did we get out of it? Nothing but want and misery! A lot of people got rich in this war, but a lot were also reduced to beggars. Our monarch, who had no idea about politics, was rushed into war by his advisors and generals, and now the people have to pay for it. We keep asking ourselves, "Did we fight poorly"? In answer to this, we can only say: "No!" It was treason and hunger that broke through the front. But when we fought, we won. Only a small piece of great Austria remains that we are allowed to call home, the "Republic of German Austria." The country is now in dire straits, but we will work hard and we will once again have a better future and, above all, never war again."[85] They had to deal with mixed feelings: on the one hand, they were happy that the war had come to an end, and that they could go home to their families. But, on the other hand, they also realized that their efforts during the war were for nothing, because the war had been lost, although they did not feel that they had lost the fight. The reduction of Austria to a small country left our individuals with a sense of lost hegemony. This led veteran associations to seek a new, bigger community along the lines of the *Frontgemeinschaft*.

Another result of what they had gone through in previous years was a radically altered experience of time and space during the war and the desire for participation and emancipation. Most veterans quickly came to the conclusion that parliamentarian democracy was not the solution to their problems. Although they did not think of democracy as we do today, they wanted to take control of their lives again. Paramilitary organizations, violence, discipline, and the *Führerkult* (leader cult) were the tools they used to express their political needs. Their action was based on a strong leader, on military discipline, and mass mobilization. The engines of change in most Habsburg successor states were the long suppressed national identities, the fuel that drove them was the violence they had experienced, and the result was the national self-determination they claimed. German-speaking

84. StmkLA, Prokosch, Vol. 7, unnumbered page.
85. Private collection of Dornik, Schaberl, 86.

Austrians and Hungarians particularly felt cheated of their promised self-determination. This was one reason why these states developed in such a violent and authoritarian manner in the 1920s and 1930s. The National Socialists as well as the other authoritarian and Fascist movements of the Interwar Years were very successful in channeling these feelings of belonging to a bigger, hegemonic, and strictly organized community.

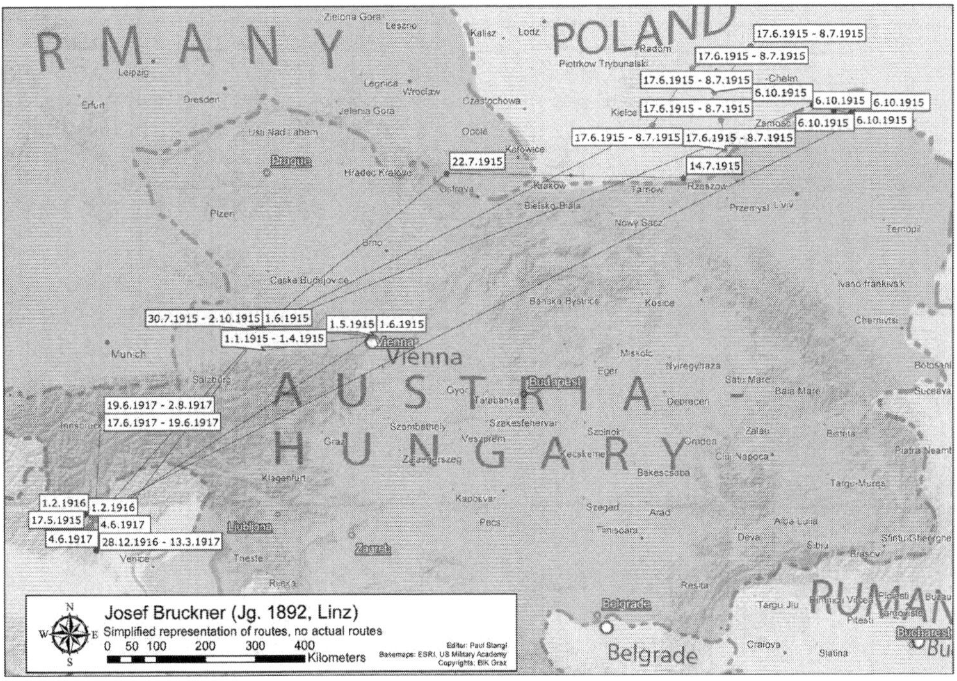

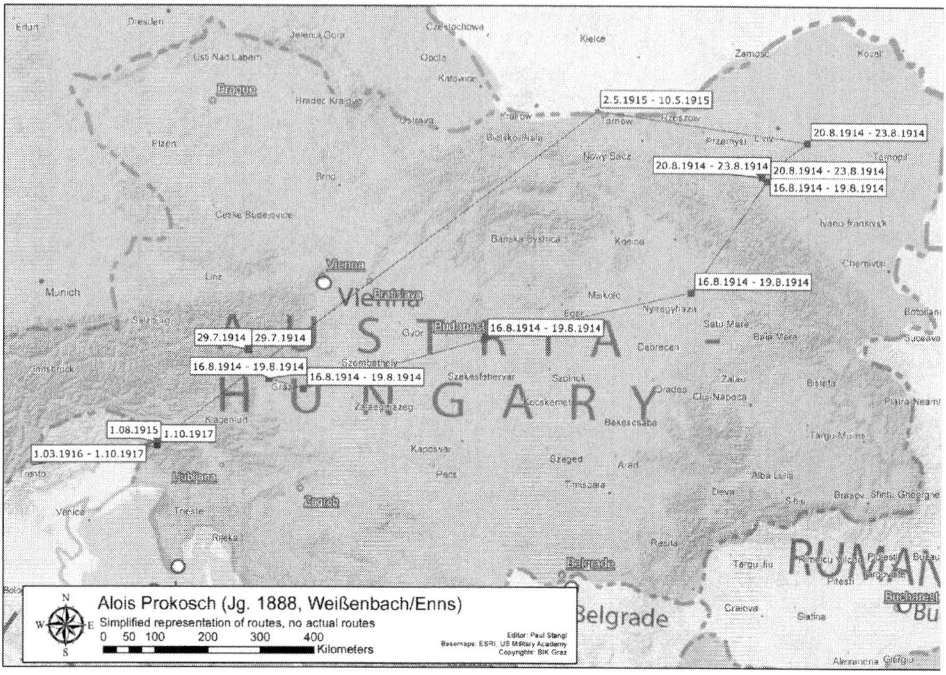
Alois Prokosch (Jg. 1888, Weißenbach/Enns)
Simplified representation of routes, no actual routes
0 50 100 200 300 400
Kilometers
Editor: Paul Stangl
Basemaps: ESRI, US Military Academy
Copyrights: BIK Graz
AUSTRIA - HUNGARY
2.5.1915 - 10.5.1915
20.8.1914 - 23.8.1914
20.8.1914 - 23.8.1914
20.8.1914 - 23.8.1914
16.8.1914 - 19.8.1914
16.8.1914 - 19.8.1914
16.8.1914 - 19.8.1914
29.7.1914
29.7.1914
16.8.1914 - 19.8.1914
16.8.1914 - 19.8.1914
1.08.1915
1.10.1917
1.03.1916 - 1.10.1917

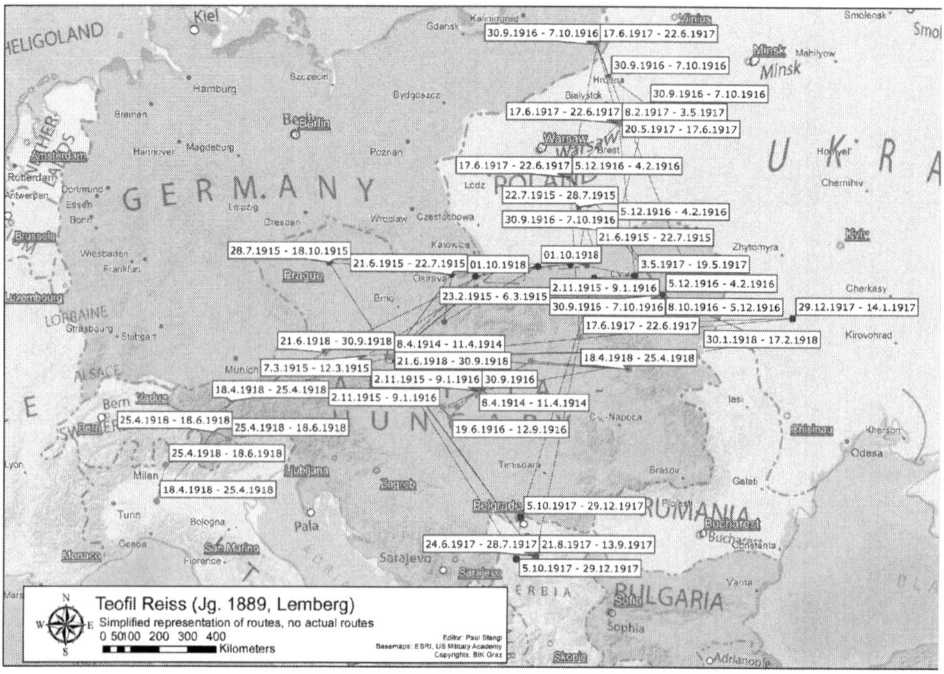
Teofil Reiss (Jg. 1889, Lemberg)
Simplified representation of routes, no actual routes
0 50100 200 300 400
Kilometers
Editor: Paul Stangl
Basemaps: ESRI, US Military Academy
Copyrights: BIK Graz
GERMANY
30.9.1916 - 7.10.1916
17.6.1917 - 22.6.1917
30.9.1916 - 7.10.1916
30.9.1916 - 7.10.1916
17.6.1917 - 22.6.1917
8.2.1917 - 3.5.1917
20.5.1917 - 17.6.1917
17.6.1917 - 22.6.1917
5.12.1916 - 4.2.1916
22.7.1915 - 28.7.1915
5.12.1916 - 4.2.1916
30.9.1916 - 7.10.1916
21.6.1915 - 22.7.1915
28.7.1915 - 18.10.1915
01.10.1918
21.6.1915 - 22.7.1915
01.10.1918
3.5.1917 - 19.5.1917
2.11.1915 - 9.1.1916
5.12.1916 - 4.2.1916
23.2.1915 - 6.3.1915
30.9.1916 - 7.10.1916
8.10.1916 - 5.12.1916
29.12.1917 - 14.1.1917
17.6.1917 - 22.6.1917
30.1.1918 - 17.2.1918
21.6.1918 - 30.9.1918
8.4.1914 - 11.4.1914
18.4.1918 - 25.4.1918
21.6.1918 - 30.9.1918
7.3.1915 - 12.3.1915
2.11.1915 - 9.1.1916
30.9.1916
18.4.1918 - 25.4.1918
2.11.1915 - 9.1.1916
8.4.1914 - 11.4.1914
25.4.1918 - 18.6.1918
25.4.1918 - 18.6.1918
19.6.1916 - 12.9.1916
25.4.1918 - 18.6.1918
18.4.1918 - 25.4.1918
5.10.1917 - 29.12.1917
24.6.1917 - 28.7.1917
21.8.1917 - 13.9.1917
5.10.1917 - 29.12.1917

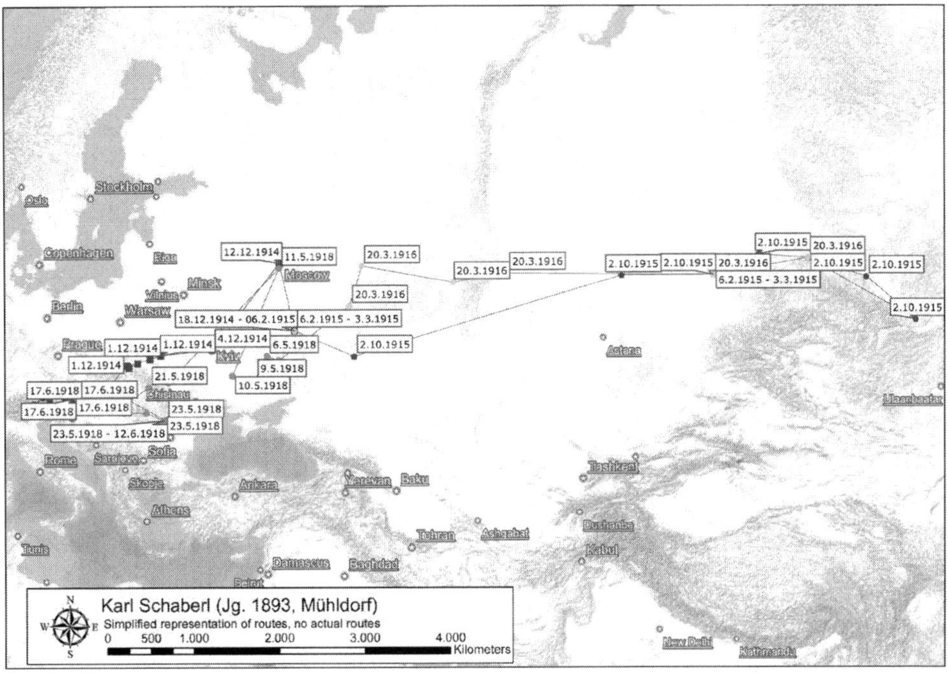
Karl Schaberl (Jg. 1893, Mühldorf)
Simplified representation of routes, no actual routes
0 500 1.000 2.000 3.000 4.000
Kilometers
12.12.1914
11.5.1918
20.3.1916
20.3.1916
20.3.1916
2.10.1915
2.10.1915
20.3.1916
2.10.1915
20.3.1916
2.10.1915
2.10.1915
6.2.1915 - 3.3.1915
2.10.1915
20.3.1916
18.12.1914 - 06.2.1915
6.2.1915 - 3.3.1915
1.12.1914
1.12.1914
4.12.1914
6.5.1918
2.10.1915
1.12.1914
9.5.1918
21.5.1918
10.5.1918
17.6.1918
17.6.1918
17.6.1918
17.6.1918
23.5.1918
23.5.1918
23.5.1918 - 12.6.1918
Oslo
Stockholm
Copenhagen
Riga
Minsk
Vilnius
Moscow
Berlin
Warsaw
Prague
Kyiv
Chisinau
Astana
Ulaanbaatar
Rome
Sarajevo
Sofia
Skopje
Ankara
Athens
Yerevan
Baku
Tashkent
Tunis
Tehran
Ashgabat
Dushanbe
Kabul
Damascus
Baghdad
Beirut
New Delhi
Kathmandu

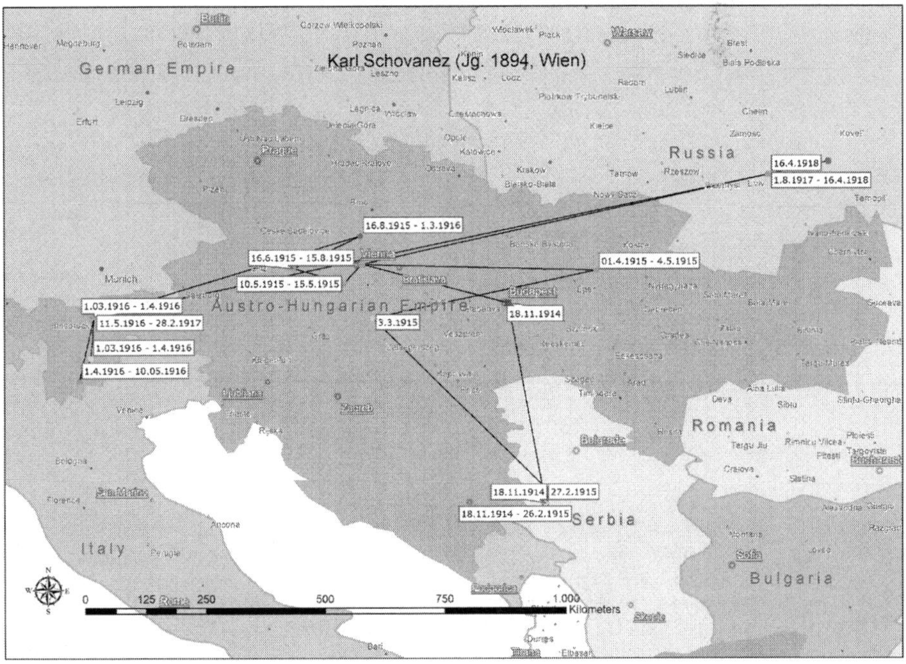
Karl Schovanez (Jg. 1894, Wien)
German Empire
Russia
Austro-Hungarian Empire
Romania
Serbia
Italy
Bulgaria
16.4.1918
1.8.1917 - 16.4.1918
16.8.1915 - 1.3.1916
16.6.1915 - 15.8.1915
01.4.1915 - 4.5.1915
10.5.1915 - 15.5.1915
1.03.1916 - 1.4.1916
11.5.1916 - 28.2.1917
3.3.1915
18.11.1914
1.03.1916 - 1.4.1916
1.4.1916 - 10.05.1916
18.11.1914
27.2.1915
18.11.1914 - 26.2.1915
Berlin
Warsaw
Prague
Vienna
Bratislava
Budapest
Munich
Ljubljana
Zagreb
Belgrade
San Marino
Sofia
Skopje
0 125 250 500 750 1.000
Kilometers

Ordinary Austrians: Common War Criminals during World War II

Winfried R. Garscha

Some of the most infamous Nazi war criminals during World War II were of Austrian descent. Among them the following perpetrators are worthy of particular mention: *Generaloberst* Alexander Löhr, commander of the unannounced air raid of the German *Luftwaffe* on Palm Sunday, 6 April 1941, that caused the death of thousands of civilians of Belgrade and destroyed the Serbian National Library with its worldwide unique medieval manuscripts. Löhr was executed by a firing squad on 26 February 1947 after a death sentence imposed by a Yugoslav military court at Belgrade.

Arthur Seyss-Inquart, *Reichskommissar* of the Netherlands, and *SS-Obergruppenführer* Hanns Albin Rauter, the two Austrians who—as chief of the civil administration and as Higher SS and Police Leader at The Hague—ordered major war crimes like large scale reprisal executions and the mass deportations of Jews and forced laborers: Seyss-Inquart was executed by hanging on 16 October 1946 (after his conviction by the International Military Tribunal for the Trial of German Major War Criminals at Nuremberg), Rauter was executed by a firing squad on 24 March 1949 (after the Dutch Special Criminal Court at The Hague had imposed a death sentence upon him).[1]

Not to mention those perpetrators, who did not commit war crimes in the proper meaning of the term, but from their desks, organized the killing of millions of people. Among them were Ernst Kaltenbrunner, chief of the *Reichssicherheitshauptamt*, a native Upper Austrian (defendant before the IMT at Nuremberg, executed by hanging on 16 October 1946), or Adolf Eichmann, who—despite his German citizenship[2]—can be regarded as Austrian: born in Solingen, Germany, he had been raised in Linz, Upper Austria, and had started his murderous career in Vienna. 1961, during the broadcasting of the main trial before the district court in Jerusalem, the public could hear him speaking German with an Austrian accent.

This essay deals with "ordinary" Austrians who committed Nazi crimes during World War II; therefore only rank and file and low rank officers

1. See the essay on Seyss-Inquart by Johannes Koll in this volume.

2. Contrary to his four younger siblings who became Austrians, after his father had adopted Austrian citizenship in the 1920s, Adolf Eichmann—being of legal age and therefore independent from his father's citizenship—remained German citizen. See Georg Kastner, "Adolf Eichmann, German Citizen," *Austrian History Yearbook*, vol. 33 (2002): 131-40.

are being presented here. The concept of "ordinary men" committing extraordinary war crimes on a daily basis in the cauldron of the Nazi war of aggression and extermination follows the findings of Christopher R. Browning in his standard work about a German police battalion and its contribution to the mass killings in Poland. His leading question was: "Why did most men in Reserve Police Battalion 101 become killers, while only a minority [...] did not?"[3] Among factors that are applicable in varying degrees he enumerates, among others, wartime brutalization, racism, careerism, deference to authority, ideological indoctrination, and conformity. He stresses that these factors apply also to war crimes at other theaters of war and other war parties. What distinguished criminal Nazi warfare in East and Southeast Europe, however, was not "battlefield frenzy" of frustrated soldiers as it was "tolerated, condoned, or tacitly (sometimes even explicitly) encouraged by elements of the command structure"[4] in so many cases elsewhere. Although such factors played a role in certain events, the key to the behavior of the policemen was "[d]istancing, not frenzy and brutalization."[5] An additional factor was political reliability: an over-proportional percentage (although still a minority) of the rank and file killers of Reserve Police Battalion 101 were members of the Nazi party. This applies also to the "ordinary" Austrian war criminals presented in this essay. Of greater importance, however, was group dynamics, as Browning shows: for most men it was easier to take part in the killing. "Why? First of all [...] nonshooters were leaving the 'dirty work' to their comrades. Since the battalion had to shoot even if individuals did not, refusing to shoot constituted refusing one's share of an unpleasant collective obligation. It was in effect an asocial act vis-à-vis one's comrades." In addition to that "stepping out could also have been seen as a form of moral reproach of one's comrades: the nonshooter was potentially indicating that he was 'too good' to do such things. Most, though not all, nonshooters intuitively tried to diffuse the criticism of their comrades that was inherent to their actions. They pleaded not that they were 'too good' but rather that they were 'too weak' to kill."[6]

Browning's conclusion was a rejection of any idea of collective predetermination that made "ordinary men" murderers: "The story of ordinary men is not the story of all men. The reserve policemen faced choices, and most of them committed terrible deeds. But those who killed cannot be absolved by the notion that anyone in the same situation would

3. Christopher R. Browing, *Ordinary men: Reserve Police Battalion 101 and the final solution in Poland* (New York: Harper Collins, 1992), 159.
4. Ibid., 160-61.
5. Ibid., 162.
6. Ibid., 184-85.

have done as they did."[7] This is true also for the cases presented in this essay. What was specifically Austrian one could observe in war crimes trials from the 1950s through the 1970s was the juries who refused to accept the simple truth that "[h]uman responsibility is ultimately an individual matter."[8] They condoned Nazi war crimes by the fact that they had been committed during a war.

From 1945 through the 1970s, the Austrian judiciary subsumed not only violation of the laws and customs of war but also participation in the Holocaust under "war crimes." On 26 June 1945 the Provisional Government of re-established Austria promulgated a special law in order to punish those Nazi crimes that were not covered by the penal code, and although war crimes as such constituted only one out of ten punishable acts described by this law, it was called "War Criminals Act." Despite Simon Wiesenthal's untiring efforts to clarify that Nazi mass atrocities in camps and killing sites were not committed as part of warfare[9], even the Jerusalem based *Simon Wiesenthal Center* continues to call the perpetrators Nazi "war" criminals. This article deals with Nazi crimes regardless their legal classification.

Not all "ordinary men" who committed these crimes, were male perpetrators. Therefore also a woman appears among the following examples.

Four types of perpetrators are exemplified:

- An SA man who was among those guards who had murdered hundreds of Hungarian Jews on their way to the Mauthausen concentration camp during the "death marches" of the last days of the war.[10]

---

7. Ibid., 188.
8. Ibid.
9. In a lecture addressed to the Union of European Journalists on 22 January 1979 in Bonn, Wiesenthal stressed that "[d]escribing the Nazi crimes as war crimes amounts to a whitewashing of the Nazi horrors and does not capture the nature of what really happened. It makes soldiers of the murderers. Yet a soldier fights against armed adversaries. He can kill and he can be killed. Those who carried out their gruesome work in the ghettos and concentration camps 'fought' at no risk to themselves. And because their fight carried no risks, around 90% of these criminals survived the war." <http://www.simon-wiesenthal-archiv.at/01_wiesenthal/05_stellungnahmen/e02_warcrimes.html#warcrimes> (10 Jan. 2012).
10. The total number of victims of the "death marches" on Austrian soil is estimated at more than 23,000 people. The vast majority of them were Hungarian Jews who had to work as forced laborers along so called Southeast Wall, a hastily built provisional fortification of ramparts and anti-tank ditches against the approaching Red Army. See Winfried R. Garscha, "Excesses of Violence in an Apocalyptic Mood: Nazi Atrocities in the Final Phase of the War—and their Presence/Absence in Public Memory and Literature," in *Crime and Madness in Modern Austria: Myth, Metaphor and Cultural Realities*, ed. Rebecca S. Thomas (Newcastle upon Tyne: Cambridge Scholars Publishing, 2008), 268-278.

- A "typical" war criminal who had committed atrocities on occupied territory—a *Feldpolizeisekretär* (which corresponded the rank of a lieutenant) who commanded an outpost of the Secret Field Police on the Greek island of Crete.
- A female guard who had served in the concentration camps Ravensbrück and Lublin-Majdanek—a native German who, in Lublin, had married an Austrian and resettled to Austria after the war. She was one of the last suspects of Nazi crimes against whom the Austrian prosecution in 2008 had instituted legal proceedings.
- As an example for "ordinary people," who had not been involved in severe atrocities, but taken part in the harassment of Jews in everyday life, this essay finishes with a fictional character who has been serving in public debates as a kind of symbolic figure for the "typical Viennese"—the notorious "Herr Karl" who was designed by Carl Merz and Helmut Qualtinger after a real character among their circle of acquaintances.

A Dumb Murderer and the Beginning of the Postwar War Crimes Trials

One month after the liberation of Vienna by the Soviet Red Army, on 15 May 1945, in the proletarian Third district (*Landstraße*) a forty year old butcher named Rudolf Kronberger showed up in an administration building used by the Soviet military authorities. He was looking for the district office of the "Auxiliary Police of the Soviet Headquarters for the City of Vienna" (*Polizeilicher Hilfsdienst für die Kommandantur der Stadt Wien*).[11] These men with red-white-red armbands had been summoned by the Red Army in order to secure water and energy supplies, to guard food stores, and to maintain public order as long as no regular police force was re-installed by the Austrian government. The auxiliary police men were in no way prepared to deal with a report as it was made by the butcher. He told them about abominable crimes of Viennese SA men that he had witnessed just six weeks before. It happened during the evacuation of a camp for Hungarian Jews who had worked as forced laborers in Engerau, a village close to the Slovak capital Bratislava. Around 2,000 Jews had been brought there from Budapest in late 1944, more than 500 among them had perished by the time of the evacuation of the camp on 29 March 1945,

11. The provisional police existed from mid-April until the re-establishment of the regular police department on 12 June 1945. Cf. Hans Hautmann, "Der polizeiliche Hilfsdienst für die Kommandantur der Stadt Wien," Quellen und Studien 2000 (Vienna: Alfred Klahr Gesellschaft 2000), 277-346.

either through starvation and diseases, or by being bludgeoned to death and/or shot by the guards. During a night march from Engerau to Deutsch Altenburg on the Danube (where the SA embarked the surviving prisoners for being brought to the Mauthausen concentration camp), another 102 men were killed.

The auxiliary policemen brought Kronberger to a Soviet officer, who questioned him. The officer then ordered the arrest of four former SA men, who Kronberger had implicated as murderers of the Hungarian Jews either in Engerau or during the evacuation march. In a first interrogation the other SA men accused Kronberger of having himself murdered numerous Jews. The Soviet occupation authorities expected Austrian police and judiciary to assume responsibility for the punishment of Nazi crimes. One week later the Soviet officer delivered all former Engerau guards he had in custody to the provisional police department of the Third district, where regular policemen started questioning the suspects. The former SA men were ready to describe in detail the atrocities they had participated in. Each of them was convinced that those Jews, whom they had shot, had been too weak and sick to survive the horrendous evacuation march. They regarded such shooting as a kind of coup de grâce. None of them showed any sign of feeling guilty. They had just followed an order to kill all those who were not able to keep the pace.

By June 1945, the Austrian judiciary began to re-organize its offices. State attorneys and examining magistrates and also criminal justices were appointed and started their first proceedings. On 22 June 1945 a state's attorney requested the institution of preliminary proceedings by the examining magistrate at the Viennese district court. He thus launched a series of proceedings that went down in Austrian legal history as the six "Engerau Trials."[12]

On 9 July 1945 the examining magistrate, an experienced judge, started a three-week long thorough investigation of all five suspects. The judge did not wait until the court administration was able to provide a recording clerk and a typewriter, but acted as his own secretary. While questioning the perpetrators, he scribbled down his handwritten protocol. It is obvious that the examining magistrate was aware that any deferment of the hearings would enable the suspects to work out their memories of the events three months before in a manner that allowed them to arrange more harmless, favorable versions.

12. Claudia Kuretsidis-Haider, *"Das Volk sitzt zu Gericht." Österreichische Justiz und NS-Verbrechen am Beispiel der Engerau-Prozesse 1945-1954* (Innsbruck: StudienVerlag, 2006). This model study abundantly quotes from the original prosecution and court documents and is being used therefore as source for the following paragraphs.

He recorded the most meaningful answers from the butcher Rudolf Kronberger, who turned out to be a rather dumb thug with sudden pangs of remorse. Kronberger depicted himself both as victim and as a leading perpetrator. On the one hand he was eager to exaggerate his actual role, to emphasize his importance as an informer; on the other hand he insisted on the fact that he himself had only implemented the orders of his superiors. He denied any responsibility or guilt: he did not act for the fun of it but out of a sense of duty only.

In his moments of remorse he concocted incredibly fanciful explanations for his deeds, e.g. that during the shootings that took place regularly in the camp, he wounded Jews with his gun only in order to help them to be transferred to a sickbay (which itself was a figment of his imagination, too). For him, killing of people was nothing that affected him personally, but something that required skills. He knew the most effective use of the pistol in order to spare bullets. And he described where and how prisoners, who turned out to be too weak to meet their workload, were killed. It seems that he was rather proud that it was he, whom the Gestapo had considered qualified to execute these killings—but maybe also his leadership role was a fantasy. He seemed to realize though that by talking about a leadership role he indicted himself. And so he stressed that he had tried to escape the impasse by telling "the Gestapo" that he had no experience in shooting people. But he was told by "the Gestapo" that he would be covered. "Thus, despite numerous sleepless nights, I had no choice but to fulfill the order I had received, and to care for the execution of the killing—if only because otherwise I had to fear to be shot myself. Luckily some comrades were ready to assume the executions themselves, but I had to be present and to report the execution."[13]

It turned out, he continued, that his nerves were not up to this task, therefore he got relieved from this duty. All these regular killings were halted after that. Kronberger suggested that it was he who had caused the official termination of the shootings. But still two men continued killing the Jews, he told the police, namely Alois Frank, a fifty year old cook, and Wilhelm Neunteufel, a 45 year old house painter.

Kronberger was bitterly disappointed that police and judiciary treated him like a criminal, whereas he regarded the disclosure of these abominable crimes as his merit only: "It would have been certainly my task to trace all the accomplices and to turn them over to the police. Instead of that the police arrested me, the one who, of my own free will, had reported these crimes to the police."[14]

13. Ibid., 75.
14. Ibid., 76.

Claudia Kuretsidis-Haider, who analyzed the handwritten protocols of the examining magistrate, summarizes Kronberger's pattern of argument in comparison with the defense strategy of the two other accused former SA men: "Whereas Kronberger tried to curry favor with the court as indispensable key witness and, by that, to divert attention from his own crimes, Frank entrenched himself behind the accusation that the confession had been squeezed out of him through threats and behind memory gaps. He was unable to recollect who had been responsible for which murders. Neunteufel by contrast showed willingness to cooperate with the court and even told the examining magistrate that he had regrets about his crimes. Yet all three admitted one or two murders at the utmost and appealed either to orders they had received or, if that seemed impossible, to the sympathy they had felt for the half-dead Jews."[15]

Kronberger's lament fit well into a pattern of his life's trajectory: after the death of his mother and the re-marriage of his father to a woman with two children, his family placed him with a farmer. He had to work as a servant at this farm, but got the opportunity, eventually, to learn the trade of the butcher. During the Austrian dictatorship 1934-1938, when the Nazi party was outlawed as illegal, his boss asked him for help to uncover the clandestine Nazis in the butcher's shop. Kronberger reported eleven out of twelve workers, who were arrested by the police as a result of his information. After the "Anschluss" 1938 he quickly tried to adjust to the new political regime. After he had been fired from the butcher's shop, Kronberger, now a member of the SA, was hired by the *Reichsbahn*, the German Railway Company. Such employments in state-owned companies constituted a kind of compensation for those clandestine Nazis, who had been subject to discrimination by the Austrian dictatorship. Kronberger was entitled to such "compensation," because he had found "witnesses" who confirmed that he had been a member of the Nazi party already in 1932, i.e. before the ban of the party 1933. As a railroader he was exempted from military service, but in 1944 he was called up as a guard on the Southeast Wall.[16] During the main trial he claimed that it was his dedication to his colleagues that had cost him his safe job.

The Austrian National Library has a press photo of the first Engerau trial in August 1945 in its Picture Archives. It shows Kronberger in leather

15. Ibid., 78.

16. The assignment of Jewish slave laborers along the Southeast Wall is described by Szabolcs Szita, "The Forced Labor of Hungarian Jews at the Fortification of the Western Border Regions of Hungary, 1944-1945," in *Studies on the Holocaust in Hungary*, ed. Randolph L. Braham (New York: Columbia University Press, 1990), 175-93; for the fate of the surviving slave laborers during the last weeks of the war see Eleonore Lappin, "Death Marches of Hungarian Jews Through Austria in the Spring of 1945," *Yad Vashem Studies* vol. 28 (2000), 203-42.

pants and a loden jacket, sitting on the dock, flanked by two policemen, apparently not understanding why he had been brought before the court as a defendant.[17] By resuming Kronberger's statements during the main trial, Kuretsidis-Haider calls him the "type of a perpetrator who was unable to understand the world any more; after all, he had always complied with the respective authorities and, by that, fulfilled his duties. Eventually he regarded himself the greatest victim both of Nazi dictatorship and of the prevailing order he had curried favor with, and which did not thank him for his compliancy."[18]

Rudolf Kronberger's August 1945 "Engerau Trial" before the Volksgericht, © Austrian National Library

The Tyrolian Downhill Racer as War Criminal

An important part of the annual ski world cup championship is the "Hahnenkamm race" at the fancy Tyrolian ski resort of Kitzbühel. The first such race took place on 28 March 1931. The winner was a 19 year old local hero: Ferdinand (called "Ferdl") Friedensbacher, single child of

17. ÖNB Bildarchiv/OEGZ, Sign. O 79/1, Austrian National Library, Vienna.
18. Kuretsidis-Haider, *"Das Volk sitzt zu Gericht,"* 367.

a landlady who farmed a chalet near Kitzbühel.[19] After his apprenticeship at an upholsterer in Kitzbühel, Friedensbacher had found only temporary appointments in his occupation. One month after his spectacular downhill victory he joined the Austrian Army, hoping to become a civil servant after his service in the mountain infantry. Four years later he was actually transferred, still as soldier, to the gendarmerie. In January 1936 he was appointed "probationary gendarme" at the sub-station Hungerburg, a neighborhood above the city of Innsbruck. There he received a mention for bravery for the imprisonment of a dangerous criminal. After the "Anschluss" in March 1938 the Hungerburg district was incorporated into the municipality of Innsbruck. There was no more need for a gendarmerie substation there since the security was now maintained by the municipal police. First Friedensbacher did not want to accept the offer for the gendarmes to move to the criminal police, but then he met a girl from Innsbruck and decided to stay. It can be assumed that his application for membership in the Nazi party was part of the arrangement with the police department. He married and became father of twins (who died soon after their birth) and, two years later, of a son.

At the criminal investigation department in Innsbruck he was appointed to the tracing division. But although soon promoted to assistant detective, he did not feel comfortable with this move from the regular to the security police. Applications of being transferred back to the regular police were, however, refused by his superiors. The records show that the main reason for this refusal was Friedensbacher's excellent reputation as a ski racer and jumper. The security police was interested in retaining him in its ski team for championships. In July 1939 he was transferred to the Gestapo division II (home security); the scope of duties of sub division II C, Friedensbacher's new office, encompassed surveying and questioning of political opponents and religious groups like Jehovah's witnesses, who refused military service. Director of division II was Werner Hilliges from Berlin, who would be appointed head of the Innsbruck Gestapo in 1943. Friedensbacher was a model policeman. He attended courses, he received awards for exemplary performance of his duties; in September 1938 he received another mention for bravery for rescuing two people from drowning.

In November 1939, after the war had begun, he was transferred to Hanover as a member of *Geheime Feldpolizei (GFP) Gruppe 611* (group 611

19. The biographical data follow Friedensbacher's police file and his questioning by the examining magistrate (1969-1970). Photocopied excerpts of the court record (LG Innsbruck 19 Vr 415/70) are stored at the Documentation Center of Austrian Resistance, Vienna (DÖW 21221).

of the Secret Field Police). The Secret Field Police—the Gestapo of the *Wehrmacht*—was divided into units of around fifty members, called "groups." In 1940 *GFP Gruppe 611* was deployed to the Netherlands, Belgium and eventually France, it combated sabotage and espionage. Head of group 611 was an Austrian, Otto Begus from Salzburg, whose role in major Nazi war crimes in Greece would be investigated by Austrian prosecutors after the war.[20] After the German conquest of the Balkans in April 1941, Begus' unit was deployed to Athens. Friedensbacher himself arrived in Athens some weeks later; he had been wounded in a railway accident in Transylvania during his transfer from France to Greece and had been sent to a military hospital in Vienna. When Friedensbacher joined *GFP Gruppe 611* again, his commander Begus had been replaced by another captain (*Feldpolizeikommissar*). Begus was posted to a special commando that began its murderous actions in the metropolitan area of Athens and Piraeus a few months later.

The Secret Field Police Group 611 (with Friedensbacher) was flown to Hania (Crete), where it replaced the SD (the Secret Service of the SS). Because the island of Crete was one of the centers of Greek resistance, the Secret Field Police command at Hania considered it necessary to establish branch offices also in the two other major towns of the island, Rethymno and Heraklion. In establishing branch offices and outposts the Secret Field Police could count on the organizational skills of the Tyrolian police officer, one out of six lieutenants (*Feldpolizeisekretäre*) of the group. Friedensbacher was sent to Heraklion, accompanied by twelve auxiliary field policemen. He installed the branch office in a confiscated private house at Heraklion's city square. After the Italian troops had withdrawn from Crete in the summer of 1943, Friedensbacher and another *Feldpolizeisekretär* were ordered to establish outposts in the Southern and Eastern parts of the island. His outpost was located in Agios Nikolaos. Friedensbacher's staff for Agios Nikolaos consisted of three auxiliary policemen, two drivers and an interpreter. The task of the outpost was to arrest suspected persons and to question the prisoners. As soon as an examination had been concluded, the

20. *Feldpolizeikommissar* (captain) Begus never got indicted for the crimes he had committed in Greece. The only punishable act that could be proved by the prosecution was his membership in the clandestine Austrian Nazi party before the "Anschluss." On 26 April 1948 he received a conviction of three years imprisonment (LG Wien Vg 11 Vr 8262/47). Information about the shooting of hostages, the murder of hundreds of civilians and other atrocities in the Athens metropolitan area can be found in Greek documents attached to the prosecution record against Otto Begus, Franz Kleedorfer, Alfred Josef Slawik and others (LG Wien Vg 8e Vr 183/53). The prosecution and court records are stored in the *Wiener Stadt- und Landesarchiv*.

prisoner was brought to Hania, where the German *Wehrmacht* had installed a court martial.

Although Friedensbacher insisted during his trial[21] that he had only issued some slaps in the face, it is unlikely that *GFP Gruppe 611* did not commit any atrocities like all the other Secret Field Police units deployed to Greece. However, the only person who accused Friedensbacher for participation in the torture of prisoners was no reliable witness: it was his interpreter who also was facing criminal investigations both by Greek and French authorities for his involvement in German war crimes. The allegation of torture and maltreatment of prisoners remained unproven, but Friedensbacher admitted that in May 1944 he had shot a thirty year old man, whom he had suspected of being chief of a clandestine resistance network. This killing action was the reason for his Austrian jury trial on 9 December 1970 (see below).

After some partisan attacks in early 1944 with considerable casualties on the German side, the Secret Field Police tried to get better intelligence through local informers. In Agios Nikolaos a young lady, who had been accused by a German soldier that she had tried to prevail upon him to desert to the Greek partisans, offered information in exchange for her release. After the arrest of all people she had identified as partisans, Friedensbacher told his interpreter to hide in the fireplace of the room the detainees were brought to. Thus he learned that one man—the pharmacist Joseph Sakkadakis—told the others how to behave during the questioning, and promised to organize an escape. Yet apart from the recognition of the young pharmacist as a kind of advisor who commanded respect by others he had no proof whatsoever. He intended to send the whole group to Hania, but expected them to be acquitted by the court martial (he was wrong: the German court imposed death sentences upon the informer and a second person). When all efforts had gone awry to persuade the pharmacist to answer a single question, Friedensbacher realized that the whole action might turn out as a dangerous failure. After a possible acquittal and release by the court martial the accused might come back later and take revenge on him. In order to prevent at least the acquittal of Sakkadakis, the suspected chief of the group, he decided to kill him. He separated the pharmacist

21. Winfried R. Garscha, "'Taten, die den allgemein anerkannten Grundsätzen des Völkerrechts und des Kriegsrechts widersprechen': Prozesse wegen Verletzung des Kriegsvölkerrechts," in *Holocaust und Kriegsverbrechen vor Gericht: Der Fall Österreich*, eds. Thomas Albrich, Winfried R. Garscha, and Martin F. Polaschek (Innsbruck: StudienVerlag 2006), 262-78 (about Friedensbacher's trial: 275-76). For additional information about this trial see <http://www.nachkriegsjustiz.at/prozesse/geschworeneng/friedensbacher.php> (10 Jan. 2012).

from the other detainees. Together with the interpreter and a driver he brought him to a place where the road ran on the top of a cliff near the ocean. There he threatened to shoot him, if he continued to refuse to answer his questions. He asked him three times, and after the third refusal he ordered him to turn around and fired two bullets of his pistol into his neck. Sakkadakis collapsed and fell over the cliff into the ocean. When Friedensbacher looked down into the water, he saw his victim drifting on the surface of the water. Because the cliff was in a restricted military area, they had encountered a patrol. The patrol reported the incident to Hania, but Friedensbacher claimed that his prisoner had been shot on the run.

In late summer of 1944 Friedensbacher was called back to Hania. Two months later the members of *GFP Gruppe 611* were flown to Athens and continued their retreat by train through Yugoslavia. In April 1945 he was sent as a billeting officer to his home province Tyrol to scout out a retreat area for his unit. When he arrived in Kitzbühel, he learned that US troops, coming from Germany, had already crossed the Tyrolian border. He deserted from the *Wehrmacht* and joined a resistance group. He probably received the help of two relatives, who had already become members of this resistance group earlier. This group had been organized in 1943 by the coal and iron salesman Max Werner, a former member of parliament who later would serve as president of Kitzbühel's tourist association for decades. Friedensbacher was one out of three officers among the seventy-three *Wehrmacht* deserters who had been members of this group.[22] His task was to find hideouts and provide food for American parachutists who had bailed out from their American bombers in the surrounding area of Kitzbühel.

After the liberation of the Tyrol, Friedensbacher served again as a gendarme for several months. When he patrolled some villages around Kitzbühel, he recognized by chance his former superior Werner Hilliges. He and some Gestapo officers had been hiding in a chalet in the Austrian Alps as so many Nazi bigwigs did at the end of the war. Friedensbacher alerted the American military police and thus contributed to Hilliges' conviction by a French military tribunal in 1948.[23] After a short period of employment

22. DÖW 06469 (a collection of papers concerning detailed information about anti Nazi resistance in Kitzbühel and other Tyrolean communities, collected in Summer 1945 to be transmitted to the Tyrolean provincial government by an Egyptian merchant living in Kitzbühel).

23. In December 1948 a French court martial in Innsbruck tried members of the Innsbruck Gestapo department who had committed atrocities in the Gestapo camp of Reichenau, close to Innsbruck. The court imposed a life sentence on Hilliges for crimes against humanity and murder. Seven years later he was released on parole, but committed suicide together with his wife in 1956.

with the municipal administration of Kitzbühel, Friedensbacher and his wife and son moved back to Innsbruck. In 1961 he returned to Kitzbühel and took over a ski school; during summers he practiced his old trade of upholsterer.

The Innsbruck trial of 1970 was the result of Greek and German war crimes cases with regard to actions of the Secret Field Police in Greece; special attention was given to its involvement in the deportation of Greek Jews to Auschwitz. The war crimes committed during the war on the island of Crete were not the main focus of the investigation and trial. On July 2, 1964 the Higher Regional Court at Athens had declared itself incompetent to prosecute German military personnel. In Germany the Bremen state attorney's office assumed prosecution of the accused Secret Field Police officers. Friedensbacher, an Austrian citizen living outside Germany, was dismissed from the proceeding. This obliged the Innsbruck state's attorney as competent prosecution office to take legal action against him.

During extensive questioning in April 1969 by the Innsbruck police department Friedensbacher told his interrogators that he accepted to have acted unlawfully in the murder of the Greek pharmacist Sakkadakis. His excuse was his young age at the time. In his statement before the examining magistrate in March 1970 he admitted that "now" he was aware that obeying the laws would have required the delivery of the suspect to the court martial. He realized that according to German martial law even during the Nazi dictatorship a shooting could only be carried out as an execution of a death sentence imposed by a court. At the time of the crime, however, he felt he was morally entitled to shoot the man as a "dangerous person," all the more since "in countless attacks" Greek resistance fighters, too, had "shot our people from behind."[24]

The court records contain no reason why the jury in the Friedensbacher trial consisted of men only. Maybe the Tyrolean judiciary at that time did not want to allow female jurors to decide the fate of men and their criminal actions in times of war. The verdict of the Tyrolese jury was that the defendant had committed manslaughter and not murder; the jurors did not see any base motives and cruelty in play. The indictment had seen Friedensbacher threatening the suspect three times to be shot on the spot as "cruel." Yet the jurors unanimously refused to accept this interpretation of the prosecutor with respect to "the prevailing specific circumstances (war, partisans) at the time."[25]

24. LG Innsbruck 19 Vr 415/70, n° 11 (interrogation of Ferdinand Friedensbacher, Innsbruck, 17 March 1970), photocopy in: DÖW 21221/4.

25. Ibid., n° 24 (finding of the jury, 9 December 1970), photocopy in: DÖW 21221/15.

The prosecution submitted a plea of nullity containing doubtful legal arguments that minimized its prospect of success (its superior authority ordered to withdraw this plea nine months later). This action of the prosecution provoked the defense to submit a statement that illustrated the reasoning of the "not cruel" plea that had convinced the jury. Friedensbacher's defense attorneys insisted that the laws and customs of war did not apply to combating partisans: "In consequence of their malicious and cruel conduct they are treated by every belligerent state as outlaws, a practice which arises from the irresistible compulsion to protect the commander's own life and that of his subordinate soldiers."[26]

By qualifying cold-blooded murder "manslaughter" as soon as the killed person was a suspected partisan, the jurors not only exonerated a local ski champion; the Austrian court exempted partisan warfare from all legal bindings and justified Nazi war crimes in general. Neither Austrian Justice nor Austrian politics saw any reason for questioning this judgment. In the two decades after the country had become independent again in 1955, Austrian courts in thirty-four cases convicted twenty Nazi criminals, and acquitted twenty-three defendants. Since 1975 no judgment whatsoever has been passed against Nazi war criminals by any Austrian court.

Almost all of these few trials leave a bad taste though: with a few exceptions the verdicts of the juries show not a glimmer of insight into the criminal character of the Nazi regime in general and of the complicity to these crimes by taking part in criminal warfare and the maintenance of concentration camps. The twenty defendants who were found guilty by the courts were sentenced because they willingly had participated in mass murder or because they had committed especially atrocious crimes from base motives. Only three received a life sentence. The acquittal of Ferdinand Friedensbacher dovetailed perfectly with this obstinate refusal of recognizing Austria's responsibility for the participation of so many Austrians in the Nazi crimes.

The defendant himself showed no sense of guilt. He conceded an infringement of martial law, but insisted on his "moral" right to do so in view of the fact that the enemy partisans, too, breached the laws and customs of war. This excuse silenced any critical assessment of the own role during World War II and reflected the general attitude of "ordinary Austrians" of that time.

26. Ibid., n° 32 (Counter statement of Kurt and Gert Strele, attorneys-at-law, to the prosecution's plea of nullity, Innsbruck, 1 February 1971), photocopy in: DÖW 21221/17.

A Female Camp Guard from the Majdanek KZ Escapes Punishment

During 1942-43 huge loads of shoes, clothing and female hair of the two million Jews murdered in the death camps located in the East of the General Government of Poland were sent to Germany from Lublin. The concentration camp of Majdanek and its sub camps had been serving as a kind of dispatch center for "Operation Reinhardt."[27] The mass killing was organized by the Austrian Nazi Odilo Globocnik, SS and Police Leader of the Lublin district, who intended to expand camp Majdanek to the biggest concentration camp in the Nazi empire. *Ostmärker* served on Globocnik's staff, mostly old comrades of his from Carinthia and Vienna. They had accompanied him to Poland after his dismissal as *Gauleiter* of Vienna. Many of these Austrians held central posts in the gruesome Nazi extermination machinery.[28]

Before shoes and clothing were delivered to Germany, they had to be cleaned and repaired or picked apart. This was done mainly by female prisoners. They had their own sector ("field") in the Majdanek KZ. They were guarded by women who were not allowed to join the SS, but served as SS-auxiliaries, called *Gefolge* ("followers").[29] The training of these SS-auxiliaries took place in Ravensbrück, the concentration camp for women north of Berlin. After their apprenticeship in Ravensbrück they were sent either to Majdanek or to Auschwitz. Both of these camps had high numbers of female prisoners and thus needed female guards.

The best known among these SS-auxiliaries was Hermine Ryan, née Braunsteiner, who had been traced by Simon Wiesenthal all the way to Queens in New York City in 1964.[30] US authorities initiated legal action against the former guard of Ravensbrück and Majdanek. Braunsteiner had

27. Majdanek was the first Nazi concentration camp liberated by Allied troops. When the Soviet and Polish soldiers, who freed the last surviving prisoners on 23 July 1944, saw the mountains of ashes and shoes, they were convinced that at least 1.5 million people perished in this extermination camp. It was only after decades of research that historiography understood that what the liberators had found, were remnants of people murdered in other camps like Sobibor and Belzec. The actual numbers are 60,000 Jewish and 20,000 non-Jewish victims. For most recent research findings see Tomasz Kranz, "Bookkeeping of Death and Prisoner Mortality at Majdanek," in *Yad Vashem Studies* 35, vol. 1 (2007): 81-110.

28. Joseph Poprzeczny, *Odilo Globocnik. Hitler's Man in the East* (Jefferson, NC, and London: McFarland, 2004), 93-143.

29. Elissa Mailänder Koslov, *Gewalt im Dienstalltag. Die SS-Aufseherinnen des Konzentrations- und Vernichtungslagers Majdanek 1942-1944* (Hamburg: Hamburger Edition, 2009).

30. "Former Nazi Camp Guard Is Now a Housewife in Queens," *The New York Times*, 14 Jul. 1964, 10 <http://www.nytimes.com/images/promos/magazine/20050306braunsteiner.pdf > (10 Jan. 2012).

been an Austrian citizen before her marriage with the American GI Ryan. The aim of the action was to revoke Braunsteiner Ryan's US citizenship and to have her deported to stand trial in a European country. The "Braunsteiner Ryan case" became the initial spark for the establishment of the Office of Special Investigations (OSI), a division of the U.S. Department of Justice.[31] Both Poland and Germany (but not Austria!) claimed Braunsteiner Ryan's extradition. Eventually she was indicted by a German prosecutor and became the main defendant in the largest trial in German criminal history: the main trial against fifteen former Majdanek camp guards in Düsseldorf (1975-81). On June 30, 1981, the German court handed down a life sentence to Hermine Ryan for "joint murder of at least hundred people" in two instances.[32]

One of the youngest guards among the SS *Gefolge* in Majdanek was Erna Wallisch, née Pfannstiel.[33] She spent a dismal youth in Thuringia. Her mother, after an attempted suicide, was sent to an asylum by her father. Similar to the case of Kronberger mentioned above, her father, after his re-marriage, asked her to leave the household. She attended for two years a school for domestic economy, spent one year at the *Reichsarbeitsdienst* (Reich Labor Service), and worked as housemaid. At the age of nineteen she read an advertisement: young single women were needed for KZ service, no education required. On October 7, 1942, after a training year in Ravensbrück, she was sent to Lublin along with other guards (among them Hermine Braunsteiner). Pfannstiel was appalled by the squalor in the camp and proved unable to cope with the circumstances there. Her personnel files contain entries about insubordination and insults against superiors; she was suspected to be potentially suicidal (fellow guards watched out for her use of the service pistol). Survivors described her as whimsical and dangerous, because she brutalized prisoners unexpectedly when she was in a bad mood. 1943 the commandant of the SS-auxiliaries, Elsa Ehrich, requested several times Pfannstiel's transfer to another concentration camp; it did not

31. In 2000 the historian Peter Black, in the 1980s and 1990s involved in tracking and prosecuting suspected war criminals within the framework of OSI, described in an interview the impact of the Braunsteiner Ryan case on US policy towards naturalized Nazi war criminals <http://www.ushmm.org/wlc/en/media_oi.php?MediaId=5593> (10 Jan. 2012).

32. Elissa Mailänder Koslov, "Der Fall Hermine Braunsteiner: Eine geschlechtergeschichtliche Studie," in *Das KZ Lublin-Majdanek und die Justiz. Strafverfolgung und verweigerte Gerechtigkeit: Polen, Deutschland und Österreich im Vergleich*, ed. Claudia Kuretsidis-Haider et al. (Graz: Clio, 2011), 223-37.

33. Winfried R. Garscha, Claudia Kuretsidis-Haider, Siegfried Sanwald, "Der Fall Majdanek in der jüngsten österreichischen Rechtsgeschichte: Die Ermittlungen gegen Erna Wallisch," in Ibid., 416-26; Florian Klenk, Stefan Apfl, "Der Fall Erna Wallisch," in *Falter* 6 Feb. 2008 (reprinted in *Das KZ Lublin-Majdanek*, ed. Kuretsidis-Haider et al., 427-37).

happen. During this time she fell in love with the Viennese SS man Georg Wallisch. She soon got pregnant and had to quit the KZ guard service in January 1944. In March 1944 she returned to the Lublin district in Poland to marry the SS man Wallisch at the German civil registry office. Her groom was released from prison for the day. Wallisch had been locked up after committing theft. He stole articles of value that had been confiscated from Jewish prisoners. First young Mrs. Wallisch stayed with her child near the Ravensbrück concentration camp; she next moved in with her sister in Thuringia; eventually she joined her husband in Vienna and gave birth to two more children. She divorced Wallisch in the 1960s and stayed on in Vienna.

Between 1963 and 1972 the state attorney's office in Graz conducted legal proceedings against former guards of the Majdanek concentration camp. In January 1973 the Austrian Ministry of Justice approved the Graz state attorney's final report of October 1972, suggesting summarily to dismiss the charges against all but one of the 64 accused guards. The exception was Erna Wallisch.

During a ten year investigation the Austrian prosecutor had been unable to indict Erna Wallisch with any crimes that were not barred by the statute of limitations. But in preparation for the Majdanek trial in Düsseldorf a German examining magistrate had interrogated Wallisch as a witness in Vienna in November 1972. On that occasion he had provoked her to admit that it was one of her duties to calm down women at Majdanek KZ who cried in front of "the hut with the showers;" they knew that the doors of the hut led to the gas chamber. Wallisch then claimed that it was Braunsteiner and Ehrich who selected the prisoners to be gassed; she herself was only responsible for maintaining "order" during the chaos of the selections on death row. The examination took place in the Viennese district court. The German magistrate and state's attorneys were both allowed to ask questions, but it was an Austrian judge who led the questioning. The Austrian judge did not see any reason for immediate legal action, which astonished the German state's attorneys. Wallisch had just admitted to have been an accomplice to the killing of prisoners in the gas chamber. During her examinations by the Graz state's attorney she had "forgotten" even the existence of a gas chamber in Majdanek. Wallisch's late avowal alerted the Graz state's attorney. In addition to that there was a request from the German judiciary concerning a possible arrest of this suspect. Therefore Erna Wallisch was the only accused against whom he did not recommend dismissal. Instead, he asked for a continuation of the proceedings against Wallisch in a Vienna court, where she resided.

The Ministry of Justice transferred Wallisch's case to Vienna immediately after the approval of the final report of the prosecution. Ten days later the Viennese state's attorney dismissed the charge, because he assessed that the statute of limitations no longer allowed to prosecute her. This assessment resulted in an interpretation of Wallisch's immediate accessory to the gassing as a "distant accompliceship."

In 2002 Efraim Zuroff, the director of the Simon Wiesenthal Institute in Jerusalem, launched the international campaign "*Operation: Last Chance*." Zuroff aimed at addressing the judiciary of those countries where unpunished Nazi criminals continued to live. The aim of the campaign was to use the last chance to bring to justice at least some of the perpetrators before their biological time clock ran out. The campaign targeted Austria particularly. Nazi criminals had been living in Austria with impunity since 1972, when the last defendant charged with Nazi crimes was convicted by a court. Moreover, as mentioned above, the last judgment by an Austrian court with respect to Nazi crimes happened in 1975, when a regular court in Austria acquitted the defendant in the only Mauthausen trial ever conducted in Austria after the dissolution of the Volksgerichte—the special courts for Nazi crimes—in 1955.

By accident, Erna Wallisch, the "ordinary" camp guard, showed up as number seven on Zuroff's "blacklist of ten most wanted Nazi criminals." Wallisch did not end up on this blacklist for the character of her crimes. She was suspected of having killed a prisoner by hitting him with a piece of wood on his head on one of her bad days. There had to be other reasons for putting her on a blacklist with leading Holocaust perpetrators such as Alois Brunner. Of course, the assumed crime had been committed in Majdanek, one of the biggest and most infamous Nazi concentration camps. It is very likely, however, that the Wiesenthal Center wanted to alert the international community to the fact that the Republic of Austria had been very uncooperative and unwilling to prosecute and convict war criminals as the Wallisch case so clearly suggested. Here was an opportunity to remind the world of the shameful record of the Austrian judiciary in the 1970s and 1980s to seriously prosecute World War II war criminals, especially those Austrians that had contributed to the killing machines in the Auschwitz, Majdanek and Mauthausen KZs.

The international media coverage of the disclosure of the Wallisch case, one of the most notorious Austrian war criminals was immense. The British historian Guy Walters published a photograph he had shot of Mrs. Wallisch, showing an old woman in her morning bathrobe with messy hair, opening the door of her house and quite displeased about the harassment administered to her at this time of the day.[34] The German tabloid newspaper *Bild* reprinted the photo with the nasty comment: "Hitler's merciless hag."[35] British newspapers were insinuating that the protection of this "murderer" by the Austrian judicial system might be an international conspiracy.[36]

The new charges against Erna Wallisch were based on the evidence of a Polish eye witness. She remembered a pregnant guard who had hit a male prisoner in the early fall of 1943 in a manner that made it likely that the man died as a result of this attack. But there were severe objections against a clear attribution of this crime to Mrs. Wallisch. In the fall of 1943 two other female guards had been pregnant at Majdanek next to Pfannstiel/Wallisch. So the identity of the alleged perpetrator was not clear. In addition, the lethal quality of the deadly blow could not be proven. Apart from the uncertainty about the age or nationality of the victim, let alone his name, nobody knew for sure that he had died from the blow. The witnesses only confirmed that they did not see their fellow prisoner after this event any more. No one knew for sure when the prisoner in question actually died. As it turned out, the key witness, a Polish survivor, had told her story in a different version some years before. Not much imagination was needed to guess the outcome of a trial based on such scanty evidence. Presumably Austrian prosecutors were relieved when Erna Wallisch died in February 2008.

The media coverage of the Wallisch case followed the same pattern observable thirty years earlier during the coverage of the Düsseldorf Majdanek mega trial. The scholar Elissa Mailänder Koslov has pointed out that men who had committed atrocities were presented as criminals in the Düsseldorf trial, whereas female perpetrators caused salacious horror in the audience. Mailänder Koslov compared the comments of the tabloid newspapers on Braunsteiner and Wallisch with the recent case of Iraqi detainees being tortured by American soldiers in the Abu Ghraib prison. While few observers remember the faces or names of the US soldiers that tortured Iraqi prisoners in Abu Ghraib, the name and face of the only female perpetrator was reported around the world.[37] It seems to be more shocking to the public at large to contemplate cases of women as perpetrators of crimes.

In her study about the SS *Gefolge* in the Majdanek KZ Mailänder Koslov recalled the fact that from 1942, when the mass gassings began, "all,

34. <http://www.wiltshiretimes.co.uk/news/1782475.how_i_found_nazi_war_criminal_suspect> (10 Jan. 2012).
35. *Bild*, 29 Jan. 2008.
36. *Daily Mail*, 2 Nov. 2007.
37. Mailänder Koslov, "Der Fall Hermine Braunsteiner," 235.

even less thuggish female guards (and SS men), were confronted, directly or indirectly, with daily killings. Also those guards who had no direct order to kill were, in carrying out the *Selektionen*, parties to the mass extermination process. Violence, dead and extermination were ubiquitous in the guards' everyday service and went over into their spare time. The smell of burning human flesh, the listening to shots, and the view of dead bodies that were collected or moved around in the camp, accompanied both workday and evening."[38]

Against this background the social dynamics of violence can be explained: "The quotidian use of force against the detainees not only served to dominate, to break in and to ruin the prisoners—a fact that had been worked out hitherto by KZ research. Not least it was directed also towards the fellow guards standing around, in order to show, what he/she was capable of. In this respect the acts of violence constituted a complex internal communication of power (Michel Foucault), self-display and self-assertion within the SS colleagues. Quite often this resulted in an escalation of brutality. These group dynamics are important for the understanding of violence. Violence, like any action, never occurs outside a social context."[39]

Within this context, "ordinary" men/women became brutal thugs. The trial records show however that even in an institution like the Majdanek KZ alternative behavior was possible. But hardly any guard abstained from violence, as Mailänder Koslov emphasized: "With their violent assaults against detainees the female guards and SS men daily maxed out their assigned tasks and competences all over again and mostly transgressed them in an arbitrary manner."[40]

Austria's "*Herr Karls*": "Ordinary Men" Harassing Viennese Jews

On 15 November 1961, a month before the Jerusalem District Court imposed its death sentence on Adolf Eichmann, Austrian public television broadcasted the one-man-play *Der Herr Karl*. It starred comedian Helmut Qualtinger, who had co-authored the play with Carl Merz.[41] The play's protagonist was an ordinary Austrian living in the time when the German Nazis controlled the *Ostmark*. "Herr Karl" was a shop assistant in his forties. He was sitting in the basement of a grocery store and was telling an

38. Mailänder Koslov, *Gewalt im Dienstalltag*, 484.
39. Ibid., 485.
40. Ibid., 491.
41. Helmut Qualtinger, *Werkausgabe*, ed. Traugott Krischke, vol. 1: *"Der Herr Karl" und andere Texte fürs Theater* (Vienna: Deuticke, 1995), 174 (ellipsis in the quotations as in the original).

imaginary young man about his experiences during the Nazi era. Whereas Eichmann, the quintessential Austrian Holocaust perpetrator, was standing trial in Jerusalem with the whole world watching, *Herr Karl*, a literary figure, acted out no "key role" in the great historical events of those days whatsoever. Qualtinger's *Herr Karl* was the representative *Mitläufer*. He was one of those many Viennese men and women who had pulled Jewish residents out of their houses and apartments after the "Anschluss" in March 1938 and forced them to clean the pavement of the streets of Vienna on their knees, often with tooth brushes:

> "Look, what they reproached us with, later on—actually that was completely different ... there was a Jew in our apartment house, a certain Tennenbaum ... otherwise a nice guy—some people had written such things against the Nazis on the pavements ... and this Tennenbaum had to wipe it clean ... not him alone ... the other Jews also, of course ... had guided him there, to mop it off ... and the janitor watched and laughed ... he was always present when there was fun somewhere."

One scene of the play made *Herr Karl* paradigmatic in his dealing with Nazi crimes and atrocities. In this scene the reaction of the typical Austrian *Mitläufer*/perpetrator was depicted. When their former victims were beginning to return home after the war, if they had been lucky enough to survive the Holocaust, postwar Vienna's Herr Karls welcomed them in a maddeningly condescending tone:

> "After the war he came back, this Tennenbaum. Not to worry, nothing happened to him ... Met him on the street. I said hello to him: '*Habediehre*, Herr Tennenbaum!' This guy didn't even look at me. I said hello to him once more: '*Die Ehre*, Herr Tennenbaum ...' Again he didn't look at me. Did I think: ... all right, well, now he's angry."

"Not to worry, nothing happened to him": *Herr Karl's* commenting on the fate of his former Jewish neighbor is archetypical for all those "ordinary men" who had contributed one way or the other to the Nazi Holocaust. It suggested both how perpetrators tried to summon survivors as witnesses for their presumed innocence, and their reproach for having survived the Holocaust at all.

Qualtinger's and Merz's play *Herr Karl* skillfully plays on all the taboos of contemporary Austrian history, still at work in the early 1960s. But at the same time he says: "Oh no, these are things, let's not go into them." *Herr Karl* only speaks frankly about the Nazi time. He does it in the manner of exposing the self-deception about the Nazi past that characterized the public conscience at the time. The "Herr Karls" did mention the word "crimes," but only when talking about Allied bombings in 1944/45 as "war crimes."

In the early 1960s television was a new phenomenon. *Herr Karl* was broadcast during the prime time evening program. Probably the majority of Austrian households with television sets saw the show. The play was a "contrast program" to the headlines in the previous months, when Austrian newspapers had reported extensively about the Eichmann trial and Austrian World War II perpetrators.

After the show, thousands of irate letters and phone calls reached the Austrian Broadcasting Company. Ordinary Austrians protested against the imposition that their lives presumably were being ridiculed in the show and complained about the "distortions" about the Nazi times. The writer and critic Hans Weigel summed up the public's reaction to the show pithily: "*Der Herr Karl* wanted to kick a certain type's leg, and a whole nation cried *ouch!*"[42] Nothing revealed the fecklessness and insensitivity of the typical Austrian ordinary *Mitläufer* more devastatingly than Qualtinger's revealing black humor.

Conclusion

In his controversy with Daniel Goldhagen's theories about ordinary Germans as "Hitler's willing executioners,"[43] Christopher Browning stressed "that the perpetrators not only had the capacity to choose but exercised that choice in various ways that covered the spectrum from enthusiastic participation, through dutiful, nominal, or regretful compliance, to differing degrees of evasion."[44] He insisted that "[t]he fundamental problem is to explain why ordinary men—shaped by a culture that had its own peculiarities but was nonetheless within the mainstream of western, Christian, and Enlightenment traditions—under specific circumstances willingly carried out the most extreme genocide in human history."[45]

Goldhagen tried to prove in his study that only "very few societies have the long-term, cultural-cognitive prerequisites to commit genocide, and that regimes can only do so when the population is overwhelmingly of one mind

42. Quoted in: Ibid., 361.
43. Daniel J. Goldhagen, *Hitler's Willing Executioners: Ordinary Germans and the Holocaust* (New York: Knopf, 1996).
44. Afterword to: Christopher R. Browing, *Ordinary Men: Reserve Police Battalion 101 and the Final Solution in Poland* (New York: Harper Perennial pb., 1998), 221.
45. Ibid., 222.

about its priority, justice, and necessity."[46] Although Goldhagen explicitly referred only to Nazi Germany, it was clear that his finding applied also to Austria under Nazi rule. Browning's finding was less decisive: "I fear that we live in a world in which war and racism are ubiquitous, in which the powers of government mobilization and legitimization are powerful and increasing, in which a sense of personal responsibility is increasingly attenuated by specialization and bureaucratization, and in which the peer group exerts tremendous pressure on behavior and sets moral norms. In such a world, I fear, modern governments that wish to commit mass murder will seldom fail in their efforts for being unable to induce 'ordinary men' to become their 'willing executioners'."[47]

The exemplary rank and file perpetrators in this essay do not show any specifics in their willingness to execute criminal orders and to participate in atrocious crimes that suggest the assumption that Austrian common Nazi war criminals distinguished themselves from ordinary Germans or collaborationists in Nazi occupied countries. Yet the unwillingness of a whole society—from the political elite to ordinary men/women who served in the juries of war crimes trials—to punish those who had committed these crimes, singled out Austria as a special case among democratic societies. It was only after the Waldheim affair of 1986-88 that Austrians began to review thoroughly their self perception and to reassess their role during World War II.[48] But this development did not concern Austrian judiciary. Until recently, Austria remained a "safe haven for Nazi criminals," as Efraim Zuroff criticized in an interview with *The Times*.[49]

46. Browning's synopsis in: Ibid., 222-23.
47. Ibid., 223.
48. Richard Mitten, *The Politics of Antisemitic Prejudice: The Waldheim Phenomenon in Austria* (Boulder: Westview Press, 1992).
49. First published by timesonline.co.uk on 16 Jun. 2008. Still accessible on the web site of the Simon Wiesenthal Center, Jerusalem <http://www.operationlastchance.org/AUSTRIA_110.67.htm> (10 Jan. 2012).

Lives behind Barbed Wire:

A Comparative View of Austrian Prisoners of War during and after World War II in Soviet and American Captivity

Günter Bischof and Barbara Stelzl-Marx[1]

Introduction

"Siberia" and the *Rheinwiesenlager* have become metaphors for the suffering of German and Austrian prisoners of war (POWs) in the World War II era. On the one hand the endless columns of exhausted, bent over, freezing figures, tracking through snow covered fields and plains, and close to collapse from hunger, thirst, and sickness, not infrequently death. On the other hand, tens of thousands of emaciated and listless men crowded into temporary enclosures—cages, under open skies, slogging around muddy fields close to the Rhine River, without shelter, toilets, food, or drink, and harassed by the guards.[2]

Of the roughly 18 million Germans who fought in Hitler's armed forces in the course of World War II some 11 million ended up in Allied captivity, about a third in Soviet hands.[3] Almost 1.3 million Austrians fought in Hitler's armies, 495,000 of them became prisoners of war at the end of the conflict. 335,500 Austrians ended up in the hands of the Western Allies (almost 140,000 in American hands) and 159,500 in Eastern Europe

1. We would like to thank Harald Knoll and Dieter Bacher for their help in preparing this essay, Rüdiger Overmans and Erwin Schmidl for some sound advice, and Eva Maltschnig for a thorough reading of the essay and saving us from some mistakes.

2. For the most solid and sober scholarly comparative account of treatment of German POWs on all fronts, see Rüdiger Overmans, "Das Schicksal der deutschen Kriegsgefangenen im Zweiten Weltkrieg," in *Der Zusammenbruch des deutschen Reiches 1945*, ed. Militärgeschichtliches Forschungsamt and Rolf-Dieter Müller, vol. 10/2: *Die Folgen des Zweiten Weltkrieges* (Das Deutsche Reich und der Zweite Weltkrieg) (Munich: dva, 2008), 379-508; see also Günter Bischof, Stefan Karner, Barbara Stelzl Marx, with the help of Edith Petschnigg, eds., *Kriegsgefangenschaft im Zweiten Weltkrieg: Gefangennahme – Lagerleben – Rückkehr* (Vienna: R. Oldenbourg, 2005); for popular German comparative account of POW treatment in East and West, based on personal stories and dwelling on the prisoners' egregious suffering and victimization, see Paul Carell and Günter Bödekker, *Die Gefangenen: Leben und Überleben deutscher Soldaten hinter Stacheldraht* (Berlin: Ullstein, 1980), now substantially updated by Rüdiger Overmans, *Soldaten hinter Stacheldraht. Deutsche Kriegsgefangene des Zweiten Weltkriegs* (Berlin: Propylaen, 2000).

3. The death rate among the POWs in Soviet captivity was high, about a third died, see Rüdiger Overmans, "'In der Hand des Feindes': Geschichtsschreibung zur Kriegsgefangenschaft von der Antike bis zum Zweiten Weltkrieg," in *In der Hand des Feindes: Kriegsgefangenschaft von der Antike bis zum Zweiten Weltkrieg*, ed. idem (Cologne: Böhlau, 1999), 1-40 (here 14).

captivity—135,000 in Soviet hands.[4] Some remained behind barbed wire after being captured for a few weeks, many for a few years, a few for ten years and more. The last Austrian POWs returned from Soviet camps in 1956 (some stragglers even returned later).[5] POWs share the searing memories of being captured, their transport into the camps, everyday life behind barbed wire with all of its psychological trauma, months and years of uncertainty, depression, hunger, deprivation, exhaustion and sickness; their waiting was interminable and for those who spent years in POW camps their return home to see their families again often meant coming back to a *Heimat* that had become distant if not foreign.[6] Approximately 16,000 Austrians died in the Soviet Union—there was no return home. 70,000 Austrians perished in Soviet camps before registration and are counted as missing. Austrians also died in American captivity in the infamous cages along the Rhine River (*Rheinwiesenlager*) and perished in French holding camps but in much smaller numbers.[7] Compared to Soviet captivity life in American POW camps in Europe was similar, in the camps of the United States quite tolerable.

Soldiering and captivity in World War II is a mass phenomenon and many soldiers spent more time behind barbed wire than at the frontlines of the war. Life in prison cages left as deep an impression on returning veterans as their fighting in the field even though historians have paid much less attention to their time of imprisonment than their spectacular military campaigns. Yet the prisoner-of-war experience left deep marks on the lives of the World War II soldiers even though these experiences were often silenced in the biography of soldiers since they came at the time when they had to cope with defeat and loss of the ideals they might have believed in. World War II veterans shared the common feeling to have sacrificed "the

4. These numbers are from contemporary statistics of the Austrian Interior Ministry, see Bundesministerium des Inneren, ed., *Das Buch des österreichischen Heimkehrers* (Vienna, 1949), and Tamara-Paula Ipavec, *Heimkehrerstatistik* (Graz, 1997), cited in Harald Knoll and Stefan Karner, "Österreichische Kriegsgefangene in westlichem Gewahrsam und ihre Repatriierung" (unpublished paper).

5. Stefan Karner, *Im Archipel GUPVI: Kriegsgefangenschaft und Internierung in der Sowjetunion 1941-1956* (Vienna: R. Oldenbourg, 1995), 201.

6. The trauma of defeat and the return home is covered by Frank Biess, *Homecomings: Returning POWs and the Legacies of Defeat in Postwar Germany* (Princeton: Princeton University Press 2006).

7. Rüdiger Overmans, "'Ein untergeordneter Eintrag im Leidensbuch der jüngeren Geschichte?': Die Rheinwiesenlager 1945," in *Kriegsgefangenschaft im Zweiten Weltkrieg: Eine vergleichende Perspektive*, eds. Günter Bischof and Rüdiger Overmans (Ternitz-Potschach: Verlag Gerhard Höller, 1999), 233-65.

best years of their lives" to war and captivity.[8] Some kept diaries during war and captivity, or recorded their wartime and POW experiences soon after their return home; some finally put their memories on paper when they retired after long and active lives. Often these private memories stayed put in family archives, few are published. When Russian archives of the Soviet era opened after the end of the Cold War, some made an effort to see their personal files, collected half a century earlier by the People's Commissariat for Interior Affairs (NKVD). All these personal files meticulously kept by the Soviet jail keepers were stamped "Top Secret" and "To Be Saved for Eternity."[9]

The German historian Lutz Niethammer has called the generation of young soldiers in the war and their children the "generation experiencing the consequences of the war" (*Kriegsfolgengeneration*).[10] Those soldiers, however, who experienced captivity probably represent a separate group and can hardly be included in the "collective identity" of this generation. There surely are commonalities of experience that may define an entire generation yet historians also have to recognize the singularity and uniqueness of individual biographies. Biography remains a step child of the historical profession in German speaking lands while it garners great popular attention in the reading public in the Anglo-American world. Even though there has been a recent "biographical boom"[11] in German and Austrian historiography too, scholarly biography remains largely ignored among historians at the universities since it does not offer a clear career path towards employment.[12]

In 1938 the German Wehrmacht invaded Austria and incorporated it in the Third Reich. With Anschluss of the *Ostmark* (later named Danube and Alpine *Gaue*) on March 14, Austrians became "Germans" from one second to the next. The Nazis incorporated the Austrian Army into the

8. See the introduction by Bischof, Karner, Stelzl-Marx, in *Kriegsgefangenschaft im Zweiten Weltkrieg*, 9-19; Rüdiger Overmans, "Das Schicksal der deutschen Kriegsgefangenen," 434.

9. See the extensive data bases of unpublished and published ego documents and the collection of copies of Soviet archival POW records in the Boltzmann Institute for the Study of the Consequences of War in Graz, Austria.

10. Lutz Niethammer, "Sind Generationen identisch?," in *Generationalität und Lebensgeschichte im 20. Jahrhundert*, Jürgen Reulecke with the help of Elisabeth Müller-Luckner, eds. (Munich: R.Oldenbourg, 2003), 1-16 (here 3).

11. Lucile Dreidemy, Katherina Prager, Elisabeth Röhrlich, Editorial, in *Zeitgeschichte* 37 (May/June 2010): 152.

12. See the introduction by Christian Klein, "Biographik zwischen Theorie und Praxis: Versuch einer Bestandsaufnahme," in *Grundlagen der Biographik: Theorie und Praxis des biographischen Schreibens*, ed. idem (Stuttgart: Verlag J.B. Melzer, 2002), 1-22 (here 12).

Wehrmacht.[13] As Nazi Germany unleashed World War II, young males from what used to be Austria were drafted in the German armed forces; eventually 1,286,000 Austrians served in Hitler's armed formations (1,075,000, the bulk of them in the Wehrmacht).[14] Like their German "comrades," these *Ostmärker* became prisoners of war of the Allies as German armies (with their soldiers from the *Ostmark*) clashed with the Soviet Red Army, and starting in November of 1942 with American and British armies in North Africa.

The first sizable group of Germans apprehended by the British and the Americans were submarine crews who fought a fierce war against Anglo-American commercial shipping and military convoys in the vast Atlantic. As the war drew on and Allied armies drew closer to the territory of the Third Reich, a growing number of German soldiers were captured by Allied armies in North Africa and Italy sometimes 20,000 per month. With the surrender of Hitler's Africa Corps in May 1943 in Tunisia, some 135,000 German soldiers flooded American, British and French POW camps in North Africa. Most of these were eventually shipped to POW camps in the United States and Canada. As Anglo-American armies invaded Sicily and Italy in the summer and fall of 1943, the Americans captured another 60,000 German soldiers. With the Normandy invasion of June 1944 and the liberation of France another 180,000 German soldiers flooded into American POW camps—initially open-field cages in France many, later shipped to American camps (and British camps in Canada and England).[15]

With the invasion of Germany and the collapse of Hitler's armies some 7 million German soldiers surrendered to the Anglo-American armies in the West. The Americans were unprepared for taking on responsibility for roughly three-and-a-half million German POWs. They squeezed a million of them into makeshift open cages in France and along the Rhine River; maybe 10,000 POWs perished in the infamous *Rheinwiesenlager*, a death rate of 1 percent among the captives.[16] By the end of the war some 380,000

13. Hermann Hagspiel, *Die Ostmark: Österreich im Großdeutschen Reich* (Vienna: Braumüller, 1995); Emmerich Tálos, Ernst Hanisch, Wolfgang Neugebauer, and Reinhard Sieder, eds., *NS-Herrschaft in Österreich: Ein Handbuch* (Vienna: Verlag für Gesellschaftskritik, 2000).

14. Based on exhaustive statistical research in the surviving personal files of the German armed forces of World War II, Rüdiger Overmans has established this figure, see the Research Note "German and Austrian Losses in World War II," in *Austrian Historical Memory and National Identity*, Günter Bischof and Anton Pelinka, eds., (Contemporary Austrian Studies, vol. 5) (New Brunswick, NJ: Transaction, 1997), 293-301.

15. For these number see Overmans, "Das Schicksal der deutschen Kriegsgefangenen," 392.

16. For a careful and sober analysis of the American treatment of German POWs in the

German POWs had been shipped to United States and were housed in some 500 camps across the country from 1943 to March 1945.[17]

The following careers of four Austrian prisoners of war (two in American and two in Soviet captivity) during and after World War II are part of the "ordinary persons" whose lives Michel Foucault intended to collect in a vast archive of humanity; he never progressed beyond the introduction.[18] Representative of the more than 30,000 Austrians shipped to POW camps in the U.S. are the Wehrmacht lieutenant Herman S. captured in North Africa in May 1943 after the collapse of Hitler's *Afrika Corps*, and the private Josef B. captured near Kaiserslautern in the battle over the Colmar bridgehead in March 1945. Representative of the 135,000 Austrians in Soviet captivity are Karl B., captured at the battle of Stalingrad in late January 1943, and Ernst H., captured in the battle over Danzig in March 1945. Based on a variety of archival sources and personal ego-documents, we will follow these parallel lives chronologically from war to capture to repatriation. The range of sources utilized to write such lives indicates

---

Rhine Meadow Camps, see ibid., 415-25. The Canadian amateur historian James Bacque published a controversial book, claiming that as many as a million German POWs died in American captivity in Europe in the weeks after the end of the war. This came as a result of a willful American (and French) policy of not taking care of the German POWs and then covering the high mortality rate up; in other words, their death was planned – the Americans allowed a quasi-mini-holocaust to happen, see *Other Losses: An investigation into the mass deaths of German prisoners of war at the hands of the French and Americans after World War II* (Toronto: Stoddart, 1989). An international group of World War II historians has rejected Bacque's charges. They maintain that the Americans were overwhelmed by the millions of German POWs at the end of the war and logistically unprepared to take care of them; moreover, Bacque's mortality rate, based on faulty reading of documents, was vastly inflated, see Günter Bischof and Stephen E. Ambrose, eds., *Eisenhower and the German POWs* (Baton Rouge, LA: Louisiana State University Press, 1992).

17. For the treatment of German (of course, including the Austrians) POWs in the United States, see Hermann Jung, *Die deutschen Kriegsgefangenen in amerikanischer Hand: USA* (Zur Geschichte der deutschen Kriegsgefangenen des Zweiten Weltkrieges, vol. 10/1) (Bielefeld: Gieseking, 1972); Arnold Krammer, *Nazi Prisoners of War in America* (New York: Stein and Day, 1979; Scarborough House Pb 1991); the chapter on World War II in Paul J. Springer, *America's Captives: Treatment of POWs from the Revolutionary War to the War on Terror* (Lawrence: University Press of Kansas, 2010), 142-62; for the fine regional studies see Robert D. Billinger, Jr., *Hitler's Soldiers in the Sunshine State* (Gainesvile: University Press of Florida, 2000); idem, *Nazi POWs in the Tar Heel State* (Gainesville: University Press of Florida, 2008); Overmans, "Schicksal der deutschen Kriegsgefangenen," in *Der Zusammenbruch des deutschen Reiches 1945*, vol. 10/2, 413-15, 430-35; for an overview of American treatment of German POWs with a focus on Austrians, see Günter Bischof, "Einige Thesen zu einer Mentalitätgeschichte deutscher Kriegsgefangenschaft in amerikanischer Gewahrsam," in *Kriegsgefangenschaft im Zweiten Weltkrieg*, eds. Bischof/Overmans, 175-212, and Robert D. Billinger, Jr., "'Austrian' POWs in America, 1942-1945," in *Zeitgeschichte* 29, no. 3 (May/June 2002): 123-32.

18. See Bernhard Fetz's introductory essay in this volume.

how difficult it is to reconstruct biographies of ordinary people who never imagined they would become historical actors of interest to historians and therefore do not tend to maintain a historical record about their existence.[19]

To the Front: Warriors

The Stalingrad POW Karl B. was born in Wels, Upper Austria on December 4, 1914, as the third of four children.[20] He passed five years of elementary and 3 years of secondary school. Since his father was on a disabled veterans pension, Karl B. entered an apprenticeship in tool-making but could not find a permanent job during the Great Depression. Like many in his age cohort he volunteered for the Austrian Army. This provided him with a minimum of financial security and daily meals.[21] A publication of the veterans' organization later noticed that for every ten applicants who wanted to join the Austrian Army, one was taken.[22]

After the Anschluss, the German Wehrmacht absorbed the entire Austrian Army and in 1941 Karl B. was promoted.[23] He was fighting in the German Wehrmacht on the Eastern front in the Charkov area.[24] In his unpublished memoirs Karl B. wrote: "After finishing the Charkov offensive

19. For a model approach of reconstructing the compelling stories of three *parallel lives* of ordinary African-Americans who were part of the great exodus of more than a million black people from the South to Northern cities, based on extensive oral histories, see Isabel Wilkerson, *The Warmth of Other Suns: The Epic Story of America's Great Migration* (New York: Vintage, 2011); the parallel lives of nine Hurricane Katrina survivors is recounted in a similar narrative style by Dan Baum in *Nine Lives: Mystery, Magic, Death, and Life in New Orleans* (New York: Spiegel & Grau, 2010). The classic biography of parallel lives is Allan Bullock, *Hitler and Stalin: Parallel Lives* (New York: Vintage, 1993).

20. Karl. B.'s story is based on his personal file from the Moscow Archives as well as letters and photos from the family archives. On top of it his grandson wrote a thesis about his imprisonment with the advice of BIK scholars, see Clemens Matthias Beham, "Der Russlandfeldzug des Zweiten Weltkrieges unter besonderer Berücksichtigung der 'Schlacht um Stalingrad' sowie die sowjetische Kriegsgefangenschaft meines Großvaters," MA Thesis, Graz 2012. Here is a case study of a member of the "third" postwar generation researching the family's wartime history, see Gerhard Botz, "Einleitung: Jenseits der Täter-Opfer-Dichotomie lebensgeschichtlich erforschen und essayistisch beschreiben," in *Schweigen und Reden einer Generation: Erinnerungsgeschichte mit Opfern, Tätern, und Mitläufern des Nationalsozialismus,* ed. idem (Vienna: Mandelbaum Verlag, 2005), 9, 15.

21. Beham, "Russlandfeldzug," 5.

22. Österreichischer Kameradschaftsbund, ed., *Kamerad in Feldgrau: Denkmal der Treue; Mahnung für alle* (Wels: Verlag Rudolf Traunau, n.D. [1955]), 162.

23. Beham, "Russlandfeldzug," 5-7.

24. The massive Eastern front is where the bulk of *Ostmärkers* fought and died and fell into captivity during World War II, see Germann, "Austrian Soldiers," 34-38; see also Bertrand Michael Baumann, *Österreicher in der Deutschen Wehrmacht: Soldatenalltag im Zweiten Weltkrieg* (Vienna: Böhlau, 2009).

in May 1942, we continued with the offensive deep into the East. The 6th Army and units of the 4th Panzer Army had been pushing towards the River Don and crossed it near Kalach in the direction of Stalingrad. On August 16, 1942, the first tank units reached the Volga River north of Stalingrad."[25]

At the end of September Karl B. and his 100th Infantry Division were transferred from the Don River to the Stalingrad front.[26] He thus entered one of the most decisive and destructive battles of World War II where the Red Army totally cut off much of General Paulus' 6th Army, parts of the 4th Army, civilian support troops, as well as Romanian and Croatian support units (some 200,000 men).[27] In December 1942 Karl B. was promoted to company leader.[28] Along with the bulk of what was left of the 6th Army, he surrendered on January 31, 1943. Only 2 days earlier Hitler had commanded General Paulus to commit suicide rather than become a prisoner of war, after promoting him to Field Marshall. The final act of the "organized mass death" was on the way.[29] By February 2, 1943, some 91,000 Wehrmacht soldiers and their allies had surrendered; a mere 6,000 of them survived their imprisonment, Karl B. one of them.[30]

Herman S. was born in Vienna in 1916 into a noble family with roots in Carniola who had served the emperor as officials and officers.[31]

25. Karl B., "Erinnerungen an Stalingrad," unpublished manuscript, Wels 1954 [no page numbers].

26. On July 6, 1942, the 100th Infantry Division was renamed the 100th *Jäger* Division, see Georg Tessin, *Verbände und Truppen der deutschen Wehrmacht und Waffen-SS im Zweiten Weltkrieg 1939-1945*, vol. 6: *Die Landstreitkräfte* (Osnabrück: Biblio Verlag, 1972), 161-63; Hans Neidhardt, *Mit Tanne und Eichenlaub: Kriegschronik der 100. Jäger-Division vormals 100. leichte Infanteriedivision* (Graz: Leopold Stocker Verlag, 1981).

27. On Stalingrad as a turning point in World War II, see Guido Knopp, *Stalingrad: Das Drama* (Munich: Wilhelm Goldmann Verlag, 2006); Wolfram Wette and Gerd R. Ueberschär, eds., *Stalingrad: Mythos und Wirklichkeit einer Schlacht* (Frankfurt am Main: Fischer Verlag, 1992); Horst Boog, Werner Rahn, Reinhard Stumpf, and Bernd Wegner, *Der globale Krieg. Die Ausweitung zum Weltkrieg und der Wechsel der Initiative 1941–1943* (Das Deutsche Reich und der Zweite Weltkrieg, vol. 6) (Stuttgart: dva, 1990); David M. Glantz and Jonathan M. House, *Armageddon in Stalingrad: September-November 1942. The Stalingrad Trilogy*, vol. 2 (Lawrence: University Press of Kansas, 2009); Anthony Beevor, *Stalingrad* (New York: Viking Press 1999).

28. Beham, "Russlandfeldzug," 19.

29. Boog et al., *Der globale Krieg*, 1057.

30. Paul Carell, *Stalingrad: Sieg und Untergang der 6. Armee* (Berlin: Ullstein, 1992) 210.

31. The information on Herman S. is based on a correspondence Günter Bischof carried on with him in the early 1990s; the information on the 1004 days he spent in Allied captivity (1943-1946) is recovered from a very detailed diary he wrote on pieces of paper in old German script while in captivity, copies of parts of which he shared with Bischof. He kept diary notes, which he managed to salvage and bring back home in spite of regular frisking and inspections while transferred from camp to camp. After his return home in February 1946, he typed up these notes and loose jottings, along with the letters he had sent to his

He graduated from high school in 1935 and joined the Austrian Army in a regiment of dragoons. From 1936 to 1938 he went through the elite Military Academy in Wiener Neustadt. He was an "excited young officer" who had also joined the *Ostmärkische Sturmscharen*, the quasi party army of the authoritarian Dollfuß-Schuschnigg regime. Like Karl B., Lieutenant Herman S. ended up in the German Wehrmacht with the transfer of the entire Austrian military into the armed forces of the Third Reich.[32] His first assignment was to the Cavalry Regiment No. 4 in East Prussia. He later stressed that he and the officer corps in that garrison were not beholden to the Nazis.[33] He was tossed with the Nazi juggernaut into the Eastern front theater, too, where in 1941 he was badly wounded. After his recovery he was transferred to North Africa to Rommel's Africa Corps and promoted to captain, where he served in high staff functions—a rare *Ostmärker* in such a position. In May 1943 the entire Africa Corps (135,000 men) and its leader General v. Arnim surrendered to the Allies. Herman S. and the staff officers of the Africa Corps chose to surrender to the British so as not to be captured by the French Gaullist forces in the area of Sidi Marie du Zid in Tunisia. The British transferred him to the Americans before the end of 1943 and he was promptly shipped to the United States.

Ernst H. was born in Vienna in 1908. After nine years of elementary and secondary school he visited a commercial school and became a clerk. From December 1937 until January 1940 he was a member of the NSDAP (National Socialist German Workers' Party) that he withdrew from when he was drawn into the German Wehrmacht on January 3, 1940. He fell into Soviet captivity during the headlong retreat of Hitler's Wehrmacht on

mother that had arrived in Vienna, into a 134-page manuscript, see personal letter Herman S. to Bischof, 15 Apr. 1991, and diary entry January 4, 1944. The diary thus represents a contemporary document with a high degree of authenticity. The detailed diary entries are at times pages long. He was a sharp observer of the world around him and also recorded the intense emotional world of a prolonged and seemingly interminable existence behind barbed wire in considerable detail. Of the letters he had received from home and collected (107 from his mother), he was allowed to take back home only 10 when he left Camp Crossville, see diary entry, October 11, 1945.

32. About the smooth integration of the Austrian Army into the German Wehrmacht, see Richard Germann, "Austrian Soldiers in World War II," in *New Perspectives on Austrians in World War II*, eds. Günter Bischof, Fritz Plasser, and Barbara Stelzl-Marx (Contemporary Austrian Studies, vol. 17) (New Brunswick, NJ: Transaction, 2009), 29-44 (here 29-31); this article is based on idem, "Österreichische Soldaten in Ost- und Südosteuropa 1941-1945: Deutsche Krieger – Nationalsozialistische Verbrecher – Österreichische Opfer?," PhD diss., University of Vienna 2006.

33. Personal letter Herman S. to Bischof, August 5, 1991.

March 19, 1945, in the Danzig area. On April 13 1945, the day the Red Army liberated Vienna, Ernst H. was interrogated and officially registered as a POW. He was retained in Soviet camps as an alleged "war criminal" until 1953.[34]

Josef B. was born on September 8, 1921, in Mellau, a small village (population 1,000) nestled among steep mountains in Vorarlberg not far from the German and Swiss borders.[35] His father returned from the Eastern front after World War with a bullet lodged in his lung, the slow corrosion of which ended his life in the mid-1930s. He grew up on a farm and was the oldest of four orphaned children. He started working after he finished eight years of elementary school in the middle of the Great Depression. It was not possible to get a regular job for a young man in rural Austria. Like many rural Austrians he supported the Dollfuß/Schuschnigg regimes and was one of the many Austrians who welcomed the Anschluss of Austria by Nazi Germany because he got a job right away in public works projects that Hitler launched all over the *Ostmark*.

His basic training was in the Tyrol region in mountain units from the Alpine region. He was trained to operate artillery—light Skoda 7.5 cm guns. In Hitler's Army people from the same region were intentionally drafted into the same units (in this case mountain troops) to strengthen unit cohesion. Josef B.'s portrait taken during basic training as a private in the German Wehrmacht shows a young man that seems to be proud of wearing his uniform. He was never a member of the Nazi Party but liked being a soldier and seems to have been impressed with the success of the German armed forces on the battlefields of Europe at this stage of the war. A tinge of self-confidence is displayed in his face. One is struck by how young and innocent he looks, like soldiers always are when they embark on their nation's wars as cannon-fodder for the tomfooleries of their leaders.

---

34. Ernst H. has left traces in the Soviet archives in a personal file as well as a file of his criminal trial due to his conviction as a "war criminal" in 1949, see personal file Ernst H.; d. 1869492, F. 460/p, RGVA (Russian State Military Archives); criminal trial file Ernst H, d. 712, op. 1,. F. 1363, NARB (National Archives of Belorussian Republic).

35. Josef B.'s wartime experience is based on informal interviews conducted by his son Gűnter Bischof. These talks were never recorded, which obviously presents pitfalls for the historian. Josef B. also sketched out his World War II experience in a short written statement that provided a basic chronology, which is in the possession of Gűnter Bischof. Between my knowledge as a historian of World War II and Josef B.'s narrations, these conversations with snippets of information accumulated over the years into a coherent narrative. At one point in the mid-1990s, I took my colleague and mentor Stephen Ambrose to meet Josef B. at his home in Mellau; I translated a long conversation between the two of them, which also left a trace in Ambrose's book *Citizen Soldiers* (1996).

Josef B. when he was drafted into the German Wehrmacht 1941, private collection

At the end of 1941, Josef B. and his comrades were transferred into battle on the most northern tip of the Eastern front, to the Arctic Circle. The Alpine boys in the mountain units were assumed to be able to take the frigid weather.[36] It was a long journey to the front, from Kufstein by

36. Austrian mountain divisions had their baptism under fire in the Narvik campaign in the

train to Aalborg in Nazi occupied Denmark. Crossing over the Skagerak to Göteborg in neutral Sweden (!), a train took them through Sweden to Kiruna and on to Narvik in Norway. By ship the soldiers were transported to Hammerfest and via the Northern Cape to Kirkenes. They walked from Kirkenes to Petsamo in Northern Finland, where they were inducted into their new unit, the Mountain Artillery Regiment 111, First Battery. Petsamo was important for the Nazi war economy as a result of its nickel mines, a raw material the Germans needed for armor plate. They walked to the front on marches for days on end.

On his twentieth birthday on September 8, 1941, his unit attacked in the direction of the Northern port of Murmansk and experienced considerable casualties. Their attack was slowed down by the roadless high tundra and they were stopped before reaching Murmansk. Another soldier from his home village of Mellau died in these attacks. They dug in in October 1941 and froze badly in frigid minus temperatures and without proper winter clothing like the rest of Hitler's Wehrmacht stopped in their advances. He spent much of the winter of 1941/42 in Strand, Norway, as a ski instructor. In February 1942 they were stationed onto the very remote Fischer Peninsula (on Russian territory), fighting on a stabilized front and lobbying artillery shells towards Murmansk. He was stationed on the Fischer Peninsula for the next two years. One reads in books such as Omer Bartov's *Hitler's Army* that the German Army on the Eastern Front became increasingly horse-drawn[37]; which was also the case in the campaign in Finland.

Finland changed sides in October 1944, as the Eastern front was collapsing in its northern extremity too. During the course of 1944, the Russians threw the German Wehrmacht out of its positions. Josef B. was lucky for the first time that he was not captured by the Red Army to enter what would have been an interminable and marginal existence in Soviet POW camps. His battery began a three-month long retreat to Morjana, Norway, marching through snow storms and roads covered with deep snow for about 1,000 km. Morjana was the endpoint of the Norwegian railroad line. Totally exhausted, his group of retreating Wehrmacht soldiers ended up in a train taking them to Moss in Southern Norway. By ship they

---

spring of 1940 in Norway and established a reputation as tough and committed Wehrmacht forces, demolishing the image of being lackadaisical soldiers (*Kamerad Schnürschuh*). "Alpine soldiering" became celebrated in the Wehrmacht, see Thomas R. Grischany, "Mental Aspects of Austrian Wehrmacht Service," in: *New Perspectives*, eds. Bischof/Plasser/Stelzl-Marx, 45-65 (here 40); this essay is based on idem "The Austrian in the German Wehrmacht, 1938-1945," PhD diss., University of Chicago, 2007.

37. Omer Bartov, *Hitler Army: Soldiers, Nazis, and War in the Third Reich* (New York: Oxford University Press, 1992).

crossed over to Aarhus in Denmark and finally got a few days rest. A train brought them to Freiburg in Southwestern Germany. In Freiburg, only some 200 km away from his home Mellau, he observed a city destroyed by Allied bombing and a war come home to the German civilian population. They crossed the Rhine river and marched towards the Colmar bridgehead, where they maneuvered against the First French Army. Without any air cover, they were pushed back over the Rhine after a week of fighting; he straggled north towards the Palatinate region. They marched during the nights and hid in forests during the days from constantly attacking Allied fighter planes. On March 19, 1945, he was captured by American forces close to Kaiserslautern not far from the French border. He was lucky not to end up in one of the Rhine Meadow camps that cropped up soon thereafter when the bulk of the German Wehrmacht fell into Anglo-American captivity in the West.

Behind Barbed Wire: Prisoners of War

The United States generally abided by the Geneva Convention with the 440,000 POWs (380,000 Germans and Austrians) that were shipped to camps in the U.S. In the case of the mass of German POWs captured towards the end of the war, the U.S. changed their status to "Defeated Enemy Personnel" (the British to "Surrendered Enemy Personnel") to circumvent the provisions of the Geneva Convention. Given that the Americans and British captured some seven million German POWs at the end of the war, they felt they no longer could strictly abide by the Geneva Convention. American logistics collapsed at the end of the war when it came to giving German POWs adequate shelter, food and medical care. The Americans had to feed some 20 million people in Europe at the end of the war and the German POWs were at the very end of the food chain. They gathered the German POWs in some 215 camps scattered over Germany and Austria. The worst treatment was meted out to the million German and Austrian POWs caged up in about a dozen camps along the Rhine River ("Rhine Meadow Camps").[38] Conditions in these camps and in their transit camps in France were at times as bad as in Soviet camps. While conditions in North African transit camps, where the Allies kept the prisoners behind barbed wire in temporary enclosures under open skies, once POWs were shipped to North American permanent camps conditions markedly improved. The Americans strictly abided by the Geneva Convention and sent all POWs home one year after the end of the war (the British and

38. Overmans, "Das Schicksal der deutschen Kriegsgefangenen," 415-25.

French repatriated their last German and Austrian POWs in 1948). The Americans and British did not separate Austrians from German POWs in their camps (the French did in some cases).

The Soviet Union had not signed the 1929 Geneva Convention and ignored its provisions for the protection of prisoners of war throughout the World War II era. Conditions in Soviet camps were dreadful during the war, especially for the first big pocket of Germans captured in Stalingrad. 90 percent of the Stalingrad POWs did not make it back. Soviet authorities during the war began a program of putting alleged German war criminals on trial and meting out numerous death sentences. Conditions for most German POWs remained bad after the war. The German POWs still retained in Soviet camps in 1949 were put on trial and convicted as alleged "war criminals" *en masse* to retain them as forced laborers. About 1,100 Austrians were convicted and sent to GULAG camps—in at least 20 cases the death sentence was meted out. In 70 percent of the cases they were convicted for "war crimes"; 18 percent for theft and sabotage; 11 percent for espionage against the Soviet Union.[39] In some cases as we shall see in this section, Austrian POWs were convicted for "mistreatment" of Soviet POWs and forced laborers on the territory of the Third Reich.[40] By 1955/1956, however, most of the German and Austrian POWs had been repatriated. During the war the Soviets started a vigorous program of "reeducation" of German POWs, selecting and indoctrinating what they considered reliable "anti-fascists" to return to Germany and Austria as cadres for the Communist parties there. The Soviets did not generally separate Austrian POWs from Germans as a matter of course except in *Antifa* camps.

Karl B., and the sorry remains of Hitler's 6th Army at Stalingrad, began their long and exhaustive killer marches between various front camps

39. Harald Knoll, "Späte Heimkehr: Als Kriegsverbrecher verurteilte österreichische Kriegsgefangene in der Sowjetunion 1944 bis 1953," in *Kriegsgefangenschaft des Zweiten Weltkrieges*, eds. Bischof/Karner/Stelzl-Marx, 167–83 (here 167–72); on the convictions of Austrian civilians by Soviet courts, see Stefan Karner and Barbara Stelzl-Marx et al, eds., *Stalins letzte Opfer: Verschleppte und erschossene Österreicher in Moskau 1950–1953* (Vienna: Oldenbourg – Böhlau, 2009); Harald Knoll and Barbara Stelzl-Marx, "Sowjetische Strafjustiz in Österreich: Verhaftungen und Verurteilungen 1945–1955," in *Die Rote Armee in Österreich: Sowjetische Besatzung 1945–1955; Beiträge,* eds. Stefan Karner and Barbara Stelzl-Marx (Graz: R. Oldenbourg Verlag, 2005), 275–322.

40. Barbara Stelzl-Marx, "Ein ganz normaler Kriegsverbrecher? Der Prozess gegen den ehemaligen Lagerkassier des Stalag XVII B Krems-Gneixendorf," in *Österreicher und Sudetendeutsche vor sowjetischen Militär- und Strafgerichten in Weißrussland 1945–1950*, eds. Stefan Karner and Vjačeslav Selemenev (Graz: Selbstverlag des Vereins zur Förderung der Forschung von Folgen nach Konflikten und Kriegen, 2007), 368–406.

in the Soviet camp system GUPVI.[41] Totally exhausted from nagging hunger pains and freezing Russian winter temperatures and weakened by three months of fighting in the Stalingrad battle, tens of thousands of the prisoners captured in Stalingrad did not survive the ordeal of these initial marches towards the base camp. After a three-week-long forced march through snow and ice deserts, Karl. B. arrived at the transit camp Nr. 50 in Frolovo.[42] Here he was first registered as a Soviet prisoner of war and went through his first physical examination. The doctors found him "healthy," which meant he was able to work. GUPVI started his personal file here, which would accompany him through all the stations of his imprisonment until repatriation in 1947.[43]

Columns of German POWs marching out of Stalingrad, 1943, © BDAK, Minsk

During the next few weeks he was transferred to various transit camps and hospitals. First to camp 366/9 in Berezinki in the area of Perm

41. GUPVI stands for "Main Administration for Prisoner and Internee Affairs," see Karner, *Archipel GUPVI*, 38.
42. On the Stalingrad camp system, see Andreas Hilger, *Deutsche Kriegsgefangene in der Sowjetunion 1941–1956: Kriegsgefangenenpolitik, Lageralltag und Erinnerung* (Essen: Klartext Verlag, 2000), 141–47.
43. Personal File Karl B., d. 884576, F. 460, RGVA, p. 34.

before the Ural mountains (1,150 km from Moscow). Between May 10 and June 20, 1943, he was in transit in cattle cars to the South to Camp 341/4 in the Sevastopol area, the Crimean Peninsula's largest city. Here he was infected with typhus and, which got him a transfer to the Zaporozhe area in the Ukraine.[44] Now his condition was so desperate that hc saw no prospect for survival. Another prisoner described the symptoms: "I was in an overcrowded hospital room, temperature 41 Celsius. I was covered with light-red, lentil-size spots all over my body. It was dreadful and the sudden fear of death struck me."[45] Family lore has it that a female Jewish doctor saved the life of Karl B.[46]

GUPVI next transferred Karl B. to a special hospital (Camp No. 2074) near Kirov on the Transsiberian Railway, 900 km east of Moscow. In Mid-August 1945 another transfer brought him to Camp No. 307/4 also in the Kirov area. During the next two years and before his return home he was transferred several times to various subcamps of Camp No. 307 and required another stay at a hospital (No. 1149).[47]

On August 15, 1945, two-and-a-half years after his capture he was finally allowed to send a card home to his wife from Camp No. 307/13. The return address was "Moscow, P.O. Box 307/13," eg. his camp number. Up until this time his family did not know whether he had survived the siege of Stalingrad. He wrote:

> My Dearest Hilda!
>
> This will be the first signal you will receive since Stalingrad that I am still alive. On January 31, 1943, I managed to save my skin by entering captivity. I am fine at this point in time, I am healthy and in good spirits. I hope that as much can be said of you, little Karl [his son born in his absence in 1941], our parents and brothers and sisters. Hitler has unleashed this terrible war, which has brought such incredible suffering to humanity. Once it is over the time will soon arrive for my return home. Until then we have to hold our heads high and be patient. My best wishes to you, little Karl, our parents and brothers and sisters from your Karl who soon will come home.
>
> Kisses, your Karl.[48]

44. Ibid., 6.
45. Quoted in Rüdiger Overmans with Ulrike Goeken-Haidl, *Soldaten hinter Stacheldraht: Deutsche Kriegsgefangene des Zweiten Weltkriegs* (Berlin: Propyläen Verlag, 2000), 136.
46. Beham, "Russlandfeldzug," 34.
47. Personal File Karl B., pp. 1-6, d. 884576, F. 460, RGVA.
48. Cited in Beham, "Russlandfeldzug," 41.

Karl B.'s personal NKVD file and the diction of the letter cited above tell us that he joined the "antifascist movement" (*Antifa*) in 1944.[49] The Soviet reeducation program aimed at turning the hostile POWs into reliable "antifascists" and "friends of the Soviet Union." The Antifa activists among the POW population organized all the education, cultural and sports programs in the camps with the help of the Soviet authorities. Since membership in the Antifa cohort gave advantages to these activists, they quickly garnered the bad reputation of being turncoats and opportunists.[50] The Antifa formed a cohort in the camp structure "on the social margins between German comrades and the Soviet holding power."[51]

In the course of his two years in Camp No. 307, Karl B. even managed to be promoted to "deputy chief of antifascist activities in the camp."[52] He had a reputation among his Soviet bosses of being "a reliable and dutiful antifascist" who was familiar with "the progressive ideas of Marxism" and commanded "authority among the POWs."[53] From July to November 1947, before his repatriation, he attended the Antifa-Academy installed for German POWs in the "Special Object No. 41 of the MVD of the Soviet Union" in Talitsy in the Ivanovo area. Graduates of this Academy were deemed to be the next generation of cadres of Communist parties in Western Europe and the guarantors of an antifascist postwar order.[54] On November 18, 1947, the leader of this special training academy Lt. Colonel Zamotaev characterized Karl B. as an "energetic young man showing initiative," "as a paragon of discipline," and "a quiet, somewhat soft, yet steady character" "who was a friend of the Soviet Union." In the beginning "he was a bit skeptical of Marxism-Leninism and the Communist Party of Austria (KPÖ), reported Zamoaev in his secret dossier, but now "he fully supports Marxism-Leninism and intends to contribute to the KPÖ." He concluded: "He gives the impression of a passionate antifascist."[55]

49. For similar letters indicating the antifascist mindset, see Wolfram Dornik, Michael Hess, and Harald Knoll, *Burgenländische Kriegsgefangene und Zivilverurteilte in der Sowjetunion 1941–1956* (Eisenstadt: Burgenländisches Landesarchiv, 2007), 83.

50. Jörg Morré, "Umerziehung in der sowjetischen Kriegsgefangenschaft: Deutsche und Österreicher in der 'Antifa'," in *Kriegsgefangenschaft des Zweiten Weltkrieges*, eds. Bischof/Karner/Stelzl-Marx, 152–66 (here 152).

51. Albrecht Lehmann, *Gefangenschaft und Heimkehr: Deutsche Kriegsgefangene in der Sowjetunion* (Munich: C. H. Beck, 1986), 50.

52. Personal file Karl B., p. 7, d. 884576, F. 460, RGVA.

53. Ibid.

54. Morré, "Umerziehung in der sowjetischen Kriegsgefangenschaft," 152; for a report on the Antifa Academy in Talizy ("the university in the swamp and jungle"), see Otto Engelberg, "Die Antifa-Schuyle Talizy: Schule des 'zwiedenkens'," in *Kriegsgefangenschaft,* eds. Wolfgang Benz and Angelika Schardt (Biographische Quellen zur deutschen Geschichte nach 1945, vol. 10) (Munich: R. Oldenbourg, 1991), 65-84 (citation 67).

55. Personal File Karl B., p. 9, d. 884576, F. 460, RGVA.

Zamotaev was mistaken. Upon his return Karl B. demonstrated no affinity with the KPÖ and even less enthusiasm vis-à-vis Marxism-Leninism. Like most of the Austrian "antifascists" he used his demonstrative enthusiasm in the Antifa as a survival strategy in the Soviet camp system. After all, the privileges of the members of the "antifascist committee" were significant—better food rations and shelter, no hard labor, chances to get out of the camp, and the prospect of early repatriation. In a situation where tens of thousands of POWs suffered and died from dystrophy—the worst kind of wasting away from starvation—a few extras slices of bread and some extra ladles of *kasha* (gruel) might make the difference between life and death.

The *Afrika Corps* Captain (*Rittmeister*) Herman S. became an Allied prisoner of war on May 12, 1943. After surrendering to the British he was transferred every few weeks to a series of transit and interrogation camps and hospitals from Tunisia to Algeria (Medjez-el-Bab, Bone, Bonfarik, Birkaden Fort l'Eau, Algier, and Alma) across the desert of North Africa and eventually transferred to the American camps in Morocco (St.Barb/Oran and Casablanca) for shipment to the USA. Officers like him were usually in camps separate from the common foot soldiers. The temporary enclosures in North Africa were under open skies. The days were uncomfortably hot and the nights characterized by freezing cold. British rations were scarce and "nagging hunger" pains regular; the food became more plentiful in later camps. Throughout his POW experience he found solace in his Catholic faith. Herman S. was suffering from a gunshot through his foot and from regular diarrhea; he also feared he was growing blind in one eye; on top of it he came down with jaundice and was treated in a hospital.[56] He played lots of bridge and chess and read whenever he could lay his hands on a book (novels, histories, English grammar) to pass the boring days. As long as he was together with German comrades he had the emotional comfort of familiar faces and a sort of unit cohesion; some of the enclosures he came through were Italian POW camps. Desperate for reliable news, the POWs passed on wild gutter rumors (*Latrinengerüchte*) about successful and failed escape attempts by POWs and the horrible and deadly conditions in Gaullist French camps. Sanitary conditions were awful in all camps and there were constant black market dealings for additional food rations. The more venturesome inmates were preparing for escapes from the camps and some did get out but where usually caught again and punished. His desperate desire for repatriation, throughout his North African journey was tempered by attending mass and holy communion, and sending letters to his mother.

56. Collective Diary entry July 26 – August 22, November 11, 1943, 29-30, 57

On July 4 he wrote to her: "This is the toughest fate that a German soldier has to suffer, but I bear it with faith in god..."[57] Herman S. specifically pointed out when British and American camp guards and personnel were Jewish refugees from Germany and Austria and repeatedly harassed the German POWs with particular contempt.[58] Attempts to persuade the British for prisoner exchanges with Nazi Germany failed, notes Herman S. who was hoping to go home in such an exchange.[59] One British officer raged: "I hate the German regime. As long as you are in North Africa you will not see a Red Cross Commission."[60] The Red Cross was supposed to inspect Allied POW camps to make sure POWs were treated according to the Geneva Convention.

On November 11, 1943, the British ("Tommies") handed Herman S. over to the Americans in Oran. Only 5 days earlier he had written a letter to his mom, expressing his hope he may be sent home on a prisoner exchange after 6 months in captivity: "[I'm] wandering from camp to camp, unfortunately mostly Italian camps [...] The food is very good here. It is in the morning and a big rainbow is in the sky. The nice time of the year is almost over—heavy rain is drumming against the sides of the tent [...] Hope to be in my final camp by Christmas [...] Hope to be introduced to a prisoner exchange commission as a result of my foot and my almost blind left eye..."[61] Instead, he ended up in American temporary enclosures in North Africa. At least the Americans gave their POWs in North Africa plenty of food (especially C-rations). Transferred in cattle cars to Casablanca, he noted again that a Sergeant, who happened to be a Jew from his native Vienna, constantly harassed the POWs. In a letter to his mom he

57. Letter to his mother, July 4, 1943 (arrived in Vienna on August 28, 1943), Diary, 21.

58. Mean Jewish camp cards seem to be a topos in the observation and memory of German POWs. There is also the topos of particularly helpful Jewish doctors in the camps. The fact is that there were few Jewish POW camps guards. Jewish exiles in the United States who joined the Army were usually trained to be utilized for POW interrogations like the well-known "Ritchie Boys" at Camp Ritchie (Hermann Freudenberger, a historian who taught for many years at Tulane University, is an example). The British used German Jewish exiles in labor units and special commandoes. We are grateful to Rűdiger Overmans for pointing out this information.

59. Hitler personally did not approve any such prisoner exchanges until later in the war, see Neville Wylie, *Barbed Wire Diplomacy: Britain, Germany, and the Politics of Prisoners of War, 1939–1945* (Oxford: Oxford University Press, 2010).

60. Diary entries June/July 1943, 5-20; most of Herman S. observations are confirmed by the North African diary entries of Kurt Glaser, "Kriegsgefangener auf drei Kontinenten," in *Kriegsgefangenschaft*, eds. Benz/Schardt; 131-43; see also Bischof, "Thesen zu einer Mentalitätsgeschichte," 178-83.

61. The letter was sent on November 6, 1943, and arrived in Vienna on March 19, 1944, Diary entries, November 4, 1943, 54-56.

wrote that the rainy season was awful but that he soon should be shipped to the U.S.: at least was back with German comrades he knew—this "made captivity more tolerable [...] I must not despair, we do not despair. Looking out of the tent I see the first snow in the high Atlas mountains [censorship had blackened out "high Atlas mountains"].[62] And in another letter his mental anguish comes through: "One must not ponder these things. I am trying to stay on the surface level with my thoughts and goals—digging too deep would end in desperation."[63]

After a brief stay in a previously empty temporary enclosure in Casablanca, where he also spent a lonely and dull Christmas, he finally embarks on his trans-Atlantic passage on a convoy from the Western coast of North Africa on the *Empress of Japan*, a Canadian passenger ship converted to troop transporter on December 26, 1943. Most of the 6 days of the passage he suffered from sea sickness and tried to overcome the ennui on the passage by playing bridge. On January 2, 1944, the convoy arrived in the port of Newport News, Virginia.[64] The next day he went through the usual rituals of being frizzed, deloused and registered: "What happens next was typically American. In record time we are deloused. We are chased from one room to the next—undressing, unfortunately a cold bath, a negro is tossing a towel, disinfection of the feet, spraying the entire body with kuprex, doctor's exam, drying in a cinema-like waiting room, dress again! —The chase continues—finger prints, signatures... A German Jew asks me why I mingle with the Germans as an Austrian. My response: the Austrians are German soldiers too..."[65] Historian Thomas Grischany confirms what Herman S. is expressing here—by 1943 Austrian soldiers had become "virtually indistinguishable" in the Wehrmacht, "in terms of how they were regarded, and in terms of how they regarded others."[66] Before midnight the POWs boarded a train (with sections for "colored people" clearly marked) and began rolling into the night towards an unknown destination. A day later they arrived in Crossville, Tennessee (west of Knoxville). As officers they refused to sweep the train before their departure ("it would be dishonorable for officers to do this kind of work").[67]

Herman S. stayed at Camp Crossville for the next 23 months until his departure for Europe in mid-November 1945. The food was plentiful

62. Letter to his mother, November 19, 1943, 59-60.
63. Letter to his mother, December 10, 1943 (arrived in Vienna on February 22, 1944), 67.
64. "*Empress of Japan*" entries, December 26, 1943, to January 2, 1944, 73-74.
65. This section begins with the heading: "AMERIKA!," see diary entry, January 3, 1944, 75.
66. Grischany, "Mental Aspects," in *New Perspectives*, eds. Bischof/Plasser/Stelzl-Marx, 54.
67. Diary entries January 3-4,, 1944, 76-77.

—too fat really, which caused liver problems for him. He was happy to meet many old comrades from North Africa again. He did not have to work and received a "pay" of 30 dollars per month as a captain. There were five sections in the camp. The inmates of section one were "Nazi-fanatics" who demanded that nobody read American newspapers, which unleashed strong protests from "straight-thinking officers interested in world events" like him. He whiled away his time playing bridge and reading "excellent" magazines *Time* and *Life* to record the progress of all British and American divisions (he termed this his "political collection"). They celebrated birthdays and at time managed to get drunk and forget their cooped-up condition. The POWS put on a performance of *Julius Caesar* with their theater group in spite of protests from the Nazi-fanatics against staging a play from Shakespeare since "he was English." They organized a hunger strike when one of their leaders was transferred from Camp Crossville. This produced further divisions along party lines among inmates ("decent" vs. "indecent"=Nazis). The hothead Nazis had to be talked out of lynching turncoats who collaborated with the Americans and exchanged intelligence. The loss of dear comrades made the "behind-barbed-wire-psychosis" worse. The letters to his mom give expression of his desire for freedom and a return home ("one day our hour of liberation has to arrive"). His uncle Andrew Schöppel apparently was the governor of Kansas and on 19 January, 1944, he wrote a letter to him addressed "Dear uncle!"[68]

In November 1945 he was scheduled for the return home. He departed Camp Crossville and was on a ship to France by the end of November. They were fed little on the ship even though the Americans "typically" threw boxes of oranges overboard while "we are hungry and Europe is hungry." Again he tried to deal with his boredom by playing bridge. On December 1, 1945, he disembarked in Le Havre, France, and at last was back on the European continent.[69]

Ernst H. fell into Soviet captivity in the Danzig area in the collapsing Eastern front on March 19, 1945, and was shipped to camp No. 168 in Minsk in White Russia. During his registration at the beginning of May 1945 the government inspector put down in his file his previous job as the chief financial officer in Camp Krems-Gneixendorf (an hour up the Danube from Vienna) during the war.[70] Krems-Gneixendorf had been one

68. Diary entries 1944/1945, 78-111 (letter to Schöppel, 80; letter to his mother, November 11, 1945, 95). Andrew Frank Schoeppel, a Republican, was indeed the 29th governor of Kansas from 1943 to 1947.
69. Diary entries, November 27 to December 1, 1945, 111.
70. Personal File Ernst H., pp. 2-3, d. 1869492, F. 460/p, RGVA.

of the largest POW camp complexes in the Third Reich and at times was holding more than 10,000 Soviet POWs.[71] He was not charged with any crimes at this point in time but transferred to a series of POW camps in Vitebsk, Bobruisk and Minsk. Like the rest of the bulk of German POWs in Soviet captivity GUPVI put him to work to rebuild the Soviet postwar economy.[72] Finally, on December 16, 1949, more than four years into his captivity, Soviet authorities apprehended him in his camp at Minsk and incarcerated him.[73]

Ernst H. became an unfortunate POW in a big wave of 1949 mass convictions of "war crimes" among the remaining German POWs. In mid-1949 the Soviet authorities began a concerted search for alleged "war criminals" among German POWs. Their conviction postponed their repatriation (in some cases it meant imprisonment and hard work for another 20 years). Prior to 1949 individual cases of German and Austrian "war criminals" were tried and convicted for war crimes. Some entered the Soviet search for and persecution of German "war criminals" in individual trials, others in mass and show trials. A big show trial was staged already during the war in Kharkov in December 1943, another in Minsk at the end of January 1946. Following the precedent he had set in the 1930s against his alleged internal opposition, Stalin had such show trials staged in ten different venues starting in 1943. Some 100 German soldiers and officers (among them two Austrians) were put on trial and 70 death sentences were meted out and executed.[74]

It is not that German soldiers were not part and parcel of the German war of aggression in the Soviet Union, involved in numerous war crimes. But Soviet courts perverted their justice system in staged trials and with their 1949 mass convictions in staged show trials. In 1949 Soviet authorities, who had not signed and did not abide by the Geneva Convention, ran

71. Stalag XVII B Krems-Gneixendorf later became famous as a result of Billy Wilder's Hollywood classic movie "Stalag 17," Barbara Stelzl-Marx, *Zwischen Fiktion und Zeitzeugenschaft: Amerikanische und sowjetische Kriegsgefangene im Stalag XVII B Krems-Gneixendorf* (Tübingen: Gunter Narr Verlag, 2000).

72. Concerning the work details among POWs in Soviet captivity, see Karner, *Im Archipel GUPVI*, 136-69.

73. Personal File Ernst H., pp. 2, 9, d. 1869492, F. 460/p, RGVA.

74. Manfred Zeidler, "Der Minsker Kriegsverbrecherprozeß vom Januar 1946: Kritische Anmerkungen zu einem sowjetischen Schauprozeß gegen deutsche Kriegsgefangene," in: *Vierteljahrshefte für Zeitgeschichte* 52, no. 2 (April 2004): 211–244; Arkadij Krupennikov, "Gerichtsverfahren gegen Kriegsverbrechen Ende der vierziger und Anfang der fünfziger Jahre," in *Die Tragödie der Gefangenschaft in Deutschland und in der Sowjetunion 1941–1956*, eds. Klaus-Dieter Müller, Konstantin Nikischkin, and Günther Wagenlehner (Cologne: Böhlau Verlag, 1998), 197–214 (here: 197-98).

out of excuses to repatriate the remaining German and Austrian POWs. Stalin ordered mass convictions for the remaining POWs to keep utilizing their forced labor in Soviet economic reconstruction. Often membership in specific units was sufficient to convict POWs who had no individual record of personal transgressions. After 1949 "Austrian" POWs no longer were a category in the Soviet camp system but only "foreign war criminals." POWs were convicted and retained for alleged "war crimes" for another 25 years and forced into hard labor.[75]

During this phase of mass convictions of German and Austrian POWs, Soviet authorities noticed in Ernst H.'s file his role in the German Stalag Krems-Gneixendorf. Soviet authorities began to question him in June 1949.[76] Stalin's perverted system of justice took a hold of his life. He was questioned again about his role in the Stalag Krems-Gneixendorf and about the dreadful conditions and work details there for Soviet POWs on December 6 and 16, 1949. The trial records show that Ernst H. denied any mistreatment of Soviet POWs. He stressed again and again that his work in the camp's financial office did not allow him any personal contacts with camp inmates.[77]

Based on article 1 of the "ukaz 43" of April 19, 1943, passed by the Supreme Soviet, in combination with Article 24 of the Soviet Penal Code ("Accessory"), he was convicted on December 25.[78] More than 70 percent of Austrian POWs 1949 trials were "Ukaz 43" convictions. "Ukaz 43" was directed towards "Measures punishing German-fascist criminals, guilty of mistreatment of Soviet civilians and Red Army POWs, as well as Soviet citizens spying and betraying the fatherland and aiding the enemy."[79]

Between May 26, 1947, to January 12, 1950, the Soviet authorities suspended the death penalty. So Ernst H. received the maximum 25-year sentence in work camps designed for the "betterment" of its inmates. The reason for his conviction was defined as: "H. served as a financial officer in the POW Stalag 17-B [XVII-B] I Krems-Gneixendorf [Ostmark]; next to prisoners of war from other countries [eg. some 4,000 American flyers shot down], 2,000 Soviet POWs were retained there, as a result of his work from 1941 to February 1943, he was part and parcel of mistreatment of

75. Karner, *Im Archipel GUPVI*, 170–79; Knoll, *Späte Heimkehr*, 175.

76. Criminal trial file Ernst H, pp. 13-15, d. 712, op. 1,. F. 1363, NARB.

77. Ibid., 15

78. Ibid., 9; Personal File Ernst H., p. 15, d. 1869492, F. 460/p, RGVA.

79. Andreas Hilger, Nikita Petrov, and Günther Wagenlehner, "Der ‚Ukaz 43': Entstehung und Problematik des Dekrets des Präsidiums des Obersten Sowjets vom 19. April 1943," in: *Sowjetische Militärtribunale*. Vol. 1:. *Die Verurteilung deutscher Kriegsgefangener 1941–1953*, eds. Andreas Hilger, Ute Schmidt, Günter Wagenlehner (Cologne: Böhlau, 2001), 177–210.

Soviet POWs."[80] Ernst H. appealed his sentence. In April 1950 a military tribunal rejected his appeal with the predictable verdict: He was "guilty of mistreatment of prisoner of war as a result of his work."[81]

The cover sheet of his personal file reflected his new status—it was changed from "prisoner of war" to "war criminal." The bureaucracy of the GUPVI dutifully stamped the place and time of his "change of registration" on his file. After his criminal conviction GUPVI transferred him to Camp No. 476 in Asbest in the Sverdlovsk area (Ekatarinburg).[82] Ernst H. spent the final three years of his imprisonment in his camp for convicted German "war criminals." During this time he repeatedly tried to get an early dismissal and repatriation, without success.[83] His personal file also contains a personal letter by his wife Ilse to the International Red Cross pleading "from the bottom of my heart for amnesty for my husband still being kept in the Soviet Union."[84]

On May 27, 1953, the Military Branch of the High Court of the Soviet Union decided that the completion of his sentence was "not necessary" and Ernst H. was to be "let go before his time was up."[85] Ernst H. returned home to Austria with the mass of convicted POWs. This was the 60th repatriation transport of Austrian POWs, the largest since January 1953.[86] The cover of Ernst H. personal was stamped a final time: on October 14, 1953, he was handed over to the Austrian Ministry of Interior in Wiener Neustadt, where most repatriation transports of Austrian POWs returning from Soviet camps ended.[87]

Josef B., who fell into Allied captivity on March 19, 1945, in the West the very same day Ernst H. was apprehended began his long imprisonment in Soviet camps in the East, began his career as a prisoner of war (POW) in Allied transit camps in France. Captured prisoners were marched (brought in trucks?) to temporary POW cages in Stenay, Eastern France. A train took them to the port city of Cherbourg, on the tip of the Normandy peninsula. Here the German POWs were caged up in a holding camp for another month. He never gave detailed descriptions about how he was treated by

80. Personal File Ernst H., p. 15, d. 1869492, F. 460/p, RGVA.

81. Ibid.; Criminal trial file Ernst H, 37, d. 712, op. 1,. F. 1363, NARB.

82. Cover of personal file, d. 1869492, F. 460/p, RGVA; on the special camps for convicted POWs, see Andreas Hilger, "Die sowjetischen Straflager für verurteilte deutsche Kriegsgefangene: Wege in eine terra incognita der Kriegsgefangenengeschichte," in: *Sowjetische Militärtribunale*, eds. Hilger/Schmidt/Wagenlehner, vol 1, 93–142 (here 104, 125).

83. Personal File Ernst H., pp. 16-17, d. 1869492, F. 460/p, RGVA.

84. Ibid., 13.

85. Ibid., 18.

86. Heimkehrerlisten, Section 14, Austrian Ministry of the Interior, see Knoll/Stelzl-Marx, "Sowjetische Strafjustiz in Österreich," 315-16.

87. Cover, Personal File Ernst H., d. 1869492, F. 460/p, RGVA.

his American captors in the French holding camps. Given the logistics of taking larger pockets of German prisoners, these French holding cages have a reputation similar to the "Rhine Meadow camps" on the Western side of the Rhine river, where half a million POWs suffered in open fields at the end of the war. The book *Facts against Falsehood*[88] suggests that Josef B. was extremely lucky a second time to be caught by the Americans in mid-March 1945. Had he been captured only a couple of weeks later, he most likely would have ended up in one of those infamous "Rhine Meadow camps" where German "Defeated Enemy Personnel" had no proper shelter and very little food and water for a number of weeks when the war ended.

After spending much of April 1945 in the Cherbourg holding camp, he was transferred by ship to a British port. He ended up on a convoy of some 80 ships crossing the Atlantic before the war was over; crossing the Atlantic took ten days. He always proudly remembered that he was one of the few prisoners not to get desperately seasick on his Atlantic crossing. His was the last convoy of German POWs shipped to the U.S. The convoy arrived in Boston on May 9, 1945, the day after the Nazis surrendered! Like all German (and Italian) POWs arriving in the U.S., the POWs immediately went through registration and a rigorous delousing process in the port of Boston.

The German POWs were put on a train and shipped to Colorado in comfortable Pullman cars. The trip from Boston to Colorado Springs took an interminable 78 hours. In mid-May 1945 Josef B. finally arrived in Camp Carson, Colorado Springs, a vast military reservation by the U.S Army.[89] He soon was transferred to one of the 25 branch camps administered by Camp Carson to work on nearby farms. Unlike the Africa Corps POWs, captured in May 1943, who were spoiled by their captors during the war (living in the "Fritz Ritz," as Americans joked), the cohort of German POWs captured at the end of the war initially were fed reduced rations for a while. With hunger pangs and behind barbed wire they were made to experience defeat. Hitler's *Afrikakorps*, the ca. 135,000 German POWs shipped to American camps after their capture in May 1943 in Tunisia. When the war ended the German POWs' very generous daily food rations were reduced to hunger rations. German POWs also were forced to watch movies with gruesome footage from the American liberation of the concentration camps in Germany. The POWs were quickly educated about the war crimes that the Nazi regime had committed during its control of Europe.

88. Günter Bischof and Stephen E. Ambrose, *Facts against Falsehood: Eisenhower and the German P.O.W.'s*. (Baton Rouge: Louisiana State University Press 1992).

89. Research report by Daniel A. Jepson, "Historical and Archaeological Perspectives on the World War II Prisoner of War Camp at Fort Carson, Colorado," Centennial Archaeology, Inc., 1990.

Josef B. and a fellow POW at Camp Carson, Colorado Springs, CO, 1945. private collection.

Farmers from the Colorado Springs area came by the branch camps of Camp Carson every day to pick up German POWs for work details. Josef B. worked on the farm of a German-American farmer who treated the POWs well because they worked hard. In his case, he harvested green beans and sugar beets in the course of the late summer and fall 1945. He regularly was done early with the daily allotment of work the farmer expected from his POW crew. The farmer drove them back to the camp after a day's work (early, if they all got done with the work ahead of time). Since Josef B. had grown up on a small dairy farm in Austria, he was familiar with farm work and liked it. He was a hard worker and the farmer appreciated his "German" work ethic. The POWs were paid 80 cents a day for their work.

After the fall harvest was in, Josef B. was transferred to work in a huge hospital kitchen in the Denver area. He worked as a dish washer. He bonded with African American cooks in the kitchen who always handed him extra food. This bonding experience of two "underdog" groups in American society is a phenomenon that is a stock theme confirmed in the extant POW literature. Black Americans generally treated German POWs well wherever they encountered them, maybe also because here was a group of white people not prejudiced against them. In the segregated American South, African Americans often envied German POWs because they were treated better than blacks in public places since they were not subject to segregated facilities in the public.[90]

Josef B.'s overall experience at Camp Carson was positive in spite of being "behind barbed wire" for a year. From his modest pay he could buy what they needed in Camp Carson's canteen store (half the pay was set aside to be paid out at the time of repatriation, the other half paid out in "cantonment tickets" for the purchase of personal items from the camp store). Among other things, he bought toiletries to bring back to Austria for his family. Josef B. always stressed in his stories about his life as a POW in the U.S. that he would have liked to stay in the United States since he caught on to the fact quickly that you get rewarded for hard work. The 1929 Geneva Convention required that POWs be retuned to their home countries. Washington bided by the Geneva Convention rules with regard to German POWs kept in the United States.

"Skoro domoi": Repatriation

When GUPVI transferred Karl B. to the Antifa-Academy "Special Object No. 41," it officially closed his personal file on July 20, 1947. At the end of the year, after he had finished his Antifa reeducation/indoctrination program, Soviet authorities transferred him to the repatriation camp Nr. 36 in Marmaros Sziget. On December 20, 1947, he arrived there at last. POWs heard the slogan "*skoro domoj*" ("soon you will be home") throughout their Soviet captivity. For Karl B. its fulfillment came with Transport No. 34 after a week-long train trip to Wiener Neutstadt, where all Austrian *Heimkehrer* (returnees) from Soviet POW camps arrived. Upon his arrival Austrian authorities handed him 50 Austrian Schillings, ten cigarettes and the information sheet "*Gruß der Heimat*" (your homeland greets you)

90. Matthias Reiß, *"Die Schwarzen waren unsere Freunde": Deutsche Kriegsgefangene in der amerikanischen Gesellschaft 1942-1946* (Paderborn: Ferdinand Schöningh 2002).

as welcome presents.[91] The government's petty material indemnification extended to returning prisoners of war was symbolic more than anything else. Of course, it could not make up for years of lost wages nor for the physical and psychological traumas incurred during years behind barbed wire.[92]

Karl B. had demonstrated keen survival instincts and talent to adapt quickly to opportunities beckoning in the Soviet camp system. The man who had pretended to be a committed communist in the Antifa reeducation camp, returned to his values as a young man upon his return and quickly found a job in the conservative state government of Upper Austria. He started his new employment on February 1, 1948, and passed the necessary exams to advance in his new life-long career over the next few years. He served as an active member of the Austrian *Stalingradbund* (League of Stalingrad Veterans) and *Heimkehrerbund* (League of Returnees) until his death in 2004. His years in Soviet captivity have remained an important topic in his family's memory of World War II.[93]

Herman S.'s repatriation journey was drawn-out and painful and lasted from December 1945 to February 1946. Instead of a quick trip home, cattle cars expedited him and the German prisoners in freezing cold to a camp in Attichy in the Bretagne, where he was incarcerated for a month (December 2 to January 4, 1946). It was an American camp and the guards took everything away they had carried with them from the U.S. (toiletries, clothing) and harassed them endlessly. They stood in line for daily body counts for hours and in endless food lines. During rain periods the camp turned into a mud field. They got enough to eat but froze every regularly through the cold winter nights in their tents that hardly protected them from the wind. They were forced to perform useless work details. Austrians were separated into their own cage and fought among themselves (conservatives vs. communists). Herman S. battled his digestion problems and diarrhea again and continued to have problems with his foot. His level of despair hit rock bottom, citing Dante's *Inferno*: "Those who enter here, cast aside all hope" ("Die ihr eintretet, lasst alle Hoffnung fahren"). Allegedly, conditions were worse than they had been in German concentration camps. He was perplexed about the Americans making all of the inmates of Attichy and

91. Beham, "Der Russlandfeldzug," 35; Heimkehrerlisten, Abteilung 14, Austrian Interior Ministry.

92. Harald Knoll, "Kriegsgefangenschaft und Heimkehr," in *"Österreich ist frei!" Der Österreichische Staatsvertrag 1955: Beitragsband zur Ausstellung auf Schloss Schallaburg 2005*, eds. Stefan Karner and Gottfried Stangler et al. (Horn: Verlag Berger, 2005), 133-36 (here 134).

93. Beham, "Der Russlandfeldzug," 35-36.

similar camps to their "arch enemies" in no time as they were constantly suffering from thirst, hunger, weakness, and harassment of every sort."[94]

Alas, Herman S.'s ordeal was not over after his departure from the detested Attichy camp as he was shipped to Stenay for another month, an American enclosure in north-eastern France with a view of the snow-covered Ardennes mountains. Stenay had the reputation of being a "hunger camp" and fully lived up to its reputation. The food distribution system was haphazard and there was never enough. Predictably, he had to deal with diarrhea again. Vying for daily rations produced "the worst kind of egotism": "Hunger gave birth to envy and naughtiness." The food system was deeply corrupted as guards sold the provisions destined for the POWs on the black market for personal enrichment. The protests of camp leaders could not change it. There were many inmates that were only "bones and skin" ("mit Haut überzogene Knochengerüste"). In spite of sleeping with layers of clothes, he continued to freeze in the frigid winter temperatures. He had not changed his under clothes since he left Camp Crossville in mid-November, for "whatever is on your body they cannot take away." Austrians and Germans were separated again at Stenay and kept fighting amongst each other.[95]

After two horrid months of moving through American temporary enclosures in France, his trip towards final repatriation home began on January 28, 1946. Living off American C-rations, trains took him through Germany and into Austria. Along the way they traded with local farmers out of the train window (soap for bread). In Linz railroad stations Catholic nuns handed them gifts of bread and coffee. On his 996th day of captivity, Herman S. was holed up again on his final stop in captivity in Ansfelden in an old SS-camp. To be dismissed from the camp someone had to pick up the inmates and confirm that a place to stay and a job was waiting for them. He bitterly complained about the Austrian authorities for doing absolutely nothing to speed up his final dismissal. On February 7, his 1004th day in captivity he was finally picked up by a friend. Regaining his freedom produced an indescribable feeling of happiness: "only he who has been unfree knows what regaining one's freedom means" ("denn wer nie unfrei gewesen ist, weiß nicht, was Wiedererlangen der Freiheit bedeutet"). On February 21 he was making it back to his native Vienna, stealthily passing as a "blind passenger" on a freight train through the Soviet zone of occupation. [96]

94. Attichy diary entries December 3, 1944, to January 4, 1946, 113-21 (Dante citation, 113).

95. Stenay diary entries, January 4 to 27, 1946, 122- 29.

96. Haid-Ansfelden diary entries, January 31 to February 7, 1946, 131-34 (quotation 133).

Herman S. soon enrolled at the University of Vienna to study ethnology. As a student he worked as a librarian at the Amerika House in Vienna. In 1953 he finished his dissertation on "The Warfare of the Plains and Eastern Forest Indians of North America" and graduated with a PhD in Ethnology. When the Austrian government began reconstituting its Army in 1955 after the withdrawal of the occupation powers, Herman S. rejoined the military. He served as a company commander in the Tyrol and later in high staff positions. He also had a tour as the Austrian military and air attaché in Switzerland. After his retirement he returned to his passion of North American Indian ethnology and finally published his dissertation (*Indianische Kriegsführung in den Plains und östlichen Waldgebieten Nordamerikas* 1984) and a number of other works, among them a study of the adoption of prisoners of war by native American tribes in North America (*Die Adoption Kriegsgefangener oder Geraubter bei den nordamerikanischen Indianern*). After his two years of American captivity, there may have been some subconscious wishful thinking involved in this study. After his retirement he returned to the U.S. annually to visit relatives in Alaska. During his retirement he also enjoyed regularly meeting former POW colleagues in a Viennese *Heurigen* to revive wartime memories. Three years of captivity (unfreedom) behind barbed wires had left a lasting impression on his mind.[97] The 86-year old Herman S. passed away in 2002.

The Soviet authorities closed Ernst H.'s personal file with his transfer to the Austria Ministry of the Interior in October 1953 after his long transport home by train and a painful chapter in his biography closed.

Josef B. was shipped home on May 9, 1946, within a year of his arrival in the U.S. Like Herman S. he disembarked in Le Havre, France. Unlike Herman S., who the Americans kept for more than another month in their dismal temporary enclosures in France, Josef B. was lucky a third time to be shipped back home to Western Austria. France, too, held back many German POWs returning from the United States for "labor reparations" in French camps and kept them for another one or two years; naturally, this outraged those whose life behind barbed wire was prolonged again. In the French internment camp of Reichenau near Innsbruck in the French zone of occupation of Austria, Josef B. was finally dismissed from his military service in June 1946. The French seized all the presents he had brought back from the U.S. for his family—useful items like toiletries one could not buy in Austrian stores at the time. On June 2, 1946, he returned back to Mellau, his hometown that he would never leave again for the rest of his

97. Information gathered from Herman S. letters and book flyers he sent me. I am also grateful to Erwin Schmidl for filling me in on his former colleague Herman S.

life and where he would raise a family of eight kids. He had served in the German Wehrmacht for a lost cause for more than five years. It is hard to say whether he ever fully came to terms with the German defeat and his "lost years" in the war.

He hardly ever talked about the war unless asked. This silence characterized an entire generation of Austrian World War II veterans. Like many of his generation who fought in the war he probably never quite got over the fact that it all ended in ignominious defeat, imprisonment and embarrassing humiliation, once the full extent of German war crimes started to become known after the war. To this date historians discuss to what extent the Wehrmacht was involved in Hitler's "criminal war of extermination" in the East. When the *Wehrmachtsausstellung* traveled through Germany and Austria in the mid-1990s, Josef B. refused to see it. His experience as a POW in thousands of miles from his home in the United States never quite left him. It easily qualified as the most "exotic" time of his life. His year in Colorado retained a special hold on his memory. He did not attend the wedding of his son in the U.S. to an American girl– he never returned to the U.S. again. Was there a lingering resentment about his captors? Yet in a fashion he did return mentally to the U.S.. In the mid-1970s he began a series of reunions with former *Wehrmacht* soldiers that all had served their imprisonment in American POW camps. As is the custom in such veterans' reunions they exchanged a lot of war stories and wallowed in the nostalgia of *temps perdu*. These men met in half a dozen such reunions every couple of years into the 1980s when most of them were retired and began to pass away. These veterans also visited Mellau during one of their reunions. Josef B. passed away at the age of 81 on June 6, 2002.

Conclusion

These biographies of Austrian prisoners of war are as remarkable in what they reveal from the documentary record as in their silences. The evidence available on all four of them is full of gaps and lacunae. The two men in Soviet captivity are documented with detailed personal files from official Soviet records, featuring predictable ideological blinders. The emotional and mental side of the dreadful captivity in Soviet camps is largely missing. Prisoners in Soviet captivity throughout their time in the POW camps lived a marginal existence—every day was a struggle for survival. Apart from the Rhine meadow and French temporary enclosures, POWs in American captivity were not threatened in their survival (in some camps inmates were killed by fellow Nazi POWs). Of course, they missed home and their families, but psychologically they were not on the margins. While we have not found official American records on the two men in American captivity, we have detailed ego records, particularly in the case of Herman S.'s rich diary. Of course, such ego documents come with their own blinders that are hard to be filled in by historians. In the case of Josef B. they are selective and constructed after the fact and thus reflect the vagaries of human memory and the silences of the forgotten or blocked out past. In the case of Herman S. they may leave out details about his political views that he did not care to write about. The Soviet captors do not care much about the physical and strained and abnormal psychological conditions of their prisoners – their records are written in cold bureaucratese. The ego documents of captives, on the other hand, may reveal the complex emotional and mental life of life behind barbed wire but tell us little about the holding powers' perspectives. The gaps in these records will never be recovered as these men have all passed away.

The collective lives of entire cohorts of Austrian POWs in Soviet and American captivity can be reconstructed from a more complete record than the lives of Ernst H., Karl B., Herman S. and Josef B. Historians have worked on the horrible conditions in the Rhine Meadow camps where the US Army was overwhelmed by the mass of humanity that fell into their hands at the end of the war and exempted them from the protection of the Geneva Convention. Changing their status to "Defeated Enemy Personnel" presumably gave their captors the wherewithal to treat them like cattle. A million German and Austrian POWs were subjected to inhuman conditions, at least for a few weeks.[98] Conditions in American temporary enclosures in France were not much better, even in 1946, as Herman S. diary exhaustively tells us.[99] Those prisoners who made it to camps in the U.S. entered the "Fritz Ritz," as American critics of the pampered German POWs called it. The political divisions between Nazis and anti-Nazis among the German POWs has been the subject of recent research. American reeducation and denazification efforts among German POWs—more subtle than the Soviet Antifa indoctrination—has been investigated in detail. The American labor

98. See the Viennese POW in the Heilbronn Camp Dr. Otto Stur's personal report to Bischof, February 23, 1990; for a composite picture of German POWs, see Paul Brägelmann, ed., *Auf den Rheinwiesen 1945: 101 Tage Kriegsgefangenschaft (*Cloppenburg: Verlag Günter Runge, 1991); see also Carrell/Böddeker, *Die Gefangenen*, 147-59.

99. Carrell/Böddeker, *Die Gefangenen*, 160-70; See also Helmut Hörner's diary published in English translation *A German Odyssey: The Journal of a German Prisoner of War* (Golden, CO: Fulcrum Publishing, 1991), and Hans Jonitz, "In amerikanischer und französischer Gefangenschaft," in *Kriegsgefangenschaft*, eds. Benz/Schardt, 85-130.

program has been analyzed.[100] The trajectory of the identity of Austrian POWs in American camps from identification with the Nazi cause towards rediscovering their Austrian identity when it was opportune has been studied.[101] Recent research has shown that soldiers from the *Ostmark*, by and large, were deeply committed to National Socialism and fought hard until the bitter end. Even if some opportunists declared themselves "Austrians who had been forced to serve the Third Reich" in POW camps, "Austrian national feeling did not seem evident on a mass basis." A slow and tender trend to (re)discover their Austrian identity was afoot in POW camps.[102] Most recently historians have found the rich new source of American interrogation records of German POWs and secret recordings of their conversations while waiting for interrogations that reveal much about the state of mind of POWs at the beginning of their captivity.[103] Herman S. and Josef B. did not end up at Fort Hunt, Virginia, where such interrogations were held and conversations were recorded. Austrian POWs in Soviet captivity, too, have also left a rich record about their awful experience in Soviet camps—their physical and mental exhaustion, their tough work details, the rigors of the Soviet camp system with lack of food and medical care, their hopeless existence in the vast spaces of the Soviet Union and the trauma they had to work through on their return home.[104] All of this information adds to fleshing out our four lives here into a prosopography —a composite picture of Austrian POWs in opposite hemispheres during World War II.

100. Springer, *America's Captives*, 151-61; Ron Robin, *Barbed-Wire College: Reeducating German POWs in the United States during World War II* (Princeton: Princeton University Press, 1996); Arthur L. Smith, Jr., *The War for the German Mind: Re-educating Hitler's Soldiers* (Providence, RI: Berghahn Books, 1996).

101. See the Editorial by Günter Bischof, and the essays by Rafael A. Zagovec, Robert D. Billinger, Jr., and Rüdiger Overmans in: *Zeitgeschichte* 29 (May/June 2002): 109-47.

102. Grischany, "Mental Aspects," 57.

103. Sönke Neitzel and Harald Welzer, *Soldaten: Protokolle vom Kämpfen, Töten und Sterben* (Frankfurt/M.: S. Fischer, 2011); Felix Römer, "Alfred Andersch abgehört: Kriegsgefangene ‚Anti-Nazis' im amerikanischen Vernehmungslager Fort Hunt," in: *Vierteljahrshefte für Zeitgeschichte* 58, no. 4 (2010): 563-98.

104. Biess, *Homecomings*; Svenja Goltermann, *Die Gesellschaft der Überlebenden: Deutsche Kriegsheimkehrer und ihre Gewalterfahrung im Zweiten Weltkrieg* (Munich: dva/Pantheon, 2011).

The Photographic Gaze—Austrian Visual Lives during the Occupation Decade:
A Cross-Section of Ordinary Austrians Photographed by American and Austrian Artists

Hans Petschar and Herbert Friedlmeier[1]

In May 1945 American troops entered Austria and soon thereafter established the Information Service Branch (ISB) of the United States Information Services (USIS) in Salzburg, the capital of the American zone of occupation. Between 1945 and 1955 the Pictorial Section of the USIS's ISB produced and archived thousands of photographs for the ISB and its various units; it also provided national and international news agencies with pictures and documentation of all aspects of the political, economic, and cultural life of the Austrian occupation.[2] The Pictorial Section of the ISB was initially operated under military control yet was eventually transformed into a civilian institution and reported on Austria under the supervision of American press officers. The ISB accumulated a large photo archive which was used by Austrian and the international media. This archive was later donated to the Picture Section in the Austrian National Library in Vienna, where this rich photographic collection is now archived.

Accomplished American photographers trained a number of young Austrian photographers and darkroom technicians who worked for USIS from 1945 to 1955 and then embarked on their own distinguished careers. The task of these photo artists was to report and document the progress in the Austrian economic recovery and to support the economic, social, and political goals of the United States in postwar Austria with detailed photographic stories. As such they constitute a rich visual history of the Austrian occupation decade. The earliest photo stories informed the Austrian population about Nazi war crimes as they became known after the war. Soon USIS's visual narratives documented in exhaustive detail the steady progress of U. S. economic, cultural, and educational policies in Austria.

In the Beginning – After the End

After the unconditional surrender of the German Wehrmacht in early May 1945, Soviet, American, British and French forces occupied

1. Günter Bischof translated this essay from German into English.

2. For a detailed presentation, see Hans Petschar, *Die junge Republik: Alltagsbilder aus Österreich 1945-1955* (Vienna: Ueberreuter, 2005). For U.S. information policy in Austria, see Oliver Rathkolb, "Politische Propaganda der amerikanischen Besatzungsmacht in Österreich 1945 bis 1950: Ein Beitrag zur Geschichte des Kalten Krieges in der Presse-, Kultur- und Rundfunkpolitik," 2 vols., Ph.D. diss., University of Vienna, 1981.

newly reconstituted Austria. Yet there is no extant visual record of the ISB celebrating the Allied victory excessively. There are no photo series documenting bombed out cities and thus visualizing total defeat. Instead, the ISB picture series from the immediate postwar period document and recapitulate the miserable and uncertain times after the war when people lived on very little and survived on scraps after six years of war. Austrians are not shown individually but collectively as a people that suffer egregiously in their struggle for survival while trying to start new lives.

On May 4, 1945, American military advance troops arrived in Salzburg. On May 14, the male ISB personnel arrived in Salzburg ready to spring into action, after a delay in Verona, Italy. During this initial phase of what has been called total occupation, the main task for the Americans was to inform and enlighten the local population about American occupation policies, including a strict order of "non-fraternization" with the locals.

On June 4, 1945, a month after the capitulation of the German forces, people throng to the show window of the Salzburg photo shop Max Mann. The ISB-Pictorial Section has appropriated this space to display a collage of first pictures of German war crimes taken in the concentration camps (Figure 1).

Figure 1

Were they "typical" Austrians that looked at those pictures? Were they distraught about the horrific record of German war crimes now on display? How much did they know about these crimes? Did they begin discussions among each other about the extent of their knowledge of these war crimes? There were people indeed who had to know a lot about Nazi war crimes from their own painful experience witnessing (or participating in) them. And then there are the victims of the Nazis. Only one-and-a-half months after her liberation from a concentration camp, Käthe Novotny dies and is buried in a Salzburg cemetery on June 15, 1945. Her coffin is carried by grieving fellow inmates from a former concentration camp, wearing the unmistakable striped "uniform" of the KZ-inmates (Figure 2).

Figure 2

Starting in late summer of 1945, when the Western occupation elements moved into the Austrian capital, the ISB-photographers began reporting from both Linz and Vienna too. This was the time when people began to remove the rubble from their bombed-out cities, for example, in front of Salzburg cathedral and the *Tiefe Graben* in Vienna's first district. In March 1946 both *Trűmmerfrauen* ("rubble ladies") (Figure 3) and veterans of the infamous Wehrmacht division *Großdeutschland* clean up bricks that will be reused under the watchful eyes of the American military police (Figure 4).

Figure 3

Figure 4

This was also a time of endless queuing. In June 1945 people line up in front of a Salzburg policy station to secure their registration cards needed to get food ration cards (Figure 5).

Figure 5 Figure 6

In the summer of 1945 women gather in a long line in Linz to collect food with their stamps. Among them is a lonely young man in his Wehrmacht uniform, probably due to lack of civilian clothing (Figure 6).

Yet people also queue in front of tobacco shops where they also can buy newspapers to squash their "hunger for information." (Figure 7)

Figure 7 Figure 8

As late as December 1947 people stand in line for some six hours in front of a branch of the *Länderbank* in Vienna to exchange three old Schillings for one new one in response to the currency reform of the Austrian government designed to stop inflation running rampant after the war during a time when wartime *Reichsmark* had not been converted to Austrian *Schillings* yet (Figure 8).

A Country Akin Serving As Refugee Center

World War II spawned an enormous concentration of human tragedy, much of it assiduously documented in the USIS-Archives, among them Jewish Displaced persons waiting for an exit visa to Palestine/Israel in the Camp *Givat Avoda* in Saalfelden, Salzburg (today the "Wallner Barracks" of the Austrian Army); refugees from all four corners of Europe waiting for visas to the United States to escape the misery of the old continent; expellees from Eastern Europe trying to make it in emergency shelters that look like abandoned railroad cars.

The former *Hotel l'Europe* next to the Salzburg railroad station also served as refugee hostel. This former luxury abode was finally torn down in 1949, after it had served the High Command of the Wehrmacht during much of the war and was severely damaged by an American bomb in 1944. In January 1949 Displaced Persons from all over Eastern Europe are still crowding its rooms, along them these two women who are trying to bring an oven into the right position to heat their place (Figure 9).

In the early 1950s the ISB-photographers change the style and substance of their visual language to send a different message. The fate of individuals moves to the forefront and the visualization of ideas and political programs becomes prominent; long narrative sequences tell these visual stories. Yoichi R. Okamoto is the key figure in initiating these visual narratives in the USIS program in postwar Austria. His visual paragons is the tradition of American photo journalism of the 1930s—famous New Deal photographers such as Dorothea Lange and James Agee who documented the hard lives of ordinary people mired in deep poverty during the great depression.[3]

Beginning in 1948, when the Marshall Plan started its programs in Western Europe, including Austria, until 1954 Okamoto directed the Vienna Bureau of the USIS Pictorial Section as "Chief" of reporters and ISB staff photographers. Okamoto was an outstanding and highly imaginative photographer himself and became the teacher of a cohort of outstanding young Austrian photo artists, among them Gottfried "Jeff" Rainer, Herbert Bayer, Fritz Mayr and Heinrich Mayr.[4]

---

3. On American photography documenting the difficult social life of the 1930s, see Gilles Mora and Beverly M. Brannan, *Les Photographes de la Farm Security Administration. Archives d'une Amérique en crise 1935 – 1943* (Paris: Seuil, 2006). The original pictures can be found in the Library of Congress.

4. Okamoto's photographic eye of Vienna was published many years later, see Yoichi R., Okamoto and Paula Okamoto, eds., *Okamoto sieht Wien: Die Stadt seit den 50er Jahren* (Vienna: Kremayr & Scheriau, 1987).

Anonymous groups of DPs, or amorphous masses of Austrians queuing up, are no longer in the focus of USIS photographers. Now portraits of individuals are at the center of the photographer's eye. The carefully written captions recorded by the USIS-staff give these people personal identities. Peter Patscheider, a Lower Austrian farmer from Plambach, is one of them. In 1940 Patscheider was forced to emigrate from the South Tyrol region of Northern Italy after being forced by the Italian fascists to opt for either his German or Italian ethnicity (Figure 10).

Figure 9

Figure 10

The Sudeten German Wollinger family had to build a new existence after their expulsion from Czechoslovakia and succeeded on the Lassnitz Heights in Styria. This picture of the Wollingers gathering in their homely living room before Christmas 1954 indicates that their farm already managed to feed the eight members of the family (Figure 11).

Figure 11

The extensive collection of pictures of the American Information Services Branch in Austria is progressively dedicated to Cold War themes starting in the early 1950s. Here the personification of the stories of individuals plays a central role too. The pictures of refugees now captured by the USIS-photographers are individuals who escaped communism in Eastern Europe. USEP (United States Escapee Program) ran refugee camp # 1002 in Wels together with the Upper Austrian government. A picture shot at the entrance of the camp's cobbler's shop displays the camp official John Daly along with the unnamed Austrian camp director and Stan Milus, the USEP's chief in Austria (Figure 12). The official markers prominently displayed at the camp bear witness to the many challenges Austria faced in taking care of tens of thousands of refugees and Displaced Persons flooding out of Eastern Europe since the end of the war.

On July 23, 1953, auto mechanic and electrician apprentices from Camp 1002 took their exams in the vocational training center in Wels. A picture shows the examining commission with the school's director Franz Rosman, Stan Milus, and Simon Wiesenthal, the chief of ORT (Organization for Rehabilitation and Training)—later to become famous as a "Nazi hunter." (Figure 13)

Figure 12

Figure 13

During the Cold War there were plenty of refugees that could be posted in pictures for propaganda and counterpropaganda purposes. When the Czech figure skating champion Miroslava Nachodska came to Vienna in January 1955 for the figure skating world championship, she decided not to return to her native Prague. Instead she got into contact with U.S. officials in Linz who soon organized a press conference for Radio Free Europe and the Voice of America. A well staged picture shows Nachodska talking to a Linz policeman who salutes her (Figure 14). Both are placed in front of a street crossing with markers indicating the distance to places, including Prague (260 km); the Czech champion looks into the opposite direction of her hometown.

Figure 14

Private and Public American Aid Programs Revive Lives and the National Economy

In November 1945, 22 leading U.S. welfare organizations founded the private aid cooperative CARE (Cooperative for American Remittances to Europe). The U.S. Army also provisioned CARE with food stocks from its depots. The first CARE packages began arriving in Austria in July 1946. In the course of the next few months clothing and medical supplies complemented the desperately needed food in these CARE packages. The U.S. Army took charge of distributing these American gift packages, often with the help of prominent people to heighten the propaganda effect of American generosity.[5] The famous American actors Joseph Cotten and Douglas Fairbanks Jr. got involved in the publicity of CARE package distributions in Austria. Cotten, who was in Vienna in 1948 as the lead actor for the shooting of *The Third Man*, gave away 15 packages to needy families in Vienna's Mariahilf dictrict, Fairbanks handed mayor Theodor Körner 25 packages at Vienna's City Hall in 1950.

Among the many photos in the USIA-Archives that are documenting CARE package distribution, two are selected here that show recipients not usually chosen for these gifts. During the festivities of Richard Meister's

5. On American aid programs in postwar Austria see Wilfried Mähr, *Der Marshall Plan in Österreich* (Graz: Styria, 1989), Günter Bischof, "Between Responsibility and Rehabilitation Austria in International Politics 1940-1950," PhD Diss., Harvard University 1989.

inauguration as *Rektor* of the University of Vienna for the academic year 1949/50, the new chancellor, along with his Deans Hans Leitmeier, Johann Kosnetter and Johann Sima, as well as Senator Johann Soelch, are closely scrutinizing a large gift of scholarly books by the American CARE-Mission to the University of Vienna (Figure 15). A picture in the same series shows Socialist Vice-Chancellor Adolf Schärf confirming the receipt of a wall of 100 CARE packages from Philipp Heller (Figure 16).

Figure 15

Figure 16

Heller is the Labor Information officer of the ECA (European Cooperation Administration) in Austria. The packages are intended for former victims of National Socialist persecution in Austria. The ECA was the governmental office founded for the organization of the Marshall Plan in Europe and usually was not involved in the distribution of these privately financed CARE packages. CARE packages surely helped many Austrians through periods of severe scarcities of food, clothing, and medical needs. But they were not destined to help overcome the structural weakness in the postwar Austrian economy, which was the inherent agenda of the Marshall Plan.

The first documentation series and photo reports of the ISB-Staff—when it was still under military control—make raising the consciousness and informing about the war crimes of National Socialism among the Austrian people a top priority. Subsequently economic, cultural and educational themes quickly rise to the top of the American agenda in Austria and inform U.S. information policies. Between 1950 and 1955 the USIS picture section systematically documents the American occupation policies in postwar Austria, including the other USIS sections. The USIS archives contain much documentation of the work of the radio station "Red-White-Red," the youth organizations AYA (Austrian Youth Activities) and 4-H (Head, Heart, Hands, Health). What is particularly well documented is the great variety of Marshall Plan projects all over Austria.

Secretary of State George C. Marshall had delivered his speech announcing a European economic recovery program on June 5, 1947. Marshall delivered his speech during the Harvard commencement ceremony, shining the light on the parlous state of the European economy with its starving population. Marshall bemoaned the "enormous complexity" of the situation which would make it extremely difficult "for the man in the street to reach a clear appreciation of the situation." For the American people, being far away from the troubled areas of the world, it would be virtually impossible to grasp the real significance of the situation "merely by reading, listening, or even seeing photographs and motion pictures."[6] Americans needed to understand the dire situation in Europe and help the European nations to stand on their own feet again—these were key elements in Marshall's famous speech. The Marshall Plan's implementation in Austria had enormous consequences for US information policies in the country. USIS's Pictorial Section produced a host of visual narratives to tell the rich story of the Marshall Plan in Austria.[7]

The editorial staff of USIS-Section naturally supported American information programs from the very beginning of the occupation, long before the Marshall Plan era, when the media coverage on the political level was increasingly aligned with the demands of the Austrian government. With the spreading of American economic aid programs to the three Western occupation zones of Austria, where the bulk of U.S. (including Marshall Plan) aid was distributed, the USIS-Picture Section systematically began to extend its coverage to all of the three Western zones. The visual narratives of the ERP programs in the Western and Southern Austrian states of Vorarlberg, Tyrol, Salzburg and Carinthia are particularly rich in the USIA-Archives. The photo stories cover river regulation, flood water protection and drainage projects, road construction and modernization of agriculture, support of the tourism industry (building of hotels and ski lifts), as well as help to individuals.[8] The staff editors narrate the story of every picture series with comprehensive captions. There are also humorous caption texts of American education programs, local festivals, and everyday lives of ordinary Austrians in the provinces.

6. A transcript of the speech and an audio file have been published on the U.S. Department of State website: http://www.america.gov/st/texttrans-english/2007/May/20070521153224MVyelwarC0.4675867.html (accessed on Feb. 2, 2012).

7. Photographs documenting the Marshall Plan are analyzed by Herbert Friedlmeier, Hans Petschar, and Michaela Pfundner, "U.S. Photography and the Marshall Plan," in Günter Bischof and Dieter Stiefel, eds., and Hannes Richter, digital ed., *Images of the Marshall Plan in Europe: Films, Photographs, Exhibits, Posters* (Innsbruck: Studien Verlag, 2009), 169-201.

8. The Marshall Plan's contribution to the reconstruction of the various sectors of the Austrian economy is analyzed in Günter Bischof, Anton Pelinka, and Dieter Stiefel, eds., *The Marshall Plan in Austria* (Contemporary Austrians Studies 8) (New Brunswick, NJ: Transaction, 2000).

Two shots show ordinary Austrians busy with improving their infrastructural needs. However, these pictures differ from the usual perspectives presented of the country's economic reconstruction. One picture shot in 1954 shows apprentices of the long distance communications school attaching wires to isolation caps; it appears as a carefully orchestrated group of people (Figure 17). Then there is the troop of eight agricultural workers regulating a local river and draining the land in Rechnitz, Burgenland, in 1950 (Figure 18).

Figure 17

Figure 18

Marshall Plan aid and counterpart funds also supported numerous medical and research facilities and production sites. In the Tyrol, both the biochemical factory in Kundl and Fritz Striede's research facility for prosthetic limbs and artificial joints in Mitterndorf/Kufstein received ERP aid. A picture documents returning Wehrmacht veterans from the war with missing limbs and shows them being fitted with artificial legs and working on improving their walking (Figure 19). Striede's facility was busy as thousands of veterans were in need of artificial limbs.

Figure 19

In this case the USIS-photographer did not apply a voyeuristic gaze but rather added a human touch to the vast figure of national and personal "*reconstruction and rehabilitation*" challenging postwar era of economic recovery.

An Iconography of Ordinary Austrians during Postwar Reconstruction

"*UdSSR: Deputierte des Volkes*" [Soviet Union: The People's Deputies] sounded the headline of a contribution to the popular *Austria Wochenschau* in 1950.[9] These were the famous "Working Heroes" of the Soviet Union – ordinary workers elected into the Soviet Chamber of People's Deputies as a result of their great work ethic. The Soviets stressed that such efforts benefitted all of society, irrespective of class background, and thus added to the progress of the Soviet experiment.

USIS photographers tried to match these Soviet icons with Austrian "Working Heroes." On August 17, 1949, Austria's most popular newspaper *Wiener Kurier* published a pictorial magazine edition entitled "*Was bringt der Marshall Plan nach Österreich?*" [What Does the Marshall Plan Contribute to Austrian Reconstruction?]. One picture depicts a worker during his cigarette break while loading coal onto a train at Vienna's Western railroad station (Figure 20). This common laborer with his shirtless muscular body, exuding confidence and strength, became an icon of Austrian reconstruction.[10]

Figure 20

9. The *Austria Wochenschau* also featured international contributions, including from the Soviet occupation element; on the *Austria Wochenschau*, see Hans Petschar and Georg Schmid, *Erinnerung & Vision: Die Legitimation Österreichs in Bildern; Eine semiohistorische Analyse der Austria Wochenschau 1949 –1960* (Graz: Adeva, 1990).

10. *Wiener Kurier Bildbeilage*, 17 Aug. 1949. Now also published in the exhibit catalogue of the Technical Museum *Österreich baut auf: Reconstruction and the Marshall Plan /Wieder-Aufbau & Marshall-Plan* (Vienna: Technical Museum, 2005), 111.

In February 1952 a miner protected by a helmet, working on the famous Styrian open-pit *Erzberg* iron mountain, shouts out warnings about falling stones after an explosion to loosen the rock. The original USIS-caption of this picture reads "ERP aids Erzberg output" and the man is termed a "typical open-pit miner." (Figure 21)

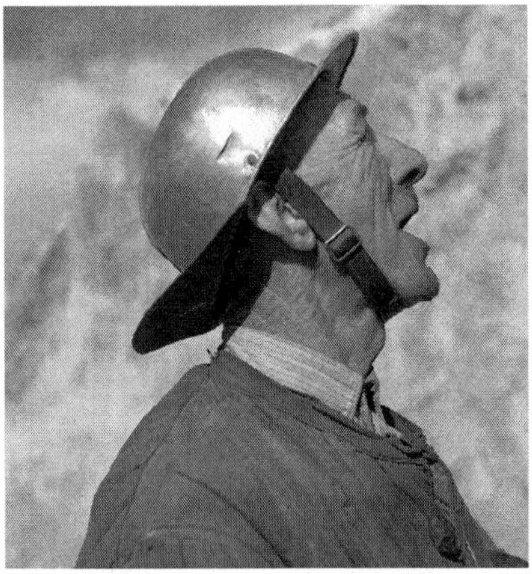

Figure 21

Figure 22

The third iconic picture displays Franz Jandl as a "typical miner" in Carinthia's remote Lavanttal brown coal mines (Figure 22). The caption of the picture stresses his pride in his job and his contribution to Austrian economic reconstruction. Carinthia's brown coal mines were supported with considerable Marshall Plan counterpart investments.

Opposite these three vibrant and ordinary Austrian workers stands classical American counterpropaganda showing a worker in the Soviet occupation zone (Figure 23). This man's picture is taken in a Soviet controlled USIA factory in Lower Austria in 1951. The unknown and unidentified man covers his face and wants to get away. It looks like the picture is posed and the man tries to slip away from dreaded American media people. The caption editorialized by American Cold warriors, however, tells a different story. The camera-shy worker doubts whether the Soviets make contributions for their employees to Austria's medical and pension funds. He also explicitly complains that the Soviet employer forced him to make "voluntary contributions" from his monthly pay to the liberation of South Korea. Both the worker and the USIS-photographer are anonymous and unnamed – they are given no identity in the American caption text. Thus this man becomes representative and iconic of thousands of Austrian workers forced to work in exploitative Soviet USIA enterprises in their Austrian zone. His fleeting image is the opposite of the burly workers exuding confidence in the Western zones.

Figure 23

Figure 24

In contrast to these "workers' heroes" four pictures are juxtaposed from the field of "cultural reconstruction." The USIS photographers do not take shots clearly establishing the identity of Austrian artists. They rather portray them in representative postures on their jobs. Part of the theme is the rebuilding of Vienna's most famous cultural sites. In 1948 the ceiling frescoes of the grand gallery of the Habsburgs' Schönbrunn Summer Palace are restored. The painter Paul Reckendorfer poses in his work place and compares his work with the original model on a slide and half of his face is covered with the magnifying glass he is using to read the slide (Figure 24).

The East Tyrolean sculptor Josef Troyer carved the new Jesus figure for the main cross of St. Stephen's cathedral. When he adjusts the head from the old cross to the new body on March 11, 1953, he is depicted doing his job by kneeling on the floor (Figure 25).

Figure 25

Figure 26

A big group of workers is mounting a 50 square meter ceiling painting in the Upper Belvedere Palace (Figure 26). In the left forefront of the picture we find the restorer and architect Oskar Lautischar. He looks up to the ceiling and pushes up the painting. His face cannot be seen. Lautischar served as the leading restoration man in the Federal Monuments Office. He had finished restoring the painting in 1949 but it could only be reinstalled in the Belvedere Palace after the restoration of the building's substance was completed.
Yoichi Okamoto's symbolical representation of the reconstruction of the famous Vienna Opera House is entirely abstract (Figure 27). In his picture composition of 1952 the ballet's soloists Margaret Bauer and Willy Dirtl serve as the background for the welder with sparks flying in the front center.

Figure 27

Go West Young Man[11]

J. William Fulbright, the U.S. Senator from Arkansas, introduced legislation in the U.S. Congress to start the Fulbright Program to exchange scholars and students. Fulbright designed this international exchange program to both provide academic education and deep cultural immersion in the public and daily life of the host country. The Austrian Fulbright Commission was founded on July 6, 1952, and the first group of "Fulbrighters" were sent in the academic year 1951/52. Many in this first group hailed from prominent Austrian families.[12]

11. The Westernization of Austria and Austrians is covered in Günter Bischof and Anton Pelinka, *The Americanization/Westernization of Austria* (Contemporary Austrian Studies 12) (New Brunswick, NJ: Transaction, 2004).
12. On the Fulbright program see the historical documentary made for the 60th anniversary of the program, *Fulbright at Sixty: The Austrian-American Fulbright Program, 1950-2010*, dir. and ed. Georg Steinböck; script Lonnie R. Johnson and Georg Steinböck, Vienna 2010.

The iconic movie *The Third Man* elevated Vienna into a prominent position. The Fulbright recipients were photographed in easily recognizable public places such as the city's remaining bastions (*Mölkerbastei*), or in front of the Palais Pallavicini on Joseph Square (the captions frequently read (a "*Third Man* house"), where key scenes of the movie were shot. The 21-yar old Josef Krainer stands on top of the bastion, shortly before his embarkation for the crossing of the Atlantic on the *Queen Elisabeth* to study at the University of Georgia in Athens (Figure 28). Krainer's father was the governor of Styria, a position Josef would succeed him in the 1980s.

Figure 28

Figure 29

Figure 30

Close by in Vienna a picture of the art historian Konrad Oberhuber, who would stay in the U.S. for 17 years, was taken (Figure 29). He was appointed director of the world famous graphic art collection *Albertina* in Vienna (1987-99).

A day before his departure to study at Harvard University, Friedrich Gleissner was posted in front of the Palais Pallavicini (Figure 30). His father Heinrich served as long term governor of Upper Austria before and after the war (1934-38, 1945-71). With his Harvard background in economics, Friedrich served as the long-term director of the foreign trade section of the Austrian Chamber of Commerce.

The Austrian Fulbright Commission was housed in Schmidgasse 14 in the Josefstadt district of Vienna. In the summer of 1953 the Fulbright Commission threw a garden party for the third group going to the U.S. in 1953/54 (Figure 31). Jens Tschebull and Egon Sohmen were in this group picture. The former became a prominent journalist in Austria and was a founder of the Austrian news magazine *Profil*. The latter made it to assistant professor of economics at Yale University, with later appointments at the Universities of Saarbrűcken and Heidelberg in Germany. He would make a name for himself as a prominent theorist of exchange rates.

Figure 31

Unlike young Austrians who came to the U.S. with the Fulbright program after the war, before the war many Austrians of Jewish descent managed to survive as refugees in the U.S. and elsewhere. Still, some of them returned to Austria after the war with the Cultural Section of the U.S. occupation element. In spite of the bad memories they harbored about Austrian prewar anti-Semitism, they contributed to Austrian cultural life by returning to their native country with the Americans. One of them was Ernst Haeusserman who would be appointed director of Vienna's *Burgtheater* (1959-68), maybe the premier theater stage in German speaking countries. In 1946 he was the programming director of the radio station *Red-White-Red* and made a program commemorating President Roosevelt. In the USIS-picture he is in an American uniform and directs the actor Raoul Aslan, who reads his script on Roosevelt (Figure 32).

Figure 32

Figure 33

Marcel Prawy, maybe the best known Austrian expert on opera and Viennese operetta, also returned to Vienna after the war as a cultural officer with the U.S. Army. Starting in 1950 he regularly organized cultural events at the Kosmos Theater in Vienna's Neubau district, whose popular programs were supported by the U.S. Cultural Section. Prawy also directed the plays of American authors such as Thornton Wilder and Tennessee Williams not yet known in postwar Austria with a traveling theater company. Above all, he made it his mission to make American musicals popular in Austria. This picture shows Prawy in front of the curtain of the Kosmos Theater displaying a Mississippi paddle wheeler (Figure 33). The program he ran had the fitting heading "From the World of American Operetta: A Trip through the American Musical Scene."

Modernizing Austria?

Austrian newspapers were full of articles about America as "the land of unlimited opportunities." The *Austria Wochenschau* too featured many commentaries and reports on this theme. It may have been a cliché to identify Americanization with modernization. In the first years after the war, however, Austrians easily were persuaded that all innovation in their society hailed from the United States. This is what they heard every day from the very successful U.S. media-and-communications juggernaut in Austria.

The youth of Austria above all embraced Americanization.[13] USIS photographers took many pictures documenting the infatuation of Austria's youth with all things American. On August 29, 1948, the 1st Battalion, 350th Infantry Regiment, organized the first "Soap Box Derby" in Austria with American rules in Vienna's 19th district. Erich Jaksch was among the children and youth participating in this event. He was allowed the wear American uniform for the occasion, with a helmet from the Military Police and all (Figure 34).

In 1949, Austria's first "4-H Club" was started with support from the Marshall Plan. Under the motto "To make the better best" Austrian kids flocked to these 4-H clubs ("4-H" standing for Head, Heart, Hands, Health). Like the symbols of the Olympic rings and the Red Cross, the 4-H logo of

13. Reinhold Wagnleitner, *Coca-Colonization and the Cold War: The Cultural Mission of the United States in Austria After the Second World War* (Chapel Hill: University of North Carolina Press, 1994), Günter Bischof, "Two Sides of the Coin: The Americanization of Austria and Austrian Anti-Americanism," in Alexander Stephan, ed., *The Americanization of Europe: Culture, Diplomacy, and Anti-Americanism after 1945* (New York: Berghahn Books, 2006), 147-81.

the 4-leaf clover was a registered trademark and became an icon. 4-H clubs appealed to the rural youngsters who were inspired to improve their skills in agricultural sciences, especially raising cattle. The appeal for 10 to 25-year olds to join the clubs surely was the generously funded programs of all sorts of leisure activities. During the annual Wels Fair kids, visibly moved by the solemn occasion, stand in front of the dais with honored guests (Figure 35). U.S. General Geoffrey Keyes, the American High Commissioner in Austria, reads their names and showers them with awards and presents.

Figure 34

Figure 35

On May 30, 1950, Austrians experienced the opening of the first self-service grocery store in the land—the supermarket being an American invention.[14] It was a branch of the cooperative *Konsumgenossenschaft* in Upper Austria. The English caption of the picture even speaks of the first "supermarket." Even those who practice traditional customs are interested in such innovation: a gentleman in traditional Austrian *Lederhosen* dress eyes the modern shop window of the new store with considerable interest (Figure 36).

Figure 36

14. Oliver Kühschhelm, "Selbstbedienung und Supermärkte," in: Susanne Breuss, ed., *Die Sinalco-Epoche: Essen, Trinken, Konsumieren nach 1945* (Vienna: Czernin Verlag, 2005), 45-60 see also Victorian de Grazia, *Irresistible Empire: America's Advance through Twentieth-Century Europe* (Cambridge, MA: Harvard University Press, 2006).

Young ladies are viewing the shop window of Vienna's Herzmansky department store on Mariahilferstraße, where "fashion for teenagers" is on display (Figure 37). Being a "teenager" was a new age category and target group for advertisers. Previously they had been categorized as "*Halbwüchsige*" (half-grown-ups).

Figure 37

Figure 38

Up until the year 1950 travel by air to destinations overseas was unknown and an extraordinary adventure. When an 87-year old lady from the Burgenland took a trip to Chicago, Illinois, to visit her relatives, this was only feasible in the Austrian imagination if "the rich uncle in America" paid for the ticket. Such a journey was very rare in April 1949 and the check-in at Vienna's Schwechat airport seems to have been quite relaxed (Figure 38).

Okamoto's Unusual Iconography of Postwar Austrians

Every age produces "typical" specimen in the collective memory of a people who may dominate the historical image of an era for two or three generations. Young Austrians today, however, have no historical memory of the characters that define the public life of the postwar years—black marketers, returning POWs (*Heimkehrer*), ladies cleaning up the rubble in the streets (*Trümmerfrauen*), and occupation soldiers from four different powers.

In all the photographs discussed so far "typical" Austrians have been depicted representing the generations living in the first postwar decade of the four-power occupation of the country. These pictures, however, are not serving a timeless cliché of the era. With these "visual lives" the USIS-photographers rather are presenting a visual narrative within a specific time horizon and historical context. They also have a straightforward political mission in an era defined by the East-West Cold War[15]: their mission was to present a very positive display of American policies in Austria, especially highlighting the benefits of American aid and the Marshall Plan for the Austrian public. They succeeded in doing this both very efficiently and appealingly.

The most important distribution channels for the rich visual imagery provided by the USIS-Pictorial Section were the ten American Information Centers in Austria (America Houses), the radio station *Rot-Weiß-Rot* (with its various magazine outlets), the lavish pictorial section of the daily newspaper *Wiener Kurier*, and above all the Information Office of the Marshall Plan's ECA Mission in Austria. The USIS-Pictorial Section was responsible for the entire production of the regular "*Wiener Kurier Bildbeilage*" (picture section). They shot the pictures, selected the ones to be published, edited them, designed the page-layout and coordinated the press run with the editor and business manager of the *Wiener Kurier*. A one-page spread was dedicated to publicize the Marshall Plan every week. This was subtle but very effective Marshall Plan propaganda.[16]

Organizationally, the ECA Division formed a separate section in the USIS-Pictorial Section. 27 percent of the total man hours expended in the Pictorial Section were devoted to the ECA mission. Add to this the labor of ten stringer photographers distributed throughout Austria, including the Russian zone. In 1950, over 1,800 photographs were taken every month to accomplish the mission of the ECA-Section, namely "to see that pictures to inform the Austrian public of what the ECA is doing are placed as extensively as possible to every available [media] outlet."[17]

What Okamoto wrote about the editorial policies of the *Wiener Kurier Bildbeilage* in his report of August 31, 1950, may stand for the entire policy and basic philosophy of the Pictorial Section of the ECA-Mission in Austria[18]:

1) Always tell the truth in pictures;

2) U.S. propaganda should be subtle, without losing the interest of the reader;

15. On the Cold War in Austria, see James Jay Carafano, *Waltzing into the Cold War. The Struggle for Occupied Austria* (College Station, Texas A&M University Press, 2002); Gűnter Bischof, *The Leverage of the Weak: Austria in the First Cold War, 1945-55* (Basingstoke: Macmillan, 1999).

16. On Marshall Plan propaganda, see the essays in Bischof/Stiefel/Richter, *Images of the Marshall Plan.*

17. Memorandum, Okamoto to Hopman, 31 Aug. 1950, p. 2, Record Group 260, National Archives and Records Administration, College Park, Maryland.

18. Ibid.

3) All picture stories will present a fundamental idea rather than straight reportage (i.e. so that the reader is left with a mental impression of an idea. Therefore an idea in propaganda is more apt to leave a lasting impression) [emphasis in the original];

4) New, modern, and even radical approaches and uses of photo technique to carry on the American tradition of journalistic progressiveness.

Yoichi R. Okamoto was the *spiritus rector* and artistic inspiration of USIS-photographers in postwar Austria. He shaped the political profile and the clearly transparent organizational structure of the Pictorial Section of the USIS picture service. More importantly, his compositional style of shooting pictures greatly influenced the photographers in the entire USIS-Section. Okamoto's gaze of Austria in large part became USIS's gaze.

Okamoto always wanted to capture the core of the human being behind the official role that was impersonated on the occasion. This he tried to accomplish in "home stories" or "personal stories." The subject of the photograph was depicted in a manner that "personalized" important events and subject matters. The traditional representation of a politician in the 1950s would have been sitting on his desk—not Okamoto's gaze. The American photo artist had become a personal friend of the popular Austrian Chancellor Leopold Figl, otherwise Okamoto's intimate visual narrative of more than 50 pictures made in 1952 would not have been possible. Figl is depicted donating blood, having a drink in a wine cellar, or with his hunting rifle in front of his trophy-wall at home (Figure 39).

Figure 39

Figure 40

A visually attractive motive can be repeated. Manfred Mautner-Markhof, Austria's best-known industrialist after the war, is similarly depicted in his living room in front of his numerous hunting trophies (Figure 40).

Okamoto is not shy in utilizing montages of pictures to heighten their visual effect. He likes symmetric arrangements in photos depicting groups of people. The Cultural Office of the City of Vienna just finished judging an USIS-poster prize competition in the fall of 1954. In Okamoto's composition the director of the office Hans Schleinzer is shown in front of the winning artists Hanno Bujatti, Hilde Zenegg, and Peppino Wieternik with their works (Figure 41).

Figure 41

Figure 42

In a similar image (Figure 42) shot in the same year the reporters for the *Rot-Weiß-Rot* radio station are arranged with their ready microphones in the form of a pyramid (Peter Doerre, Ernst Hellebrand, Viktor Fit, and Gerhard Stappen).

The next four pictures were also taken in 1954. Okamoto liked to experiment with tricks and montage techniques in depicting his colleagues in the *Rot-Weiß-Rot* radio station. The star reporter for sports Heribert Meisel is shown in the studio with soccer balls whizzing all around him (Figure 43), while the composer and conductor Alexander Steinbrecher, who directed the station's music programs, is surrounded by telephones, sheets of puzzles, and pencils (Figure 44).

Figure 43

Figure 44

The Austrian Gottfried "Jeff" Rainer was one of Okamoto's best known artist-apprentices. An unusual picture shows Rainer shooting ladies' legs advertising nylons with the well-known actress Nadja Tiller as the model. Okamoto cannot help but document the compositional framing of the entire scene in the studio (Figure 45).

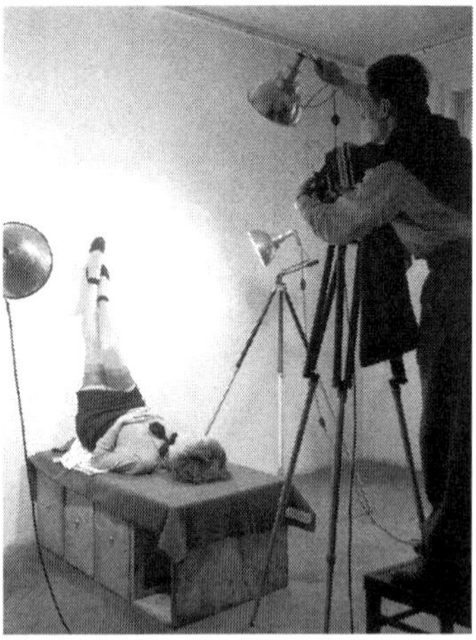

Figure 45

Figure 46

Finally, a team of USIS photographers are shown during one of their regular office meetings. Their boss Yoichi R. Okamoto is shown in typical American fashion unceremoniously placing his foot up on the desk (Figure 46). The group is discussing a set of newly printed pictures. In the background their upcoming schedule is on the wall. They are getting ready to fan out into Vienna for new photo shoots. For a fleeting moment the Austro-American USIS-picture team, documenting with such professional skill and passion the visual lives of Austrians after the war, leaves a lasting impression.

Conclusion

In this concise overview of representative pictures chosen from the USIS-collection one may easily notice a continuous development, namely Americans becoming more familiar with the country and its people every day. In 1945 when "non-fraternization" with the native population was still the order of the day for US military personnel, intimate "home stories" about an Austrian chancellor or a captain of industry would not have been possible. In the first few months of the occupation pictures of people removing the rubble and standing in long lines for the necessities of life are common; individuals submerged in anonymous crowds—the common gate of Austrian humanity—define these early pictures.

With the arrival of the Marshall Plan in Austria, the USIS Pictorial Section changed its mission fundamentally. Now more than a quarter of its staff resources were utilized to document the blessings of Marshall Plan aid in the reconstruction of Austrian industry, agriculture and tourism. The archetypical visual representation of the Marshall Plan in Austria is its modernizing effect on Austria.

In 1948 Yoichi Okamoto took over the USIS-bureau in Vienna—at the time the Marshall Plan got under way. Retrospectively, he was often called the "*chronicler of cultural life in Austria.*" But he and his staff, whom he taught professional photographic skills, also portrayed ordinary workers and craftsmen and their personal recovery as if they were an essential part of Austrian cultural life. Okamoto became friendly with Austrian people and leaders, especially with Leopold Figl. No Austrian media people got access to the Chancellor's private life as did Okamoto. His preference for experimental visual compositions is often documented along with journalistic colleagues from the U.S. Information Service Branch. In his function as chief of the USIS-Pictorial Branch Okamoto shaped both the political profile and mission of his unit. He made it his goal to present via visual means a positive display of American policies in Austria. In the process he also captured the core of the *homo Austriacus* – both his personal stories and his ideas.

During the early Cold War in Austria USIS-photographers changed their photographic style. The fate of individuals became part of a political statement. On the one hand refugees are photographed and their individuality is recorded by name and where they came from. On the other hand "typical Austrians" are portrayed both as representatives of different professions and of Austrian culture and life. Their visual lives in the Western zones are compared and contrasted with the fate of their compatriots in the Russian zone. Between 1945 to 1955, USIS-photographers documented all aspects of Austrian life after World War II and left a rich visual archive of the period for posterity. It was their task to report and document the progress of Austria's recovery and to "sell" via media stories and subtle visual strategies the benefits and the implicit political values of the American aid program to the Austrian, European and American publics at once. USIS-photographs not only preserved a rich memory of postwar Austria. They also established a rich corpus of Austrian visual history and a paradigmatic source for the study of "visual power politics."[19]

19. We suggest to use the concept of "visual power politics" to stress the crucial role that images and visual strategies have played in the construction and implementation of soft power politics.

Balancing Between Autonomy and Dependence Family Farming and Agrarian Change in Lower Austria, 1945–1980

Ernst Langthaler[1]

Conventional View: Peasants into Farmers

"The most dramatic change of the second half of this century, and the one which permanently cuts us off from the world of the past, is the death of the peasantry,"[2] Eric Hobsbawn states in his famous world history of the twentieth century, *Age of Extremes*. There is no doubt that rural society after the Second World War experienced a dramatic change;[3] however, the issue of "de-peasantization" raises serious concern, above all with regard to tendencies of "re-peasantization" in the neo-liberal era.[4] The answer to the question whether the peasantry in Europe and other parts of the world rapidly passed away from the mid-twentieth century onwards or whether it has somehow survived—or even been reborn—depends on how we define the "peasant." According to Eric Wolf, "peasants" are neither "primitives" nor "farmers." What distinguishes them from "primitives" is their subordination to political and economic forces such as bureaucratic nation-states and capitalist markets; what distinguishes them from "farmers" is their focus on agricultural production for household self-consumption rather than entrepreneurial engagement in factor and product markets.[5] Hobsbawm's dictum of the "death of the peasantry" obviously follows this definition;

---

1. This article is a result of the research project *Farming Styles in Austria, 1940s-1980s* (FWF P20922-G15) which was conducted at the Institute of Rural History in St. Pölten from January 2009 to December 2011 (director: Ernst Langthaler, collaborators: Rita Garstenauer, Benjamin Schiemer, Ulrich Schwarz and Sophie Tod). I would like to thank the project collaborators for providing first drafts of the final report; furthermore, my thanks go to Alexander Mejstrik (Geometric Data Analysis) and Reinhard Sieder (Documentary Method) for methodological consulting, as well as Inge Fink of the University of New Orleans English Department for the expert translation from German into English.
2. Eric Hobsbawm, *Age of Extremes: The Short Twentieth Century, 1914-1991* (London: Michael Joseph, 1994), 289.
3. See Ernst Langthaler, "Landwirtschaft vor und in der Globalisierung," in *Globalgeschichte 1800-2010*, eds. Reinhard Sieder and Ernst Langthaler (Vienna: Böhlau, 2010), 135-69.
4. See Jan Douwe van der Ploeg, *The New Peasantries: Struggles for Autonomy and Sustainability in an Era of Empire and Globalization* (London and Sterling, VA: Earthscan, 2008); idem, "The Peasantries of the Twenty-First Century: the Commoditisation Debate Revisited," in *Journal of Peasant Studies* 37, no. 1 (2010): 1-30.
5. See Eric Wolf, *Peasants* (Englewood Cliffs, NJ: Prentice Hall, 1966), 2-3.

the storyline goes something like this: the majority of subsistence-oriented "peasants" disappeared through *proletarization* of land-owning families, i.e. they became wage labourers; the residual minority disappeared through *accumulation* of land and capital, i.e. they became commercial "farmers" (in capitalist countries) or "production cooperatives" (in socialist countries), both closely tied to the agribusiness complex.[6] The conversion of "peasants" into "farmers" in the second half of the twentieth century has also been widely adopted by Austrian historiographers; to quote a recent handbook, "aus Bauern wurden agrartechnisch orientierte Farmer."[7]

The master narrative of post-war agrarian change, rooted in the debates on the "agrarian question" (*Agrarfrage*) in Europe from the late-nineteenth century onwards,[8] is to be questioned from different angles. First of all, the storyline of rural "class differentiation"[9] does not fit perfectly with empirical data on agrarian change in post-war Austria. As late as 1960, most of the agricultural area consisted of small and medium family farms; nearly two thirds of the farm holders managed less than 10 hectares.[10] Though the concentration of farmland slightly rose in the following decades, the decline of the number of farms, as well as the increase of the agricultural area per farm between 1960 and 1980, was below average compared to other industrialized countries (Table 1). In addition to the empirical evidence, the theory of the history of everyday life (*Alltagsgeschichte*) reveals that the master narrative outlined above undervalues or even ignores the fact that individual and collective actors' agency vis-à-vis the political and economic forces of agrarian "structural change" (*Strukturwandel*) played a crucial role.[11] Proponents of both empirical and theoretical considerations argue against conceptualizing agrarian change in post-war Austria as a one-way

6. See Henry Bernstein, *Class Dynamics of Agrarian Change* (Halifax and Sterling, VA: Fernwood and Kumarian, 2010).

7. Ernst Hanisch, *Der lange Schatten des Staates. Österreichische Gesellschaftsgeschichte im 20. Jahrhundert* (Vienna: Ueberreuter, 1994), 100. However, other passages of the book argue more ambivalently (ibid., 61): "Es war weniger der Typus 'Bauer,' der verschwand – auch wenn er sich mehr in Richtung 'Farmer' und 'Nebenerwerbsbauer' entwickelte –, es war die ländliche Unterschicht, Knecht und Dirn, die von den anderen Sektoren aufgesogen wurde." On agricultural development in twentieth century Austria in general see Ernst Bruckmüller et al., *Geschichte der österreichischen Land- und Forstwirtschaft im 20. Jahrhundert*, 2 vols. (Vienna: Ueberreuter, 2002-03).

8. See Karl Kautsky, *The Agrarian Question* (Winchester, MA: Zwan Publications, 1988 [1899]).

9. See Bernstein, *Agrarian Change*, 104-12.

10. See Österreichisches Statistisches Zentralamt (ÖSTAT), ed., *Republik Österreich 1945-1995* (Vienna: Österreichische Staatsdruckerei, 1995), 176.

11. See Alf Lüdtke, ed., *The History of Everyday Life: Reconstructing Historical Experiences and Ways of Life* (Princeton, NJ: Princeton University Press, 1995).

street to accumulation and proletarization, according to the dictum "get big or get out" (*Wachsen oder Weichen*).[12] We had better re-conceptualize agrarian change with regard to the many ways in which farming systems[13] and their corresponding farming styles[14] developed in the spectrum between productivist and non-productivist thought and action.[15] In short, the crucial question with regard to agrarian change in post-war Austria is not why the peasantry passed away, but why relatively large fractions of it survived longer than they did elsewhere. The search for an answer inevitably takes us to a more realist notion of farming families beyond the ideal-typical dichotomy of "peasant" and "farmer."

Table 1: Agrarian change in selected industrialized countries, 1960-80

Country	number of farms (in 1,000)			agricultural area per farm (in hectares)		
	1960	1980	index (1960=100)	1960	1980	index (1960=100)
Austria	397	303	76	10.2	12.1	119
Denmark	194	120	62	16.1	24.3	151
France	1,994	1.262	63	17.3	25.2	146
German (FRG)	1,618	928	57	8.8	14.2	162
Italy	4,294	3,532	82	4.3	5.0	116
Japan	6,057	4,661	77	1.0	1.2	117
The Netherlands	301	143	48	7.7	14.2	185
Spain	3,008	2,134	71	10.9	14.8	135
UK	396	281	71	50.2	65.7	131
USA	3,711	2,227	60	118.6	193.2	163
Total	21,970	15,591	71	26.2	35.7	136

Source: own calculations according to Hayami and Ruttan, *Agricultural Development*, 457–465; the figures for Austria have been corrected according to ÖSTAT, ed., *Republik Österreich*, 175.

This actor-centered concept of agrarian change, which is both empirically and theoretically grounded, has far-reaching methodological consequences: rather than aggregated data referring to abstract entities (communes, regions, nation-states etc.), we need disaggregated sources

12. The phrase "get big or get out" was coined by the US-American Secretary of Agriculture Ezra Taft Benson in the 1950s. One of his successors in the 1970s, Earl Butz, proclaimed in a similar way: "adopt or die." See Paul Roberts, *The End of Food: The Coming Crisis of the World Food Industry* (London: Bloomsbury, 2008), 120. On the synonymous German dictum *Wachsen oder Weichen* see Hermann Priebe, *Die subventionierte Unvernunft: Landwirtschaft und Naturhaushalt (*Berlin: Siedler, 1985), 86.

13. See John S. Caldwell, "Farming Systems," in *Encyclopedia of Agricultural Science*, vol. 2, eds. Charles J. Arntzen and Ellen M. Ritter (San Diego: Academic Press, 1994), 129-38.

14. See Jan Douwe van der Ploeg, *The Virtual Farmer: Past, Present and Future of the Dutch Peasantry* (Assen: Royal van Gorcum, 2003), 101-41.

15. See Geoff A. Wilson, *Multifunctional Agriculture: A Transition Theory Perspective* (Wallingford and Cambridge, MA: CABI publishing, 2007), 271-320.

tracing everyday practices of concrete actors. Moreover, we need to analyze these sources with the aid of mixed methods, therefore exploring both quantitative and qualitative aspects of agrarian change. This is the methodological design the following case study adopts. It draws on two sets of sources: first, a series of farm files (*Betriebskarten*) with farm-level data (land use, livestock, machinery, labor force, yields etc.) from the 1940s to the 1980s;[16] second, a couple of narrative interviews with farm owners of both sexes from different generations.[17] Both sets of sources refer to two regions in the province of Lower Austria, broadly covering the spectrum of agricultural landscapes in post-war Austria: the Mank region in the hilly and mountainous area between the northern fringe of the Alps and the Danube valley and the Mödling region in the basin south of the city of Vienna. A combination of quantitative (Geometric Data Analysis)[18] and qualitative methods (Documentary Method)[19] enables the assessment of agrarian change from different perspectives, long shots as well as close ups. The results of this investigation call for a revision of the picture of agrarian change in post-war Austria as outlined by conventional historiography.

Long Shot: Family Farming Systems

The farms we investigated in the Mank and Mödling regions can be ordered with regard to their similarities and differences in a multi-dimensional space of agrosystems: the more they resemble each other, the closer they are; the more they differ from each other, the further apart from each other they are. The most important spatial dimension, first and foremost a representation of the choice of region, indicates the embedding of agrosystems into their natural environment; it marks the advantages and disadvantages of the farms' locations with regard to topography and traffic

16. See Niederösterreichisches Landesarchiv (NÖLA), inventories *Bezirksbauernkammer Mank* and *Mödling*, boxes *Hof- und Betriebskarten*. The farm file surveys 1944/46, 1952, 1959/69, 1970/71 and 1982/83 of ten communes in the two regions were fed into an Access database (subsequently Farming Styles Database) from which 3,561 datasets of farming units were exported to be analysed with XLSTAT.

17. Twenty-seven narrative interviews with former, current and designated owners of family farms of both sexes were conducted in the regions of Mank and Mödling during winter 2010/11. The quotations refer to the transcriptions of the digital recordings which were analysed with Atlas.ti.

18. See Brigitte Le Roux and Henry Rouhanet, *Geometric Data Analysis: From Correspondence Analysis to Structured Data Analysis* (New York: Kluwer Academic Publishers, 2004).

19. See Ralf Bohnsack, Iris Nentwig-Gesemann und Arnd-Michael Nohl, eds., *Die dokumentarische Methode und ihre Forschungspraxis: Grundlagen qualitativer Sozialforschung*, 2nd ed. (Wiesbaden: Verlag für Sozialwissenschaften, 2007).

infrastructure, as well as the resulting focuses of land and livestock use. The farm holders in the Mödling region, such as those in the community of Guntramsdorf, find themselves in a relatively advantageous location. They enjoy a warm, dry climate with a growing season of more than 250 days; the hilly terrain, as well as the proximity to the Vienna market, supports an intensive use of the land for viticulture, root cropping, and grain farming. Areas like the community of Plankenstein in the Mank region, which are located higher up in the mountains and further away from the railroad line, are situated less fortunately. The cool and moist climate, a growing season of barely more than 200 days per year, topographical inclines that can be extreme in some cases, and a tentative connection to the traffic infrastructure force the mountain farmers to use the land more extensively through grassland farming and forestry; the considerable number of cattle and dairy cows is proportional to the weight of feed grown on the land.[20] All in all, the first dimension of the space of agrosystems includes the natural and transportation-related conditions, which curtail the farm holders' leeways with regard to land and livestock use.

The second dimension concerns the embedding of agrosystems into the social environment, the years and decades of the "farm expansion" (*Betriebsaufstockung*), as contemporary jargon would have it, of the farms' resource base through factor markets. The farm holders go about expansion in two ways: initially, they increase the machinery, especially tractors, in absolute numbers and relative to the farmland. This capital intensive or "internal expansion" goes hand in hand with an extensive or "external expansion" through farm enlargement,[21] which comprises both agricultural area and livestock.[22] Farm expansion through factor markets for capital, land, and livestock extends to product markets through the agro-industrial processing of cash crops, such as sugar beets in the Mödling region and

20. On the natural and transport conditions as well as land and livestock use in the two regions see Erik Arnberger, ed., *Atlas von Niederösterreich (und Wien)* (Vienna: Freytag-Berndt und Artaria, 1951-58), fol. 12 (relief), 14-21 (climate and phenology), 22-23 (soil types), 66-94 (agriculture and forestry), 106-110 (railways and streets).
21. On the definition of "external" and "internal expansion" (*innere* and *äußere Aufstockung*) see Hansueli Herrmann, *Bauern im Wandel: Agrarischer Strukturwandel, bäuerliches Verhalten und bewusstseinsmässige Verarbeitung am Beispiel einer Agglomerationsgemeinde* (Küssnacht ZH) 1945-1980 (Zurich: Chronos, 1990), 59-60. Accordingly, "internal expansion" means more intensive uses of land and livestock; "external expansion" means farm enlargement. Additionally, we have also included the machinery in this definition.
22. See Robert Eastwood, Michael Lipton and Andrew Newell, "Farm Size," in *Handbook of Agricultural Economics*, vol. 4, eds. Prabhu Pingali and Robert Evenson (Amsterdam: Elsevier, 2010), 3323-97; Prabhu Pingali, "Agricultural Mechanization," in *Handbook of Agricultural Economics*, vol. 3, eds. Robert Evenson and idem (Amsterdam: Elsevier, 2007), 2779-2805.

fed cattle in the Mank region. In short, the second dimension of the space of agrosystems consists of the bundle of interdependent aspects of capital intensification, farm concentration, and specialization,[23] which restrict the farm holders' leeways and push them toward market-dependency.[24]

While the first two dimensions of the multi-dimensional space describe the external relationship between agrosystems and the natural and social environment, the third most important spatial dimension refers to internal connections: the internal integration of the farms' resource flows.[25] Small-scale agrosystems with a low rate of integration—viticulture in the Mödling region, part-time farming in the Mank region—form a contrast to large-scale farming, which integrates arable with stock farming, often in combination with the employment of farmhands, a system characteristic of the community of Achau in the Mödling region and the community of Bischofstetten in the Mank region. Farms with strong internal integration boast many resources: they grow lots of grain, especially bread grain; they raise cattle and horses; they employ many workers, especially male and female farmhands. Quality complements quantity: these resources are internally renewed through the production of organic manure to fertilize plants, through the production of food crops to feed humans and animals, through the breeding of horses, fed cattle, and dairy cows, and through the recruitment of workers through networks of family, kinship, and neighborhood. Despite its self-sufficiency, large-scale mixed farming is market oriented as a large surplus of plant and animal products, including cash crops such as sugar beets, are sold. However, the self-controlled (re-) production of much of the farm's material and energy base through the internal recycling of resources makes it less dependent on the market and thus the state and increases the farm holders' rooms of maneuver.[26] Up until the middle of the century, the owners of such large-scale farms were often regarded (by themselves and others) as "gentlemen farmers" (*Herrenbauern*), whose autonomy derived from their local and regional status as owners of land and horses and as employers of the rural population, as well as from their reserved attitude toward supra-regional dependency on political-economic forces.[27]

23. See Brian Ilbery and Ian Bowler, "From agricultural productivism to post-productivism," in *The Geography of Rural Change*, ed. Brian Ilbery (London: Longman, 1998), 57-84.
24. See van der Ploeg, *Virtual Farmer*, 55-57.
25. On the debate on "integration" as a couterpart of "industrialization" in the 1970s see Hans Bach, *Landbau und Umwelt: Industrialisierung der Agrarwirtschaft oder integrierter Landbau*, Schriftenreihe des Institutes für Raumordnung und Umweltgestaltung 6 (Linz: Trauner, 1978).
26. See van der Ploeg, *Virtual Farmer*, 55-57.
27. On the type of the "gentleman farmer" (*Herrenbauer*) see Norbert Ortmayr, "Ländliches Gesinde in Oberösterreich 1918-1938," in *Familienstruktur und Arbeitsorganisation in*

The three most important dimensions of the multi-dimensional space—(un-)favorable location, farm expansion, and internal integration—come together to determine the character of a farming system: the external relationship with its natural and social environment and its internal dynamics.[28] Seen from this perspective, an agrosystem is an area of tension where the "powers of one-sidedness" (*Kräfte der Einseitigkeit*, e.g. topography and traffic infrastructure), the "powers of multi-sidedness" (*Kräfte der Vielseitigkeit*, e.g. the equilibrium of fertilizer, feed, and work) and the "powers of economic development" (*Kräfte der Wirtschaftsentwicklung*, e.g. technological innovations) interact with each other.[29] Each one of these aspects determines the corridors between non-productivist and productivist thinking and acting: on the one hand, the better the location of a farm, the more independent it is from markets, and the more it is internally integrated, the more leeways the farm holder has to manage his or her resources. On the other hand, an unfortunate location, increased dependence on markets, and weakened internal integration restrict the opportunities for farm development.[30] In a historical perspective, it seems that from the mid-1940s to the 1980s, the trend toward market-dependent farm expansion increased while internal integration declined; as a result, the farm holders' rooms of maneuver must have constricted during this time. However, this is still a rough sketch; fine grained views of the space of agrosystems give a more detailed picture (Figure 1).

Let us start with the field that is suspended between the first and second dimension and that shows the three-dimensional space of agrosystems from the front; it depicts the interplay between (un-)fortunate location and farm expansion. The diagonals refer to the ideal-typical horizons of farm development: the *viable farm* (*entwicklungsfähiger Betrieb*), the focus of the agrarian-technocratic discourse in the 1960s, is to be found on the upper left; its opposite, the *vulnerable farm* (*Notstandsbetrieb*), on the lower right; the *developed farm in an unfavorable location* on the upper right; the *underdeveloped farm in a favorable location* on the lower left.[31]

ländlichen Gesellschaften, eds. Josef Ehmer and Michael Mitterauer (Vienna: Böhlau, 1986), 325–416; Karl Kaser and Karl Stocker, *Bäuerliches Leben in der Oststeiermark seit 1848*, vol. 2: *Die verspätete Revolution* (Vienna: Böhlau, 1988), 50-57.

28. See Ernst Langthaler, "Agrarsysteme ohne Akteure? Sozialökonomische und sozialökologische Modelle in der Agrargeschichte," in *Grüne Revolutionen: Agrarsysteme und Umwelt im 19. und 20. Jahrhundert,* eds. Andreas Dix and Ernst Langthaler, Jahrbuch für Geschichte des ländlichen Raumes 3 (Innsbruck: Studienverlag, 2006), 216-38.

29. See Bernd Andreae, *Betriebsformen in der Landwirtschaft* (Stuttgart: Ulmer, 1964), 16-31.

30. See van der Ploeg, *Virtual Farmer*, 55–57.

31. On the "viable farm" (*entwicklungsfähiger Betrieb*) as an ideal of Austrian agrarian structural policy in the 1960s and 1970s see Melanie Kröger, *Die Modernisierung der Landwirtschaft: Eine vergleichende Untersuchung der Agrarpolitik Deutschlands und Österreichs*

The cloud of dots refers to the real expressions of farming systems; its margins—the corridors of the pathways of farm development—shift in several stages: in 1944/46 we see a regionally balanced distribution, with the farms in the favorable Mank locations sticking out with regard to size and mechanization. By 1952, we see a significant imbalance in favor of technologically developed medium-sized and large farms in the plains and hills of Mödling; by 1959/60, this balance has increased further, probably as a result of the active real-estate market in the Vienna region. By 1970/71, and consecutively by 1982/83, the catch-up development of Mank farms, especially those in favorable locations, established some balance. However, increasing farm expansion and the resulting dependency on factor and product

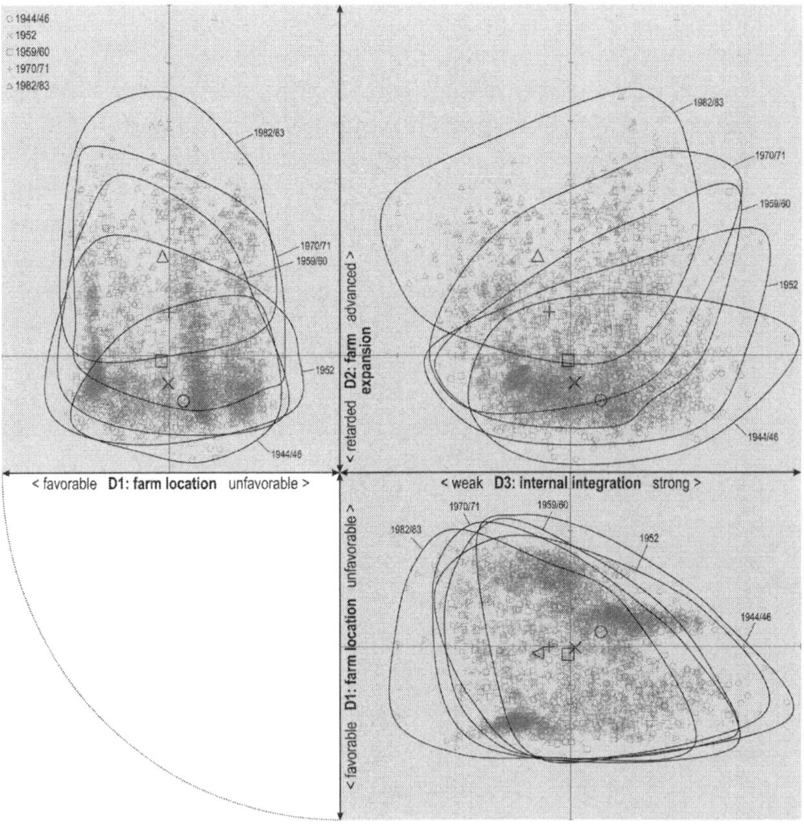

Figure 1: The space of agrosystems in the regions of Mank and Mödling, 1944/46–1982/8, source: Principal Components Analysis (data matrix: 60 variables over 3.561 investigations) based upon the Farming Styles Database.

---

nach 1945 (Berlin: Logos, 2006), 301-311.

markets narrowed the leeways for farm development, especially in unfavorable locations; this is shown in the columnar compression of farms toward the top. On the other hand, farms less oriented toward mechanization and expansion found additional room to move; this can be seen in the even distribution at the bottom. All in all, the distance between the "pioneers" and the "laggards" of the productivist transition increased through the decades.

The field suspended by the third and second dimension opens the side view of the three-dimensional space; here the relationship between internal integration and farm expansion becomes clear. The diagonal lines refer to *internal expansion* on the upper left as the productivist horizon per se; the *old peasant economy* as its opposite on the lower right; *external expansion* on the upper right; and the *old smallholder economy* on the lower left. Between these ideal types, the dots, which indicate the real characteristics of agrosystems, show an apparently paradoxical interplay: on the one hand, the large mixed-farming operations expanded most aggressively from the 1950s on; their quantitative and qualitative resources gave them a head start in the first phase of their campaign for mechanization. On the other hand, through the decades, they slowly but steadily moved away from the agrarian mixed-farming profile. However, the growing gap between self-controlled, labor-intensive internal and dependent, capital-intensive market integration did not lead to "get big or get out"; the productivist vanishing point of maximal expansion and minimal internal integration remained an elusive ideal. On the contrary, many farms managed to navigate the widening gap between these issues; those with moderate to strong internal integration accumulated the most land, livestock, and machines.

The field formed by the third and first dimension shows the three-dimensional space of agrosystems from above; here internal integration and farm location work together. The diagonals indicate the ideal types of *part-time farming in unfavorable locations* on the upper left; *full-time mixed farming in favorable locations* on the lower right; *mixed farming in unfavorable locations* on the upper right; and *specialization in favorable locations* on the lower left. The dots from the years in which the data was collected show an extremely uneven, triangular distribution of real agrosystems. As early as 1944/46, an almost impenetrable barrier restricted the possibilities for expansion for Mank farms in mountain locations; during the next decades, as technology replaced human and animal labor, this barrier moved slowly in the direction of weakened internal integration. The integration of arable farming and animal husbandry, which gave a good deal of autonomy to medium-sized and large farms in the plains, did not thrive in the mountains. The farms' dependency on unfavorable topography and transportation infrastructure limited their room to maneuver, but not completely. Mountain farming families sought to strengthen internal integration—and thus their ability to control their own resources—by growing feed and breeding young cattle. In addition, the integration of individual family members in the industrial labor market partially compensated for the farm's unfavorable location as a part of the wages was re-invested in the family operation.

Close Ups: Family Farming Styles

The overview of the space of agrosystems has revealed the ways in which farms developed. In two case studies, I will now examine the paths taken by farming actors in their daily work, and the management styles they used, in greater detail.[32] In the mid-1940s, the Huber[33] family farm in Plankenstein in the Mank region, situated about 500 meters above sea level and twelve kilometers from the next train station, showed typical characteristics of a mountain farm: 18.3 hectares of cultivated land—six tenth pasture, three tenth fields, and one tenth forest—and 11.4 units of livestock—twelve heads of cattle, including two oxen and six dairy cows, some pigs, sheep, and two dozen laying hens—put the farm in the medium-sized category. While labor-saving machines were lacking, the owner couple did all the manual labor with two farmhands, one male, the other female; occasionally, day laborers would help out. Annually, the farm produced about twenty hundredweights of hay, 6,000 liters of milk, and occasionally some wood for the market; the rest of the production, including three to four pigs for slaughter, served the needs of the people and animals on the farm. Until the beginning of the 1950s, the farm had retained its shape: it had become a family enterprise, consisting of the farm holder's wife—the farm holder, an alcoholic, had died prematurely—, two sons, and a daughter. The production of rye and oats had increased, and two draft horses had joined the oxen in the stable. In all other ways, however, the use of land and livestock and the—very modest—amount of machinery were the same as they had been at the end of the war.

However, in 1954, a disastrous fire that consumed the house and barn severely tested the family's improvisational skills. In this emergency situation, the neighborhood network showed its mettle: man and beast found shelter in neighboring farms; and the neighbors lent the family machines and tools for daily tasks. In the meantime, the farm owner

32. Criteria of selection were, first, the continuity of farming from the mid-1940s to the mid-1980s and, second, the agrosystemic diversity of the cases.
33. The actual name was replaced by a pseudonym.

planned the reconstruction of the buildings, supported by the son who was designated to take over the farm. Because the insurance money did not cover the cost of reconstruction, the family had to take out a mortgage. Besides the client and the builder, the reconstruction of the stable involved other people—neighbors, presumably, who took a lively interest—as the later wife of the heir to the property remembers: "The Schmoll [builder] had been planning a larger farmstead. [...] the others cried out and said, you can never pay for that. [...] Now he has made the whole thing smaller." To a farmer's daughter from the more technologically advanced plains, the mountain world she had married into seemed to be hopelessly behind the times. Her perception of the backwardness had its effects: rebuilding the stable smaller for twelve heads of cattle and two horses turned out to be an obstacle later on; "in ten years, it was too small."[34] This story illustrates the ambivalent nature of personal networks in the countryside: they provide a family with vital resources in emergency situations, but also control the extent of the investments.

By the end of the 1950s, the farm, now at the point of being handed over to the heirs, showed subtle signs of change: the family had slightly expanded the amount of farmland at the cost of pasture land; the livestock had increased by adding more dairy cows, pigs, and chickens; small machines, among them an electric motor, had been added. Overall, however, the farming system resembled the one of two decades ago very closely. The change in management started in 1960, when the "machine-crazy"[35] adult son and his wife took over the farm. The young couple changed the use of the land completely: they significantly increased their farm by leasing fields; they increased pastureland—especially meadows—at the cost of farmland; on the remaining farmland, they grew wheat and barley because oats were no longer needed once they stopped keeping horses. Moreover, they doubled their herd of dairy cows, increasing it to 12 cows. The expansion of land and livestock was driven by the acquisition of machines, and especially of a tractor by means of a low-interest loan, a move derided by the neighbors. Together with a tube milking plant, a manure spreader, a forage wagon, and other machines, they created a fully mechanized grassland farm. The farm holder's wife explains the connection as a "chain" between mechanization and expansion: "the machines had to be paid for, didn't they? Now you had to increase your livestock, [...] you had to make more money."[36] In short, the tractor, like a Trojan horse,[37] smuggled in the need for farm expansion.

34. Interview with E. D. on 27 January 2011, transcription, 75.
35. Interview with M. H. on 15 February 2011, transcription, 27.
36. Interview with E. D. on 27 January 2011, transcription, 37.
37. See Pierre Bourdieu, *Wie die Kultur zum Bauern kommt: Über Bildung, Schule und Politik*

In the 1960s, growth took off on the Huber farm. Besides the quantity of resources, the quality of using them counted as well. Because the farming couple were careful about keeping their stables clean, they escaped the epidemic of bovine tuberculosis, which forced their neighbors to renew their livestock. Soon, however, the farm had reached the limits of its expansion: the additional cattle filled the stable to capacity and forced its eventual enlargement; in addition, there was no more pastureland available for lease, which would have served as fodder for the cattle. The "chain" between mechanization and expansion grew taut and threatened to choke the farming family. To earn additional income, the man took a job in the timber industry and offered other farmers his machine services for a fee. In addition, his family tried to limit their expenses as much as they could; because, as his wife tells it, money was a "rare commodity," she made her daughters' clothes herself.[38]

However, the problem of expansion could not be solved by means of working part-time jobs and limiting consumer expenses. The family sought the advice of an expert; and the advisor from the chamber of agriculture, who had already brokered the loan for the tractor, had a solution: "internal" instead of "external expansion." He advised the farm owners to join a cattle-breeding syndicate to increase the dairy cow's productivity through breeding methods. This brought higher yields in their own stable but also insured that their young livestock sold at top prices (Figure 2).[39] This course of action determined the management style of the farming couple, which has, by now, become middle-aged, until the beginning of the 1980s: they expanded their pastures yet again by leasing more land; they expanded their livestock, especially young female cattle for breeding; they purchased a still more powerful tractor, in addition to other machines. The fully mechanized, expanded farm, specializing in dairy production and the breeding of dairy cattle, became a sign of economic advancement for its owners, an accomplishment that seemed even more glamorous in contrast with the bleak 1950s. The farm holder's wife, now grown old, proudly summarizes their accomplishments: in 1960, she and her husband started out with seven heads of cattle; three decades later, they handed over 50 heads to their daughter and son in law. However, the economic gain came at a great social cost; they paid for their advancement with "work"—a term indicating increased effort and a lower standard of living.[40]

(Hamburg: Junius, 2001), 16.

38. Interview with E. D. on 27 January 2011, transcription, 12.

39. Interview with E. D. on 27 January 2011, transcription, 93.

40. Interview with E. D. on 27 January 2011, transcription, 40.

Figure 2: Franz Huber presenting one of his breeding heifers at an auction of cattle, 1972, source: Huber private collection, Plankenstein.

Let us now turn to Guntramsdorf in the Mödling region, where the gentle slopes of the Vienna Woods meet the Vienna Basin. There, at about 200 meters above sea level, close to the railroad, the Meier[41] family owned a "beautiful farm." 48.8 hectares of farmland—almost all of it the best arable land with a patch of pasture—and 15.9 units of livestock—four horses, twelve heads of cattle, among them five dairy cows, eight breeding and feeding pigs, one sheep and a dozen chickens—formed a sizable basis of resources. After the owner of the farm had lost his life at the end of the war, under circumstances which were never fully explained, his son, with the help of the widow and a daughter, managed the farm; they employed two male farmhands. A sizeable number of machines stood at the ready—tractor, reaper-binder, electrical motor, etc. Even though we lack exact numbers as to the farm's market production, we assume that it consisted of a mix of bread grain and milk as sources of income; the modest number of pigs indicates that they were probably used to feed the multi-person household. At the beginning of the 1950s, the young farm leader took a decisive step in the direction of cash-crop production: he increased the farm's arable land by several hectares, promoted the production of grain, especially barley, (re-)

41. The actual name was replaced by a pseudonym.

introduced sugar beets, and greatly expanded his livestock, especially the number of dairy cows and pigs. At the same time, he more than doubled the machinery; he purchased a second tractor and the first combine (Figure 3).

Figure 3: Franz Meier with members of his family operating the new tractor-drawn combine, around 1952, source: Meier private collection, Guntramsdorf.

His sister had already got a small vineyard; as a result, she could no longer work on her brother's farm. So he employed a milker in addition to the two farmhands and, at peak times, hired four day laborers to get the work done. This "big leap" was followed by a period of high-level consolidation until 1959/60: even though a vineyard was added, the overall area of the farm declined slightly; in the fields, sugar beets replaced potatoes and fodder beets entirely; the livestock, despite the focus on feeding horses and pigs, had declined because the family no longer kept dairy cows; a number of machines were added.

The expansion and consolidation of the farm in the late 1940s and 1950s, to a great extent, was the result of the farm owner's aptness at applying his resources with maximum added value to the product markets: by renting out his machines' labor and transportation services outside of the farm, such as in the reconstruction of factories destroyed by the war, he brought in additional income; the sale of wine, milk, and meat to local distributors, to customers in the farm-owned pub, and to consumers in the largely urban and industrialized region made even better profits. Deftly, the farm owner took advantage of market regulations, which were more rigid with regard to grain and milk than to meat; he focused on the areas with the largest negotiation margins, without however giving up any of his other endeavors. The great gusto with which he negotiated business deals face-to-face with his business partners is still part of the stories he tells today: "in the old days, we sat down together, the butcher and I, and made deals. I demanded this much, he demanded that much. Then we found out who was the better tactician."[42] The division of labor with his mother and sisters at first, then with his wife, who managed the house and stable, as well as hiring farmhands for the field work, which was already mostly mechanized, allowed the young farm owner to pursue his passion for market activities. His virtuosity in finding profitable opportunities on the product markets served an important function besides his intentions of finding a "good bargain," namely to limit the risks on the factor markets. For example, he financed his large machine purchases not through expansive bank loans but paid for them with his accumulated savings. His son sums up his father's strategy: "we never took out a loan to buy a machine. If we didn't have the money, we waited a year, didn't we? And if we had the money, we made sure to get the best product on the market at the time. And then we used it for a very long time."[43]

At the beginning of the 1970s, it became clear that the consolidation of the 1950s was but a moment of rest before another "leap forward": the cultivated area—almost entirely arable land for bread grain, barley, and sugar beets; the rest vineyards—had grown some more. The livestock had almost doubled to about 5,000 hens through the addition of an egg farm—the source of the oldest daughter's income—and a pig feeding plant with over 100 pigs; as the retired farm holder puts it today, the lucrative business of selling eggs and pork to corporate and private clients "drove away" the farm's cattle in the long run.[44] In order to manage this enormous expansion with two full-time workers, the married couple, and the help of the growing children, the farm owners pushed toward the full mechanization of the farm, which now boasted four tractors. In addition, they tried to minimize the risk of debt by not taking out loans for new purchases and by using machines as long as possible.

Farm and family were inextricably linked in the Meier's management style. The accumulation of land served the purpose of providing a living for the five children—vineyards and lots on which to build their homes for the daughters, farmland for the sons. Up until the early 1980s, the Meier dynasty had divided its land into three operations to save on taxes: the father

42. Interview with F. G. on 14 December 2011, transcription, 13.
43. Interview with F. G. jr. on 14 December 2011, transcription, 13.
44. Interview with F. G. on 14 December 2011, transcription, 21.

still managed the central farm with 41.4 hectares of arable land—mostly grain and sugar beet fields, some vineyards—and 20.1 units of livestock—laying hens and feeding pigs. The oldest son owned a grain and sugar beets farm without any livestock of 19.1 hectares, half of which was leased. The second-oldest son managed an equally livestock-free wine and grain farm of 4.9 hectares, most of which was leased. The three formally independent operations were held together by the informal net of cooperation between the father and his two sons, especially with regard to machine usage. This network was strongest in the first two of the three operations; they practically formed a unit with a fluent change of generations in farm management. So far, this last act of a decades-long family farm development lets us conclude that the Meiers made no difference between farm economy and family politics; they considered making a profit in the markets not as an end in itself but as a means to equip the family members with resources that would need effort and gain income.

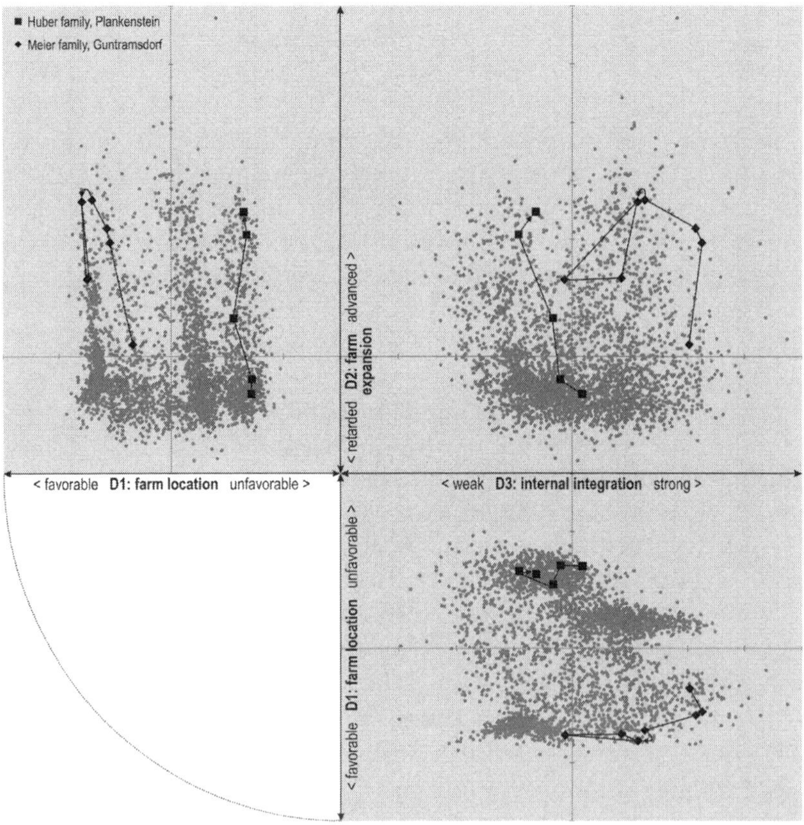

Figure 4: Development pathways of the Huber and Meier farms, 1944/46-1982/83, source: Principal Components Analyses (data matrix: 60 variables over 3.561 investigations) based upon the Farming Styles Database.

The Huber and Meier family farms took different paths in the space of agrosystems (Figure 4). The Huber farm was located in a relatively unfavorable place (dimension 1). However, the farm grew steadily, first through "external" and then through "internal expansion," accommodated by increasing mechanization; the "big leap" in this direction happened in the 1960s, when the young farming couple made drastic changes in farm management (dimension 2). In the course of expansion, the farm's initial medium degree of internal integration diminished slightly (dimension 3). By comparison, the Meier farm started out with better location and traffic conditions (dimension 1). The accumulation of land, livestock, and machines in the late 1940s and 1950s was followed, in the 1960s, by a clear turn in the direction of specialized egg and pork farming, a trend that continued in the 1970s in the division of the farm between the father and his two sons (dimension 2). The initially high internal integration of the cattle-heavy farm diminished rapidly over the course of the decades (dimension 3). Of course, the two cases do not represent all farms, especially not those that ceased to operate in the course of time; but they show different styles of farming—*labor-based internal expansion* in the case of the Huber farm, *family-oriented market sovereignty* in the case of the Meier farm. These styles probably influenced the thought and action in other cases where the family managed to continue the existence of the farm over decades.

Revised Picture: Resilience Through Hybridity

The crucial question this article tried to answer is why the peasantry—which was rhetorically sentenced to death by the advocates of liberal or socialist modernization from the late-nineteenth century onwards and by current mainstream historiography—survived the post-war agrarian change in surpisingly high numbers. A long shot of a number of family farming systems in two Lower Austrian regions and two close-ups of farming styles of two land-owning families have revealed the actors' everyday struggle for survival (as seen from the point of view of practice theory)[45] or the resilience of their farm-household systems (as regarded from the perspective of systems theory).[46] Accordingly, for explaining and understanding the actor-induced resilience of family farming systems, two

45. See James C. Scott, *Weapons of the Weak: Everyday Forms of Peasant Resistance* (New Haven: Yale University Press, 1985).
46. See Fikret Berkes and Carl Folke, eds., *Linking Social and Ecological Systems: Management Practices and Social Mechanisms for Building Resilience* (Cambridge: Cambridge University Press, 1998).

flows of resources have to be taken into account: first, the external upstream and downstream flows of commodities from and to markets; second, the internal (re-)production of a self-controlled resource base (Figure 5).[47] The resilience of the family farming system depends on the relation between these resource flows and the corresponding "modes of ordering"[48]: the more subordination to factor and product markets gains hegemony, the more class differentiation between accumulation and proletarization takes effect; vice versa, the more the farm's self-controlled resource base is strengthened, the more the family members are able to cope with unfavorable conditions of the political-economic system in their life-worlds. Accordingly, the resilient family farming system in bureaucratic and capitalist environments resembles a *Stehaufmännchen*; metaphorically speaking, *family farms wobble, but they don't fall down*.

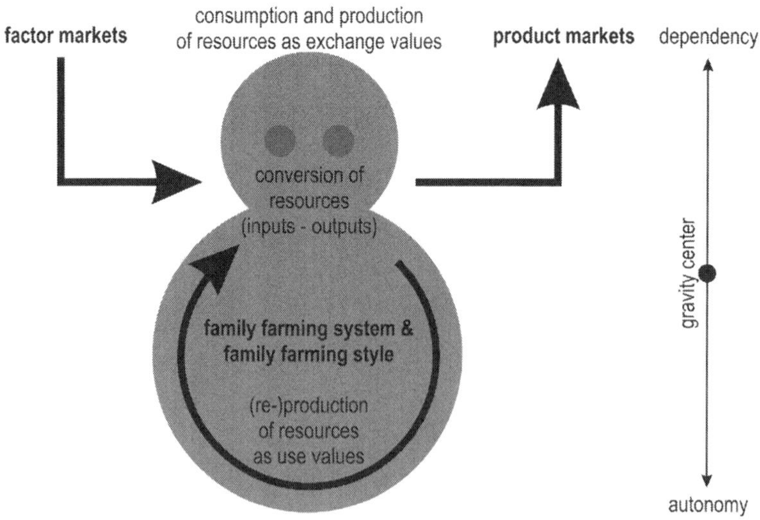

Figure 5: Style-specific resource flows in the family farming system, source: own design adapted from van der Ploeg, New Peasantries, 153.

We must not attribute the ability of family farms to survive under unfavorable conditions to a time-transcending "peasant's essence"; on the contrary, the resilience of the family farming system is permanently being

47. See van der Ploeg, *New Peasantries*, 152-57.
48. On the distinction between (static) "order" and (dynamic) "ordering" see John Law, *Organizing Modernity* (Oxford and Cambridge: Blackwell, 1994).

(re-)constructed in everyday life by the actors' farming styles as shown by the Huber and Meier families, as well as by other case studies.[49] Our studies have revealed a multitude of strategies suited to reduce market dependency in favor of family autonomy: first, strategies with regard to the family as an inter-personal network include, among others, the negotiation of a collective "orientating pattern"[50] of farm management and family life in order to gain a sufficient degree of acceptance by the individuals of the household; the flexible application of family labor, especially that of female members,[51] in order to save transaction costs; the permanent or at least temporary reduction of the family's standard of living in order to save expenses for consumer goods; the gaining of income outside of the farm to reduce the dependency on farm income; co-operation with local and regional actors in order to activate social capital. Second, strategies with regard to the self-controlled resource base of the farming enterprise comprise, among others, working carefully with organic and inorganic resources in order to minimize the risk of animal diseases, crop failures and mechanical breakdowns; adapting to the ecological niche of the farm location in order to enhance co-production between man and nature; integrating different branches of farming in order to gain synergy. Third, strategies with regard to factor and product markets comprise, among others, avoiding too much debt from investment credits in order to maintain the leeway of decision-making; diversifying the produce in order to counterbalance price fluctuations; marketing products directly to consumers in order to add value. All these strategies tend to deepen the gravity center of the family farm, therefore decreasing market dependency and increasing family autonomy.

The most crucial feature of these family farming styles is their hybrid character, which overcomes the dichotomy of "peasants" running household and "farmers" managing enterprises. The Hubers, Meiers and others run households and manage enterprises at the same time. On the one hand, they acquire technology and other commodities from factor markets and deliver food and other commodities to product markets; on the other hand, they manage to control market dependency to a certain degree by maintaining a

49. In our research project eight cases of family farming systems in total have been reconstructed on the basis of narrative interviews and additional sources.

50. See Ralf Bohnsack, "Orientierungsmuster," in *Hauptbegriffe Qualitativer Sozialforschung: Ein Wörterbuch,* eds. Ralf Bohnsack, Winfried Marotzki and Michael Meuser (Opladen: Leske und Budrich, 2003), 132-33.

51. On the role of rural women as providers of flexible laborforce see Ingrid Bauer, "Zwischen Goldhaube und Telehaus: Modernisierung der Geschlechterverhältnisse im ländlichen Raum," in *Salzburg: Zwischen Globalisierung und Goldhaube,* eds. Ernst Hanisch and Robert Kriechbaumer (Vienna: Böhlau, 1997), 210-39.

self-controlled resource base. This combination of strategies lets them keep the balance between dependency and autonomy. Thus—and most ironically—these farming families can successfully act like "farmers" because they successfully act like "peasants." Needless to say, maintaining the balance between dependency and autonomy is neither always harmonious nor necessarily successful; it may involve severe conflicts, and it may eventually fail.[52] However, the cases of the Hubers, Meiers and others highlight a crucial aspect of Austria's path of post-war agrarian change: besides other factors,[53] it is the hybridity of family farming styles that increases the resilience of family farming systems in the challenging environment of post-war "organized capitalism."

52. As a case study emphasizing the "decline of the peasant economy" see Christa Müller, *Von der lokalen Ökonomie zum globalisierten Dorf: Bäuerliche Überlebensstrategien zwischen Weltmarktintegration und Regionalisierung* (Frankfurt am Main: Campus, 1998), 88-139; a more differentiated account is provided by Thomas Fliege, *Bauernfamilien zwischen Tradition und Moderne: Eine Ethnographie bäuerlicher Lebensstile* (Frankfurt am Main: Campus, 1998).
53. See Kröger, *Modernisierung*, 395-418.

Attitudinal Lives: A Survey of Austrian Students Attitudes towards Muslims and Jews, Vergangenheitsbewaeltigung and World War II, and Democratic Dispositions

Petra Ziegler, Yvonne Schuermann-Zehetner,

Regina Fritz, Alexander Salzmann and Oliver Rathkolb

Introduction

On the basis of "Authoritarianism, History and Democratic Dispositions in Austria, the Czech Republic, Hungary and Poland," a study conducted by the Institute of Contemporary History of the University of Vienna and SORA, and the surveys carried out repeatedly in Germany by the Friedrich Ebert Foundation on the topic of "Rechtsextreme Einstellungen in Deutschland" (Extreme Right Attitudes in Germany), an online survey of Austrian students was carried out between 1 March and 10 April 2011, focused on the topics of globalization, authoritarianism, anomia, coming to terms with national history and democratic disposition.

The survey had two objectives: it aimed, on one hand, to ascertain how students felt about varying questions related to the above topics and, on the other, to test whether a sufficient number of students could be reached via online survey.

This survey was designed to be a preliminary step to conducting further surveys among students of *Fachhochschulen* (universities of applied science) and *Pädagogische Hochschulen* (Teacher Training Colleges) in Austria, in order to compare the results with the results obtained from university students as well as from the population at large as encapsulated in the Institute of Contemporary History/SORA project.

Procedure

In the development of the questionnaire, a test was tried out on students to establish what kinds of questionnaire items were likely to function and what was the optimum questionnaire length. In selecting the questionnaire items, tried and tested statements from the 2007 survey (SORA and Institute of Contemporary History) were relied upon; these were supplemented by selected items from the surveys conducted by the

Friedrich Ebert Foundation (Germany), e.g. regarding globalization. The items took the form of short, concise statements designed to provoke an unambiguous response. On the basis of the results of a test survey, which was conducted between December 2010 and January 2011, the questionnaire for students was revised and finalized.

At the beginning of the summer term 2011 the questionnaire was sent via e-mail to 175,000 students[1]. In addition to a brief outline of the project, the e-mail included a link to the survey, which enabled students to access and fill out the questionnaire. On completion a cookie was deposited in the students' browsers to ensure that no one could fill out the questionnaire more than once.

Evaluation of the data began with comprehensive reliability and validity tests. Only a very small number of items could not be included on account of insufficient reliability (e.g. the questionnaire item "Die internationalen Finanzmärkte sind Schuld an der weltweit wachsenden Ungleichheit" [The international financial markets are to blame for the worldwide growth of inequality]). In all other cases satisfactory values were achieved with regard to reliability and validity, which was also due to the fact that the questionnaire items used for the survey had already performed satisfactorily in the past.

Methodology

The questionnaire was programed using the open-source program "LimeSurvey." This program contains all survey and questionnaire formats in common use and enables user-friendly programing and presentation. In addition to this, all data can be summarized via LimeSurvey and fed to evaluation programs such as SPSS or Excel.

The survey was conducted online, i.e. the students themselves filled in the questionnaires without the guidance of an interviewer, as opposed to telephone surveys. The fact that there was no interviewer can also be viewed positively, as the influence and the socially desirable responses could be minimized. Online surveys have their advantages and disadvantages, the most important of which should be mentioned here. Some advantages are that

- online surveys take little time to carry out and are cost-effective. Large-scale surveys cost decidedly less than telephone surveys and

1. According to Statistik Austria, the total number of students at public universities in the winter term 2010/11 was close to 217,000. Statistik Austria: Universitäten, Studium http://www.statistik.at/web_de/statistiken/bildung_und_kultur/formales_bildungswesen/universitaeten_studium/index.html (accessed on 10 Jan. 2012).

the results are available in a shorter time and can be accessed at any point for the analysis of interim results.
- as there is no manual processing of data the likelihood of recording errors is reduced.
- the quality of data obtained online is usually high and data obtained in a standardized way can be used for comparisons for a longer amount of time.
- interviewees themselves decide when they want to fill out the survey.

Among other disadvantages of online surveys, above all the issue of representativity must be discussed: Particularly in the early days of online surveys in the 1990s, this was one of the main objections against online surveys, as polling companies did not have sufficiently large panels of interviewees at their disposal and/or found it impossible to compose samples for an e-mail survey that were representative of the entire population. Even today (2012) large gaps persist above the age of 64, which prevents online surveys from achieving a satisfactory degree of representativity of the total population. In the case of younger population groups (up to 29 years of age) it is possible to achieve a high degree of interviewee representativity, as practically 100% of this population segment is online. The survey carried out among students may therefore claim to have achieved representativity as 100% of students have a unet e-mail address at their disposal, which they moreover use a great deal particularly at the beginning of the term to register for lectures, etc.

Other disadvantages of online surveys are:
- A high percentage of people who do not carry the survey out to completion may lead to a drop in the realization of a sample's potential, which would have a negative effect on the representativity of the results. This is why incentives are frequently brought into play to motivate interviewees to fill out the whole survey. Incentives were also used for this survey among students: three copies of the above-mentioned study conducted by the Institute of Contemporary History and SORA[2] were raffled off among all participants.
- There was a certain danger that questionnaires were filled out several times by the same individuals. The survey did include as one of its features the deposition of a cookie but this could be sidestepped by an individual with the requisite knowledge who

2. Oliver Rathkolb, Günther Ogris, *Authoritarianism, History and Democratic Dispositions in Austria, Poland, Hungary and the Czech Republic* (Innsbruck: Studienverlag, 2010).

> is determined to do so. It is therefore impossible to exclude that possibility altogether. However, the results of the survey were based on more than 14,500 completed questionnaires, a number large enough that the odd multiple filing would not affect the results.[3]

All in all, the difficulties inherent to online surveys have been taken into account and neutralized as far as possible. As all members of the young population group at the center of the survey were 100% reachable via e-mail, the representativity of the results is guaranteed.

Results–Socio-demographics, Fields of Study, Universities

As regards age, the majority of students in the poll were between 22 and 25 years old (38%), 25% were between 26 and 30, 18% between 18 and 21, 11% were older than 35, and 8% were between 31 and 35.

In terms of gender 61% were female, 39% male. As it is usual in online surveys for more women to participate than men, this distribution made sense.

In terms of nationality the majority of participants in the survey were Austrian (86%), 8% were German and 2% Italian (predominantly South Tyroleans, who are exempt in Austria from the tuition fees they would have to pay in Italy).

In terms of fields of study, a clear majority came from the humanities (38%), 23% from economics and law, 16% from "MINT" subjects (Math, Computer Sciences, Natural Sciences and Technology/Engineering), 17% study social sciences and 6% of the students were studying to become teachers.

In terms of universities an absolute majority (55%) of students attended one of the universities in Vienna, 13% studied in Graz and Innsbruck respectively, 11% in Linz and 5% in Salzburg. 4% had enrolled at more than one university. At Klagenfurt University the questionnaire was not distributed, which is why Klagenfurt is not represented in this survey.

---

3. For advantages and disadvantages and for methodological considerations in general see also: Samuel D. Gosling, Simine Vazire, Sanjay Srivastava, Oliver P. John: "Should we trust webbased studies? A comparative analysis of six preconceptions about Internet questionnaires," *American Psychologist* 59, no. 2 (2004): 93-104; Sanjay Srivastava, Oliver P. John, Samuel D. Gosling, Jeff Potter, "Development of personality in early and middle adulthood: Set like plaster or persistent change?," *Journal of Personality and Social Psychology* 84, no. 5 (2003): 1041–1053; Nikolaus Jackob, Harald Schoen, Thomas Zerback, eds., *Sozialforschung im Internet: Methodologie und Praxis der Online-Befragung* (Wiesbaden: VS Verlag, 2009); Don A. Dillman, Jolene D. Smyth, Leah Melani Christian, *Internet, mail, and mixed-mode surveys: the tailored design method* (New York: Wiley, 2009).

Group-focused Enmity

The extent of group-focused enmity among Austrian students was examined in the present survey, focusing on 14 items. Questions referring to the construction of mosques and synagogues, the acceptance of religious laws and fears about immigrants—reflected for instance in the fear of rising crime rates and of increasing competition in the job market—addressed topics that were the subject of increasingly heated public debates in the past. As a characteristic group-specific prejudice, the topic "Jews – Capitalism," was also included in the survey. In addition to this, attitudes relating to the rights of traditional minorities and the opening of the borders in 1989 were also part of the survey.

Immigration

The survey results revealed a predominantly positive attitude among students towards migrants: 87% of respondents were in favor of the immigration of Muslims, only 4% were against it. Among law and economics students the rate of acceptance was somewhat lower: 7% came out against the immigration of Muslims.

As many as 61% of students saw the fall of the borders of 1989 as advantageous, with men (70%) taking a considerably more positive view than women (55%), who demonstrated a significantly higher degree of scepticism.

Responses to the particularly relevant question concerning competition in the job market gave no indication of misgivings in that respect on the part of students: 83% rejected the idea that immigrants compete with Austrians for jobs, only 4% of students showed themselves concerned about the possibility of facing a shortage of jobs due to immigration.

In topical questions regarding national and individual security, 18% of students felt that immigrants cause the crime rate to rise. On the other hand, more than half (51%) did not take this view and 28% of respondents were undecided on this point. A comparison of these results with those of the survey carried out by SORA in November/December 2007 on the topic "Authoritarianism in Austria und Central Europe" and the data of a survey of European values published in 2008 by Christian Friesl, Regina Polak and Ursula Hamachers-Zuba illustrates how significantly the results obtained from these two groups of respondents differ: accordingly as many as 26% of Austria's population overall agreed with the statement that immigrants take away jobs from people born in Austria; only 47% disagreed. The proportion of the total population who in 2007 saw immigrants as the cause of the rise of crime-related problems in Austria was, at 51%, nearly three times as high as it was among students. Only 23% did not share this attitude and merely 2% were undecided on this issue.[4] A year later, in 2008, about two-thirds, 69% to be precise, shared this opinion.[5]

Muslims

The present survey also contained items designed to test the incidence of Islamophobia among students. 15% endorsed the statement that "the great number of Muslims sometimes makes them feel as if they were foreigners in their own country." The right of the Muslim population to freely practice their religion was assessed by two items, namely "Muslims in Austria should be entitled to live according to their religious laws," which elicited a response of 74% in favor, and a question about the right to build mosques (72% in favor), which meant in overall terms that almost three-quarters of students supported these rights. There is a noteworthy difference in the rejections: 13% of respondents were against the construction of mosques, 8% were against Muslims living according to their religious laws in Austria. What is also noteworthy are differences between the fields of study. A significantly higher proportion of law students and students of economics—11%—rejected the right of Muslims to live according to their own religious laws than was the case e.g. with students of the social sciences (5%).

A comparison of the results of the student survey with Austria's total population highlights significant differences: in the latter survey, only 35% were in favor of Muslims practicing their religion freely, the same proportion, 35%, rejected it and roughly a quarter of respondents were undecided on this point. The right to build mosques was rejected by a clear majority of 57%, with only 25% in favor.[6] In the Federal Republic of Germany, according to the data polled by the Friedrich Ebert Foundation in 2010 in the entire country, 58.4% of the total population rejected free religious practice for Muslims, Friedrich Ebert Foundation found in (former) East Germany that this view was shared by up to 75.7% of the population.[7] These results could be linked to the polemical public debates about the construction of mosques and/or of minarets.

4. SORA data set from 2007, independent analysis of the Austrian data (November 2011).
5. Christian Friesl, Ursula Hamachers-Zuba, and Regina Polak, eds., *Die Österreicherinnen. Wertewandel 1990-2008* (Wien: Czernin Verlag, 2009), 260.
6. SORA data set from 2007, independent analysis of the Austrian data (November 2011).
7. Oliver Decker et al., *Die Mitte in der Krise: Rechtsextreme Einstellungen in Deutschland 2010* (Berlin: Friedrich-Ebert-Stiftung, 2010), 134, 144.

Fig. 1: Immigrants take away jobs from people who were born in Austria (in %)

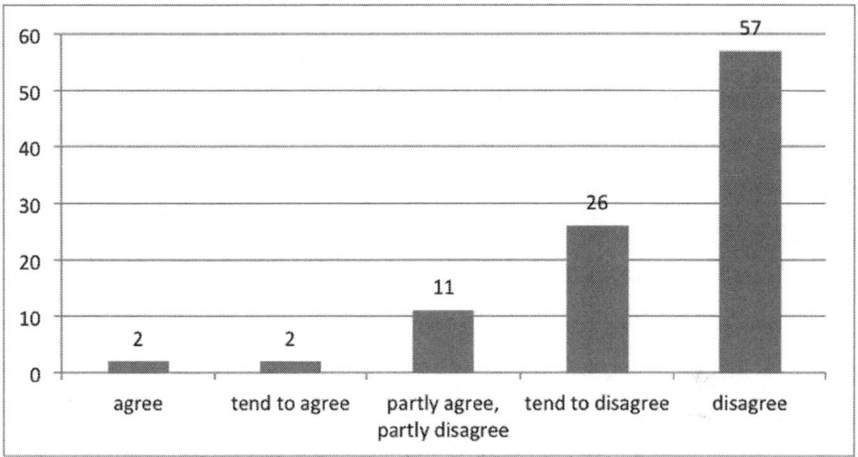

Source: Our own data/survey, March - April 2011

Jews

As becomes clear from a comparison, freedom of religious expression for the Jewish population received much greater acceptance than was the case vis-à-vis Muslims. Both the question about the right to build synagogues and the question about Jews' rights to live according to the laws of their religion were endorsed by 83% of Austrian students. While 4% would deny freedom of religion to Jews, rejection of visible changes in the outward appearance of Austrian towns as the result e.g. of the construction of synagogues was more pronounced (6%). Again law students and students of economics were more pronounced in their rejection (10%) than the students of the other fields of study. The prejudice "Jews are to blame for the excesses of capitalism," which is deeply rooted in traditional anti-Semitism, was overwhelmingly rejected by 94% of the students. Only 2% of respondents agreed with this statement.

Rights of Traditional Minorities

In their responses to items about the rights of Austria's traditional minorities such as Carinthia's Slovenes and Burgenland's Croats, 90% of Austrian students came out in favor of the foundation of associations and organizations dedicated to the promotion of their respective cultures. Another 72% endorsed newspapers, radio broadcasts and TV programs in the languages of the minorities and their participation through political representatives in local, regional and national governments. An interesting result of the study is linked to the issue of the language of instruction: with only 49% in favor, less than half of the respondents endorsed the right to have school taught in the language of the respective minority. The proposition was completely rejected by 30%, 20% were undecided. The high rejection rate and the large number of undecided respondents revealed a significantly lower level of tolerance towards minorities in this particular respect.

The survey results on the topic of "Group-focused Enmity" revealed a comparatively low tendency towards xenophobic attitudes among students compared to the Austrian public as a whole. This allows for the conclusion that the higher the level of the respondents' formal education, the more tolerant and open respondents are likely to be towards immigrants and minorities, and they are less likely to display anti-Semitic and islamophobic attitudes. In the direct comparison, there appears to be a higher degree of acceptance of Jews than of Muslims.

Coming to Terms With History

The perception of history among Austrian students and more specifically the way and extent they are coming to terms with Austria's contemporary history was examined using 5 items. This complex focused on key positions on certain aspects related to Austria's Nazi era history. Ultimately, personal attitudes towards Austria's more recent history, i.e. the individual perception of history, may be considered a potential indicator of authoritarian, anti-Islamic and anti-Semitic attitudes.[8]

The survey showed that on issues that may be regarded as key themes of attempts to come to terms with Austria's history—such as the "victim thesis," the drawing of a final line (Schlussstrich) under debates on World War II and the Holocaust, the significance of Austrian resistance against Nazi rule for the liberation of the country and the shared responsibility of Austrians for the fate of the Jews—Austrian students generally support historical perceptions that are closer to the current state of historical research than is the case with the population at large.

8. See Oliver Rathkolb, "Die 'longue durée' autoritärer Einstellungen der österreichischen Gesellschaft 1978 und 2004/2008," in *Politische Gewalt und Machtausübung im 20. Jahrhundert Zeitgeschichte, Zeitgeschehen und Kontroversen, Festschrift für Gerhard Botz*, eds. Heinrich Berger, Melanie Dejnega, Regina Fritz and Alexander Prenninger (Vienna: Böhlau, 2011), 403-417.

Victim Thesis and shared Responsibility for the Persecution of the Jews 1938/45

Starting with the country's liberation in 1945, the so-called "victim thesis" formed an integral part of Austria's way of dealing with its Nazi past for over 40 years. The victim thesis served, on one hand, as a political tool in negotiations with the Allies and, on the other, as an identity generating construct in the context of creating a post-totalitarian Austrian post-war society or rather as a reintegrating element for large segments of the population. Responsibility for Nazi crimes was externalized, not viewed as part of Austria's past, and the blame for them was shifted to the Federal Republic of Germany. This made National Socialism "an event outside Austria's actual development,"[9] and official Austria was able to position itself as a victim behind the "shield" of the discourse of German responsibility.

It was only when the Waldheim Affair erupted in the second half of the 1980s that "victim thesis" began to erode. It was modified to a perpetrator-victim thesis or respectively a shared responsibility thesis – the acknowledgement that the Nazi era had not only seen Austrians as victims (and Austria herself as the first victim) but also as perpetrators in large numbers has since begun to spread across Austria's party political landscape, following seminal speeches by Franz Vranitzky (1991) and Thomas Klestil (1994), albeit in varying forms corresponding to with the parties' respective milieux.

The "victim thesis" nevertheless continues to be endorsed by large parts of the population and a pervasive ambiguity is evident: in the 2007 SORA survey, as many as 36.5% of respondents identified with the statement that Austria was the first victim of National Socialism, only 25% tended to reject that statement. A notably high number of respondents, 23.1%, was unable or unwilling to respond to this point, 15.4% were undecided[10], which may be interpreted as evidence of a process of reorientation in dealing with the Nazi past that is still ongoing in large parts of the population.

The issue of the shared responsibility of Austrians for the fate of the Jews between 1938 and 1945 on the other hand showed a more differentiated picture: Almost 57% of the population acknowledged in 2007 the shared responsibility of Austrians, only 13.7% rejected the idea, as many as 29.7%

9. M. Rainer Lepsius, *Demokratie in Deutschland: Soziologisch-historische Konstellationsanalysen; Ausgewählte Aufsätze,* (Göttingen: Vandenhoeck & Ruprecht, 1993), 232 (Translation by the authors).
10. SORA data set from 2007, independent analysis of the Austrian data (November 2011).

were undecided or did not respond.[11] A combination of the two responses points to an acceptance of the perpetrator-victim thesis: on one hand, the (individual) shared responsibility of Austrians for Nazi crimes is accepted, while, on the other, Austria's role as a victim is still met with acceptance or, respectively, large parts of the population are still undecided on this point.

The same items that were used in the SORA survey of Austria's total population elicited significantly different responses from Austrian students. The question of whether Austria was the first victim of National Socialism received tentative support from only 10% of students, while a clear majority of 63% rejected Austria's role as a victim. Even more pronounced was the students' endorsement of the shared responsibility of Austrians for the persecution of the Jews: 82% agreed and only 2% of students rejected the idea of Austrian responsibility. The clearer rejection of the "victim thesis" in comparison with the total population and the high acceptance of shared responsibility for Nazi crimes may perhaps be accounted for by the fact that the peer group of the students in the survey grew up in the political/historical environment of the post-Waldheim years and have greater than average levels of education.

Fig. 2: Austrian men and women were co-responsible for the fate of the Jews between 1938 and 1945 (in %)

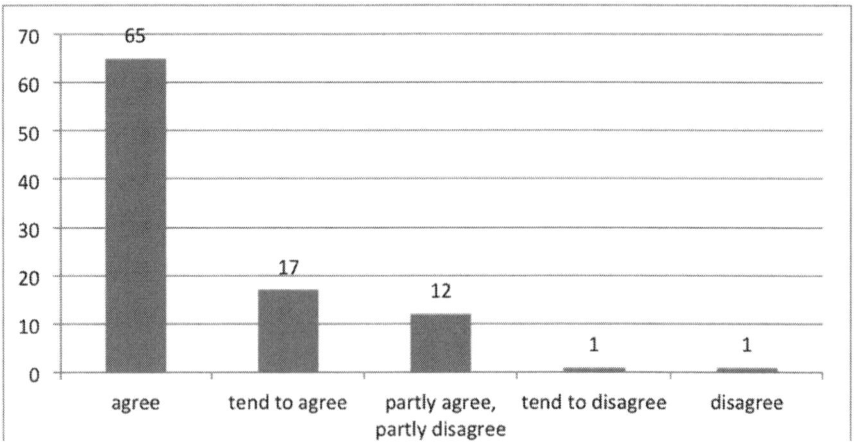

Source: Our own data/survey, March - April 2011

11. Ibid.

Resistance

In Austria's postwar discourse the emphasis on the national resistance to Nazi Germany, coupled with the victim myth, represented an important identity generating element. This had its roots in a resolution by the Allied foreign ministers in the Moscow Declaration (1943), in which Austria was recognized as the first victim of the Third Reich. At the same time the document served as a reminder for Austria "that she has a responsibility, which she cannot evade, for participation in the war at the side of Hitlerite Germany, and that in the final settlement account will inevitably be taken of her own contribution to her liberation."[12] It was therefore in Austria's political interest to make her own contribution in her liberation appear as large as possible. In contrast to the victim thesis, the "resistance myth" has not yet been publicly deconstructed and debated. This might be the reason why there is still substantial support both in the population at large and among students for the idea that resistance was in fact significant: 45% of students endorsed the statement that Austrian resistance against the rule of the Nazis was a significant factor in the country's liberation, 20% tended to disagree. There was again a remarkably high percentage of those undecided and/or not responding (16% "Partly agree, partly disagree" and 19% "Don't know"). In the SORA survey as many as 51.5% of the total population[13] endorsed the significance of resistance.

Expropriation

There is hardly another topic related to the Nazi era that was as present in the media over the last few years as the hotly debated restitution of works of art that had been stolen from their Jewish owners during World War II. Countless media reports reminded the public in this context of the practice of the systematic expropriation of Austrian Jews (Aryanization). 44% of Austrian students endorsed the statement that many Austrians extracted a personal profit from the murder of the Jews, 20% disagreed with this statement. A high percentage of undecided respondents could be noted here as well (36% "It depends" or "Don't know"). In the SORA survey a roughly identical percentage of the Austrian population endorsed the statement that "[m]any Austrians extracted a personal profit from the murder of the Jews": 44.8% saw the material benefit Austrians drew from the extermination of the Jews as a fact, and the rejection of this statement was roughly the same as among the students at 19.3%.[14] These survey results confirm the view of

12. Moscow Conference, October 1943, Joint Four Nation Declaration, online at: http://www.ibiblio.org/pha/policy/1943/431000a.html (accessed 24 Feb. 2012).
13. SORA data set from 2007, independent analysis of the Austrian data (November 2011).
14. Ibid.

the Austrian historian Heidemarie Uhl that "the question of who moved into the "aryanized" flats, shops etc. formerly owned by the more than 65,000 murdered and the roughly 130,000 expelled Austrian Jews after 1945 and of what happened to their assets [...] continues to have a lasting potential for causing distress in view of the continued effects of guilt and of restitution that failed to take place."[15]

Drawing a *Schlussstrich*

In their response to the question whether a *Schlussstrich* (engl. Übersetzung) should be drawn under discussions of World War II, a large percentage of Austrian students signaled disagreement. While in the SORA survey 51.1% agreed that discussion should come to an end and only 34.6% disagreed with this proposition[16], only 15% of Austrian students came out in favor of drawing a *Schlussstrich* under debates about World War II, 71% disagreed or tended to disagree. It is noteworthy that only 7% of students of the social sciences advocated drawing a Schlussstrich, whereas, among students of economics and law (21%) and the MINT subjects (Math, Computer Sciences, Natural Sciences and Engineering) (20%), roughly one fifth of respondents favored an end of the discussions.

Democratic Dispositions

Since 1945, there have repeatedly been surveys, which try to gauge the attitudes in society towards democracy. The first analysis of the kind came in 1947 and was concentrated on the US zones in Salzburg, Upper Austria and parts of Vienna – with ambivalent results and an approval of monarchy by over 15% to 28% of the respondents.[17]

In 2011, on the other hand, the general acceptance of democracy was high both among students as well as among the population at large (in 2007), despite an awareness of problems: 85% of the students supported democracy compared to a low level of rejection of 6% (in society as a whole the percentages add up to 86.5% versus 3.5%[18]). In a comparable EU-survey of values, the percentage supporting democracy was ever greater: in 1998, 96%, in 2008, 92%.[19]

---

15. Heidemarie Uhl, "Österreich: Vom Opfermythos zur Mitverantwortungsthese; Die Transformationen des österreichischen Gedächtnisses," in *Mythen der Nationen: 1945 – Arena der Erinnerungen, Band II*, ed. Monika Flacke (Mainz: Philipp von Zabern Verlag, 2004), 481-508, here 499. (Translation by the authors).

16. SORA data set from 2007, independent analysis of the Austrian data (November 2011).

17. Klaus-Dieter Mulley, Sebastian Meissl, Oliver Rathkolb, eds., *Verdrängte Schuld, Verfehlte Sühne* (Vienna: Verlag für Geschichte und Politik, 1986), 74.

18. Rathkolb, Ogris, eds., *Authoritarianism* (Vienna: Studienverlag, 2010).

19. Sieglinde Rosenberger, Gilg Seeber, "Kritische Einstellungen: BürgerInnen zu

At the same time, the trend towards supporting the demand for a government of experts, although the legitimisation of the experts by means of democratic elections would no longer be possible, increased, even among students. 33% of the students agreed with the statement that experts should decide over what is best for the country; 30% disagreed. At 36%, the majority was undecided on this point. An interesting aspect is that men agreed notably more frequently than women: 38% compared with 29%. It should be noted that, in the 2007 survey, the agreement with the statement was higher on the one hand, but the rejection of it was more clearly negative at 41.9% on the other.

It is generally worth noting that in Austria the choice of wording can strongly influence the rates of approval or disapproval. Whereas, in 1999, 15.7% considered the statement "There should be a strong leader (*Führer*), who does not need to bother with a parliament or elections," good or very good (2.9%), in the same survey 19.6% agreed when it was formulated as "a strong man." In 2008, almost 20% of respondents even voted for the "strong leader" (*Führer*).

In this central question, a higher level of education in the end provides a critical barrier against the longing (*Sehnsucht*) for a *Führer*-dictatorship: Only 5% of the students wished for a strong leader (*Führer*), 88% rejected the idea – here the trends in favour of a *Führer* figure were definitely higher in society as a whole – in the Rathkolb/Ogris survey from 2008 71.6 % were against and 14.4 % were for a strong *Führer*.

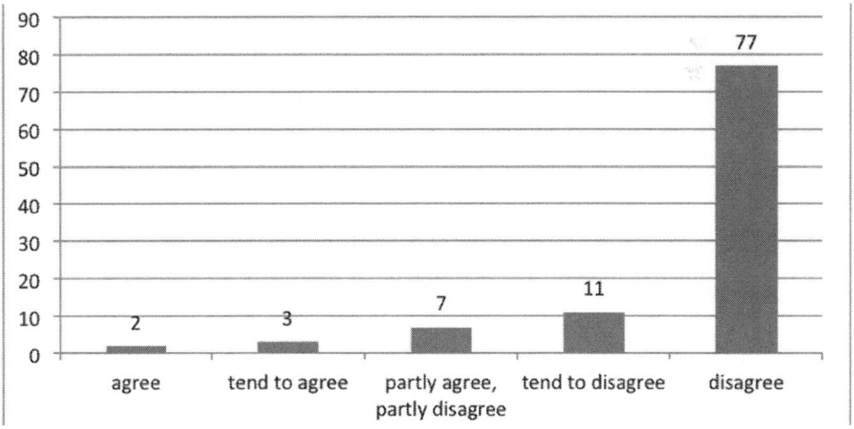

Fig. 3: There should be a strong leader (*Führer*), who does not need to bother with a Parliament or elections (in %)

Source: Our Own Data, March – April 2011

Demokratie, Politik, Migration," in *Zukunft. Werte. Europa: die europäische Wertestudie: 1990 - 2010; Österreich im Vergleich,* ed. Regina Polak (Vienna: Böhlau, 2011), 65-190.

New Authoritarianism

Another important indicator for democratic dispositions is the basic attitude of the people towards state incursions on civil liberties and the rights of citizens. Ralf Dahrendorf discussed in 2006 the consequences of the September 11th attacks on civil liberties against the backdrop of massive state incursions in the fight against terrorism[20]. He saw in that a "new authoritarianism," where individual liberties were curtailed by arguments of security and replaced by the thesis "Security equals freedom."

In 2007, 13.2%, for example, considered banning public protests/ assemblies justified, 66.2% argued against it. As regards covert online searches of PCs, 49.5% were against it, 24.3% were in favour. 16.5% argued against video surveillance of public spaces, 60.2% argued for it.

In this area, students proved themselves much more resistant than the rest of society in Austria. The questions regarding whether certain measures of the government would be justified, a general ban on strikes and assemblies was rejected very clearly: between 94% and 96% considered these measures not justified. Covert online searches of private computers were rejected by 80% and the surveillance of phone calls was rejected by 75%. On the other hand, video surveillance of public spaces was only rejected by 39%, 34% supported it. It is notable, however, that only 23% of students of the social and cultural sciences supported video surveillance of public spaces, in comparison with 45% of those studying economics or law.

Conclusion

The result of this online survey among Austrian students did not only produce a remarkable high turnout, but confirmed the thesis that educated Austrians follow the historiographic turn towards a critical perception of the active role of many Austrians in the National Socialist movement, World War II and the Holocaust more closely than the rest of the society. Here, however, students from the medical university did not all answer the survey, and students of law and business tended to be less prepared to distance themselves from the old victim's myth, but still showed significantly higher awareness concerning these questions. Student cohorts from the humanities and social sciences also tended to be more outspoken to resist authoritarian trends and strongly embrace democratic values and democracy as such and here again the higher educational background diminishes traditional negative prejudices vis-à-vis Jews or—which tend to become a hot issue in Austria—against Muslims.

---

20. Ralf Dahrendorf, Der 11. September und der neue Autoritarismus, online: www.project-syndicate.org/commentary/dahrendorf54/German (accessed on 21 Jan. 2012).

Book Reviews

Ernst Hanisch, *Der große Illusionist: Otto Bauer, 1881-1938* (Vienna: Böhlau Verlag, 2011)

Peter Berger

In many respects, Otto Bauer's personality and career were as much opposed to the Austrian cliché as one would imagine. Throughout his relatively short lifespan he lacked every hedonistic trait usually associated with Austrians (and the Viennese in particular). As a schoolboy, few if any of his classmates outperformed him in work discipline, intellectual curiosity, and talent. His career as a noted publicist and Marxist social critic began when he was barely twenty-six. Just a year earlier he had earned a PhD in law and state sciences (*Staatswissenschaften*) at the University of Vienna. Bauer's academic studies were interrupted by one year of military service and a sequence of monthly training courses for reserve officers. On the eve of the First World War he held the rank of lieutenant of the reserve in a regiment that was quickly deployed at the Russian front. In clashes with the Tsar's troops he displayed an unusual fighting spirit and, as a result of his bravery, suffered three years of detention in a POW-camp in Siberia. Shortly after his release in 1917 (made possible by the tacit collaboration of Russia's new Bolshevik leadership and the Austrian Social Democrats, who intervened in favor of their young comrade), the Habsburg Empire collapsed under dramatic circumstances, and Bauer launched his career as social democratic politician. He briefly held the post of Foreign Secretary in Austria's first Republican cabinet under Karl Renner, another prominent Socialist, while at the same time being his party's chief whip in the Austrian Lower House and a regular contributor to the *Arbeiter-Zeitung*, the Social Democratic daily paper whose literary quality and circulation were far above average. In another journalistic capacity Bauer acted as one of three editors-in-chief of *Der Kampf*, the Austro-Marxist monthly defining the party line. When the Democratic Left chose for an opposition role in 1920, never to regain government participation (until, in 1933-34, it was forcibly removed from Austria's political stage), Bauer continued to be a political multi-functionary, prolific publicist and pamphleteer, in short: a workaholic. Being a chain smoker, he refused drinking even a symbolic glass of Austrian wine both at official occasions and privately. When he appealed to his fellow minister Joseph A. Schumpeter in 1919 to discuss financial aspects of foreign policy with him (Schumpeter held the finance portfolio in the Renner government), his invitation contained the usual reference to "a little wine or tea" one would have during the talks – but, clearly, the wine would be Schumpeter's and the tea Bauer's.

All this said, there is another, very typically Austrian Otto Bauer. His parents were model fin-de-siècle burghers, Habsburg Monarchy style. Father Philipp Bauer owned textile factories in Northern Bohemia, close to the German (Saxon) border, but the head offices of his company were located in the Emperor's capital, Vienna. Otto's mother Katharina, née Gerber, reportedly held a stake in the firm. Both Philipp and Katharina were Jewish, and both seem to have been proud of their son's scholastic and intellectual performance – and only moderately disappointed of his decision to become a professing anti-capitalist of the Marxist creed. After all, it was not uncommon for the offspring of wealthy manufacturers to refuse stepping into the paternal footprints, and once the decision to trade business for politics or journalism was made by a young Jew, the choice of a spiritual home or Weltanschauung was extremely limited. In fact, only Socialists and Communists avoided making political Anti-Semitism a pivotal point of their party programs. Otto Bauer's father seems to have been quite non-political, and so was Otto's sister, Ida, known to Freudians—though under the pseudonym Dora—as the object of a prominent case study on neurosis. The psycho-analytical connection involved father Bauer as well, whose fits of dementia and paralysis were diagnosed by Sigmund Freud as consequences of syphilitic contagion.

Like many Austrians of his time, young Otto Bauer held views on his fatherland that were slightly schizophrenic. During his childhood years his family changed residence a couple of times, so that Otto's career as a pupil was broken into stages at Vienna, Meran/Merano in South Tyrol, and Reichenberg/Liberec in the Czech lands. Everywhere he seems to have been imbued by his (ethnically German) teachers with a deep feeling of attachment to German classical culture, epitomized in the plays and writings of Goethe, Schiller, Herder, and Kant. Later, Otto added Karl Marx to his private list of German spiritual-intellectual giants. Being enthusiastic about the German nation—or any other nation present in the multi-ethnic Habsburg state—not necessarily contradicted an Austrian's loyalty to the Empire as such or the figure of the Emperor. And indeed a majority of Francis Joseph's subjects were loyal to the Monarch, sometimes to the point of sacrificing their lives for him in the First World War, a fate that could easily have been Bauer's. When he discovered Marxian Socialism for himself in his late teenage years, the challenge was to reconcile this new utopia with his state patriotism, German nationalism, and an emotional awareness of his Jewish background. Bauer, unlike other leading figures of

Austrian Socialism never rescinded his membership in Vienna's Israelite Community, for reasons which he once explained to a non-Jewish fellow socialist: "You have never heard someone muttering 'filthy Jew' behind your back!" It may well be true that Bauer's multi-faceted identity helped shape his deeply entrenched, and again very Austrian, tendency towards personal and political compromise, and his utter reluctance to accept violence as a means of practical politics. On the surface, however, Bauer the practical politician appeared—ironically enough—as the exact opposite of an appeaser, due to his scornful and occasionally radical language directed in the 1920s and 1930s against the political Right, and especially its petty bourgeois elements. It seems obvious that the roots of Bauer's alleged and much-reviled arrogance and aggressiveness lay in his being intellectually superior to most of interwar Austria's political personnel, and in his tragic failure to grasp how a battle of words could easily lead to feelings of mutual hatred and even physical violence – especially if an opponent did not share his own conviction that "intellectual arguments are here to save men from killing each other." (The quote is from the Austrian philosopher, Karl Popper.)

It will be clear to the reader by now that giving an account of the life and achievements of Otto Bauer, no matter to what extent we consider them "Austrian" in character, is a tricky and ungrateful task. While he was alive, Bauer fascinated his many admirers and antagonized his even more numerous critics. Following his tragic death in French exile, shortly after Hitler's Anschluss of Austria in March 1938, the memories he evoked remained highly ambiguous. On the political Left in post-1945 Austria he came to be widely remembered as a betrayer of the cause of Social Democracy, cowardly abandoning his comrades who in utmost despair, though ultimately in vain, bode armed resistance to the assault of Austro-Fascism. (Indeed Bauer slipped out of Austria and into the Czechoslovak Republic on the second day of the infamous Civil War of February 1934, while clashes between the red *Schutzbund* and Austria's regular army and *Heimwehr* forces continued in Vienna and elsewhere.) A number of surviving old-style Social Democrats continued to revere him for his masterly Marxist analyses of socio-political developments of his times. Much later, his writings earned Bauer the respect and adoration of a young generation of student protesters who in 1968 hit the streets of Europe, opposing what they saw as a decadent and incompetent political caste compromised by its stubborn refusal to finally confront the ghosts of a fascist (or colonialist) past.[1] For Austrian postwar conservatives Otto Bauer was the bête noire

1. An assessment of Otto Bauer's importance for the modern political Left can be found in

of interwar politics, a man who constantly spoke revolution (but backed away from every opportunity to accomplish one), an irresponsible verbal rabble rouser and intransigent enemy of the propertied classes. When Ernst Hanisch, Professor Emeritus of History at the University of Salzburg, chose to become Bauer's first non-contemporary (and non-Socialist) biographer, he must have been fully aware of the potential pitfalls of his interest in a highly controversial personality. Having had the endurance to finish his biographical project is the first thing for which Hanisch deserves praise.

But then, of course, writing a prominent political figure's biography holds out a host of professional rewards for those who dare doing so. As Hanisch himself admits in a brief introductory chapter to his study, times are definitely over when scholars emphasizing the human factor in history met with nothing but contempt on the part of "structural" historians. From the late 1960s until way into the 1980s it seemed a foregone conclusion that coming to an understanding of a period's social, cultural, and political characteristics required amassing a formidable wealth of statistical material, to be presented in almost unintelligible volumes full of sparsely commented tables and graphs. Today it goes largely uncontested that a representative historical agent's life, so long as it is well told, reveals as much about his or her times as any structural study does. And Otto Bauer's life must be considered representative indeed. While he was active as a writer-commentator and politician, his ancestral region of East Central Europe experienced the rise of nationalism, socialism, and fascism; the death struggle and final demise of three multi-national Empires (Russia, Austria-Hungary, and Ottoman Turkey); Lenin's November revolution; the territorial changes following the peace treaties of Paris, and the economic consequences of these treaties—inflation, economic nationalism, and the disruption of traditional industrial and trade ties, to name but a few; the coming of the Great Depression and, in its wake, the explosion of mass unemployment, anti-Jewish resentment, and National Socialist propaganda; and finally, Hitler's successful bid for power in Germany (and later in Austria), accompanied by early preparations for a war of revenge that would, in the eyes of the Germans, undo the injustice suffered by the Reich in 1918 and the subsequent years. Bauer's role in all this was, of course limited, since for most of the time he was but an opposition leader in a small, peripheral country. But his relatively minor international stature is compensated for a large part by the astonishing plethora of writings which he left behind.[2] Hanisch skillfully exploits Bauer's work to

Walther Baier, Lisbeth N. Trallori, Derek Weber, eds., *Otto Bauer und der Austromarxismus* (Berlin: Karl Dietz Verlag, 2008).

2. There exists an edition of Bauer's works from the 1970s: Otto Bauer, *Werkausgabe*,

shed light on both events and currents of thought of his times, thereby admitting that any decision about which texts to comment and which to omit in a biography must inevitably be arbitrary and dependent on the biographer's own personality and views.

In 1907, in his mid-twenties, Bauer published his study on (Austria's) Nationality Question and Social Democracy (*Nationalitätenfrage und Sozialdemokratie*), a work that instantly established his reputation as a Marxist thinker and solid socio-economist. Hanisch's discussion of this *Coup de force* is one of the key elements in his account of Bauer's formative years. In his first book Bauer already exhibited all the merits and shortcomings that were to characterize his writings throughout the next three decades. He used short, expressive sentences which made for an unmistakable literary style. Ample statistical material served to support his verbal argumentation. Bauer's theoretical approach was that of a historian steeped in Marxian theory. His readers surely benefited, and still benefit, from the evocative power inherent in the historical method, so long as it is skillfully employed. But they might also have been repelled by the unshakeable conviction of a dyed-in-the-wool Marxist that history held its own laws and hence could easily be predicted. (In fact, throughout his life most of Bauer's historical forecasts proved utterly wrong.) *Nationalitätenfrage und Sozialdemokratie* can also serve as an early example of Bauer's penchant to argue in one direction, while keeping the door open for other options—a trait that caused his critics (who were not always as malicious as Lenin or Stalin who both commented on the nationality book) to dub him "the man of the either-or." Thus, Bauer in 1907 would in principle defend the continuing coexistence of at least six nationalities under the constitutional and economic umbrella of Cisleithanian Austria. But at the same time he made it clear that, should the Habsburg state be destroyed by an "irresponsible policy of catastrophic dimensions," the escape route for Austria's ethnic Germans would lead them into "a unified, democratic state of the entire German nation." In Bauer's view (of 1907), the preferred road to salvation for Habsburg Austria as a political entity was that of granting the members of each and every nationality their "personal autonomy" as opposed to the territorial autonomy envisioned by classical statecraft. Since in Austrian reality it would be impossible to redraw the map of ethnical settlement along the lines of clearly separated territories for each nation, there was no other way than making every single *person* "autonomous," meaning to allow him or her to opt for adherence to a defined ethnic body, and then democratically elect this nationality's cultural representatives. Political matters were to

---

Volumes 1-9 (Vienna: Europaverlag, 1975-1980).

remain in the jurisdiction of the Viennese central government. Less than a dozen years after these ideas were put to print the Habsburg Empire was gone, while Otto Bauer had become Foreign Secretary of a tiny Austrian Republic and a radical advocate of Anschluss, Austria's peaceful unification with Weimar Germany.

At the time of his promotion to the leading post in Austrian diplomacy, Bauer was thirty-seven, a married man (his wife Helene Gumplowicz, divorced from the lawyer, Max Landau, with whom she had three children, was ten years Bauer's senior), and a brightly shining intellectual star of his Social Democratic Party. As Foreign Secretary, Bauer resembled a white elephant. Foreign Affairs under Habsburg used to be an aristocratic domain, with only now and then a converted and ennobled Jew among its personnel. Most of the older career diplomats left the service when it became republican, and those who stayed sneered at the "very Jewish-looking," if indisputably talented young "Bolshevik" who rightfully claimed to be their boss. Bauer's anachronistic tenure at the *Ballhausplatz* lasted no longer than eight months. Shortly before the opening of the Paris peace conference in summer 1919 he offered his resignation to the President of Austria's National Assembly. The official reason given for this move was that his holding on to the job would result in a harsher treatment of Austria by the Allied Powers than otherwise (since the French in particular mistrusted an Austrian chief diplomat who was openly pro-Anschluss and, moreover, sympathetic to Hungary's Communist government under Béla Kun.) Privately, Bauer must have been extremely disappointed by the failure of a round of talks in spring 1919 with his German homologue at the *Wilhelmstraße*, Count Brockdorff-Rantzau, talks that in his eyes were supposed to prepare the ground for Austro-German unification. The German Minister, however, had been less than enthusiastic about the pressure put upon him by the impatient Bauer. Also, a secret initiative by Bauer to convince Italy of the wisdom of returning occupied South Tyrol to the Austrians brought no tangible result. His semi-voluntary departure from the Foreign Ministry gave Bauer more room for maneuver in other fields of activity, notably his party work, and his journalistic endeavors. As a retired Foreign Secretary and insightful witness of Austria's difficulties to digest the consequences of the Saint-Germain peace treaty, he wrote his second influential chef d'oeuvre in the Marxian-historical vein, titled "The Austrian Revolution" (*Die österreichische Revolution*, 1923).

Hanisch discusses this work in great detail, a handsome analogy to his treatment of "*Nationalitätenfrage und Sozialdemokratie*" earlier in his book. Again, he praises Bauer for his knowledgeable, thick description of social and political trends, this time in post-World War I, Republican Austria. According to Bauer the country in 1918/19 underwent a threefold revolution—national, democratic, and social—to stop short of being transformed into a Soviet Republic governed by "workers' councils," as had happened in Hungary. Communist ambitions met with stubborn and ultimately successful resistance by the Social Democratic Party, with Otto Bauer himself in a leading role as advocate of moderation. But instead of an all-out victory of the moderate Left, Austria from late 1919 until mid-1922 experienced something that Bauer called "an equilibrium of power wielded by the [bourgeois and proletarian] classes" (*Gleichgewicht der Klassenkräfte*). The roots of this somewhat surprising development lay in the recovery of bourgeois political strength, which in turn was made possible by, among other factors, the waning threat of a Russian-inspired communist onslaught on Central Europe. The slow but steady resurgence of political conservatism in Austria benefited from the Social Democrats' decision in fall 1920 to discontinue their coalition with the Christian Socials—a move strongly supported by Otto Bauer and later considered a major gaffe by historians sympathetic to the Socialist cause. In 1922, a bipartisan government of Catholics and Pan-Germans, led by Ignaz Seipel, definitely tipped the scale in favor of continued bourgeois-peasant leadership, when it managed to put an end to Austria's rampant inflation by securing an internationally guaranteed loan under the auspices of the League of Nations. Seipel's readiness to accept Western financial interference (or tutelage, as those opposed to the loan package preferred to call it) blocked the road to a heavy taxation of wealth which the Austrian Left had proposed, along with foreign financial assistance, to achieve budget equilibrium. More important, Seipel could henceforth rely on the support of Austria's creditors and the League of Nations in his continued efforts to minimize Social Democratic influence on government policies. In *Die österreichische Revolution*, Bauer acknowledges the superior tactical skills displayed by Seipel during the League-of-Nations loan episode. Bauer's own party initially resisted the Geneva Protocols of 1922, the international treaty in which the conditions for foreign financial assistance were laid down. But then it lost its nerves and, by lending unconditional parliamentary support to a constitutional reform which the foreign creditors had deemed necessary, it in fact betrayed its own voters. Hanisch shows little understanding for the Social Democrats' ambiguous handling of the foreign loan issue while other historians, like Charles A. Gulick, see it as a proof of the party's ultimate willingness to accept responsibility for the state. However that may be, the year 1922 marked a turning point both for the Democratic Left and for Otto Bauer.

In the decade to come he would preach to his followers the gospel of historical materialism and the unavoidable final triumph of the proletariat. Meanwhile his party, though generally successful at the polls, dramatically failed to reassert its grip on Austrian domestic politics, a development caused in part by Bauer's ambiguous performance as a practical politician.

Arguably, the most interesting parts of Hanisch's biography are those in which he juxtaposes Bauer the staunch believer in "scientific" Socialism, and Bauer the man of missed opportunities in day-to-day politics. In his capacity of Socialist theoretician Bauer penned down the Social Democratic party program of 1926, a key document of Austro-Marxist reasoning and, in Hanisch's opinion, also a proof of its author's political illusionism. An oft-quoted paragraph of the program raised the specter of a dictatorship of the working class, calling it a legitimate instrument to overcome (violent) bourgeois resistance against reforms in the Socialist vein, should such resistance occur. Clearly, Bauer did not envisage the impending deliberate destruction of Austrian democracy at the hands of his own comrades. But his mention of even the slightest possibility that a workers' revolution might happen sufficed to reinforce conservative prejudice against the Social Democrats, and adversely affected Austria's internal stability.

Less than a year later, on July 15, 1927, an angry crowd set fire to the Palace of Justice near Vienna's Ringstraße. The riots followed a jury's acquittal of right-wing militants who had shot and killed two innocent bystanders of a Socialist rally at the Burgenland village of Schattendorf. The Palace of Justice incident, which cost 57 workers' lives, was triggered by an emotional condemnation of the Schattendorf verdict in the *Arbeiter-Zeitung*. But once the crowds hit the street the party leadership proved ill-fit to control them, and totally unable to prevent the murderous intervention by Viennese police. Otto Bauer's role in the events of July 15 was peripheral, Hanisch tells us. The night before, he seems to have deliberately avoided meeting representatives of the Viennese electricity works who wanted instructions for the probable case of forthcoming labor unrest. This, says Hanisch, was only a minor gaffe, if it happened at all. Bauer's decisive historical miscalculation came in the aftermath of July 15, when the Social Democratic Trade Unions, in agreement with the party leadership, called a general strike in Vienna and a strike of public transportation workers all over Austria to force the resignation of Federal Chancellor Ignaz Seipel. The strike failed to achieve anything except authorization by the government of a new Viennese city guard manned with Social Democratic personnel. For the party and Bauer himself July 1927 turned out to be a momentous defeat, despite successful efforts after the event to strengthen the Social Democrats' armed wing against paramilitary units of the anti-democratic Right.

In 1931 Bauer celebrated his fiftieth birthday, while Austria suffered the severest crisis of its short Republican history when in May of that year the country's largest bank, the Credit-Anstalt, declared itself insolvent. In the ensuing, extended fight to keep the bank alive, Austria's conservative governments opted for a factual nationalization of the entire financial sector and for a renewed call on international lenders to avoid state bankruptcy by means of another League of Nations loan. Shortly before the global recession, triggered by Wall Street's Black Friday, made itself felt in Austria, Bauer began writing a study on the phenomenon of the capitalist crisis titled *Rationalisierung – Fehlrationalisierung*. The manuscript went into print at a time when the Austrian Left was bitterly divided about how to counter the adverse economic effects of the financial crisis, notably mass unemployment and an exploding national budget deficit. Eventually, the Social Democratic fraction in Parliament supported a rigorous cutback of state expenses and pro-cyclical policies of deflation designed to keep Austria within the international gold standard. The party rank and file and the Social Democratic trade unions, whose support for a Keynesian strategy to combat the depression was already strong in the early 1930s, were consoled by Bauer *cum suis* with predictions of an impending collapse of the capitalist regime as such, and with hollow rhetoric directed against the alleged dictatorship in Austria of international finance, or the "crimes" against humanity of the Austrian bourgeoisie and its right-wing stooges in government. Not before 1933, says Hanisch, did Otto Bauer reluctantly perform a "Keynesian turn" to propose a publicly financed program of job-creation for 200,000 people. Even then, in his heart, he was convinced of the incurability of capitalism's shortcomings as identified in the above-mentioned book on rationalization.[3] Capitalism, in Bauer's view, depended on the permanent "renewal, enlargement, and technical improvement of the means of production," but industry seemed incapable of spreading investments into such improvement evenly over time. With rationalization expenses compressed into relatively short phases followed by long periods without significant investment, the business cycle and employment were prone to wild swings. Whenever a financial crisis reinforced the downward

3. A recent discussion of "Rationalisierung-Fehlrationalisierung" can be found in Günter Chaloupek, Harald Hagemann, Andreas Resch, eds., *Rationalisierung und Massenarbeitslosigkeit: Otto Bauers Theorie der Rationalisierung im Kontext der Zeit* (Graz: Leykam, 2009).

movement of the business cycle, mass unemployment would become particularly painful. In the long run Bauer saw no other remedy than replacement of the free market-mechanism with a Soviet style planned economy. This was once more a great illusion, as Hanisch puts it, and a dangerous one too since it caused those without jobs who expected practical help from politics to turn away from Democratic Socialism and subscribe to aggressive Nazi propaganda.

When in the middle of the Credit-Anstalt drama Engelbert Dollfuß became head of the Austrian government, the stage was set for the fatal showdown between this energetic veteran of World War I and former minister of agriculture, and Otto Bauer, in all but name leader of the Austrian Left. During the 1920s, the politician-priest Ignaz Seipel had been Bauer's Christian Social antipode. These two men respected each other, despite their frequent clashes on the parliamentary floor and as negotiators for their respective parties. On the occasion of Seipel's death in 1932 Bauer held a moving speech in which he paid homage to the prelate's impressive political stature. Dealings between Bauer and Dollfuß lacked this element of mutual appreciation, and in the course of the latter's tenure as Chancellor their relation moved from bad to worse. During an infamous parliamentary skirmish over the prosecution of Credit-Anstalt directors who were found guilty of fraud Bauer accused Dollfuß of ideological tergiversations. The Chancellor retaliated, calling Bauer a notorious anti-democrat and Bolshevik. This happened in fall 1932. On March 4, 1933, Dollfuß took advantage of the confusion created by the simultaneous resignation of three presidents of the Lower House of Parliament (following disagreement over the outcome of a vote), and proceeded to install an extra-parliamentary regime. Hanisch leaves no doubt that the prime motive for Dollfuß to choose the authoritarian path was his anxiety about a looming National Socialist victory at the polls. This line of reasoning echoes Bauer's contemporary judgment of the events of March 1933. In the months following the Dollfuß coup d'état the Social Democrats, alarmed by Hitler's success in Germany, signaled their willingness to compromise with the government in matters of constitutional reform, so long as emergency powers, to be used against Austrian Nazis, remained a temporary affair. But the Chancellor failed to respond to such overtures, fearing that even limited cooperation with the Democratic Left would drain public support for his regime and work into the Nazis' hands. Instead, Dollfuß relied on a strategy of attrition applied simultaneously against both the Social Democrats and Hitler's Austrian followers. The Social Democratic *Schutzbund* was declared illegal, police and army were dispatched to search workers' homes for hidden weapons, and "Red" Vienna suffered depletion of its financial reserves at the hands of the federal government. At the same time, the Austrian National Socialist Party fell under a legal ban, its members were excluded from the civil service, and detention camps or even the death penalty awaited those who had committed acts of violence. However, there was an important difference between the war fought against "the Reds" and the measures directed against the Nazis. As Emil Fey, the *Heimwehr* minister responsible for state security affairs put it: "Battling the Bolsheviks is our pleasure, while it is only our sense of duty, and an instinct of self-preservation that causes us to fight the Nazis, too."[4]

In the face of mounting aggression, the Democratic Left was torn between conciliatory gestures and preparations for the worst. In one of his memorable speeches Otto Bauer defined the limits not to be transgressed by the government if it wished to avoid military action by *Schutzbund* forces. The workers were ready to take up arms, said Bauer, if Austria was pushed down the road to Fascism. And he continued with the ominous announcement that, should the party leadership be coerced into inaction, the proletariat would act on its own behalf. In the morning of February 12, 1934 *Schutzbund* men in Linz, Upper Austria, took the liberty of interpreting Bauer's words their own way. They fired a Stengun at police units positioned in front of the local Social Democratic Party headquarters. This was the beginning of Austria's short and bloody Civil War, and doubtlessly of the darkest days in Otto Bauer's political life as well.

For an assessment of Bauer's conduct during the critical February days of 1934 his biographer is compelled to resort to speculative psychology. Official documents are as sparse as eyewitness reports, and most of the latter are heavily biased. Bauer and Julius Deutsch, supreme commander of the *Schutzbund*, both published their story of the events, but both had reasons to obscure potentially embarrassing details. What Hanisch derives from his sources and conjectures is a sympathetic understanding of Bauer's role in the revolt, but no whitewashing of a man who certainly failed to live up to the expectations of his comrades in arms. Hanisch gives Bauer credit for not having authorized the shooting in Linz of February 12. Unable to hold back the determined local *Schutzbund* leader Richard Bernaschek (who later accused Bauer, in an unmistakably anti-Semitic language, of treachery), he must have been stricken by a sudden attack of panic, says Hanisch. Bauer spent the hours until noon of the next day in fruitless

4. Quoted from Peter Huemer, *Sektionschef Robert Hecht und die Zerstörung der Demokratie in Österreich* (Vienna: Verlag für Geschichte und Politik, 1975), 223. Translation by the author.

attempts at coordinating military actions at Vienna. When he definitely lost touch with the *Schutzbund* units under siege in various parts of the town, he and Deutsch made their escape across the Czechoslovak border in a car provided by that country's ambassador, Zdenek Fierlinger. Deutsch later claimed to have been wounded in combat (this turned out to be untrue), while Bauer, in an article written after the event and titled "The insurrection of the Austrian workers," post-dated his flight to February 15 (instead of 13), presumably to create the impression of having held out with the Viennese workers until the complete breakdown of the *Schutzbund* rebellion. Along with Bauer and Deutsch, the editorial offices and printing presses of the *Arbeiter-Zeitung* were now domiciled at Brünn/Brno, Moravia. Henceforth, the paper would be smuggled into Austria (where its distribution was prohibited), and it would contain fiery condemnations of Dollfuß and the regime from the pen of Otto Bauer. Not too far in the future, Bauer assured his readers, a popular revolutionary movement would put an end to Austro-Fascism and replace it with the dictatorship of the proletariat gradually to be transformed into a genuine workers' democracy. In one of the rare emotional statements of his biography, Hanisch calls this prophesy the nadir of Bauer's political and intellectual career.

After its defeat in February 1934 the once so proud Austrian Social Democratic Party was in shambles. Part of its cadres defected either to the Communists or the Nazis. Those who stayed engaged in bitter infighting over various issues: the appropriate name for an underground Socialist movement in Austria, the wisdom or folly of forming an alliance with the Communists, the proper way to confront Austrian Nazism, and the desirability of infiltrating the trade unions functioning within the framework of Austria's Catholic corporatism. The exiled former party mandarins in Brno continued to exert a certain influence in all these discussions, the more so since the *Auslandsbüro der österreichischen Sozialisten* (ALÖS), run by Bauer and Deutsch, managed those financial assets that the party had been able to move out of Austria. But compared to Bauer's political weight prior to 1934 his new status was clearly reduced. The Czechoslovak government, in which Socialists held a stake, made it clear from the very beginning that it would not tolerate armed aggression against Austria organized by Socialist exiles. They were free to agitate against the Austrian regime, but within boundaries set by Prague's desire for "neutral" relations with its Southern neighbor. Apart from Czechoslovak anxieties, there were other factors which undermined Bauer's position as a leader-in-exile. His vision of the ALÖS as a catalyst for the reunification of Austrian Socialism, and his expectations of the Dollfuß-Schuschnigg regime being swept away, "in the short perspective," by a united front of Socialism and Communism, proved untenable. Hanisch says little about the stress to which Bauer's health was exposed due to overwork, his chain smoking, and feelings of personal abandonment. But it seems clear that the Bauer of Brno was a tired man, despite his relatively young age. In his state of exhaustion he published a last great book titled "In between two World Wars?" (*Zwischen zwei Weltkriegen?*). Most of it was written before the events of February 1934. Hanisch mentions the volume briefly in the context of Bauer's writings about the Great Depression, but disdainfully brushes aside what Bauer said in 1936 about the chances for a new and potentially hyper-destructive global conflagration, followed by the Soviet Union's ascent to superpower status upon the defeat of Nazi Germany, and by the rise of a Socialist world-system. From today's standpoint this was again a bad prognosis. But Europeans who lived to see the Cold War unfolding would probably not have rejected it out of hand as Hanisch does.

From 1936 onward, Bauer was primarily concerned with developments in his native Austria. Understandably, the assassination by Nazi conspirators of Dollfuß in June 1934 failed to stir his empathy. But when Austria's new Chancellor Kurt Schuschnigg in July 1936 decided to return to business as usual with Nazi Germany despite Hitler's obvious involvement in the plot against Dollfuß, Bauer correctly anticipated the threat to Austrian independence emanating from a German military leadership bent on encircling and attacking Czechoslovakia, and subsequently the Soviet Union. Always a staunch believer in Anschluss, defined as the peaceful unification of Austria with Germany, the Otto Bauer of 1936-38 steadfastly refused to consider sacrificing Austrian sovereignty under pressure from the Third Reich. As late as March 10, 1938—two days before Hitler's troops crossed the Northern borders of Austria—Bauer appealed to "his" workers to support Schuschnigg's plan for a plebiscite, and thus "block the road to Vienna for Nazi barbarianism." In a rather astounding volte-face after Hitler's triumph, Bauer dropped the demand that Austria be independent and declared that the Nazis should and would be removed by an "all-German" Socialist revolution. With the Anschluss accomplished, Brno and Czechoslovakia offered scant safety for Bauer and his friends. The ALÖS was quickly moved to Paris. There, Otto Bauer died from a heart attack on July 5, 1938, two months before his fifty-seventh birthday.

Upon perusal of Hanisch's biography of Bauer, one is left with the impression that its hero was a highly gifted but also a tragic personality. Bauer's tomb at Vienna's Central Cemetery, erected on the occasion of the return of his ashes from France to Austria in 1948, bears no inscription except his name and that of his spouse Helene. But one could imagine it adorned with the epitaph that Austria's hapless ruler Joseph II allegedly wanted for himself: "Here lies a man who failed in all he undertook." Hanisch is forthright enough to let us know that, in his opinion, Bauer's misfortunes were to Austria's advantage. He underscores his argument with the highly speculative notion that, had Bauer survived World War II and again lived in Austria as an active politician, he might have surrendered his Socialist Party and his country to the Communists, just as many post-1945 Socialist leaders in East Central Europe did. Whatever one thinks of such hypothesizing, one can hardly escape the conclusion that Bauer's life and deeds warranted an in-depth study, and that Hanisch's book, despite occasional lax editing[5], will serve as a benchmark for a long time to come.

5. In this reviewer's copy, all the footnotes of the introductory chapter were missing. Furthermore, names are spelled incorrectly (eg. Schiller-Marmorek instead of Schiller Marmorek), financial terms are confused (a loan, in German: *Anleihe*, becomes *Anlage*, which means investment, p. 281); etc., etc.

Ein österreichischer General gegen Hitler: Feldmarschalleutnant Alfred Jansa; Erinnerungen, ed. Peter Broucek (Vienna: Böhlau, 2011)

Alexander N. Lassner

Scholars of the Austrian First Republic and the *Standesstaat* have known for decades that the Austrian Chief of the General Staff, Field Marshall Alfred Jansa, wrote a memoir that the Jansa family would not allow to be seen or published. Now, at long last, that work has been published by Böhlau Verlag in a massive eight-hundred and thirty page volume. The memoir, *Ein österreichischer General gegen Hitler*, will very likely represent the last significant documentary contribution to the field of interwar (1919 - 1939) Austrian history by a major political figure from that period. Jansa's name will ring familiar to those scholars who study central European politics and diplomacy during the time when Austria struggled to maintain its independence against Nazi Germany, most especially through Jansa's association with Austrian defense planning against an attack by the Third Reich. But the memoir is interesting for other reasons as well, perhaps most significantly for the author's recollections of his time in the Austro-Hungarian Army as a general staff liaison officer in World War I, and as the Austrian Military Attaché to Berlin. The book is also remarkable for the span of time it covers, during which Jansa worked and lived under five different forms of government in Austria.

The book begins with a standard introduction by the editor, Peter Broucek, a well known Austrian military historian and archivist from the *Österreichisches Staatsarchiv*. However, the foreword is not followed by the memoir itself, but by a rather strange and out of place essay written by Broucek. Not only is the essay unnecessary, but the interpretation is flawed and distortive. The editor fails to align the essay with the periods of Jansa's life as outlined in the memoir, giving the impression that the Austrian officer's later life is the period worthy of serious attention. Broucek is not writing an "*Einführung in die militärisch-politische Lage Österreichs*," despite that being the title of the essay, nor is he writing an introduction to the history of the Austrian *Bundesheer*. What he has written is a wandering discussion on the Austian *Bundesheer* during the period of the First Republic and the *Standesstaat*, with a shifting focus on rearmament, operational planning and a dash of political context.

The result is unsatisfying: Broucek provides no new interpretations here and substantially less information than in his previously published works, and he continues to ignore English and Italian language scholarship on the subject. Making matters worse, when he does bring new evidence to bear, such as his discovery of the German minutes of talks between Austrian Chancellor Kurt Schuschnigg and Italian *Capo del Governo* Benito Mussolini in May of 1935, Broucek uses it in a way that conforms to his long held views on the Dollfuß and Schuschnigg regimes' actions, and, in so doing, distorts the evidence. Thus, for example, Broucek stresses Schuschnigg's desire for Hungarian military aid and positive orientation towards Italy in the discussions with Mussolini (p. 92).

Yet the Italian and Austrian records of the same meeting (the Austrian document from Broucek's own *Österreichisches Staatsarchiv*), of which the author should be well aware, tell a very different story. Schuschnigg explicitly and repeatedly refused at this and other meetings to be drawn into Italian and Hungarian security arrangements, including explicit rejections of Mussolini's proposals, and no amount of wishing this evidence away or ignoring it away will make Broucek correct.[1] The Italian and Austrian

1. As both the Austrian and Italian archival documents show, Mussolini also wanted to know if Schuschnigg was favorably disposed towards an Italo-Austrian-Hungarian-Yugoslavian "alignment" (*Zusammengehen*). Schuschnigg's position accorded with the recent tenor of Austro-Yugoslav talks. Thus he held that the Italo-Yugoslav rapprochement was "vital for Austria" and that:

> "the big concern for Austria up to now has been that of having to face not only an attack from Bavaria but also from Yugoslavia. If Italian troops would have had to come to the aid [*soccorso*] of Austria, they could have faced a Yugoslavian penetration in Carinthia. So the Italian-Yugoslav agreement avoids this."

Nevertheless, the chancellor expressed trepidation that the Yugoslavian government was already too firmly linked to Germany and that Berlin's anti-Austrian propaganda in Belgrade was severe. Here, the Duce disagreed, believing instead that the Yugoslav leadership saw the danger that Nazi propaganda posed to Yugoslavia. Indeed, on this issue both leaders were sensitive to Berlin's subversive propaganda efforts in Italian South Tyrol and in Austria.

Talks centered on Nazi Germany. Mussolini estimated that the Third Reich would not be rearmed fully for another two to three years, and he wanted to know if the Austrian government would accept unilateral Italian military assistance in the case of an outright German assault on Austria. Schuschnigg was under no illusions, stating that the "biggest problem" for Austria was always the same: "the threat from Germany." The Reich, he expounded, "will always have as a goal of its politics, explicitly or not, the absorption of Austria." Military action by the Reich against Austria would likely take one of two forms. In the first instance the "Austrian Legion"—which Schuschnigg estimated at 29,000 "armed, motorized, and anxious men"—might attack. In this case Austrian armed forces alone had to and would defend the country.

Here we come to the crux of the matter of what Broucek leaves out of his account. Schuschnigg noted that if the German *Wehrmacht* attacked outright matters would be completely different:

documents—and not whatever partial information and rumor the Nazis managed to find out—must be considered the more reliable and definitive sources. Overall, as the historian Martin Moll has correctly observed, Broucek's essay has not done the memoir any favors.[2]

Indeed, one is left wondering why the editor's essay should be here at all. It is usual practice for a memoir to have a short introductory chapter by the editor introducing it to the reader and giving some orientation as to its importance and place in the literature; this Broucek has done well. It is highly unusual, however, for an editor to write a miniature history to be squeezed in between his own introduction and the memoir itself. One cannot escape the impression here that Broucek has used Jansa's memoir to give himself a platform to advance a particular interpretation of historical events, and thereby prejudice the readers evaluations of the memoir being presented. Given the inherent problematic nature of memoirs as sources, Broucek makes a bad problem worse.[3]

> "In this case there are only two choices: to submit or to rely on European aid. The first choice is out of the question, so in this scenario we are compelled to put forward a claim for help. Thus we are of the view that, with respect to the current foreign political situation, [Austria] cannot rely on unilateral Italian assistance. The other powers also [would] have to stand up for the territorial *status quo* in central Europe directly and immediately."

In order to avoid German aggression, it was crucial to conclude the CEP (which included Britain, France, and Italy) for its "preventative effect" (*Präventivwirkung*), and in order that "the Austrian question would be understood as a European question with all the consequences…." Alexander N. Lassner, "Peace at Hitler's Price: Austria, Europe and the Anschluß," (PhD. diss., Ohio State University, 2000), 116-19. See also the broad argument contained in Ibid., Chapter 3, Chapter 4, Chapter 5.

2. http://www.koeblergerhard.de/ZRG129Internetrezensionen2012/EinoesterreichischerGeneralgegenHitler.htm, accessed 28 Feb. 2012

3. Perhaps the most regularly cited sources among historians are memoirs. They are compact, often available in translation, and easily obtainable at libraries or for purchase. Moreover, they purport to give the reader an inside look into the workings of the world with which the author was most intimately connected. It is all too common, however, for the authors of memoirs to obscure the very events that they profess to describe. The chief problem is the idea of a memoir itself: *ex post facto* writing is done with the knowledge of the results of the actions, policies, and/or decisions under discussion. The negative impact of such knowledge upon the accuracy of memoirs can hardly be overestimated. With reputations at stake, authors are prone towards self-aggrandizement, the concealing of guilt, and the shifting of blame. Tactics include distortions, outright lies, and the omission of unpleasant evidence. Baruch Fischoff, "Hindsight is not Equal to Foresight: The Effect of Outcome Knowledge on Judgement under Uncertainty," *Journal of Experimental Psychology: Human Perception and Performance* 1, no. 2 (1975): 288-99; S.A. Hawkins and R. Hastie, "Hindsight: Biased Judgements of Past Events after the Outcomes are Known," *Psychological Bulletin* 107, no. 3 (1990): 817-29; Philip E. Tetlock and Aaron Belkin, eds., "Counterfactual Thought Experiments in World Politics: Logical, Methodological, and Psychological Perspectives," in *Counterfactual Thought Experiments in World Politics: Logical, Methodological, and Psychological*

The memoir itself can be roughly divided into four sections: Jansa's childhood and entrance into the Austro-Hungarian Army; his service in World War I; his time as an officer in the *Bundesheer* of the Austrian First Republic and *Standestaat*, to include his service as military attaché in Berlin and Chief of the General Staff until the Anschluß; and, finally, his attempts to survive during World War II and in post war Europe. All are interesting, though not all are equally important.

Jansa's recounting of his life as a child and young adult are necessarily of lesser significance to historians of World War I and of the Interwar Period. Yet the story is fascinating, nonetheless. It is quickly apparent that Jansa was born into a relatively impoverished petite noble family living in spartan accommodations. The author spends almost no time discussing his lineage (as opposed to, for example, the lengthy family pedigrees that one finds in the memoir of Egon and Heinrich Berger Waldenegg or in that of Ernst Rüdiger Starhemberg), for although Jansa was close to his parents, the family on the father's side seems to have been estranged (p. 129). Throughout the author's childhood the family moved often due to his father's responsibilities as an officer in the Austro-Hungarian Army, and Jansa lived in a variety of ethnically diverse cities. As a consequence of the family's persistent money troubles, he eventually went, cost free, to a military academy and was commissioned a Lieutenant in the Austro-Hungarian Army (1902). What is most interesting in these introductory chapters is the snap-shot of life that emerges in the multi-ethnic and polyglot Empire (see, for example, pp. 125-29). Here one sees—albeit in gentle form—the internal tensions within the state, from competing and developing nationalism, to the ethnic prejudices: his mother, for example, advised him most stringently against marrying a Hungarian (p. 155).

Life did not fall into a steady routine from the time Jansa joined his first regiment until the outbreak of World War I. By competitive exam he was chosen to attend the *Kriegsschule* (the rough contemporary American equivalent is a Command and General Staff College) in order to become a staff officer, where, evidently, he had his critics (pp. 177-79). After graduating in 1910 and being promoted to the rank of Captain in 1912, Jansa ended up becoming an operations staff officer for Field Marshall

Perspectives (Princeton: Princeton University Press, 1996), 1-38.

Recently, one historian has commented precisely upon such tendencies in connection with the memoirs of leading members of the Austro-Hungarian political and military leadership in World War One. Too often the memoir has become both apologia and propaganda for its author. Holger H. Herwig, "Of Men and Myths: The Use and Abuse of History and the Great War," in *The Great War and the Twentieth Century*, ed. J. Winter, Geoffrey Parker, Mary Habeck, (New Haven: Yale University Press, 2000), 299-330.

Oskar Potiorek, the military governor of Bosnia and thereafter commander of the Austro-Hungarian 6th Army. As one of Potiorek's staff officers, Jansa was involved in further refining already existing theater strategy and operational planning against Serbia.[4] The author has interesting things to say about the dysfunctionality of Potiorek's command, his aloofness from his soldiers and officers, and the substandard decision making of Potiorek himself; decision making that Jansa claims to have opposed and tried to change (pp. 213, 231, 233, 235-237, 247, 251).[5]

Perhaps the most remarkable claim that the author makes is that a significant part of the blame for the initial disasters that Austro-Hungarian armed forces experienced in 1914 is attributable to the baleful influence on Potiorek by his Adjutant, Colonel Erik Merizzi. Specifically, Jansa argues that Merizzi systematically prevented coordination and advice from reaching Potiorek and "*planmäßig vergiftet*" ("regularly poisoned") Potiorek's relationship with Chief of the General Staff FM Franz Conrad Hötzendorf (pp. 209-212, 222, 225). This exaggerates the centrality of one critical command relationship in the Austro-Hungarian defeats of 1914, but it is an important detail given the significantly different conceptions of operations against Serbia entertained by Conrad and Potiorek. As military historians are making clear, command relationships are critical and sometimes decisive in operational success or failure.[6]

The author saw duty as a staff officer on all three main Austrian fronts of the war (Balkan, Italian, Russian) and his memoir has value as a source for looking at ethnicity, nationalism and linguistic fractures within the Austro-Hungarian military units in which Jansa served (pp. 167, 237, 240,

---

4. A rough contemporary American Army equivalent of Jansa position and extent of responsibility would be the rank of Major/Lieutenant Colonel at the US Army Europe G3 and G5 level (operational tasking, planning and execution), although Jansa was only a Captain at the time, and the staff on which he worked was much smaller.

5. For example, Jansa's view of Potiorek's aloofness accords with the portrait we have from Rudolf Jeřábek, *Potiorek: General im Schatten von Sarajevo* (Vienna: Verlag Styria, 1991), 30.

6. A truly outstanding work of scholarship that illuminates the kinds of problems that arose in British and French commands during World War I is that by Elizabeth Greenhalgh. Elizabeth Greenhalgh, *Victory through Coalition: Britain and France during the First World War* (Cambridge: Cambridge University Press, 2005).

The 1991 Gulf War proves a comparative contemporary example of competition and friction in a coalition and between services in the same military. See: Michael R. Gordon and Bernard E. Trainor, *The Generals' War: The Inside Story of the Conflict in the Gulf* (Toronto: Little Brown and Company, 1995); Rick Atkinson, *Crusade: The Untold Story of the Persian Gulf War* (Boston: Mariner Books, 1994). Especially instructive and illuminating as to the issues of dysfunctional command relationships between services—which is not dissimilar to that between national coalition partners—is the four hour documentary on the Gulf War by Frontline http://www.pbs.org/wgbh/pages/frontline/gulf/, accessed 28 Feb. 2012.

283, 416-17, 425). But the more intriguing part of his experiences in World War I concerns his repeated assignments as a liaison officer to the Germans and to the Bulgarians. In particular Jansa served directly under the newly promoted FM August Mackensen and his chief of staff Major General Hans Seekt in the newly formed Army Group Mackensen.

There is a well developed literature, though uneven in coverage, on the problematic relations between German and Austro-Hungarian armed forces in World War I, and the consequences of tensions on grand strategy and operational planning.[7] Jansa's experiences fit the general historiographical picture that has been developed of Austro-Hungarian and German friction and duplicity during the war, even while adding new details to that depiction.[8] Unsurprisingly the author's sympathies are firmly Austrian: he is critical of Mackensen's attitude and prejudices towards Austria-Hungary, and, although there is also camaraderie between the two sides, he relates specific examples of the manner in which Germany regularly placed its own interests above those of Austria-Hungary (pp. 243, 244, 261, 265, 278, 280, 288, 295, 297, 301-302, 313-14). Military historians studying the formation and workings of wartime coalitions and alliances on the model laid down by Elizabeth Greenhalgh will find useful what Jansa has to say here.[9]

7. The scholarship that focuses on the Austro-Hungarian - German alliance tends to focus on the prewar and early war period. Some of the better examples of studies that focus specifically on the Austro-Hungarian - German alliance relationships, especially those of planning and command relationships include, H. Otto, "Zum strategisch-operativen Zusammenwirken des deutschen und österreichisch-ungarischen Generalstabes bei der Vorbereitung des ersten Weltkrieges," in *Zeitschrift für Militärgeschichte* II (Deutscher Militärverlag, 1963), 426; Gordon Craig, "The World War I Alliance of the Central Powers in Retrospect: The Military Cohesion of the Alliance," *Journal of Modern History* 37 (summer, 1965): 341; Norman Stone, "The Austro-German Alliance, 1914-1918" in *Coalition Warfare: An Uneasy Accord* (Ontario: Wilfrid Laurier Universiy Press, 1983), 17. Less detailed, but still interesting, is Richard L. DiNardo and Daniel J. Hughes, "Germany and Coalition Warfare in the World Wars: A Comparative Study," in *War in History* 8, no. 2 (2001): 166-90.

More generally, Holger Afflerbach has recently written a biography of Falkenhayn that includes many very interesting details as regards the dysfunctional alliance. Holger Afflerbach, *Falkenhayn, Politisches Denken und Handeln im Kaiserreich* (Munich: R. Oldenbourg, 1994). Manfried Rauchensteiner and Holger Herwig's magisterial works provide much information on the problems affecting the Austro-Hungarian and German alliance. Manfried Rauchensteiner, *Der Tod des Doppeladlers: Österreich-Ungarn und der Erste Weltkrieg* (Graz: Verlag Styria, 1993); Holger Herwig, *The First World War: Germany and Austria-Hungary 1914-1918* (London: Edward Arnold, 1997).

8. Jansa's memoir, while of lesser interest, nonetheless fits well with the very few other such memoirs covering Austro-Hungarian and German command relationships and planning. See, for example, Josef Stürgkh, *Im deutschen Hauptquartier* (Leipzig: List, 1921) and August von Cramon, *Unser österreich-ungarischer Bundesgenosse im Weltkrieg: Erinnerungen aus meiner vierjährigen Tätigkeit als bevollmächtigter deutscher General beim k. und k. Armeeobercommando* (Berlin: Mittler, 1920).

9. Greenhalgh, *Victory through Coalition*, passim.

There is a final aspect of Jansa's World War I recollections that will intrigue military historians. This has to do with the infantry and artillery revolutions in military affairs (RMAs) that took place in World War I in tactical and operational concepts. Although numerous studies have been written which look at the Great Powers' RMAs and military effectiveness during the Great War, virtually nothing of a similar nature has been done for Austria-Hungary.[10] For example, the first volume of Allan R. Millett and William Murray's groundbreaking co-edited three volume series, *Military Effectiveness: The First World War* ignores the Austro-Hungarian case while including extensive and detailed chapters on her allies and enemies.[11]

Jansa's memoir illustrates the degree to which the Austro-Hungarians were aware of the ongoing changes in infantry and artillery doctrine, the author going so far as to attended a German *Sturmkurs* in 1917 set up to train German troops in the changing infantry doctrine (pp. 302, 315, 345). And although Jansa tends to lay a lot of blame for Austro-Hungarian military failures on materiel deficits (pp. 244, 255, 295, 302) he ultimately wrote up his views on the changing combined arms doctrine, though this document is not included in the memoir (p. 409). Unfortunately, the editor seems unaware of the potential importance of this document and does not comment as to whether or not it is still extant. If it does exist and can be located, it would be of considerable value to any study on Austro-Hungarian military effectiveness during World War I.

With the collapse of the Austro-Hungarian Empire Jansa found employ in the newly formed *Bundesheer* of the Austrian First Republic and the *Standesstaat*. The author's sympathies were decidedly not with the Socialists and their paramilitary forces in the First Republic, yet, rather surprisingly,

10. As Macgregor Knox and Williamson Murray persuasively argue, it is critical to distinguish between two types of revolutions: "military revolutions" which are driven by vast social, economic and political changes and "revolutions in military affairs (RMAs) which can be created and driven by military organizations themselves and which are not necessarily linked to evolving technology. MacGreggor Knox and Williamson Murray eds., *The Dynamics of Military Revolution 1300-2050* (Cambridge: Cambridge University Press, 2001), 1-14; 176-77.

The RMAs of the Central Powers in World War I were primarily doctrinal, while those of the Allies were more a mix of doctrinal and technological. See especially, Bruce I. Gudmundsson, *Stormtrooper Tactics: Innovation in the German Army 1914-1918* (Connecticut: Praeger Publishers, 1982); Timothy T. Lupfer, *The Dynamics of Doctrine: The Changes in German Tactical Doctrine During the First World War*, Leavenworth Papers No. 4 (Fort Leavenworth Kansas: US Army Command and General Staff College, 1981); Shelford Bidwell and Dominick Graham, *Fire-Power: The British Army Weapons and Theories of War 1904-1945* (London: Unwin Hyman, 1985); Allan R. Millett and Williamson Murray eds., *Military Effectiveness: The First World War*, vol. I (Boston: Unwin Hyman, 1989).

11. Ibid.

he was less sympathetic to the aristocratic elements than one might expect (pp. 465, 491-492, 731-734). His focus during the early interwar period seems to have been on trying to train the best possible armed forces despite the ever-present dearth of funds from the government in Vienna (pp. 452, 465, 474-75).

With the rise of Hitler and the National Socialist Party, but prior to the Nazi *Machtergreifung* in Germany, one sees thc author drawn into the fight against Nazi led attempts to subvert Austrian armed forces (p. 488). Obtaining and reading a copy of *Mein Kampf* confirmed Jansa in his opposition to Hitler, and it was in no small part a consequence of his anti-Nazism that Jansa was made the Austrian Military and Air Attaché to Germany and Switzerland from 1933 to 1935. Given the missing archival documents in the *Österreichisches Staatsarchiv* covering his period in Berlin, this chapter of the book is a welcome source that includes useful particulars, even if there is no momentous revelation here.[12] Jansa evaluates many of the key Austrian personalities in Berlin and in Vienna and his relationship to them, including Ambassador to Berlin Stefan Tauschitz, Political Director Theodor Hornbostel, Chancellor Kurt Schuschnigg, and Secretary for Defense Willhelm Zehner. Of these men, Jansa makes his most stinging critique about Zehner, and has his most interesting conversations with Schuschnigg, to whom Jansa declared that there were only two possibilities for Austria: "*bedingungslose Unterwerfung oder Kampf*" (pp. 526, 549, 573-74). The chapter also includes some details on the author's impressions and evaluations of German maneuvers and military personalities, such as German Chief of Staff, General Ludwig Beck (pp. 523-24, 552-53, 561).

The most significant aspect of Jansa's chapter on his time in Berlin, however, has to do with his growing recognition of the danger that Nazi Germany presented Austria. The development of these views was partly a consequence of his own observations of Nazi leadership, the oppressive police state as he observed it in Berlin, and the assassination of Austrian Chancellor Engelbert Dollfuß by Austrian Nazis with the connivance and support of Nazi Germany (pp. 523-24, 539, 540-49, 552, 560, 569-70). But Jansa's hardening views of the Nazi regime were also buttressed and developed though his talks with American and British Ambassadors and Military attachés in Berlin and Vienna (pp. 554-55).[13] By the time Jansa

12. Almost no Austrian documents regarding Jansa's period as military attaché in Berlin survived German archival purges in 1938 and after, as well as the destructiveness of the war.
13. The U.S. National Archives and the Foreign Relations of the United States (FRUS) published documents contain the most important documentary evidence for American ambassador George Messersmith's views on the Nazis, views that he shared and discussed regularly with high ranking Austrians, to include Jansa.

returned to Vienna, he understood the regime in Berlin to be one of brutal violence run by a murderer (pp. 552, 568).

This brings us to the most significant part of the author's memoirs, namely his time serving as Chief of Staff for the Austrian armed forces. Unfortunately, as greatly as historians may have waited to see this part of the memoir, the eighty-seven pages prove thoroughly underwhelming. There is little here that cannot be found in the archival sources located in Austria, France, Germany, the United States, Italy and Hungary, and there are very important details that Jansa leaves out of account or of which he is unaware. Thus, for example, while Jansa spends a great deal of time discussing operational planning and arming of the Austrian armed forces for use against the Third Reich (pp. 602-603, 620-29), he avoids entirely any mention of contingency planning against Czechoslovakia stemming from a potential Italo-German ultimatum to Austria combined with the November/December 1937 pressure by Hungarian heads of state for Austria to participate in the destruction of Czechoslovakia. This is a serious and somewhat puzzling omission, as Jansa declared at the time that joining Hungary and Germany in order to plan an attack on Czechoslovakia would be nothing short of suicide for the existence of Austria, and nothing came of the planning.[14]

As regards the issues of which Jansa is unaware, none will be more potentially misleading to scholars who rely on this memoir than the interactions of Jansa with leading Italian political and military figures in mid-1936. Here, every one of Jansa's details tells only part of a much larger and more important story that can only be answered by extensive work in the Italian, Hungarian and Austrian archives, from the question of why Italy did not ship promised military material to Austria in 1936-1937, to the comments made to Jansa by *Il Duce* as to a possible German-Italian

---

On 25 October 1934 Messersmith wrote Washington: "terroristic policy ... is one of the principles of National Socialism .... [and] such men that did prosecute [Nazis] would be dealt with [,] with the barbarity and intolerance with which National Socialism has treated its opponents in Germany." Lassner, "Peace at Hitler's Price," 55-56.

14. In the late summer and fall of 1936, Hungarian leaders—enthused by the conclusion of the July 1936 Austro-German *Abkommen*, and privately hoping that Austria would ultimately accede to their plans for future war against Czechoslovakia—requested that Schuschnigg join them in Berchtesgaden to meet with Hitler, in order to help advance Hungarian revisionism, and acquiesce to the expansion of the Roman Protocols by concluding an Austro-Italian-Hungarian military agreement. Vienna rejected these proposals, aware that they were but precursors to Budapest's ardently desired bloc of Germany-Italy-Austria-Hungary. By November 1937 the Hungarians were explicitly and repeatedly pressuring the Austrians to join in the destruction of Czechoslovakia. The very same Hungarian statesmen claimed to have the permission and backing of Germany in putting forth this request to Austria. Lassner, "Peace at Hitler's Price," 296-316.

"*Zusammengehen*" against Great Britain (pp. 628-35). What Jansa never properly understood (pp. 613, 632) is that Mussolini had always considered Germany as a possible ally to correct the *vittoria mutilata* (mutilated victory) imposed on Italy by Britain and France after World War I. After the British sanctions on Italy at the end of 1935, Mussolini steered Italy secretly and purposefully towards alliance with Nazi Germany for purposes of Italian territorial aggrandizement. In this, *Il Duce* wanted to bring Austria along as an authoritarian and pro-Italian ally, quite unrealistically, as it turned out.[15]

More useful are Jansa's comments on the July 1936 Austro-German *Abkommen*. His views here accord with a shifting interpretation of the significance of the *Abkommen* and the Schuschnigg regime's intentions in signing that agreement. The *Abkommen* was created with purposeful ambiguity and contradiction by both sides. On the Austrian side this was because Schuschnigg and his collaborators believed that they could mire the Nazis in endless legal arguments and maneuvers in interpreting the *Abkommen* and thereby win time for international matters to tilt back into a more pro-Austrian path, or at the very least, *to avoid Nazi German military aggression when it came, as Schuschnigg believed that it ultimately would.* On the German side, this was because Adolf Hitler and his cronies believed that they could attain their ends through pro-German interpretations and purposeful subversion of the *Abkommen* backed by the coercive might of the *Wehrmacht*.[16] Thus, Jansa reveals that although he and Hornbostel

15. For the full story to these and other issues that Jansa brings up with respect to Italy see Ibid., chapter 10, chapter 11.

16. See, Gabriele Volsansky's *Pakt auf Zeit: Das Deutsch-Österreichische Juli-Abkommen 1936*, (Vienna: Böhlau Verlag, 2001), 32-35, 46-47, 71-72, 185-99, 223-24; Lassner, "Peace at Hitler's Price," chapter 6, chapter 7.

The key to understanding the contradiction and ambiguity purposefully built into the *Abkommen* lies in the Schuschnigg government's understanding the international strategic situation. The senior members of that regime understood early on that Nazi Germany would eventually use force to seize and digest portions of central Europe in particular as a preliminary to a major war, and Schuschnigg and his closest collaborators understood that Austria was first on the German menu after the remilitarization of the Rhineland.

What Volsansky fails to discuss satisfactorily (and here she is the victim of her limited sources and, more significantly, the limited scope of her work) is *why* the *Abkommen* ended up taking the contradictory and ambiguous form that it did. The majority of the participants in drafting the *Abkommen* were diplomats and lawyers, so there was hardly a lack of understanding on the drafters' part about the meaning of the words that they chose to use, or which phrases were unclear and which phrases were exact. Indeed, the endless bickering and wordsmithing that went into the actual creation of the agreement—which Volsansky herself portrays—shows that these men were quite aware of each distinction and/or ambiguity that they included. Moreover, Schuschnigg understood what liars he was dealing with in the likes of Adolf Hitler, Hermann Göring, Papen and others, and he hardly became their dupe by permitting them to include wording that he, Schuschnigg, did not recognize as being subject

were against the conclusion of the agreement, he, Jansa, understood the argument in favor of its conclusion and the inherent flexibility of the agreement. He further believed that Schuschnigg could and would restrict its interpretation and not deviate from the previous held political line vis-à-vis Nazi Germany (pp. 643-45). Here, the author's memoir indicates that he miscalculated: he describes with disappointment his and Hornbostel's gradual estrangement from the Austrian chancellor, as Schuschnigg's began to give ground in interpreting the *Abkommen*. In the end, Schuschnigg and Zehner were not even willing to defend Jansa's use of a state car to take care of his two daughters, after the death of Jansa's wife (pp. 648, 653, 658-59). Jansa became aware of his impending retirement from rumors in late 1937, and he was officially informed in January 1938 (pp. 664, 667). Unsurprisingly, Jansa is very critical of Schuschnigg's handling of matters in 1937-1938, going so far as to state that Austria would have been better served by Dollfuß, who, in Jansa's opinion, would have fought Hitler with military force if needed. Jansa, at any rate, clearly viewed the Austrian armed forces as a deterrent that would actually be used, if need be, against the armed might of Nazi Germany. Although he did not believe that Austria could win a hot war, he did believe that a sustained defense would give time for the Great Britain, France and Italy force Germany to withdraw (pp. 619, 676). Given the actual strategic situation in January 1938, however, this must be judged extremely unlikely.

The last chapter of the author's memoir is the least significant for the historian, though it remains interesting. Jansa details his questioning at the hands of the Gestapo and the measures that he and his family took to survive World War II (pp. 682, 701). After the war Jansa was publically hailed for his role in the defense of Austria, and was even consulted by Austrian Chancellor Leopold Figl on matters of national security (pp. 718, 721-23, 725). But Jansa soon made the conscious decision to devote himself to his daughters and family life, and to fade away. Overall, *Ein österreichischer General gegen Hitler* is a worthwhile and interesting addition to the literature on Austria in the twentieth century. Although not without significant shortcomings, most of these applicable to all memoirs, Jansa's work holds up better than most.

to wide interpretation. Ibid., chapter 6, chapter 7.

Evan Burr Bukey, *Jews and Intermarriage in Nazi Austria* (Cambridge: Cambridge University Press, 2011)

Gerald Steinacher

In February 1943 a large crowd of "Aryan" women in Berlin waited publicly and persistently for the release of their Jewish husbands from the hands of the Gestapo. The events of these "Rosenstraße protests" were in the subject of a 2003 film, which helped popularize a widely ignored topic: the fate of husbands, wives and children in the unions between Jews and Gentiles or what the Nazis called "mixed marriages," Evan Burr Bukey, a University of Arkansas Emeritus Professor of History, opens his important book with the surprising fact that almost 90 percent of Austrian Jews in mixed marriages survived the Holocaust. The secret diaries of Victor Klemperer—a professor of Romance languages who happened to be of Jewish ancestry—were published in 1998-1999 and provided an emotional but also detailed account of the experience he and his gentile wife had in Dresden. But how could they survive the onslaught?

The infamous Nuremberg laws of 1935 forbade marriages and sexual relationships between Jews and citizens of "German or kindred blood." But what was Jewish and what was German? And who was considered a Jew in the eyes of Hitler? It is surprising that the Nazis themselves struggled with the answers to these questions from the start to the end of the Thousand-Year Reich. Based on social Darwinism and "völkisch" ideology (racial extreme nationalism) from the late 19th century, the Nazis defined Jews as a race. However, there of course were no "racial markers" to distinguish German Jews from German Gentiles. The Nuremberg laws' definition of racial identity was therefore based solely on religious criteria. Nazi law makers classified people with three or four grandparents of Jewish faith as "Jewish." People with less than three grandparents of Jewish faith were considered "*Mischlinge*"—mixed-blood people. "*Mischlinge*" were not considered "racial Jews" unless they were officially members of a Jewish religious community (p. xv).

The existence of intermarried couples and their "*Mischlinge*" children not only challenged Nazi thinking but also showed its absurdity. The huge *bureaucracy* of the Nazi state and its ideologists constantly struggled with definitions, as to who was or was not a Jew (p. 199). As Bukey remarks, "the idea of being part-Jewish and part-German made little sense in a society based on notions of discrete races" (p. 80). This "problem" was of big concern to the Nazi leadership. It was widely discussed at the notorious Wannsee Conference on January 20, 1942 (p. 2) and continued to be an issue until the collapse of the Nazi state. The Nazi leadership often approached the question of mixed marriages and "*Mischlinge*" with hesitation. Hitler and Goebbels seem to have feared unrest in the society, especially among Aryan family members and relatives. Hitler and the Nazi leadership paid close attention to public opinion, which seems unusual for a totalitarian regime. Though Himmler and Heydrich had very different opinions of how to deal with Jews in mixed marriages, Hitler remained cautious. As a consequence of this stalemate Jewish partners in intermarried couples were often spared from deportation and extermination. This does not mean that partners in mixed marriages and their children were left in peace. The regime harassed them in various ways, discriminated and banned them from public life wherever possible, and fired them from academic jobs at Universities and from the civil service sector.

Ninety percent of Austria's Jews lived in Vienna and many of them were no doubt aware of the widespread virulent anti-Semitism in the city since the 19th century. In fact, Vienna was arguably the most anti-Semitic city in Central Europe having been governed by Karl Lueger and having been the place where Hitler's early ideology was formed. However, in March 1938 when the German *Wehrmacht* rolled into Austria and the Austrian Nazis roamed the streets, the city's close to 170,000 Jewish residents were taken by surprise. The "Anschluss" triggered a wave of anti-Semitic violence in Austria that surprised even the German Nazis. Angry Viennese mobs forced Jews to scrub the cobblestones with tooth brushes and then beat them. The seizure of Austria bolstered the persecution of Jewish communities all over Hitler's Germany. This new wave of open violence reached its first peak in the pogroms of November 1938, *cynically* labeled by Nazi propaganda as "*Kristallnacht*" (night of the broken glass).

In the wake of the "Anschluss" SS Untersturmführer Adolf Eichmann arrived in Vienna. There he opened his office of "emigration," robbing Jewish families of their cash and apartments before forcing them out of the country. The exodus of Austrian Jews included such prominent "non-Aryan" refugees like Sigmund Freud, Franz Werfel, Richard Tauber, and Raul Hilberg. While much is known and researched about this persecuted group, we know relatively little about the fate of gentiles and their Jewish spouses and children. Jews in Germany had years to adapt to the escalating anti-Jewish legislation and harassment. In Austria the "Anschluss" changed Jewish life overnight and in May 1938 the Nuremberg Laws went into effect. As a consequence Viennese Jews and citizens of Jewish descent lost their jobs and were forced out of their rented apartments in a matter of weeks. Intermarried couples in Vienna had to "make life and death decisions overnight" (p. 4). Austrian families of "mixed blood" immediately became outsiders, excluded from the Aryan *"Volksgemeinschaft."*

Bukey makes it very clear that one cannot easily generalize the many different situations of intermarried couples. The spectrum ranged from tolerance, to discrimination, and to severe persecution. Several prominent musicians and other cultural icons such as Franz Lehar and Theo Lingen received protection for their Jewish wives; others, like the popular film comedian Hans Moser, were not as lucky. The pianist Paul Wittgenstein, an older brother of the philosopher Ludwig Wittgenstein, managed to improve the "racial family status" by paying a huge bribe. Hitler himself signed a decree classifying the Wittgensteins "*Mischlinge* of the first decree." Günther Nenning, a prominent journalist in post-war Austria, remembered that his Jewish mother was unharmed, while his "Aryan" father continued to run the family business (p. 117). Other relatives were not so lucky—they were deported to "the East."

The Nazis wanted to correct the "abnormality" of intermarriage and "*Mischlinge.*" The most logical approach was to convince or pressure Aryans to divorce their Jewish or partially Jewish spouses. The Nazis had little success with this approach and marital loyalty often proved to be stronger than ideology. Only a few Austrian intermarriage couples therefore divorced. External pressure played an obvious role in motivating some spouses to file for divorce, but it is not clear to what extent. According to Bukey, nearly all of the dissolved marriages appear to have been unstable or in crisis long before the "Anschluss." Traditional marriage offences such as adultery, domestic violence and alcoholism seemed to have been important factors in divorces, but "probing the 'real reasons' for divorce in any society is a daunting, if not impossible task" (p. 136).

Given the patriarchal structure of German law, the marriage of a gentile man and a woman, who was Jewish or classified as Jewish under the Nuremberg laws, was generally considered a "privileged mixed marriage." The couple faced less discrimination and persecution than Jews in "non-privileged" unions, who were subjected to expropriation, ghettoization, forced labor, having to wear the Star of David, and allocation of much smaller rations. Widowed Jewish women normally lost their "privileged" status with the death of their gentile husbands. Friedensreich Hundertwasser, the well known Viennese artist, recalled how he shielded the household from Nazi assaults as proud Hitler Youth Member, while his widowed Jewish mother hastened through the streets as a pariah: "I didn't realize the perversity of the whole thing," he later wrote. "While my mother went shopping with a Yellow Star, I ran around with a swastika" (p. 118). The sons and daughters of mixed couples often wanted to be part of the mainstream group. They simply wanted to "fit in" and join the Hitler Youth.

Given the vagueness of certain Nazi classifications, *"Mischlinge"* could appeal to Nazi authorities to change their "racial status" and many did. The strength of Bukey's book rests with his research into those Viennese who either persevered or who "upgraded" their racial status in the Aryan *Volksgemeinschaft.* This is a particularly fascinating chapter in Bukey's book, providing clear evidence about the Nazi regime's internal contradictions. Gaps in the family tree and paternity disputes were used to challenge the labeling of the guardians of the race. Bukey identified and carefully analyzed archival material of the District kinship office and the Viennese court of Civil affairs at the *Wiener Stadt- und Landesarchiv.* One example is the case of Kurt Sandor, a highly decorated veteran of the Hitler movement, who found out about the Jewish identity of his grandmother only in 1941. He suffered no negative consequences to fear, because his "German blooded" status was recognized in no time at all (p. 38).

One way to improve one's "racial status" was to deny the legal (Jewish) father's biological paternity. For example, children/wives claimed that the deceased legal (Jewish) father/husband was impotent or *syphilitic* and that the biological father was an *Aryan* man. Witness reports, rumors, testimony of *Aryan* relatives or affidavits sometimes supported such claims. The majority of those attempting to improve their racial status were successful: "Moreover, well over half of the petitioners emerged from chambers for all intents and purposes reclassified as 'persons of German blood'" (p. 78). A simple description of one's physical appearance was labeled as "hereditary and racial scientific examination" and it was the way to determine a person's biological ancestry and often used to solve paternity disputes. But unlike modern day DNA tests, the work of so-called racial scientists was pseudo-scientific. It is of no surprise, that even these Nazi scientists could not prove what was not there. Therefore, they rarely found "morphological evidence of Jewish decent." As a consequence, they could wholeheartedly attest to the petitioner's "German-blooded" status.

The concept of a "German blooded" citizen is older than the Third Reich and even more astonishingly, it survived the end of the Reich for decades. Bukey does not talk about this interesting fact, but traces of this notion can be found in the post-1945 German citizenship law. According to these laws the right of citizenship was also based on German ancestry (*deutsche Volkszugehörigkeit*), especially for ethnic Germans from all over Europe. At the end of his excellent book, Bukey reminds us of the post-war fate of intermarried couples and their children: "Among family members with close ties to Judaism, ... Nazi persecution awakened or reinforced a sense of Jewish identity. This explains why a number of them emigrated to Israel or the United States after the war. The others appear to have devoted themselves to rebuilding their lives in the Second Austrian Republic, quietly keeping their counsel, occasionally seeking restitution, and, in the privacy of their homes, grieving for family members who had fallen as soldiers of the German Wehrmacht, lost their lives to Allied bombardment, or perished in the Holocaust" (p. 199).

In his informative and well-written book Bukey shows us some of the many contradictions in Nazi "*Weltanschauung*" and describes how these contradictions helped save lives in a totalitarian murderous regime. Close to ninety percent of the intermarried Viennese Jews survived the Nazi rule. Meanwhile, the history of their post-war fate in an Austrian Republic, which official memory ignored the perpetrator role of Austrians in war and Holocaust, still awaits to be written.

Dirk Rupnow and Heidemarie Uhl, eds., *Zeitgeschichte ausstellen in Österreich: Museen–Gedenkstätten–Ausstellungen* (Vienna: Böhlau, 2011)

Berthold Molden

In the growing literature on the function of historical representation in museums and exhibitions, the recent volume edited by Dirk Rupnow and Heidemarie Uhl delivers the first profound status report on Austria. The editors identify systematic research into the musealization of Austrian contemporary history as an "evident desideratum" (p. 10) and offer this book as a collective counter effort. Its contributions were mostly penned by historians who are both interested in exhibitionary categories such as curatorial strategies, story lines, display and the hegemonies of representation, and well informed in the current theory of their analysis. Some of them, like Ulrike Felber, Dirk Rupnow, Monika Sommer or Renate Wonisch, are either themselves curators or working in museological contexts. Hence this blend of cultural history, social memory studies and critical museology is the central feature of the book.

Both editors are engaged analysts in debates about Austrian politics of history. Rupnow, currently director of the Institute of Contemporary History at the University of Innsbruck, started his career with a study of the Jewish Central Museum in Prague and its role for historical memory in the Third Reich and has researched, published and lectured extensively on related subjects. Heidemarie Uhl, historian at the Austrian Academy of Sciences, is widely renown as a leading scholar in Austrian memory studies. They intend their volume to be a critical intervention and inventory at a moment they take as a twofold watershed in Austrian cultural memory: on the one hand, an Austrian "House of History" (or rather the lack thereof) is once again being discussed and, on the other, the Austrian exhibition in Auschwitz-Birkenau as well as the Mauthausen memorial are just being revised. Accordingly, the book focuses on two key issues in the labyrinth of the Austrian "exhibitionary complex" (Tony Bennett)—the mnemonic representation of Nazi-victims, resistance and perpetrators; and the different modes of narrating and displaying the history of Austria's First and Second Republic as well as the Austrofascist period in local, regional, and national shows. Interestingly, the order of articles in the book does not indicate these focal points.

The issues of National Socialism, its victims and its collaborators comprise five articles. First, the eminent specialist Bertrand Perz analyzes the KZ-memorials in Mauthausen, Gusen and Melk. He mainly concentrates on the history of the exhibition concepts in Mauthausen since the Soviet authorities handed over the site to Austria in 1947, under the condition that a memorial be constructed there, up to the current revision of the exhibition. Perz emphasizes the divergence between the marginal attention given to the Mauthausen memorial inside Austria and the much stronger reception abroad. He shows how non-Austrian victims were only slowly included in the story line and how the wording and display have always been subject to the hegemonic political discourse: in the case of Austria at least until the Waldheim affair in 1986, this meant the "victim-doctrine" blinding out Austrian responsibility for Nazi crimes. It was therefore little surprising that the 1990s (and the steady retirement of survivors from the educational boards) caused changes in the curatorial debates on memory that still continue.

Brigitte Bailer-Galanda's text on the Austrian memorial in the Auschwitz-Birkenau State Museum follows a similar pattern, from the establishment of the site in 1978 to its current re-conceptualization. As in various other chapters of the book it becomes evident that the "erosion of national historical myths" (p. 160)—again, the Austrian victim-narration—was a European process triggered by previous political changes. Maria Rest's article on the memorial site and contemporary history museum in the former concentration camp Ebensee, on the other hand, focuses on the challenges faced by a local initiative that managed to secure its funding only in the 1990s. And Peter Larndorfer gives insight into Austria's sole permanent exhibition on National Socialism at the Dokumentationsarchiv des Österreichischen Widerstandes. In its permanent and hence institutional character, this show stands in contrast with the temporary touring exhibition "Vernichtungskrieg. Verbrechen der Wehrmacht," of which its two editions were sponsored by the Hamburg Institute for Social Research in the 1990s and are analyzed in this volume by Alexander Pollak. While the former represents more of an insider tip in Austria and the Dokumentationsarchiv is rather known for its research and archival work and for editing the Handbook of Austrian Right-Wing Extremism, the so-called "Wehrmachtsausstellung" abruptly changed Austrian historical memory (or at least the discourse about it) by an effective deconstruction of the "innocent Wehrmacht" myth.

The other articles of the book broach different representations of Austrian (mainly 20th Century) history of longer diachronic range. Hannes

Leidinger and Verena Moritz deal with the Heeresgeschichtliches Museum and its changeable history. Going back to 1869 and situated in a building designed as barracks to control post-1848 bourgeois-revolutionary Vienna, the museum was the first one to house a permanent historical exhibition on the period of 1918-1945, which was opened in 1998. Although the museum is often characterized as antiquated and dusty, Leidinger and Moritz see the exhibition "Republik und Diktatur" as a "landmark" in Austrian exhibitionary history (p. 44). In her essay, Regina Wonisch is able to show that the Technisches Museum, generally not associated with this topic, does indeed reflect aspects of contemporary life and history when seen from a curatorial perspective. The same is true for the issue picked up by Jennifer Jordan: the relationship of food, identity and contemporary history as displayed in four selected exhibitions which "display contemporary history —though sometimes unnoticeably" (p. 394).

Two chapters tackle important anniversary exhibitions. Karin Liebhart writes on the 1996 "millennium exhibition." The 1000th anniversary of the first documented use of Ostarrîchi was sorts of a reenactment of the Second Republic's earliest identity politics in 1946—even though the curators of the 1996 show denied this. Ulrike Felber's take on the exhibition in the Austrian parliament celebrating the 90th anniversary of the proclamation of the republic points out how the storyline excludes Austrians with migratory backgrounds and thus homogenizes national identity. This case in particular also demonstrates public alliances with tendentially xenophobic mass media. Felber also refers to the massive public staging of history politics in the so called "Gedankenjahr" (as an allegory to "Gedenkjahr/ Anniversary Year") 2005—the multiple anniversary of 1945 (liberation), 1955 (state treaty) and 1995 (EU accession). This is, together with a mention in Rupnow's final chapter, the only reference to one of two issues that constitute a surprising absence in this book: the anniversaries of 2005 and 2009 (20 years since the fall of the Iron Curtain).

However, these events have been amply covered in other publications and the volume at hand presents new material instead. Two articles shed light on little known museums and exhibitions and contextualize them in Austrian historical discourse. Richard Hufschmied contributes a meticulous account of the virtually unknown Museum der Ersten und Zweiten Republik, which was conceived by then president Karl Renner in 1946 and moved between different patronages and host institutions until it was finally dissolved in 1998. But while Renner's concept was meant to reconcile the conflictive heritage of Austrian politics, other exhibitions, although conceived at a much later time, when historiography and museology had already provided a critical apparatus, were less balanced. The ideological charge of historical exhibitions when connected with memorials to polarizing political figures becomes evident in Lucile Dreidemy's analysis of the small town museum in the birthplace of the Austrofascist chancellor Engelbert Dollfuß. Financed mainly by ÖVP-politicians, the museum displays a seemingly objective, yet glorifying image of the man who replaced the First Republic by an authoritarian corporate state in 1933 and was shot 16 months later in a failed Nazi coup.

In a related, but comparative focus, Monika Sommer writes about the role of contemporary history in Austrian State Museums, i.e. the Landesmuseen in each federal state. Sommer gives a survey over 9 of the 10 museums of this network, which interestingly includes the Landesmuseum in South Tyrol, Italy. Instead of on-site analyses of each museum's exhibitions on 20th Century history, she follows their specific self-representations in the texts and images of a recent book edited by the Austrian State Museums. Although contemporary history and its political controversies do not constitute their main topic, Sommer assesses that they have revisited their former self-image as art cabinets and treasuries dedicated to solely positive identity politics. From a very informed vantage point, she dissects the historical interventions during "Linz09," the Upper Austrian capital's year as a "European Capital of Culture." Also from a comparative perspective, Gerald Lamprecht depicts the history of Jewish museums during the Second Republic. Museums in Vienna, Eisenstadt and Hohenems as well as the Institute for Jewish History in Austria, located in St. Pölten, illustrate the difficult relationship of large parts of the political elites with Austrian-Jewish history. The 2005 exhibition "Jetzt ist er bös, der Tennenbaum" at the Jewish Museum Vienna may be the most telling example, and all the more visible in the context of national collective self-mystification in 2005.

In the final chapter on Austria as a "Nation without Museum," Dirk Rupnow covers much ground of Austrian museum history, from the Habsburg monarchy up to the present, and brings together many of the issues tackled in the book. The data-rich and yet synthetic article revolves around the fact that Austria lacks a national history museum and concentrates on the controversies about the construction of such a museum since 1945, particularly the recent discussions on a "Austrian House of History." Rupnow frames the Austrian debates in a European context and highlights how Austria does neither fit into the pattern of universalist, Enlightenment-inspired concepts exemplified in British and French museums nor into the catch-up nationalism of 19th Century Germany: the Habsburg monarchy did create museums for different regional and non-

German identities in its realm, but no explicitly historical museums for the Empire as such.

Beyond Austria's strained relationship to German history, Rupnow shows how the transnational impact of European debates on national concepts is in itself an echo of the "Germanization" of historical (and in this case, museological) discourse in Europe. The soon-to-be-opened "House of European History," which is highly controversial precisely because it is suspected to promote the German-dominated vision of European integration, may serve as a projection screen for the inability of Austria's traditional political parties (Social Democrats and Christian Democrats) to sponsor a critical institution dedicated to Austrian history. "As vague as the term 'Europe,' which remains historically changing and open to different definitions, is the term "Austria,'" Rupnow observes (p. 461), and ends the book by summing up the problematic of reducing history to simple narratives: "To press 'Austrian history' into one 'house' remains a challenge" (p. 463).

Ingrid Schramm and Michael Hansel, eds., *Hilde Spiel und der literarische Salon* (Innsbruck: Studienverlag, 2011)

Maria-Regina Kecht

On the occasion of Hilde Spiel's 100th birthday—she was born in Vienna on October 19, 1911—a team of researchers working at the Literary Archive of the Austrian National Library (ÖNB) put together a volume celebrating the contributions of this highly productive and influential Austrian writer and critic. Since Hilde Spiel's *Nachlass* is housed in the Literary Archive, it seems quite obvious that the current director, the scholar Bernhard Fetz, and his colleagues would want to commemorate Spiel through a special publication. It is much less understandable, however, why the book, which they also presented to the public with a certain fanfare, would be so decidedly unimpressive and contribute little to the knowledge base of the relevant scholarly community. (Was the project conceived too late to solicit well-matched and solid contributions? Did too many invited contributors decline the request and the editors had to scramble for texts? Did the deadline result in rushed work?)

No doubt, the volume pays tribute to Hilde Spiel's accomplishments and her status in the cultural landscape of Austria—and this in a variety of ways that reflect Spiel's multiple talents and her own sense of her cultural mission. The chosen title "Hilde Spiel und der literarische Salon" already evokes the writer's incredible talent to gather notable intellectuals and artists at her place—no matter where she resided—and stimulate the exchange of ideas and emergence of collaborative initiatives. The title also makes a reference Spiel would have appreciated very much. It draws a parallel between Spiel and Fanny Baronin von Arnstein, the famous and influential Jewish *salonière* of the late 18th/early 19th century, about whom Spiel wrote a much-praised biography. The concept of a literary salon attracting numerous (meritorious) individuals whose diverse perspectives and opinions—shared through spirited conversations—lead to intellectual or cultural progress in the public sphere is replicated in the organization of this commemorative volume. At least in its intent. Among the ten contributions, we find very short pieces (as reprints) by the writers Julian Schutting and Peter Turrini; personal reminiscences by cultural critics such as Ulrich Weinzierl or Hans Neunzig; and some (more or less) scholarly essays by Austrian Studies experts. The quality of the individual pieces is quite uneven; and if the different voices in the collection are supposed to capture the different sides of Hilde Spiel's achievements, then one must commend the effort despite the shortcomings.

In his introduction Bernhard Fetz emphasizes Spiel's highly influential role as a translator—not only of languages but, more importantly, of cultural perspectives. Her émigré status in Britain motivated Spiel to act as an intermediary between the Anglo-Saxon and the German-speaking worlds: starting journalistic writing in English, acquiring excellent translation skills while presenting works from English literature to a German/Austrian audience, representing Austrian intellectual life in various social and professional contexts, including the international P.E.N. club. This talent as a "cross-cultural communicator" characterizes Hilde Spiel's approach to all her activities—from her pre-war years in London to her immediate post-war assignment as war correspondent in Berlin and to her multiple engagements as a *femme de lettres* in Austria over three decades since the 60s. Fetz delineates Spiel's biography in terms of her impressive networking abilities—making a clear reference to the book's title—and endorses the volume as a "kritische Hommage […] und als Beitrag zu den dampfenden 'Namensküchen' eines vergangenen, wiewohl nachwirkenden Literaturbetriebs" (p. 9).

Julian Schutting is the first among the ten contributors, who enthusiastically praises Spiel's extraordinary gift for language and her powerful mastery of style, whether this pertains to her literary translations, her journalistic writings, her theater reviews, or her oral statements in television debates. Schutting is one of the many Austrian writers who was granted Hilde Spiel's mentoring and who is appreciative of the intellectual encounters at her gatherings in her house at Wolfgangsee.

In her description of the Viennese literary salon of the fin-de-siècle, the British scholar Deborah Holmes provides the initial framework of reference for our understanding of Spiel's cultural role. She argues that even though the male-dominated coffeehouse culture around 1900 actually replaced the female space of the salon of the 19th century, Hilde Spiel had biographical, social, and intellectual reasons to admire and emulate the famous *salonières* Alma Mahler-Werfel, Bertha Zuckerkandl, and Eugenie Schwarzwald. Spiel was one of the young Viennese women who attended a Schwarzwald school and graduated with "Matura" in 1929. She personally got to know the legendary founder and despite a rather critical assessment of Schwarzwald's personality, Spiel always emphasized the influence this visionary woman had on her development. Holmes's essay highlights the experiential and intellectual links between Spiel and Schwarzwald.

Another angle of approaching Spiel's accomplishments is offered by Ingrid Schramm, who depicts the social and cultural scene Fanny von Arnstein created as the "Madame de Staël of Vienna." It is Spiel's biography of Fanny von Arnstein that allows the co-editor Schramm to choose this thematic focus. She paints a vivid portrait of this educated, multitalented, and publicly influential Jewish woman, who demonstrated her strength by refusing to convert to Catholicism, thus contributing substantially to the emancipation of the Viennese Jews. Hilde Spiel, who had high regard for the intellectual and aesthetic sensibilities of Fanny von Arnstein and her ability to draw the Viennese elite to her residence, clearly tried to follow in her footsteps—and some would argue, successfully.

If Schramm's essay is only indirectly about Spiel, the subsequent contribution by Hans A. Neunzig (responsible for the Spiel *Nachlass*) makes the conceptual link between Arnstein and Hilde Spiel quite clear: both possessed incredible talent for establishing connections and crossing boundaries. Neunzig's flattering reminiscence of "Hilde Spiels literarische Netzwerke" (p. 55) provides a kind of anecdotal journey from Spiel's early successes as a writer in the late twenties to her special promotion of young Austrian writers in the seventies and eighties. And at each stage of her life, Spiel thrives amidst circles of artists and intellectuals she adroitly brings together. Exemplary is the period in Berlin soon after WWII: "Unzählig ist die Zahl der Begegnungen mit Künstlern, ob Schriftstellern, Musikern, Theaterleuten, zu nennen, berühmten und weniger berühmten, Politikern aller Couleur und Vertretern aller vier Besatzungsmächte, die jene zwei Jahre des Berliner Aufenthalts bestimmten" (p. 64).

Almost as if to set the picture straight, the essay of the Germanist Esther Schneider Handschin takes a less favorable view of Spiel's activities during those years in Berlin. The credibility of her critical assessment is, so it seems to this reader, undermined by a consistently moralizing tone. Schneider Handschin perceives a double standard and hypocrisy in the careers (and life styles) Spiel and her first husband Peter de Mendelssohn established after the war. She acknowledges that Spiel contributed substantially to the cultural re-awakening of postwar Berlin—particularly in her role as theater critic for the paper *Welt*: "Als Gastgeberin und Theaterkritikerin leistete sie einen Beitrag zur Verständigung zwischen den Deutschen und den Besatzungsmächten sowie zum kulturellen Wiederaufbau Berlins" (p. 76). However, she finds fault with the nepotistical job assignment (P. de Mendelssohn was chief editor of *Welt*), the contradiction between progressive, liberal views and an elitist, snobbish lifestyle, as well as with the murkiness of Spiel's ethical judgment regarding German/Austrian guilt.

The Austrian literary critic Evelyne Polt-Heinzl largely concurs with Schneider Handschin's fundamentally critical depiction of Spiel's career. In her essay "Hilde Spiel—Ein Lebensentwurf zwischen Kaffeehaus und Salon," Polt-Heinzl discerns great ambition and opportunism in Spiel's professional decision-making. As much as one may empathize with Spiel's astute recognition that women tend to get deleted from literary history if they cannot acquire some institutional position of power (e.g. presidency of the P.E.N. club)—and thus understand her passionate pursuit of "Verankerung in der Institutionengeschichte" (p. 97)—one cannot endorse Spiel's calculated career climbing and her adoption of typically male patterns of behavior. This is certainly a different aspect of networking; one that other contributors to this volume do not point out. (It is interesting in this context that Spiel definitely promoted young male authors, such as Bernhard or Turrini, whereas she did not establish bonds of solidarity with female writers, such as Bachmann or Aichinger.)

A collection of pictures separates the above-presented essays from the final two contributions, both of which take up Spiel's life and work in the Salzkammergut and Salzburg. The editors of the volume, Schramm and Hansel, are clearly in awe of the long list of Who's Who in Austria that is recorded in the guest book of Hilde Spiel's house at Wolfgangsee. "Nationale und internationale Persönlichkeiten aus Kunst und Kultur, Musik, Film und der Medienlandschaft gaben sich von 1955 bis 1986 sozusagen die Klinke in die Hand" (p. 116). The reader learns a great deal about all the socializing that took place in Spiel's home but is given specific information—spiced up with anecdotes—about Spiel's amicable interactions with Lernet-Holenia, Doderer, and Bernhard on the one hand, and her great dislike for Canetti on the other.

Christa Gürtler's concluding essay focuses on Spiel's Salzburg years as a critic of the Summer Festival. Once again, a salon-like space, in this case, the Café Bazar on the river Salzach, is Spiel's social environment. It's a site that has attracted dozens of writers and artists over decades: "Georg Trakl saß gerne im 'Bazar,' Stefan Zweig hatte einen Stammtisch und traf sich manchmal mit Carl Zuckmayer, Karl Heinrich Waggerl blieb jahrzehntelang Stammgast" (p. 142). Gürtler sketches four sorts of dialogue that are connected to the Salzburg phase of Spiel and can always be linked back to the Café Bazar. She describes in more detail than Polt-Heinzl the ambivalent attitude Spiel demonstrated towards Bachmann and her work. She discusses the epistolary friendship Spiel kept up with the composer Gottfried von Einem. She presents Spiel's strong advocacy on behalf of Thomas Bernhard, and she comments on Spiel's passionate insistence that the *Salzburger Festspiele* return to the initial focus on drama (rather than music) notwithstanding the organizers' and politicians' opposition. In contrast to some of her female colleagues in this volume, Gürtler attests Spiel good ethical judgment.

Ulrich Weinzierl, who succeeded Spiel as Austrian "Kulturkorrespondent" for the daily *Frankfurter Allgemeine Zeitung (FAZ)*, adds a brief epilogue to the volume combining reminiscence with eulogy.

Connoisseurs of Austrian literature will not benefit much from this collection of essays because it does not really offer any new information about Spiel. If somebody wants to dwell on "the world of yesterday" and nostalgically indulge in cultural retrospection, s/he is likely to find this Hilde Spiel celebration enjoyable and perhaps also edifying.

Manfried Rauchensteiner, ed., *Zwischen den Blöcken: NATO, Warschauer Pakt und Österreich* (Vienna: Böhlau, 2010)

Thomas Nowotny

The quest for Austria's security: the role of the military

History demonstrated that war has a momentum of its own and it carries you away from all thoughtful intentions.

(George F Kennan as quoted in the New York Review of Books Dec. 8th 2011, p. 8)

The book under review deals with Austria's security policy in the time between 1945 and the end of the Twentieth Century. Contrary to what the title might suggest, the book does not review Austria's overall strategy "between the blocks." It mainly deals with the state, the policies and politics of the Austrian military. Just three of the thirteen contributions—one on foreign policy, one on external trade, and one on the impact of the main media—address some of the non-military dimensions of Austria's security policy.

Peter Jankowitsch (pp. 451-96), a former minister of foreign affairs is author of the chapter on "The Problem of Equidistance—the Second Austrian Republic in Search for Foreign Policy Guidelines." His main aim is to refute conservative critics of Austria's foreign policy which these critics picture as unprincipled efforts of "triangulation" between the two power blocks, lacking substance and moral content. Jankowitsch succeeds well by pointing, in particular, to the Austrian stance at the United Nations and at the Conference for European Security and Cooperation – CSCE. The positions taken in these settings testify to an independent[1], though essentially "Western" orientation of Austria's foreign policy. However, Peter Jankowitsch does not to address the broader question as to the function of foreign policy in service of Austria's overall security policy.

In 1956 already, one of Austria's most prominent leaders, Chancellor Julius Raab had perceived of that function as the central one, reminding

1. This independence had nonetheless limits where an independent Austrian voice would have clashed with the innermost core security interests of one of the two blocks. But as the track record proves, such limits had to be respected on very rare occasions only. In 1956, for example, they did not impede Austria from taking the initiative at the UN for a vote criticizing the Soviet Union for its invasion of Hungary.

the military that "Austria cannot wage war ….and its defense therefore has to be political mainly."[2] Later on, this was emphasized again by Austrian Chancellor Bruno Kreisky, claiming that foreign policy could add more to the country's security than anything the military would be able to provide. Foreign countries, and the great powers in particular, should be given a stake in the continued independence and integrity of the republic.

That aim was served making the country a "nct provider" of stability and a promoter of global cooperation; and by establishing Vienna as headquarters for international organizations as well as the venue for important international political encounters.[3] The same goal was served by some massive foreign direct investment, such as the one by giant US "General Motors" that built a vast engine and transmission factory at a site only 30 kilometers West of the "Iron Curtain." This was not just another, if welcome addition to Austria's industrial capacities. It also added to Austria's external security as this important US corporation and with it the US had a stake in keeping the factory safe and running and keep Austria functioning as a state.

Mutually beneficial foreign trade will also keep alive the interest of trading partners in the continued and secure existence of their counterpart. That was of particular relevance in relations to the Communist countries. As one of the authors—Andreas Resch (pp. 497-56)—demonstrates, all during the time of the Cold War, Austria had been an important trading partner to these countries. In terms of this trade, Austria thus was relevant to the Communist "COMECON" countries, and this not in spite, but because of its being "Western." Austria was a trading partner they did not desire to be without, and a partner which they wished to hang on to.

This might be one of the reasons for the muted reaction of Communist countries against Austria's complete integration into the "Western" Coordinating Committee—COCOM regime. This US led regime restricted the export of certain high technology products to Communist countries if—in a rather broad interpretation—such technology could also have military uses. Just as Austria, all of the other European neutral countries also had no choice but to implement this US-imposed regime though it had no base in legally binding resolutions of the UN Security Council.[4]

2. The Austrian Chancellor Julius Raab in a session of the *Landesverteidigungsrat* (National Defense Council) on February 25th 1958.

3. On this matter, see for example Eric Frey, "Konferenzplatz Wien: Vienna as an International Conference Site," in *Global Austria*, Contemporary Austrian Studies vol. 20, eds. Günter Bischof, Fritz Plasser, Anton Pelinka, and Alexander Smith (New Orleans: UNO Press, 2011), 147-60.

4. This has not remained the only instance of US pressure exercised to tangible effect while

Austria's trade with the "East," constituted only a minor and a shrinking part of its overall foreign trade. By far more relevant as the base for Austria's wealth was its trade with the West. When probing into the contribution of foreign trade to Austria's security, it is therefore not sufficient—as Andreas Resch does—to just deal with the relatively minor contribution made by "Eastern" trade. In part, the growing "Westernization" of Austria's economy and of its foreign trade was a quasi automatic consequence of economic dynamics and of Austria having opted for a "Western" economic model. But "Westernization" also was the consequence of policy choices that attached Austria more firmly to Western markets and institutions. Without these options having been taken, the economic development of Austria would not have been as rapid; and Austria's inner and external security would not have been anchored that well.

Security policy also has to be anchored in public opinion which is both reflected in, and shaped by public media. As Berthold Molden (pp. 687 ff) demonstrates, the Austrian ones were thoroughly pro-Western, and often stridently so.[5] Repeatedly, they had to be shielded in their independence against Eastern allegations of their having jeopardized the country's permanent neutrality. This held true, in particular, for the public Austrian radio and television ORF with its emissions being received in wide swaths of adjoining Communist Czechoslovakia and Hungary. They had a share in de-legitimizing Communist rule.

In signing the State Treaty in 1955 and in accepting Austria's neutrality, the Western Allies had made a trade-off. They had exchanged a military disadvantage—namely the military evacuation of their zones of occupation —against the advantage of having a high visibility, pro-Western country sticking out deep into the flanks of an ideologically hostile power. Doing that, the Western Allies had, however, not neglected the military aspect of Austria's future status. At this time already, when Austria regained its full independence, the military dimension of Austria's neutrality had been of concern to them. It remained so up to the time of the collapse of the Eastern military alliance. Their concern over Austria's being weak in military terms subtracted from otherwise good relations.

circumventing procedures prescribed by international law. This demonstrates not just the might of the US "hegemon"; but also the fact that the international economy functions on a level of its own, disconnected to a large extent from the web of legally binding international norms, such as those embodied in formal treaties or in resolutions of the UN Security Council.

5. In parts, this is due to their origins. Some of the more important media had been founded or supported by the Western occupying powers. Such was the case for the two mass circulation dailies, as well as for radio station "Red White Red," established by the US and later merged into the Austrian Broadcasting Company - ORF.

The idea that Austria could regain full independence by becoming neutral and by following a "Swiss" pattern of neutrality found its expression in the Moscow Memorandum of April 1955 that opened the way to the State Treaty. In this memorandum, the Swiss model had expressly been mentioned as such. Would Austria have truly followed this Swiss model of neutrality, it should have invested heavily in defense. US military would have applauded. They always had feared that a dangerous military vacuum might emerge once they would have withdrawn their troops from Austria. It is for this reason that right up to the signing of the State Treaty, the US military even opposed the very idea of an Austrian independence. In this they were motivated not just by an unselfish concern for the future internal and external security of Austria. They had other motives too. Their troops in the Western part of the country helped them to secure the transit over the Alpine passes that connect the Southern sphere of NATO with its Central part. They wanted to retain control over this line of communication that was essential to them.

It was for these concerns that in the time before April 1955 already, the United States had supported and equipped in its zone of occupation an unofficial Austrian military force, thinly veiled as *B-Gendarmerie*.[6] It had become operative in 1952 with the official mission of securing internal security. In case of a "big" East-West war, however, it was also to function as part of NATO.

When finally overruled in their resistance to Austrian independence, the US military did their best to provide for a future, viable Austrian defense. The nascent army was given equipment from the stocks of the American occupation forces as they left the country. US military also succeeded in attaching conditions to their consenting to Austria's independence. The armament of the future army should be NATO compatible; and though in flagrant violation of neutrality, flights of military NATO aircraft in the corridor between Southern Germany and Northern Italy should be tolerated, provided that these flights were at great height and occurred at night mainly. In the case of an East-West war, the operative mission of the Austrian armed forces remained those that had been the ones of the *B-Gendarmerie*. They would retreat in fighting towards the West, vacating the largest and most populous part of the country in order to join up with NATO in the Alps.

---

6. Setting up this military or quasi-military force stood in contradiction to a prior agreement according to which Austria would have no military forces as long as a State Treaty had not been signed. The setting up of the B- Gendarmeries had undercut that commitment. The creation of the B- Gendarmerie had its counterpart, however, in the equally illegal setting up of a similar, thinly veiled military unit (*Bewaffnete Volkspolizei*) in Eastern Germany.

Like the Austrian the Swiss military too, might have seen their ultimate function as being a kind of auxiliary to NATO. In this "limited" sphere of neutrality policy, the two countries might have been similar indeed and in this respect Austria's neutrality might indeed have been patterned after the Swiss model. But otherwise, the Swiss model was swiftly discarded by Austria. Unlike Switzerland, Austria quickly acceded to the United Nations[7] and to the Council of Europe.[8] Unlike Switzerland, it also failed to invest more heavily in its military. Its expenditures on defense were lower too, than those of neutral Sweden and neutral Finland, this gap being wide. In the Seventies for example, Switzerland spent 68 US Dollars per capita on defense and Sweden 128 US Dollars per capita, whereas in Austria these per capita expenses amounted to 20 US Dollars only. Different too, was the size of forces if measured in terms of the percentage of the population that could be mobilized for defense. In the seventies[9] Austria could mobilize just two percent of its population, whereas Switzerland and Sweden could each one mobilize ten percent of their population for defense.

This underfunding of the military has several causes. One of them is the historic memory of a nation that has not won a single war since 1866, and that suffered enormously in the last two world wars. As in Japan and in Germany, this experience in the last big war had bred reticence towards military adventure and towards the military in general. This is a sentiment not shared in the three other European neutral countries.[10] With Finland

7. In a strictly formal/ legal sense, membership with the UN is incompatible with permanent neutrality, as even neutrals are bound to implement economic sanctions imposed by the UN Security Council. In practical terms, that caveat has been irrelevant in the times of Cold War, as the Soviet Union would have vetoed any decision of the UN Security Council that would have damaged its core interests. Austria therefore never ran the danger of having to support one sided UN sanctions against the Soviet Union that would have called into question its neutrality, officially defined as permanent and as directed against all sides, but which, in practice had been neutrality between the East and the West mainly.

8. With both of these steps having been in preparation well before the signing of the State Treaty and the re-gaining of full sovereignty. Not only was membership valued as symbol and—to a certain extent—as guarantor of the newly reclaimed sovereignty. It also corresponds to a more "activist approach" to international affairs, partly rooted in the desire to be seen and to be recognized; partly rooted in a national tradition quite different from the Swiss one.

9. That is before the reform of the Austrian army which was started in the seventies and which that shifted the emphasis towards a militia system. If fully implemented—which it never was—the reform would have resulted in an army which after full mobilization would have numbered 300,000 soldiers; that is about 4.5 percent of the Austrian population.

10. Actually, not four but five European states claim a status of being neutral: next to Switzerland Austria, Sweden and Finland, Ireland too defines itself in such terms. Its neutrality is, however, a special one, having its base in the political goal of distancing itself from the United Kingdom to which it had been attached up to the 20th century.

having been successful—at least for a while—in a battle against the Soviet Union; with Sweden having retained its neutrality[11] in World War II; and with Switzerland firmly convinced that it had been its strong military mainly which had kept Hitler from invading the country.

Austria's neutrality also differs from the Swiss one inasmuch, as the latter had been "guaranteed" in the *acts of the Congress of Vienna.* As explained by Michael Gehler (pp. 89-134), such a guarantee for thc integrity of Austrian territory had originally been envisaged in the Moscow Memorandum,[12] with the Soviet side declaring itself willing to participate in a four power guarantee for the integrity of Austria's territory. However, it soon became obvious that the three former Western occupying powers were not willing to grant a guarantee worth its name. They stood ready to offer a mere "pseudo"-guarantee, with the promise to seize the UN Security Council should the integrity of Austria's territory be threatened or violated.[13] In the end, the three Western powers failed to officially table even this minimal offer they had agreed upon among themselves. On their side, neither Russia nor Austria pursued that matter any further. Austria had come to fear that such a pseudo guarantee would detract more from its external security than it could add, as it could legitimize outside interference and limit Austria's freedom of action while bringing symbolic help at best.

If a motive at all, their being unwilling to "guarantee a military vacuum"[14] must have been a minor cause of their negative attitude. Other factors were more compelling by far, as we may be certain that a guarantee would not have been granted even if Austria would have provided credible proof for its

11. Defined not as a legally binding permanent neutrality but as a de facto non-adherence to military pacts.

12. In negotiations for the Moscow Memorandum the issue of guarantees had surfaced with the Soviet side asking what kind of guarantees Austria could offer against the danger of a new Anschluss with (Western-) Germany. The Austrian answered that such reassurance could be provided by a "guarantee similar to the guarantee offered to Switzerland by the Congress of Vienna."

13. In connection with the Hungarian uprising and its subsequent repression by Soviet troops, that readiness echoed in a November 15, 1958 declaration of the US State Department, stating that any violation of Austria's integrity would be considered a "serious threat to world peace" which the UN Security Council could act upon; but was unlikely to act upon given the fact that the Soviet Union could block any decision of this body by its veto. An even milder version of this "guarantee" was offered by the US on occasion of the invasion of Czechoslovakia by Soviet (Warsaw Pact) troops in 1968, with the US Secretary of State declaring that the US would have "an interest in Austria (as well as in Switzerland, Yugoslavia, Romania and Albania—the latter three not being the kind of company Austria aspired to be in).

14. These are the words of the UK ambassador negotiating the issue with his two Western colleagues in Vienna. This wording is used by Michael Gehler as a heading for the special chapter on the issue of a guarantee.

resolve to vastly increase military efforts. For one, providing to a non-NATO country a guarantee equal to the one offered to NATO members would have undermined NATO cohesion as it would have promoted neutralism[15] instead of military solidarity. A guarantee was, however, refused not just for these political reasons, but for military reasons too. The three Allies simply would not have been in a position to live up to such a promise. In the case of a "big East West War," Warsaw Pact forces were assumed to use their numerical superiority for a rapid dash over Northern Germany and perhaps through the Fulda gap in central Germany, so as to reach the Atlantic ports in order to prevent them being used for landing US reinforcements.[16] With NATO troops thus concentrated on this front in Northern and North-Central Germany, not much military might was left so as to secure the front in Southeastern Germany. The relatively weak forces there were given the task of securing the flanks for the decisive action further North; and they were given the task to slow any hostile advance over these flanks by retreating in fighting to the Rhine river where defense could be made to last longer.

So what was the role assigned to Austria's military in the NATO scenario? The role remained the same as the one assigned to the *B-Gendarmerie* already. Austrian forces were supposed to retreat in fighting to the fortress in the Western Alps where they were to join up with NATO forces. Yet when reaching this retreat in the Alps, the majority of Austrian soldiers would have been killed already. It even was uncertain whether, when having reached the Central Alps, NATO troops would still be there to rescue them. NATO forces were assumed not to defend these alpine regions at great length but to preserve their strength to be able to offer stronger resistance after having retreated to the Rhine. Nonetheless and in spite of that, Austria's military planned for that hopeless mission; evidently oblivious of the fact that such plans failed to match basic interests of the Austrian republic and of its citizens.

As Friedrich Korkitsch (pp. 387-450) demonstrates in his contribution, this dilemma became most obvious in the scenario for nuclear warfare. By now it is certain that battle plans for both sides included the use of nuclear weapons: on one side in order to stem the advance of Warsaw Pact forces; and on the other side in order to break the resistance of NATO forces.[17]

---

15. In particular, as posing the danger of weakening and undermining Germany's resolve to be a firm part of a military alliance and toying with the idea of neutrality instead.

16. In the 1980s strategies on both sides changed somewhat, with the Warsaw Pact forces opting for a more defensive stance, and with NATO's FOFA strategy including "defensive" airstrike deep into Warsaw Pact territory.

17. As of the late 1970s, the role of nuclear weapons became deemphasized as the risk

Regardless of what the Austrian military did, or did not do, they would have become targets of these weapons. Would they offer stiff resistance, they and all civilians in their vicinity would be obliterated by "Eastern Nukes." Would they yield and open the way to the advance of Warsaw Pact forces, they and the surrounding Austrian civilians would meet the same fate as targets of "Western Nukes."

It is in Eastern Austria where the majority of its citizens live. The three largest cities—Vienna, Graz and Linz—are located there, each in close distance to the "Iron Curtain" with assault ready Warsaw Pact troops being amassed behind. Over the comparatively flat terrain heavily armed units would have reached those cities within a few hours. Assuming as hopeless the task of an effective defense of these cities and of the flat, close to the borders terrain of Eastern Austria, the army would have left a clear majority of Austria's population at foreign mercy, at best offering some token resistance to the hostile advance so as to gain time for the government to escape towards the sparsely populated, mountainous West.

In all of the above we have used the scenario of the "big" war which was of prime concern to the military in both of the mutually hostile alliances. Yet the likelihood of such a disaster actually occurring was remote as both sides had come to accept that maintaining the status quo was the best they could hope for. Still unlikely, but less so than the "big war," was the eventuality of a military action just against the Austrian Republic alone. In times of seriously heightened tensions, both sides could have found a military rationale for reconquering their former zones of occupation. For both sides, this would have brought a straightening of front lines with ensuing improvement in their position for an eventual showdown in an all out war. This advantage would have been greater for the Western side, as it would have regained military control over the Austrian mountain passes and with it control over the important communication between Southern and Central NATO. Seen from this narrow perspective of immediate tactical advantage, one has to assume that in the case of a war limited to Austria alone, Western military would have had few incentives for coming to the rescue to the Austrian troops fighting the Warsaw Pact forces in the East of the country. For these Eastern forces, the Austrian army would have hardly been a match. In the final days of the Warsaw Pact, about 5,600 tanks were stationed in Czechoslovakia alone. They could have entered Austria across a 450 mile frontier and penetrated over relatively easy terrain reaching the Danube and Vienna in very short time. But would the Warsaw Pact

---

involved in their actual use—and in the threat of their actual use—began to outweigh their military usefulness.

forces really have re-occupied the former Soviet zone of occupation, this would have given a pretext to the Western forces for doing the same in the Western part of Austria. Western military would have much profited from being given this chance. As a look at the map of Europe shows, Western Austria forms a longish East-West sliver along the main ridges of the Alps, vastly extending NATO's Eastern front lines and blocking the logistics between NATO Forces in Northern Italy and Southern Germany. From a purely military perspective, the Western Allies therefore could have even seen an advantage in a possible military action of the Warsaw pact directed against Austria alone. On the other side, the military advantage obtained by the Warsaw Pact through an occupation of Eastern Austrian would have been minor in comparison. It would have gained control over a territory it would have been able to conquer easily in the case of the "big war"; and that within days if not hours.

Two strategic conclusions derive from such scenarios:

- First: at the signing of the State Treaty, the political advantages gained for the West by Austria's independence weighed heavier than the disadvantages of withdrawing their troops from the Western part of the country. For the future Western support of Austria, political considerations would continue to be more relevant than purely military ones.
- Second: in order to maintain the Eastern interest in Austria's territorial integrity the Austrian military should demonstrate willingness to remain independent enough and resolved to also defend the country in the West in order to secure Austrian control over the North-South mountain passes.

The already dire situation of the Austrian military worsened in the early seventies that is at a time of the onset of a 13 years exclusive rule of Social Democrats and of their Chancellor Bruno Kreisky. It was at that time that many developments converged that called into question the concepts of the Austrian military. East-West tensions had lessened and the eternal "enemy in the East" now appeared less threatening. A certain smugness had come to prevail that made it increasingly difficult to mobilize the population by visions of an external, mortal threat. Also, the youth revolt of 1968 still resounded through Austria, with sentiments averse to the military and averse to their American godfather.

But the weakening position of Austria's military was due too, to their internal failings. Hundreds of thousands of young men had already passed through the nine months of obligatory military service.[18] Many returned to civilian life with negative feelings about their experiences, with days and weeks having been wasted without them having been given any sensible tasks. These draftees experienced an officer corps still largely formed by experience in World War II.[19] They obtained firsthand insights into deficiencies in both equipment and training. Only a tiny percentage of these young men had later on been made of effective use in the reserve. For the rest, the investment made in their training was often wasted.

Political/public support for the military remained weak also because the strategic and operative concepts of the military leadership did not make sense. It did not provide an answer as to how someone weaker in military terms could defend against an overpowering enemy. It did not provide an answer as to how to protect the majority of Austria`s population living in the Eastern, flatter parts of the country. It did not provide for a military defense of the transit corridors over the Western Alps—a defense which would have been necessary in order to maintain Warsaw Pact countries interested in the integrity of Austria's territory. It did not provide for a full use of all of these young men that had passed through their military service without having been made part of effective reserves. It did not take account of the fact that Austria would never be in a position to provide air cover to its troops; and—more generally—military planning still was based on the notion of the Austrian army functioning as kind of NATO auxiliary[20] and not as the defensive shield of a neutral country.

---

18. Among them, I myself who, at the time of being drafted, had become attaché in the diplomatic service already. The transition from purposeful, intense professional life to the stultifying emptiness of a life in the military barracks was a very depressing experience (alleviated later on by my being transferred to the precursor of the military academy).

19. My friend Anton Pelinka—a frequent contributor to this journal—told me about an incident during his own military service when the commanding officer instructed the recruits to simulate "clearing of terrain infested by guerilla fighters." This is what the German army had been instructed to do in Yugoslavia during World War II. In Austria and for the Austrian army, the roles would have to be reversed. The Austrians should have been the guerilla fighters, defending against an overpowering, armor-clad occupier.

20. From 1958 on, Austria had taken measures to make its military neutrality less obviously one-sided. Flights of NATO military aircraft over Austria's territory which had been tolerated in the past were prohibited. Arms purchases were increasingly made in other European neutral countries and some even in Warsaw Pact countries.

Nonetheless NATO ties remained close. One example being the "Königswarte listening station" located on the Eastern slope of Austria's easternmost hill, with its electronic devices capable to intercept the military radio transmissions deep in Warsaw Pact territory. The installation was paid for and equipped by the US with Austrian military not even in a position to decipher the listening tapes which were sent directly to Western Germany.

All that dissatisfaction coagulated in the somewhat rash project of the new Social Democratic government of Bruno Kreisky to reduce obligatory military service from nine months to six—a move which, if not accompanied by drastic changes in concepts and structures of the military, would have further weakened an already weak defense capacity. Now in charge of government, the Social Democrats found themselves in a quandary. They could not renege on their promise to reduce obligatory military service. On the other side, they wished to avoid blame for undermining Austria's military defense.

One minister of defense quit when failing to bridge that gap. After some troubled months, rescue came from a professional soldier—General Emil Spannocchi. His concept of a *Raumverteidigung* offered a plausible vision for resolving the dilemma and his concept was retained by government. *Raumverteidigung* is a plan for "asymmetric warfare." It is not a prescription for guerilla war—though it borrows some of its elements. It does not provide for a defense along a linear front but for a defense in various clusters spread over the country.[21] Assuming an "open sky" with Austria not being able to provide air-cover, vulnerable long distance movements of troops and equipment were to be avoided. The bulk of the fighting would be done by the rather static Landwehr composed of reservists mainly; and, in addition, by more mobile infantry units (*Jägerbrigaden*). These two elements would be complemented by the *Bereitschaftstruppe*—that is by a military organized and equipped in a more traditional manner.

The main asset of the *Raumverteidigung* was the uncertainty it imposed unto the calculations of any military adversary. The adversary would not know in advance whom to fight first, how and with how much of his own assets. For him, the Austrian forces became difficult to locate and difficult to fight. The adversary thus could not precisely calculate the military costs of an advance through Austrian territory (*Durchmarschpreis*); nor the prize of permanently occupying the country (*Aufenthaltspreis*). The prize could be high in terms of losses; but high too, in terms of time lost in an advance towards the West.

All that highly recommended the new concept of *Raumverteidigung*. Yet it never became fully implemented, one of the reasons being that the ministry of defense continued to be starved of funds. The original plans

21. There are personal and historic reasons for Bruno Kreisky responding so positively to the proposals of General Emil Spannocchi to switch to an asymmetric version of warfare. Kreisky had internalized lessons from the 1934 Austrian civil war. These were reinforced when he served as an assistant to the Austrian president (and ex-general) Theodor Körner in 1951/1953. Theodor Körner was one of the first in the military to recommend that strategy to weaker belligerents.

foresaw a mobilized strength of 300,000 soldiers. That number still would not have been sufficient.[22] Nonetheless even that less ambitious goal of 300,000 mobilized soldiers had not been met, and was reduced in the following years.

In their contributions on military maneuvers and on war games, Manfried Rauchensteiner (pp. 253-324) and Hannes Phillip (pp. 325-86) provide evidence for some progress having been achieved nevertheless by the switch towards the *Raumverteidigung*. But even so, the Austrian defense capacities sufficed for nothing more than for the maintenance of internal security and for some in limited actions[23] during crisis situations. Even in their reformed version, Austrian forces would have had to capitulate rather early to the superior forces of any potential enemy. Not all of that can be blamed on politicians underfunding the Austrian military. To no small extent, they have to blame themselves.

Right from the start, the implementation of the concept of *Raumverteidigung* had become embroiled in bureaucratic infighting among leading military. Many of them preferred to stick to traditional concepts and, as a consequence, they supported the conventionally organized *Bereitschaftstruppe* to the detriment of the militia in the Landwehr. Funds that would have been needed for a realization of the militia concept were also channeled into the purchase of equipment such as additional tanks and troop carriers that had little function in a meaningful *Raumverteidigung*. Especially disastrous in its impact on the budget of the army was the purchase of 24 supersonic fighter planes. Basically unarmed,[24] they had

22. The Swiss—with a smaller population and with a country more easily defended than Austria with its vast East West extension—they could mobilize twice that number. According to this rough calculation, the mobilized strength of the Austrian army would have had to amount to 900,000 soldiers if the army should have been given a true chance of being effective in the defense of the territory.

23. Such as securing frontiers as they did in 1956 at Hungarian border.

24. The State Treaty contains a provision (similar to provision in peace treaties with other European nations) that forbade Austria the possession of "rockets." This was interpreted to apply to both anti-tank and air to air, as well as to air to surface missiles. A fighter plane equipped with board canons or machine guns only, was however defenseless against fighter planes equipped with air to air missiles (as all fighter planes nowadays are). The lack of such weapons seriously handicapped the whole of Austria's defense efforts. One of the contributors to the book under review claims that this deficiency too, was due to the negligence of politicians who had not pressed hard enough for an interpretation of the State Treaty that would have allowed Austria to acquire these weapons (whose effectiveness had been proven in the 1973 Arab – Israeli war). The reproach is not substantiated by facts. The ministers of defense and even the heads of government had tried repeatedly to seek from the Soviet side consent to such an interpretation of the relevant clauses of the State Treaty. After all, these articles in the State Treaty have their origin in the Allied experience with the long-range German rockets in World War II. But these had been offensive weapons

no military value and only a symbolic value at best. To set things in their proper perspective: this purchase came at a time when the army could keep just 80 percent of that stock of ammunition that would have been required for an effective defense lasting a mere three days.[25]

Such quarrels among the various fractions of the Austrian military became mute with the disappearance of the East-West conflict and the dissolution of the Warsaw pact. The scenario of East-West war[26] that had provided the base for Austria's military planning became defunct. For the first time in its long history, Austria was able to breathe freely, no longer being threatened by any military enemy. Not just the military doctrine, but the complete Austrian security doctrine had to be revised.

In a short period of transition between the 1989 and 1991 some plans were floated in neighboring countries that would have expanded Austrian neutrality into a neutral, Central European zone. Other concepts went even further. They envisaged the disappearance not just of the Warsaw Pact but of NATO too, with both alliances being replaced by a Pan-European security system. These remained visions and dreams. Instead, NATO membership was extended to all of Austria's former Communist neighbors. Austria had to decide on whether to follow their example. In the end it did not. The option of full NATO membership was rejected, though at first sight and in the mid-1990s still, such a step must have seemed logical.

Historically, neutrality has its origins in the attempt of countries located at a dividing line between contending powers to extricate themselves from the confrontation between these opponents. One should assume that with the disappearance of such antagonism, motives for being neutral should disappear too. This argument had indeed echoed in Austria with the then Vice-Chancellor Wolfgang Schüssel giving it prominence in declaring neutrality obsolete. Austria should become a full member of NATO.[27] It

---

unlike the anti-tank and surface -to-air missiles which clearly were of a defensive nature. Yet such Austrian entreaties yielded no results. At that time, some of the Austrian military had suggested that Austria should go ahead anyhow, disregarding Soviet objections. But wiser politics prevailed. Acting in clear violation of the State Treaty would have permitted the Soviet Union to start a procedure provided for in the treaty, with Austria slipping into the role of the accused and becoming object again and pawn in the East West gamble and confrontation. That was not a price worth paying. Anyhow, at the dusk of the Communist era, Austria was then in a position to acquire these defensive short range missiles.

25. I noted as significant a phrase in the contribution of Hannes Philipp who reveals this detail but adds that this state of affairs was troubling not in itself but because no proper attention had been given to gaining quick and secure access to ammunition "stored beyond the Austrian borders."

26. Or of a preemptive East West war on Austria's territory alone.

27. But this was not an opinion of conservatives only. Some on the liberal Left chimed in too (as for example the prominent Social Democrat Joseph Cap).

was bound to be affected by NATO decisions anyhow. It thus would be prudent to take a seat at the table where such decisions were being made.

Notwithstanding these seemingly solid arguments, the step for full NATO membership was never taken, the main reason being a public opinion that overwhelmingly favored retaining neutrality in preference to membership in a military alliance. With NATO's attention having shifted to "out of area" actions, substance was provided to the fear that such a NATO membership could oblige the country to join in military adventures it considers hopeless, or that it disapproves of. Another more opaque motive for rejecting NATO membership should not be dismissed either. Membership in a military alliance provides a certain tilt to a nation's overall security and foreign policy, shifting it closer to military options.[28] It is noteworthy that similar considerations also prevailed in the other European neutral countries. Neither of them joined NATO.

In the case of Austria, a further motive intruded. The notion of being "permanently neutral" had become interwoven with the country's sense of identity. Neutrality had served to cement[29] the then still fragile notion of a distinct Austrian nationhood.[30] In fact, Austria's national day commemorates the anniversary of the date when, on 26 October 1955, the country declared its permanent neutrality and enshrined it in its constitution.

The termination of the Cold War also opened for Austria the way to membership in the European Union. This Union is more than a mere joint organ of fully sovereign states because states had to yield up parts of the sovereignty when becoming Union members. Yet the neutrality as it had been defined by Austria after 1955 was still based on the concept of a full, unlimited sovereignty. When entering the European Union Austria thus had to abandon this former and more encompassing definition of neutrality. It was replaced by a new definition that whittled neutrality down to a bare minimum: to the non participation in war; to non-membership

28. That is a likely but not a necessary consequence—as demonstrated by NATO member Norway with its very active policies of promoting peace and negotiated solutions to conflicts.

29. It confirmed the Austria's identity in particular by stressing neutral Austria being different from NATO member Germany. Stressing differences to Germany was essential if seen against the historic background of early 20th century, when many Austrians had failed to identify with their newly created, smallish successor state to the Austrian empire and had considered themselves as kind of Germans in exile.

30. Enthusiasm for NATO that had been widespread among Austrian conservatives in particular, was dampened further by the "Western" countries deciding on some sort of sanctions when, after the breakup of the "big" left-right coalition, the leading conservative party—ÖVP—teamed up with the populist/nationalist Freedom Party to form a new governing coalition. The Freedom Party is difficult to classify under traditional categories. But it certainly also represents tendencies evident in some European parties of the extreme, and potentially non-democratic European Right such as the "Vlaams Belang" in Belgium.

in a military alliance; and to a ban on foreign troops being stationed on the nation's territory.

These low criteria for defining Austria as "neutral" were lowered even further in the course of Austria's EU membership. The EU "Amsterdam Treaty" which Austrian ratified in July of 1998 provided for a strengthening of joint European Defense and Security policies. For Austria, this ratification implied the acceptance of the so called Petersberg Tasks and among them the task to "make peace." "Making peace" is a euphemism for participating—for altruistic reasons perhaps, but for participating nonetheless—in acts of warfare. Clearly, this is not compatible with the status of a permanently neutral country, even if this neutrality is given its most minimal interpretation. That being obvious, the Austrian constitutional law that defined neutrality was changed accordingly with the insertion of a new article (Art. 23 j). Henceforth, even the participation in such actions of the European Union could not have been interpreted as violating neutrality.[31]

Such contortions should not be seen as mendacious maneuvers and as attempts to have the cake and eat it too—to have EU membership and for getting by at minimal costs and without joining common efforts. Repeatedly, Austria had made clear that by adhering to the EU, it did not wish its status as a neutral to become an obstacle for Union efforts towards gaining greater coherence and integration. It would therefore refrain from blocking an extension of EU integration unto the field of defense and security policies.[32] But not only would it refrain from blocking relevant EU actions. It would also stand ready to join in them. The track record demonstrates that these have not been mere words and empty promises. Austria had made tangible contributions, in particular, to EU campaigns intended to stop and resolve conflicts in the area of what once had been Yugoslavia. It still participates, for example, with a 500 soldier contingent in the stabilization of the Kosovo.

At the price of not being covered by NATOs security guarantees, and at the price of not participating directly in NATO decisions that might affect them, the other European neutrals and Austria as well had abstained from full NATO membership. But they opted for tying themselves to NATO in less stringent ways, namely by PfP – Partnership for Peace agreements. In principle, Austria seeks to join in international security efforts through

31. Substantiating a quip of one of my colleagues: neutrality is what the European neutrals define it to be.

32. As Austria, most other midsized and smaller members of the Union are also ready to strengthen the common to the detriment of the national; and that in particular even in the realm of security policies. Bigger EU member still might harbor more illusions about their capacity to affect outcomes when acting alone.

European security institutions and security policies mainly. Relations to NATO remain essential nonetheless, as projects to create a proper European defense force that could act in full independence from NATO have failed to materialized to any great extent. The European Union might be able to make its own strategic/military decisions. But for implementing them, it will need NATO resources (including the NATO command and planning structures). This obliges the EU country Austria into a constructive and structured relationship with NATO.

In the time of the Cold War, Western complaints found some echo that pictured Austria as being a parasitic "free rider" profiting from Western military efforts, while providing little in return. But as we have seen, greater Austrian military efforts would not have benefitted Austria. They also would have added little to Europe's security. Austria therefore sought security more through its internal and external policies—and among the latter through efforts to strengthen a world order based on multilateralism with the United Nations at its center; with very targeted efforts, for example to widen the impact of international law or to promote arms control. But right from the beginning, it also contributed to that aim by putting military contingents at the service of the United Nations. It has remained a major provider of such assistance, with substantial and cost intensive participation missions on the Balkans, in Africa (Congo, Chad) and the Middle East (the Golan Heights between Syria and Israel; or now, in the most recent past: the Lebanon).

In 2007 the Swiss minister of foreign affairs Micheline Calmy-Rey envisaged for her country a more activist foreign policy with the full use of the political space provided for her country in the United Nations and in the European institutions, with solidarity and not standoffishness becoming the guiding principle. In her view, Switzerland should now come to "practice a kind of neutrality as it had been practiced by Austria since 1955." History thus has come around full circle, since fifty-two years earlier, Austria, on its turn, had proposed to follow the Swiss example in its security policies.

Annual Review

Austria 2011

Government reshuffle

State Secretary for Integration

Styria – Reform Agenda

Political scandals and corruption

WKR and "the new Jews"

Economic and statistical Data

Reinhold Gärtner

Government reshuffle

In April 2011, Josef Pröll, vice chancellor and Minister of Finance, declared his retreat from politics. This would not be a decision against political activity but one for family and health, he said. During the months before, Pröll had been suffering from pulmonary embolism.

Pröll had succeeded Wilhelm Molterer as vice chancellor and chairman of ÖVP in 2008 and his successor is Michael Spindelegger. Pröll's farewell to politics was part of a general government reshuffle of ÖVP (2011-04-21): Maria Fekter (former Minister of the Interior) became Minister of Finance; Johanna Mikl-Leitner (former member of the government of Lower Austria) was appointed Minister of the Interior. Beatrix Karl (former Minister of Science and Research) replaced the unlucky Claudia Bandion-Ortner as Minister of Justice. The new Minister of Science and Research is Karlheinz Töchterle, until then principal of the University of Innsbruck.

Wolfgang Waldner was sworn in as new State Secretary in the Ministry for European and International Affairs and both Reinhold Lopatka and Christine Marek left the government (Marek in November 2010 already).[1]

1. < http://www.austria.gv.at/site/1/Default.aspx>.

State Secretary for Integration

One interesting point in this government reshuffle was the creation of a new State Secretary for Integration within the Ministry of the Interior[2]. The then 24 year old Sebastian Kurz was appointed the new State Secretary for Integration. The creation of this State Secretary was an important signal for better integration of people with migrant background in Austria.

The first migrant workers of the Second republic came to Austria in the early 1960s (especially from Turkey and the former Yugoslavia). But for decades, there had been no measures for real integration at all. Contrary, in the late 1980s this topic was more and more negatively emotionalized by right wing populists in Austria (and many other European countries).

Until now, Austria has not had a real integration policy. Migrants came to Austria but were expected to leave again after a few years. But already in the 1970s it was obvious that this rotation didn't work.

On January 1st 2011 there were 8,404,252 people living in Austria, 1,543,289 with migration background—these people were either born in foreign countries (1,138,724) or born in Austria but had parents who were born in foreign countries (second generation of migrants; 404,565). In addition, those born in Austria are not necessarily Austrian citizens. Austria follows the *ius sanguinis*, which means that new born children get the citizenship of their parents (or their mother respectively) and not the citizenship of the country in which they were born (*ius soli*, as in the USA). As a result of this there are 137,079 people living in Austria who were born here but don't have the Austrian citizenship.

In Austria there are some 220,000 people with German background (some 75,000 of them meanwhile are Austrian citizens); 210,000 are from Serbia, Montenegro and Kosovo (again some 75,000 of them are Austrian citizens) and some 185,000 have Turkish background (some 70,000 of them are Austrian citizens).

Styria – Reform Agenda

On June 30th 2011, the Styrian government announced a reform of administration. This agenda shall bring reforms in politics, administration and communities and it is planned to be implemented until 2015.

Politics:

- Reduction of the country parliament from 56 to 48 MPs

2. <http://www.bmi.gv.at/cms/BMI/sts/start.aspx>.

- Reduction of the Graz city council from 56 to 48 members
- Reduction of the Graz Senate from 9 to 7 members
- New Creation of the country government

The country government was until then built proportionally. All political parties which were part of the country parliament and had a percentage of some 10% of the seats sent members to the government. This proportional creation of the country government is still adopted in Burgenland, Carinthia, Upper and Lower Austria. It was changed in Salzburg and the Tyrol in 1998 and it was never adopted in Vorarlberg. Vienna is a special case as both country and community and has both executive and non-executive city councilors.

Administration:

- New organization of counties

Styria consists of 16 counties and 2 branches (Expositur Bad Aussee and Expositur Gröbming) as part of Austria's biggest county, Liezen in upper Styria. Expositur Bad Aussee will be closed down and there will be an office of Liezen county in Bad Aussee.

On January 12th 2012 the two counties Knittelfeld and Judenburg were consolidated to the county Murtal. Both counties have long historical connections and Knittelfeld has become an own county as late as 1945. The new county is Styria's second largest (area 1,676 km^2) and the fifth largest respectively as far as population is concerned (74,500).

- New organization of the office of the Styrian government

Some aspects will be the reduction of organizational units and the evaluation of outsourcings and advisory boards.

Communities:

Styria consists of 542 communities, 76 of them are very small ones with less than 500 and only five with more than 10,000 inhabitants. The second part of the project "Regionext" should bring a clear reduction of the number of communities and thus the establishing of economically strong and professional community centers. Among the criteria will be closed areas of settlement; better community structures, emotional affiliation of the population and the structure of interior institutions.

Political Scandals and Corruption

In February 2011, Ernst Strasser (ÖVP), member of the EU-Parliament, aroused indignation. Two *Sunday Times* journalists recorded a talk with Strasser about lobbying. Strasser is seen and heard on this video as follows:

"(S:) In five years I will have an office here in Brussels because this is now, this is a wonderful opportunity to learn all the people, to have my own network and to, to use this network for my, for my, for my companies. ... This is a very good combination. And I see it now in Austria after one year. There are a lot of people, they need something in competition, or whatever, yes, sport and health, and education and whatever. And when you go there as a MEP, this is something, it opens a door in another way as you go in there as a lobbyist, yes? Of course I'm a lobbyist, yes, and I'm open for that, yes?

> *(Q:) So you say you have two roles really. Well, you've got several roles, haven't you? You're a lobbyist and you're also an MEP.*
>
> *(S:) Yes, but erm*
>
> *(Q:) How does that work together?*
>
> *(S:) Oh, it works very well. And so I only, I only, I have one chance to lie, yes? So I will be very, very careful on this because if you once lie, you are dead, yes? And I don't want to be, and I want to build up my network. And want to use it after my time as an MEP."*

On the reporters' question if he declares his commercial clients on the European Parliament's register of interests Strasser answers:

> *"You will not find in my papers something because I have to protect my clients.*
>
> *(Q:) I see. How would it work with us? How would it work with us if you were on our advisory board?*
>
> *(S:) If I have a contract that I help you to do your things, this is confidential.*
>
> *(Q:) You don't have to register it?*
>
> *(S:) No, no. You know, the problem is, a lobbyist is a lobbyist, yes? And a lobbyist has some special smell. It's true to be said I am myself something like that. So we have to be very careful. But the fee, so my clients pay me for a year 100.000 Euro, yes. I now have five – hopefully from tomorrow, six clients where I make such an advisor. Hopefully tomorrow six. Not, not. You are not included. You are the seventh."*[3]

3. <http://www.youtube.com/watch?v=DJxD-ysedbk&feature=related>.

After that, Strasser had to resign as MEP. Later on, Strasser said that he thought the two journalists were part of a secret service and that he wanted to reveal their activities. A lawsuit might bring this affair to light in spring 2012.

Another ÖVP-MEP had to resign in March 2012: Hella Ranner faced accusations of fraud.

And since 2009 Austria's courts have been trying to solve another dubious affair: The sale of 60,000 federal apartments by BUWOG (Bauen und Wohnen GmbH) and the former minister of finance, Karl Heinz Grasser, assisted by Walter Meischberger and Peter Hochegger. Meischberger and Hochegger got € 9.9 Million premium for their assistance in the sale.

Transparency International pointed out in December 2011 that Austria fell down to position 16 worldwide (compared to position 10 in 2005). Corruption in Austria would meanwhile arouse international attention.[4]

WKR and "the new Jews"

WKR—Wiener Korporationsring—is the umbrella association of more than 20 right wing students' fraternities in Vienna and is a party-affiliated organization to FPÖ. As every year, WKR organized the WKR-Ball, 2012 on the 27th of January (Remembrance Day of the liberation of the concentration camp of Auschwitz-Birkenau). And as in previous years, there were demonstrations against the ball on the one hand, and right wing extremists from around Europe who visited the ball, on the other hand —among them Marine Le Pen (Front National), Kent Ekeroth (Swedish Democrats) and Philip Claeys (Vlaams Belang).

During the event, Heinz Christian Strache (FPÖ) said to a journalist that the visitors had been molested by demonstrators—so "we are the new Jews" ("Wir sind die neuen Juden"). Attacks against premises of fraternities would have been "similar to the criminal acts of Novemberpogrom" ("Das war wie die Reichskristallnacht") and finally another FPÖ-representative said that those working for this ball would get the Jewish badge ("Wer für diesen Ball arbeitet, bekommt gleich den Judenstern aufgedrückt").[5]

WKR and its organizations must by no means be equated with CV (Cartellverband). CV is an umbrella association of catholic student fraternities who is a party-affiliated organization to ÖVP. WKR—and Freiheitlicher Akademikerverband as its Austrian equivalent—still can be

4. <http://www.ti-austria.at/ti-allgemein/corruption-perceptions-index.html>.

5. Der Standard, 29.01.2012; <http://derstandard.at/1326504057390/Reportage-Der-letzte-Tanz-der-neuen-Juden-in-der-Hofburg>.

partly characterized as right wing extremist and one of its members, Martin Graf (Burschenschaft Olympia), is 3rd president of Nationalrat, the first chamber of the Austrian parliament.

Economic and Statistical Data

Inflation was at 3.3 percent in 2011 (compared to 1.9 percent in 2010), HVPI was at 3.6 percent (compared to 1.7 percent in 2010). The public deficit amounted 4.4 percent in 2010 (4.1percent in 2009) and public debts amounted to 71.8 percent in 2010 (69.5 percent in 2009).

In 2010, GNP was at € 34.120 per capita (compared to € 32.860 in 2009); economic growth was 2.3 percent in 2010 (compared to 3.8 in 2009).

In 2010, imports amounted € 113.652 million (€ 82.345 million from the EU-27) and exports amounted € 109.372 million (€ 77.145 million to the E.U.). Imports from NAFTA were € 3.836 million; exports to NAFTA € 6.087 million.

In 2010 4,096,400 people in Austria were employed (according to the Labor Force Concept; on average 4,077,700 in 2009; the rate of unemployment was at 4.4 percent in 2010 (on average 4.8 percent in 2009).

At the beginning of 2011, 8,404,252 people were living in Austria, among them 927,612 foreigners (and among them 359,300 from EU-27). In 2010 78,742 children were born alive in Austria and 77,199 people died. Life expectancy is at 77.9 years (men) and 83.5 (women).

List of Authors

Günter Bischof is a university research professor of history and director of CenterAustria at the University of New Orleans.

Peter Berger is professor of history and head of the Institute for Economic and Social History at the Vienna University of Economics and Business.

Jason Dawsey is a Ph.D. candidate in Modern European history at the University of Chicago.

John Deak is an assistant professor of History and a fellow of the Nanovic Institute for European Studies at the University of Notre Dame.

Wolfram Dornik is a senior researcher at the Ludwig Boltzmann-Institute for Research on the Consequences of War in Graz.

Martin Eichtinger is an ambassador and director general for cultural policy in the Austrian Federal Ministry for European and International Affairs.

Bernhard Fetz is director of the Literary Archives of the Austrian National Library and associate professor at the Department of German studies at the University of Vienna.

Herbert Friedlmeier is a librarian and senior curator of the USIS collection at the Austrian National Library.

Regina Fritz is a researcher at the Institute of Contemporary History (Munich/Berlin) and lecturer in the Institute of Contemporary History of the University of Vienna.

Winfried R. Garscha is an archivist at the Documentation Center of Austrian Resistance (DÖW) and co-director of the Austrian Research Agency for Post-War Justice (Forschungsstelle Nachkriegsjustiz), Vienna.

Reinhold Gärtner is a professor at the Department of Political Science, University of Innsbruck.

Ernst Hanisch is a professor emeritus of modern Austrian History of the University of Salzburg.

Gabriella Hauch is a professor of modern history/the history of women and gender history at the University of Vienna.

Deborah Holmes is a lecturer in German at the University of Kent, UK, where she is a specialist in Austrian culture and literature of the late nineteenth and early twentieth centuries.

Maria-Regina Kecht is a professor of German Literature and is currently serving as Academic Director of Webster University Vienna.

Johannes Koll has been a post-doctoral researcher at the Institute of Social and Economic History at the University of Economics and Business Administration in Vienna from 2007 to 2011.

Ernst Langthaler is director of the Institute of Rural History in St. Pölten and was visiting professor at the Universities of Innsbruck and Vienna.

Alexander N. Lassner is an associate professor at the Department of Strategy, US Air War College, in Montgomery, Alabama.

Eva Maltschnig is a doctoral candidate in the Institute of Social and Economic History at the Vienna University of Economics and Business Administration; in 2011/2012 she was the Austrian Ministry of Science fellow at CenterAustria at the University of New Orleans.

Stefan Maurer is a literary scholar in Vienna, currently working on a project about Austrian Literature and the Cold War on the University of Vienna as a doctoral candidate.

Berthold Molden is researcher and lecturer at the University of Vienna and the 2012/2013 Marshall Plan Chair at the University of New Orleans.

Thomas Nowotny is a retired Austrian diplomat and lecturer for political science at the University of Vienna.

Hans Petschar is a historian and the director of the Picture Archives and Graphics Department at the Austrian National Library.

Fritz Plasser is professor of political science and dean of the faculty of political science and sociology at the University of Innsbruck.

Timothy Edward Pytell is an associate professor of history at California State University San Bernardino.

Oliver Rathkolb is professor of history and head of the Department of Contemporary History at the University of Vienna.

Elisabeth Röhrlich is postdoctoral researcher and lecturer at the Department of Contemporary History at the University of Vienna.

Alexander Salzmann is an independent historian in Vienna.

Yvonne Schürmann-Zehetner is an independent scholar in Vienna.

Gerald Steinacher is an assistant professor of history and holocaust studies at the University of Nebraska in Lincoln.

Barbara Stelzl-Marx is deputy director at Ludwig Boltzmann Institute for Research on War Consequences (BIK) in Graz and a lecturer at the University of Graz.

Philipp Strobl is a lector at the University of Economics in Bratislava.

Helmut Wohnout is a director of department in the Austrian Federal Chancellery and the executive director of the Karl von Vogelsang-Institute in Vienna; he is also an adjunct lecturer of Austrian history at the University of Graz.

Petra Ziegler is a project manager and researcher in the business consulting firm 3s Unternehmensberatung in Vienna.

Contemporary Austrian Studies

Günter Bischof and Fritz Plasser, Editors

Volume 1 (1992)
Austria in the New Europe

Volume 2 (1993)
The Kreisky Era in Austria
Oliver Rathkolb, Guest Editor

Volume 3 (1994)
Austria in the Nineteen Fifties
Rolf Steininger, Guest Editor

Volume 4 (1995)
Austro-Corporatism: Past—Present—Future

Volume 5 (1996)
Austrian Historical Memory & National Identity

Volume 6 (1997)
Women in Austria
Erika Thurner, Guest Editor

Volume 7 (1998)
The Vranitzky Era in Austria
Ferdinand Karlhofer, Guest Editor

Volume 8 (1999)
The Marshall Plan in Austria
Dieter Stiefel, Guest Editor

Volume 9 (2000)
Neutrality in Austria
Ruth Wodak, Guest Editor

Volume 10 (2001)
Austria and the EU
Michael Gehler, Guest Editor

Volume 11 (2002)
The Dollfuss/Schuschnigg Era in Austria: A Reassessment
Alexander Lassner, Guest Editor

Volume 12 (2003)
The Americanization/Westernization of Austria

Volume 13 (2004)
Religion in Austria
Hermann Denz, Guest Editor

Volume 14 (2005)
Austrian Foreign Policy in Historical Perspective
Michael Gehler, Guest Editor

Volume 15 (2006)
Sexuality in Austria
Dagmar Herzog, Guest Editor

Volume 16 (2007)
The Changing Austrian Voter

Volume 17 (2008)
New Perspectives on Austrians and World War II
Barbara Stelzl-Marx, Guest Editor

Volume 18 (2009)
The Schüssel Era in Austria

Volume 19 (2010)
From Empire to Republic: Post-World War I Austria

Volume 20 (2011)
Global Austria: Austria's Place in Europe and the World
Alexander Smith, Guest Editor

Also Available from UNO PRESS

General Titles

**Sometimes Courage Looks Like Crazy: A Journalist's Story* by Kim Bondy, 978-1-60801-058-5 (2011)

Post-Katrina Brazucas: Brazilian Immigrants in New Orleans by Annie Gibson, 978-1-60801-070-7 (2011)

The Saratoga Collection, edited by Terrence Sanders, 978-1-60801-061-5 (2011)

**The Garden Path: The Miseducation of a City,* by Andre Perry, 978-1-60801-048-6 (2011)

Before (During) After: Louisiana Photographers Visual Reactions to Hurricane Katrina, edited by Elizabeth Kleinveld, 978-1-60801-023-3 (2010)

**Beyond the Islands* by Alicia Yánez Cossío, translated by Amalia Gladhart, 978-1-60801-043-1 (2010)

**Writer in Residence: Memoir of a Literary Translator* by Mark Spitzer, 978-1-60801-020-2 (2010)

**The Fox's Window* by Naoko Awa, translated by Toshiya Kamei, 978-1-60801-006-6 (2010)

Black Santa by Jamie Bernstein, 978-1-60801-022-6 (2010)

Dream-crowned (Traumgekrönt) by Rainer Maria Rilke, translated by Lorne Mook, 978-1-60801-041-7 (2010)

**Voices Rising II: More Stories from the Katrina Narrative Project* edited by Rebeca Antoine, 978-0-9706190-8-2 (2010)

**Rowing to Sweden: Essays on Faith, Love, Politics, and Movies* by Fredrick Barton, 978-1-60801-001-1 (2010)

Dogs in My Life: The New Orleans Photographs of John Tibule Mendes, 978-1-60801-005-9 (2010)

New Orleans: The Underground Guide by Michael Patrick Welch & Alison Fensterstock, 978-1-60801-019-6 (2010)

Understanding the Music Business: A Comprehensive View edited by Harmon Greenblatt & Irwin Steinberg, 978-1-60801-004-2 (2010)

**The Gravedigger* by Rob Magnuson Smith, 978-1-60801-010-3 (2010)

Portraits: Photographs in New Orleans 1998-2009 by Jonathan Traviesa, 978-0-9706190-5-1 (2009)

**I hope it's not over, and good-by: Selected Poems of Everette Maddox* by Everette Maddox, 978-1-60801-000-4 (2009)

Theoretical Killings: Essays & Accidents by Steven Church, 978-0-9706190-6-8 (2009)

**Voices Rising: Stories from the Katrina Narrative Project* edited by Rebeca Antoine, 978-0-9728143-6-2 (2008)

On Higher Ground: The University of New Orleans at Fifty by Dr. Robert Dupont, 978-0-9728143-5-5 (2008)

The Change Cycle Handbook by Will Lannes, 978-0-9728143-9-3 (2008)

Us Four Plus Four: Eight Russian Poets Conversing translated by Don Mager, 978-0-9706190-4-4 (2008)

The El Cholo Feeling Passes by Fredrick Barton, 978-0-9728143-2-4 (2003)

A House Divided by Fredrick Barton, 978-0-9728143-1-7 (2003)

William Christenberry: Art & Family by J. Richard Gruber, 978-0-9706190-0-6 (2000)

The Neighborhood Story Project

New Orleans in 19 Movements by Thurgood Marshall Early College High School, 978-1-60801-069-1 (2011)

The Combination by Ashley Nelson, 978-1-60801-055-4 (2010)

The House of Dance and Feathers: A Museum by Ronald W. Lewis by Rachel Breunlin & Ronald W. Lewis, 978-0-9706190-7-5 (2009)

Beyond the Bricks by Daron Crawford & Pernell Russell, 978-1-60801-016-5 (2010)

Aunt Alice Vs. Bob Marley by Kareem Kennedy, 978-1-60801-013-4 (2010)

Signed, The President by Kenneth Phillips, 978-1-60801-015-8 (2010)

Houses of Beauty: From Englishtown to the Seventh Ward by Susan Henry, 978-1-60801-014-1 (2010)

Coming Out the Door for the Ninth Ward edited by Rachel Breunlin, 978-0-9706190-9-9 (2006)

Cornerstones: Celebrating the Everyday Monuments & Gathering Places of New Orleans edited by Rachel Breunlin, 978-0-9706190-3-7 (2008)

The Engaged Writes Series

Medea and Her War Machines by Ioan Flora, translated by Adam J. Sorkin, 978-1-60801-067-7 (2011)

Together by Julius Chingono and John Eppel, 978-1-60801-049-3 (2011)

Vegetal Sex (O Sexo Vegetal) by Sergio Medeiros, translated by Raymond L.Bianchi, 978-1-60801-046-2 (2010)

**Wounded Days (Los Días Heridos)* by Leticia Luna, translated by Toshiya Kamei, 978-1-60801-042-4 (2010)

When the Water Came: Evacuees of Hurricane Katrina by Cynthia Hogue & Rebecca Ross, 978-1-60801-012-7 (2010)

**A Passenger from the West* by Nabile Farès, translated by Peter Thompson, 978-1-60801-008-0 (2010)

**Everybody Knows What Time It Is* by Reginald Martin, 978-1-60801-011-0 (2010)

**Green Fields: Crime, Punishment, & a Boyhood Between* by Bob Cowser, Jr., 978-1-60801-018-9 (2010)

**Open Correspondence: An Epistolary Dialogue* by Abdelkébir Khatibi and Rita El Khayat, translated by Safoi Babana-Hampton, Valérie K. Orlando, Mary Vogl, 978-1-60801-021-9 (2010)

Gravestones (Lápidas) by Antonio Gamoneda, translated by Donald Wellman, 978-1-60801-002-8 (2009)

Hearing Your Story: Songs of History and Life for Sand Roses by Nabile Farès translated by Peter Thompson, 978-0-9728143-7-9 (2008)

The Katrina Papers: A Journal of Trauma and Recovery by Jerry W. Ward, Jr., 978-0-9728143-3-1 (2008)

Contemporary Poetry

California Redemption Values by Kevin Opstedal, 978-1-60801-066-0 (2011)

Atlanta Poets Group Anthology: The Lattice Inside by Atlanta Poets Group, 978-1-60801-064-6 (2011)

Makebelieve by Caitlin Scholl, 978-1-60801-056-1 (2011)

Dear Oxygen: New and Selected Poems by Lewis MacAdams, edited by Kevin Opstedal, 978-1-60801-059-2 (2011)

Only More So by Tony Lopez, 978-1-60801-057-8 (2011)

Enridged by Brian Richards, 978-1-60801-047-9 (2011)

A Gallery of Ghosts by John Gery, 978-0-9728143-4-8 (2008)

The Ezra Pound Center for Literature

The Poets of the Sala Capizucchi (I Poeti della Sala Capizucchi) edited by Caterina Ricciardi and John Gery, 978-1-60801-068-4 (2011)

Trespassing, by Patrizia de Rachewiltz, 978-1-60801-060-8 (2011)

**The Imagist Poem: Modern Poetry in Miniature* edited by William Pratt, 978-0-9728143-8-6 (2008)

Contemporary Austrian Studies

Global Austria: Austria's Place in Europe and the World, Günter Bischof, Fritz Plasser (Eds.), Alexander Smith, Guest Editor, 978-1-60801-062-2 (2011)

From Empire to Republic: Post-World-War-I Austria Volume 19 edited by Günter Bischof, Fritz Plasser and Peter Berger, 978-1-60801-025-7 (2010)

The Schüssel Era in Austria Volume 18 edited by Günter Bischof & Fritz Plasser, 978-1-60801-009-7 (2009)

*Also available as E-book